Mobile Communication Systems for Private Networks

IEEE Press
445 Hoes Lane
Piscataway, NJ 08854

Mobile Communication Systems for Private Networks

Srinivasan Balasubramanian

IEEE Press
WILEY

Published by John Wiley & Sons, Inc., Hoboken, New Jersey.
Published simultaneously in Canada.

Library of Congress Cataloging-in-Publication Data applied for:
Hardback ISBN: 978139201785

Cover Design: Wiley
Cover Image: © metamorworks/Shutterstock

Set in 9.5/12.5pt STIXTwoText by Straive, Pondicherry, India

To my dear parents,

I deeply appreciate the guidance and sacrifices you have done for me, which have profoundly shaped not just who I am but also the values I hold dear. You both have etched a blueprint of moral and ethical living into my heart through the eloquence of your actions, and every decision I make carries the imprint of your wisdom. Your unwavering commitment to integrity and kindness has been, and will continue to be, a light guiding me on the path of righteousness, even in the darkest of hours. Beyond financial support, you invested in my future not just with resources but with your boundless faith in my potential. Your belief in me has propelled me to reach heights I once deemed unreachable. You never allowed me to settle for mediocrity, always urging me to push beyond my comfort zone, strive for excellence, and reach for the stars. In your eyes, I saw reflections of my untapped potential, and in your encouragement, I found the courage to chase my wildest ambitions.

With deepest gratitude, respect, and boundless love,

Srinivasan Balasubramanian

Contents

Foreword by Mehmet

Private cellular networks mark a significant milestone in today's rapidly evolving technological landscape. These networks are gaining a lot of momentum, and they are expected to play an increasingly significant role in the future of enterprise wireless connectivity.

It is my great pleasure to introduce this comprehensive and insightful book authored by my esteemed colleague, Srini Balasubramanian. With decades of expertise in cellular wireless communications together with his hands-on experience in private networks, Srini adeptly explains all the critical technical aspects with the right level of detail. This book delves into the intricacies of private networks, shedding light on their transformative potential.

Mastering private network technology requires a solid understanding of wireless communications, 3GPP standards, and enterprise networking. It is often quite challenging to gather all the relevant information from different sources. Furthermore, private network requirements are quite different than those of traditional mobile operator networks. In traditional cellular networks, a mobile operator can have radio access network (RAN) solution, core network solution, and operations support system or business support system (OSS/BSS) solutions from different vendors and integrate all the components using well-defined standards and operate the network. However, in private network space enterprises, information technology or operational technology (IT/OT) departments typically need a turn-key solution that integrates well with their existing local area network (LAN). Thus, integration with enterprise dynamic host configuration protocol (DHCP) servers, network access controls (NACs), and firewalls becomes crucial requirements for successful and scalable deployments. Also, device management in private cellular networks has quite unique requirements, including device life-cycle management, integration with enterprise virtual local area networks (VLANs), and the creation of network slices.

In his book, Srini does an excellent job in guiding the reader through necessary pieces as he meticulously explores the various facets of private networks from foundational principles to practical applications. I am confident that readers will find this book to be an invaluable resource, one that not only educates but also inspires.

Mehmet Yavuz, CTO, Celona Inc.

Foreword by Masoud

The recent movements toward enhancing digital life have motivated significant change in the direction of telecommunications industry so that the development of digital enterprise networks and private wireless networks has become the cornerstone of advanced wireless technologies such as 5G new radio (NR) and 6G. As a result, technology ecosystems such as third-generation partnership projects (3GPP) have initiated in-depth studies to promote private wireless networks. Advanced private wireless and enterprise use cases require wireless connectivity to deliver high throughput, high bandwidth, broad coverage, low latency, very high reliability, and enhanced security, which are not necessarily delivered by existing Wi-Fi networks. The 3GPP community has offered solutions to support these use cases as part of its 5G NR and 5G advanced solutions such as massive Internet of Things (IoT) communications, cloud storage and computing, and AI. Moreover, private 5G wireless networks may require custom design to meet the desired performance levels and service demands. However, the basis of any wireless system is the spectrum, and therefore, the policymakers have promoted studies to secure proper spectrum ranges for the digital enterprise development. The Citizen Broadband Radio Service (CBRS) has created a dynamic spectrum-sharing platform that enhances the proliferation of private and enterprise wireless systems by relaxing the significant financial burden of securing exclusive license spectrum.

During the development of CBRS network features for private and enterprise wireless use cases, and as the chair of OnGo Alliance (previously known as CBRS Alliance) Network Services Task Group (NSTG), I had the privilege of working with Srinivasan Balasubramanian, who was instrumental in the development of nonpublic networks (NPN) in the spectrum-sharing platform. Before joining the CBRS development effort, he had at least two decades of theoretical expertise as well as hands-on experience in cellular and private wireless communications, with a deep knowledge of 3GPP long-term evolution (LTE) and 5G NR advanced technologies. These experiences and knowledge have enabled him to write a comprehensive and insightful book in the field of private and enterprise wireless networks. Titled *Mobile Communication Systems for Private Networks*, this book serves as a master guide, offering all the essential technical details and design criteria required for a deep understanding of the design and development of private wireless networks. Therefore, this book can be considered as a comprehensive source for those who want to develop and design enterprise wireless networks.

The topics covered in the book extend from use case definition, spectrum management, and security frameworks to network architecture for both mobile network operator (MNO)-integrated and standalone nonpublic networks. It also includes radio and RAN planning, core network design, roaming design, enhanced quality of service (QoS), artificial intelligence (AI) or machine learning (ML) integration, and device management plans for enterprise and private wireless networks. Moreover,

Srini has covered the coexistence and integration of private cellular networks with other wireless solutions such as cellular and Wi-Fi networks. This is essential in providing high scalability to organizations to manage and make the best use of all three networks: public, Wi-Fi, and nonpublic networks.

I am confident that all readers – network architects, RAN developers, network planners, spectrum engineers, IT professionals, and business leaders – will find the topics in this book insightful and useful. The book is a crucial source for understanding the strategic implications of deploying private networks on business and product development strategies.

Masoud Olfat, Vice President of Technology and Ecosystem Development, Federated Wireless Inc.
Chair, Network Services Task Group, and member of board of directors, OnGo Alliance
Chair, WinnForum CBRS and 6GHz Test and Certification WG

Foreword by Sree

In today's rapidly evolving digital landscape, the need for robust, secure, and scalable communication networks is more critical than ever. Enterprise private cellular networks offer unparalleled opportunities for innovation, efficiency, and competitive advantage, allowing organizations to tailor connectivity solutions to meet their unique needs.

This book, *Mobile Communication Systems for Private Networks*, serves as a comprehensive guide for understanding, designing, and implementing private cellular networks within the enterprise context. It is intended for network architects, IT professionals, business leaders, and technology enthusiasts who seek to deepen their knowledge and stay ahead in this dynamic field.

Private cellular networks can profoundly impact various industries, from manufacturing and logistics to health care and smart cities. These networks enable new levels of operational efficiency, data security, and real-time decision-making capabilities. The convergence of 5G technology, the IoT, and edge computing is driving this transformation, creating a landscape where connectivity is not just a utility but a strategic asset.

A significant aspect of this evolving landscape is the coexistence and integration of private cellular networks with existing Wi-Fi networks. While Wi-Fi remains a dominant force in enterprise networking, private cellular networks offer complementary benefits such as enhanced security, broader coverage, and more reliable connectivity. Understanding how to strategically deploy and manage both Wi-Fi and private cellular networks will be crucial for maximizing an organization's communication infrastructure.

The device baseband and telephony frameworks can significantly impact the adoption and uptake of private networks in both enterprise and consumer spaces. Special care must be taken to ensure that private networks are suitably discovered, onboarded, and given priority with respect to other radio access, depending on the use cases and user profiles. There is tremendous opportunity for innovation here and room to differentiate services as exposed to the end user.

The chapters that follow will delve into the architectural principles, technological components, and practical considerations necessary for building and managing private cellular networks. The book also explores topics such as spectrum management, network planning, security frameworks, performance optimization, coexistence strategies with Wi-Fi networks, and the integration of AI/ML for enhanced QoS. Real-world case studies and best practices mentioned illustrate the tangible benefits and challenges associated with deploying these networks in various scenarios.

In addition to the technical insights, this book addresses the strategic implications of adopting private cellular networks. It highlights the need for a forward-thinking approach that aligns with an organization's broader digital strategy, emphasizing the importance of collaboration between IT and business units. The adoption of private cellular networks requires careful planning and investment to ensure that they complement existing technologies and deliver measurable business value. This strategic foresight is critical in driving digital transformation and maintaining a competitive edge.

As we stand at the forefront of this exciting technological development, it is crucial to stay informed and agile. This book is a testament to the expertise and experiences of the author, who has had a stellar career pursuing advancements in the field of wireless communications and networking. Srini's insights will undoubtedly provide valuable guidance to anyone seeking to harness the power of private cellular networks.

I invite you to immerse yourself in the rich content of this book, to explore the possibilities and challenges it presents, and to envision the future of connectivity in your organization.

Sree Vallath, Wireless Technologies, Apple Inc.

Foreword by Ariful

I became acquainted with Srinivasan Balasubramanian through his contributions to the Technical Work Groups within the OnGo Alliance, where we engaged in discussions and advocated for 4G/5G technologies that would power the next generation of public and private networks utilizing the CBRS spectrum. I have long admired the ideas he introduced to the industry, and I am genuinely pleased to learn that he has chosen to write this book to reach a broader audience.

There is no doubt that wireless communication is undergoing a profound transformation, driven by the growing demand for high-speed, reliable, and secure connectivity in diverse settings. This book, focusing on the deployment of private networks based on LTE and 5G NR technologies, offers a timely and comprehensive guide to this rapidly evolving field.

An important catalyst for private networks would be how regulatory bodies shape the national spectrum strategies to strike a balance between dedicated spectrum and localized and shared spectrum allocation. These strategies must be driven by the need to support diverse use cases and deployment scenarios for private networks while ensuring efficient spectrum utilization and minimizing interference between public and private networks. This book highlights CBRS as a prime example of shared spectrum, enabling dynamic allocation and operation for individual enterprises. It also discusses spectrum allocation in different countries, with many adopting localized allocation policies. It underscores the importance of the evolution of spectrum management for both private and public networks, including interference mitigation and fair sharing, especially with the increasing demand for reliable and high-performance wireless connectivity in various industries.

As Srini points out, the successful implementation of private networks requires a deep understanding of the underlying technologies and their unique challenges. This book addresses this need by providing a clear and accessible overview of LTE and 5G NR, as well as the specific considerations for deploying these technologies in private network settings.

Whether you are a network engineer, IT professional, or business leader, this book will equip you with the knowledge and insights to navigate the complex landscape of private networks and harness their full potential. The author's insight, highlighting the critical decision points, makes this book an invaluable resource for anyone seeking to stay ahead of the curve in this exciting field.

Ariful Hannan, Solution Architect, Telecom Industry, Google Inc.

Preface

Looking back at my career working in the wireless field, the initial enterprise work environment I was in used tethered (ethernet) connectivity, switching to a hybrid mode and using wireless only when tethered connectivity was not available, and finally switching to operating with only wireless connectivity. Both the reliability and the ubiquitous availability of wireless connectivity have become basic necessities now. My initial foray into wireless was on 3GPP2, developing 1xRTT and High Rate Packet Data (HRDP) systems, and I still remember attending wireless conferences discussing contributions using printed copies, given the lack of connectivity while traveling to a site to meet.

Wireless voice solutions were the first to arrive and were mainly focused on cellular wide-area coverage-based support, creating the cellular industry. Voice service remained the main service that dominated the wireless industry even up to the third generation, even though data connectivity was introduced. The data connectivity through wireless was expensive to deploy, required high subscription costs, and was very restricted in its use. The barrier was broken with the 4G long-term evolution (LTE) technology, where data connectivity became a more accessible commodity. While cellular technology was evolving for wide-area coverage, the void of wireless connectivity for in-building home and enterprise data connectivity was filled by Wi-Fi. Given the low costs to both deploy and manage, Wi-Fi became the go-to choice for shorter-range connectivity. This resulted in the enterprise connectivity solutions industry growing in parallel with the cellular industry.

The Wi-Fi standards have made strides to meet enterprise demands. Since its introduction in 1997, the ongoing evolution of the Institute of Electrical and Electronics Engineers (IEEE) 802.11 Wi-Fi standards has led to much faster data transmission rates, longer ranges, and more reliable and secure connections. IEEE 802.11ax™, or Wi-Fi 6, is the most recent standard in the IEEE 802.11 series, published in 2022. Wi-Fi 6E is an extension of the Wi-Fi 6 standard (which is based on the 802.11ax standard) that operates in the 6 GHz frequency band. It provides additional spectrum for Wi-Fi devices, enabling higher data rates, lower latency, and less interference compared to operating in the crowded 2.4 GHz and 5 GHz bands. Wi-Fi 7 is the next generation of wireless network technology that is being developed in the standards and brings with it some fundamental technical improvements over its predecessors.

One of the key aspects of Wi-Fi was its reliance on the use of unlicensed spectrum. Wi-Fi became and still is synonymous with "free," at least from a user perspective. This is certainly true when compared to the costs for data connectivity on a cellular platform. 4G LTE, and now 5G NR, has provided definitions for the use of 3GPP technologies in an unlicensed spectrum. It relied on a licensed spectrum as an anchor, and the unlicensed spectrum was used to augment the capacity and is termed as licensed assisted access (LAA). Given that the base stations for both licensed and unlicensed services needed to be deployed in close proximity, this was more suitable for small cell solutions. The support of small cells in a licensed spectrum required sophisticated spectrum sharing between the macro and small cells, which made it difficult for market adoption.

All radio and telecommunications use waves of different frequencies (measured in Megahertz [MHz] and Gigahertz [GHz]) to carry data. These frequencies are grouped together to form bands, and multiple bands combine to form a spectrum of radio waves. Every successive generation of telecom has its fixed spectrum, and its bands are allocated to telecommunication companies for commercial use. Spectrum resource availability has become the biggest bottleneck, with wireless service providers paying huge sums of money to acquire spectrum resources and going through bidding wars involving large amounts of money. 3GPP-defined 4G/5G systems offer higher reliability when compared to Wi-Fi in terms of providing service guarantees and also deliver improved system capacity with the available spectrum. For this technology to be supported in an enterprise environment, a specific spectrum needs to be made available. Exclusive spectrum purchases by the smaller entities (both in geographic footprint and financial capacity) meant that an innovative approach was needed to address this demand. This naturally lent itself to the definition of shared spectrum use by these smaller entities.

In 2015, the Federal Communications Commission (FCC) developed a framework for the shared commercial use of the 3,550–3,700 MHz band (3.5 GHz band). The Citizens Broadband Radio Service (CBRS) was established with a tiered access and authorization framework to accommodate shared federal and non-federal use of the band. Wi-Fi uses unlicensed spectrum within the 2.4 GHz and 5 GHz frequency ranges, while CBRS uses shared spectrum within the 3.55 GHz and 3.70 GHz range that is regulated by a central entity and referred to as lightly licensed. The CBRS spectrum is divided into three tiers, each requiring specific licenses with strict priority based on the users (base station deployments by an enterprise) belonging to a tier. The creation of this shared spectrum use has generated momentum for lower-cost, smaller deployments using 4G LTE and 5G NR technologies on individual campuses, which can be deployed and managed similarly to Wi-Fi networks. With the CBRS spectrum serving as an example, several countries have defined procedures for smaller entities to acquire spectrum for enterprise-level operations, with more and more countries following suit. The amount of spectrum bandwidth allocated varies across different countries, but it is definitely a trend that is here to stay, providing smaller footprint spectrum usage that is readily available. Much of the focus is on optimally managing the spectrum to avoid interference between the deployed smaller networks and to enable fair sharing of the available spectrum. This aspect is actively evolving, with real-time demand-based spectrum management being envisioned.

As of the writing of this book, private network deployments are well underway, with implementations across several verticals, including educational institutions such as colleges and K-12 schools, offices, hospitals, ports, manufacturing industries, big-box retail, warehouses, mining, and many more. The use of 4G LTE/5G NR has enabled increased capacity, higher reliability, and fewer network nodes compared to Wi-Fi, supporting enterprise functions. The 3GPP standards body envisioned a set of features to support private networks and introduced these in Release 16 (published in July 2020) and Release 17 (January 2022). Most, if not all, private networks deployed now use Release 15 (June 2018), which is the initial release where 5G NR support is defined. Given that the end-user device availability was limited to Release 15 initially, and demand for private networks was growing, deployments needed to accommodate support for Release 15 devices. It turns out that many use cases can be addressed using Release 15. Advanced scenarios of macro network operators deploying smaller footprint networks and seamlessly transitioning across macro and small cell networks require the features introduced in Release 16 and beyond. Macro network operators are actively entering this space, given that users spend a lot of time indoors and there is a lack of good coverage provided by the macro network in buildings. Distributed antenna systems (DAS) exist but are very costly to deploy. However, where DAS solutions are deployed, they can be leveraged to support both licensed and shared spectrum.

The macro network operators are used to managing complex networks and actively tune the parameters to maximize the performance of the network, accommodating different user types. 4G LTE/5G NR systems are defined to accommodate complex scenarios and are inherently difficult to manage. Enterprise networks typically have Wi-Fi support and are very simple to deploy and manage. Take a home setting where the public at large can go and buy an access point, plug it in, and get it functioning in a matter of minutes. Granted that enterprise environments are a lot more complex, ensuring that there are no hidden spots where coverage is needed, supporting the required load, and managing the security of the system while also overseeing the enterprise applications are challenging. Now, bringing in a complex system like 4G LTE/5G NR and deploying it in the same environment becomes a tall order. The enterprise folks are not going to budge from the fact that managing this 3GPP-based network is much more complex than a Wi-Fi system. In fact, even if it is as straightforward as a Wi-Fi network, it still means the enterprise information technology (IT) has to manage yet another network and an additional screen to stare at. Both the deployment and the management of the 3GPP systems for enterprises need to be simplified enough not to scare away an enterprise entity from adopting it.

At this historic crossroad, it is strongly believed that a book on covering 4G/5G technology and its adoption into private networks will serve as an enlightening guideline to spur interest and enable increased adoption among different enterprises. Such a book will also attract a broad audience in both academia and industry, creating a great platform for both experimentation and exploration of newer use cases in the market. To ensure that enterprises of all sizes understand and consider support for 4G/5G private networks, this book tries to pull together the complex details of the LTE and NR systems and distill them into the key aspects that will both allow the reader to understand the broad concepts and also sufficiently appreciate the nuances involved while keeping the material as easy to read as possible. There are many books that go into great detail on the technology aspects, with individual books on finer topics. I have tried to bring all this together in a concise manner in this book and have hopefully found the right balance. This book, addressing private networks, may well be the first of its kind, and I hope it serves its intended purpose. This book is written in 28 chapters organized into three parts.

Part I Laying the Foundation: This section of the book lays the foundation by providing the technological details of 3GPP 4G LTE and 5G NR systems. These are broader concepts that apply equally to a macro network as well as to a private network. The same technological concepts are applied to private networks, subjecting them to the constraints of a smaller network. Private networks also pose a different set of problems not directly experienced by macro networks, and techniques defined in these systems are leveraged to adequately address the required scenarios. The relevant knobs in these systems are captured, and the reader is requested to use that frame of mind when applying them to private networks.

LTE Fundamentals: This captures the essence of 4G LTE networks. Evolved UMTS terrestrial radio access (E-UTRAN) refers to fourth-generation wireless technology defined by 3GPP (third-generation partnership project). It is the radio access network (RAN) of LTE, which is the standard for 4G wireless communication. Starting with the network architecture, the protocol stacks across the network nodes and the end-user equipment (UE) are shown. This broadcast signals, along with the system acquisition and camping procedures, are described. The physical channel structure for both Frequency Division Duplex (FDD) and time division duplex (TDD) operations is illustrated. The signaling procedures of interactions between the UE and network for establishing connectivity and providing UE capability information for the network to appropriately configure the UE for operation are presented. The UE packet data operations on the downlink (DL) and uplink (UL) are described. The UE mobility procedures and the use of the timing advance procedures to appropriately coordinate the transmission on the DL and UL are shown.

5G NR Fundamentals: This chapter covers the key aspects of 5G NR. Given that NR is a direct evolution from the LTE system, this chapter assumes the fundamentals shown in LTE equally apply to NR as well. The focus of this chapter is to address the key enhancements/changes relative to the LTE system that are introduced into 5G NR. It covers the key functions introduced in NR from a radio network and core network perspective, including scalable numerology and frame structure, including the definition of self-contained slots. The supported bandwidths, along with the sub-carrier spacing (SCS) and bandwidth part operations, are captured. The use of different waveforms and slot formats is presented. Beamforming is an important aspect of NR and is captured here. The evolution of RAN architecture, along with the bandwidth requirements across hops for the key RAN split options, is shown. The RAN–core interconnection options, with the simultaneous operation of LTE and NR together with the evolved packet core (EPC)/5th generation core (5GC), are shown. The comparisons and differences with 4G LTE are covered where relevant.

NR Physical Layer: The NR physical layer continues the wireless evolution using LTE as a basis. The same waveforms are used in 5G NR as in 4G LTE. Enhancements have been made to accommodate wider bandwidth, a completely new band with mmWave, and additional RF, physical layer, and associated Medium Access Control (MAC) layer techniques. In fact, many of the logical and physical channel definition nomenclature is directly carried over from LTE to NR. Newer reference signals are introduced for improved operations for both DL and UL. It covers the 5G NR reference signals and channels. It addresses cell acquisition and initial access procedures. The Random Access Channel (RACH) procedures that are contention-based and contention-free are presented. The data traffic operations for both DL and UL are also addressed. Note that the focus is again on showing the key aspects where NR differs from LTE, and the underlying operations based on LTE definitions continue to remain true.

Beamforming and Massive MIMO: Beamforming offers significant benefits to both the network and UE, enabling larger system capacity and higher individual UE throughput. There are sufficient challenges to supporting beamforming, which forms the basis for supporting multiple input multiple output (MIMO) systems and further extending it to massive MIMO (M-MIMO). This section discusses the motivation behind beamforming in 5G NR and covers the aspects of beam management and massive MIMO operations. The basic procedures involved in beamforming techniques are described. With private networks and shorter ranges of communication, apart from being mostly indoor and in limited mobility scenarios, it naturally lends itself to applying beamforming for improved system performance. Beamforming is primarily used to compensate for propagation loss and improve coverage. This includes both single-user and multi-user MIMO techniques. Beam management supports intra-cell beam transitions and mobility across cells while maintaining the optimum connection for radio link operation. M-MIMO operation is supported by large antenna arrays. M-MIMO is typically enabled with 32, 64, 128, and even 256 array elements. The large antenna array allows for fully digital steerable antennas, providing the flexibility to serve many users simultaneously.

NR Millimeter Wave: The low-band and mid-band spectrum are already very congested, and wider bandwidths introduced in 5G require larger spectrum space to leverage the full capability of 5G. It is intended that mmWave can fulfill the demand for enhanced mobile broadband (eMBB) and novel 5G use cases that require more spectrum. There are several advantages and challenges associated with using higher frequencies. With higher frequencies, antenna size becomes very small, and a larger antenna array can be supported, allowing for higher gain. With more antennas, it supports directivity, enabling better beamforming. Along similar lines, it does come with its own set of challenges as well. Higher frequencies imply an inferior link budget, bringing with them significant deployment challenges. 5G mmWave operation is defined to be between 24,250 MHz and 52,600 MHz. The mitigative techniques required for operating on mmWave channels using antenna arrays and the need for phase noise cancellation are discussed in this chapter.

NR Unlicensed: Apart from licensed spectrum, leveraging unlicensed spectrum will allow for a more comprehensive approach to wireless support. The notion that cellular technology requires licensed, clean channels for operation is not sufficient. Enabling alternative technologies for data connectivity in unlicensed spectrum, beyond Wi-Fi, can be useful depending on the service requirements and the associated quality of service (QoS) that needs to be met. 3GPP has defined NR standards to realize this vision and has outlined different techniques such as SCS, flexible frame structures, and others. The use of self-contained Time Transmit Interval (TTI), which allows for unlicensed operations by contending for the channel in a single slot and completing the grant, data transmission, and acknowledgment within a single transmission interval, is described. This primarily opened up the use of unlicensed channels for LTE/NR support. Both LAA with LTE and NR operation on unlicensed spectrum (NR-U) have yet to gain traction in the market. This chapter is structured to show the enabling technological aspects that support NR operations in unlicensed spectrum. A quick comparison of LAA and NR is also presented.

NR Mobility: This section details the 5G NR modes of idle, inactive, and connected mobility in stand-alone (SA) mode. Aspects of non-stand-alone (NSA) mode are captured to provide sufficient context; however, they are not relevant to private networks since NSA mode is not supported in such deployments. From a mobility perspective, idle mode and inactive mode behave the same way, except for some signaling procedures that involve reading broadcast messages and access procedures. The exceptions as they apply to inactive mode are explicitly noted. For connected mobility, measurement event triggers related to mobility and transitions are captured. Intra-NR mobility in NSA mode requires specific treatment, and the associated procedures are addressed. Inter-RAT in a private network setting, transitioning across NR and LTE, is considered for multi-mode campus deployments that support both LTE and NR. The context of L3 mobility, along with lower-layer beam mobility and related procedures, is also addressed, with a brief mention of forward-looking concepts introduced in 3GPP Release 18 for multi–transmission received points (mTRP) using L1/L2 triggered mobility (LTM).

NR Protocols: The NR protocol stack is very similar to the LTE protocol layers. To aid in faster packet processing due to the shorter time intervals compared to LTE, some changes have been introduced. Support is provided to perform just-in-time packet formation, and due to the large payload sizes supported, packets can be processed as they are received without having to wait for the full payload. Some functions are moved between the Radio Link Control (RLC) and Packet Data Convergence Protocol (PDCP) layers to enable higher reliability. Additionally, a new layer called the service data adaptation protocol (SDAP) layer has been introduced for better handling of QoS flows by separating the RAN and core network functions, as well as supporting quick QoS flow activation. The SDAP layer is applicable only when the UE is operating in 5G NR SA mode. The focus is on highlighting the key differences compared to the LTE protocol layers. Most of the changes are in the user plane to accommodate just-in-time packet formation, given the smaller slot sizes in NR compared to LTE. The protocol stacks for signaling traffic and user plane traffic are captured. The additional user plane protocol aspects introduced in NR, relative to LTE, are discussed and include PDCP duplication, SDAP protocol layer support, and MAC layer packet multiplexing.

Standards: This chapter presents a high-level view of the different standards bodies, their working group structures, and some of the relevant specifications employed to design, develop, and deploy enterprise private networks. The focus is on the standards definitions that apply to private networks. 3GPP standards provide the fundamental technological basis for 4G/5G private networks. WInnForum and OnGo Alliance address the operations on the CBRS band. The Small Cell Forum provides the architectural and network interfaces for small cell-based private network deployments. The Global System for Mobile Communications (GSMA) standards provide definitions for credential management and basic services like VoIP, VT, and Short Message Service (SMS) operations on IP Multimedia Subsystem (IMS). They also provide specifications for connectivity to the EPC and 5GC networks via the Wi-Fi system. Ongoing efforts to support Telco cloud are also referenced. The 5GACIA standards leverage 3GPP standards and provide specifications for protocols and functions for industrial IoT (IIoT) operations. The open RAN realizations, including the RAN functional split options and the interfacing protocols, apart from the RAN intelligent controller (RIC) specifications, are provided by this standards body. The suggested RAN architectures are also absorbed into the 3GPP specifications. The National Spectrum Consortium (NSC) forum discusses spectrum policies and allocation methodologies in the United States of America (USA).

Part II Technological Framework: Part II of the book provides the reader with technological frameworks for the RAN and core network realizations for private network building, expanding upon the fundamentals introduced in Part I. As part of covering the RAN aspects, topics such as spectrum, fundamentals of delivering the requisite QoS with the RAN scheduler, open RAN including RIC, RAN slicing, self-organizing of the RAN, and techniques for fractional frequency reuse (FFR) are discussed. As part of the core, the convergence with EPC and 5GC, the interfaces across the different nodes in the network, and security, including integration with enterprise systems and network slices, are discussed. The realization of neutral host network (NHN) for macro network users to camp on the deployed private network, particularly for in-building scenarios using these private network techniques based on the RAN and core extensions for private networks, is also discussed. The 3GPP-defined procedure for non-public networks (NPN), supporting stand-alone NPN (SNPN), and public network integrated NPN (PNI-NPN), is introduced for completeness, even though these techniques have not yet seen market adoption. Device provisioning, a critical aspect regulating access to the enterprise campus, is addressed by providing a viable method for credential creation and distribution, adapting to the varying sizes of different enterprises.

Radio Access Network Aspects

Global Private Spectrum Allocations: Traditional spectrum allocations primarily assumed nationwide coverage requirements. This required nationwide coverage, and the spectrum policies were naturally driven to meet the needs of such large deployments. Over the wireless generations, the adoption of different spectrum regions has been enabled, starting with the low band below 3 GHz, moving into the mid-band spectrum between 3 GHz and 6 GHz, and looking further into the mmWave spectrum from 24 GHz to 51 GHz as the high band. With the demand for reliable availability of spectrum for localized use in smaller footprints for enterprises to support cellular technologies for campus coverage, the concept of shared spectrum was born. Globally, several countries have enabled spectrum allocations in small, localized regions that can be requested from a governing body, most of it done through static allocations for a period of time. This chapter discusses the need for and allocations in the different countries, with more and more countries following through and planning for such spectrum allocations.

CBRS Fundamentals: There are several benefits to shared spectrum usage. One of the benefits of shared spectrum is that the spectrum costs can be shared. This is because multiple users can share the same spectrum, which means that there is less need for each user to have their own spectrum. Sharing allows for improved efficiency of radio spectrum usage, as the demands of peak usage vary in time between the networks sharing the spectrum. Shared spectrum can also help to improve the QoS for radio users. The Citizen Broadband Radio Service (CBRS) is an innovative spectrum management approach that allows for localized allocation and operation for individual enterprises. This section details the operations of the CBRS band, together with the regulatory aspects involved, to support dynamic allocation, arbitrating across the different networks within a given locale. This is an early venture into spectrum management and a fantastic experiment that is proving to be successful based on the traction it is getting in the market.

RAN Scheduler: The scheduler function in the RAN allows for managing the radio resources by providing grants for transmitting and receiving packets over the air by the different users and applications active for the individual user. This section addresses the aspects of a typical RAN scheduler implementation. It also suggests the knobs that would be good to make available, along with the scheduler properties that they invoke and the performance implications. The scheduler realizes different priority levels based on the QoS associated with the applications supporting guaranteed bitrates, throughputs, delays, jitter, and packet error rates, while retaining fairness across the different users and flows. Accommodations are made to support different classes of users, including enterprise users and inbound roaming users, as well as macro network offloads when the private network also supports an NHN. The caveats of downlink and uplink scheduling are also addressed.

RAN Intelligent Controller (RIC): Artificial intelligence/machine learning (AI/ML) is actively being employed to address optimizations in many fields, and it is an active area of research ongoing in several wireless standards forums, including 3GPP and O-RAN. Private networks lend themselves more to predictable patterns of behavior on services used, including the time of day and day of the week, which are custom to the individual enterprises and even localized to specific locations within a given enterprise. The types of verticals in private networks are numerous, and tuning them individually will not allow for a scalable solution. Employing AI/ML for both the RAN and certain aspects of the core networks is becoming essential. These learnings can potentially be applied to macro networks as well, including transitions across macro and private networks. With distributed antenna systems (DAS) used for in-building deployment of private networks using licensed spectrum by managed service providers (MSPs), a role many current Macro Network Operator (MNOs) are taking on, the learnings for such solutions together with operations with shared spectrum use will provide ample room for optimizations using AI/ML. The metrics collection with the Network Data Analytics Function (NWDAF) (5G network data analytics function) and the integration of the RIC operations with the metrics collected from both the UE reports and network nodes are discussed as the starting point for data collection to enable the AI/ML functions to be developed for RAN and core network and operations, administration, and management (OAM) optimizations. The RIC discussed in this chapter is a framework that can be employed, and the insights gained across private network verticals, with typical models developed through learnings potentially across participating network and UE vendors, will allow for significantly improved private network operations.

Enterprise RAN Slice: Effective management of radio resources is a key aspect that differentiates the different network solutions. Functionally, this is realized by the RAN scheduler implementation. Even in macro networks, there are different tiers of users (e.g. gold, silver, bronze) that require RAN resources to be prioritized based on the user group. This is typically managed by supporting different weights applied to the scheduling function of the individual groups. In private networks, the RAN resources, based on the supported functions, need to be shared among enterprise users, enterprise visitors, and NHN users offloaded from the macro networks. Even within each of these categories, there will be different grades of users, and the resources will be appropriately made available based on the category of the user. With different entities establishing contracts, there is a notion of reserving a finite amount of resource availability to be guaranteed. This chapter suggests the aspects involved in regulating the RAN resources, the criteria that need to be considered to retain fairness while optimally using the RAN resources, and suggests an implementation that can achieve these goals while avoiding rigid resource allocations. This allows for capitalizing on the user population from different categories and the types of traffic exchanged.

Self-organizing Networks (SON): Self-organizing networks (SON) is a broad notion referencing approaches used to partition radio resource allocation among the different radio nodes in the system, as well as tuning the operational parameters. The primary resource that is required to be managed is the spectrum allocation. In private networks, small cells are used and require orthogonal frequency allocation across the neighboring cells to avoid inter-cell and cross-link interference. A graph algorithm is typically used for this purpose, and a brief introduction to graph theory is provided here, along with the optimization problem addressed using this approach. A typical illustration of a private network deployment, including the indoor and outdoor cells that will be deployed, is shown, highlighting the overlapping regions and the need for orthogonal frequency allocation. In the CBRS system, users (network deployments) interact with the central entity, the spectrum access system (SAS), to dynamically acquire spectrum for individual sites in a private network deployment. This is a more complex system, and the procedures described for SON will be much simpler with static allocations of spectrum provided for a campus to operate its private network. The chapter describes the procedures for balancing the spectrum allocations once the allowed set of channels for individual cells is provided by the SAS. Power allocations can be adapted, but it tends to be very complex to determine the interference level at the SAS, and hence the actual spectrum that can be allocated. Therefore, a fixed power is used for both indoor and outdoor cells in these computations. The TDD patterns for identifying the DL and UL slots also determine the system behaviors. Apart from these, there are other RAN operational parameters that are managed as part of the SON procedures but are not directly covered in this chapter.

Fractional Frequency Reuse (FFR) Techniques: This chapter covers the concept of FFR. There are several network configurations where FFR can be used, although it initially began with the sharing of the spectrum between a macro cell and a set of small cells within the same footprint, and even between two macro cells. With the increasing scarcity of shared spectrum usage for private networks and the shifting load across the small cells, the dynamic rebalancing of the resources can play a key role in meeting the SLO/SLA requirements for a given enterprise. This chapter introduces the different variants of the FFR. The rebalancing of resources when a higher-tier user claims the spectrum in the CBRS spectrum and tiered user levels is discussed, as is the need to leverage FFR. A scheduler-based approach to handle FFR is discussed as a proposal. The concept of inter-cell interference cancellation (ICIC) is also introduced.

Cellular Core Network

Converged Core: Traditionally, the core network refers to the functions that are not part of the radio network. With the advent of cloud computing, edge computing, multi-access edge computing (MEC), and the more recent evolution of the Telco cloud and open RAN, the functions supported in a core platform now feature a wide range of varying configurations. Like RAN functions, the separation of control and user plane functions also applies to the core network. This section details the converged core's functional constitution and provides a view into its architectural variants. The 4G EPC and 5GC architectures and detailed interface interconnects are discussed. Given that these functions can be realized in software and run on generic compute, the grouping of the EPC and 5GC functions and nodes to run them can be supported in a converged core and scaled to the demands of each enterprise. The evolution from the 4G networks to the 5G networks is illustrated with consideration of the functional grouping involved. Some of the key concepts of slices, QoS, Traffic Detection Function (TDF), framed routes, and other such topics are explicitly treated. The core–RAN interconnect is fundamental to the nature of traffic management, with enterprise deployments supporting LTE-only, NR-only, and LTE + NR systems that accommodate both NSA mode and SA modes of operation.

Network Interfaces: This section covers the protocol stacks used for the different interfaces for both LTE/EPC and 5G NR/5GC networks. The connectivity between the radio nodes eNB/gNB and the packet core network is described. The individual interfaces between the nodes within the packet core networks are presented, providing justifications for the protocols used where relevant. The end-to-end information exchange for signaling and user plane traffic is shown for completeness. The LTE/EPC and 5G NR/5GC are discussed independently. However, as described in the converged core section, the network functions and interfaces are integrated for a combined implementation while retaining the integrity of the individual interfaces. This section focuses on the protocol stack used for information exchange across the interfaces. The 5G NR/5GC network is presented, assuming the context introduced for LTE/EPC, and the evolution of the 5G NR/5GC networks is presented, providing the reasoning behind the choices being made. 5GC inter-function information exchange is significantly simplified, given that HTTP/2 is used as a generic definition for protocol structure, with the information exchange performed using JavaScript Object Notation (JSON), making the interactions among these nodes generic and allowing for significant reuse in the implementations.

Security: Connectivity with public MNO networks requires high security to ensure that the users are authenticated and authorized for connectivity. For enterprise private network connectivity, both the user credential authentication and the access into the enterprise network need to be protected, and even more attention to detail is needed to avoid any breaches with the introduction of 4G/5G networks. Given that 4G/5G networks are supported in an enterprise in addition to other forms of connectivity, including Wi-Fi, this creates another surface of attack. The tenets of zero trust from National Institute of Standards and Technology (NIST) are presented, and the details of the 3GPP-defined security procedure that meets these goals are presented. The procedures for primary authentication for associating with the 4G/5G networks are covered, and the use of secondary authentication for further verification of the user connectivity into specific domains of the enterprises is presented. The deployment and interconnection of the network functions with secure connectivity, including the location and relocation of the functions to accommodate proximity to the RAN node and dynamic loading, are discussed. The network slice uses the isolation of the traffic types to allow for increased security in the core, and enterprise applications are also addressed. The security key derivations for the different network nodes to use for the individual user and the dynamic refresh of the key, while retaining the persistent context in the home authenticating network and the visited networks, are covered. A comparison with the Wi-Fi security and the methods of integrating the 3GPP security nodes of HSS/UDM with the Wi-Fi Remote Authentication Dial-In User Service (RADIUS) server for unified credential management is suggested.

Network Slices: At a high level, network slices are nothing but resource allocation into the appropriate IP domain in the different hops of the network, from the enterprise core to the radio nodes, and including the over-the-air traffic scheduling for each admitted UE data flow to meet their QoS guarantees.

The definition and resource allocation are more focused on the core network and do not directly involve the RAN network. The RAN is impacted indirectly based on the QoS flows and their associated QCIs that need to be supported within the network slice. The realization of these network slices is the subject addressed in this section. A brief introduction to the QoS mechanisms defined in 3GPP is provided, and the network slice concept is discussed as an extension to the QoS realization to support packet prioritization and isolation in the different hops of the private network. The actual realization of the QoS guarantees is typically implementation-specific and has requirements that need to be met at both the RAN and EPC/5GC enterprise core, as well as at the node interconnects, including the routers, bridges, and interface cards supporting the transportation of the packets between the UE and the far-end service, including the enterprise application servers. The individual sections of the RAN and core network in the book provide suggestive approaches that should sufficiently point the reader in the right direction, apart from motivating aspects that need to be considered as part of the realization. The chapter also ties together the pieces of QoS, network slice, RAN slice, and VLAN association to enable enterprise applications, users, and QoS flow in a private network.

Neutral Host Networks

Neutral Host Network: The fundamental concept of an NHN is enabled by sharing a network deployment across users of all types and subscriptions without requiring explicit roaming agreements and supporting direct camping. Sharing comes in different forms for a given campus network. This can be passive, without requiring active or dynamic management (e.g. tower, rooftop, power, cabinets, lighting, air conditioning). The more interesting form is active sharing, which adapts to real-time conditions and the user population demanding access to the network. Active sharing involves the sharing of antennas, access networks, transmission, spectrum, Radio Frequency (RF) design/planning, core networks, and air conditioning. Our focus in this chapter is to cover a specific form of active sharing, which is NHN. A lack of seamless mobile coverage and poor user experience is common in many indoor venues. It requires a business arrangement for the macro network operators to allow for their network identifiers to be broadcast on the NHN. This allows generic users to enter in-building scenarios and leverage this NHN coverage extension without having to leave the building or obtain other explicit subscription to access the enterprise-deployed network. The enterprise users may be provisioned with private network credentials, as well as with devices supporting dual-SIM operations with both macro network and enterprise network credentials. The goal is to achieve five-bar service from a radio perspective and support sufficient user throughput/capacity to allow for seamless operations across the macro, NHN, and private networks for different services. This chapter motivates the need for NHNs and suggests ways to leverage enterprise deployments of private networks for neutral host operation, addressing coverage and capacity issues currently seen with macro network deployments, particularly for in-building scenarios.

Admission and Congestion Control: Traditional admission control for individual users/services is done using static resource reservations. This typically involves allocating the maximum resource needs associated with a given service. Depending on the algorithm of choice and the headroom allocated for variability in the services, it either overestimates or underestimates network capacity planning. Resource reservations are typically made only for Guaranteed Bitrate (GBR) bearers (QoS flows with guaranteed bitrates), in addition to the resource reservations made for common channel operations for both DL and UL. Any leftover resources during scheduling are taken up by the non-GBR bearers, and the users/flows are proportionally served in real time. There are several other techniques for admission and congestion control that are well known and employed based on the scheduler metrics and the associated thresholds that are targeted to be met. This chapter focuses more on the enterprise networks, both private and NHNs and suggests some possible optimizations that can be considered for implementation. Individual campus deployments have a lot of variability. These include campus types: carpeted/non-carpeted, types of users, types of services, times of usage, expected service levels, device types, and types of partnerships, including interworking with MNO networks. Several of these behaviors can be learned for optimized performance and may even extend to demand-based pricing. The goal is to manage system loading dynamically, adjusting admission/congestion control based on real-time analytics. This chapter covers some suggested approaches on managing the users with macro network subscriptions to transition across the macro and NHN networks while being aware of the coverage and loading conditions of the two networks.

Nonpublic Networks: An NPN is a 5G system (5GS) deployed for non-public use (see 3GPP TS 22.261). This definition of NPN in 3GPP was intended to address the enterprise network deployments. Inasmuch as the enterprise private networks are enabled for neutral host operation to support macro network users, the macro networks can be utilized to service the enterprise's needs. In fact, one of the key envisioned use cases of network slices is to enable the macro network to support connectivity into the enterprise networks. Given the momentum for enterprise networks in the market and the lack of availability of 3GPP Rel-16-based UEs, where the NPN feature is defined, the LTE and NR private networks were based on the 3GPP Rel-15 procedures. This has been fairly sufficient to address the needs of the market, and we are now at a point where deliberations are ongoing on the benefits of introducing the Rel-16 NPN procedures. The Rel-16 features are required to allow for a macro network to be utilized to provide service to an enterprise, which could include using the large macro network cells or explicitly deployed smaller cells on campuses, using both shared and licensed spectrum by the macro network operators. In this chapter, we will go through the basic definition of NPN, the network architectures, the identifiers used, and the UE behaviors in discovering, camping, and operating on these networks.

Device Provisioning: For LTE and NR private networks, given that the end-user devices that operate on the macro network needs to be leveraged, the same type of credentials need to be provisioned in these devices, and the corresponding authentication information must be stored in the EPC/5GC in the network. The existing procedures for (e)SIM credential management are repurposed for this. However, a major obstacle needs to be addressed when supporting the functions used for macro networks to be applied to private networks. The credential management system for macro networks is typically geared up to handle millions of users, and even when supporting specific classes of users for a macro network operator, the number of users tends to run into the millions for each of those categories. Some tricks are needed to allow this toolkit to scale for enterprises of different sizes, ranging from a few dozen users to a few tens of thousands of users. There are also enterprise-specific identifiers that may need to be accommodated when distributing the credentials to ensure that the end-user devices attempt access on known networks where valid attach/registration is possible. The different methods of Subscriber Identity/Identification Module (SIM) credentials provisioning and the associated use case scenarios are discussed. Note that, apart from the SIM credential provisioning and distribution using Mobile Data Management (MDM), certificate-based credentials for supporting TLS/TTLS-based authentication and integration with the campus RADIUS server are also possible. These certificates can be stored in the SIM or in a secure location on the device.

Part III Enterprise Applications: This section of the book takes typical use cases and details the aspects that need to be considered for each of these deployment verticals. There are several industry verticals that want to introduce private networks, with each solving a different set of problems. Special types of networks that accommodate atypical devices like autonomous guided vehicles (AGVs) and headless devices like IoT and security video cameras exist, and based on traffic and mobility type, network designs need to be planned for support. Based on the type of network, coexisting with Wi-Fi may be required to support seamless mobility across LTE, NR, and Wi-Fi networks deployed on the same enterprise campus. It is possible for Wi-Fi to be simultaneously connected with LTE/NR, and maintaining service continuity without breaks becomes a primary aspect to address apart from throughput augmentation. Roaming across independently deployed private networks may need to be supported.

IIoT Protocols: There are several industrial implementations dating back several decades. Starting with the wired connectivity, it is evolving into more flexible wireless connectivity. The protocol realizations and the reliability maintenance with the wireless connectivity are also evolving together with it. This chapter introduces the communication protocols, the connectivity methods, a unified architecture, and a framework for reliable data exchange in industrial and automation systems. The subsequent chapter discusses the mechanisms of integrating these protocols into a 5G LAN private network.

This chapter addresses the protocols relevant to IIoT deployments. Based on the 5GACIA and ISA-95 standards bodies, there is a lot of convergence in the protocols suggested for use in the industrial environment. Many lingering protocols from the 1970s and 1980s are implemented and actively used even today. These are not going to be replaced overnight and will require coexisting with private network support, potentially integrated at some level.

IIoT with DetNet and TSN: 3GPP specified 5G support for Time Sensitive Network (TSN) in Release 16, with further enhancements in Release 17, to allow seamless integration of a 5GS with TSN networks. In integrated networks like this, a 5G system will be perceived as IEEE-compliant virtual Ethernet-TSN bridges. 3GPP TS 22.104 and IEC/IEEE 60802 have described many important industrial automation use cases. The specification discusses the integration of 5G with TSN for typical industrial use cases, namely control-to-control, control-to-device, and device-to-compute communications. Industrial automation applications include safety light curtains to protect areas, AGVs/mobile robots, discrete manufacturing and process automation, and the coordination of multiple controllers for a task to be executed together. More advanced use cases of a camera assisted robot arm-based sorting, with image reconstruction for 3D analysis for AGV mobility. This can be supported as a control-to-controller function or controller-to-device function. Although the relevant pieces of the technology definitions exist, there are still gaps in terms of what is achievable relative to the actual demands of the IIoT. Deterministic networks (DetNet) bring us a little closer to allowing for the integration of communication technology (CT), IT, and operational technology (OP) to meet the requirements. The ISA-95 standards body defines these aspects. This chapter discusses the integration of these IIoT protocols with the 5G system.

Private Network Verticals: This chapter goes over several of the typical private network verticals and addresses the aspects that need to be considered for each. I have used a use case model to provide the relevant context for each of the private network verticals, along with some examples. For some of these verticals, additional solutions need to be put in place, and where relevant, these approaches are discussed. Some of these can be customized using the existing standards, while others require standardization for solutions that can be applied across the industry. The required performance criteria to measure and manage are identified for the individual verticals. Some key technological concepts are highlighted for the verticals from Part I and Part II in case the reader wishes to review them. This chapter describes some of the known verticals supported by private networks. By no means are private network applications to be limited to these verticals. This is a fast-evolving field, and service demands for these verticals will only grow, including the emergence of other creative verticals in the market. The use cases of ad hoc networks, campus emergencies, big-box retail, collaborating organizations, conference centers, educational institutions, and offices are covered as some exemplary verticals.

Looking Ahead: Private networks are one of the key growth areas for wireless communications. This book has detailed the fundamentals of LTE and NR systems, covered the key technological aspects involved in deploying private networks, and illustrated some potential use cases and industry verticals that are currently in play. All this is very much in its infancy and will rapidly evolve as the demands of the market change. This chapter provides some leading thoughts on where the standards and the industry are heading and includes pointers for where the reader can pursue further investigations. The spectrum aspects, AI/ML, and some potential use case evolutions, including private network integration, digital twins, the Metaverse, and the use of blockchains, are discussed. With costs for these deployments being a primary driver, aspects of commoditizing LTE and NR devices in both the network and end-user devices are presented.

Acknowledgments

I am profoundly grateful to the many individuals whose support, insights, and dedication have brought this book to life.

To my esteemed colleagues at Qualcomm, Ericsson, ViaSat, Celona, and Apple, both past and present – your deep technical discussions, invaluable feedback, and unwavering support have shaped my understanding and fueled my passion for wireless technologies throughout my career. I would like to especially thank the team at Celona, where I worked on private networks, and extend my gratitude to Celona's CTO, Mehmet Yavuz, and CEO, Rajeev Shah, for allowing me to be part of their journey on private networks. I learned a lot through the process.I am also very grateful for my interactions with the team at Apple, where I received excellent support in making end-user device-based improvements to support private network operations. I am also thankful for the colleagues I subsequently joined and now work alongside. I appreciate my manager at Apple, Sree Vallath, for his support and for allowing me to pursue writing this book while working at Apple.

I extend my sincerest gratitude to the members of standards organizations OnGo Alliance, WInnForum, MFA, Small Cell Forum, 3GPP, GSMA, and 5GACIA. Your keen interest in my contributions, commitment to enhancing and refining them, and our strong collaboration and friendships have been instrumental in transforming theoretical concepts into practical, viable solutions for private networks. I am grateful for your professionalism, the insights you have shared with me, and the strong friendships we have built. A special thanks to the OnGo Alliance and WInnForum teams for pursuing such forward-looking and innovative spectrum sharing and management within the CBRS band, paving the way for private networks. I would also like to acknowledge the SAS vendors, Google and Federated Wireless, for defining and enabling the market with their products for spectrum sharing across the United States, distilling a complex problem into a viable approach. Your collective efforts have not only enriched my professional journey but also significantly contributed to advancing wireless communications.

I also want to thank my wife, Shubha, and my son, Suraj, for their support and for bringing out the best in me. I am deeply grateful for conversations with my mom, who provided me with constant guidance, kept me motivated throughout the process, and reminded me of how my dad would have approached it.

I would also like to acknowledge Kavipria Ramachandran, Sandra Grayson, and Becky Cowan at Wiley for their guidance and continuous support in refining the book and helping me get it published.

Thank you to all the colleagues I have worked with over the years. Your collective efforts have not only enriched my professional journey but have also significantly contributed to advancing wireless communications as a whole.

Thank you for your collaboration, encouragement, and tireless dedication.
Warm regards,
Srinivasan Balasubramanian

Introduction

Welcome!

There are several books that cover 4G long-term evolution (LTE) and 5G new radio (NR) in great technical depth, providing the architecture and features as defined in the 3rd Generation Partnership Project (3GPP) standards. A single book is not sufficient to capture all the concepts from both 4G LTE and 5G NR wireless systems, given the immense nuances added to the specifications to allow for extracting the maximum capacity while enabling the individual end-user devices to perform optimally in these networks.

There are books that provide information on Wi-Fi as a technology along with its evolution. There are also books that cover enterprise network management, which is centered on Wi-Fi deployments as well as the Internet protocol (IP) domain, security, and user credential management. This is fairly entrenched area with several areas and levels of certification courses to allow individuals to become accustomed to designing, deploying, and managing Wi-Fi networks.

The compute resources are evolving, and there is a shift toward using generic off-the-shelf hardware where possible and using the customized solutions with hardening only where such generic compute cannot be directly utilized. There is also a trend toward network compute resource evolution, including cloud-based deployments, which is modifying the nature of the network deployments. There are generic cloud-level software designs that are common knowledge now. Each cloud platform offers a suite of services along with documentation and training to leverage these capabilities efficiently.

With the current trend of private networks with 4G LTE and 5G NR networks gaining traction, there is a significant gap in bringing the concepts of all these domains together. The revolution driving this shift in enterprise connectivity to enable improved operations is fundamental. Although in-building small cell deployments are already enabled, primarily through distributed antenna system (DAS) solutions, these were extensions to macro networks. Leveraging 4G/5G connectivity for enterprise operations allows for support increased reliability, enabling applications that cannot be immediately realized only using Wi-Fi solutions. Augmenting with the 4G/5G-based solutions has become very compelling, even for basic applications like internet/intranet packet connectivity, and is no longer seen as a luxury that is required only for specialized applications.

I hope to bridge these gaps by distilling the key aspects of information by demystifying the foundational technological aspects, and building on these foundations to address the aspects needed for enterprise networks. I have tried a simpler representation, focusing on the crux needed to understand the context without dwelling on every minute detail. The intent is to allow the reader to obtain sufficient knowledge of the concepts to both understand the bounds of a 4G/5G enterprise network systems and be equipped to tackle any of the design or deployment scenarios involved. In that regard, the attempt is to hit the right level of technical depth, providing sufficient understanding of the technological concepts and the problem domains to focus on for an enterprise private network.

Where possible, figures are used for representation and have minimally provided the required context surrounding the view graph. The pictures have a lot of details captured, and it is quite possible that the reader may not be able to absorb all the information represented in the individual pictures in a single read. The intent is to allow for gaining an initial understanding first, and the reader, upon further revisiting, may gain additional insights.

The book is focused on explaining the concepts, and the performance studies are not covered. The required performance aspects that can be conducted are captured in the individual areas where relevant. Many of the performance aspects are not very different from the attributes of a macro network except for two key aspects: first, the small cell deployment, both indoor and outdoor, within an enterprise campus, and second, the core network integration with the enterprise core and the use of the localized computing to support enterprise application services. The required performance criteria tend to be specific to each enterprise, and service agreements need to be in place to collect the required metrics to determine if the defined key performance indicators (KPIs) associated with the individual enterprise applications are met.

Although end-user device levels are required to accommodate enterprise private networks, from a wireless technology layers perspective, leveraging the existing realizations of device operation for macro network operations is required given that the private network ecosystem is not sufficiently mature and the volumes are small enough not to demand independent configuration. Apart from describing the air interfaces as introductory foundation material, the book focuses on network functions, particularly from the 4G LTE and 5G NR network infrastructure support needed.

Given that Wi-Fi deployments in enterprise markets are quite commonplace now, the book tries to demystify the 4G/5G aspects, allowing the reader to treat these wireless technologies like Wi-Fi in terms of the simplicity while retaining the required complexity to gain from the sophistication offered by the 4G/5G wireless systems.

The standards bodies have provided definitions for small cells, flexible radio access network (RAN) architectures, neutral host networks (NHNs), non-public networks (NPNs), and several other aspects. All of this is still in the preliminary stages, and as more of the market realization of the enterprise private networks progresses, typical problems will become visible, requiring the specifications to address viable solutions. The solutions required may be specific to private networks, and explicit solutions for operations with such networks will likely be necessary and required in the future. In the meantime, some proprietary realizations, potentially with some sub-optimality, may happen and cannot be avoided.

Providing the foundations and bringing together the technological framework will not be sufficient without providing practical ways to use this information for typical deployments. With that in mind, the typical industry verticals that are currently using enterprise private networks are captured in the book.

Given that the focus of the book will be on infrastructure, it will be good to define it at a high level. Infrastructure is a combination of hardware and software components that make up the enterprise campus deployment, including the radio nodes, core network functions, and the compute platforms such as servers, storage, network devices, virtual local area network (VLAN) or virtual eXtensible local area network (VxLAN), application services, firewalls, routers, bridges, etc. As part of the infrastructure, it also needs to support device provisioning to allow for access management and policy enforcement by enterprise information technology (IT). Orchestration to manage the network nodes with both localized and central control for the enterprise IT, the network vendor, and the managed service provider is necessary to monitor the real-time operations of the system and adjust the parameterizations to adapt the network conditions for viable use of the system. Automation of these functions, where possible, should be planned given the need for scalability. Employing lessons from one deployment in other deployment scenarios, together with the use of artificial intelligence (AI), is required to better manage and optimize the network operations.

Enterprise architecture design and implementation is not a one-time event but rather an ongoing iterative process. Even at initial deployment, proposals are made and adjusted both prior to and after installation. Depending on the enterprise, extensive acceptance tests may need to be performed prior to launch. After deployment, constant monitoring of the network is required to ensure the proper operations and determine if the required service-level objectives (SLOs) are met. Enterprise requirements change over time, and the network must be adaptable enough to predict and dynamically accommodate such changes. Typically, the complexity of the use cases increases as time progresses, and network upgrades to support these scenarios will be required. Traceability will be key to the process and customer satisfaction.

Enterprise networks are deployed as a service offering that includes everything from radio frequency (RF) planning, core network deployment, enterprise IT integration, deployment of the node, spectrum management, and eventually managing the quality of service (QoS) requirements of the enterprise application. The network is designed to meet the specific criteria of the individual enterprises, and a solution offering is made to the enterprise as a proposal. The enterprise network is designed more as network-as-a-service (NaaS), and the process involves defining an adaptable solution architecture. Modular and reusable solutions are assumed to be fundamental for scalability and adaptability. The process starts by identifying business requirements, including determining the value streams associated with the business functions. The network is designed by putting together the required nodes and functions to bring together a viable solution. The technology choice becomes key, and it is important not to rush to the latest and greatest to avoid overdesigning the solution proposal. Putting together the relevant documentation and management framework through the orchestration layers is essential to avoid the enterprise from giving up on the operations of the deployed solution.

Figure 1 illustrates a set of functions that need to be supported in an enterprise private network. The figure is shown as a jigsaw puzzle to highlight the complex set of pieces that need to fit together to form the system. This is also not the exhaustive set of functions needed but is more exemplary of what is required. All this can be daunting to grasp. The intent of the book (hopefully) is that the reader will be able to gather all the pieces involved and bring them together to form a complete picture – ideally, without having to cut corners!

The book is divided into three parts.

Part I covers the 4G and 5G wireless technology aspects, providing the required foundation putting the reader in the required frame of mind on the type of wireless systems involved and how to leverage their strengths. Both the radio and core network aspects are addressed. There is a rich body of literature that covers the LTE and NR fundamentals in great detail. The intent in this section is to capture the various aspects in sufficient detail, allowing the reader to grasp the concepts without being overwhelmed. It is a balance and trade-off that I have chosen regarding the topics and level of depth to keep the reader engaged. This is a starting point, hopefully with sufficient representation, and is not intended to be a complete reference to the LTE and NR-based systems. Note that the private networks deployed employ all of these aspects described, and the context provided should mostly be sufficient to design, deploy, and manage private networks.

Figure 1 Enterprise private network functions are like a jigsaw puzzle.

There are other surrounding aspects, including interfacing with the system and other enabling functions. Some of these functions, as they apply to the enterprise private network, are implicitly brought about in Part II discussions on the individual topics discussed. Part I also provides a set of standards bodies, their working group structures, and the relevant (key) specifications. The reader should visit these sites, given that the specifications are constantly evolving, and newer and more detailed information can be obtained by directly reviewing the specifications. The focus is to highlight the standards bodies, working forums, and specifications that are relevant for private networks. Additionally, the specific additions made for private networks are also captured. The topics covered in Part I of the book are captured in Figure 2.

Part II of the book builds on the foundation provided by Part I. The topics covered in Part II are depicted in Figure 3.

RAN aspects are covered, starting with the private network spectrum, which really started this technological wave of private network deployments. Citizen Broadband Radio Service (CBRS) shared band of operation in the United States of America (USA), which started the effort in 2016, is an initial foray into shared spectrum use that is being mimicked across the globe now. CBRS has more dynamic aspects with tiered services that is very advanced in its dynamic spectrum sharing ability used in the USA, while the rest of the world is currently starting off with a more static allocation of spectrum. Although part of the spectrum, given the leading-edge procedures for handling dynamic spectrum sharing with common arbiters and tiered usage, this requires explicit treatment and is captured in an independent chapter. The small cell has significant restrictions both from an RF and a compute resource perspective, and specific choices are required to be included in the RAN scheduler to accommodate such an environment. The RAN intelligent controller (RIC), together with AI concepts, allows for more sophisticated RAN optimization algorithms to be supported through learning and adaptations that cater to individual enterprise network demands. Given that the RAN resource will need to accommodate diverse types of users on an enterprise network, notwithstanding the neutral host users, RAN slicing allows for better resource allocation and addresses meeting the required SLO. Apart from obtaining the requisite spectrum, the allocation of the spectrum to individual access points in the enterprise network needs to be managed to avoid interference, and this is achieved using self-organizing networks (SONs) realizations.

The cellular core network concepts forming the converged fourth generation evolved packet core (EPC) and fifth generation core (5GC) are discussed, along with an illustration of the individual nodes and functions of the EPC and 5GC. The key network interfaces supporting inter-node interactions are discussed. Security is a key function, and this section discusses the zero trust (ZT) aspects, showing how the 4G and, even more so, the 5G network function definitions bring it closer to full ZT realization. Network slices allow for isolations which provide security and also allow for addressing QoS functions from the core network, avoiding congestion when required. NHN is a key function that allows the macro network operators (MNOs) to extend their footprint to in-building scenarios and potentially offload, enabling users to experience improved coverage in weak and no-coverage scenarios for a given MNO. The NHN function, improved camping with geofencing, is presented as a potential forward-looking concept. NPN allows MNOs to provide in-building service using their network for enterprises to leverage without having to deploy their own networks. The different industrial internet-of-things (IIoT) protocols and their applications for a factory are covered. Significant benefits are already being seen with its use in different industrial environments. However, given that each situation has a distinct set of aspects that need to be addressed, significant interactions are required between the network vendor and the industrial manufacturing entity to deploy and manage the network to see the eventual benefits from the use of such deployments. Device provisioning is a key aspect that impacts all enterprises, and careful

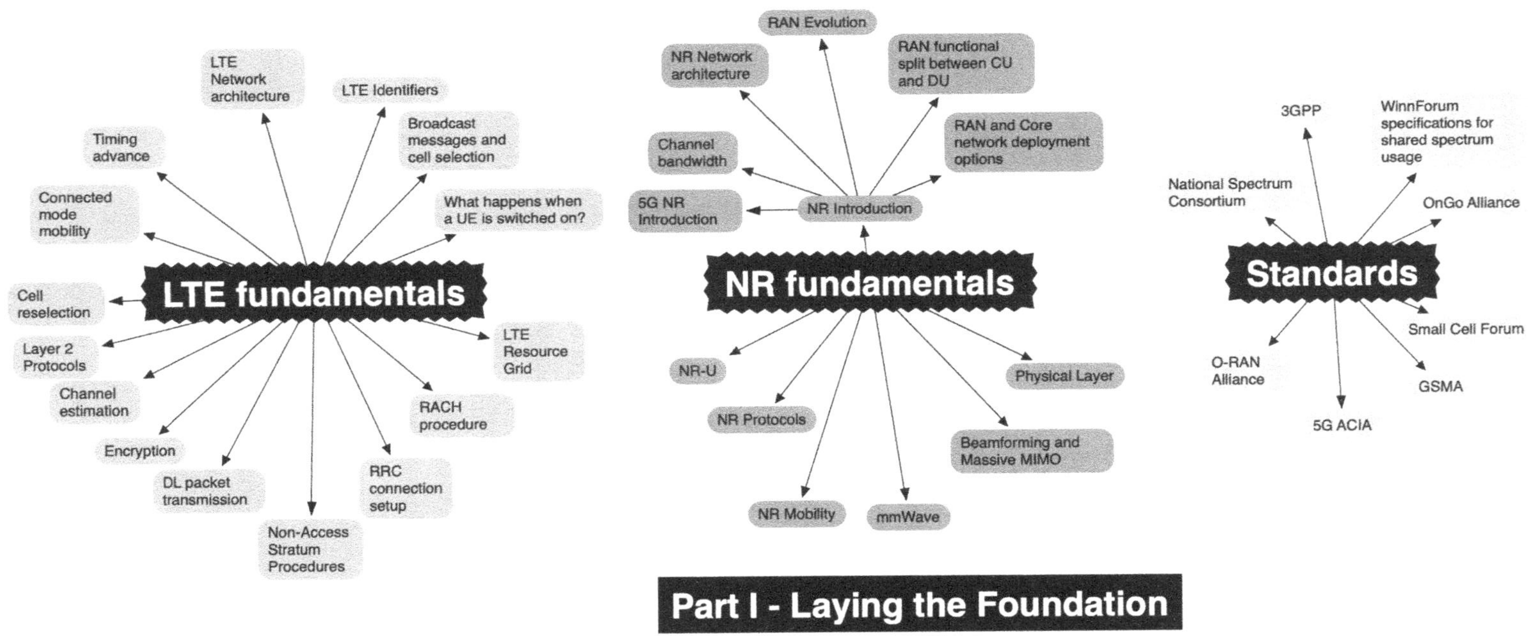

Figure 2 Part I: Laying the foundation.

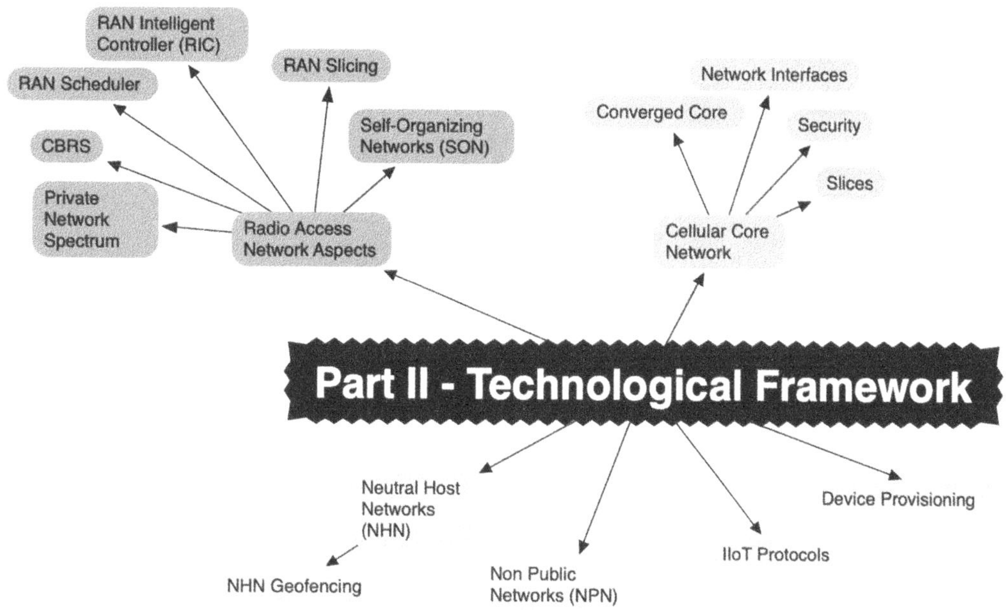

Figure 3 Part II: Technological framework.

management of subscriptions and policies, along with exposure functions to allow enterprise-level enforcements, is fundamental for any deployment.

Part III takes typical use cases and details the aspects that need to be considered for each of these deployment verticals. There are several industry verticals that want to introduce private networks, each solving different problems. Special types of networks that accommodate atypical devices like autonomous guided vehicles (AGVs) and headless devices like IoT devices and security video cameras exist, and based on traffic and mobility type, network designs need to be planned for support. Based on the type of network, coexisting with Wi-Fi may be required to support seamless mobility across LTE, NR, and Wi-Fi networks deployed on the same enterprise campus. It is possible for Wi-Fi to be simultaneously connected with LTE/NR, and maintaining service continuity without breaks becomes a primary aspect to address, apart from throughput augmentation. Roaming across independently deployed private networks may need to be supported. The topics covered in Part III of the book are captured in Figure 4.

Enterprise private networks are both a technology and a movement. The technology leverages the definition of 4G/5G systems already provided by the different standards bodies, with 3GPP as the main entity driving that forward. The definitions were mainly focused on macro networks. Further extensions to handle smaller enterprise networks were needed, and that is happening in several standards bodies now. Small cells have been around for a while; however, these were intended to be managed and operated by the MNOs, and there was little incentive to provide good indoor or ubiquitous coverage. For larger buildings, a very costly DAS-based solution is used, and DAS continues to have traction due to the use of licensed spectrum, but these are high-maintenance and costly networks to deploy.

Central to the movement are the shared spectrum allocations. They allow for both smaller footprint allocations and dynamic modifications to the allocations. The adaptations can be based on both deployed networks and the services and types of users supported by these networks.

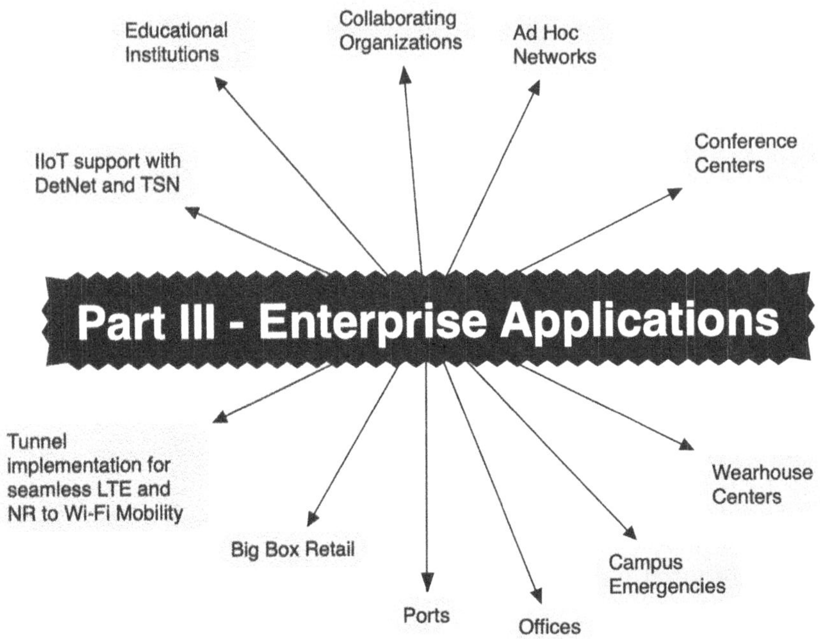

Figure 4 Part III: Enterprise applications.

All this started with the CBRS spectrum definitions for shared use established by the U.S. Government Federal Communications Commission (FCC): https://www.fcc.gov/wireless/bureau-divisions/mobility-division/35-ghz-band/35-ghz-band-overview. It allowed the incumbents to continue to use the spectrum and, given the sparse use, demand for the channel only when needed. Local (countywide) licensed allocation is supported while still leaving room for generic lightly licensed (unlicensed with authorization from a central entity) access. This allowed individual enterprises to not just rely on Wi-Fi but take the sophistication such as reliable QoS offered by 4G/5G networks, into their campuses and retain control on the operations of the network. This fundamentally changed the dynamics of the market.

From its initial start in 2016, it took several years to both define and deploy the framework involved to manage across the entire country of the USA for dynamic spectrum allocation in a localized manner. Once in place, enterprise private networks have become the primary greenfield deployments supporting the growth of 4G/5G networks.

The evolution is primarily on the network side, reusing the existing market-supported 4G/5G end-user devices. They are currently based on 3GPP Release 15, which seems to address the current market demands for private networks. Given that, this book focuses on highlighting the technological aspects driving the private network deployments using the 3GPP Release 15 as a baseline and further augmented by the specification definitions from other standards bodies that leverage the 3GPP definitions. The Release 16 and beyond context are also described, providing the relevant context for the reader to track the potential evolution path(s) for private networks, although these features are not being absorbed for private network deployments.

There are several specialized devices, including AGV, video surveillance, and industrial devices, that are being supported with 4G/5G and have already seen significant performance benefits, enabling use cases never before possible. Several improvements to device modem operations to efficiently find and camp on these enterprise networks are introduced. With further market adoption, there is potential for significant improvements to be considered from both the network and the end-user devices, which will follow a natural evolution process.

Throughout the book, I have used figures to illustrate the concepts being discussed and have chosen not to explicitly describe all associated details in textual form for brevity. Adequate context for the individual pictures is provided to enable understanding of the figures. Hopefully, it is easier to make a quick pass through the material, and I request the reader to revisit the figures for a possible deeper understanding.

It should be exciting to watch what the next few years bring to the field of enterprise private networks!

Part I

Laying the Foundation

I.1

LTE Fundamentals

I.1.1 Introduction

Long-term evolution forms the basis for 4G wireless networks. The fundamentals captured in the chapter equally apply to macro networks as much as to private networks. The current private networks are deployed based on 3GPP Release-15 as the baseline and use the existing user equipment (UE) without modifications, relying on the devices already deployed in the market. The use of existing end-user devices for private network operation is a necessity for quicker adoption of the private networks, and mandating specialized devices will be impractical. The number of devices available in the market for macro networks is numerous, and the users mainly purchase the devices for connectivity with the macro networks and will implicitly expect the private network to host these devices. Developing specialized devices will also be cost-ineffective due to the volume involved, and no individual enterprise will be able to finance the development of such devices.

Evolved Universal Mobile Telecommunications System (UMTS) terrestrial radio access (E-UTRAN) refers to fourth-generation wireless technology defined by the third-generation partnership project (3GPP). It is the radio access network (RAN) of LTE, which is the standard for 4G wireless communication. The intent of the LTE fundamentals chapter and the New Radio (NR) fundamentals chapters is to expound on the basics involved in 4G/5G technology, which is the main goal of Part I of this book. Sufficient focus is provided to the relevant topics, and these underlying concepts will, in some form, directly or indirectly, be required for private network design and deployment.

The basis for private network deployments is the fundamentals explained here. Without this knowledge, deploying private networks will not be possible. Except for the footprint sizes and use of indoor and outdoor cells accounting for multipath in the Radio Frequency (RF) signals, the behavior must mimic the macro network operations. Note that the distributed antenna solutions (DAS) used as indoor solutions leverage the LTE/NR specifications as is, which is the same for small cells.

The private network market has been kindled by the advent of shared spectrum and localized spectrum allocation rather than nationwide spectrum grants. Independent of the type of spectrum used, the behavior of the LTE and NR systems remains the same, whether in macro networks that are based on large cells (~10 km [about 6.21 mi] radius) or in private networks that are based on small cells (~50–150 m).

This caveat applies to the rest of the book. The concepts captured are intended to apply to private networks. It is possible, and highly likely, that the concepts discussed equally apply to macro

Mobile Communication Systems for Private Networks, First Edition. Srinivasan Balasubramanian.

networks. The intent is to bring together the relevant key concepts as they apply to private networks and not to focus only on the delta aspects from the macro networks, where the private network is handled differently.

I.1.2 LTE Network Architecture

This section captures the high-level views of the LTE network architecture, focusing on the end user to the edge of the wireless network (end-to-edge), which is connected to the internet protocol (IP) backbone, whether intranet/internet.

Figure I.1.1 illustrates the end-to-edge architecture with the UE connected to the LTE network via the Uu (radio wireless interface), communicating with the evolved Node B (eNB), which is the LTE radio base station. The eNB connects to the core network nodes in the evolved packet core (EPC). The eNB is connected to the mobility management entity (MME) for control signaling and the serving gateway (SGW)/packet gateway (PGW) for user plane (data) traffic. The policy and charging rules function (PCRF) is a control node in the EPC that regulates the activity for the different users in the system. The application function (AF) consists of applications/services (e.g. email service, web page) that the UE interacts with to exchange content. The UE connects via the intranet/internet to access these servers.

Figure I.1.2 provides the nomenclature and names of the interfaces of the interacting nodes in the LTE RAN and the EPC.

Figure I.1.3 provides a view of the functional separation among the RAN and EPC nodes.

Figure I.1.4 provides the protocol stack with the different layers involved as the user plane (data) traffic traverses from the UE all the way to the servers, taking hops through the eNB, SGW, and PGW into the IP core. The IP layer is the interfacing layer to the transport layer of TCP/UDP/RTP layers, to which the application layers connect to the wireless protocol stack. Packet data convergence protocol (PDCP) is the first LTE protocol defined layer with which the IP layer interacts. The radio link control (RLC) manages the segmentation and reassembly. The PDCP

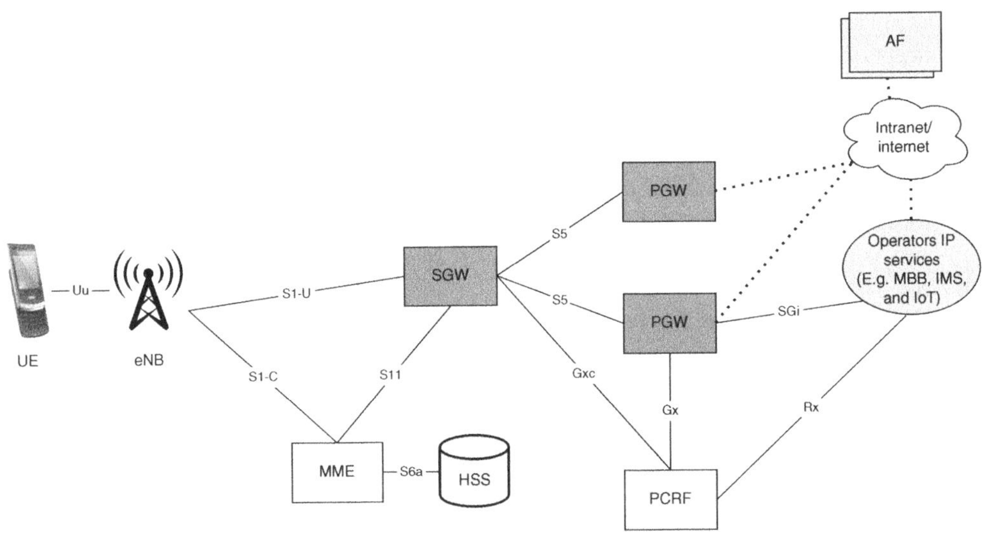

Figure I.1.1 LTE network high-level end-to-end architecture.

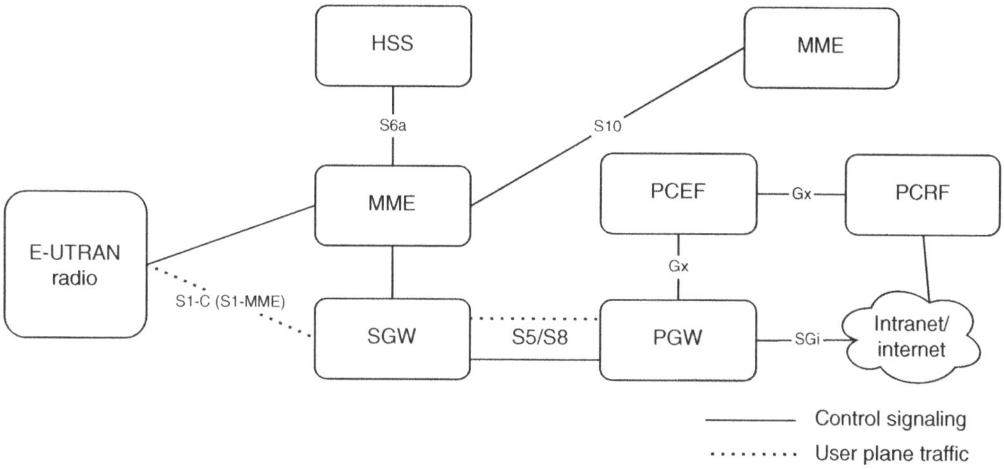

Figure I.1.2 LTE/EPC interfaces.

and RLC layers and medium access control (MAC) constitute the L2 (layer 2) of the LTE protocol stack. MAC adapts to the radio conditions and forms appropriately sized packets based on the grants provided to the physical layer by the network. The network nodes interact with each other using the generic tunneling protocol (GTP). GTP-U is used for exchanging user plane packets and uses user datagram protocol (UDP)/IP via L1/L2, which typically tends to be ethernet connectivity across the nodes.

Figure I.1.5 provides the protocol layers for the UE and network exchanging control information. GTP-C (control plane) is used in the network to exchange control information, and it is treated with a higher priority than GTP-U packets.

I.1.3 LTE Identifiers

This section provides the LTE identifiers used at the UE, RAN, and core network nodes.

International Mobile Subscriber Identity (IMSI) is used to identify the subscription in the UE. Globally Unique Temporary Identifier (GUTI) is the globally unique identifier of the UE, stored in the EPC core network. S-TMSI is a temporary subscriber identifier used until the user is authenticated by the network. International Mobile Equipment Identity Software Version (IMEISV) is the mobile station equipment identifier and includes the software version loaded on the device. Figure I.1.6 provides details on how these identifiers are derived.

Figure I.1.7 shows the Tracking Area Identity (TAI) and PDN-ID. The TAI is used to recognize a group of cells in the network, typically serving as the paging zone. The UE is required to inform the network when it transitions from one TAI to another. The PDN-ID is used to identify the packet data gateway, and thus the IP core connectivity desired by the UE, including IPv4 and/or IPv6.

Figure I.1.8 provides the different radio network temporary identifiers (RNTIs) used by the RAN node to schedule individual UEs and send broadcast messages addressing all UEs. When addressing specific UEs, this can be done using temporary, semi-persistent (grants that remain until revoked), or permanent identifiers. For broadcast, it can page (P-RNTI) or use random access

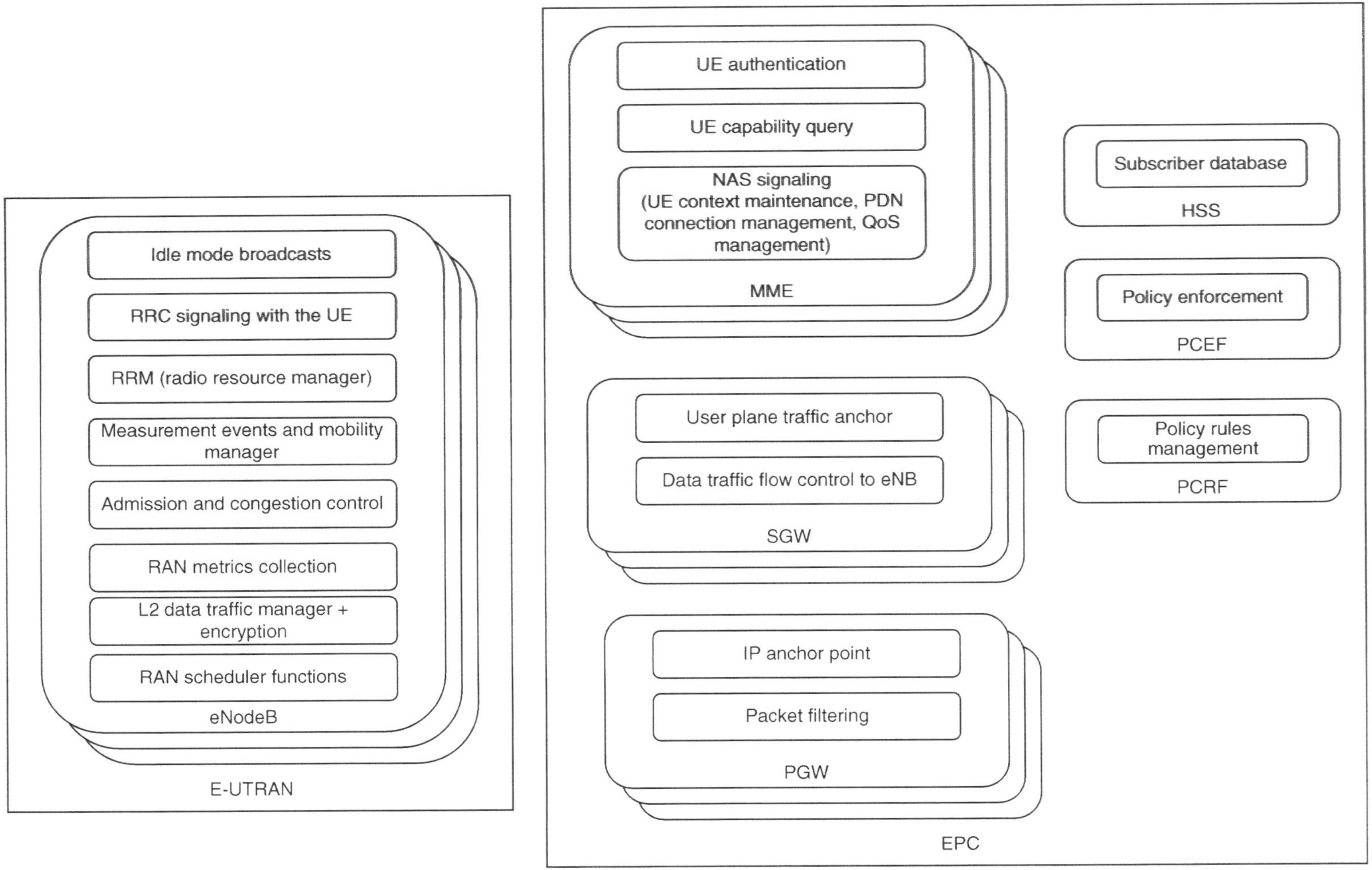

Figure I.1.3 Functional split between the E-UTRAN and the EPC.

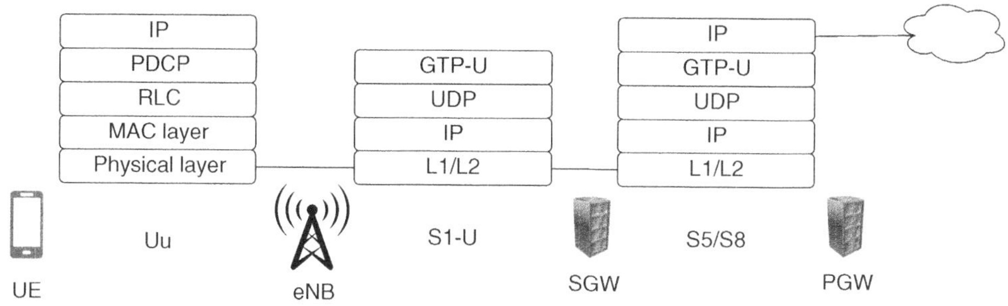

Interface

- Uu - Radio interface 36.201 (physical layer); 36.321(MAC layer); 36.322 (RLC); 36.323 (PDCP)
- S1 - 36.411 (physical layer); 36.414 (data transport)

Terms

- MAC – Medium access control
- RLC – Radio link control
- PDCP – Packet data convergence protocol
- IP – Internet protocol
- GTP – GPRS tunneling protocol
- GTP-U – GTP user plane

Figure I.1.4 E-UTRAN protocol stack: user plane.

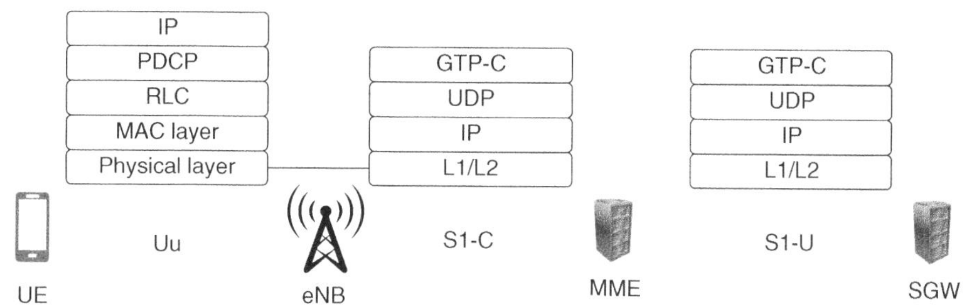

Interface

- Uu - RRC (36.331)
- S1 - 36.412 (signaling transport); 36.413 (application protocol)

Terms

- MAC - Medium access control
- RLC - Radio link control
- PDCP - Packet data convergence protocol
- IP - Internet protocol
- GTP - GPRS tunneling protocol
- GTP-C- GTP control plane
- RRC - Radio resource control

Figure I.1.5 E-UTRAN protocol stack: control plane.

(RA-RTNI), which are used to provide responses to random access (RA) from the UEs or carry system information (system information radio network temporary identifier [SI-RNTI]).

Figure I.1.9 provides the identifiers used to recognize the packet associated with a given UE in the network using the LTE network identifiers. These identifiers are used at the end points of the different hops in the network, including RAN and core network nodes. The LTE bearer identifiers allow for segregating the flows within a UE so that they are given the appropriate QoS treatment (e.g. VoIP and best-effort generic internet traffic).

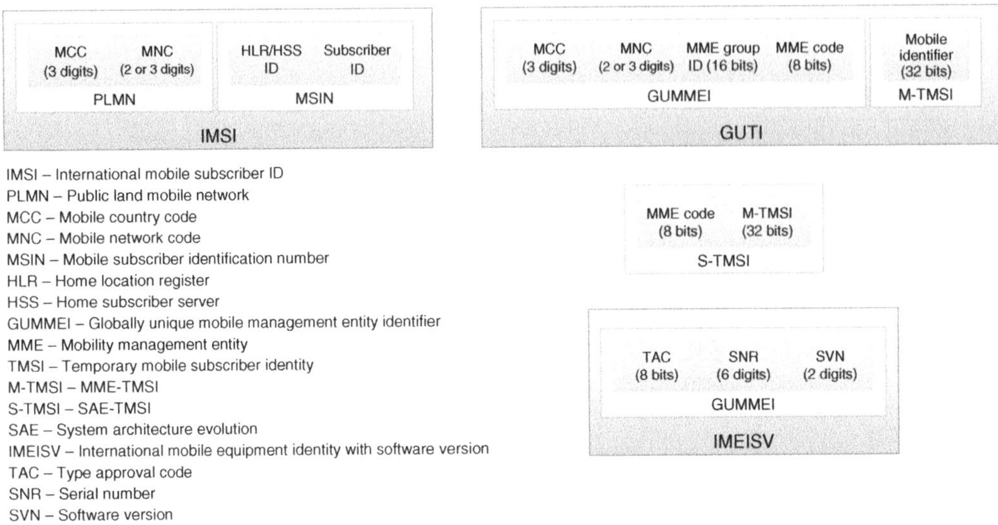

Figure I.1.6 E-UTRAN identifiers IMSI, GUTI, S-TMSI, and IMEISV.

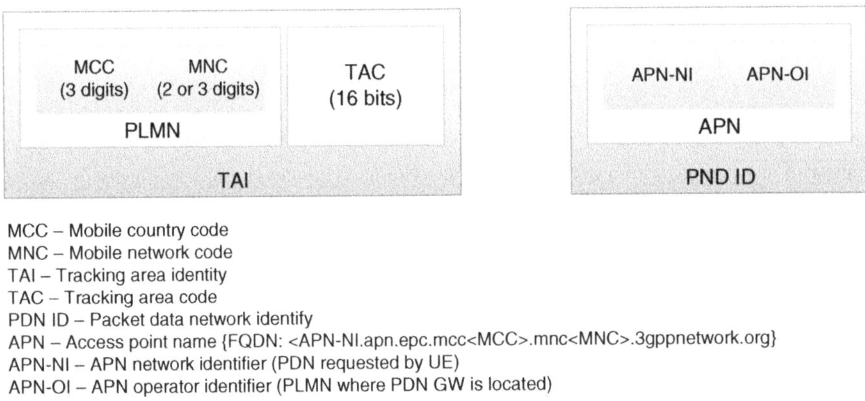

Figure I.1.7 E-UTRAN identifiers TAI, PDN-ID.

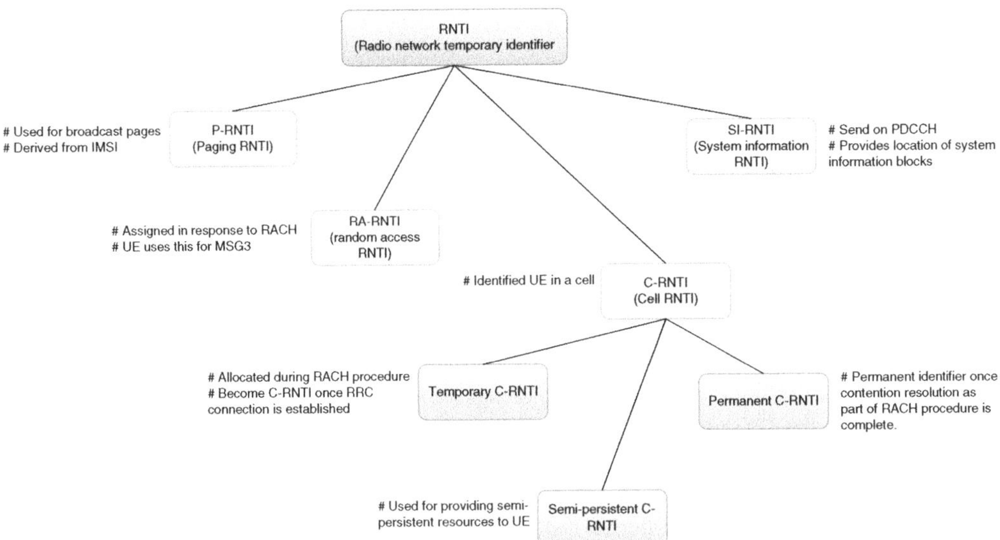

Figure I.1.8 E-UTRAN RNTI types.

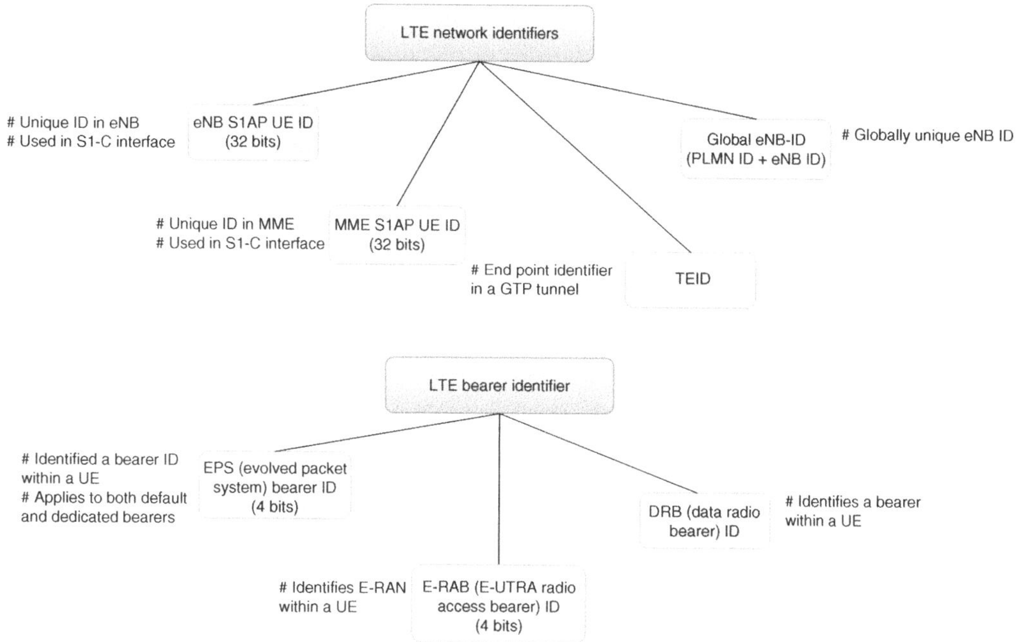

Figure I.1.9 E-UTRAN protocol stack: control plane.

I.1.4 Broadcast Signals/Messages and Cell Selection

This section details the broadcast reference signals that the eNB sends and the UE uses to lock onto the cell and measure signal strength for camping suitability. The UE also receives broadcast information via the system information blocks (SIBs) to obtain the required operating parameters, which provide system identifiers and random access channel (RACH) parameters. These allow the UE to both check if it is a valid system and determine the transmit power needed to initiate a connection with the network. This process is broadly termed "the system selection procedure" used by the UE.

I.1.4.1 Information Used by UE for System Selection

Information element	Description
EHPLMN	Equivalent HPLMN (Home PLMN): It contains a list of PLMNs that can be regarded as Home PLMNs.
HPLMNwAcT	"HPLMN with Access Technology." It stores the HPLMN and a list of available access technologies. This parameter contains the list of (PLMN, access technology) pairs.
PLMNwACT	"User Controlled PLMN with Access Technology." This parameter contains the list of (PLMN, access technology) pairs. This information is determined by the user and defines the user's preferred PLMNs in priority order.

(Continued)

Information element	Description
OPLMN	Operator-controlled PLMN selector with access technology. This parameter is set by the network operator. This is where the network operator adds other networks that have roaming agreements. This parameter contains a list of (PLMN, access technology) pairs.
Forbidden PLMN	PLMNs where the UE encountered failures and marked them as forbidden in volatile memory.
Tracking area code reject	Tracking Area Update (TAU) rejects from the network with back-off based on error codes are retained in volatile memory.
• EF_HPPLMN	Higher-priority PLMN search period

I.1.5 What Happens When a UE Is Switched On?

I.1.5.1 System Acquisition

The LTE UE searches for two synchronization signals to detect and identify the cell: the primary synchronization signal (PSS) and the secondary synchronization signal (SSS). Once the cell is identified, the UE reads the broadcast channel (BCH) to obtain the system information carried in the SIB. The Physical Broadcast Channel (PBCH) carries the master information block (MIB), and the physical downlink (DL) shared channel (PDSCH) carries the SIBs. After the UE has acquired the cell, it proceeds to attach to the network, communicating via the eNB (evolved node B) to the MME.

Figure I.1.10 shows the PSS and SSS system acquisition signals are transmitted from the eNB that is used by the UE to find the network radio access nodes.

I.1.5.2 Synchronization Signals (PSS and SSS) – Frequency Division Duplex

Figure I.1.11 shows the PSS transmissions as part of the cell broadcast reference signals for FDD channels. The PSS is mapped to the last OFDM symbol in slots 0 and 10.

Figure I.1.12 shows the PSS transmissions as part of the cell broadcast reference signals for TDD channels. The PSS is mapped to the third OFDM symbol in subframes 1 and 6.

PSS and SSS are used by the UE to acquire frequency and timing. They are used for carrier frequency determination, Orthogonal Frequency Division Multiplexing (OFDM) symbol, subframe, and frame timing determination. Their signatures are also used to determine the cell ID of a given cell (1 of 504 physical cell identifiers [PCIs]). PSS is used to determine the subframe timing and supports three indices (0, 1, 2). The SSS is used to determine the frame timing and provides 168 unique cell ID group (CIG) numbers.

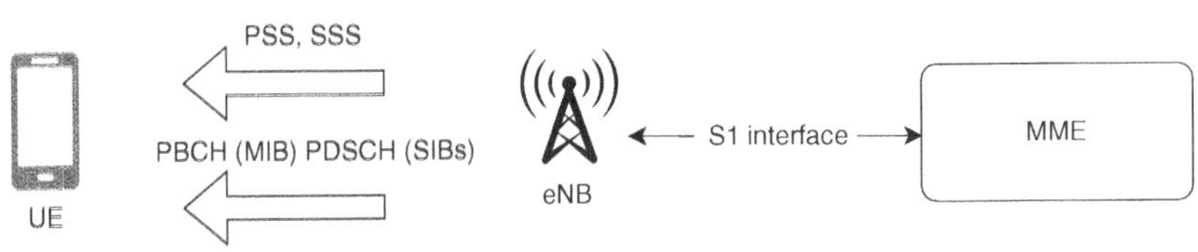

Figure I.1.10 PSS and SSS system acquisition signals are transmitted from the eNB.

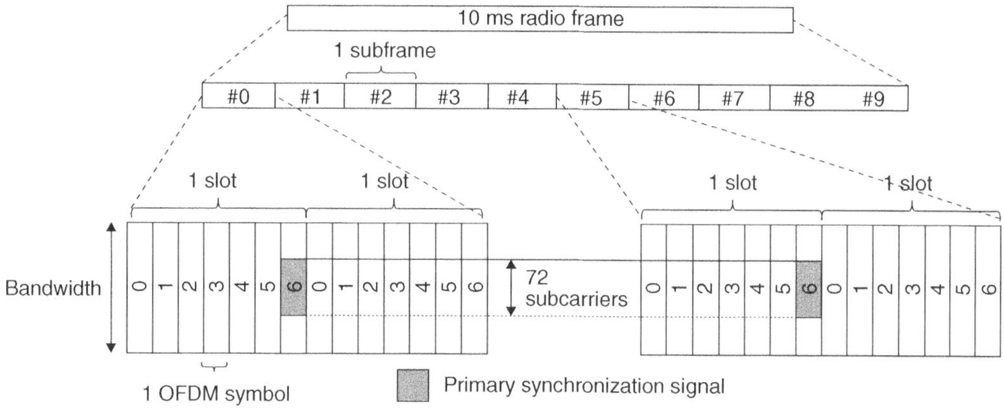

Figure I.1.11 FDD – the PSS is mapped to the last OFDM symbol in slots 0 and 10.

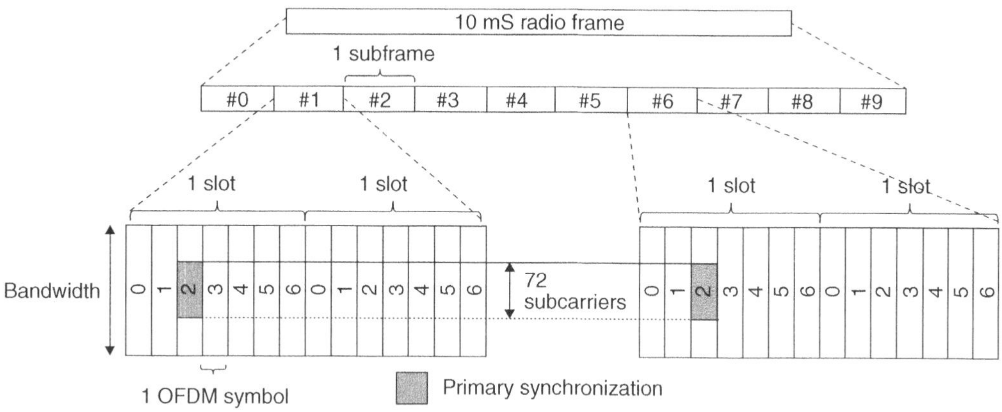

Figure I.1.12 TDD – the PSS is mapped to the third OFDM symbol in subframes 1 and 6.

I.1.5.3 Cell Identity Arrangement

The physical cell identity, *NcellID*, is defined by the equation:

$$N_{ID}^{CELL} = 3N_{ID}^{(1)} + N_{ID}^{(2)}$$

- $N_{ID}^{(1)}$ is the physical layer cell identity group (0–167).
- $N_{ID}^{(2)}$ is the identity within the group (0–2).

This arrangement creates 504 unique physical cell identities.

The PSS is linked to the cell identity within the group ($N_{ID}^{(2)}$). The SSS is linked to the cell identity group ($N_{ID}^{(1)}$) and the cell identity within the group ($N_{ID}^{(2)}$).

You can obtain $N_{ID}^{(2)}$ by successfully demodulating the PSS. The SSS can then be demodulated and combined with knowledge of $N_{ID}^{(2)}$ to obtain $N_{ID}^{(1)}$. Once you establish the values of $N_{ID}^{(1)}$ and $N_{ID}^{(2)}$, you can determine the cell identity (N_{ID}^{CELL}). Figure I.1.13 shows how the Cell ID is derived from the PSS and SSS signals transmitted by the RAN.

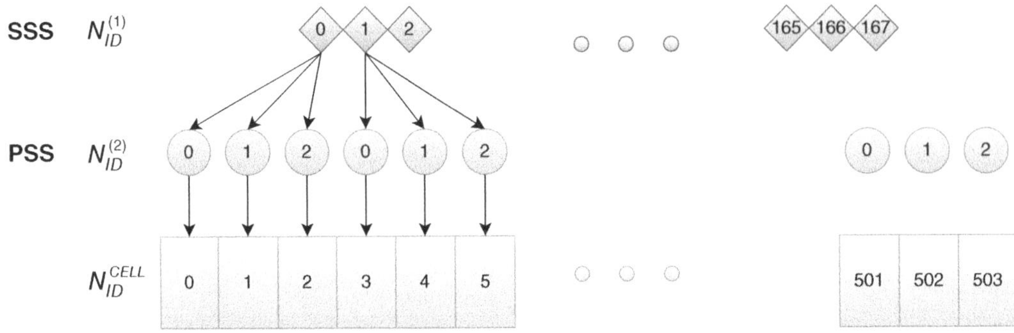

Figure I.1.13 Cell ID derivation from the PSS and SSS signals transmitted by the RAN.

PCIs in LTE networks provide a pseudo-unique value for identifying eNodeBs in a deployed carrier network. The PCI value is derived from two synchronization reference signals – PSS and SSS. The PSS supports three values: 0, 1, or 2. The SSS supports values between 0 and 167. The PCI value is [PSS + 3 × SSS], resulting in a value between 0 and 503. With a limited 504 values for all eNBs to be supported in the network, PCIs must be reused. The reuse is strategically planned and separated sufficiently far to avoid the UE seeing two eNBs using the same PCI value.

I.1.5.3.1 Initial Acquisition Procedure Details

When the UE is switched on, it searches for a strong cell by monitoring the DL broadcast signals and starts with rough frequency synchronization. The UE scans a provisioned set of bands/frequencies looking for a valid pilot. The UE determines the strongest signal based on the scans performed and examines the PSS signature in that channel. The UE uses the PSS to determine the carrier frequency, cell ID index, subframe timing (1 ms-level timing), and also the cyclic prefix length. Subsequent to that, the UE acquires the SSS, determines the frame-level timing, and identifies the CIG. Together with the cell ID index and CIG, the UE determines the physical cell ID. The UE then reads the PBCH channel to receive the MIB and obtains the essential cell information. It then reads the physical DL control channel (PDCCH) or PDSCH to receive the other SIBs. SIB1 provides the cell identifiers, and the UE determines if it is a valid cell for the UE to camp on. Once that is ascertained, the UE uses the SIB2 parameters to perform a RA to connect to the network.

The PBCH is transmitted in subframe 0 in every frame and uses the first four OFDM symbols in the second slot (slot #1) in the six resource blocks (RBs) immediately after the PSS/SSS. The allocation for the PBCH is the same for both frequency division duplex (FDD) and time division duplex (TDD). The MIB is broadcast every 40 ms in four bursts at a very low data rate so that even the UEs at the cell edge can receive the broadcast message (note that the information transmitted every 10 ms is self-decodable). The MIB information specifies the minimum required information, and the UE receives the remaining information from the PDSCH. The MIB provides the DL bandwidth, Physical HybridARQ Indicator Channel (PHICH) configuration (which indicates where the PDCCH channel is transmitted, which is the control channel that provides the scheduling information for the PDSCH to receive the remaining SIBs), apart from the system frame number (SFN). The SFN, together with the hyper frame number (HFN), allows the UE to determine the paging cycle to establish the wake-up timing for the UE to receive incoming pages.

The UE, after receiving the MIB, proceeds to receive the SIBs. SIB1 repeats every 80 ms. The other SIBs are transmitted with a lower periodicity. Note that the UE can go into a connected mode and request that the SIBs be delivered as dedicated messages to the UE on demand. The SIBs are scheduled on the PDSCH using the SI-RNTI.

I.1.5.3.2 LTE System Information Block 1 (SIB1)

It contains essential cell-specific information: cell selection, cell access, and SI scheduling. It includes cell identity, tracking area code, and PLMN for initial network connection.

Information elements		
Cell access information	PLMN ID list (up to six entries)	PLMN ID
		Cell reserved for operator's use
	Tracking area code	
	Cell identity	
	Cell barred	
	Intra-frequency cell reselection allowed	
	Closed Subscriber Group (CSG) indication	
	CSG identity	
Cell selection information	Qrxlevmin	
	Qrxlevmin offset	
Pmax		
Frequency band indicator		
Scheduling information list	SI periodicity (8, 16, . . . 512 radio frames)	
	SIB mapping (1–32 instances)	SIB type
TDD configuration	Subframe assignment (UL–DL configuration)	
	Special subframe pattern (special subframe configuration)	
System information window length (1, 2, 5, 10, 15, 20, 40 ms)		
System information value tag		
IP Multimedia Subsystem (IMS) emergency support		
Release nine extension	Cell selection information	Qqualmin
		Qqualmin offset

I.1.5.3.3 LTE System Information Block 2 (SIB2)

It contains RACH, access barring, uplink (UL) frequency information, and multicast/broadcast single frequency network (MBSFN) configuration. It also offers details about the RACH-related info, timers, and UL power control.

Information elements	
Access Class (AC) barring for emergency calls	
AC barring for Mobile Originated (MO) signaling	ß
	Barring the following time (4, 8, 16, 32, . . . 512 seconds)
	Barring special AC

(*Continued*)

Information elements		
Radio resource configuration	RACH configuration	Number of RA preambles
		Size of RA preamble group A
		Message size group A
		Message power offset group B
		Power ramping step
		Preamble: initial received target power
		Preamble trans max
		RA response window size
		MAC connection resolution timer
		Max HARQ Msg3Tx
	Broadcast control channel (BCCH) configuration	Modification period coefficient

SIB	Information carried
MIB	Physical layer information of the LTE cell, which in turn helps receive further SIs, i.e. system bandwidth
SIB1	Information about whether the UE can access the LTE cell. It also defines the scheduling of the other SIBs and carries the cell ID, MCC, MNC, TAC, and SIB mapping.
SIB2	Common channel, as well as shared channel information. It also carries radio resource control (RRC), UL power control, preamble power ramping, UL cyclic prefix length, subframe hopping, and UL EARFCN.
SIB3	Cell reselection information as well as intra-frequency cell reselection information.
SIB4	Intra-frequency neighbors (on the same frequency); they carry the serving cell and neighbor cell frequencies required for cell reselection, as well as handover between the same Radio Access Technology (RAT) base stations (GSM BTS1 to GSM BTS2) and different RAT base stations (GSM to WCDMA, GSM to LTE, or between WCDMA and LTE, etc.). It covers E-UTRA and other RATs as mentioned.
SIB5	Inter-frequency neighbors (on different frequencies); they carry E-UTRA LTE frequencies and other neighboring cell frequencies from other RATs. The purpose is cell reselection and handover.
SIB6	WCDMA neighbor information; that is, it carries serving - Universal Terrestrial Radio Access (UTRA) and neighbor cell frequencies useful for cell reselection.
SIB7	GSM neighbors information; that is, it carries GSM EDGE Radio Access Network (GERAN) frequencies as well as GERAN neighbor cell frequencies. It is used for cell reselection as well as handover purposes.
SIB8	CDMA-2000 Evolution Data Optimized (EVDO) frequencies and CDMA-2000 neighbor cell frequencies
SIB9	Home eNodeB identifier (HNBID)
SIB10	Earthquake and Tsunami Warning System (ETWS) primary notification
SIB11	ETWS secondary notification

I.1.6 LTE Resource Grid

The LTE resource grid is used to define the locations where the broadcast signals/messages and the UE-specific scheduling are performed. This provides the actual physical resources to determine the cell capacity and the UE-level throughput that is achievable, subject to the UE's radio channel conditions in the system. Both FDD and TDD resource grids are captured below. The representation is provided for a 3 MHz bandwidth, and with increased bandwidth, the control and broadcast regions will remain the same; however, more RBs will be available for scheduling individual users. LTE supports a maximum bandwidth of a 20 MHz channel.

I.1.6.1 LTE TDD Resource Grid

Figure I.1.14 A sample LTE TDD resource grid with 3MHz as the channel bandwidth illustrating the different physical layer channels. Table I.1.1 provides the parameter used to generate this LTE TDD sample frame.

I.1.6.2 LTE FDD Resource Grid

Figure I.1.15 A sample LTE FDD resource grid with 3MHz as the channel bandwidth illustrating the different physical layer channels. Table I.1.2 provides the parameter used to generate this LTE FDD sample frame.

I.1.7 RACH Procedure

Figure I.1.16 provides the steps used by the UE to perform RA to the network to initiate RRC connection setup procedures. A RA is required when the network is not aware of the UE, and once the contention resolution is completed—accounting for scenarios in which multiple UEs access the network at the same time—the UE is provided a temporary identifier (C-RNTI) to use for subsequent communication that is dedicated to the UE for the duration of the connection on the eNB.

I.1.8 RRC Connection Setup

Figure I.1.17 captures the same procedures as the RACH mechanism and adds details on the messages, including non-access stratum messages (NAS), which are part of the subsequent steps executed once the RRC connection setup is completed.

I.1.9 Non-access Stratum Procedures

This section details the NAS procedures. The UE sends the NAS signaling messages as payloads in RRC signaling messages, which are transported to the EPC core network via the eNB. The UE and the network go through mutual authentication procedures, and the UE is assigned an IP address after successful authentication. The UE subsequently exchanges data traffic using the assigned IP address. The attach procedures are captured in Figure I.1.18.

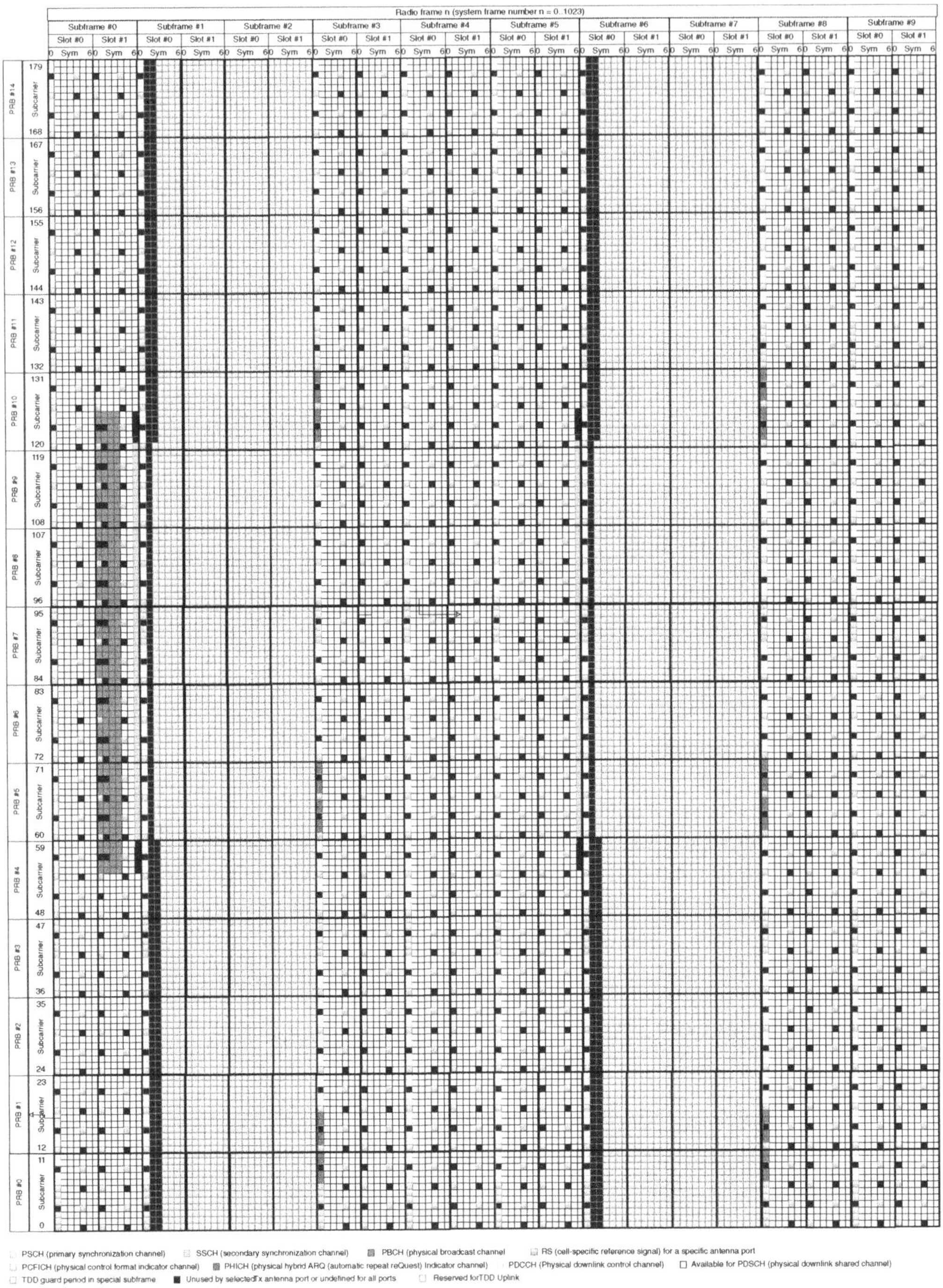

Figure I.1.14 A sample LTE TDD resource grid with the above-identified parameters.

I.1.9.1 UE Attach Procedure

Figure I.1.18 provides the steps involved in the UE LTE attach procedures, which involves finding and accessing the LTE network, performing mutual authentication, providing the UE capability to the network, obtaining an IP address allocation and starting to exchange user data traffic.

Table I.1.1 Parameter for LTE TDD sample frame generation.

Frame parameters	Value
Duplexing mode	TDD: frame structure type 2
TDD UL/DL configuration (from SIB1 in PDSCH)	2: (DL I UL I special subframes: [0,3-5,8-9 I 2,7 I 1,6])
TDD special subframe configuration (from SIB1 in PDSCH)	0: (3 DwPTS symbols, 1 UpPTS symbol); (note: no PDSCH allowed in DwPTS of this duration)
MBSFN subframe: (from SIB2 in PDSCH): none	N/A
Channel bandwidth (from MIB in PBCH)	3 MHz: (15 PRBs, 180 subcarriers)
Cyclic prefix	Normal: (7 symbols per slot, 8 PHICH resources per PHICH group)
Tx antenna port/number of ports	0/2
Physical layer cell ID (0–503) (from PSCH and SSCH)	0: (ID group: 0, ID: 0, RS frequency shift: 0)
Control format indicator (CFI) (from PCFICH)	1: (1 PDCCH symbol, 26/20 PDCCH REGs, 2/2 CCEs) (Warning: no room for common search space if there are fewer than 4 CCEs.)
CFI for TDD subframes 1 and 6 (from PCFICH)	1: (1 PDCCH symbol, 26 PDCCH REGs, 2 CCEs) (Warning: no room for common search space if fewer than 4 CCEs.)
PHICH duration (from MIB in PBCH)	Normal: (one symbol)

Table I.1.2 Parameter for LTE FDD sample frame generation.

Frame parameters	Value
Duplexing mode	FDD: frame structure type 1
MBSFN subframe (from SIB2 in PDSCH): none	N/A
Channel bandwidth (from MIB in PBCH)	3 MHz: (15 PRBs, 180 subcarriers)
Cyclic prefix	Normal: (7 symbols per slot, 8 PHICH resources per PHICH group)
Tx antenna port/number of ports	0/2
Physical layer cell ID (0–503) (from PSCH and SSCH)	0: (ID group: 0, ID: 0, RS frequency shift: 0)
Control format indicator (CFI) (from PCFICH)	1: (1 PDCCH symbol. 26/20 PDCCH REGs, 2/2 CCEs) (Warning: No room for a common search space if there are fewer than 4 CCEs.)
PHICH Ng factor (from MIB in PBCH)	1: (2 PHICH groups, 8 REGs, and 16 PHICH resources)
PHICH duration (from MIB in PBCH)	Normal: (1 symbol)

I.1.9.2 UE Capability Exchange

UE capability information is sent by the UE in response to the UE capability inquiry message from the network when the UE attaches to the network. The network may query the UE at a subsequent point as well to obtain the UE capabilities. The network queries the UE, providing the aspects of the UE capabilities that it is interested in for the UE's operation with that network. The response from the UE contains all the information that the UE is capable of, subject to the masks provided by the network.

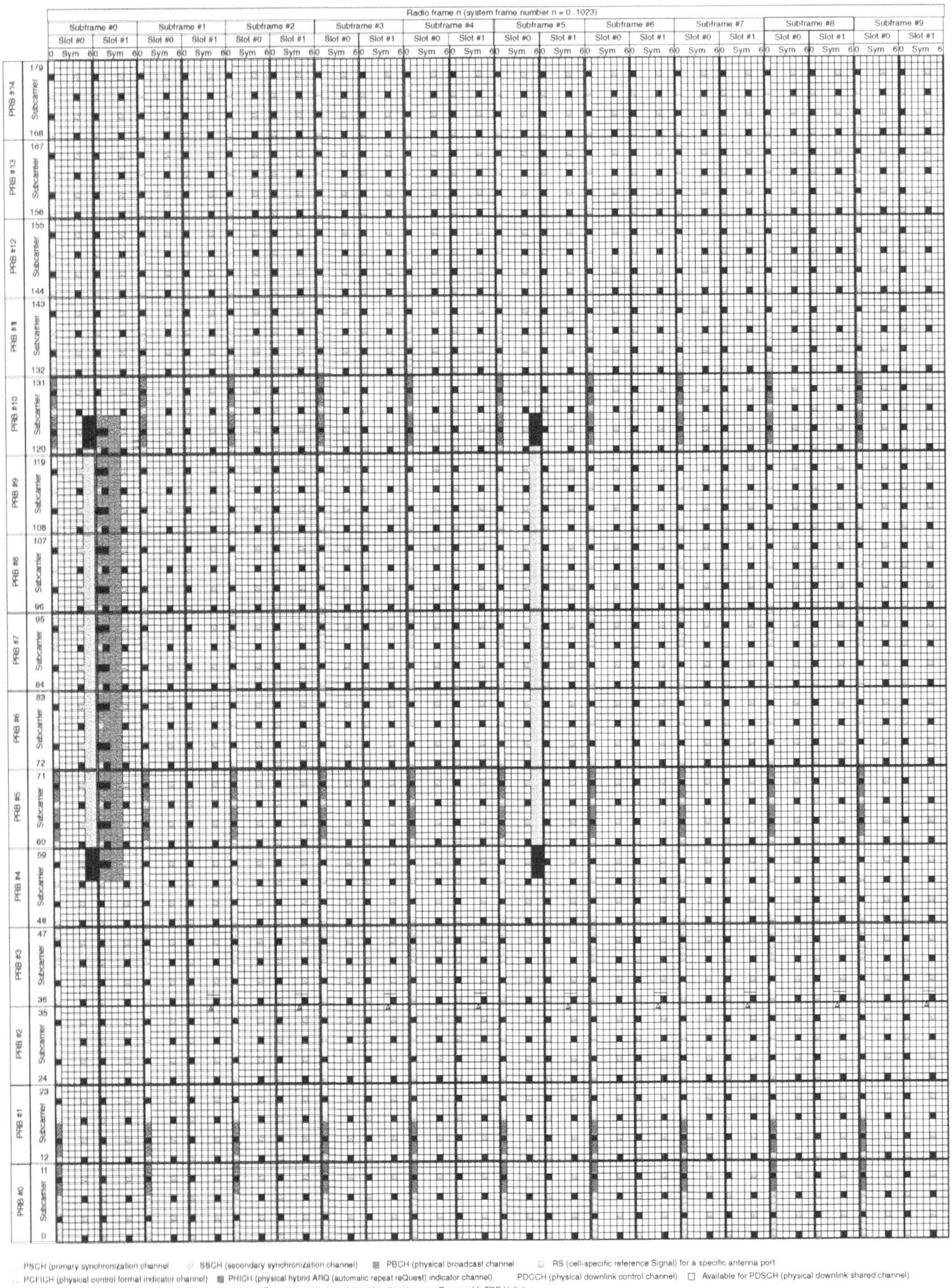

Figure I.1.15 A sample LTE FDD resource grid with the above-identified parameters.

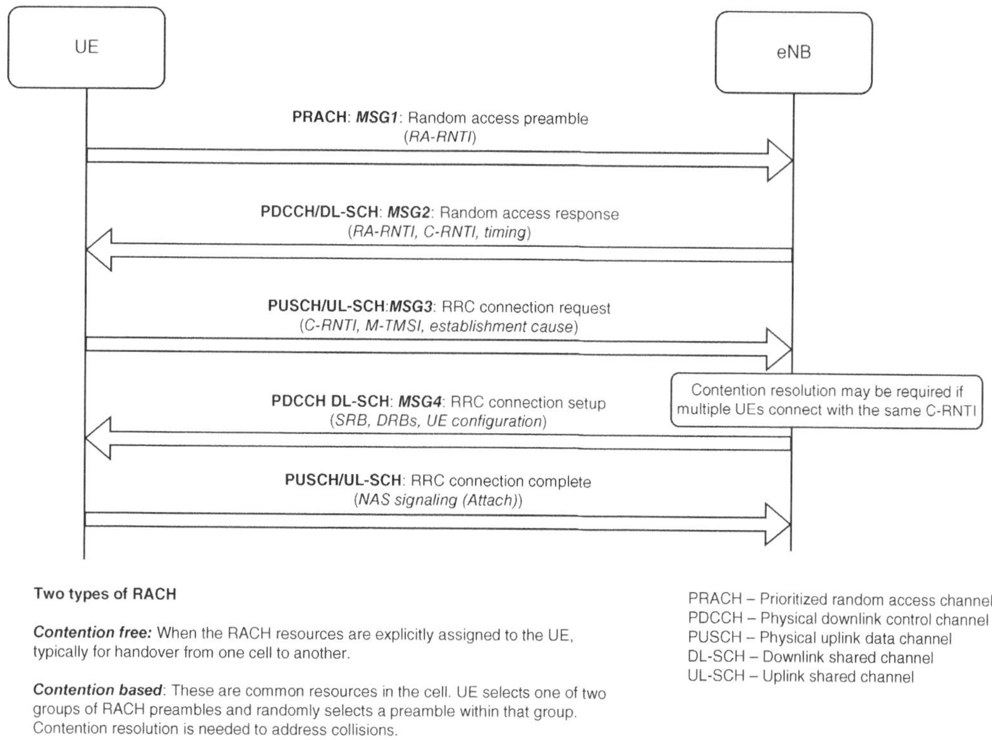

Figure I.1.16 LTE RACH procedures.

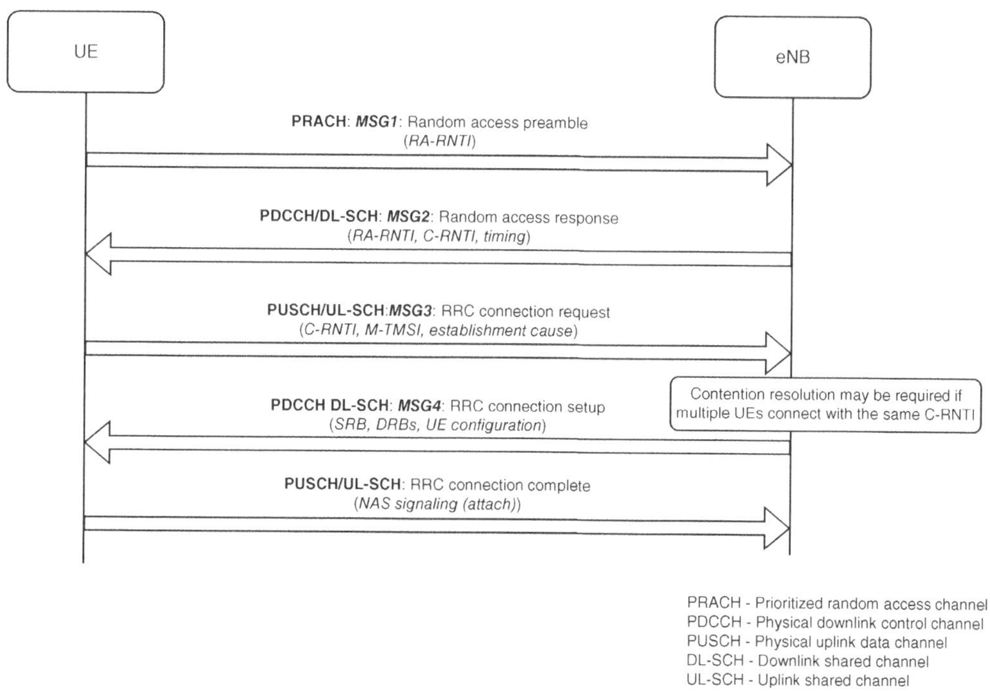

Figure I.1.17 LTE RRC connection setup procedure.

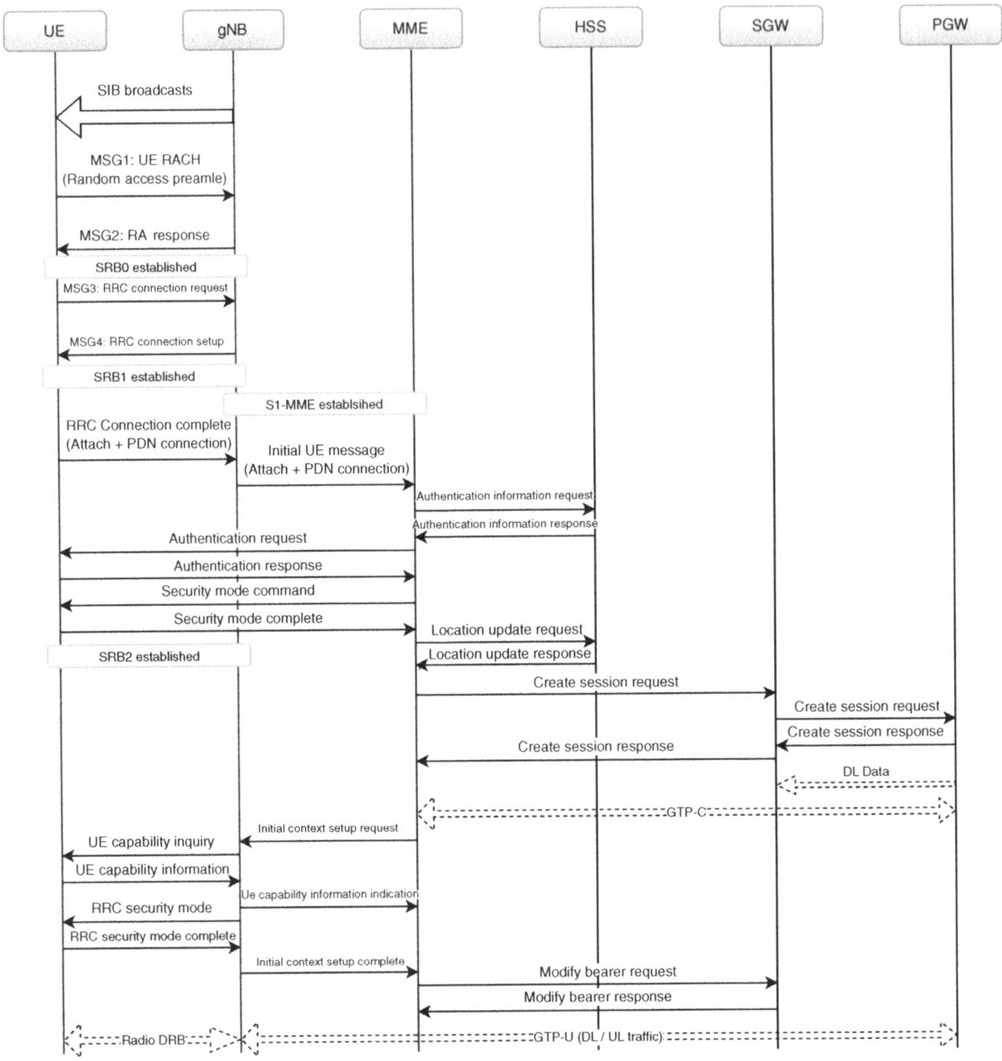

Figure I.1.18 UE LTE attach procedures.

For enterprise private networks, the UE is required to operate on a limited set of bands, sometimes even just one. For example, the Citizen Broadband Radio Service (CBRS) band in the USA or n77 in the United Kingdom. Also, the UE may be required to support only LTE or only NR, and when the enterprise campus supports both 4G and 5G, support for both LTE and NR needs to be reported. The enterprise campuses do not require 2G/3G networks.

I.1.9.2.1 Supported Bands on LTE, UMTS, and GSM Technologies

The list of supported LTE bands is reported in the "supportedBandListEUTRA." The list of supported WCDMA and GSM bands is reported in the information element (IE) "interRAT-Parameters" under "utraFDD" and "geran," respectively. Figure I.1.19 provides the structure of the UE capability information reported to the network.

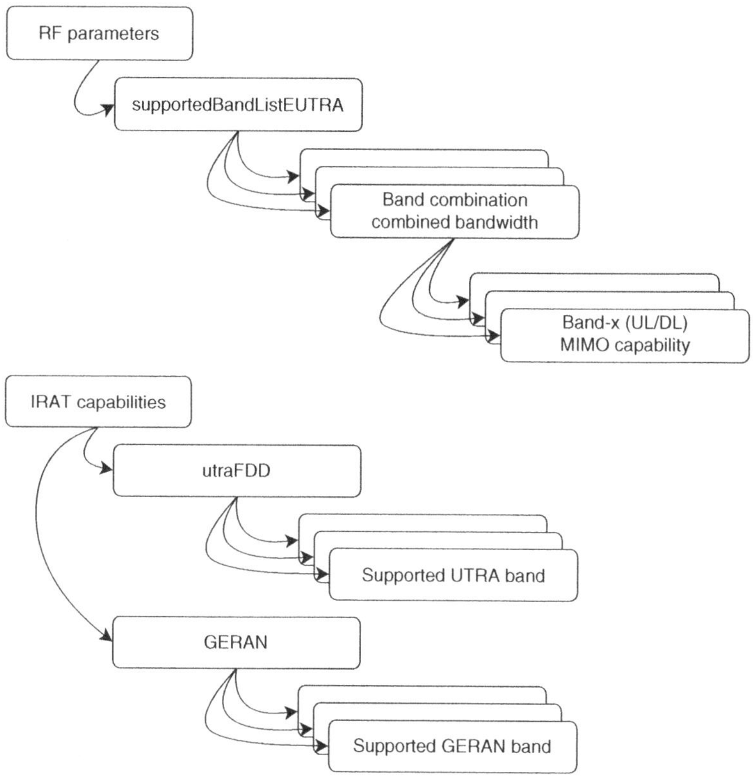

Figure I.1.19 UE capability information.

I.1.9.2.2 UE Category

3GPP Release 8 defines five LTE UE categories depending on maximum peak data rate and Multiple Input Multiple Output (MIMO) capabilities support. With 3GPP Release 10, called LTE Advanced, three new categories have been introduced, followed by four more with Release 11, two more with Release 14, and five more with Release 15.

Maximum data rates shown are for 20 MHz of channel bandwidth. Categories 6 and above include data rates from combining multiple 20 MHz channels. Maximum data rates will be lower if less bandwidth is utilized.

These are L1 transport data rates, not including the different protocol layers overhead. Depending on cell bandwidth, cell load (number of simultaneous users), network configuration, the performance of the UE used, propagation conditions, etc., practical data rates will vary.

The 3.0 Gbps/1.5 Gbps data rate specified as Category 8 is near the peak aggregate data rate for a base station sector. A more realistic maximum data rate for a single user is 1.2 Gbps (DL) and 600 Mbps (UL).

LTE UE Category Rationale

- LTE utilizes the LTE UE or UE categories or classes to define the performance specifications of LTE devices and enables LTE base stations to communicate effectively with them, knowing their performance levels. Some LTE UE categories such as LTE Cat 3, LTE Cat 4, and LTE Cat 0 are widely quoted and used. Other UE categories such as LTE Cat 7 and LTE Cat 8 are much newer.
- In the same way that a variety of other systems adopted distinct categories for the handsets or UE, there are also 3G LTE UE categories. These LTE categories define the standards to which a particular handset, dongle, or other equipment will operate.

- The LTE categories, or UE classes, are needed to ensure that the base station, or eNodeB (eNB), can communicate correctly with the UE. By relaying the LTE UE category information to the base station, it can determine the performance of the UE and communicate with it accordingly.
- As the LTE category defines the overall performance and capabilities of the UE, it is possible for the eNB to communicate using the capabilities that it knows the UE possesses. Accordingly, the eNB will not communicate beyond the performance of the UE.

User equipment category	Max. L1 data rate downlink (Mbps)	Max. number of DL MIMO layers	Max. L1 data rate uplink (Mbps)	3GPP release
NB1	0.68	1	1.0	Rel 13
M1	1.0	1	1.0	
0	1.0	1	1.0	Rel 12
1	10.3	1	5.2	Rel 8
2	51.0	2	25.5	
3	102.0	2	51.0	
4	150.8	2	51.0	
5	299.6	4	75.4	
6	301.5	2 or 4	51.0	Rel 10
7	301.5	2 or 4	102.0	
8	2,998.6	8	1,497.8	
9	452.2	2 or 4	51.0	Rel 11
10	452.2	2 or 4	102.0	
11	603.0	2 or 4	51.0	
12	603.0	2 or 4	102.0	
13	391.7	2 or 4	150.8	Rel 12
14	391.7	8	9,585	
15	750	2 or 4	226	
16	979	2 or 4	105	
17	25,065	8	2,119	Rel 13
18	1,174	2 or 4 or 8	211	
19	1,566	2 or 4 or 8	13,563	
20	2,000	2 or 4 or 8	315	Rel 14
21	1,400	2 or 4	300	
22	2,350	2 or 4 or 8	422	Rel 15
23	2,700	2 or 4 or 8	528	
24	3,000	2 or 4 or 8	633	
25	3,200	2 or 4 or 8	739	
26	3,500	2 or 4 or 8	844	

256QAM Downlink and 64QAM in Uplink

We can check the "UE capability information" for the list of LTE bands supporting 256QAM in the DL and 64QAM in the UL. By default, when 256QAM DL and 64QAM UL are supported by any device, the support is available on all bands. The supported LTE bands in the

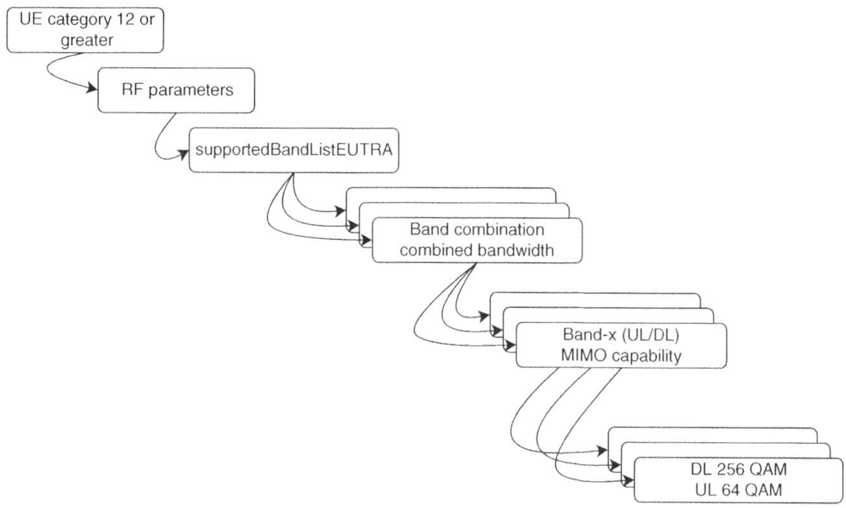

Figure I.1.20 UE RF capability.

Figure I.1.21 Dynamic UE capability.

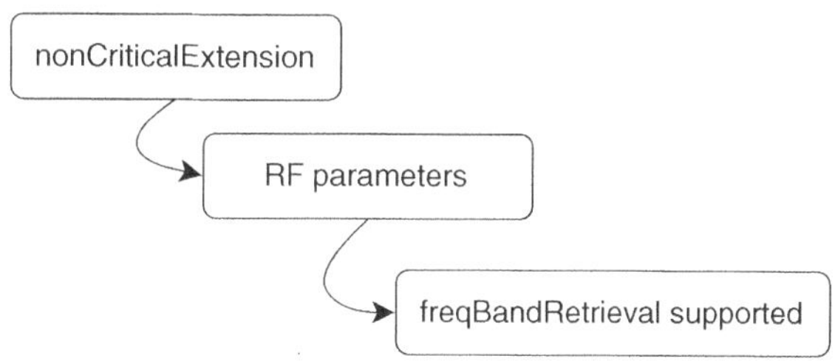

IE "supportedBandListEUTRA" are mapped sequentially to the IE "supportedBandListEUTRA-v1250." Figure I.1.20 provides the structure representing the UE's RF capabilities.

I.1.9.2.3 Dynamic UE Capability

There is a new method to save the length of LTE CA band combinations, which will, in turn, reduce the length of the "UECapabilityInformation" message sent by the UE. If the IE "freqBandRetrieval-r11" is reported by the UE in the capability, then it means dynamic UE capability is supported. Figure I.1.21 shows the structure of the information provided as part of the dynamic UE capability.

I.1.9.2.4 Feature Group Indicator

Feature group indicator (FGI) is a special IE within the UE capability information message. FGI primarily carries information about radio protocol aspects. The indexing starts from index 1, which is the leftmost bit in the field. Index 1–32 is for Release 8, Indexes from 33 to 64 are for Release 9, and Indexes from 101 to 132 are for release 10. The UE is allowed to signal different values for FDD and TDD.

The meaning of each FGI bit is defined in the 3GPP specification 36.331.

- featureGroupIndicators: 36.331 Annex B, Table B.1-1
- featureGroupIndRel9Add: 36.331 Annex B, Table B.1-1a
- featureGroupIndRel10: 36.331 Annex C, Table C.1-1

A few exemplary entries are shown below. Please refer to the tables defined in the standards references mentioned above for the full details.

Index of indicator (bit number)	Definition (description of the supported functionality when the indicator is set to one)	Notes	If indicated "Yes," the feature shall be implemented and successfully tested for this version of the specification	FDD/ TDD diff
1 (leftmost bit)	• Intra-subframe frequency hopping for Physical Uplink Shared Channel (PUSCH) scheduled by a UL grant • DL Control Information (DCI) format 3a (transmit power control [TPC] commands for Physical Uplink Control Channel (PUCCH) and PUSCH with single-bit power adjustments) • Aperiodic CQI/PMI/RI reporting on PUSCH: Mode 2-0 – UE-selected subband CQI without Pre-coding Matrix Indicator (PMI) • Aperiodic CQI/PMI/RI reporting on PUSCH: Mode 2-2 – UE-selected subband CQI with multiple PMI	• Set to 1 by category M1 and M2 UEs that have implemented and successfully tested "Aperiodic CQI/PMI/RI reporting on PUSCH: Mode 2-0 – UE-selected subband CQI without PMI"		Yes
2	• Simultaneous CQI and acknowledgment/ negative acknowledgment (ACK/NACK) on PUCCH, i.e. PUCCH format 2a and 2b • Absolute TPC command for PUSCH • Resource allocation type 1 for PDSCH • Periodic CQI/PMI/RI reporting on PUCCH: Mode 2-0 – UE-selected subband CQI without PMI • Periodic CQI/PMI/RI reporting on PUCCH: Mode 2-1 – UE-selected subband CQI with single PMI	• If a category M1 or M2 UE does not support this feature group, this bit shall be set to 0.		Yes
3	• 5 bit RLC UM SN • 7 bit PDCP SN	• It can only be set to 1 if the UE has set bit number 7 to 1.	Yes, if UE supports VoLTE, Mission-Critical Push-To-Talk (MCPTT), or both. Yes, if UE supports Single Radio Voice Call Continuity (SRVCC) to EUTRAN from GERAN.	No

4	• Short discontinuous reception (DRX) cycle	• It can only be set to 1 if the UE has set bit number 5 to 1. • Not supported by category M1 or M2 UE		Yes
5	• Long DRX cycle • DRX command MAC control element		Yes	No
6	• Prioritized bit rate		Yes	No
7	• RLC UM	• It can only be set to 0 if the UE neither supports VoLTE nor MCPTT	Yes, if UE supports VoLTE, MCPTT, or both. Yes, if UE supports SRVCC to EUTRAN from GERAN.	No
8	• EUTRA RRC_CONNECTED to UTRA FDD or UTRA TDD CELL_DCH PS handover if the UE supports either Universal Terrestrial Radio Access Network (UTRAN) FDD or UTRAN TDD • EUTRA RRC_CONNECTED to UTRA FDD CELL_DCH PS handover if the UE supports both UTRAN FDD and UTRAN TDD	• It can only be set to 1 if the UE has set bit number 22 to 1	Yes (except for categories M1 and M2 UEs) for FDD, if the UE supports UTRA FDD.	Yes
9	• EUTRA RRC_CONNECTED to GERAN GSM_Dedicated handover	• Related to SR-VCC • It can only be set to 1 if the UE has set bit number 23 to 1	Yes (except for category M1 and M2 UEs) if the UE supports SRVCC to EUTRAN from GERAN.	Yes
10	• EUTRA RRC_CONNECTED to GERAN (Packet_) idle by cell change order • EUTRA RRC_CONNECTED to GERAN (Packet) idle by cell change order with network-assisted cell change (NACC)			Yes

I.1.9.2.5 Clarification for Mobility from EUTRAN and Inter-frequency Handover Within EUTRAN

Feature	GERAN	UTRAN	HRPD	1×RTT	EUTRAN
A. Measurements and cell reselection procedure in E-UTRA idle mode	Supported if GERAN band support is indicated	Supported if UTRAN band support is indicated	Supported if CDMA2000 HRPD band support is indicated	Supported if CDMA2000 1×RTT band support is indicated	Supported for compatible bands
B. RRC release with the blind redirection procedure in E-UTRA connected mode	Supported if GERAN band support is indicated	Supported if UTRAN band support is indicated	Supported if CDMA2000 HRPD band support is indicated	Supported if CDMA2000 1×RTT band support is indicated	Supported for compatible bands
C. Cell change order (with or without) network-assisted cell change in E-UTRA connected mode	Group 10	NA	NA	NA	NA
D. Inter-frequency/RAT measurements, reporting, and measurement reporting event B2 (for inter-RAT) in E-UTRA connected mode	Group 23	Group 22/39	Group 26	Group 24	Group 25
E. Inter-frequency/RAT handover procedure in E-UTRA connected mode	Group 9 (GSM_ connected handover) Separate UE capability bit defined in 3GPP TS 36.306 for PS handover	Group 8/38 (PS handover) or Group 27/40 (SRVCC handover)	Group 12	Group 11	Group 13 (within FDD or TDD) Group 30 (between FDD and TDD)

I.1.10 DL Packet Transmission

I.1.10.1 Downlink Scheduled Operation Overview

Figure I.1.22 provides the steps involved in the eNB scheduling the UE in the DL (data traffic from the network to the UE). The PDCCH provides the DL grant to identify the resources for the PDSCH, where the data traffic is sent to UE. The UE indicates hybrid automatic repeat request (HARQ) positive acknowledgment (ACK) or negative acknowledgment (NACK) to the network based on its ability to successfully decode the packet from the network. If the UE indicates an ACK, the network assumes the UE received the packet successfully and moves to schedule subsequent packets. If the UE indicates a NACK, the network sends the packet to the UE again. The UE combines the information received across multiple transmissions for the same packet and attempts to decode the packet. The network attempts to send the same packet a finite number of times and gives up afterward. The RLC layer subsequently tries to resend the packet after all the HARQ attempts at the physical layer have failed.

I.1.10.2 Hybrid Automatic Repeat Request in LTE

Figure I.1.23 shows the systematic and parity bits and the packets forming for the each of the Hybrid ARQ (HARQ) transmission process supporting 4 IR (incremental redundancy) packets. The UE receives the different IR transmissions version and combines them to receive the decode the packet.

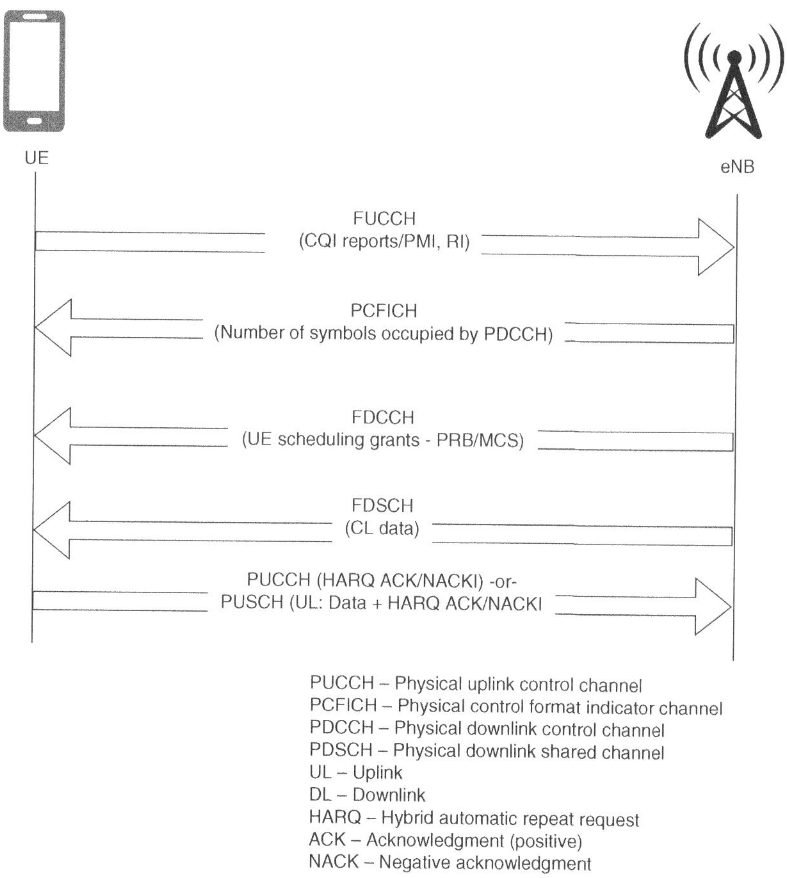

Figure I.1.22 UE downlink scheduling procedure.

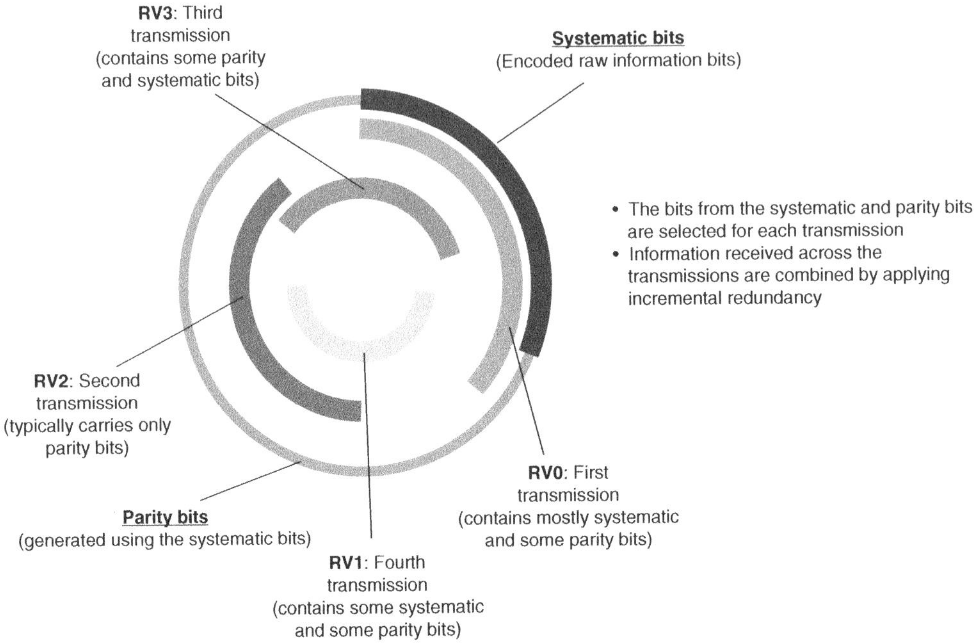

Figure I.1.23 Hybrid ARQ (HARQ) process.

The circle consists of systematic and parity bits. Hybrid ARQ or HARQ is a combination of high-rate forward error correction (FEC) and automatic repeat request (ARQ) error control. In standard ARQ, redundant bits are added to the data to be transmitted using an error-detecting (ED) code such as a cyclic redundancy check (CRC). Receivers detecting a corrupted message will request a new message from the sender. In HARQ, the original data is encoded with an FEC code, and the parity bits are either immediately sent along with the message or only transmitted upon request when a receiver detects an erroneous message. The FEC code is chosen to correct an expected subset of all errors that may occur, while the ARQ method is used as a fallback to correct errors that are uncorrectable using only the redundancy sent in the initial transmission. The HARQ procedure allows for the packets to be recovered through redundant transmissions at the physical layer without relying on the higher layers to resend the packet.

$$\textbf{FEC} = \left(\textbf{Forward Error Correction}\right)/\textbf{Soft Combining}.$$

FEC is a technique used in HARQ in LTE networks to improve the reliability of data transmission. FEC is a process in which redundant data is added to the original data before transmission. The additional data allows the receiver to detect and correct errors without the need for retransmissions.

In LTE, the FEC technique is implemented using a convolutional code, which is a type of error-correcting code. The convolutional code adds parity bits to the original data before transmission, enabling the receiver to detect and correct errors. The addition of the parity bits increases the size of the data transmitted, but it also improves the reliability of the data transmission.

The use of FEC in HARQ allows for more efficient and reliable data transmission, as it reduces the need for retransmission of data, which can result in increased latency and reduced throughput. In LTE networks, the combination of FEC and ARQ in the form of HARQ allows for efficient data transmission and error correction.

Figures I.1.24 and I.1.25 provide the HARQ sequence of repeats for the DL and UL HARQ processes, respectively.

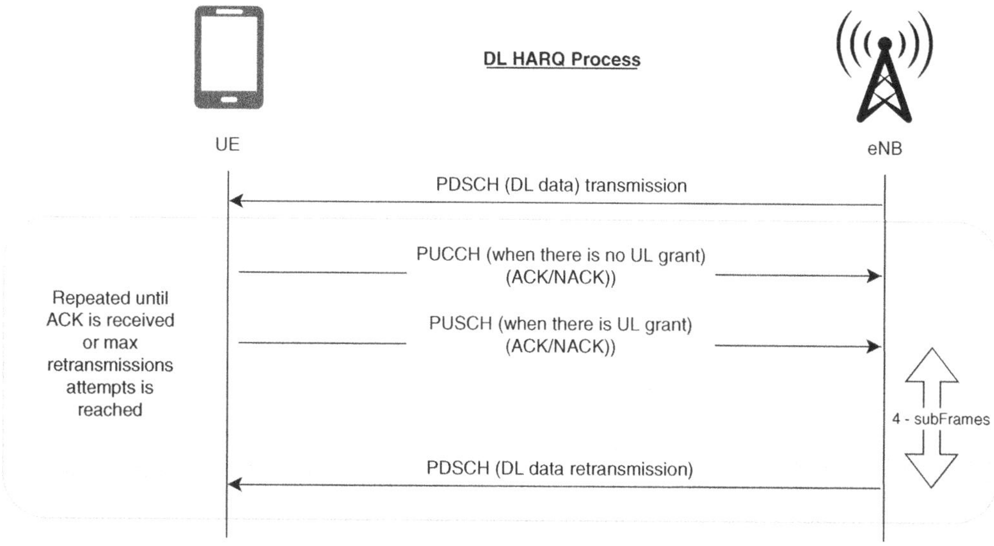

Figure I.1.24 DL HARQ process.

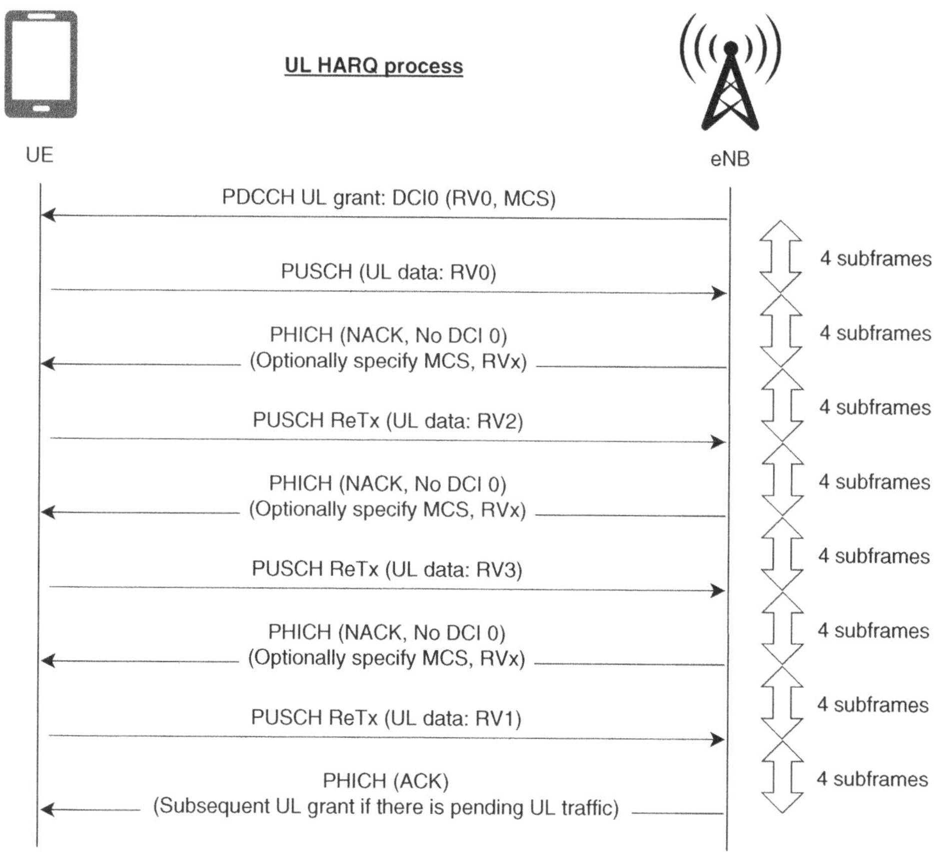

Figure I.1.25 UL HARQ process.

HARQ type	Description
Chase combining (Type 1 HARQ)	• The same information and parity bits are retransmitted each time. • Uses repetition coding to increase the Eb/No at the receiver, employing the maximal ratio combination (MRC) technique, proportionally summing it across all the received payloads for the same packet before passing it to the encoder. • Each transmission includes data + error detection (ED) bits + FEC bits. • If the channel quality is poor and not all errors can be corrected, the receiver asks for retransmission. • FEC adds a large overhead.
Incremental redundancy (Type #2 HARQ/ Type #3 HARQ)	• Each transmission includes information as data + error detection (ED) bits + FEC bits. • However, the information in the individual transmissions of the same packet is a different subset of data: ED and FEC. • In Type #2 HARQ, each retransmission of the packet includes redundant information, and the receiver uses all the transmissions received to form the packets. • In Type 3 HARQ, each retransmission is self-decodable, and retransmissions are made only if the channel conditions are not good and the data was not decoded correctly.

I.1.10.2.1 HARQ Processes

The HARQ process relies on receiving an ACK for the packets. If the sender sends a packet and then waits for the ACK before sending another packet, it is called a stop-and-wait (SAW) process. This increases the round-trip time (sender and receiver processing time + propagation delays). Therefore, multiple SAW processes are used in LTE. For example, when one SAW process is waiting for an ACK, another SAW process can send data. These SAW processes are also known as HARQ processes.

In LTE, in FDD, the RTT is 8 ms. The question arises: why are there eight HARQ processes? The answer is as follows: consider the case of DL. When the eNodeB sends data, the UE takes 3 ms for processing, so it sends an ACK/NACK 4 ms later. Similarly, after receiving the ACK/NACK, the eNodeB takes 3 ms for processing and sends a new transmission/retransmission, totaling of 8 ms. Hence, in FDD, there are 8 HARQ processes, so it takes 8 ms for a process to send data and receive an ACK/NACK, followed by a new transmission/retransmission 8 ms later, corresponding to an RTT of 8 ms. The max number of retransmissions for a MAC PDU is 4.

A HARQ entity and HARQ processes are maintained at both the eNodeB and the UE. During DL assignment, the eNodeB sends an new data indicator (NDI) bit through the PDCCH (DCI) to inform the UE whether the data is new or a retransmission. If the NDI bit is toggled, that is, different from the one sent in the previous transmission, it means new data is transmitted in the DL for the given HARQ process. If DCI 0, that is, an UL grant, is sent in the PDCCH and the NDI bit is toggled, this means the UE should transmit new data. Figure I.1.26 illustrates the HARQ process.

Overall architecture of LTE HARQ – MAC function

- Refer to 3GPP 36.321 sections 5.4.2.1 and 5.4.2.2 for a detailed description of the mechanism.
- A slightly different mode of the HARQ process is used depending on whether it is for FDD or TDD, and whether it is for UL or DL. However, I will only discuss the FDD case.
- In FDD, we are using eight HARQ processes.

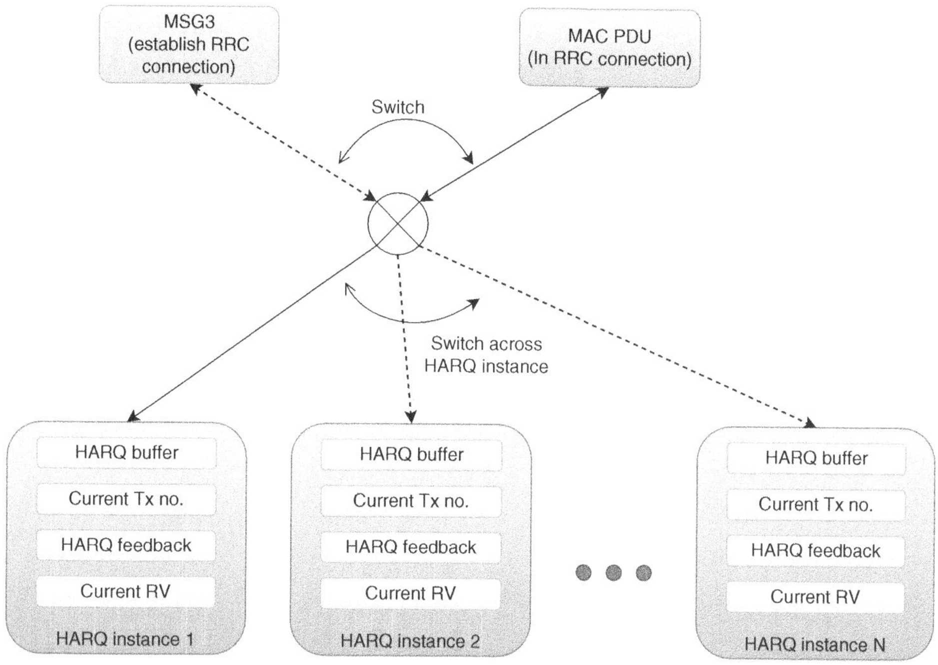

Figure I.1.26 LTE HARQ process.

i) For DL: asynchronous process
   a) it can use the eight HARQ processes in any order (asynchronous process).
   b) The UE does not have any prior knowledge of HARQ process information for DL data until it receives it. Therefore, the network sends this information (process ID, redundancy version [RV]) in the PDCCH (DCI; refer to DCI section of this site).
ii) For UL: synchronous process
   a) it has to use the specific process in a specific subframe (synchronous process). UE must use the same HARQ process number every eight subframes.
   b) Since UE has to use a specific HARQ process ID at a specific subframe, the receiver (eNode B) knows exactly which HARQ process comes when. Additionally, the eNodeB can also know about RV because the UL grant (DCI 0) from the eNodeB can specify RV using the modulation coding scheme (MCS) field.
   c) It has two modes of operation: adaptive and nonadaptive HARQ.

I.1.10.2.2 HARQ Procedure During Downlink Transmission

When the eNodeB sends data to the UE through PDSCH, the UE determines its correctness by checking the CRC and reporting it to the eNodeB through the ACK/NACK bit. If the UE also has data to send and receives a grant, it will send ACK/NACK on PUSCH along with the data; otherwise, it will send it on PUCCH. The eNodeB can use eight HARQ processes in any order (asynchronous HARQ); that is, retransmissions can occur at any time relative to the initial transmission. Figure I.1.27 provides a pictorial representation of the sequence of the steps involved with the LTE DL HARQ process.

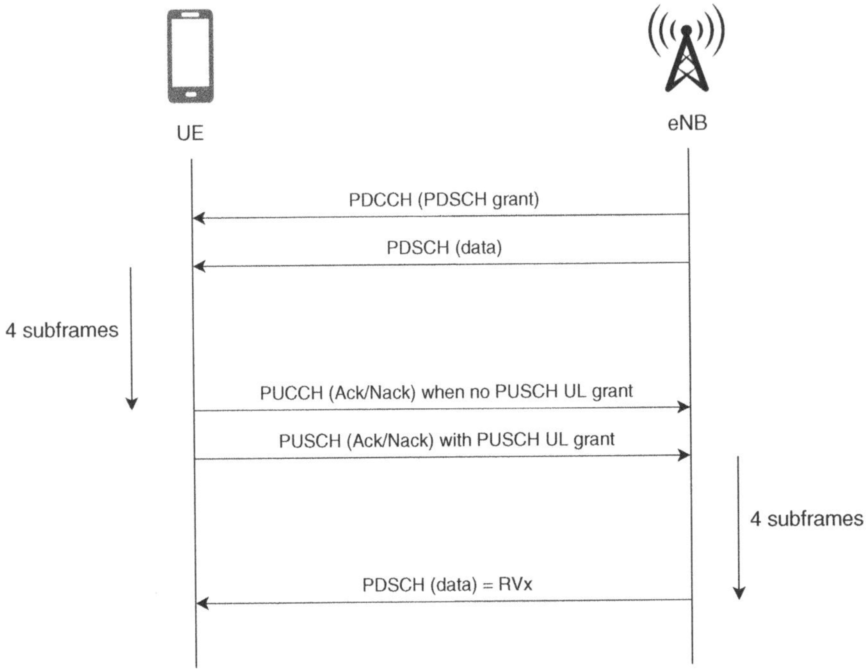

Figure I.1.27 LTE DL HARQ process.

Therefore, it needs to send the HARQ ID for the UE to determine the original transmission corresponding to which the retransmission is happening. The HARQ ID is sent in the PDCCH. DL supports adaptive transmission; that is, resources are allocated afresh each time and sent on the PDCCH. RV and MCS are notified in DCI 0. RV values are predefined in specifications (0, 2, 3, 1). CURRENT_IRV is an index into this sequence.

- Maintain several HARQ processes.
- Analyze the search space to find a DL grant on the PDCCH.
- Send HARQ information to the UE through the PDSCH; send the HARQ process ID and RV on the PDCCH.
- UE receives the data and finds the HARQ process number from the PDCCH. If it is a retransmission, it performs soft combining of this data with the data stored in the buffer from the last time. If it were a new transmission, it buffers the data and checks the CRC. It requires 3 ms for processing, after which it takes 4 ms. If it has data to send and has a grant, it will send UL data along with ACK/NACK on PUSCH; otherwise, it sends ACK/NACK on PUCCH.

I.1.10.3 CQI/PMI/RI Reporting Overview

UE provides control information to the eNB and uses the PUCCH (when there is no scheduled UL PUSCH grant available) and the PUSCH (control information multiplexed together with UL data traffic) to transmit.

Figure I.1.28 illustrates the channel state information reported on the PUCCH/PUSCH channels on the UL.

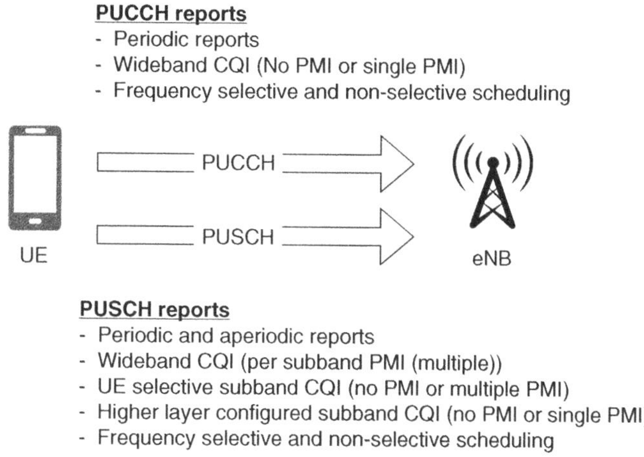

Figure I.1.28 PUCCH/PUSCH reports.

I.1.11 UL Packet Transmission

I.1.11.1 Uplink Scheduled Operation – Link Adaptation

Figure I.1.29 illustrates the uplink scheduled operation showing the link adaptation procedure.

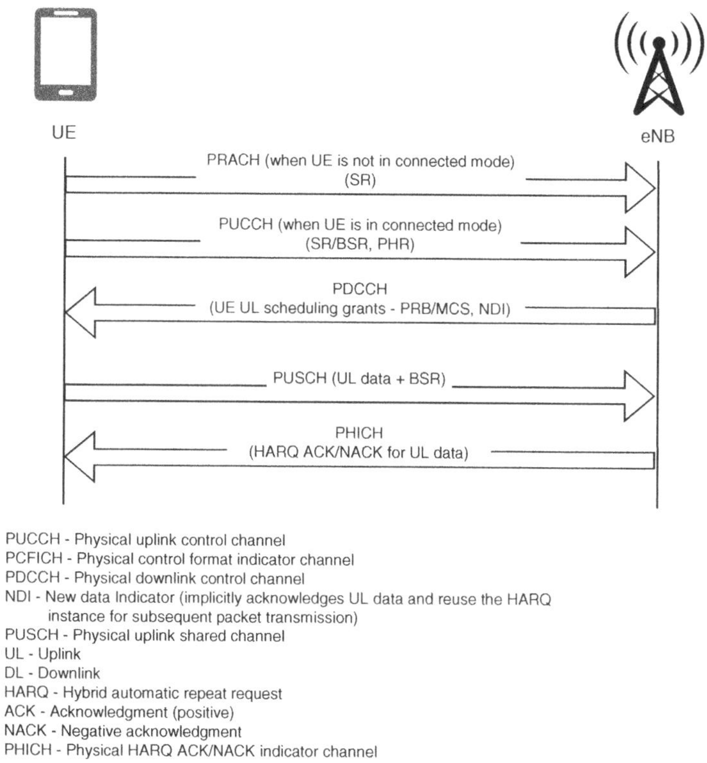

Figure I.1.29 Uplink scheduled operation – link adaptation.

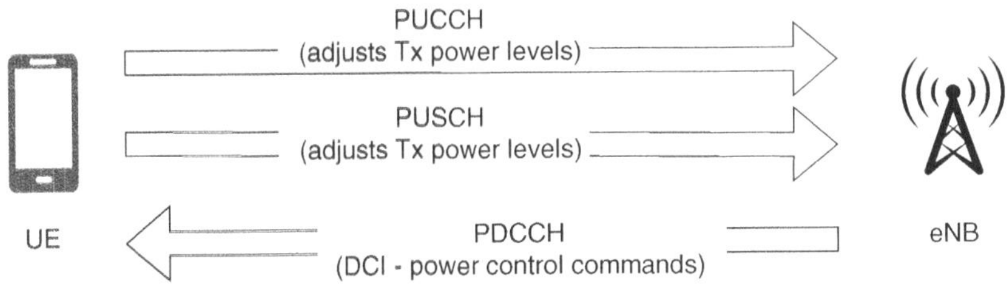

Figure I.1.30 Uplink power control of PUCCH and PUSCH.

I.1.11.2 Uplink Closed Loop Power Control

The PUCCH and PUSCH require power control to avoid interference with other users while optimally completing the link. The eNB continuously monitors the link by measuring the reference signals and packet error rate (PER) experienced on the channel. The UE is associated with only one cell/eNB at a time – the serving cell. The eNB sends TPC commands using DCI over the PDCCH. The UE adjusts the transmit power level based on the power control commands provided. Figure I.1.30 show this uplink power control of PUCCH and PUSCH process.

I.1.11.3 HARQ Procedure During Uplink Transmission

When UE sends data in the UL through PUSCH, eNB has to determine its correctness using CRC and inform UE about the ACK/NACK. eNodeB sends ACK/NACK through PHICH. Each HARQ process uses a round-robin fashion to transmit HARQ; hence, each transmission and retransmission can be determined from SFN and SF. UE does not need to send information about RV (synchronous HARQ).

UL can be used for adaptive or nonadaptive retransmission. In adaptive UL transmission, MCS and RV are determined from DCI 0. In nonadaptive UL transmission, the transmission attributes remain the same as in the previous transmission. RVs are assigned according to a predefined sequence: 0, 2, 3, 1. The variable CURRENT_IRV is an index into this sequence. When the eNB does not send a DCI 0 but sends a NACK on PHICH, the UE performs nonadaptive retransmission.

- Maintain several HARQ processes.
- Analyze the search space to find an UL grant, that is, DCI 0 on PDCCH.
- Calculate the HARQ process number corresponding to this subframe.
- Route HARQ information to it.
- eNB receives the data on PUSCH and calculates the HARQ process number from the TTI where the UL transmission is scheduled. If it were a retransmission, it performs soft combining of this data with the data stored in the buffer from the last time. If it were a new transmission, it buffers the data and checks the CRC. It requires 3 ms for processing; after 4 ms, it sends ACK/NACK on PHICH.

I.1.11.3.1 Adaptive UL HARQ Process

Here, the transmission attributes, such as MCS, RV, and the subcarrier on which transmission is going to occur, do not remain the same during each retransmission but are notified by the sender. These attributes can be changed according to radio channel conditions; hence, they again provide flexibility but increase overhead. Figure I.1.31 illustrates the adaptive UL HARQ process.

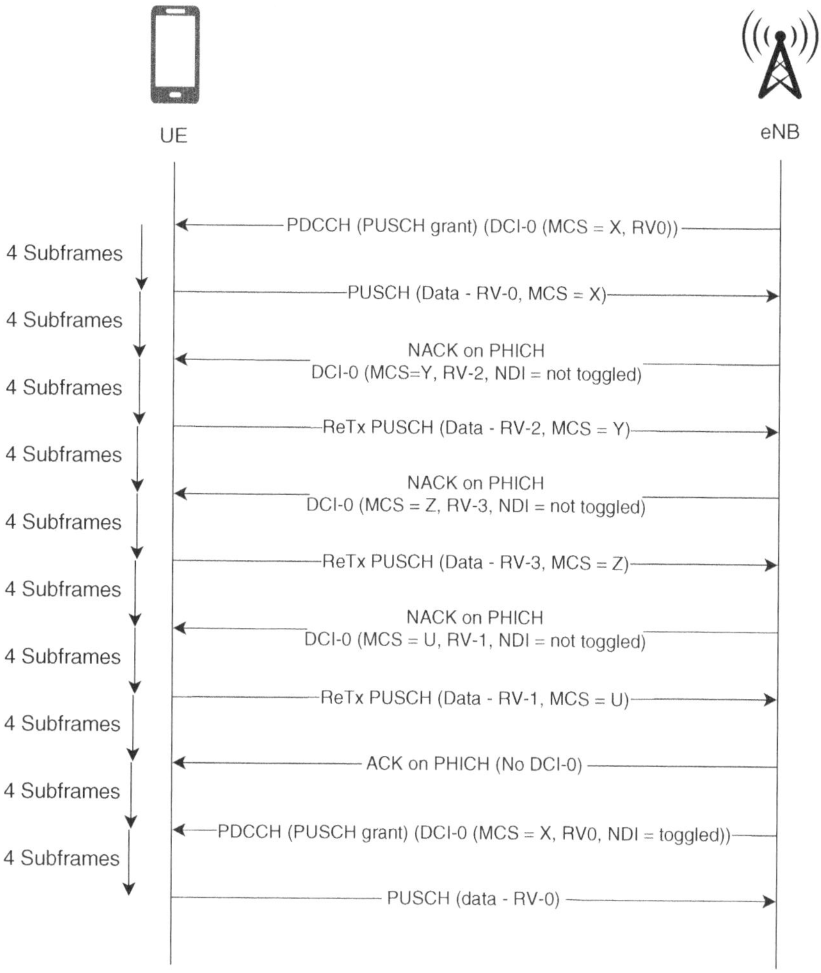

Figure I.1.31 Adaptive UL HARQ process.

UE performs "adaptive retransmission" if it detects DCI 0 with NDI not toggled. (In this case, UE does not care about "HARQ feedback (PHICH)"; it retransmits based on DCI 0 information.)

I.1.11.3.2 Nonadaptive UL HARQ Process

Here, the transmission attributes remain the same during each retransmission. The UE performs "nonadaptive retransmission" if it receives "HARQ feedback (PHICH = NACK)" but does not get DCI 0. In this case, the UE retransmits the PUSCH in predefined RV and MCS without the information from DCI 0. Figure I.1.32 illustrates the nonadaptive UL HARQ process.

I.1.12 Encryption

The UE uses signaling radio bearer (SRB) to exchange control signaling information. When the UE initiates a RACH to connect to the network, the signaling messages exchanged are done using signaling radio bearer 0 (SRB0). SRB0 is used to transfer RRC messages that utilize the common control

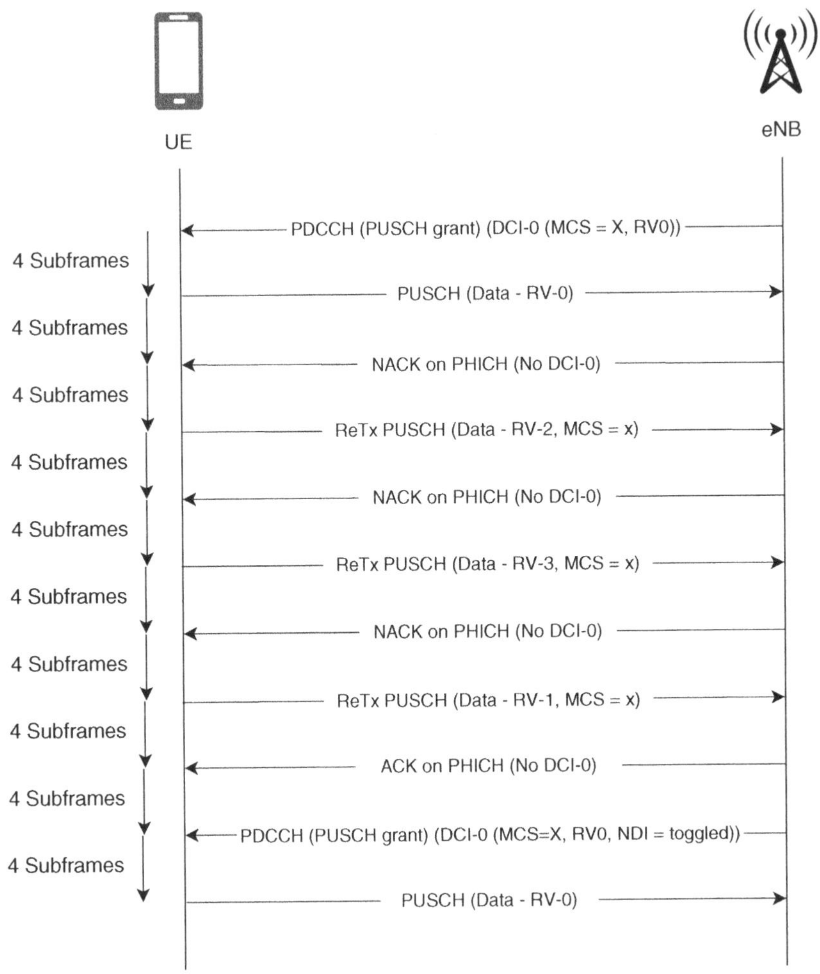

Figure I.1.32 Nonadaptive UL HARQ process.

channel (CCCH) and does not have any encryption. Once the UE is RRC connected to the eNB, SRB1 is established, and encryption between the UE and eNB can be performed. SRB1 is used to transfer RRC messages that utilize the dedicated control channel (DCCH). SRB1 is also used to encapsulate NAS messages if SRB2 has not been configured. The UE uses SRB1 to perform UE authentication, transporting messages to the MME. Once the UE is authenticated, SRB2 is established, which supports full encryption. SRB2 is used to transfer RRC messages that use the DCCH channel and encapsulate a NAS message. SRB2 has a lower priority than SRB1, and it is always configured after security activation. SRB0 uses transparent mode RLC, while SRB1 and SRB2 use acknowledged mode RLC.

LTE SRB type	DL/UL	RRC message	RLC mode
LTE SRB0 (CCCH)	DL	RRC connection setup RRC connection reject RRC connection reestablishment RRC connection reestablishment reject	Transparent
LTE SRB0 (CCCH)	UL	RRC connection request RRC connection reestablishment request	Transparent

LTE SRB type	DL/UL	RRC message	RLC mode
LTE SRB1 (DCCH)	DL	RRC connection reconfiguration RRC connection release Security mode command UE capability inquiry DL information transfer (if no SRB-2) Mobility from EUTRA command Handover from the EUTRA preparation request Circuit-Switch (CS) fallback parameter response CDMA2000 Counter check	Acknowledged
LTE SRB1 (DCCH)	UL	RRC connection setup complete Security mode is complete Security mode failure RRC connection reconfiguration is complete RRC connection reestablishment is complete Measurement report UE capability information UL information transfer (if no SRB2) UL handover preparation transfer CS fallback parameters request for CDMA2000 Counter check response	Acknowledged
LTE SRB2 (DCCH)	DL	DL information transfer	Acknowledged
LTE SRB2 (DCCH)	UL	UL information transfer	Acknowledged

I.1.13 Channel Estimation

Channel estimation is fundamental for the information exchange between the UE and the network. A proper estimation of the channel allows the UE to be scheduled on the DL and UL with the appropriate MCS, which is the packet encoding used for transmission. A conservative MCS is used in poorer radio conditions; however, a lower MCS implies less throughput on the channel. A trade-off is required to ensure that the UE has an optimal choice of MCS to reduce the PER on the channel while retaining the maximum possible throughput.

The DL reference signal that is typically transmitted at a fixed power level is used by the UE to estimate the performance achievable on the channel. The measured estimates are sent to the eNB for scheduling, potentially for both DL and UL. Similarly, the UE transmits a reference signal on the UL that the network can use for channel estimation. For TDD channels, given that the DL and UL operate on the same spectrum, unlike FDD, the network uses these UL reference signals to schedule the UE for both UL and DL, apart from using the channel estimation reports provided by the UE. In addition to using channel estimation reports, the network also uses the residual PER to assess the performance of the channel and adapts the MCS as needed to schedule a UE.

The relevant DL and UL reference signals are provided below.

I.1.13.1 DL Reference Signals

Five types of DL reference signals are defined:

- Cell-specific reference signals (CRS)
- MBSFN reference signals
- UE-specific reference signals (DMRS)
- Positioning reference signals (PRS)
- Channel State Information (CSI) reference signals (CSI-RS)

I.1.13.2 UL Reference Signals

- UL physical reference signals are used within the Physical Layer (PHY) layer and do not convey information from higher layers. There are two main types of sounding reference signals and demodulation reference signals, as mentioned below.
- Demodulation reference signal:
  - This facilitates coherent demodulation and is associated with the transmission of PUSCH or PUCCH. It is transmitted in the fourth SC-FDMA symbol of the slot and is the same size as the assigned resource.
- Sounding reference signal:
  - This is used to facilitate frequency-dependent scheduling and is not associated with the transmission of PUSCH or PUCCH. Both variants of the UL reference signal are based on Zadoff-Chu sequences.
  - Sounding Reference Signal (SRS) are of two types based on periodicity. The minimum periodicity of SRS is 2 ms, and the maximum is about 320 ms.
- The similarity between SRS and Demodulation Reference Signal (DMRS) is that both use constant amplitude zero autocorrelation (CAZAC) sequences.

Reference signal type	Direction	Modulation	Position	Function
DL-RS	Used in the downlink	QPSK	First and third from the last OFDM symbol in each slot, with a six-subcarrier difference between them in the symbol	These pilot subcarriers are used for channel estimation by the UE
DMRS	Used in the uplink		Fourth SC-FDMA symbol of the slot	Channel estimation
SRS	Used in the UL	Zadoff-Chu	Transmitted on the last SC-FDMA symbol of each subframe or once after two slots	Channel sounding – understanding channel quality and subsequently addressing frequency selective fading

I.1.13.3 Channel Estimation

- Used for
  - Scheduling for both DL and UL
  - Triggers and measurement reporting for access and mobility
- The measurement of the reference signals is used for mobility – both the current serving cell and its neighbors
  - Reference Signal Received Power (RSRP) or Reference Signal Received Quality (RSRQ)
- For MIMO/beamforming and MCS selection for scheduling
  - CQI reported from the UE is used for DL
- SRS or residual Block Error Rate (BLER) is used for the UL

I.1.14 Layer 2 Protocols

The LTE layer 2 protocols include the MAC layer, RLC layer, and PDCP layer.

I.1.14.1 LTE MAC

Figure I.1.33 provides the MAC structure overview, UE side. This illustration is from 3GPP TS 36.321, figure 4.2.1-1.

LTE MAC functions	Description
Multiplexing and demultiplexing	The multiplexing and demultiplexing entity is in charge of forming and decoding the MAC PDUs. It performs multiplexing and demultiplexing of data from several logical channels into and from one transport channel.
Logical channel prioritization	When the radio resources for a new transmission are allocated, the logical channel prioritization manages the multiplexing and demultiplexing functions to generate MAC PDUs from the MAC SDUs. The logical channel prioritization also determines how much data from each configured logical channel should be included in each MAC PDU whenever radio resources for a new transmission are available.
HARQ	The HARQ function performs the "transmit" and "receive" HARQ operations. The transmit HARQ operation includes the transmission of transport blocks and, if necessary, the retransmission of the transport blocks, as well as the reception and processing of HARQ ACK/NACK signaling. The receive HARQ operation includes the reception of transport blocks, the combining and decoding of the received transport blocks, and the generation of HARQ ACK/NACK signaling.
Control	The control function is responsible for several functions, including DRX, resource requests, alignment of the UL timing, power headroom reporting, and so on. The random access (RA) procedure is used to request UL radio resources to transmit UL data when the UE does not have any dedicated UL transmission resources or to respond to the network's request.

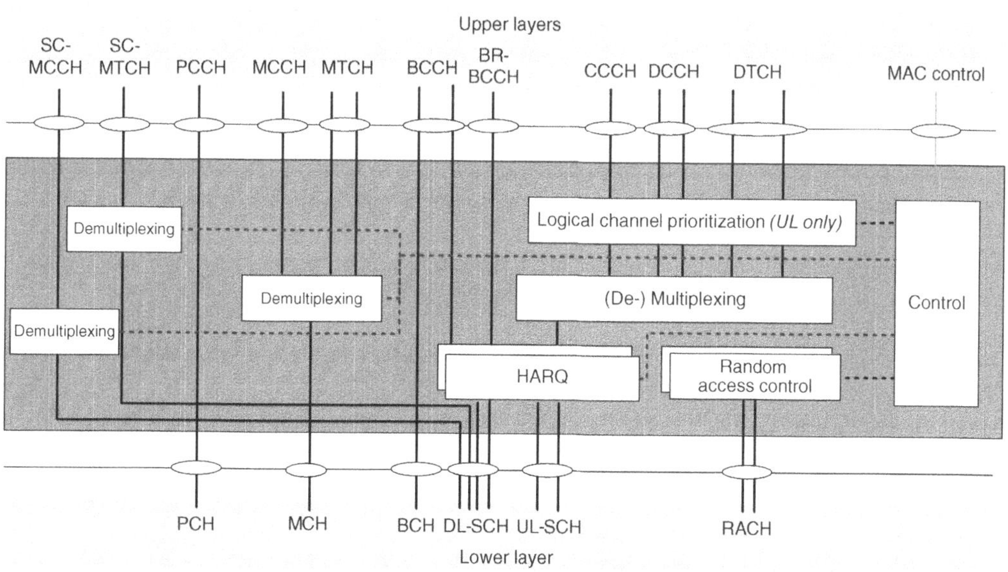

Figure I.1.33 MAC structure overview, UE side (from 3GPP TS 36.321, figure 4.2.1-1).

The LTE MAC functions include mapping between logical channels and transport channels, as well as multiplexing MAC SDUs from one or different logical channels onto transport blocks (TB) to be delivered to the physical layer on transport channels. It also supports the demultiplexing of MAC SDUs from one or different logical channels from TBs delivered from the physical layer on transport channels. The MAC function handles the scheduling information reporting and error correction through HARQ. Priority handling between UEs by means of dynamic scheduling and priority handling between the logical channels of one UE is a fundamental MAC function for managing control signaling and QoS functions. Based on the packets handled, the transport format selection is performed.

I.1.14.1.1 Transport Channels and Logical Channel

LTE is based entirely on shared BCHs and contains no dedicated channels carrying data to specific UEs, enabling a packet-switched end-to-end architecture. This improves the efficiency of the radio interface and can support dynamic resource allocation between different UEs, depending on their traffic/QoS requirements and their respective channel conditions. MAC procedures used for L2-level operations include the RA procedure, DL/UL-SCH data transfer, paging channel (PCH) reception, BCH reception, DRX, MAC reconfiguration, and MAC reset. The operations are structured using logical and transport channels for functional realization.

Logical channels provide services at the Service Access Point (SAP) between the MAC and RLC layers, while transport channels provide services at the SAP between the MAC and PHY layers.

Logical Channels

Table I.1.3 provide the list of LTE logical control channels along with the context / relevance of these channels. Table I.1.4 captures the LTE logical traffic channels.

Transport Channels

Transport channels exist between the MAC and physical layer. The transport channels are used by the PHY to offer services to its upper layer, that is, the MAC. Table I.1.5 provides the LTE downlink (DL) transport channels and Table I.1.6 provides the LTE uplink (UL) transport channels.

Table I.1.3 The LTE logical control channels.

Logical control channels	Description
Broadcast control channel (BCCH)	BCCH is a DL channel used to carry broadcast system control information (e.g. SIBs)
Multicast control channel (MCCH)	A point-to-multipoint DL channel is used for transmitting control information to UEs in the cell. It is used only by UEs that receive multicast/broadcast services.
Paging control channel (PCCH)	PCCH is a DL control channel that carries paging information such as control information during mobile-terminated calls.
Common control channel (CCCH)	CCCH is used to carry control information between the UE and the network when the RRC connection is not available. CCCH is a bidirectional channel. CCCH is used during the RA procedure.
Dedicated control channel (DCCH)	A point-to-point, bidirectional channel that transmits dedicated control information between a UE and the network. This channel is used when the RRC connection is available; that is, the UE is attached to the network.

Table I.1.4 LTE logical traffic channels.

Logical traffic channels	Description
Dedicated traffic channel (DTCH)	A point-to-point, bidirectional channel used between a given UE and the network. It can exist in both UL and DL.
Multicast traffic channel (MTCH)	A unidirectional, point-to-multipoint data channel that transmits traffic data from the network to UEs. It is associated with the multicast/broadcast service.

Table I.1.5 LTE DL transport channels.

DL transport channels	Description
Broadcast channel (BCH)	BCH is associated with the BCCH logical channel and is used to broadcast system information over the entire coverage area of the cell. BCH has a predefined transport format.
Downlink shared channel (DL-SCH)	DL-SCH is used to transfer both DL traffic data and control data. DL-SCH supports HARQ, dynamic link adaptation, dynamic and semi-persistent resource allocation, UE DRX, and multicast/broadcast transmission. DL-SCH can be broadcast throughout the entire cell.
Paging channel (PCH)	PCH is only associated with the PCCH logical channel. The PCH channel supports DRX to enable UE power saving and can be used in the entire cell coverage area.
Multicast channel (MCH)	Associated with MCCH and MTCH are logical channels for the multicast/broadcast service. It supports multicast/broadcast single frequency network (MBSFN) transmission, which transmits the same information on the same radio resources from multiple synchronized base stations to multiple UEs.

Table I.1.6 LTE UL transport channels.

UL transport channels	Description
Uplink shared channel (UL-SCH)	UL-SCH works similarly to DL-SCH but in the UL. It supports HARQ, both dynamic and semi-static resource allocation, dynamic link adaptation, and beamforming. It can be associated with CCCH, DCCH, and DTCH logical channels.
Random access channel (RACH)	RACH is not associated with any logical channels and is used for transmitting a small amount of data; for example, RACH can be used in the case of initial access.

A transport channel is characterized by how and with what characteristics data is transferred over the radio interface; that is, the channel coding scheme, the modulation scheme, and antenna mapping. Transport channels can be of two types depending on the direction of use: DL transport channels and UL transport channels.

I.1.14.1.2 MAC PDU – Protocol Data Unit

A MAC PDU consists of a MAC header, zero or more MAC service data units (MAC SDUs), zero or more MAC control elements, and optionally padding. MAC PDUs are byte-aligned, meaning they are multiples of 8 bits. MAC headers and SDUs are of variable sizes. MAC SDUs (RLC PDUs) are also byte-aligned. A MAC PDU subheader consists of the six header fields R/R/E/LCID/F/L, except for the last subheader in the MAC PDU and for fixed-sized MAC control elements. The last subheader in the MAC PDU and the subheaders for fixed-sized MAC control elements consist solely of the four header fields: R/R/E/LCID. A MAC PDU subheader corresponding to padding consists of the four header fields: R/R/E/LCID. MAC PDU subheaders have the same order as the corresponding MAC SDUs, MAC control elements, and padding. MAC control elements are always placed before any MAC SDU. Figure I.1.34 provides the data structure for the MAC PDU.

I.1.14.1.3 Radio Link Control

The following set of figures are used to illustrate the structure and operations of the Radio Link Control (RLC) layer. Some of these figures are directly borrowed from the 3GPP specification and included here to provide the relevant context to the reader. Figure I.1.35 provides an overview of the model of the RLC sublayer (3GPP TS 36.322, figure 4.2.1-1). Figure I.1.36 shows the behavior as the RLC RRC connection is setup. Figure I.1.37 shows the RLC interactions with other layersfor uplink (UL)

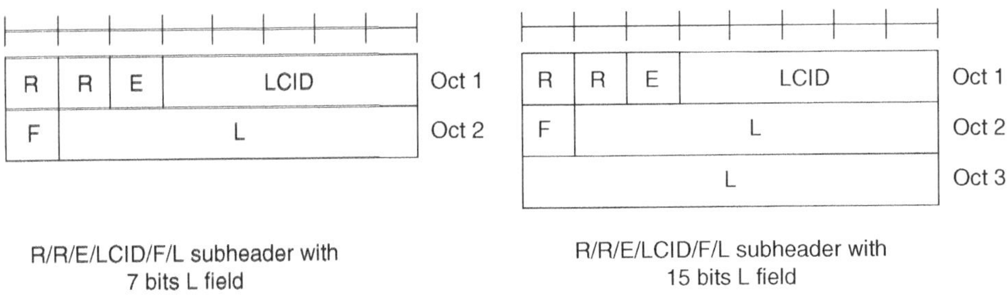

Figure I.1.34 MAC PDU.

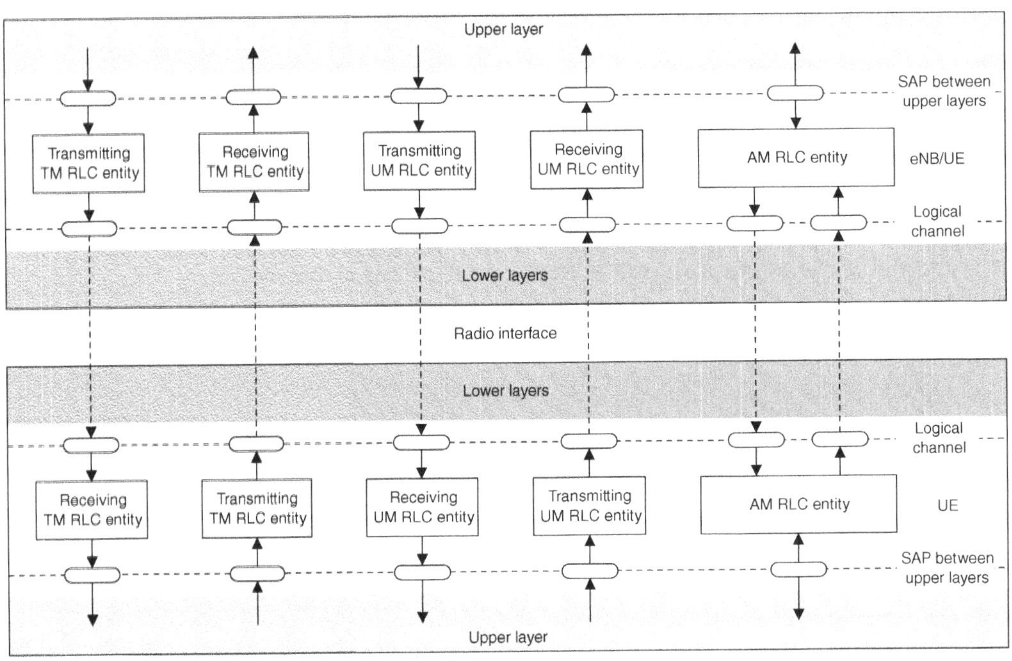

Figure I.1.35 Overview of the model of the RLC sublayer (3GPP TS 36.322, figure 4.2.1-1).

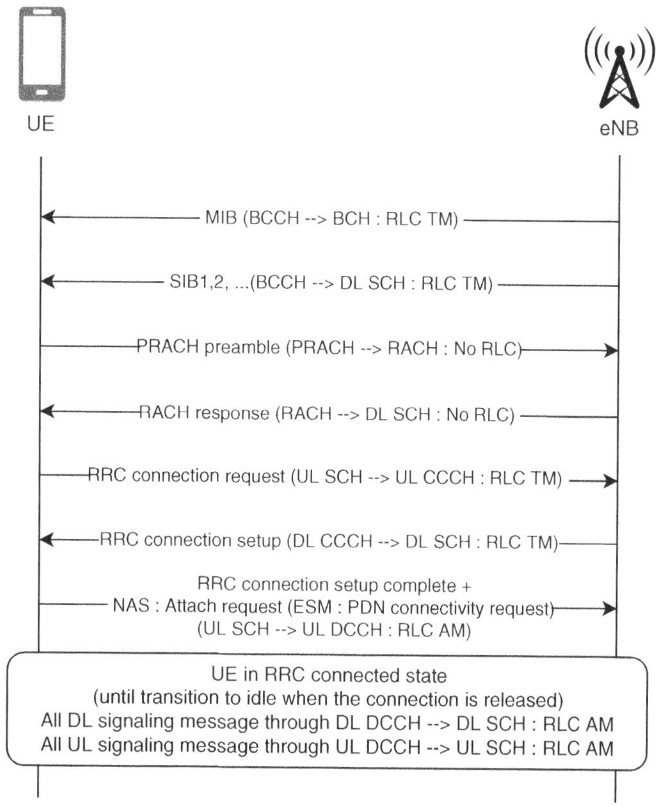

Figure I.1.36 RLC during RRC connection setup.

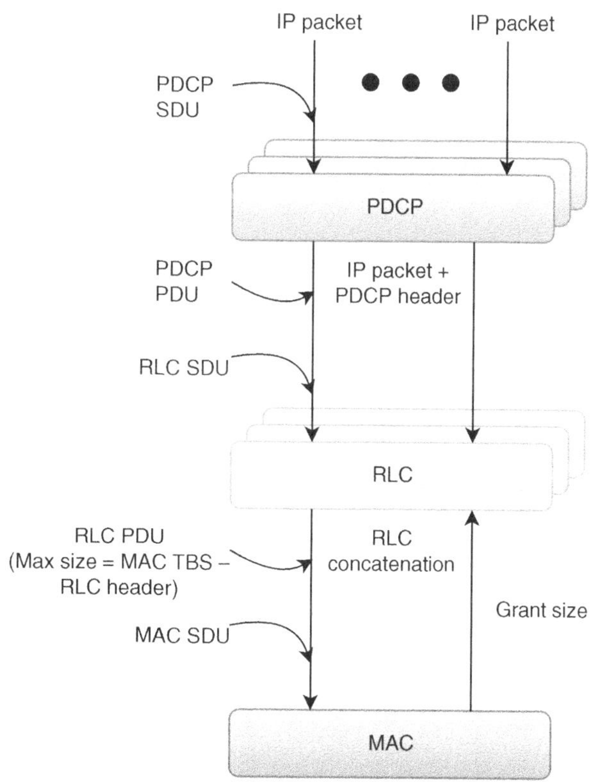

Figure I.1.37 RLC interaction with other layers – UL.

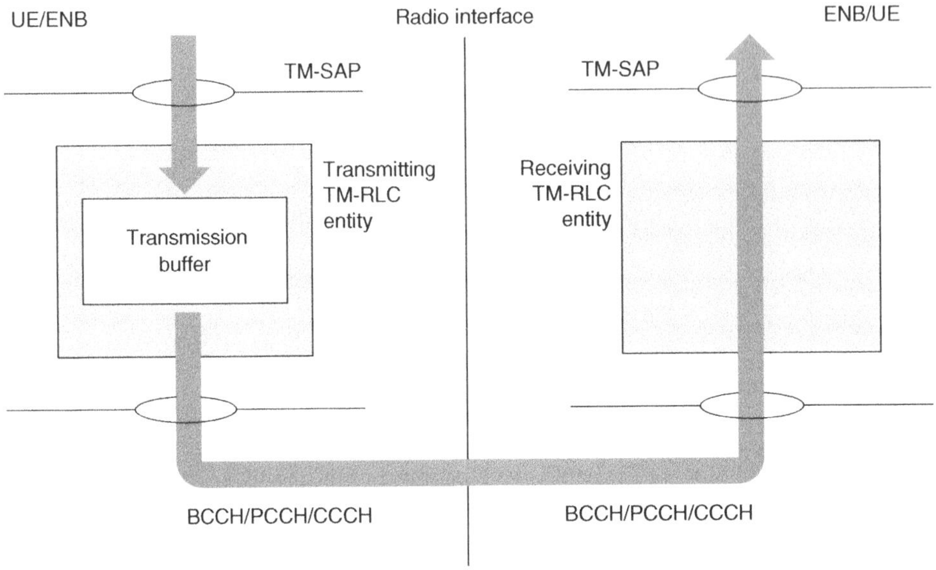

Figure I.1.38 Model of two transparent mode peer entities (from 3GPP TS 36.322, figure 4.2.1.1.1-1).

operations as seen from the UE perspective. Figure I.1.38 show the model of two transparent mode peer entities (from 3GPP TS 36.322, figure 4.2.1.1.1-1). Figure I.1.39 shows the model of two unacknowledged mode peer entities (from 3GPP TS 36.322, figure 4.2.1.2.1-1). Figure I.1.40 shows the model of two acknowledged mode peer entities (from 3GPP TS 36.322, figure 4.2.1.3.1-1).

I.1.14.1.4 Packet Data Convergence Protocol

The data coming into the (eNB or UE) first goes through PDCP and then gets into RLC (DL path). Data waiting in RLC trying to go out to the outside world must go through PDCP to reach the outside world (UL path). PDCP supports the functions listed below.

- Transfer of data (C-plane and U-plane) between the RLC and the higher U-plane interface
- Maintenance of PDCP sequence number (SN)
- Transfer of SN status (for use upon handover)
- Robust header compression (RoHC)
- In-sequence delivery of upper-layer PDUs at the reestablishment of the lower layer
- Elimination of duplicates of lower-layer SDUs at the reestablishment of the lower layer for RLC AM
- Ciphering and deciphering of C-plane and U-plane data
- Integrity protection and integrity verification of C-plane data
- Timer-based discard
- Duplicate discard
- For split and LTE/WLAN Aggregation (LWA) bearers, routing, and reordering

Figure I.1.41 shows the PDCP layer, structure view (from 3GPP TS 36.323, figure 4.2.1.1). Figure I.1.42 shows the PDCP layer, functional view (from 3GPP TS 36.323, figure 4.2.2.1).

I.1.14.1.5 PDCP Data PDUs

Figure I.1.43 shows the PDCP data PDUs data structure.

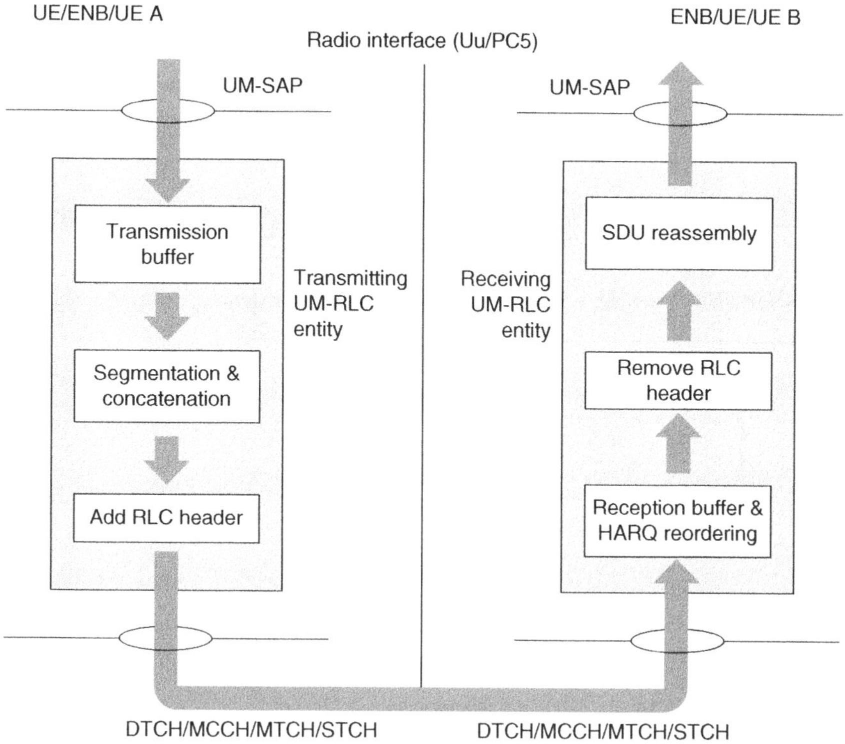

Figure I.1.39 Model of two unacknowledged mode peer entities (from 3GPP TS 36.322, figure 4.2.1.2.1-1).

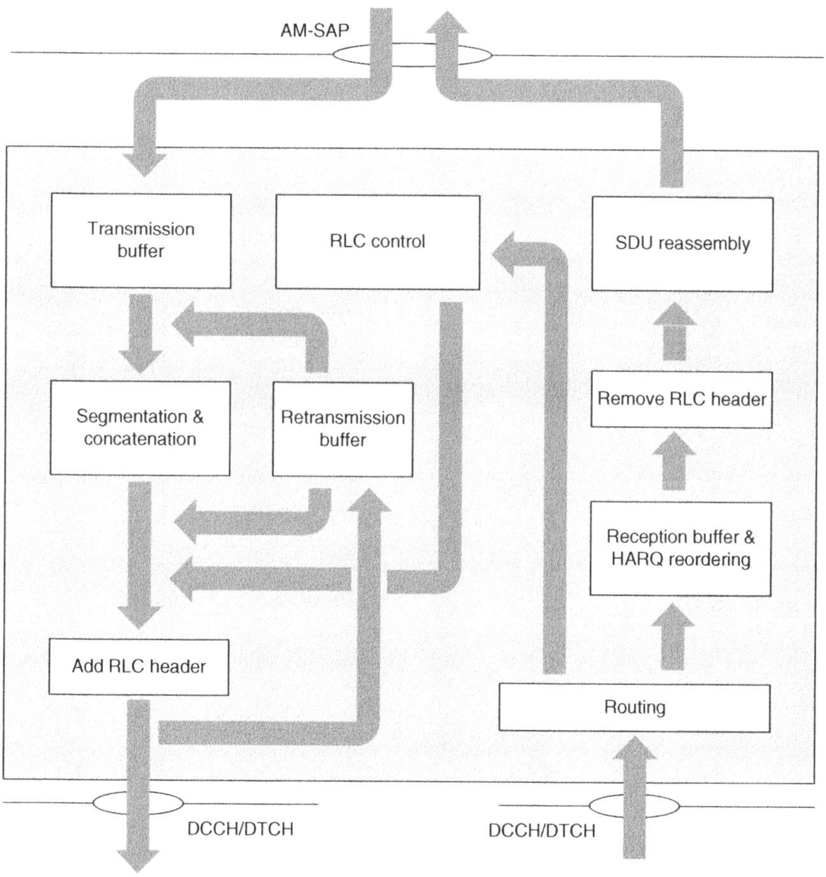

Figure I.1.40 Model of two acknowledged mode peer entities (from 3GPP TS 36.322, figure 4.2.1.3.1-1).

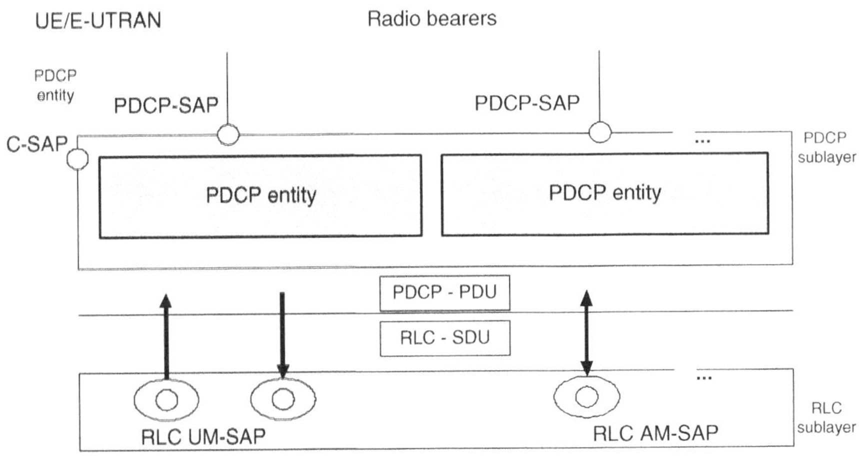

Figure I.1.41 PDCP layer, structure view (from 3GPP TS 36.323, figure 4.2.1.1).

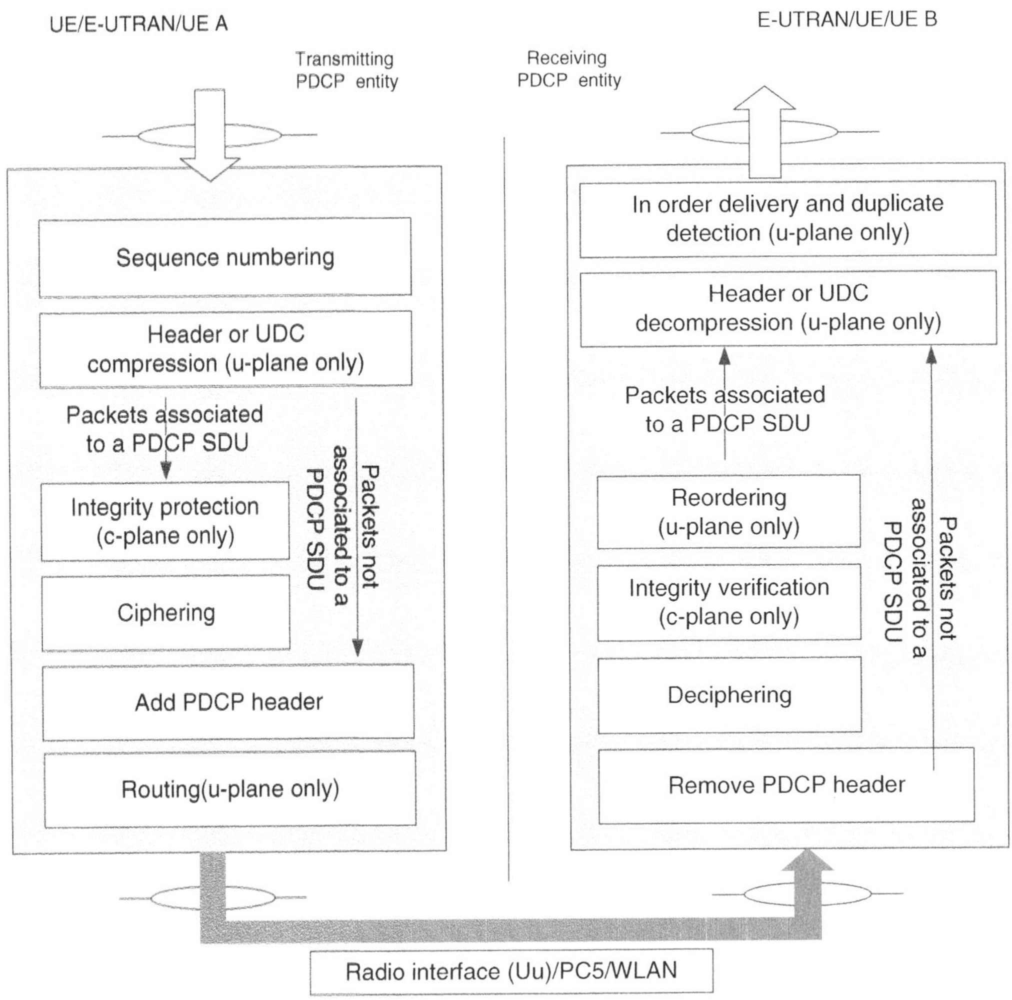

Figure I.1.42 PDCP layer, functional view (from 3GPP TS 36.323, figure 4.2.2.1).

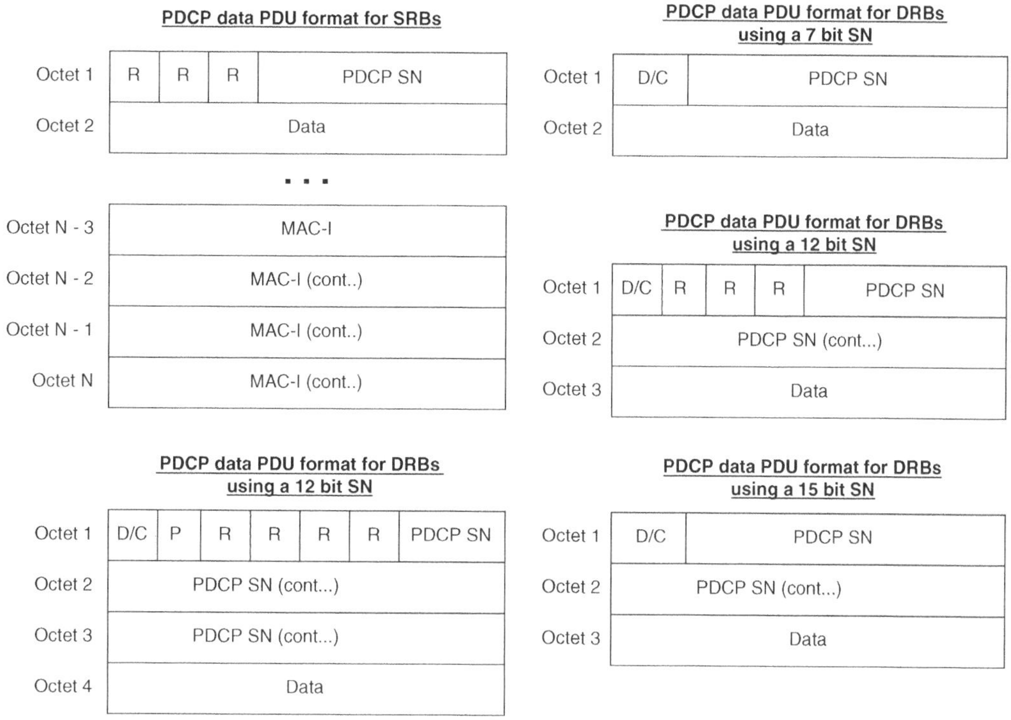

Figure I.1.43 PDCP data PDUs.

I.1.14.1.6 PDCP Control PDUs

Figure I.1.44 shows the PDCP control PDUs data structure.

Integrity Protection Process

Figure I.1.45 illustrates the integrity protection process.

I.1.14.2 Robust Header Compression

RoHC provides a mechanism to perform header compression at the transmitter and decompression at the receiver to reduce the overhead caused by headers at the Open Systems Interconnection (OSI) network, transport, and application layers, For example IP (network layer), TCP (transport layer), and RTP (application layer). See 3GPP TS 33.323 for more details on RoHC. RoHC operates in different modes. Table I.1.7 provides the various RoHC modes. Table I.1.8 provides the different RoHC states to which compressor transitions based on the operating mode and feedback received from the decompressor. Figure I.1.46 illustrates the RoHC state transitions associated with the RoHC operating modes. Table I.1.9 provides the set of RoHC profiles defined in 3GPP, specifying the headers that are compressed. Figure I.1.47 shows the RoHC state transitions in U, O, and R modes at the RoHC compressor.

I.1.15 Cell Reselection

Cell reselection is the process by which the UE measures the DL reference signals and determines the best cell to camp on at any given time. There are times when the current cell is "good enough" and the neighboring cell is not stronger than a certain threshold; in such cases, the UE continues

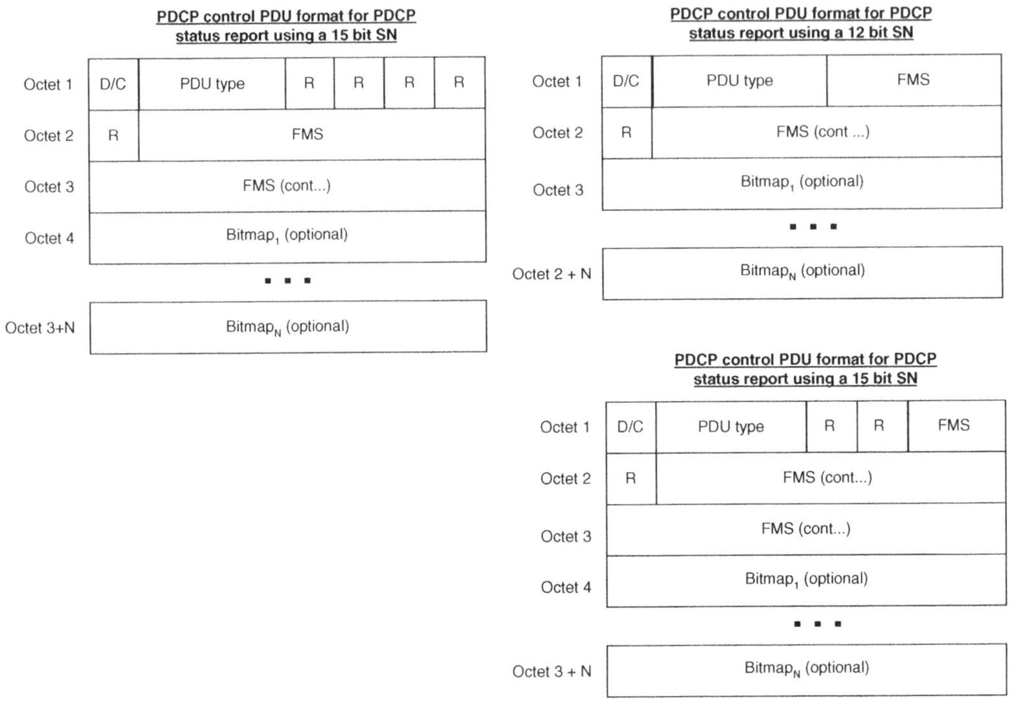

Figure I.1.44 PDCP control PDUs.

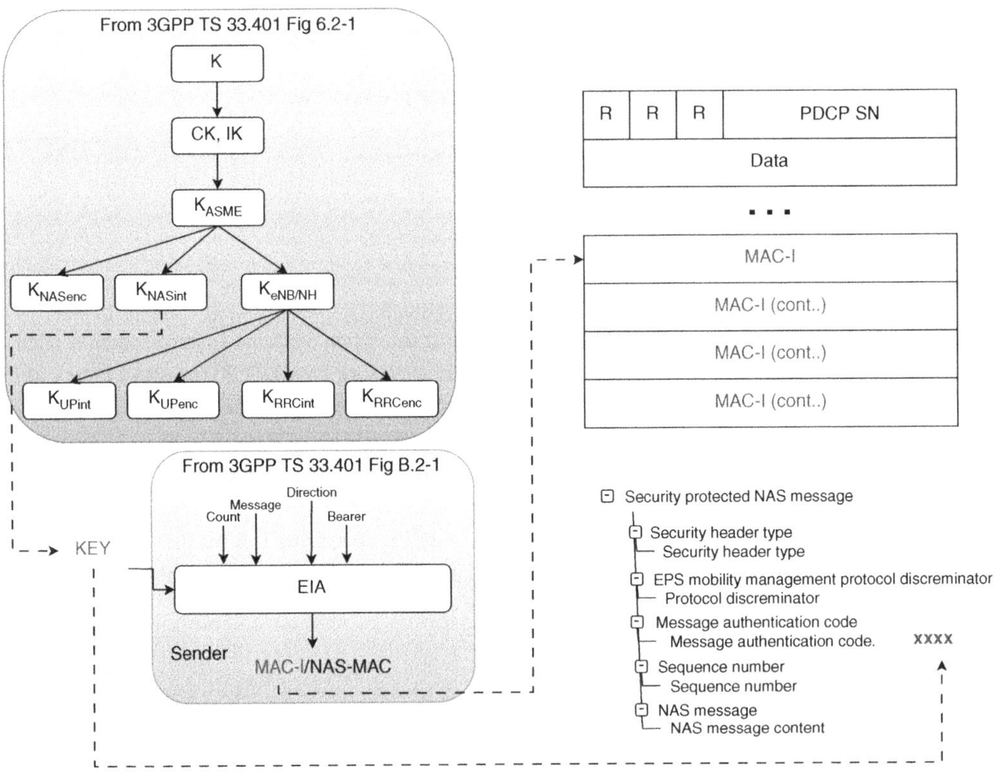

Figure I.1.45 Integrity protection process.

Table I.1.7 RoHC operating modes.

RoHC mode	Description
Unidirectional mode (U-mode)	Packets are only sent in one direction from the compressor to the decompressor. This mode is usable over links where feedback from the decompressor to the compressor is not possible or desirable.
Bidirectional optimistic mode (O-mode)	This is like U-mode. In addition, a feedback channel is used to send error recovery requests. Acknowledgments of significant context updates from the decompressor to the compressor may be optionally sent. This mode is used to maximize compression efficiency with spare usage of the feedback channel. It works well on less noisy channels.
Bidirectional reliable mode (R-mode)	The feedback channel is used more actively to maintain the compressor and decompressor always in synchronization to ensure that the two do not go out of sync. This mode is required for noisy environments, or the channel can become noisy. This mode is typically used for wireless connections.

Table I.1.8 RoHC states.

RoHC states	Description
Initialization and refresh (IR) state	The compressor has just been created and reset. Full IP packet headers are sent.
First order (FO) state	The compressor has detected and stored the static fields (such as IP addresses and port numbers) on both sides of the connection. The compressor is also sending dynamic packet field differences in the FO state.
Second-order (SO) state	The compressor is suppressing all dynamic fields such as RTP sequence numbers (SNs). The compressor sends only a logical SN and a partial checksum to cause the other side to predictively generate and verify the headers of the next expected packet.

to camp on the current cell and transitions only when that threshold is crossed. The transition threshold is regulated by the network through broadcast SIB parameters, which specify these based on infra-frequency and inter-frequency neighbors.

Given that the private networks are deployed with the neighboring cells typically using orthogonal frequencies, the neighbor scans typically tend to be inter-frequency scans. For the macro network, neighbor scans and transitions are typically horizontal (intra-frequency) transitions.

I.1.15.1 LTE to LTE Intra-frequency Measurement

- **S_INTRA_SEARCH:** This parameter is the threshold value for intra-frequency measurement; that is, it is used to trigger intra-frequency measurements.
  - The actual value in dB is obtained by multiplying by 2.
  - It corresponds to the parameter s-IntraSearch specified in SIB3 Settings: 31, 62 dB,
- Measurement rules for intra-frequency cell reselection
  - Serving_Srxlev > Sintrasearch
    - Do not perform intra-frequency measurement; for example, if the measured RSRP of the serving cell is −80 dBm

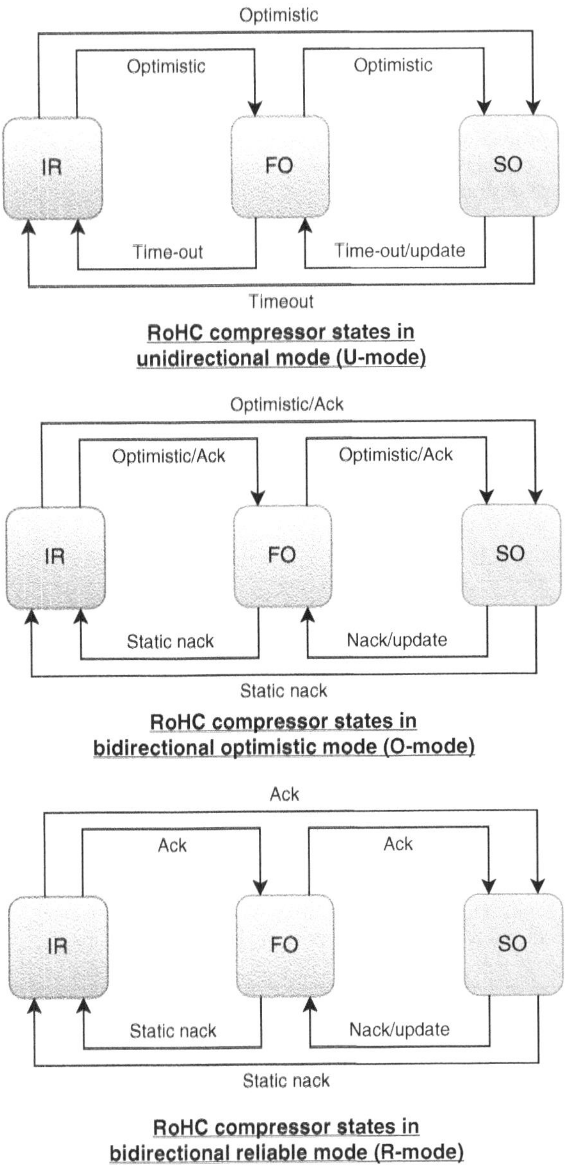

Figure I.1.46 RoHC state transitions in U, O, and R modes.

- Then Srxlev = −80 + 128 = 48 [Srxlev = Qrxlevmeas – Qrxlevmin (−128)]
- Srxlev is 48, which is > 31 (Sintrasearch value). Do not perform intra-frequency measurement.

– Serving_Srxlev <= Sintrasearch
  - Perform RSRP measurement; for example, if the measured RSRP of the serving cell is −100 dBm
  - Then Srxlev = −100 + 128 = 28
  - Srxlev is 28, which is <31 (Sintrasearch value)

- Perform intra-frequency RSRP measurement and condition for reselection:
- RSRP serving Cell + Qhyst< RSRP neighbor cell – Qoffset during Treselection

Table I.1.9 RoHC profiles.

Profile identifier	Usage	Reference
0 x 0000	No compression	RFC 4995
0 x 0001	RTP/UDP/IP	RFC 3095, RFC 4815
0 x 0002	UDP/IP	RFC 3095, RFC 4815
0 x 0003	ESP/IP	RFC 3095, RFC 4815
0 x 0004	IP	RFC 3843, RFC 4815
0 x 0006	TCP/IP	RFC 4996
0 x 0101	RTP/UDP/IP	RFC 5225
0 x 0102	UDP/IP	RFC 5225
0 x 0103	ESP/IP	RFC 5225
0 x 0104	IP	RFC 5225

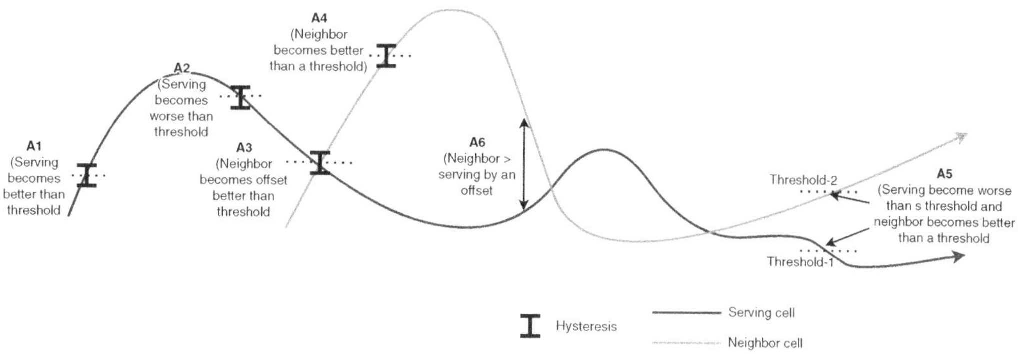

Figure I.1.47 Handover thresholds.

I.1.15.2 LTE to LTE Non-intra-frequency Measurement

- If the serving cell's evaluation result is as follows, the UE may not perform non-intra-frequency measurement.
  - SrxLev > s-NonIntraSearchP
  - Squal > s-NonIntraSearchQ
  - Note: If neither of s-NonIntraSearchP nor s-NonIntraSearchQ is specified, the UE applies the default value (s-NonIntraSearchP = infinity, s-NonIntraSearchQ = 0 based on 36.331).
- If the serving cell's evaluation result does not meet the following criteria, the UE performs a non-intra-frequency measurement.
  - SrxLev > s-NonIntraSearchP
  - Squal > s-NonIntraSearchQ
  - Note: If neither s-NonIntraSearchP nor s-NonIntraSearchQ is specified, UE applies the default value (s-NonIntraSearchP = Infinity, s-NonIntraSearchQ = 0 based on 36.331). This implies that if neither of s-NonIntraSearchP and s-NonIntraSearchQ is specified, UE always performs NonIntra frequency measurement.

I.1.15.3 Cell Reselection: SIB1

```
c1: systemInformationBlockType1 (1)
            systemInformationBlockType1
                cellAccessRelatedInfo
                    plmn-IdentityList: 1 item
                        Item 0
                            PLMN-IdentityInfo
                                plmn-Identity
                                    <...>
                                cellReservedForOperatorUse:
                                  notReserved (1)
                    trackingAreaCode: 0001
                    cellIdentity: 00000000
                    cellBarred: notBarred (1)
                    intraFreqReselection: allowed (0)
                    .... ..0. csg-Indication: False
                cellSelectionInfo
                    q-RxLevMin: -130dBm (-65)
                p-Max: 23dBm
                freqBandIndicator: 4
                schedulingInfoList: 3 items
                    <...>
                si-WindowLength: ms20 (5)
                systemInfoValueTag: 0
                nonCriticalExtension
```

I.1.15.4 Cell Reselection: SIB3

```
sib-TypeAndInfo item: sib3 (1)
    sib3
        cellReselectionInfoCommon
            q-Hyst: dB0 (0)
        cellReselectionServingFreqInfo
            s-NonIntraSearch: 62dB (31)
            threshServingLow: 62dB (31)
            cellReselectionPriority: 7
        intraFreqCellReselectionInfo
            q-RxLevMin: -140dBm (-70)
            s-IntraSearch: 62dB (31)
            .0.. .... presenceAntennaPort1: False
            neighCellConfig: Not all neighbor cells
                             have the same MBSFN subframe allocation
as serving cell (0)
            t-ReselectionEUTRA: 0s
        lateNonCriticalExtension: <MISSING>
```

```
        s-IntraSearch-v920
            s-IntraSearchP-r9: 62dB (31)
            s-IntraSearchQ-r9: 0dB
        s-NonIntraSearch-v920
            s-NonIntraSearchP-r9: 62dB (31)
            s-NonIntraSearchQ-r9: 0dB
        q-QualMin-r9: -34dB
        threshServingLowQ-r9: 0dB
```

I.1.15.5 Cell Reselection: SIB4

```
sib-TypeAndInfo item: sib4 (2)
    sib4
        intraFreqNeighCellList: 1 item
            Item 0
                IntraFreqNeighCellInfo
                    physCellId: 1
                    q-OffsetCell: dB3 (18)
```

I.1.15.6 Cell Reselection: SIB5

```
sib-TypeAndInfo item: sib5 (3)
    sib5
        interFreqCarrierFreqList: 1 item
            Item 0
                InterFreqCarrierFreqInfo
                    dl-CarrierFreq: 5790
                    q-RxLevMin: -110dBm (-55)
                    p-Max: 23dBm
                    t-ReselectionEUTRA: 0s
                    threshX-High: 4dB (2)
                    threshX-Low: 2dB (1)
                    allowedMeasBandwidth: mbw25 (2)
                    .... .0.. presenceAntennaPort1: False
                    cellReselectionPriority: 4
                    neighCellConfig: No MBSFN subframes are present
in all neighbor cells (1)
                    q-OffsetFreq: dB3 (18)
```

I.1.16 Connected Mode Mobility

I.1.16.1 Handover Thresholds

Figure I.1.48 provides a visual representation of the handover thresholds and the events types that get triggered based on either going above or below the threshold based on the event type measuring the serving and neighbor cells.

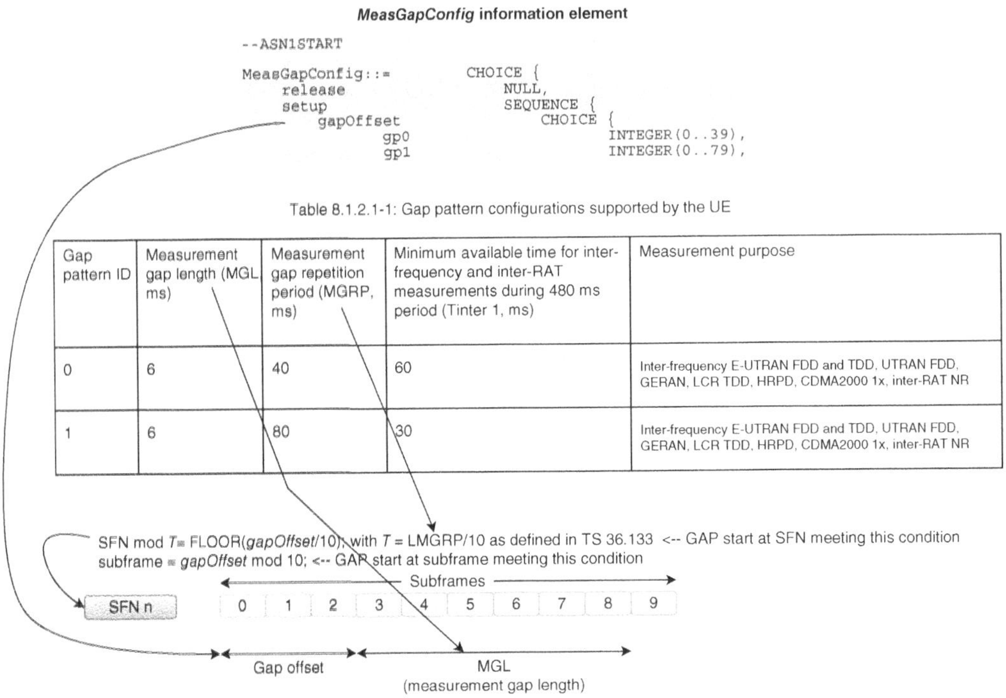

Figure I.1.48 Measurement gap.

I.1.16.2 Measurement Gap

When the UE is operating in connected mode, the eNB needs to provide gaps during which the UE is not scheduled for both DL and UL traffic, allowing time for the UE to perform inter-frequency neighbor measurements. Prior to handover (the network command to transition the UE from one cell to another) in connected mode, the network requests the UE to perform measurements, and based on the UE's measurement reports, the network determines the appropriate cell to hand over the UE. Such handovers are required, given that the UE may go out of coverage from the current cell of operation, and the RRC connection needs to be maintained for continued operations.

For private networks, given that the neighboring cells are typically deployed on orthogonal frequencies, inter-frequency scans are required, implying that the measurement gaps need to be configured in the UE to support mobility within the enterprise campus.

- Before the handover, UE normally measures the cell power (signal quality) of the target cell and reports it to the network so that the network can decide whether to allow UE to hand over to the target cell or not.
  - It is not a big issue to measure the signal quality of the target cell if the target cell is at the same frequency as the current cell (intra-frequency measurement).
  - But there would be an issue when the target cell is at a different frequency from the current cell (inter-frequency measurement).
    - Just in terms of logical sense from a viewpoint, the simplest solution for inter-frequency measurement would be to implement two RF transceivers on the UE. However, there are

some practical problems with this kind of two-transceiver solution. One of the problems is the cost issue. It would require additional costs to implement the additional transceiver. The other problem would be the possible interference between the current frequency and the target frequency, especially when the current frequency and the target frequency are close to each other.

- They developed a special technique called "measurement gap." The idea behind the measurement gap is to create a brief interval during which no transmission or reception occurs. Since no signal transmission and reception happen during the gap, the UE can switch to the target cell, perform the signal quality measurement, and return to the current cell.

- To make this work seamlessly, there should be a well-established agreement between UE and the network about the gap definition (e.g. starting position of the gap, gap length, and number of gaps), and this agreement is established by MeasGapConfig IE of the RRC connection reconfiguration message.

Figure I.1.49 show the measurement gap definition and how the UE uses these gaps to perform inter-frequency measurements while operating in connected mode on a given channel.

I.1.16.3 Scheduling Data Around the Measurement Gap

One of the complications regarding the measurement gap is how to schedule data transmission around the gap. The situation is more complicated than you may think because we must consider not only the data transmission itself but also the scheduling grant and ACK/NACK transmission. One of the possible scheduling examples around the measurement gap is as follows. Figure I.1.50 shows the opportunities for data transmissions around the measurement gap that can be supported.

I.1.16.4 Handover (HO) Procedure

Figures I.1.51 and I.1.52 show the steps involved in transitioning the UE from one cell to another. The S1-AP procedure uses the core network to exchange messages between the source and target eNB to perform the handover. The X2-based handover uses direct communication between the source and target eNBs to perform the handover. Figure I.1.51 shows the procedures involved with S1-AP-based handover. Figure I.1.52 shows the procedures involved with X2-based handover.

In private networks, given that the core network is very close to the eNBs, there are no significant performance benefits to using an X2-based HO unlike in the macro network. Private networks are typically implemented using S1-AP-based HO.

I.1.17 Timing Advance

Timing advance (TA) is used to control the UL transmission timing of individual UEs. It helps to ensure that UL transmissions from all UEs are synchronized when received by the base station.

UL frame number i for transmission from the UE shall start at $T_{TA} = (N_{TA} + N_{TA,offset}) \cdot T_c$ before the start of the corresponding DL frame at the UE.

The figure below illustrates the concept of TA and the UL/DL timing at both the Base Station (BS) and UE sides.

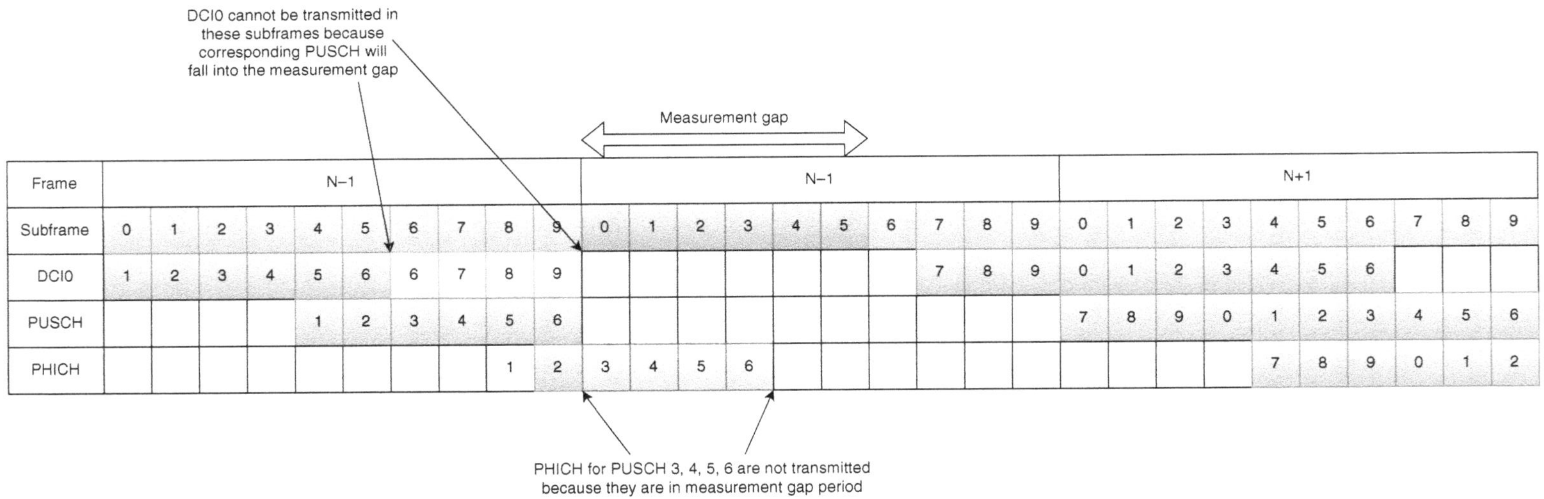

Figure I.1.49 Data transmission around the measurement gap.

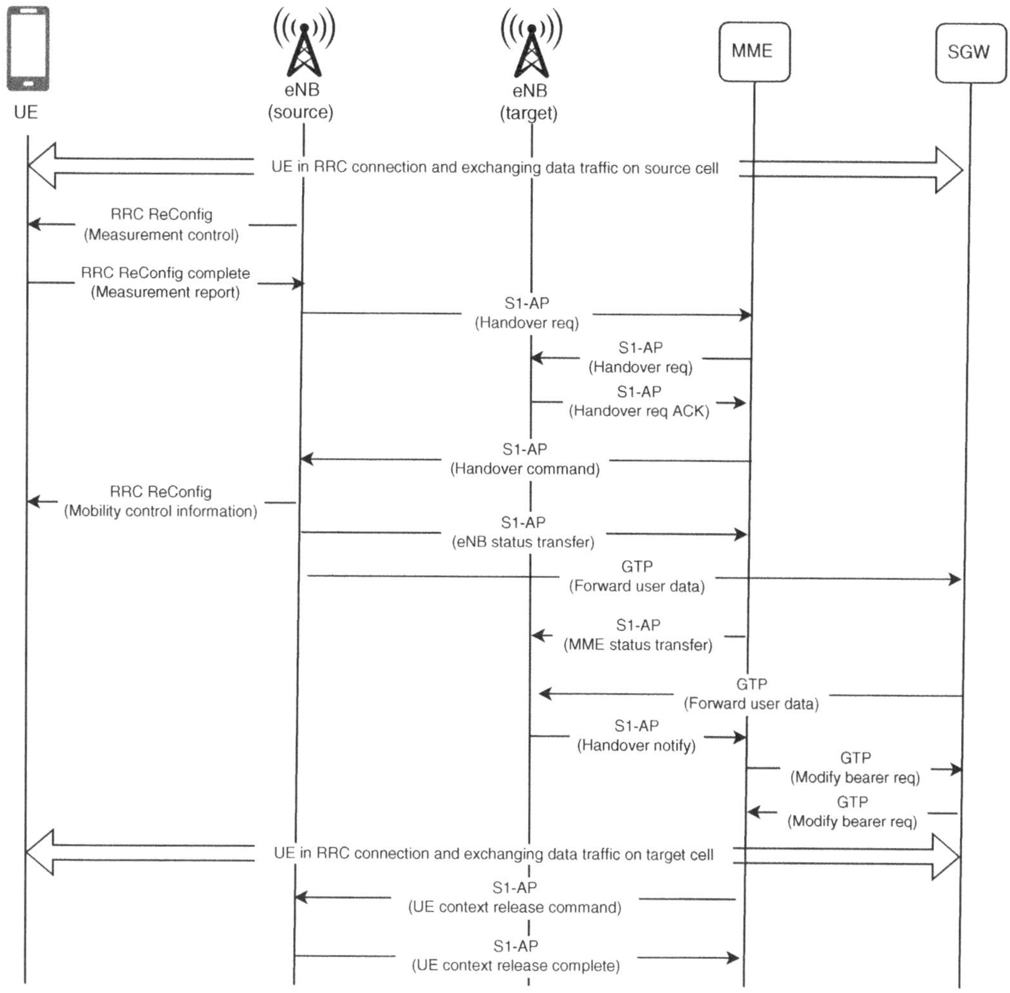

Figure I.1.50 S1-AP-based handover.

- UEs closer to BS have shorter propagation delays and hence smaller TAs.
- UEs further away from BS have a longer propagation delay and, hence, a larger TA.
- TA shall account for the round-trip propagation delay, hence $2 \cdot t_{prop}$. In addition, it also includes a timing offset, $t_{offset} = N_{TA,offset} \cdot T_c$. The purpose is for a TDD base station to activate its transmitter after an UL frame.
- Seen from UE side:
  - The reference point for the UE initial transmit timing control requirement shall be the DL timing of the reference cell minus $(N_{TA} + N_{TA,offset} \cdot T_c)$, which is TA.
  - The DL timing is defined as the time when the first detected path (in time) of the corresponding DL frame is received from the reference cell.
- Seen from the BS side, the time difference between an UL radio frame and the corresponding DL radio frame is t_{offset}, which is the same for all UEs attached to it. The propagation delay is already compensated on the UE side by TA.
- N_{TA} for Physical Random Access Channel (PRACH) equals 0.

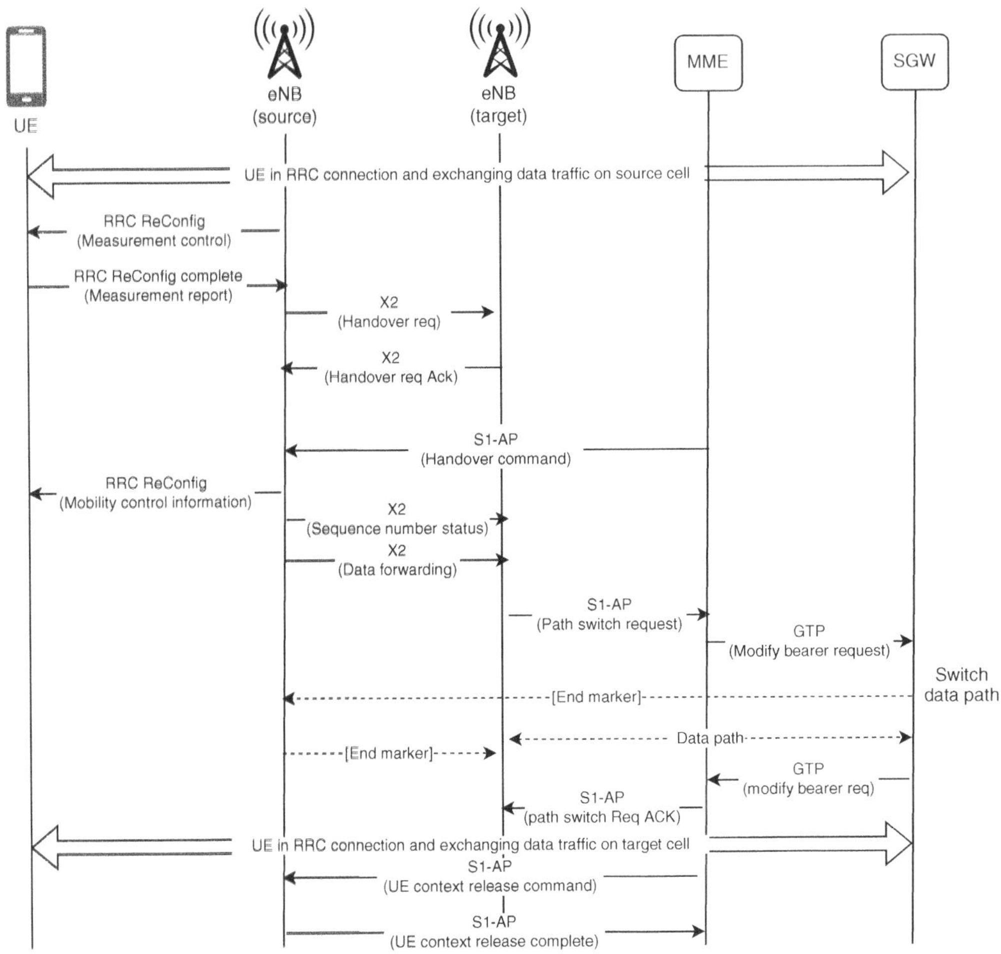

Figure I.1.51 X2-based handover.

Note: $T_c = 1/(480\,\text{kHz} \cdot 4096) = 0.509\,\text{ns}$

Figure I.1.52 shows the need for timing advance and how this addresses UE successfully completing the UL transmissions without getting intefered with higher powered DL transmissions.

I.1.18 Summary

This section provides an overview of the 4G LTE technology. This is not meant to be an exhaustive treatment of the material. However, this provides the reader with sufficient information to understand the higher details of LTE and appreciate the nuances involved. Armed with this level of detail, the reader will be able to identify the relevant topics when designing a network or working to debug an issue in the network, as well as how to go about researching additional specifics to address a problem at hand. LTE is a 4G technology and forms the basis for the OFDM-based systems being defined for 5G and 6G as well. Forming a good foundation with LTE will allow the user to apply this knowledge to other subsequent generations of wireless standards without loss of

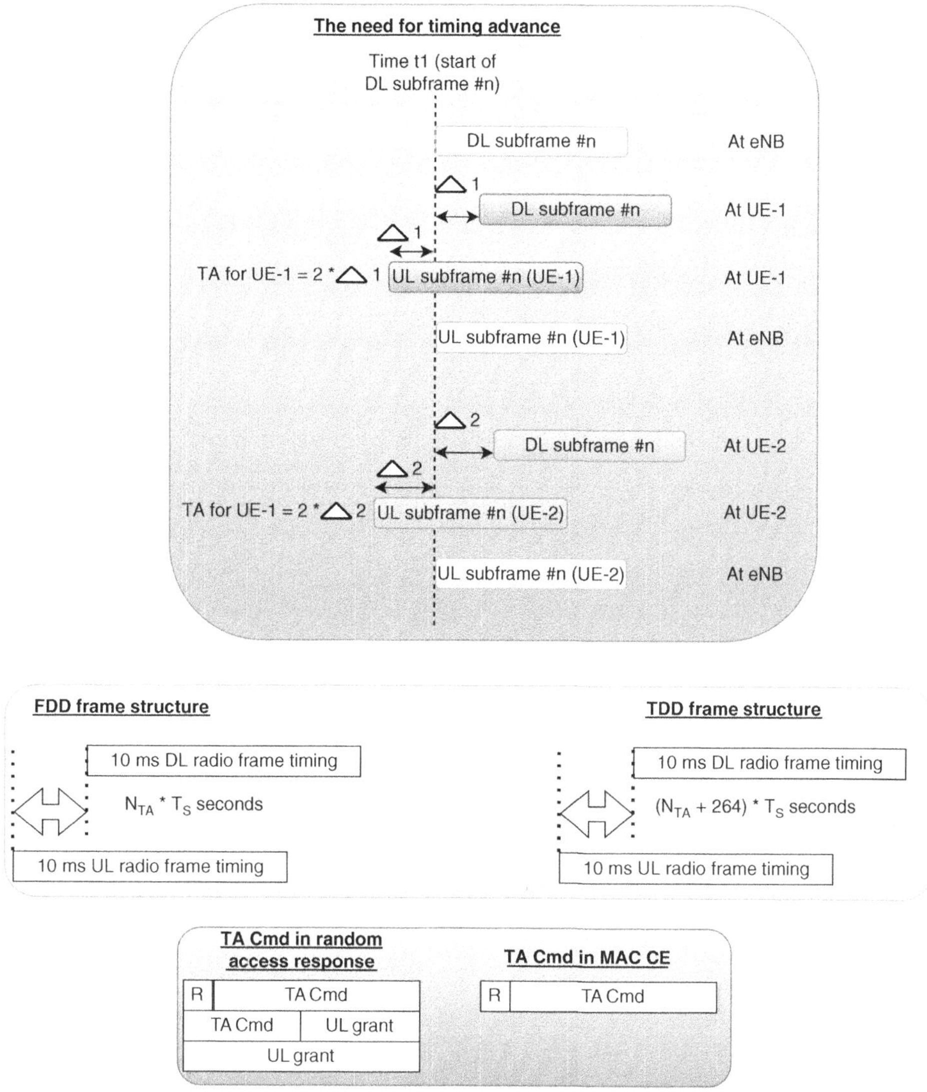

Figure I.1.52 Timing advance.

context. Many of the mechanisms are reused as is in 5G and possibly 6G, with specific adaptations to the finer timelines and some feature sophistication added for improved performance.

Reference

See Part-I "Standards" section for a list of references to the 3GPP LTE specifications.

Part I.2

NR Fundamentals

I.2.1

5G NR Fundamentals

I.2.1.1 5G NR Introduction

This chapter covers the key aspects of 5G new radio (NR). It is mainly addressed using pictures to illustrate the different aspects involved. It covers the key functions introduced in NR from both a radio network and a core network perspective. Comparisons and differences with 4G long-term evolution (LTE) are shown where relevant. Some explanatory text is provided where the figures do not directly capture the details, providing some additional context to the reader.

Given that NR is a direct evolution of the LTE system, this chapter assumes that the fundamentals shown in LTE equally apply to NR as well. The focus of this chapter is to address the key enhancements and changes relative to the LTE system that are introduced in 5G NR. Figure I.2.1.1 provides the key motivators for 5G NR. See the references called out at the end of this chapter for a summary of the 3GPP spectation releases 15, 16, 17, and 18 that capture the key aspects of the features introduced in each of the 3GPP NR releases.

Private networks are typically limited by the spectrum available. Although NR supports up to 100 MHz for each channel (LTE supports a maximum of 20 MHz), the demands of the private network, due to its short range and the number of user equipment (UE) camped on the system, mean that smaller bandwidths tend to be sufficient. For typical campus deployments, LTE-based operations are largely equivalent to what can be achieved with NR. There are specialized deployments that require low-latency communications like industrial IoT (IIoT); however, there is no immediate drive to deploy 5G NR networks in enterprises. However, the technology enhancements being done both in the UE and the macro networks are almost exclusively on the NR side. Given that, there is a motivation to get to NR deployments for enterprise campuses as well. The higher-end and more sophisticated devices all support 5G NR now, so it would be worthwhile to move to NR to take advantage and go with the flow in the wireless industry.

Figure I.2.1.2 shows the deployment options with LTE and NR coexisting. For the evolution from 4G LTE to 5G NR, these gradual steps were needed in the macro networks, with the macro network also supporting NR stand-alone (SA) mode without requiring an LTE leg to stand on. For enterprise campuses, and with the limitation of the spectrum available, it typically allows for either LTE- or NR-based networks to be supported. Given that, enterprise campuses either operate with LTE + EPC *or* NR + 5GC, each in SA mode. The non-stand-alone (NSA) modes typically do not apply to private networks.

One of the key aspects introduced into NR is a scalable orthogonal frequency-division multiplexing (OFDM) numerology. LTE supports a fixed 15 kHz subcarrier spacing (SCS), and given the

Mobile Communication Systems for Private Networks, First Edition. Srinivasan Balasubramanian.

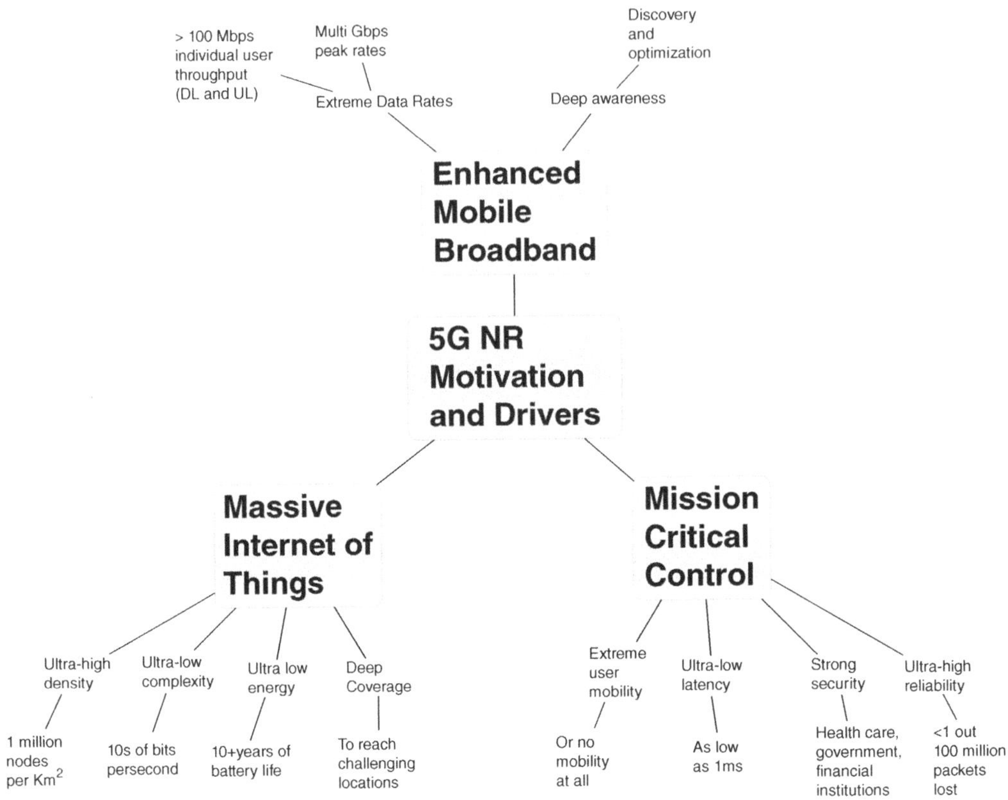

Figure I.2.1.1 Motivation and drivers for 5G NR.

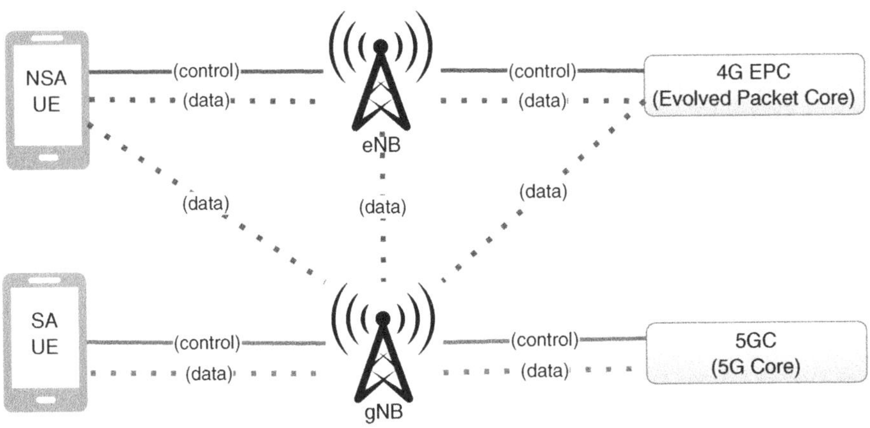

Figure I.2.1.2 5G NR deployment options.

20 MHz upper limit to the channel, the FFT (fast Fourier transform)/IFFT (inverse FFT) hardware and computation needs are fairly limited. Note that 7.5 kHz SCS is supported for multicast channels in LTE, but it currently has limited use in the market.

With much larger bandwidths supported in NR and a wide array of spectrum (low band – sub 3 GHz, mid band – 3–6 GHz, and high band in millimeter wave [mmWave] in the 24–52 GHz range),

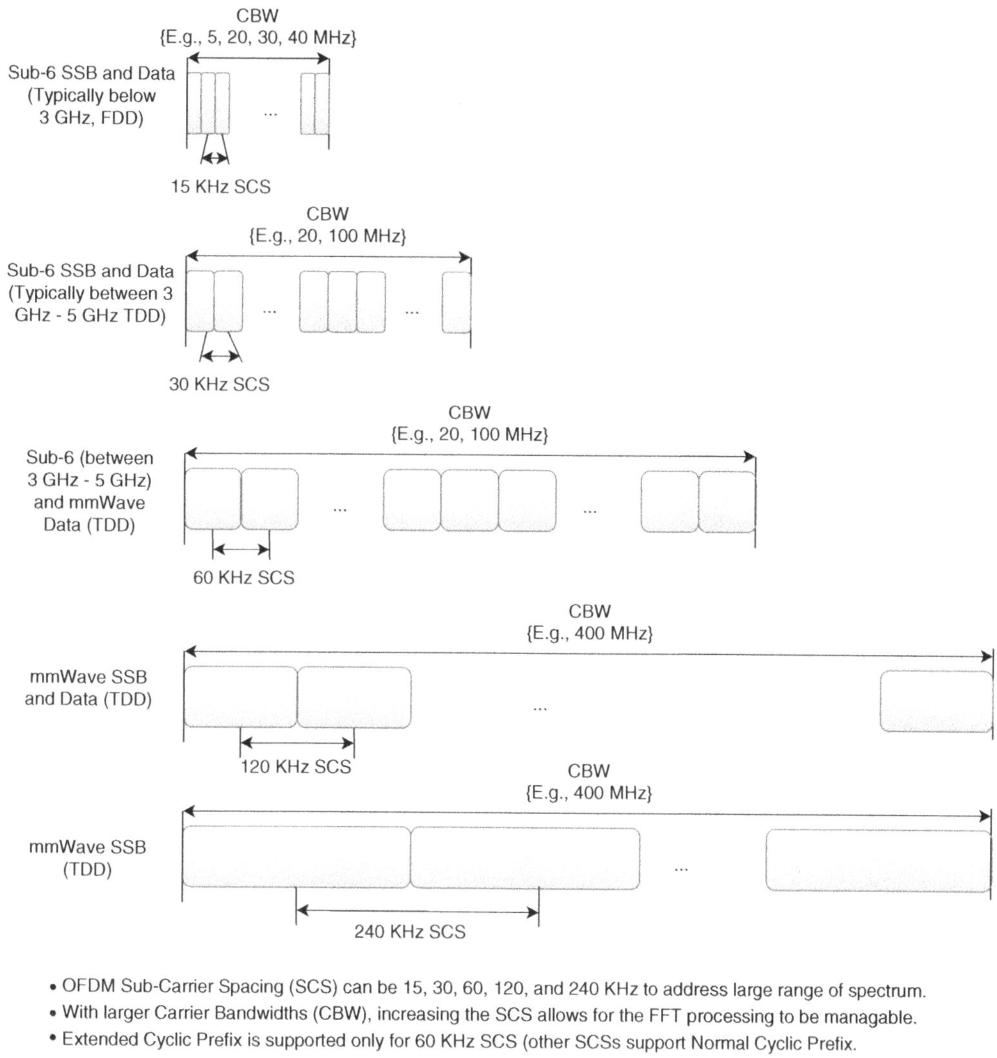

Figure I.2.1.3 Scalable 5G NR OFDM numerology.

a more flexible approach is needed. NR, in addition to the 15 kHz SCS, also supports 30, 60, 120, and 240 kHz, applied based on the low, mid, and high spectrum and the channel type used for NR operations. Figure I.2.1.3 illustrates the different SCS and highlights the spectrum where it is typically used.

Although the time domain of 10 ms for a frame and 1 ms for a subframe is retained the same as in LTE, the number of slots available for each SCS is doubled with the doubling of the SCS used. This is illustrated in Figure I.2.1.4. A slot is a typical schedulable unit together with a set of tones in the frequency domain.

In addition, NR introduced a self-contained slot where the grant, data transmission, and acknowledgment are supported in a single slot. This is mainly intended to operate in channels where the transmitter needs to contend for the channel resource. This also allows for quicker hybrid automatic repeat request (HARQ) feedback for repeating the packet for low-latency communications. This is illustrated in Figure I.2.1.5. Self-contained slots are typically not employed in the market now and may apply to IIoT scenarios.

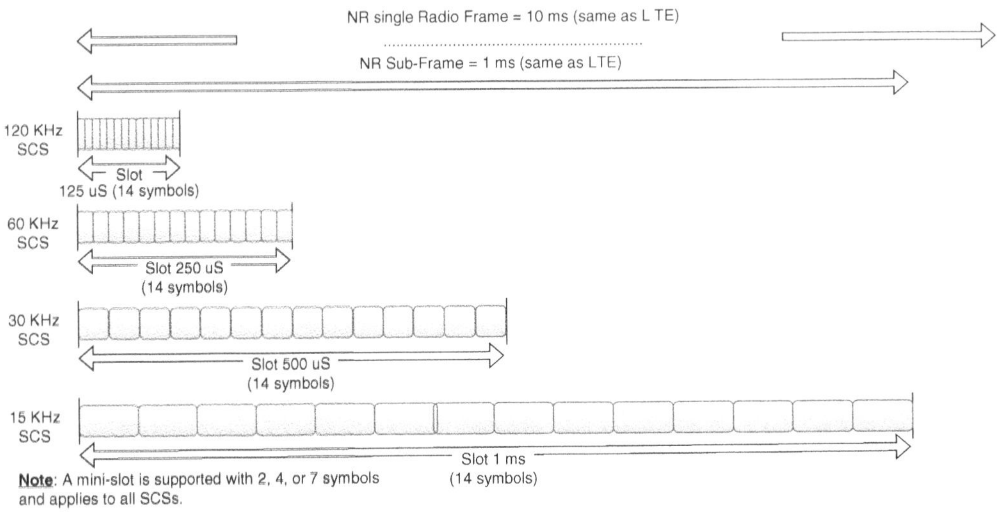

Figure I.2.1.4 NR frame structure.

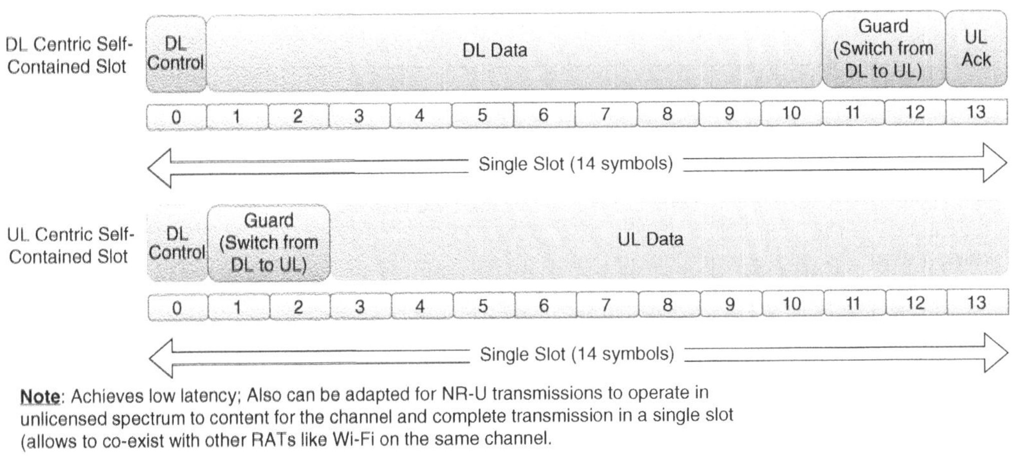

Figure I.2.1.5 NR self-contained slots.

I.2.1.2 Channel Bandwidth

Figure I.2.1.6 provides the NR channel bandwidths and the number of resource blocks (RBs) available for the configurations. Resource blocks are fundamental schedulable units.

Figure I.2.1.7 provides an example of bandwidth parts (BWPs) that can be configured in the UE. These BWPs are subsets of the carrier bandwidth (CBW). A given UE can be provisioned with up to four BWPs at a given time, and the network and the UE operate in one BWP at a given time. The network can switch the UE to operate from one BWP to another based on different conditions. For example, a power-saving BWP, which can be as small as 5 MHz (typically 20 MHz), is used when the UE does not have much traffic, and when the UE is in active traffic, it is switched to a BWP that is set to the full CBW.

OFDM waveforms demonstrate great resiliency in frequency-selective channels. By attaching a copy of the end of the OFDM symbol to the beginning of the symbol (a cyclic prefix), a receiver can better tolerate synchronization errors and prevent inter-symbol interference (ISI). Two waveforms,

	SCS (KHz)	Min BW (MHz)	Max BW (MHz)	Max RBs
Sub-6 GHz (FR1)	15	5	50	270
	30	5	100	273
	60	10	100	135

	SCS (KHz)	Min BW (MHz)	Max BW (MHz)	Max RBs
mmWave (FR2)	60	50	200	264
	120	50	400	264

Note: Resource Block (RB) is 12 consecutive OFDM carriers independent of SCS. This implies for a given CBW, the number of RBs vary based on SCS used on the channel,

Figure I.2.1.6 Number of resource blocks (RBs) associated with channel bandwidth (CBW).

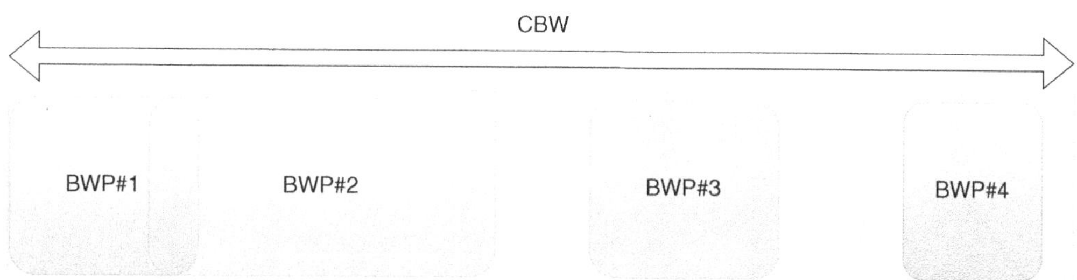

Note:

- Up to 4 Bandwidth Parts (BWPs) can be configured for a given UE. Only one can be active at a given time.
- Each BWP can be in a different frequency location, support different SCS, and Bandwidth sizes.
- Helps with power save for the UE and also support devices with RF not support the full CBW bandwidth

Figure I.2.1.7 NR bandwidth parts (BWPs).

cyclic prefix OFDM (CP-OFDM) and discrete Fourier transform OFDM (DFT-s-OFDM), are supported in both LTE and NR.

OFDM waveforms suffer from high peak-to-average power ratios (PAPR). DFT-s-OFDM provides higher-efficient uplink (UL). Using DFT-s-OFDM, the transmitter modulates all subcarriers with the same data. It lowers the peak-to-average ratio while retaining the multipath interference resilience and flexible subcarrier frequency allocation that OFDM provides. While the PAPR with CP-OFDM may be 11–13 dB, with DFT-s-OFDM, it is only 6–9 dB. The two UL waveforms are illustrated in Figure I.2.1.8.

In LTE, there are a set of time division duplex (TDD) configurations specified in the standards. The eNB selects a specific TDD format to operate with. There are also three types of TDD slots: downlink (DL) slot, UL slot, and switching slot. The switching slot is needed when there is a

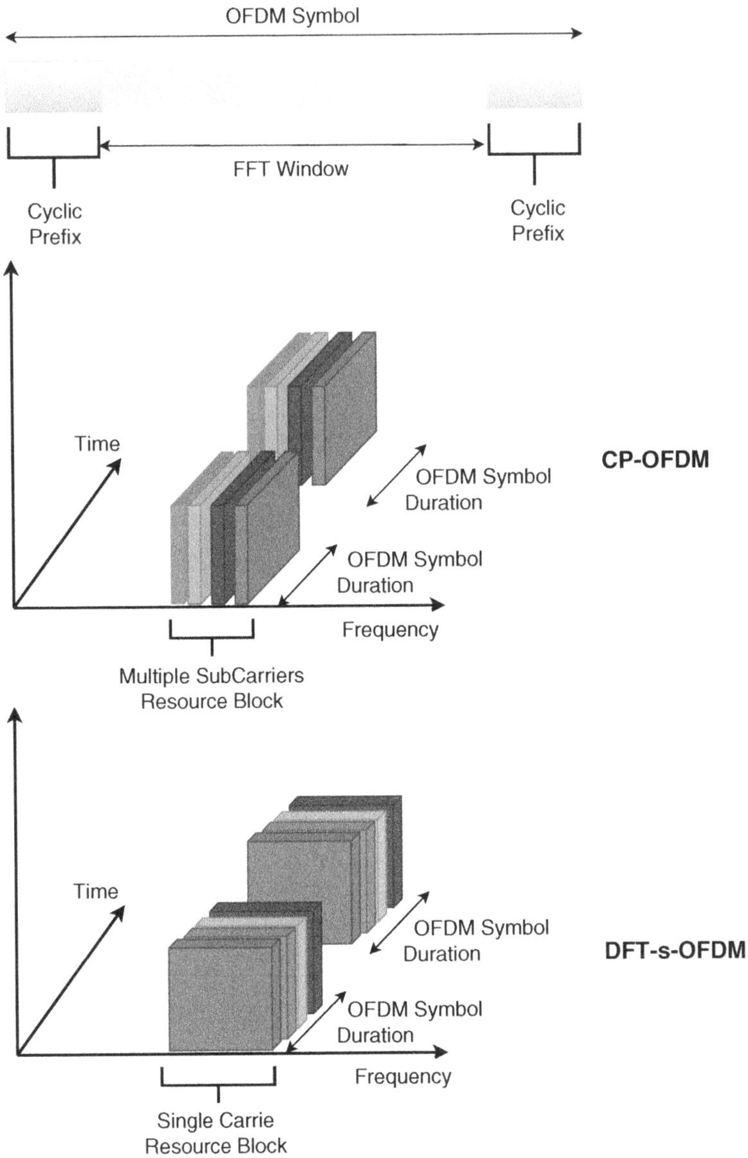

Figure I.2.1.8 NR waveforms = CP-OFDM and DFT-s-OFDM.

transition from DL to UL to prevent UE UL transmissions from being interfered with by the DL transmissions. The switching slot has 14 symbols, and there are several patterns with a certain number of DL symbols, followed by several gap symbols, and then followed by UL symbols.

In NR, an additional flexible slot is introduced. Based on the real-time changes in configuration, the flexible slot can be used as a DL slot or an UL slot. Additionally, NR allows for the slot patterns to be configurable, ranging from all DL slots to all UL slots. NR also supports slot patterns specified with a time interval of repetition. Figure I.2.1.9 provides the typical TDD slot configuration. Figure I.2.1.10 specifies the dynamic slot formats, with the network being able to switch from one format to another dynamically.

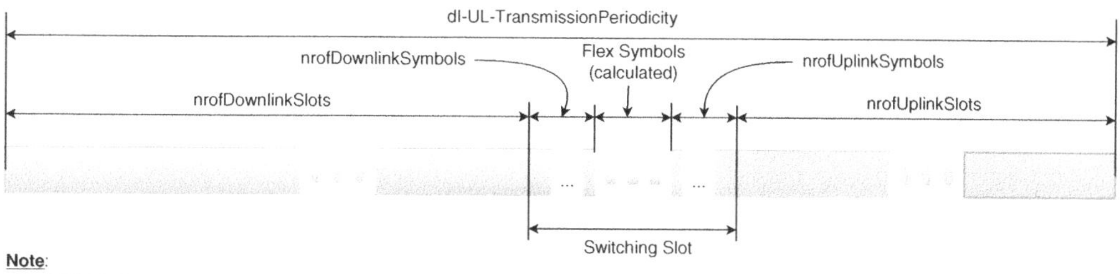

Note:

- TDD-UL-DL-configurationCommon can be configured in different ways depending on the specific requirements of the network (DL centric / UL centric).
- Ensure sufficient Guard time for DL-to-UL Switching Gap
- PRACH Occasion resources allocated in the slots/symbols where UL is configured.

Figure I.2.1.9 TDD UL/DL common configuration.

The use of beams, although supported in LTE as well, became a lot more prevalent and even necessary in NR. The network supports a set of beams, and the UE selects the strongest beam to operate with. With TDD spectrum operation, where many of the 5G NR systems are deployed, beam reciprocity can be employed, given that the same spectrum is used for both DL and UL. The UE performs beam sweeping to select the best beam. Associated with each beam is a set of random access channel (RACH) resources specified. When the UE RACH-es on these resources, the network implicitly knows the beam selected by the UE. This is illustrated in Figure I.2.1.11.

One of the additional benefits of using beams is performing beam refinement. When the UE is in a fairly static location, the beam can be made narrower and pointed at the UE. This both allows for coverage to be extended and supports higher modulation and coding scheme (MCS) and hence higher throughput for a given UE. With such beam refinement, part of the cell can be isolated, and the same resource (time and frequency) can be reused spatially, enabling MU-MIMO (multiuser multiple input multiple output) to serve multiple users simultaneously. Such beam refinement allows for mMIMO (massive multiple input multiple output) antenna techniques to be supported. This is illustrated in Figure I.2.1.11.

I.2.1.3 NR Network Architecture

The NR network is designed right from the beginning to accommodate some fundamental principles. Separating the control and user plane functions allows for the two to be scaled and architected independently. This is referred to as control and user plane separation (CUPS). The second principle is to support the network with minimal runtime context to allow for quicker recovery from a network function/node crash. This allows for high-availability functions to be easily introduced into the network design. A high-level view is shown in Figure I.2.1.12. The LTE network architecture (Figure I.2.1.13) is listed here again to allow for the reader to compare it with the NR network architecture (Figure I.2.1.14). The LTE nodes have a mix of control and user planes, while the NR architecture and functional separation implicitly follow the CUPS architecture. See the Part II converged core chapter for a description of the different nodes/functions and the evolution of the LTE evolved packet core (EPC) functions to the corresponding NR 5GC functions. Table I.2.1.1 provides comparisons between the two architectures.

Figure I.2.1.15 provides a view of all the NR and 5GC functions and the interfaces interconnecting the functions/nodes. This view is introduced to show the parts of the 5GC systems involved. From a private network perspective, many of these functions are coalesced into a single function

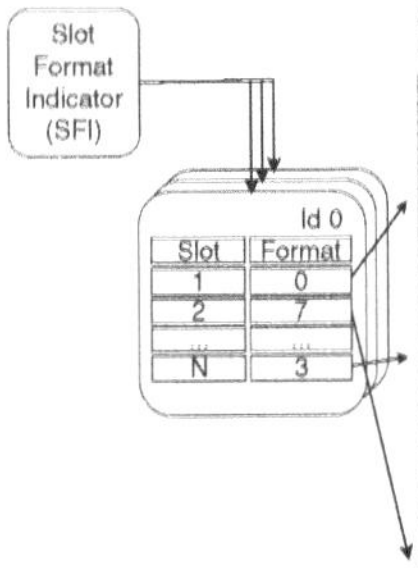

Note:

- RRC configures the UE with multiple slotFormatCombinations
- Each combination is a lot of formats for a number of consecutive slots
- Dynamic SFI is provided on PDCCH for upcoming slots (SFI-RNTI)

3GPP TS 38.213 v15.7 -Table 11.1.1-1: Slot formats for normal cyclic prefix>
D : Downlink, U : Uplink, F : Flexible

	Symbol Number in a slot													
Format	0	1	2	3	4	5	6	7	8	9	10	11	12	13
0	D	D	D	D	D	D	D	D	D	D	D	D	D	D
1	U	U	U	U	U	U	U	U	U	U	U	U	U	U
2	F	F	F	F	F	F	F	F	F	F	F	F	F	F
3	D	D	D	D	D	D	D	D	D	D	D	D	D	F
4	D	D	D	D	D	D	D	D	D	D	D	D	F	F
5	D	D	D	D	D	D	D	D	D	D	D	F	F	F
6	D	D	D	D	D	D	D	D	D	D	F	F	F	F
7	D	D	D	D	D	D	D	D	D	F	F	F	F	F
8	F	F	F	F	F	F	F	F	F	F	F	F	F	U
9	F	F	F	F	F	F	F	F	F	F	F	F	U	U
10	F	U	U	U	U	U	U	U	U	U	U	U	U	U
11	F	F	U	U	U	U	U	U	U	U	U	U	U	U
12	F	F	F	U	U	U	U	U	U	U	U	U	U	U
13	F	F	F	F	U	U	U	U	U	U	U	U	U	U
14	F	F	F	F	F	U	U	U	U	U	U	U	U	U
15	F	F	F	F	F	F	U	U	U	U	U	U	U	U
16	D	F	F	F	F	F	F	F	F	F	F	F	F	F
17	D	D	F	F	F	F	F	F	F	F	F	F	F	F
18	D	D	D	F	F	F	F	F	F	F	F	F	F	F
19	D	F	F	F	F	F	F	F	F	F	F	F	F	U
20	D	D	F	F	F	F	F	F	F	F	F	F	F	U
21	D	D	D	F	F	F	F	F	F	F	F	F	F	U
22	D	F	F	F	F	F	F	F	F	F	F	F	U	U
23	D	D	F	F	F	F	F	F	F	F	F	F	U	U
24	D	D	D	F	F	F	F	F	F	F	F	F	U	U
8	D	F	F	F	F	F	F	F	F	F	F	U	U	U
26	D	D	F	F	F	F	F	F	F	F	F	U	U	U
27	D	D	D	F	F	F	F	F	F	F	F	U	U	U
28	D	D	D	D	D	D	D	D	D	D	D	D	F	U
29	D	D	D	D	D	D	D	D	D	D	D	F	F	U
30	D	D	D	D	D	D	D	D	D	D	F	F	F	U
31	D	D	D	D	D	D	D	D	D	D	D	F	U	U
32	D	D	D	D	D	D	D	D	D	D	F	F	U	U
33	D	D	D	D	D	D	D	D	D	F	F	F	U	U
34	D	F	U	U	U	U	U	U	U	U	U	U	U	U
35	D	D	F	U	U	U	U	U	U	U	U	U	U	U
36	D	D	D	F	U	U	U	U	U	U	U	U	U	U
37	D	F	F	U	U	U	U	U	U	U	U	U	U	U
38	D	D	F	F	U	U	U	U	U	U	U	U	U	U
39	D	D	D	F	F	U	U	U	U	U	U	U	U	U
40	D	F	F	F	U	U	U	U	U	U	U	U	U	U
41	D	D	F	F	F	U	U	U	U	U	U	U	U	U
42	D	D	D	F	F	F	U	U	U	U	U	U	U	U
43	D	D	D	D	D	D	D	D	D	F	F	F	F	U
44	D	D	D	D	D	D	F	F	F	F	F	F	U	U
45	D	D	D	D	D	D	F	F	U	U	U	U	U	U
46	D	D	D	D	D	F	U	D	D	D	D	D	F	U
47	D	D	F	U	U	U	U	D	D	F	U	U	U	U
48	D	F	U	U	U	U	U	D	F	U	U	U	U	U
49	D	D	D	D	F	F	U	D	D	D	D	F	F	U
50	D	D	F	F	U	U	U	D	D	F	F	U	U	U
51	D	F	F	U	U	U	U	D	F	F	U	U	U	U
52	D	F	F	F	F	F	U	D	F	F	F	F	F	U
53	D	D	F	F			U	D	D	F	F			U
54	F	F	F	F	F	F	f	D	D	D	D	D	D	D
55	D	D	F	F	F	U	U	U	D	D	D	D	D	D
62-254	Reserved													
255	UE determines the slot format for the slot based on tdd-UL-DL-Configuration Common, or tdd-ULDL- Configuration Dedicated and, if any, on detected DCI formats													

Figure I.2.1.10 Dynamic slot format indication.

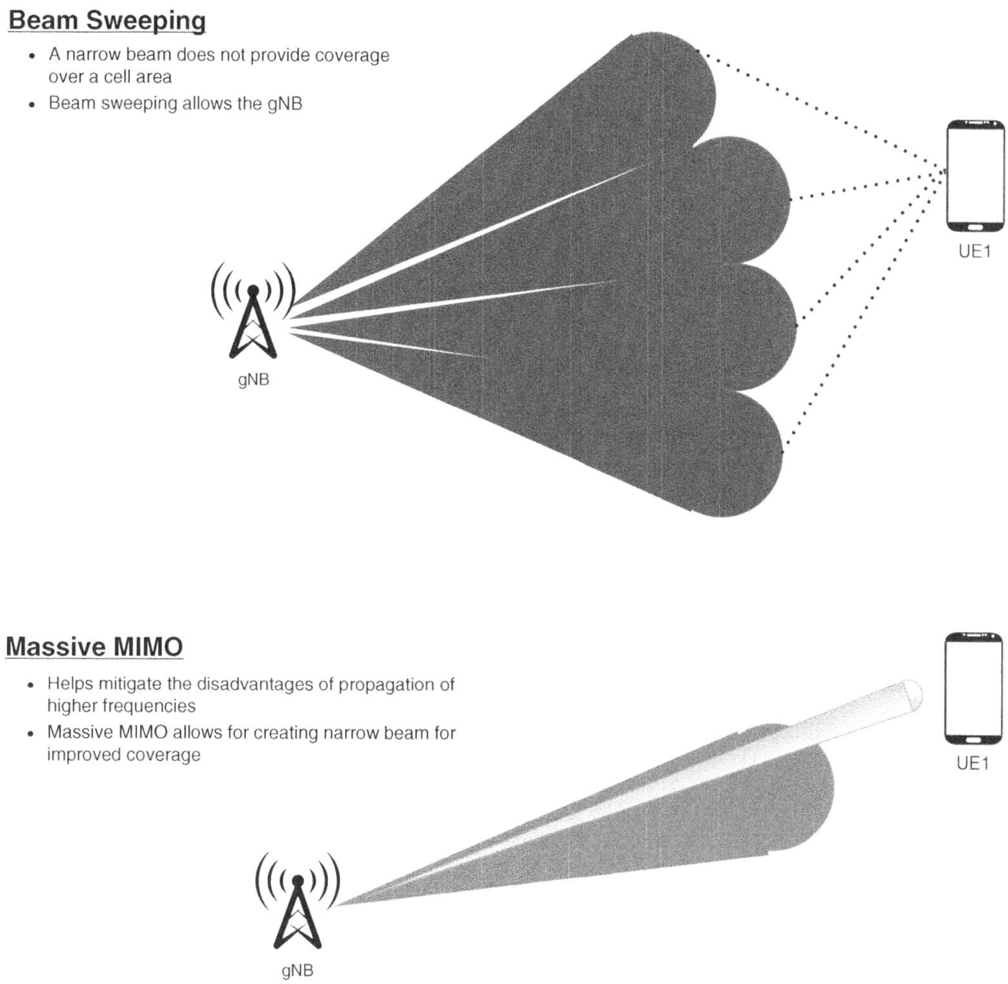

Figure I.2.1.11 Massive MIMO and beam sweeping.

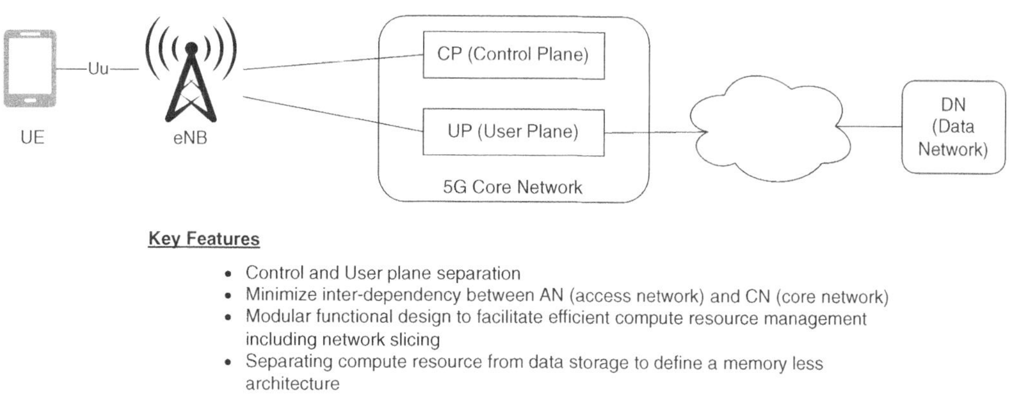

Figure I.2.1.12 Motivation for NR system architecture.

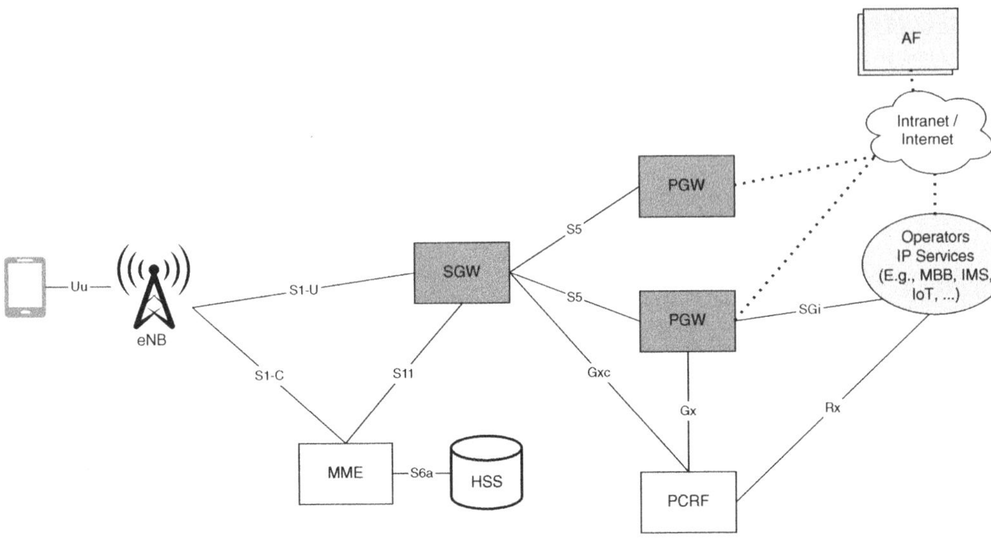

Figure I.2.1.13 LTE EPC architecture.

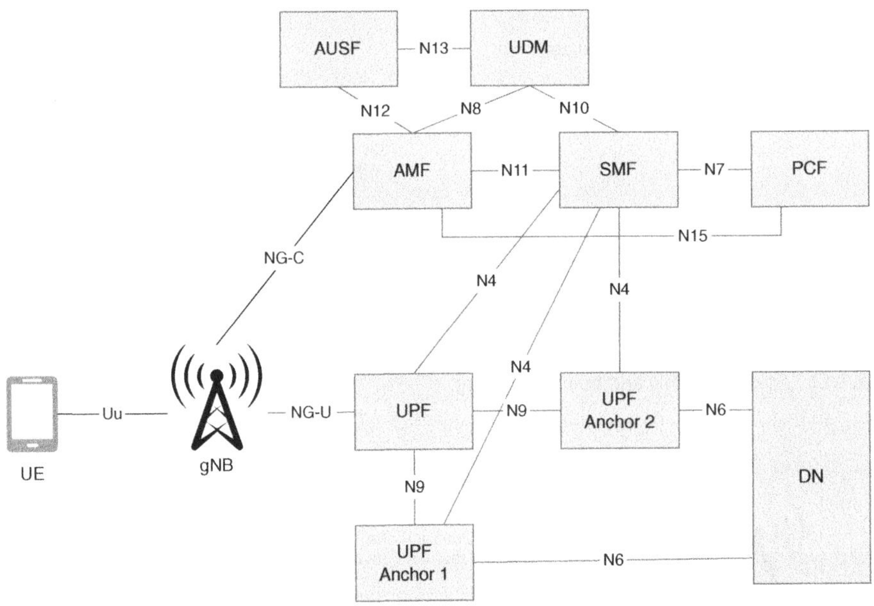

Figure I.2.1.14 NR 5G-C architecture.

with the interface absorbed into the component realization. These functions are described in detail in the "Converged Core" chapter in Part II of the book.

Figure I.2.1.16 provides the interacting functions involved in supporting a network slice. The network slice concept is introduced in NR 5GC to allow for isolation of specific users and traffic types. This allows for narrower view into the core network allowing specialized features to be supported. The network slices allow for additional authentication from the UE to be enforced. While the radio access network (RAN) aspect remains unified, the network slice allows for tighter control over quality of service (QoS), regulating the hop-to-hop delays in the core network

Table I.2.1.1 Comparisons of LTE EPC and NR 5GC.

LTE EPC	NR 5GC
MME handles both the mobility management function and the session management function	The mobility management functions are handled by the access and mobility management function (AMF) and are separated from the session management functions that are handled by the SMF.
The user plane functions are handled by the S-GW and P-GW	User plane function (UPF) is a generic function that handles all user plane functions. It includes more sophisticated anchor UPF and intermediary UPF for flexible address assignments and route definitions.
Control and user plane operations are handled by a common function	The control and user plane separation (CUPS) architecture supports the independent scalability of the required compute resources, including the location of the functions for optimal performance.
It is a point-to-point architecture with explicitly defined pairwise interacting interfaces between nodes	Supports a service-based architecture with a pub-sub (publish-subscribe) model and network routing function (NRF), where any node/function can reach any other node/function.

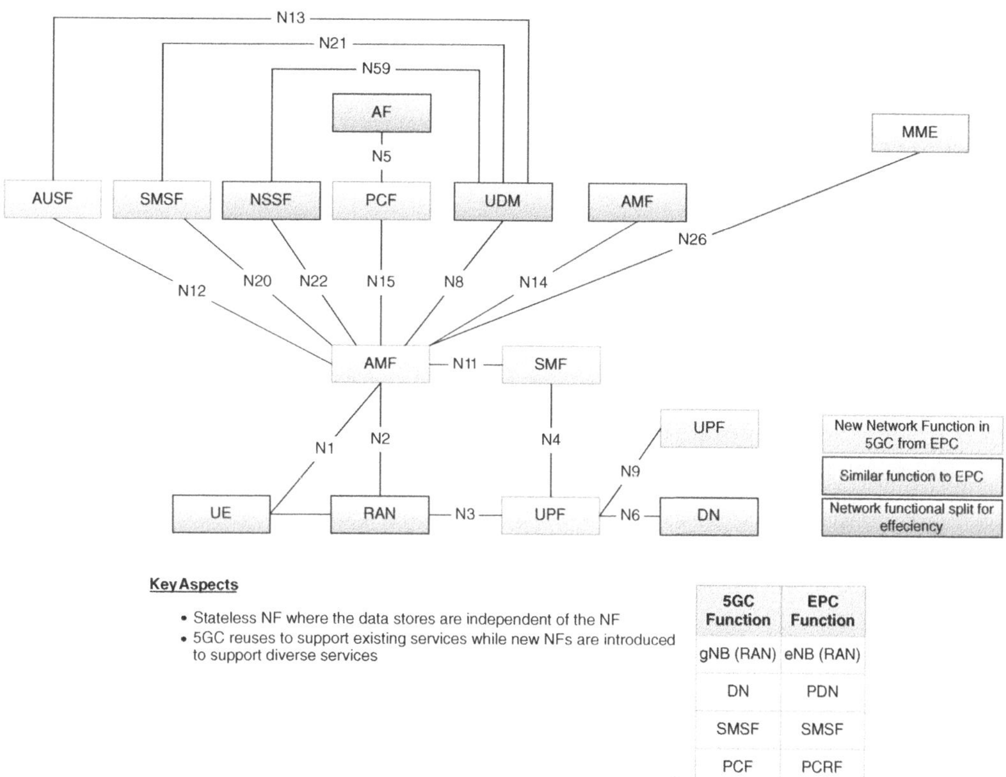

Figure I.2.1.15 NR architecture overview.

to better manage the mixing of different traffic types. Slices are also envisioned as an approach to isolate resources in a macro network to provide service to an enterprise (see "Non-public Networks" chapter in Part II of the book, particularly public network integrated non-public networks [PNI-NPN]).

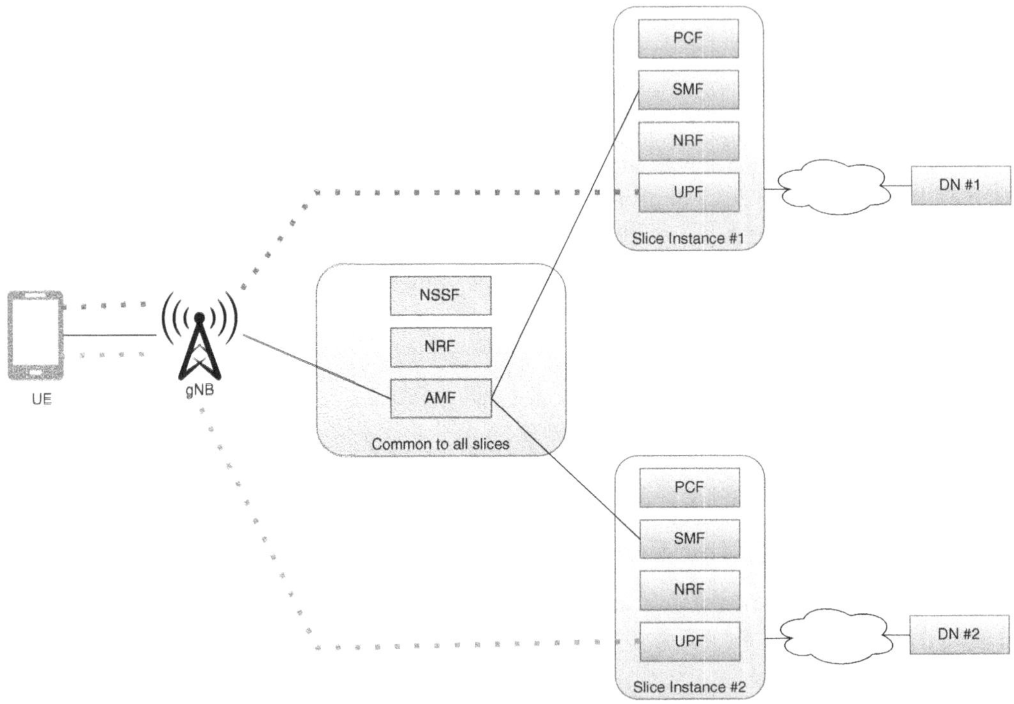

Figure I.2.1.16 Network slices and architectural separation across slices.

The 5G NR network features in 5GC are evolved to support advanced technologies like network functions virtualization (NFV), software-defined networking (SDN), network slicing, and multi-access edge computing (MEC). The software is written to be generic so that it can run on a variety of hardware platforms, potentially off-the-shelf. These network functions are expected to be housed in different cloud platforms, including using compute resources deployed close to the access points (eNB/gNB) where the users are served. The expectation is that based on the costs, the scalability is handled by dynamically moving the functions across private compute, metro cloud, demilitarized zone (DMZ), and public cloud based on the predicted load.

I.2.1.4 RAN Evolution

Traditionally, the radio base stations are built with all the radio functions, including the protocol stacks, integrated into a single node, with much of the hardware customized by each deployment vendor. This single integrated box is sometimes also referred to as a "fat AP" (fat access point that supports all required RAN functions). With the evolution of the compute resources and the need to leverage off-the-shelf compute resources, a functional split of the RAN function is being considered. See 3GPP TR 38.801, Section 11, RAN logical architecture for NR, which describes the different RAN split options and introduces the concept of central unit (CU) and distributed unit (DU) for RAN. Different deployment environments require vastly different ways to realize the end-to-end operations, and a single choice may not be suitable for all scenarios, requiring a more flexible approach.

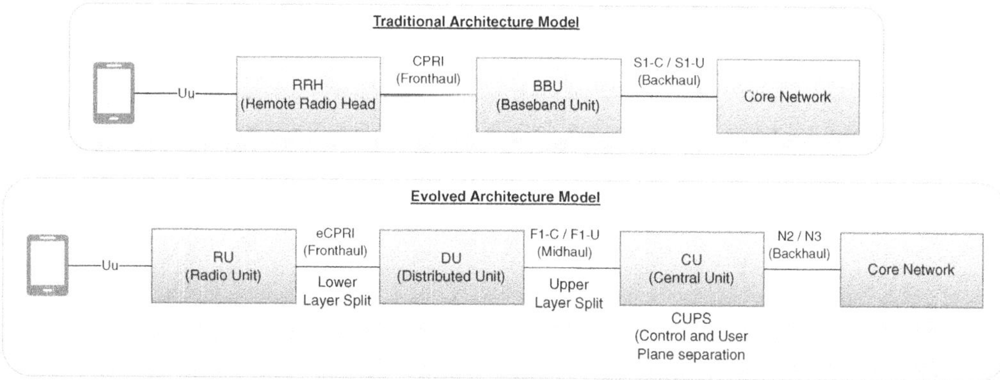

Figure I.2.1.17 Evolution of RAN architecture.

Figure I.2.1.17 provides a high-level view of the RAN architecture evolution. This illustrates a few key aspects. The baseband unit is divided into the CU and DU. The baseband to radio unit (RU) evolved from common public radio interface (CPRI) to enhanced CPRI (eCPRI) to both accommodate higher throughput and avoid requiring tight timing alignment between the two. The functional separation between CU, DU, and RU is intended to be flexible to adapt to the deployment scenarios based on end-to-end use case realization, QoS requirements, available compute resources, network interwork cabling/routers/bridges support with the required throughput, and the integration with the core network/enterprise. The CU and potentially even the DU can largely be supported with generic compute resources. The RU tends to be customized based on the RF bands, number of component carriers, and RF techniques like MIMO and beamforming that need to be supported. The front haul with the eCPRI and the functional separation between the CU, DU, and RU will be the key determining factors for the RAN network architecture. The eCPRI standard is a successor to CPRI, which was defined for the original centralized RAN (C-RAN)/fat-AP configuration. Developed by the eCPRI forum, this protocol makes more efficient use of bandwidth than its predecessor and is packet-based, meaning that it can be framed within Ethernet, avoiding the need for dedicated fiber. With tight timing requirements removed in eCPRI relative to CPRI, the Ethernet interface can support other traffic apart from what is carried for eCPRI activity. The section below discusses the different RAN split options, which are also referred to as the "disaggregation of the RAN." Some of the key motivations for disaggregating the RAN stem from having to mix and match different vendors and hardware platforms from an open RAN perspective. This architecture provides a great advantage even from a single vendor perspective to take their solutions into different markets. Although the intent is to truly have an open architecture, the complexity of integrating the modules is quite high and requires a lot of expertise in the actual realization of the individual functions for network-level optimizations to be performed, particularly given that individual vendors build custom features to position themselves better in the market. The integration effort is still reliant on the network vendors supplying these functions/nodes and becomes a key factor in defining a solution for a specific deployment.

CU consists of control and user plane protocol stacks that can be flexibly deployed with the functions collocated or distributed based on the deployment needs. A given gNB typically can be structured to have a central unit control plane (CU-CP), a central unit user plane (CU-UP), and one or more DUs. A DU is associated with and managed by only one CU-CP but can be connected to multiple CU-UPs based on the bearers and where the user plane traffic is exchanged. The CU–DU interface is IP-based. The E1 interface is used for bearer management and load balancing.

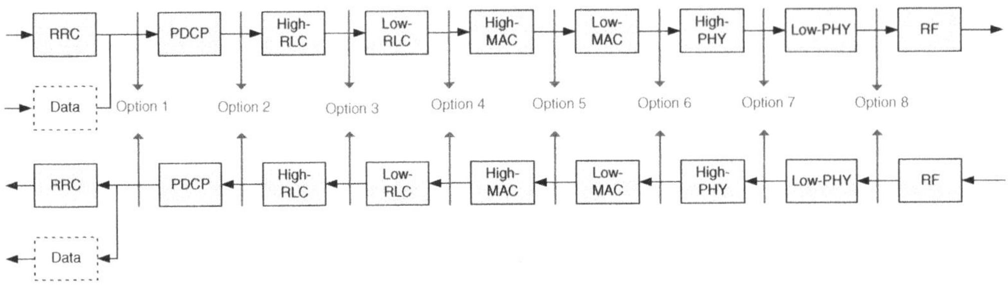

Figure I.2.1.18 Function split between central and distributed unit (3GPP TR 38.801, figure 11.1.1-1).

The F1-C interface is used for radio resource control (RRC) control signaling procedures, interface establishment, and gNB and individual UE context management. The F1-U interface is used for user plane traffic.

I.2.1.4.1 RAN Functional Split Between Central Unit and Distributed Unit

The O-RAN alliance defined a set of split options that has since been absorbed into 3GPP as well. The RAN split options are shown in Figure I.2.1.18, which primarily cover the functional separation between the CU and DU. These split options apply to both macro networks and private networks supporting small cells. Based on the QoS demands, capacity requirements, and compute and connectivity support available on the enterprise campus, different split options can be enabled for private networks. LTE nodes are typically deployed as "fat AP" (access point), implying that all the RAN functions are built into one box. With the evolution of generic compute platforms, NR is inherently architected to support RU, which acts as a transmit-receive point (TRP), DU, where the RAN scheduling, mobility, and other real-time functions are supported, and CU, which mainly acts as the RAN context for the UE as it moves across DUs/RUs.

A detailed explanation of the individual RAN split options is described in Table I.2.1.2.

This section details the different split options. Typical deployments support Option 2, Option 6, and Option 7.x, with the throughput requirements on the RAN node interconnects increasing from Option 1 to Option 8. The throughput demands on the cables interconnecting these RAN nodes are also shown.

I.2.1.4.1.1 Sample Fronthaul Bandwidth Calculations

One of the key aspects that needs to be addressed as part of deploying networks is the cabling and connectivity support required to manage the bandwidth requirements. This aspect becomes very critical with the much higher throughputs supported by 5G NR, running into gigabits per second in terms of the user throughput experienced. Supporting such throughput requires the network interconnects to support the overheads that include the transport packet headers, which ensure the context of the users/user flows between the CU and DU. Additionally, based on the level of encoding performed prior to the transport of the information in symbols, the required capacity on the cables can be several multiples of the user bitrate that needs to be supported. The parameters used to perform these computations and the DL and UL capacity requirements on the cabling between CU and DU for the key set of RAN split options are captured in the sections below.

The intent is to derive the required throughput for the cabling for the different options, which will have a direct impact on the dedicated cabling requirement and the costs of the deployments.

Table I.2.1.2 Descriptions of the RAN split options.

Functional split option	Description
Option 1 (1A-like split)	The function split in this option is similar to the 1A architecture in DC. RRC is in the central unit. Packet data convergence protocol (PDCP), radio link control (RLC), medium access control (MAC), the physical layer (PHY), and radio frequency (RF) are in the distributed unit.
Option 2 (3C-like split)	The function split in this option is similar to the 3C architecture in DC. RRC and PDCP are in the central unit, while RLC, MAC, PHY, and RF are in the distributed unit. This option may be a base for an X2-like design due to its similarity on the U-plane, but some functionality may be different, e.g., C-plane, since some new procedures may be needed. There are two possible variants available for this option. • Option 2-1 split U-plane only (3C-like split): In this split option, RRC and PDCP are in the central unit, while RLC, MAC, PHY, and RF are in the distributed unit. • Option 2-2: In this split option, RRC and PDCP are in the central unit. RLC, MAC, PHY, and RF are in the distributed unit. In addition, this option can be achieved by separating the RRC and PDCP for the CP stack and the PDCP for the UP stack into different central entities.
Option 3 (intra RLC split)	Low RLC (a partial function of RLC), MAC, PHY, and RF are in the distributed unit. PDCP and high RLC (the other partial function of RLC) are in the central unit. In this option, two approaches are taken based on the real-time/non-real-time functions split, which are as follows: • Option 3-1 split based on automatic repeat request (ARQ) o Low RLC may consist of segmentation functions; o High RLC may be composed of ARQ and other RLC functions; o This option splits the RLC sublayer into high RLC and low RLC sublayers such that for RLC Acknowledge Mode operation, all RLC functions may be performed at the high RLC sublayer residing in the central unit, while the segmentation may be performed at the low RLC sublayer residing in the distributed unit. Here, high RLC segments the RLC PDU based on the status reports, while low RLC segments the RLC PDU into the available MAC PDU resources. • Option 3-2 split based on TX RLC and RX RLC o Low RLC may be composed of the transmitting TM RLC entity, the transmitting UM RLC entity, a transmitting side of AM, and the routing function of a receiving side of AM, which are related to downlink transmission. o High RLC may be composed of the receiving TM RLC entity, the receiving UM RLC entity, and a receiving side of AM, except for the routing function and reception of RLC status reports, which are related to uplink transmission.
Option 4 (RLC-MAC split)	MAC, PHY, and RF are in the distributed unit. PDCP and RLC are in the central unit.

(Continued)

Table I.2.1.2 (Continued)

Functional split option	Description
Option 5 (intra MAC split)	RF, PHY, and some parts of the MAC layer (e.g., HARQ) are in the distributed unit. The upper layer is in the central unit. This option assumes the following distribution: • RF, PHY, and lower part of the MAC layer (low-MAC) are in the distributed unit • The higher part of the MAC layer (high-MAC), RLC, and PDCP are in the central unit Therefore, by splitting the MAC layer into two entities (e.g., high-MAC and low-MAC), the services and functions provided by the MAC layer will be located in the central unit (CU), in the distributed unit (DU), or in both. An example of this kind of distribution is given below. • In the high-MAC sublayer, the centralized scheduling in the high-MAC sublayer will be in charge of the control of multiple low-MAC sublayers. It takes high-level centralized scheduling decisions. The inter-cell interference coordination in the high-MAC sublayer will be in charge of interference coordination methods such as JP/CS CoMP. • In the low-MAC sublayer, the time-critical functions in the low-MAC sublayer include the functions with stringent delay requirements (e.g., HARQ) or the functions where performance is proportional to latency (e.g., radio channel and signal measurements from PHY, random access control). It reduces the delay requirements on the fronthaul interface. Radio-specific functions in the low-MAC sublayer can perform scheduling-related information processing and reporting. It can also measure/estimate the activities on the configured operations or the served UE's statistics and report periodically or as requested to the high-MAC sublayer.
Option 6 (MAC-PHY split)	The PHY and RF are in the distributed unit, while the upper layers are in the central unit. The MAC and upper layers are in the central unit (CU). The PHY layer and RF are in the DU. The interface between the CU and DUs carries data, configuration, and scheduling-related information (e.g., MCS, layer mapping, beamforming, antenna configuration, RB allocation, etc.) and measurements.
Option 7 (intra PHY split)	Part of PHY function and RF is in the distributed unit. Upper layers are in the central unit. Multiple realizations of this option are possible, including asymmetrical options that allow obtaining the benefits of different sub-options for UL and DL independently. This option requires some kind of compression technique to reduce transport bandwidth requirements between the DU and CU. In the UL, FFT and CP removal reside in the DU, and the two subvariants, 7-1 and 7-2, are described below. The remaining functions reside in the CU. In the downlink, iFFT and CP addition reside in the DU, and the rest of the PHY resides in the CU.

Table I.2.1.2 (Continued)

Functional split option	Description
	Considering the above, there are three subvariants available for this option, described as below • Option 7-1 In this option – In the UL, o DU: ▪ FFT ▪ CP removal and ▪ possibly physical random access channel (PRACH) filtering functions o CU: the rest of PHY functions. – In the DL o DU: ▪ iFFT ▪ CP addition functions o CU: the rest of PHY functions. • Option 7-2 In this option – In the UL: o DU: ▪ FFT ▪ CP removal ▪ resource de-mapping and possibly pre-filtering functions o CU: the rest of PHY functions – In the DL: o DU: ▪ iFFT ▪ CP addition ▪ resource mapping and pre-coding functions o CU: the rest of PHY functions • Option 7-3: – (Only for DL): Only the encoder resides in the CU, and the rest of the PHY functions reside in the DU.
Option 8 (PHY-RF split)	RF functionality is in the distributed unit, and the upper layer is in the central unit. This option allows to separate the RF and the PHY layers. This split permits the centralization of processes at all protocol layer levels, resulting in very tight coordination of the RAN. This allows for efficient support of functions such as CoMP, MIMO, load balancing, and mobility.

NOTE: The options represented consist of a non-exhaustive list. The assumption about protocols and function definitions was based on what was available during the study phase in the 3GPP 38.801 specification definition.

Parameter Set

Parameter set	Channel BW (MHz)	Modulation scheme	Number of MIMO layer	IQ bitwidth (bit)	Number of antenna ports
TR 38.801 [3]	100 (DL/UL)	DL:256QAM UL:64QAM (NOTE 1)	DL: 8 UL: 8	DL: 2×(7~16) UL: 2×(10~16)	32 (DL/UL)
#1	100 (DL/UL)	256QAM (DL/UL)	DL: 8 UL: 4	DL: 2×16 UL: 2×16 (NOTE 2)	32 (DL/UL)
#2					8 (DL/UL)
#3	200 (DL/UL)				32 (DL/UL)
#4					8 (DL/UL)
#5	400 (DL/UL)				32 (DL/UL)
#6					8 (DL/UL)

NOTE 1: While table A-2 in 3GPP TR 38.801 states "256QAM" for UL, the calculation in table A-1 in 3GPP TR 38.801 is based on 64QAM.

NOTE 2: For IQ bit width, only 2×16 is used (for parameters set #1-6) since the intention is to show the maximum values.

Option 6

Downlink			
Parameter	**Description**	**Higher range value**	**Units**
A0	Peak data rate of LTE reference	150.000	Mbps
B1	System BW scaling	5.000	(100 MHz/20 MHz)
C1	MIMO layer scaling	4.000	(8 layer/2 layer)
D1	QAM scaling	1.333	(8 bits per symbol/6 bits per symbol)
E1	Overhead (accounts for scheduling/control signaling)	133.000	Mbps
A1	Required FH BW (Gbps) for TR 38.801	4.133	Gbps

Parameter	Description	Parameter set #1	Parameter set #2	Parameter set #3	Parameter set #4	Parameter set #5	Parameter set #6	Units
B2	System BW scaling	1	1	2	2	4	4	X MHz/100 MHz
C2	MIMO layer scaling	1	1	1	1	1	1	(8 layer/8 layer)
D2	QAM scaling	1	1	1	1	1	1	(8 bits per symbol/8 bits per symbol)
E2	Spectrum usage scaling	1.1	1.1	1.1	1.1	1.1	1.1	(99%/90%)
F2	Margin for an upper-bound estimation	1.2	1.2	1.2	1.2	1.2	1.2	(120%/100%)
A2	Required FH BW (Gbps) for TR 38.801	5.456	5.456	10.911	10.911	21.822	21.822	Gbps

Uplink

Parameter	Description	Higher range value	Units
A0	Peak data rate of LTE reference	50.000	Mbps
B1	System BW scaling	5.000	(100 MHz/20 MHz)
C1	MIMO layer scaling	8.000	(8 layer/1 layer)
D1	QAM scaling	1.500	(6 bits per symbol/4 bits per symbol)
E1	Overhead (accounts for scheduling/control signaling)	2,640.000	Mbps
A1	Required FH BW (Gbps) for TR 38.801	5.640	Gbps

(*Continued*)

Uplink								
Parameter	**Description**	**Higher range value**	**Units**					
Parameter	**Description**	**Parameter set #1**	**Parameter set #2**	**Parameter set #3**	**Parameter set #4**	**Parameter set #5**	**Parameter set #6**	**Units**
B2	System BW scaling	1	1	2	2	4	4	X MHz/100 MHz
C2	MIMO layer scaling	0.5	0.5	0.5	0.5	0.5	0.5	(4 layer/8 layer)
D2	QAM scaling	1.333	1.333	1.333	1.333	1.333	1.333	(8 bits per symbol/6 bits per symbol)
E2	Spectrum usage scaling	1.1	1.1	1.1	1.1	1.1	1.1	(99%/90%)
F2	Margin for an upper-bound estimation	1.2	1.2	1.2	1.2	1.2	1.2	(120%/100%)
A2	Required FH BW (Gbps) for TR 38.801	4.963	4.963	9.926	9.926	19.853	19.853	Gbps

Option 7.1

Downlink			
Parameter	**Description**	**Higher range value**	**Units**
B1	Number of subcarriers of LTE reference for 20 MHz	1,200.000	1,200 SC/20 MHz
C1	System BW scaling	5.000	(100 MHz/20 MHz)
D1	OFDM symbol rate	14.000	14 symbol/ms
E1	Antenna port	32.000	Antenna ports
F1	IQ bitwidth	32	2 × 16 bits
G1	Overhead (accounts for scheduling and control signaling)	121.000	Mbps
A1	Required FH BW (Gbps) for TR 38.801	86.137	Gbps

Parameter	Description	Parameter set #1	Parameter set #2	Parameter set #3	Parameter set #4	Parameter set #5	Parameter set #6	Units
B2	System BW scaling	1	1	2	2	4	4	X MHz/100 MHz
C2	Number of Ant port scaling	0.25	0.25	1	0.25	1	0.25	([8 Ant, 32 Ant]/32 Ant)
D2	IQ bitwidth scaling	1	1	1	1	1	1	(2×16 bits/2×16 bits)
E2	Spectrum usage scaling	1.1	1.1	1.1	1.1	1.1	1.1	(99%/90%)
F2	Margin for an upper-bound estimation	1.2	1.2	1.2	1.2	1.2	1.2	(120%/100%)
A2	Required FH BW (Gbps) for TR 38.801	28.425	28.425	227.402	56.850	454.803	113.701	Gbps

Uplink			
Parameter	**Description**	**Higher range value**	**Units**
B1	Number of subcarrier of LTE reference for 20 MHz	1,200.000	1,200 SC/20 MHz
C1	System BW scaling	5.000	(100 MHz/20 MHz)
D1	OFDM symbol rate	14.000	14 symbol/ms
E1	Antenna port	32.000	Antenna ports
F1	IQ bitwidth	32	2×16 bits
G1	Overhead (accounts for scheduling/control signaling)	80.000	Mbps
A1	Required FH BW (Gbps) for TR 38.801	86.096	Gbps

Parameter	Description	Parameter set #1	Parameter set #2	Parameter set #3	Parameter set #4	Parameter set #5	Parameter set #6	Units
B2	System BW scaling	1	1	2	2	4	4	X MHz/100 MHz
C2	Number of Ant port scalings	0.25	0.25	1	0.25	1	0.25	([8 Ant, 32 Ant]/32 Ant)

(*Continued*)

Uplink									
Parameter	**Description**	**Higher range value**	**Units**						
D2	IQ bitwidth scaling	1	1	1	1	1	1	(2×16 bits/2×16 bits)
E2	Spectrum usage scaling	1.1	1.1	1.1	1.1	1.1	1.1	(99%/90%)
F2	Margin for an upper-bound estimation	1.2	1.2	1.2	1.2	1.2	1.2	(120%/100%)
A2	Required FH BW (Gbps) for TR 38.801	28.412	28.412	227.293	56.823	454.587	113.647	Gbps

Option 7.2

Downlink			
Parameter	**Description**	**Higher range value**	**Units**
B1	Number of subcarrier of LTE reference in a 20 MHz bandwidth	1,200.000	1,200 SC/20 MHz
C1	System BW scaling	5.000	(100 MHz/20 MHz)
D1	OFDM symbol rate	14.000	14 symbol/ms
E1	MIMO layer	8.000	8 layer
F1	IQ bitwidth	32	2×16 bits
G1	Overhead (accounts for scheduling/control signaling)	713.900	Mbps
A1	Required FH BW (Gbps) for TR 38.801	22.218	Gbps

Parameter	Description	Parameter set #1	Parameter set #2	Parameter set #3	Parameter set #4	Parameter set #5	Parameter set #6	Units
B2	System BW scaling	1	1	2	2	4	4	X MHz/100 MHz
C2	MIMO layer scaling	1	1	1	1	1	1	(8 layer/8 layer)
D2	IQ bitwidth scaling	1	1	1	1	1	1	(2×16 bits/2×16 bits)
E2	Spectrum usage scaling	1.1	1.1	1.1	1.1	1.1	1.1	(99%/90%)
F2	Margin for an upper-bound estimation	1.2	1.2	1.2	1.2	1.2	1.2	(120%/100%)
A2	Required FH BW (Gbps) for TR 38.801	29.328	29.328	58.655	58.655	117.311	117.311	Gbps

Uplink			
Parameter	**Description**	**Higher range value**	**Units**
B1	Number of subcarrier of LTE reference in 20 MHz	1,200.000	1,200 SC/20 MHz
C1	System BW scaling	5.000	(100 MHz/20 MHz)
D1	OFDM symbol rate	14.000	14 symbol/ms
E1	MIMO layer	8.000	8 layer
F1	IQ bitwidth	32	2×16 bits
G1	Overhead (accounts for scheduling/control signaling)	120.000	Mbps
A1	Required FH BW (Gbps) for TR 38.801	21.624	Gbps

(*Continued*)

Parameter	Description	Parameter set #1	Parameter set #2	Parameter set #3	Parameter set #4	Parameter set #5	Parameter set #6	Units
B2	System BW scaling	1	1	2	2	4	4	X MHz/100 MHz
C2	MIMO layer scaling	0.5	0.5	0.5	0.5	0.5	0.5	(4 layer/8 layer)
D2	IQ bitwidth scaling	1	1	1	1	1	1	(2×16 bits/2×16 bits)
E2	Spectrum usage scaling	1.1	1.1	1.1	1.1	1.1	1.1	(99%/90%)
F2	Margin for an upper-bound estimation	1.2	1.2	1.2	1.2	1.2	1.2	(120%/100%)
A2	Required FH BW (Gbps) for TR 38.801	14.272	14.272	28.544	28.544	57.087	57.087	Gbps

Option 7.3

Downlink			
Parameter	**Description**	**Higher range value**	**Units**
A0	Peak data rate of LTE reference	150.000	Mbps
B1	System BW scaling	5.000	(100 MHz/20 MHz)
C1	MIMO layer scaling	4.000	(8 layer/2 layer)
D1	QAM scaling	1.333	(8 bits per symbol/6 bits per symbol)
E1	Overhead (accounts for scheduling/control signaling)	133.000	Mbps
A1	Required FH BW (Gbps) for TR 38.801	4.133	Gbps

Parameter	Description	Parameter set #1	Parameter set #2	Parameter set #3	Parameter set #4	Parameter set #5	Parameter set #6	Units
B2	System BW scaling	1	1	2	2	4	4	X MHz/100 MHz
C2	MIMO layer scaling	1	1	1	1	1	1	(8 layer/8 layer)
D2	QAM scaling	1	1	1	1	1	1	(8 bits per symbol/8 bits per symbol)
E2	Spectrum usage scaling	1.1	1.1	1.1	1.1	1.1	1.1	(99%/90%)
F2	Margin for an upper-bound estimation	1.2	1.2	1.2	1.2	1.2	1.2	(120%/100%)
A2	Required FH BW (Gbps) for TR 38.801	5.456	5.456	10.911	10.911	21.822	21.822	Gbps

Uplink			
Parameter	**Description**	**Higher range value**	**Units**
A0	Peak data rate of LTE reference	50.000	Mbps
B1	System BW scaling	5.000	(100 MHz/20 MHz)
C1	MIMO layer scaling	8.000	(8 layer/1 layer)
D1	QAM scaling	1.500	(6 bits per symbol/4 bits per symbol)
E1	Overhead (accounts for scheduling/control signaling)	2,640.000	Mbps
A1	Required FH BW (Gbps) for TR 38.801	5.640	Gbps

(*Continued*)

Parameter	Description	Parameter set #1	Parameter set #2	Parameter set #3	Parameter set #4	Parameter set #5	Parameter set #6	Units
B2	System BW scaling	1	1	2	2	4	4	X MHz/100 MHz
C2	MIMO layer scaling	0.5	0.5	0.5	0.5	0.5	0.5	(4 layer/8 layer)
D2	QAM scaling	1.333	1.333	1.333	1.333	1.333	1.333	(8 bits per symbol/6 bits per symbol)
E2	Spectrum usage scaling	1.1	1.1	1.1	1.1	1.1	1.1	(99%/90%)
F2	Margin for an upper-bound estimation	1.2	1.2	1.2	1.2	1.2	1.2	(120%/100%)
A2	Required FH BW (Gbps) for TR 38.801	4.963	4.963	9.926	9.926	19.853	19.853	Gbps

I.2.1.4.2 RAN and Core Network Deployment Options

This section covers the different options for interconnecting the LTE and NR RAN nodes with the EPC and 5GC core networks. For private networks, only two of the options are relevant: Option (1) LTE eNB connecting to the EPC and Option (2) NR gNB connecting to the 5GC. The other options are employed in the macro network with the LTE and NR coexisting and the network evolving from EPC to 5GC. Figure I.2.1.19 provides an illustration showing the interconnects based on the options between eNB/gNB and EPC/5GC. Table I.2.1.3 provides a brief description of the LTE/NR RAN interconnect options with the EPC/5GC core network.

Figure I.2.1.20 illustrates the LTE and NR operating in dual-connectivity mode and the associated terminologies involved. This dual connectivity typically will not apply to private networks, given that an enterprise campus will support an LTE/EPC network or NR/5GC network.

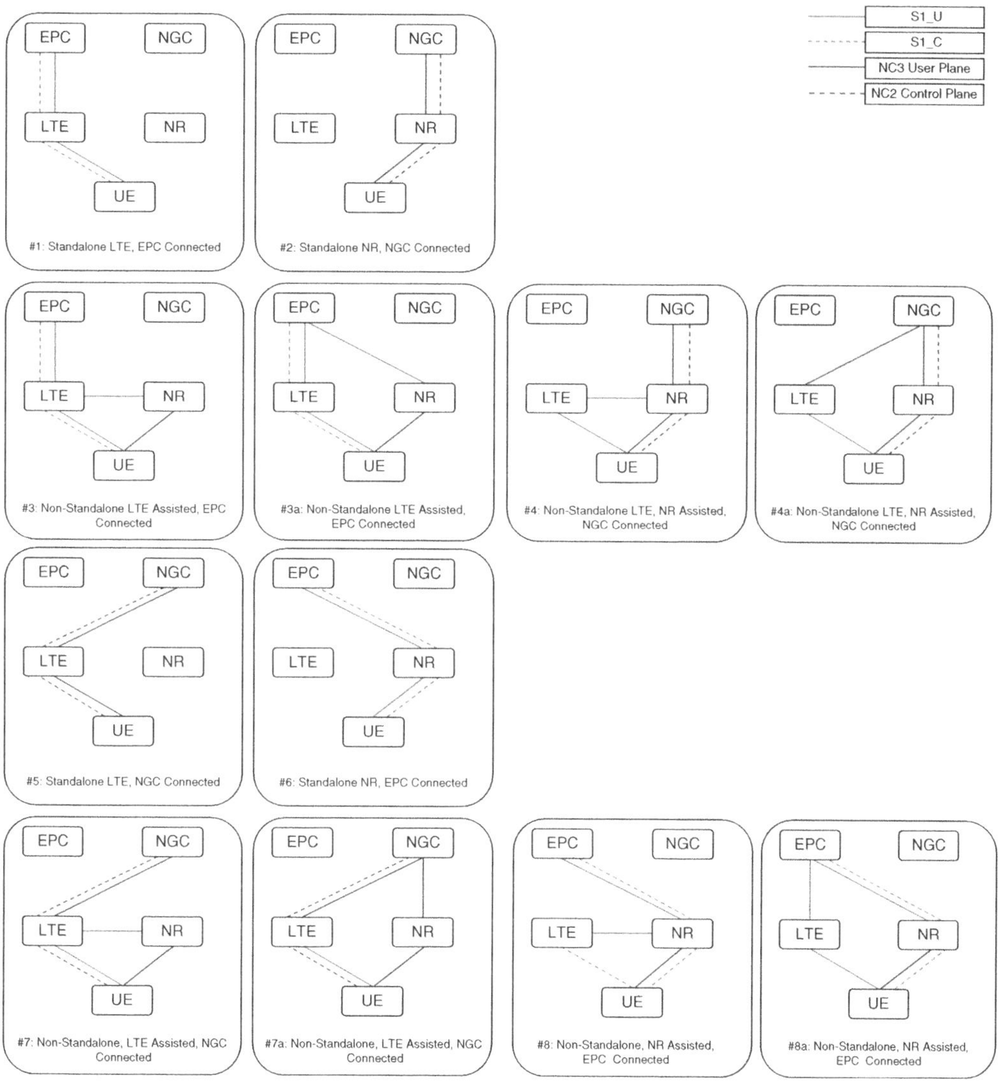

Figure I.2.1.19 LTE/NR RAN – core network interconnect variants.

Table I.2.1.3 LTE/NR RAN – core network interconnect variants.

Deployment option	RAN	Core networks	Description
Stand-alone – Option 1	eNB	EPC	LTE-only operation
Stand-alone – Option 2	gNB	5GC	NR SA mode operation
Stand-alone – Option 5	NG-eNB (eLTE)	5GC	Supports the changes needed in the eNB to connect to a 5GC
Stand-alone – Option 6	gNB	EPC	The gNB is connected to the EPC in stand-alone mode. This option is not commercially used.
Non-stand-alone – Option 3, 3a, 3x	NG-eNB, eNB	EPC	Architecture was used to introduce NR to the markets with LTE as the anchor/ master cell group (MCG) and NR as the secondary carrier group (SCG).
Non-stand-alone – Option 4, 4a	NG-eNB, gNB	5GC	gNB is the anchor, with MCG and eNB as SCG.
Non-stand-alone – Option 7, 7a, 7x	NG-eNB, gNB	5GC	Evolved eNB (eLTE) as anchor (MCG) with NR as SCG.
Non-stand-alone – Option 8, 8a	eNB, gNB	EPC	NR as MCG and LTE as SCG supporting NR-assisted camping. This option is not used commercially.

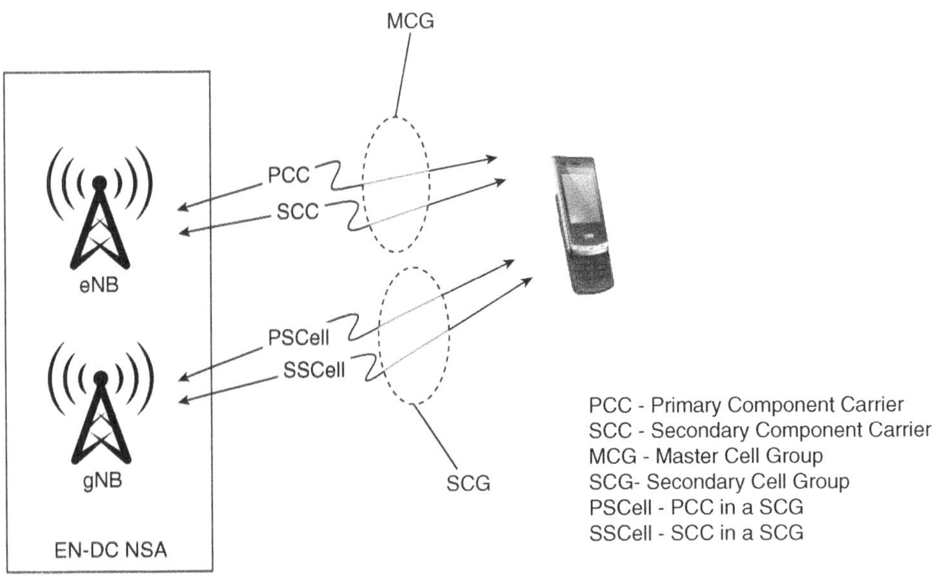

Figure I.2.1.20 Dual-connectivity terminology.

Figure I.2.1.21 shows the protocol stack communicating across the LTE and NR systems for signaling traffic for the NSA dual-connectivity option, and Figure I.2.1.22 shows the user plane protocol stack for the same.

Figure I.2.1.23 shows the control and user plane stacks for NR SA mode of operation. This will be the configuration used for NR-based private network deployments, independent of the RAN split option used in the network.

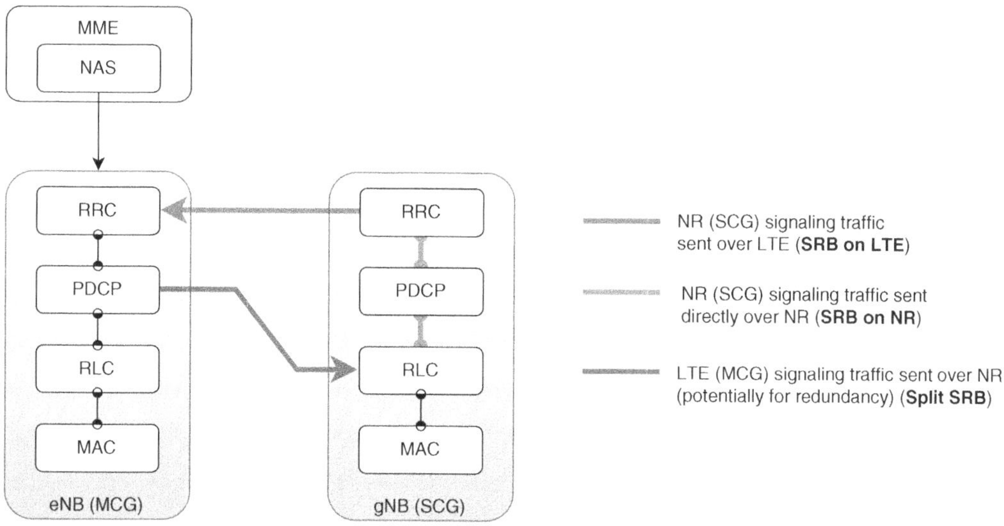

Figure I.2.1.21 Signaling radio bearer with dual connectivity.

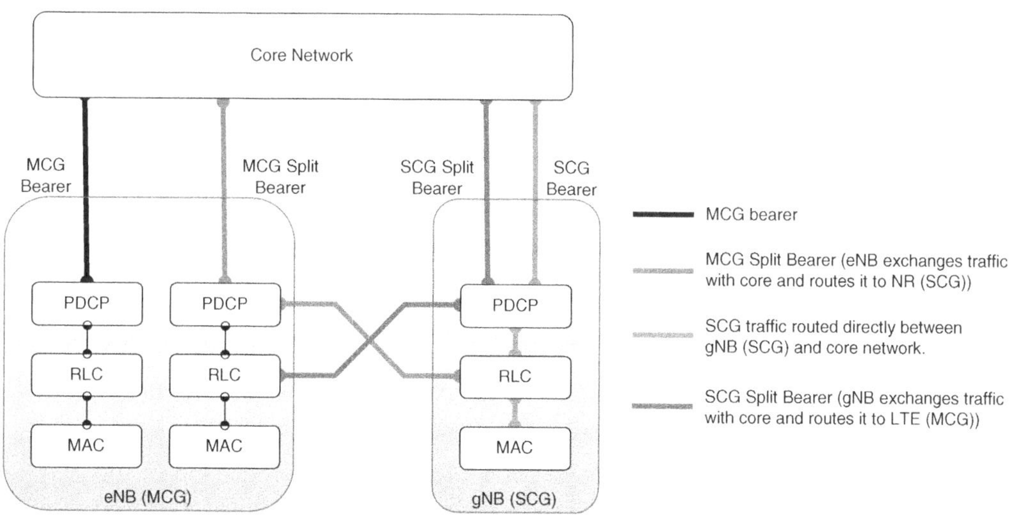

Figure I.2.1.22 User plane traffic handling with dual connectivity.

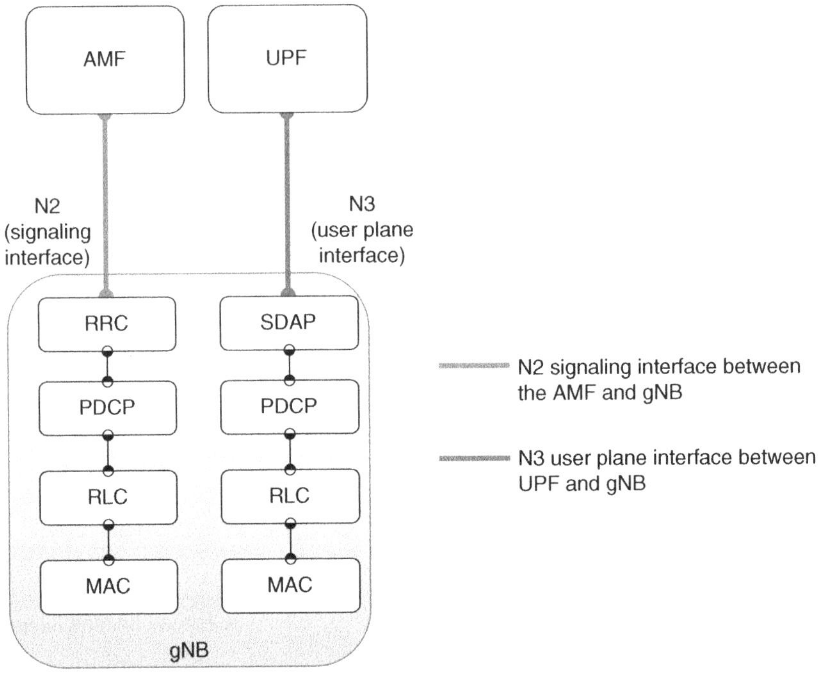

Figure I.2.1.23 NR SA mode signaling and user plane traffic handling.

I.2.1.5 Summary

The 5G NR key radio aspects are described. The importance of a disaggregated RAN is discussed, and possible architectural variants along with the aspects that need to be considered for deployments are shown. The CUPS for generic hardware use for network functions scalability is described. Additionally, the network function separation from the data stores for a memory-less deployment is shown to enable high availability and dynamic scaling that adapts to system load. The RAN–core network interconnect variants are shown, describing the different options.

References

See the Standards section for a list of references to the 3GPP NR specifications. There are many 3GPP specifications. A more concise, relevant set of specifications is highlighted as a starting point for the reader to explore further. The references below are to the 3GPP releases (from release 15 to 18) and provide summary descriptions of the features and work items, serving as a good overview.

1 3GPP Release 15: 3GPP TR 21.915 Release 15 Description; Summary of Rel-15 Work Items
2 3GPP Release 16: 3GPP TR 21.916 Release 16 Description; Summary of Rel-16 Work Items
3 3GPP Release 17: 3GPP TR 21.917 Release 17 Description; Summary of Rel-17 Work Items
4 3GPP Release 18: 3GPP TR 21.918 Release 18 Description; Summary of Rel-18 Work Items

I.2.2

NR Physical Layer

I.2.2.1 Introduction

The new radio (NR) physical layer continues the wireless evolution using long-term evolution (LTE) as a basis. Unlike 3G code division multiple access (CDMA) to 4G OFMD switch and using a completely different technological basis starting with the waveform, 4G to 5G is a more seamless transition. The same waveforms are used with 5G NR as with 4G LTE. Enhancements are done to accommodate wider bandwidth, a completely new band with mmWave, and the inclusion of additional radio frequency (RF), physical layer, and the associated medium access control (MAC) layer techniques. In fact, much of the logical and physical channel definition nomenclature is directly carried over from LTE into NR. Newer reference signals are introduced for improved operations for both downlink (DL) and uplink (UL).

This section is described using illustrations. It covers the 5G NR reference signals and channels. It addresses cell acquisition and initial access procedures that account for both beamforming and dynamic locations where the cell reference signals are located, which are fundamentally different in NR relative to LTE. The random-access channel (RACH) procedures that are contention-based and contention-free are shown. The data traffic operations for both DL and UL are also addressed. Note that the focus, again, is to show the key aspects where NR differs from LTE, while underlying operations based on LTE definitions continue to remain true [1].

I.2.2.2 Physical Channels and Reference Signals

The physical, logical, and transport channels, and the relationships between them, are shown in Figure I.2.2.1.

I.2.2.2.1 5G NR Logical Channels

There are several different logical channels that are used within the 5G NR radio access network. Some of these will be familiar names from the 4G LTE system, as the names have been carried over.

Mobile Communication Systems for Private Networks, First Edition. Srinivasan Balasubramanian.

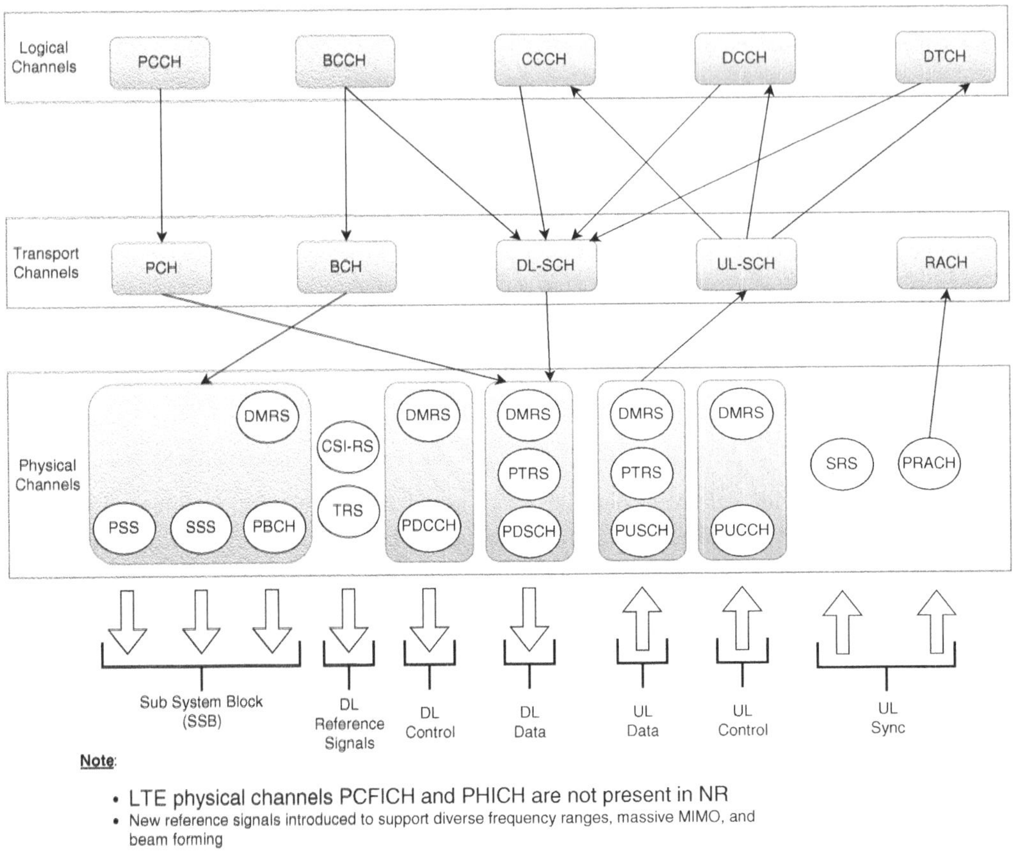

Figure I.2.2.1 5G NR physical reference signals and channels.

- ***Broadcast Control Channel (BCCH):*** The BCCH is used within the downlink, and it is used for sending broadcast-style information to the user equipment (UE) within that cell. The system information transmitted by the 5G NR BCCH is divided into different blocks:
  - *Master Information Block (MIB):* There is one MIB, and it is mapped onto the broadcast channel (BCH) transport channel and then to the physical broadcast channel (PBCH) physical channel.
  - *System Information Block (SIB):* There are several SIBs. These are mapped onto the DL-SCH transport channel and then onto the physical downlink shared channel (PDSCH) physical channel.
- ***Paging Control Channel (PCCH):*** This is a downlink channel. It is used to page the UEs whose location at the cell level is not known to the network. As a result, the paging message needs to be transmitted in multiple cells. The PCCH is mapped to the paging channel (PCH) transport channel and then to the PDSCH physical channel.
- ***Common Control Channel (CCCH):*** This 5G channel is used on both the downlink and uplink for transmitting control information to and from the user equipment or mobiles. The channel is used for initial access, i.e., those mobiles that do not have a radio resource control (RRC) connection.

- ***Dedicated Control Channel (DCCH):*** The DCCH is used within the uplink and downlink to carry dedicated control information between the UE or mobile and the network. It is used by the UE and the network after a radio resource control (RRC) connection has been established.
- ***Dedicated Traffic Channel (DTCH):*** This 5G channel is present in both the uplink and downlink. It is dedicated to one UE and is used for carrying user information to and from a specific UE and the network.

I.2.2.2.2 5G NR Transport Channels

There are five different transport channels. Some are used on the uplink, others on the downlink, and some can be used on both.

- ***Broadcast Channel (BCH):*** The BCH 5G channel is used in the downlink only for transmitting the BCCH system information, and specifically the MIB, information. In order for the data to be utilized, it has a specific format.
- ***Paging Channel (PCH):*** The PCH is used for carrying paging information from the PCCH logical channel. The PCH supports discontinuous reception (DRX) to enable the UE to save battery power by waking up at a specific time to receive the PCH.

  To ensure that the PCH is received by all mobiles/UEs in the cell, the PCH must be broadcast over the entire cell as a single message. When beamforming is used, this can be done using several different PCH instances.
- ***Downlink Shared Channel (DL-SCH):*** As the name indicates, this is a downlink-only channel. It is the main transport channel used for transmitting downlink data and supports all the key 5G NR features. These include dynamic rate adaptation, hybrid automatic repeat request (HARQ), channel-aware scheduling, and spatial multiplexing.

  The DL-SCH is also used for transmitting some parts of the BCCH system information, specifically the SIB. Each UE has a DL-SCH for each cell to which it is connected.
- ***Uplink Shared Channel (UL-SCH):*** This is the uplink counterpart to the DL-SCH, that is, the uplink transport channel used for the transmission of uplink data.
- ***Random-Access Channel (RACH):*** The RACH is a transport channel that carries the random-access preamble used to overcome the message collisions that can occur when UEs access the system simultaneously.

I.2.2.2.3 5G NR Physical Layer Data Channels

The 5G physical channels are used to transport information over the actual radio interface. They have the transport channels mapped onto them, as seen in the diagrams, but they also include various physical layer data required for the maintenance and optimization of the radio communication link between the UE and the base station.

The 5G mobile communication physical layer channels resemble those of 4G LTE, but PHICH and PCHCH have been removed. The HARQ operation has also been updated to be more flexible. Additionally, the downlink control channel, physical downlink control channel (PDCCH), is now administered by layer 3 procedures.

There are three physical channels for both the uplink and downlink:

5G NR Downlink Physical Channels

- ***Physical downlink shared channel (PDSCH):*** The 5G NR PDSCH carries data-sharing capacity on a time and frequency basis. The PDSCH physical channel carries a variety of data items: user data, UE-specific higher layer control messages mapped down from higher channels, SIBs, and paging.

  The PDSCH uses an adaptive modulation format dependent on the link conditions, i.e., signal-to-noise ratio. It also uses a flexible coding scheme. The combination of these means that there is flexible coding and data rate.
- ***Physical downlink control channel (PDCCH):*** As the name implies, the 5G PDCCH carries downlink control data. Its primary function is scheduling the downlink transmissions on the PDSCH and also the uplink data transmissions on the physical uplink shared channel (PUSCH).

  The PDCCH uses quadrature phase shift keying (QPSK) as its modulation format and polar coding as the coding scheme, except for small packets of data.
- ***Physical broadcast channel (PBCH):*** This 5G channel is part of the synchronization signal block. Its function is to provide UEs with the MIB. Another function of the PBCH in conjunction with the control channel is to support the synchronization of time and frequency. This aids in cell acquisition, selection, and re-selection.

  The PBCH uses a fixed data format, and there is one block that extends over a transmission time interval (TTI) of 80 ms.

  The PBCH uses QPSK modulation, and it transmits a cell-specific demodulation reference signal, a demod reference signals (DMRS) pattern that can be used to aid beamforming.

5G NR Uplink Physical Channels

- ***Physical random-access channel (PRACH):*** This 5G channel, the PRACH, is used for channel access. It transmits an initial random-access preamble consisting of sequences that may be of two different lengths:
  - A long sequence is 839, which is applied to the subcarrier spacings of 1.25 and 5 kHz
  - Short sequence lengths of 139 are applied to subcarrier spacings of 15 and 30 kHz (FR1 bands) and 60 and 120 kHz (FR2 bands).
- ***Physical uplink shared channel (PUSCH):*** The 5G PUSCH is the counterpart of the PDSCH. It is used to carry data from the UL-SCH and its higher-mapped channels on a frequency- and time-shared basis.

  Like the PDSCH, the PUSCH also has a very flexible format. The allocation of frequency resources is undertaken using resource blocks (RBs), along with a flexible modulation and coding scheme (MCS) dependent upon the link signal-to-noise ratio.

  To support the channel link estimation and demodulation, the PUSCH contains DMRS signals.
- ***Physical uplink control channel (PUCCH):*** The 5G PUCCH carries the uplink control data. It is also possible that, dependent on the resource allocation, the uplink control information (UCI) or data may also be sent on the PUSCH, even though in the downlink direction, control information is always sent on the PDCCH.

I.2.2.2.4 Comparing LTE and NR Reference Signals

The LTE physical control format indicator channel (PCFICH) channel indicates the location and format of the PDCCH channel carried at the beginning of each frame. For NR, this is no longer required, given that the common search space (CSS) and UE dedicated search space are specified

Table I.2.2.1 Comparing reference signals between LTE and NR.

Reference signal usage	4G LTE	5G NR	Description
DL channel state information	CRS[a] CSI-RS	CSI-RS	Used for channel state feedback and beam management Up to 32 ports supported
UL channel state information	SRS	SRS	UL channel estimation and UL beam management Used for channel reciprocity-based DL scheduling in TDD
Data channel demodulation	CRS, DMRS	DMRS	Used for coherent demodulation of DL channels (transmitted with PBCH, PDCCH, and PDSCH) Front-loaded for faster decoding Up to 8 ports for SU-MIMO and 12 ports for MU-MIMO
Control channel demodulation	CRS	DMRS	Coherent demodulation Front-loaded
Phase tracking (mmWave)	–	PTRS	Used for phase noise compensation Dense in the time domain compared to the frequency domain
Time and frequency tracking	CRS	TRS	Used for time and frequency tracking Configured in conjunction with the subsystem block (SSB) to assist UE
Beam management	–	SSB, CSI-RS	Reference signal measurements for switching beams
Radio link monitoring	CRS	CSI-RS, SSB	Used primarily to detect and declare radio link failures (RLF)
RRM measurement	CRS	CSI-RS, SSB	Signal strength reporting is used for load balancing.

[a] LTE's always-on cell-specific reference signal (CRS) is replaced with multiple UE-specific on-demand RS signals in 5G NR.
PTRS: phase tracking reference signal; TDD: time division duplex.

through the SIBs, and the UE uses that to demodulate the PDCCH channel. The LTE PHICH is not used in NR, and the new grant provided on the PDCCH for the same HARQ instance is treated implicitly as an acknowledgment by the UE (Table I.2.2.1).

I.2.2.3 NR UE Acquisition

Given that NR systems have beam-formed operations and do not have the reference signal supported on a central frequency but can appear anywhere in the CBW (carrier bandwidth), modifications to the UE procedures relative to LTE are needed. The UE performs raster jumps (e.g., 200 kHz) within supported NR bands to detect the SSB that carries the synchronization signals, primary synchronization signal (PSS) and secondary synchronization signal (SSS). The SSB also supports the PBCH, which has the management information block (MIB) and DMRS (used for channel estimation). The UE selects the strongest beam and communicates with the network on the selected beam. Figure I.2.2.2 illustrates the procedure where the UE is already associated with LTE

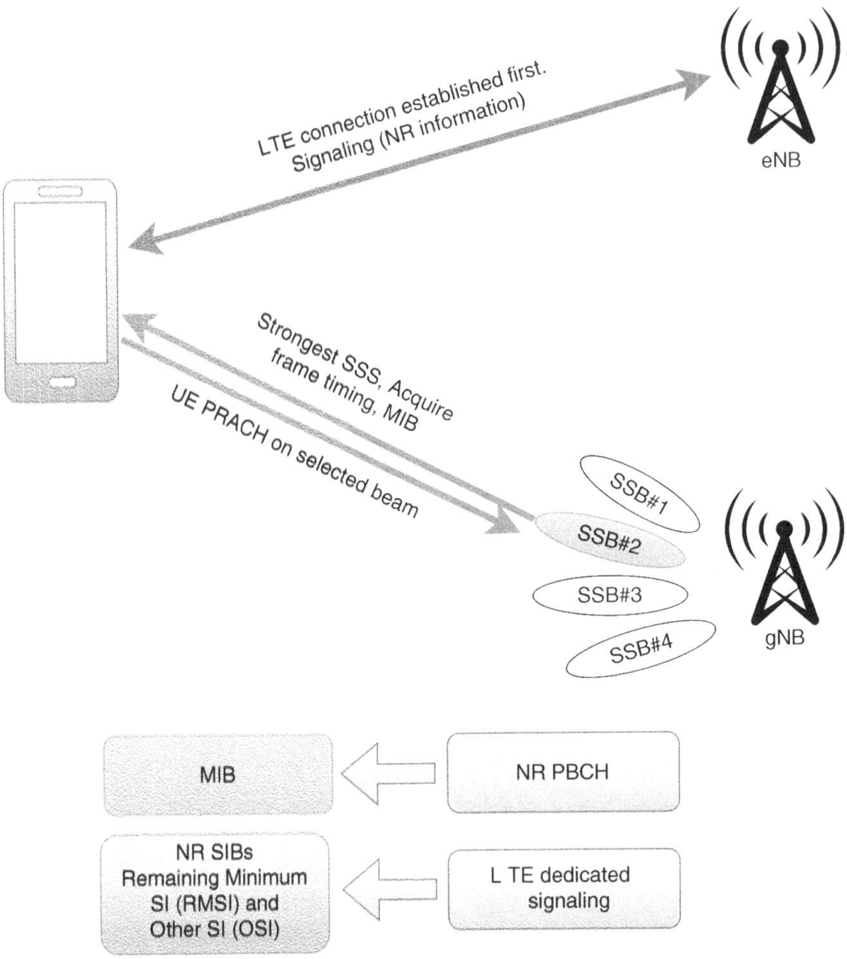

Figure I.2.2.2 5G NR UE cell acquisition in non-stand-alone (NSA) mode.

as the master cell group (MCG) in RRC connected mode, and the network adds the NR as the secondary cell group (SCG) in non-stand-alone (NSA) mode. This mode of operation typically does not apply to private network operations. Figure I.2.2.3 provides the system acquisition procedure for NR stand-alone (SA) mode, which applies to NR private networks. Figure I.2.2.4 provides the structure of the SSB and how the SSBs are transmitted in a time-division manner, lopping through the individual beams. The UE has to monitor a given beam and account for the time duration the gNode base station (gNB) takes to transition across the beams. Different base stations use different periodicities, but it is often sufficient to allow the UE to detect the SSBs, e.g., once every 20 ms for an omni-sector beam, or sweeping across four beams with SSB transmission switching every 8 ms.

Figure I.2.2.5 specifies how the RACH resources are indicated to the UE. Typically, long preambles are used. For very small cells, unlike the small cells deployed for private networks, Figure I.2.2.6 shows the four-step RACH procedure. The steps remain the same as with LTE. However, with the use of beams, the UE finds the strongest beam and initiates random access on the RACH resources identified by the beam. The RACH resources used by the UE implicitly point to the DL beam selected by the UE.

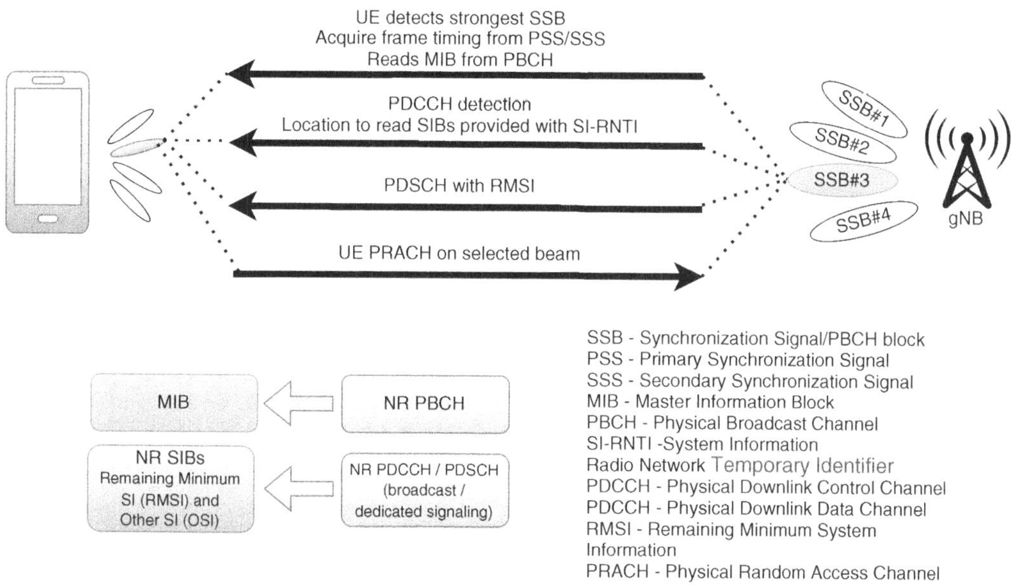

Figure I.2.2.3 5G NR UE cell acquisition in stand-alone (SA) mode.

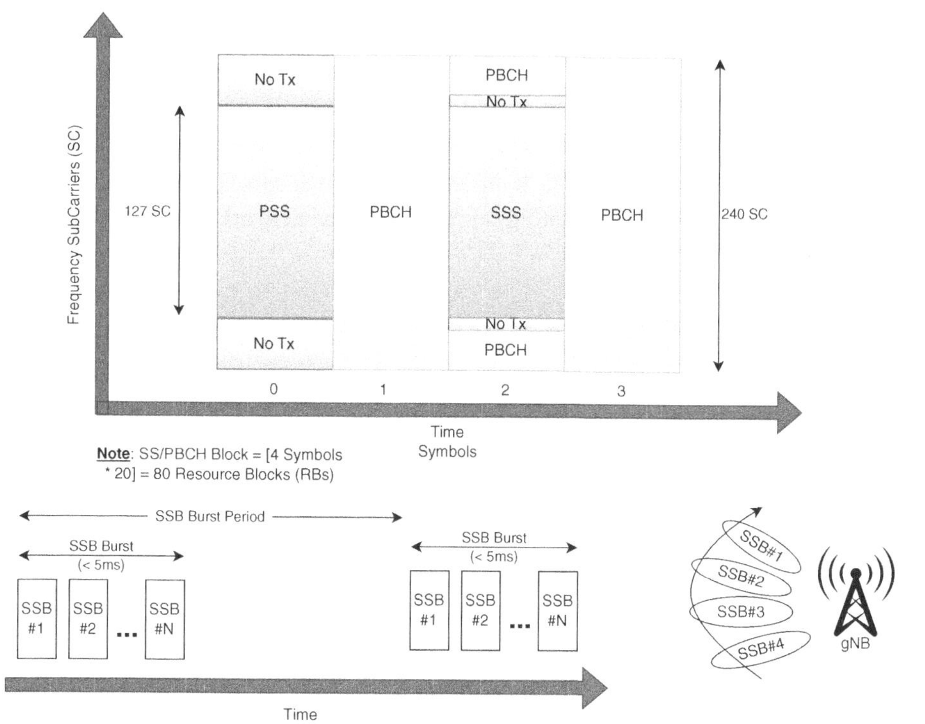

Carrier Frequency	SubCarrier Spacing (SCS)	Max No. SSBs within the SS Burst Set
f≤3GHz	15 kHz, 30kHz	4
3GHz < f ≤6GHz	15 kHz, 30kHz	8
f > 6GHz	120 kHz, 240 kHz	64

Note:

- Maximum number of SSBs in the burst set depends on the carrier frequency. Higher frequency =>narrower beam => more SS blocks needed
- SS Block Index in each beam to help UE in identifying a particular beam
- UE assumes SSB periodicity as 20 ms for initial acquisition. SSB Burst transmitted in regular intervals with configurable periodicity (5 ms to 160 ms)

Figure I.2.2.4 SSB transmission.

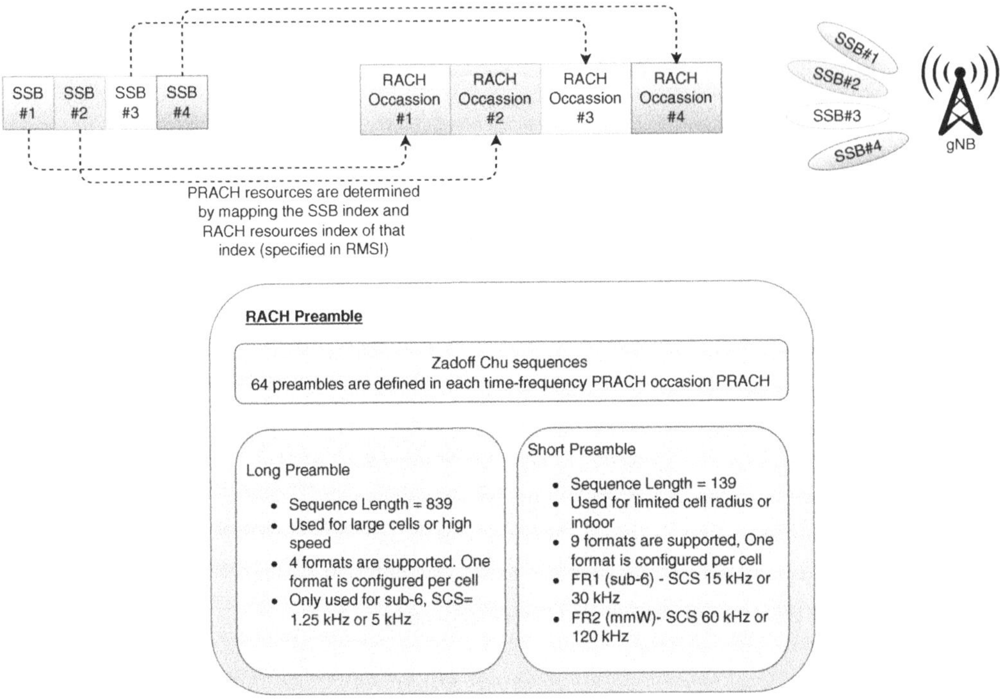

Figure I.2.2.5 NR RACH resources.

Figure I.2.2.7 shows a new procedure introduced in NR. The initial random access and the contention resolution are addressed in a single request/response procedure. This approach works well when there is a low UE population initiating connections to the network.

I.2.2.4 Control Resource Set

CORESET stands for COntrol Resource SET. It is a set of time-frequency resources on the NR downlink resource grid where a PDCCH may be transmitted. These are used to transmit downlink control information (DCI) messages, which instruct the UE on how to receive and process the data transmitted on the downlink by providing the time and frequency locations of the downlink data channels, the MCSs used, and the transmit power.

Figure I.2.2.8 provides an illustration of NR CORESET, along with its justification and use. CORESETs are semi-statically configured by the network and communicated to the UE via RRC reconfiguration messages.

Search space is an area within a CORESET that the UE monitors to detect a specific PDCCH to receive DL control information (DCI). Common search space is used to transmit PDCCHs for all UEs in the cell. The UE-specific search space (USS) is used to transmit PDCCHs for specific UEs. Which search space the UE has to monitor is defined by the radio network temporary identifier (RNTI) type or RRC configuration summarized below. See 3GPP TS 38.213-10.1. The size of a search space is determined by the aggregation level (AL). The aggregation level is a parameter that specifies how many control channel elements (CCEs) are grouped together to form a PDCCH candidate. The higher the aggregation level, the larger the search space will be. The number of

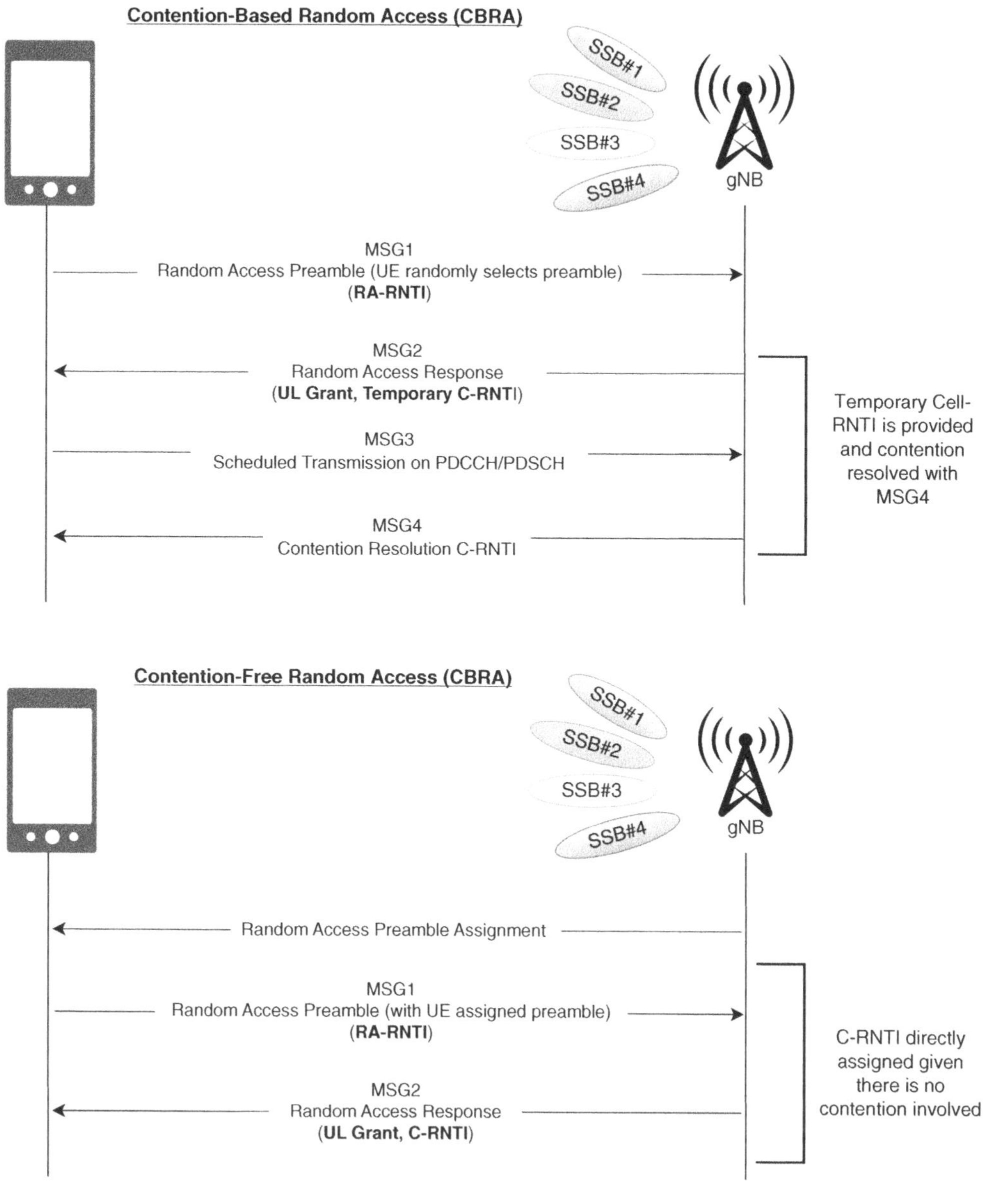

Figure I.2.2.6 RACH procedure (four steps).

CORESETs within a channel bandwidth (CBW) depends on how many CORESETs are configured in each bandwidth part (BWP) and how many BWPs are configured in the CBW. The larger the CORESET, the more CCEs are available to send DCI messages. This is because each CCE is made up of a group of physical resource blocks (PRBs) and symbols.

The PDCCH is a physical control channel in 5G NR that is used to transmit DCI to UEs. It is built on top of the following building blocks:

- CCEs
- Each CCE consists of six resource-element groups (REGs).

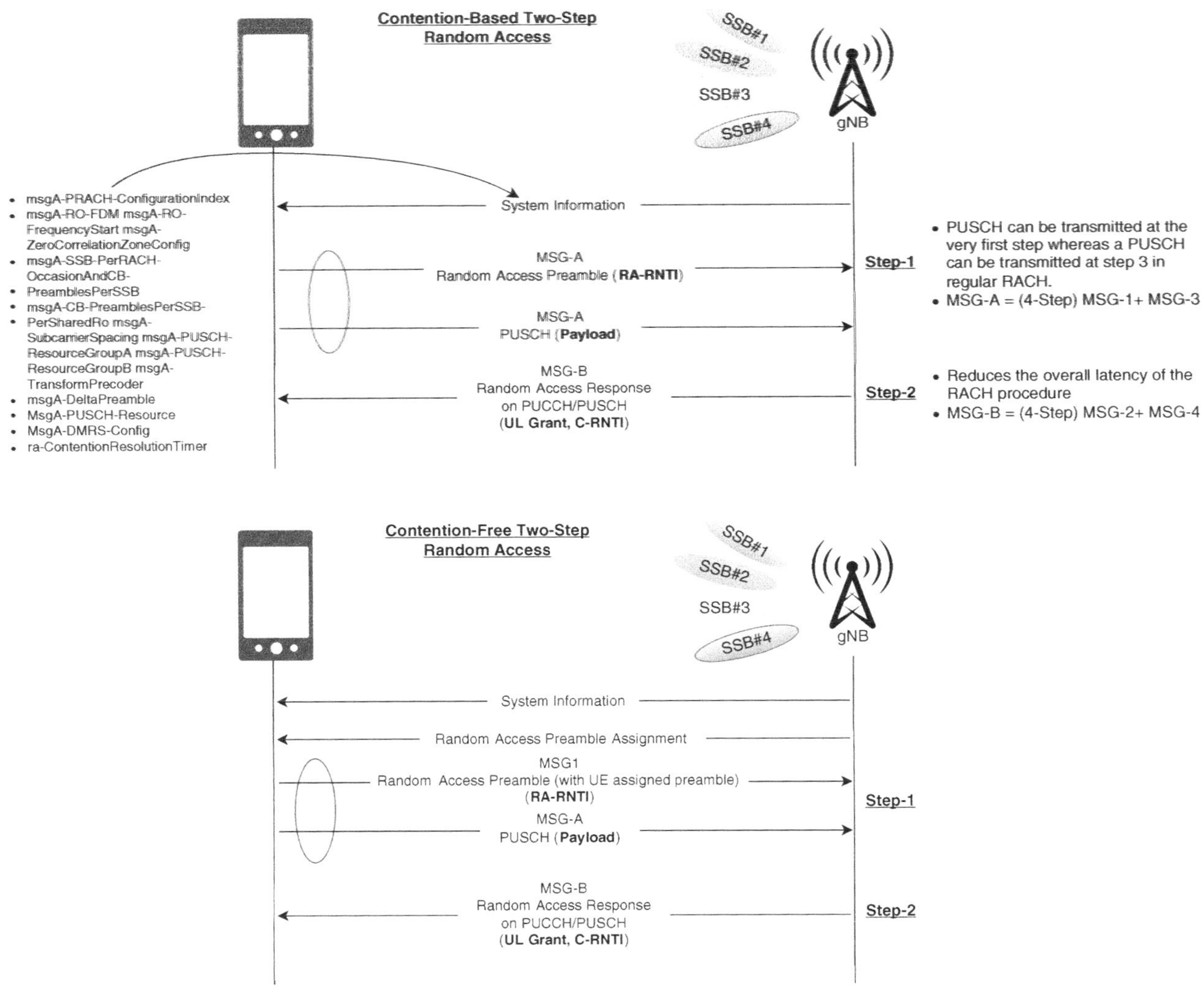

Figure I.2.2.7 SSB transmission (two steps).

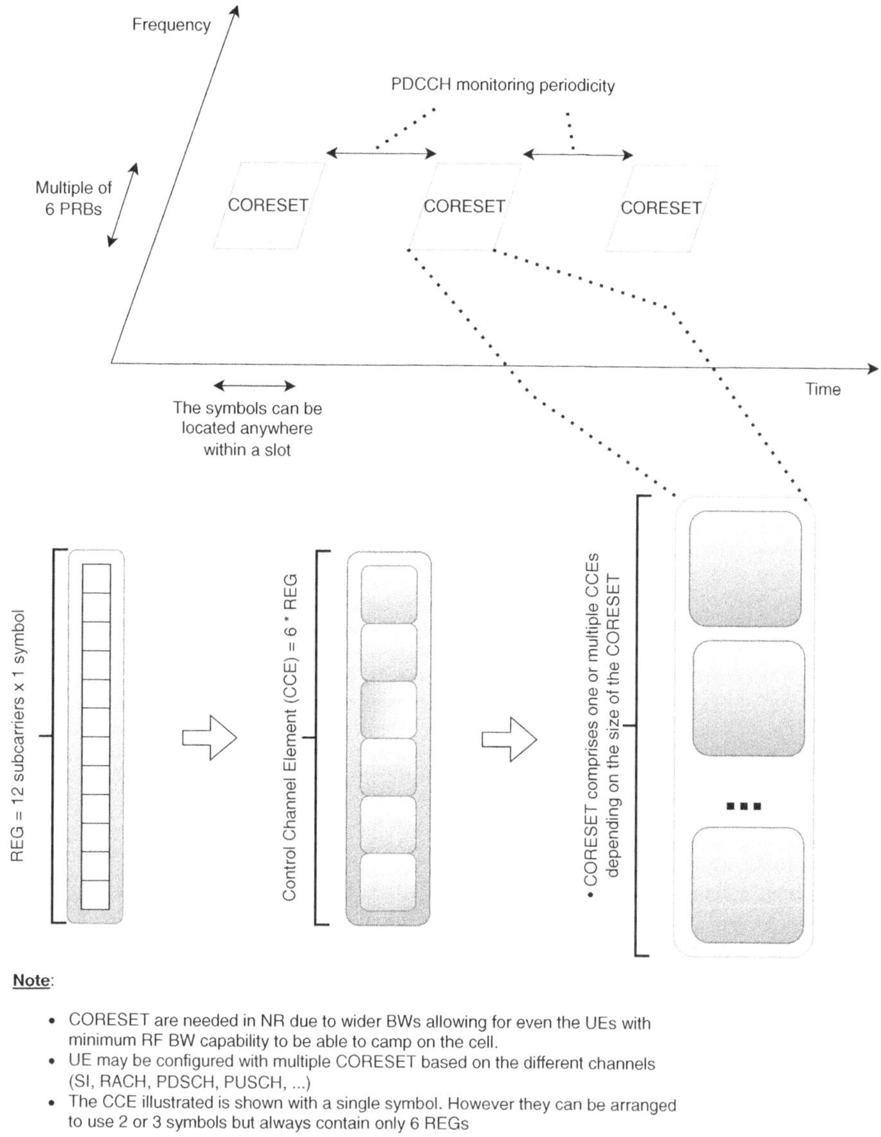

Figure I.2.2.8 PDCCH CORESET.

- A REG is equal to one resource block during one orthogonal frequency-division multiplexing (OFDM) symbol (12 REs).
- An resource element (RE) is equal to one subcarrier in one OFDM symbol.

The AL defines the number of CCEs that will be used for DCI transmission. Note that an aggregation level = 6 REG and REG = 12 REs, so one aggregation level equals 72 REs.

There is a special type of coreset called CORESET 0. This coreset is the one transmitting PDCCH for SIB1 scheduling. CORESET 0 cannot be specified by RRC since it should be used before any RRC is transmitted and hence is defined by a predefined process with a predefined set of parameters and is defined in the MIB broadcast as part of the SSB.

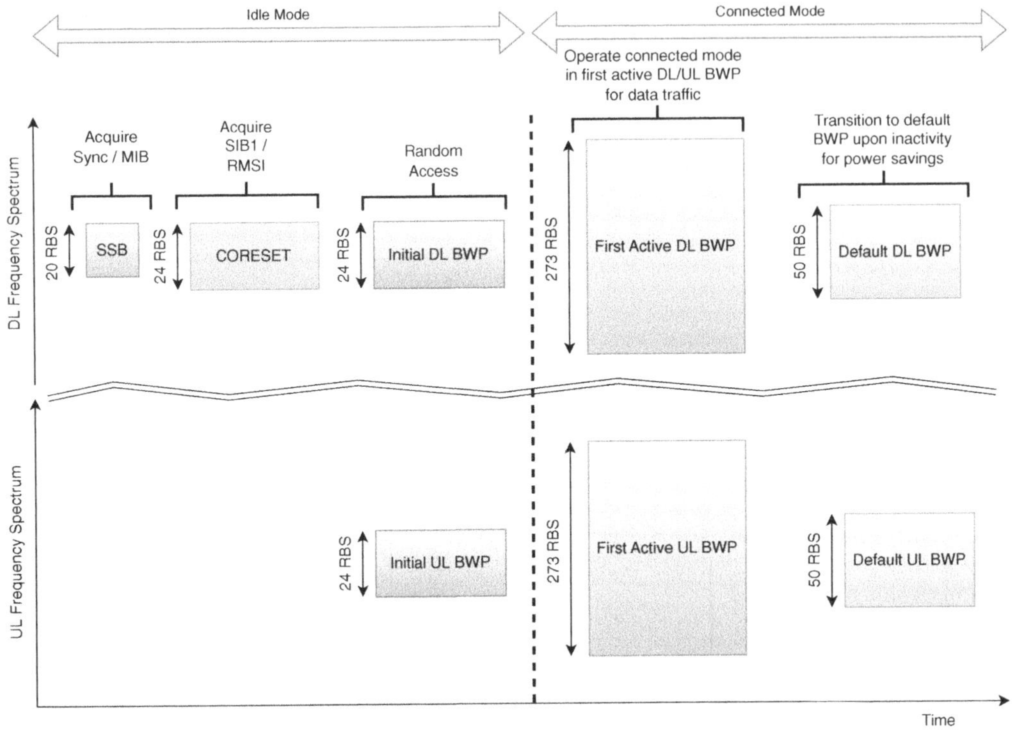

Figure I.2.2.9 UE BWP adaptation for idle and connected-mode operations.

Figure I.2.2.9 illustrates the BWP, which is a subset of a CBW. It is a contiguous set of PRBs on a given carrier. These RBs (resource blocks) are identified from a contiguous subset of the common resource blocks for a given numerology (u). Each BWP defined for a numerology is defined using the three parameters of subcarrier spacing, symbol duration, and cyclic prefix (CP) length.

The UE can be configured with a maximum of four BWPs for DL and UL, but at any given point in time, only one BWP is active for DL and one for UL. It enables UEs to operate in narrow bandwidths when operating on the full CBW is not required. The BWP is configured by specifying the numerology (u), bandwidth size, frequency location (NR-ARFCN [absolute frequency channel number]), and CORESET.

The UE operates within a given active BWP. With respect to DL, the UE monitors only the BWP space to receive PDSCH, PDCCH, CSI-RS, or tracking reference signal (TRS). Each DL BWP includes at least one CORESET with USS. For a primary carrier, at least one of the configured DL BWPs includes one CORESET with CSS for the UEs to find and camp on the system.

With respect to the uplink, the UE is expected to transmit PUSCH or PUCCH only within an active BWP. There are exceptions where a UE may perform radio resource management (RRM) measurements or transmit a SRS outside of its active BWP via a measurement gap.

See 3GPP TS 38.321-5.15 for BWP operation. Based on the current need for bandwidth (e.g., using full bandwidth for peak traffic and using smaller bandwidth for UE power-saving operations), the UE's active BWP may be changed. BWP switching can be done based on the techniques listed below. RRC procedures are useful for providing full BWP configuration and allocation, MAC CE allows for controlled switching, and DCI enables quicker switches, although it can encounter increased errors. The timer-based switch allows for a UE autonomous method to enable the UE to enter power-saving mode due to inactivity on wider bandwidth operations without requiring network control.

- Dedicated RRC signaling
- Over the PDCCH channel, DCI – DCI 0_1 (UL grant) and DCI 1_0 (DL scheduling)
- By bwp-inactivityTimer – ServingCellConfig.bwp-InactivityTimer
- By MAC CE (control element)

I.2.2.5 NR UE Scheduling

This section describes the DL and UL scheduling operations for NR. Table I.2.2.2 provides the list of downlink commands sent from the gNB to the UE. Table I.2.2.3 provides a comparison of the LTE and NR data channels and resource management methods.

Table I.2.2.2 Downlink control information (DCI) formats (from 3GPP TS38.212 – Table 7.3.1-1).

DCI contains information that the UE needs to identify and decode RBs in that subframe and includes the following:

- modulation and coding scheme (MCS) information
- redundancy version (RV) parameters for the hybrid ARQ protocol
- the CRC of the DCI is scrambled with the RNTI that is used to address the scheduled message to the UE

DCI format	Usage
Format 0_0	Scheduling of PUSCH in one cell
Format 0_1	Scheduling of PUSCH in one cell DCI format 0_1 with CRC scrambled by C-RNTI DCI format 0_1 with CRC scrambled by CS-RNTI
Format 1_0	Scheduling of PDSCH in one cell DCI format 1_0 with CRC scrambled by C-RNTI DCI format 1_0 with CRC scrambled by C-RNTI for PDCCH order DCI format 1_0 with CRC scrambled by RA-RNTI DCI format 1_0 with CRC scrambled by TC-RNTI DCI format 1_0 with CRC scrambled by SI-RNTI DCI format 1_0 with CRC scrambled by P-RNTI
Format 1_1	Scheduling of PDSCH in one cell
Format 2_0	Notifying a group of UEs about the slot format
Format 2_1	Notifying a group of UEs of the PRB(s) and OFDM symbol(s) where a UE may assume that no transmission is intended for it
Format 2_2	Transmission of TPC commands for PUCCH and PUSCH
Format 2_3	Transmission of a group of TPC commands for SRS transmissions by one or more UEs
Format 2_4	Notifying the PRB(s) and OFDM symbol(s) where the UE cancels the corresponding UL transmission
Format 2_5	Notifying about the availability of soft resources
Format 2_6	Notifying the power-saving information outside of DRX active time for one or more UEs
Format 3_0	Scheduling of NR sidelink in one cell
Format 3_1	Scheduling of LTE sidelink in one cell

TPC: transmit power control.

Table I.2.2.3 Comparison of LTE and NR data channels.

		LTE	NR
TDD configuration	UL/DL scheduling	Subframe level	Symbol level
	TDD config switching	RRC	Both RRC & DCI
Data channels	DL/UL data	PDSCH/PUSCH	PDSCH/PUSCH
	Channel coding	Turbo code	LDPC for PDSCH/PUSCH
	Waveform	DL: CP-OFDM UL: DFT-s-OFDM	DL: CP-OFDM UL: CP-OFDM and DFT-s-OFDM (RRC and DCI level switching)
Resource management	Frequency resources	Full carrier bandwidth	BWP
	Transmission time interval for scheduling	Subframe/ mini-slot	Slot/mini-slot/multi-slot
	Scheduling resource preemption	Not supported	Supported

Figure I.2.2.10 provides the mechanism of DL scheduling in NR. Figure I.2.2.11 illustrates the DL HARQ procedure. Both of these aspects remain the same as with LTE, except for the use of the specific BWP that the UE is currently associated with in terms of the resources that can be used to schedule the UE. The UE can be configured with up to four BWPs; however, the UE can be associated with only one active BWP at a given time.

Figure I.2.2.12 provides the UL scheduling mechanisms supporting both configured grants (same as semi-persistent grants in LTE) and regular UL grants. Figure I.2.2.13 provides the UL HARQ sequence/process. The main difference is that in UL with PDCCH carrying UL grants for new packets on a given HARQ instance, it is treated as an implicit acknowledgment for the previous packet transmitted on the same HARQ instance. Also, the UL HARQ operation is synchronous in LTE, while the NR UL is scheduled explicitly by the network for each HARQ retransmission.

I.2.2.6 NR PUCCH Operations

PUCCH is an uplink physical control channel that carries UCI. As DCI is carried by PDCCH, UCI is carried by PUCCH. A significant difference between DCI and UCI is that UCI can be carried either by PUCCH or PUSCH depending on the situation, whereas DCI can be carried only by PDCCH (not by PDSCH in any case).

A short PUCCH format may consist of one or two symbols. A long PUCCH format may span multiple symbols and slots. Multiple long PUCCH formats may be defined (e.g., four symbols, a slot, and multiple slots). A long PUCCH format may be useful for larger payload HARQ-ACK feedback, - information (CSI) feedback, etc. Figure I.2.2.14 provides an illustration of the NR PUCCH structure, and Table I.2.2.4 provides a brief description, including the number of bits used to represent the information.

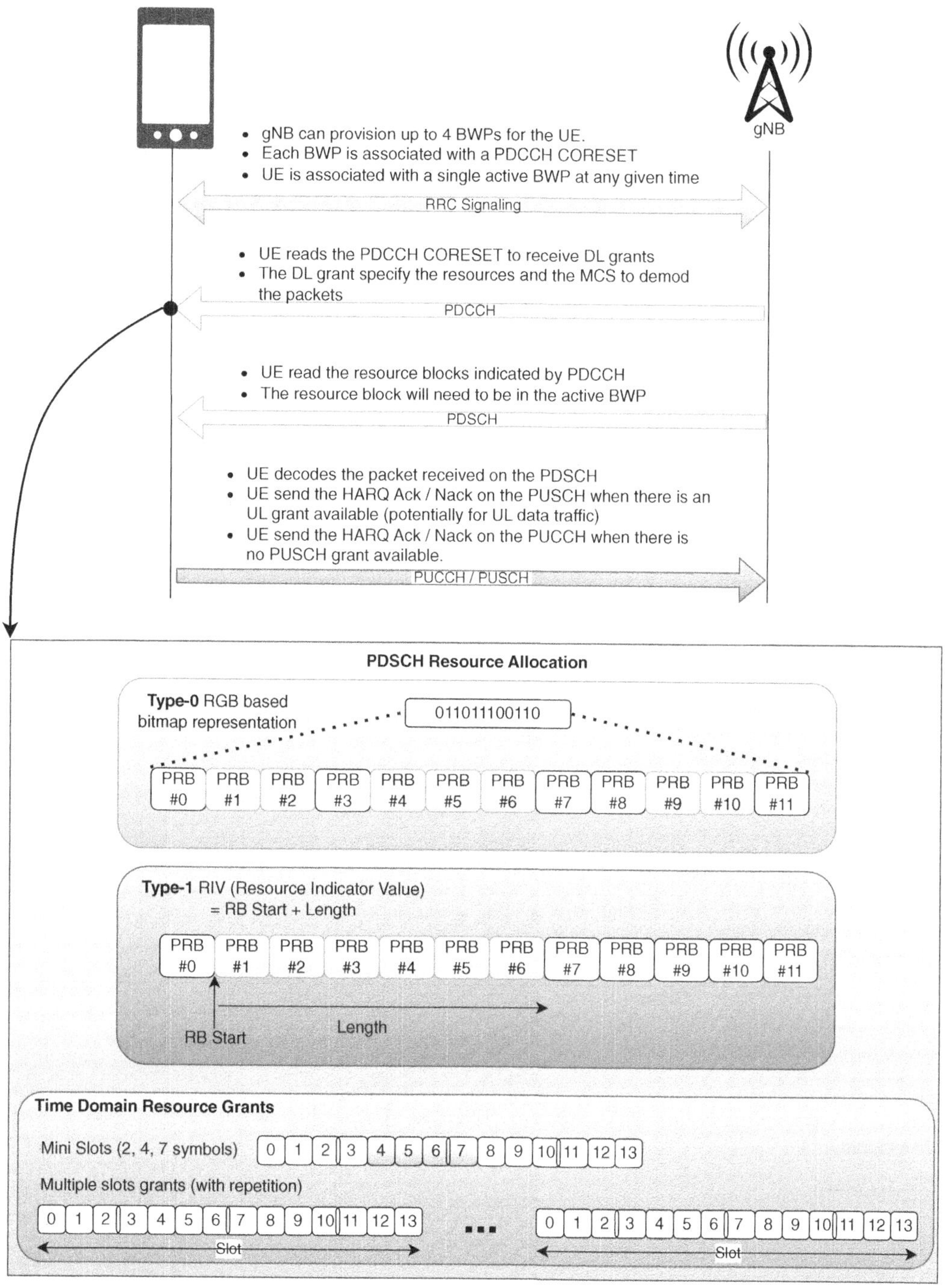

Figure I.2.2.10 NR DL packet scheduling.

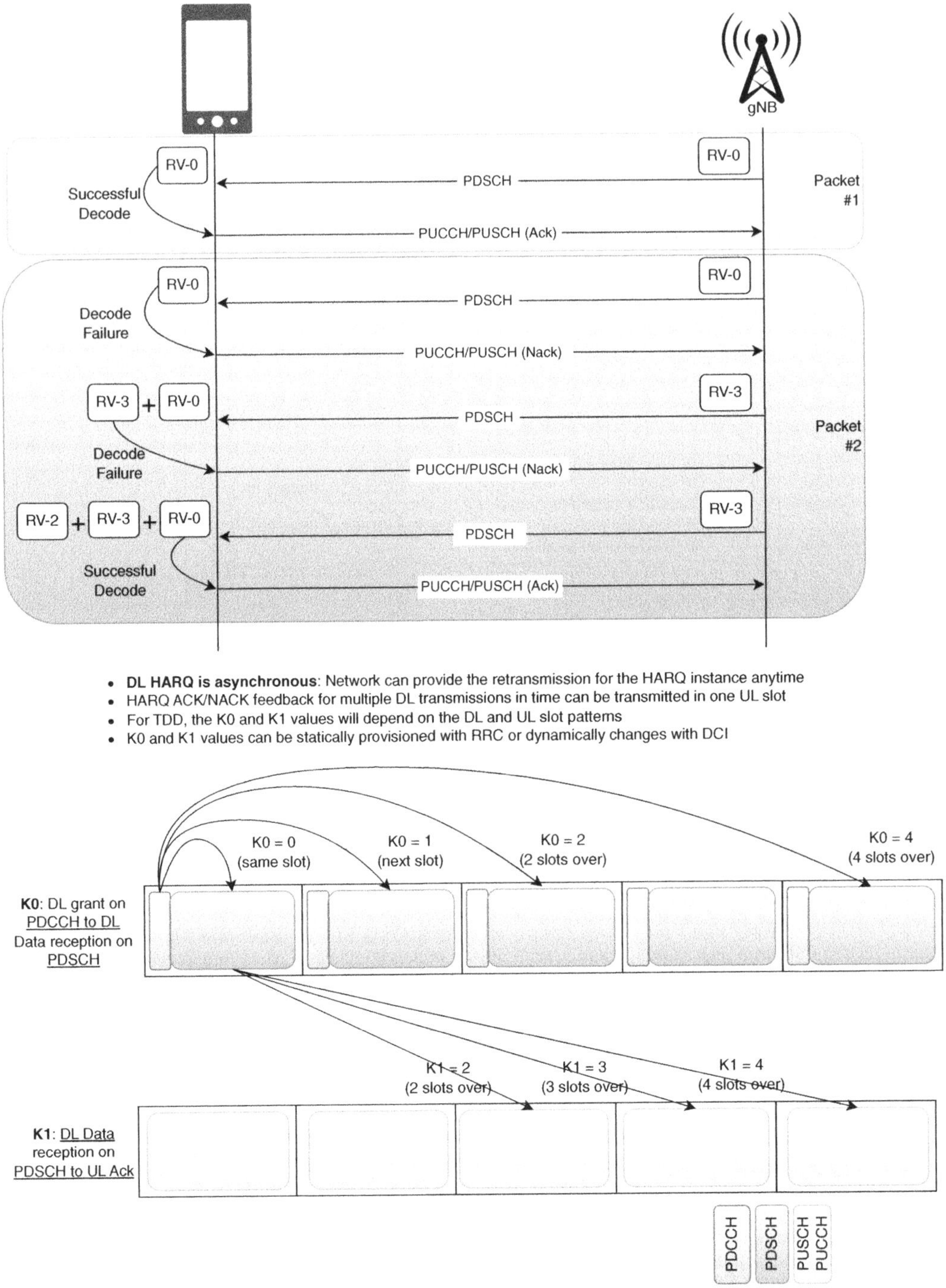

Figure I.2.2.11 DL HARQ process.

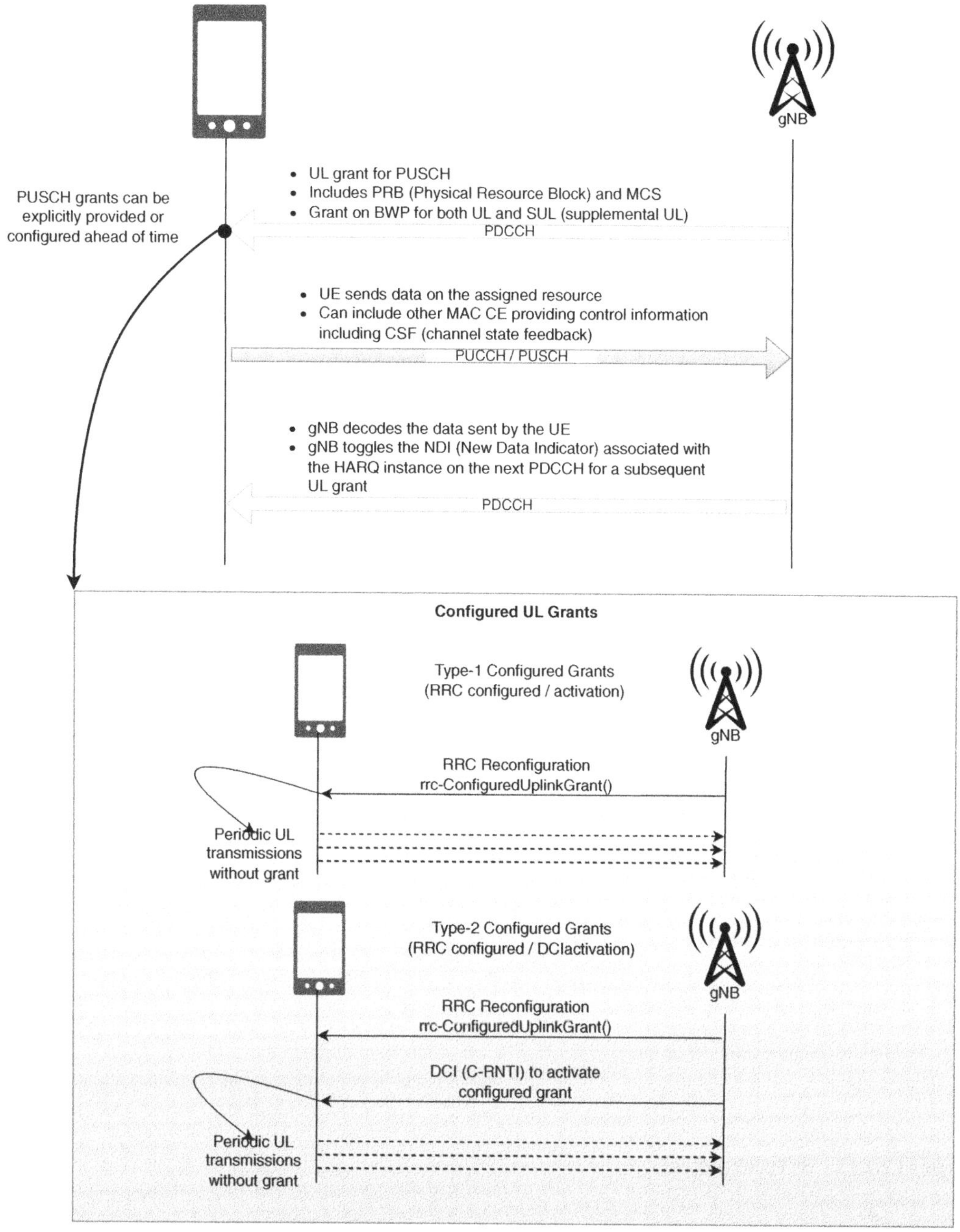

Figure I.2.2.12 NR UL packet scheduling.

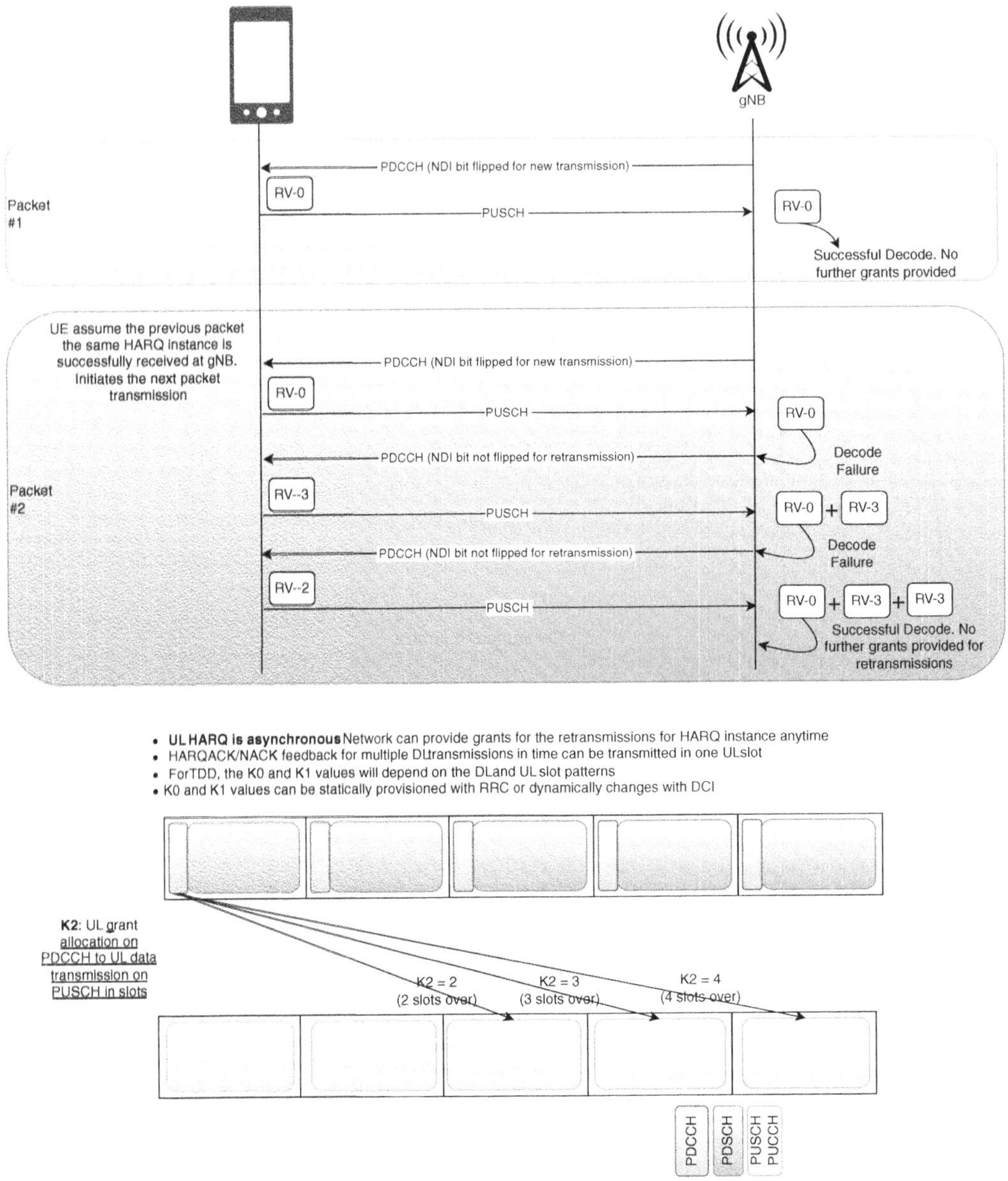

Figure I.2.2.13 UL HARQ process.

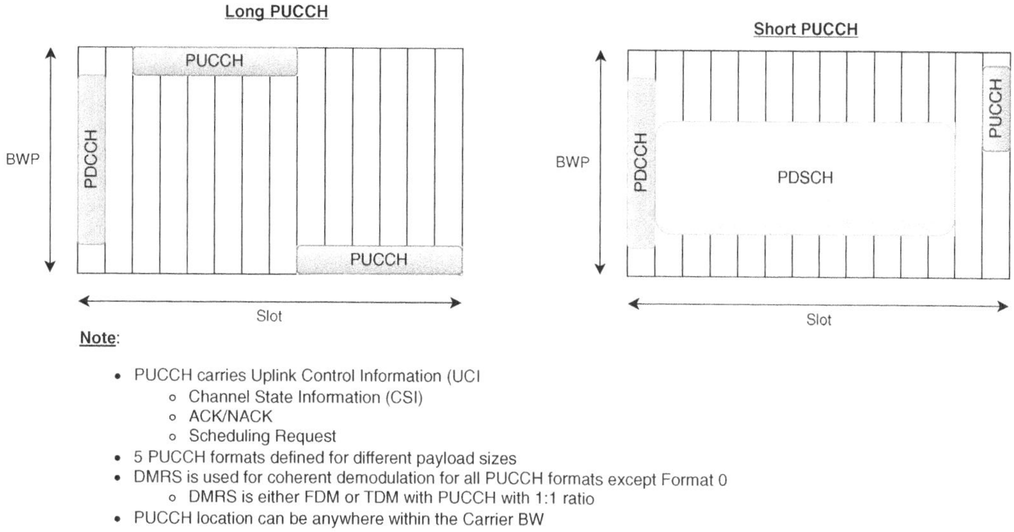

Figure I.2.2.14 NR PUCCH structure.

Table I.2.2.4 Short and long PUCCH formats.

PUCCH format	Length of OFDM symbols	Number of bits	Description
0	1–2	≤2	Short PUCCH format with 1–2 bits of UCI
1	4–14	≤2	Long PUCCH format with 1–2 bits of UCI (TD-OCC)
2	1–2	>2	Short PUCCH format with >2 bits of UCI
3	4–14	>2	Long PUCCH format with >2 bits UCI and no multiplexing capability
4	4–14	>2	Long PUCCH format with >2 bits UCI and no multiplexing capability

I.2.2.7 NR MIMO Operations

This section captures the multiple-input multiple-output (MIMO) operations for DL and UL, including the feedback mechanisms for MIMO supported through CSI feedback from the UE to the network.

See the MIMO and beamforming chapter in Part I for a more detailed treatment of these aspects. SU-MIMO (single-user MIMO) is intended to target multiple streams to the same UE. MIMO beamforming is supported by both digital and analog beamforming. See Figure I.2.2.15 for an illustration.

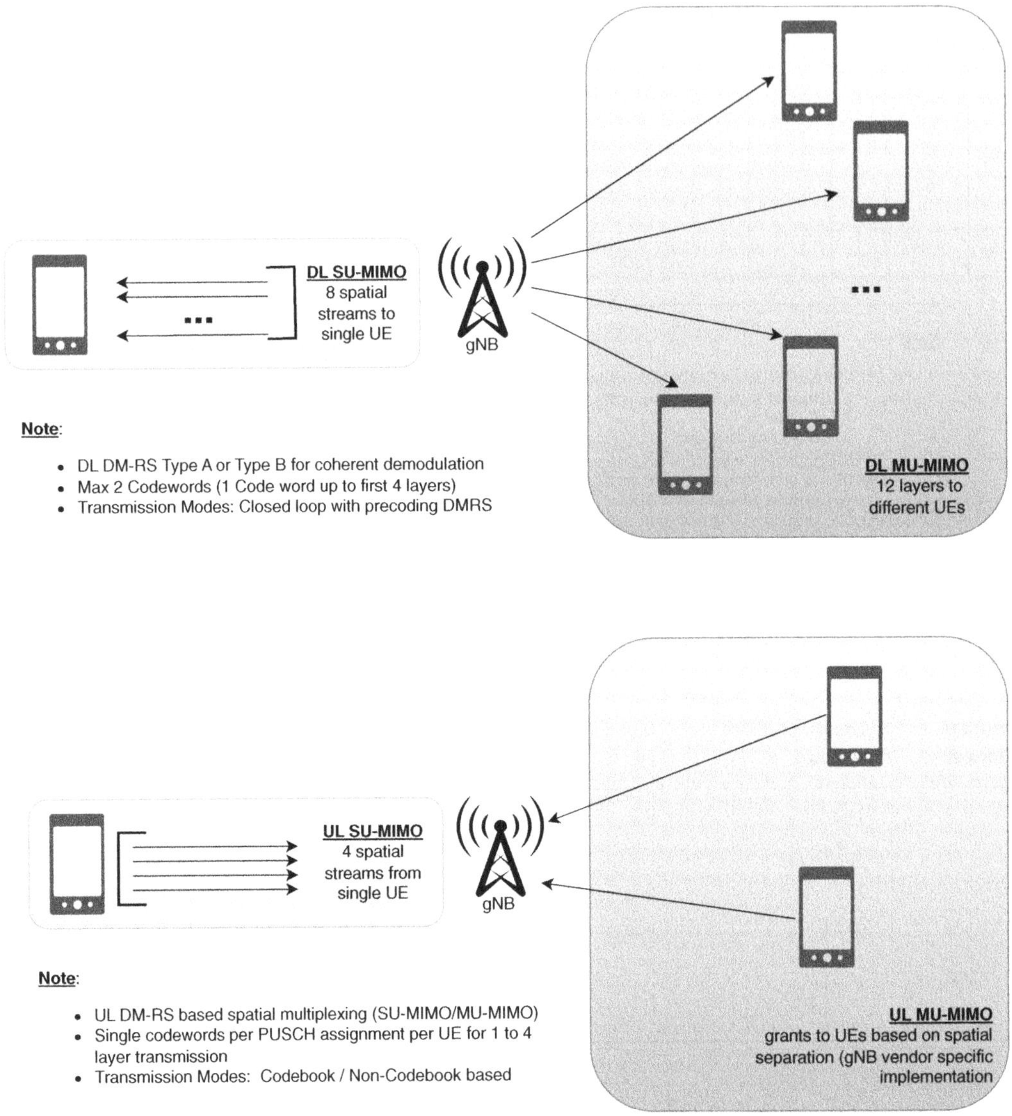

Figure I.2.2.15 DL/UL MIMO.

The type-1 codebook feedback supports basic digital beamforming and relies on analog beamforming. The type-2 codebook allows for finer control of digital beamforming in addition to supporting analog beamforming. See Figure I.2.2.16 for an illustration.

I.2.2.8 NR Power Control

This section lists the type of power control (open or closed loop) applied to the different NR channels between the UE and network (see Table I.2.2.5).

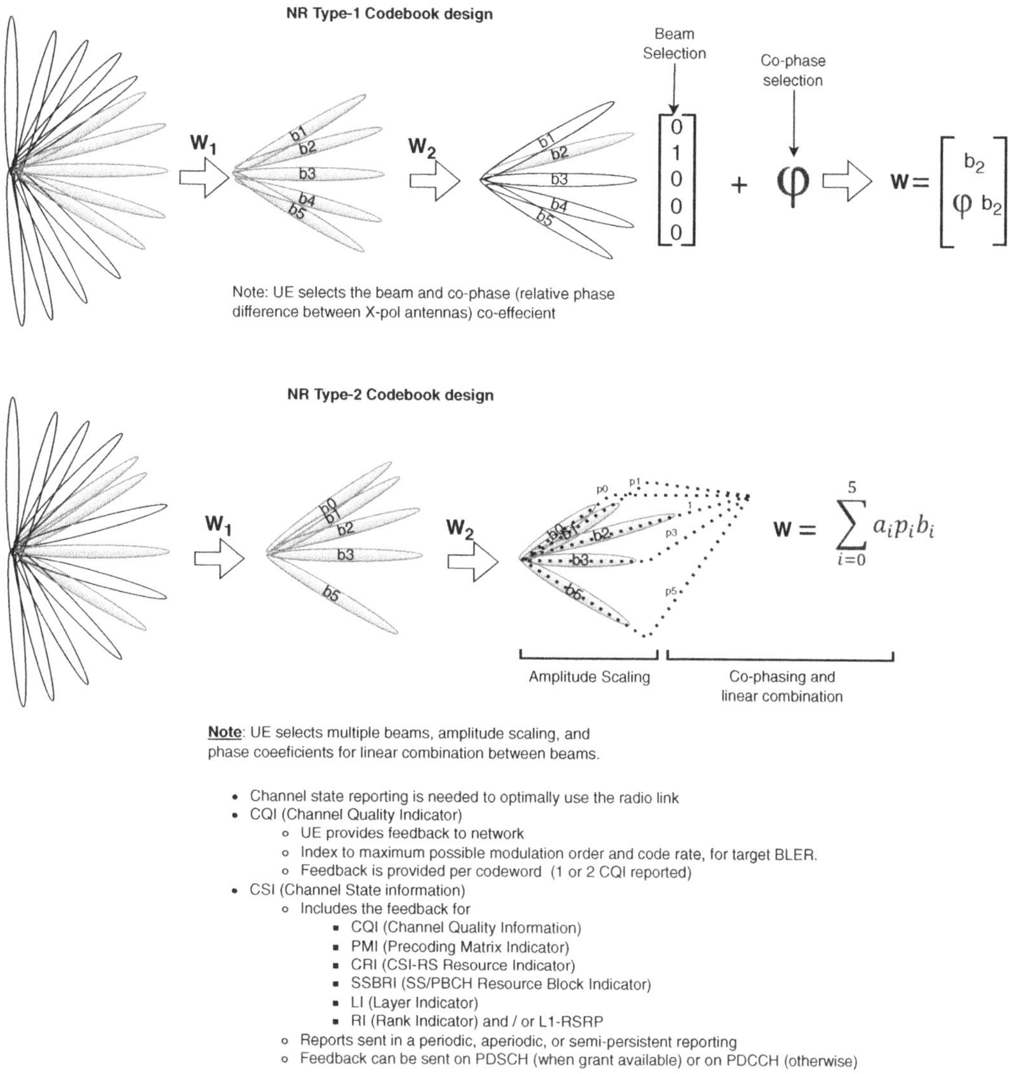

Figure I.2.2.16 CSI (channel state information) reporting.

Table I.2.2.5 UL power control.

Power control

- Parameters signaled through RRC
- Applies to all UL channels
- Beam-based: two closed-loop power controls for PUCCH/PUSCH and separate power control per beam indicated by SRI

UL physical channel	Power control type
PRACH	Open loop with power ramping and beam switching
PUCCH	Two closed loop
PUSCH with grant	Open loop
PUSCH without grant	Open loop
SRS	Closed loop (separated PC with PUSCH PC)

I.2.2.9 Summary

This chapter covers the 5G NR physical reference signals and channels. With that defined, the 5G NR UE cell acquisition in NSA mode and SA mode is described, including the steps involved in finding and retrieving information from the reference signals. More specifically, receiving the SSB transmissions and handling NR RACH resources are described with the four-step and two-step RACH procedures. The PDCCH CORESET and how the control information is delivered to the UE in the DL are also described. The UL control information reporting using the PUCCH/PUSCH, including the details of the PUCCH structure, is described. The wider channel bandwidth, the need to support smaller BWP, and the UE BWP adaptation for idle and connected mode operations are illustrated. The NR DL/UL packet scheduling and HARQ process are described. The fundamental use of multiple antenna techniques in 5G NR and the aspects of DL/UL MIMO are shown. All of this is governed by the UE reporting of CSI to enable the scheduling, with the basic type-1 reporting and the more advanced type-2 reporting described.

A comparison of LTE and NR reference signals and data channels is also shown for the reader to leverage their understanding of LTE and map the differences that need to be noted in NR. The DCI formats, short and long PUCCH formats, and the UL power control details are also presented.

Reference

1 3GPP TS **38.201: NR; Physical layer; General description.**

I.2.3

Beamforming and Massive MIMO

I.2.3.1 Introduction

Beamforming offers significant benefits to both the network and UE, enabling larger system capacity and higher individual user equipment (UE) throughput. There are significant challenges in supporting beamforming, which forms the basis for supporting multiple input multiple output (MIMO) systems and further extending them to massive MIMO (M-MIMO). This section discusses the motivation behind beamforming in 5G new radio (NR). The basic procedures involved in beamforming techniques are described.

With private networks and shorter communication ranges, apart from being mostly indoor and involving limited mobility scenarios, it naturally lends itself to applying beamforming for improved system performance. This includes both single-user and multiuser MIMO techniques. Given the limitations in the spectrum availability for private networks, using MIMO techniques will allow for better meeting the service level objective (SLO)/ service level agreement (SLA) demands of an enterprise campus.

I.2.3.1.1 Beamforming Techniques

Beamforming is primarily used to compensate for propagation loss and improve coverage. By regulating the width and direction of the beam, it allows for improving spectrum efficiency by spatial reuse. Beamforming is realized at the base stations and UEs using large antenna array sizes. Using the antenna array, high directivity and focused energy can be performed. By regulating the phase and power applied to the individual antenna elements, the capability to perform complex beamforming can be supported. With these beamforming techniques, a very narrow, pointed main lobe can be generated. This results in the signal to noise interference ratio (SINR) on downlink (DL) and uplink (UL) being drastically improved, increasing system capacity by reducing interference to the intra-cell user, supporting spatial reuse, and improving coverage for the individual UE, thus resulting in higher throughput.

Mobile Communication Systems for Private Networks, First Edition. Srinivasan Balasubramanian.

I.2.3.1.2 Types of Beamforming

Based on the complexity of the hardware and firmware functions, the following forms of beamforming can be supported.

Beamforming type	Description
Analog	*Analog beamforming is implemented using phase shifters and attenuators per radiator, with a single RF path to the transceiver in the array. Although a certain amount of control can be exercised, the beamforming with this approach tends to be fixed. However, it has less complexity in its implementation.*
Digital	*Digital signal manipulation with separate RF paths (baseband processing, precoding,* etc.*) per radiator provides higher degrees of freedom. The digital beamforming is very flexible, including receiving feedback from the receiver to apply the appropriate precoding matrix to the individual RF paths. The complexity increases significantly with increased RF paths.*
Hybrid	*A combination of analog and digital beamforming involves multiple radiators per RF path to reduce spatial and cost concerns. Most implementations will employ an appropriate mix of digital and analog beamforming, trading the required flexibility for the manageable complexity in both implementation and usability in the deployments.*

I.2.3.1.3 SU-MIMO versus MU-MIMO

In single-user MIMO (SU-MIMO) operation, both the base station and UE have multiple antenna ports and antennas. Each of the antenna ports supports independent data streams. This allows for multiple data streams to be transmitted simultaneously to the UE using the same time/frequency resources, doubling (2×2 MIMO) or quadrupling (4×4 MIMO) the peak throughput of a single user. Long-term evolution (LTE) networks were initially deployed by supporting SU-MIMO.

In multi-user MIMO (MU-MIMO), the base station sends multiple data streams, one per UE, using the same time-frequency resources. MU-MIMO increases the total cell throughput capacity by serving multiple users simultaneously using the same radio resources. The base station has multiple antenna ports, with one antenna port supporting each UE.

I.2.3.2 Beamforming – Spatial Diversity

Beamforming fundamentally offers spatial diversity by focusing the beams on specific directions. In particular, the beams are focused on specific UEs, knowing their location relative to the base station. When the beams serving the individual UEs are sufficiently spatially separated, the same radio resources can be used to serve both UEs at the same time, allowing for improved system throughput. Figure I.2.3.1 provides a high-level view of the spatial diversity achieved through beamforming, which allows for the network to schedule more than one UE using the same radio resources simultaneously.

I.2.3.2.1 Digital Beamforming

Digital beamforming is realized at the antenna element level or at the sub-array level. Architecturally, there are many digital receivers, with one receiver at each of the radiating elements of the antenna.

Figure I.2.3.1 Beamforming: Spatial diversity.

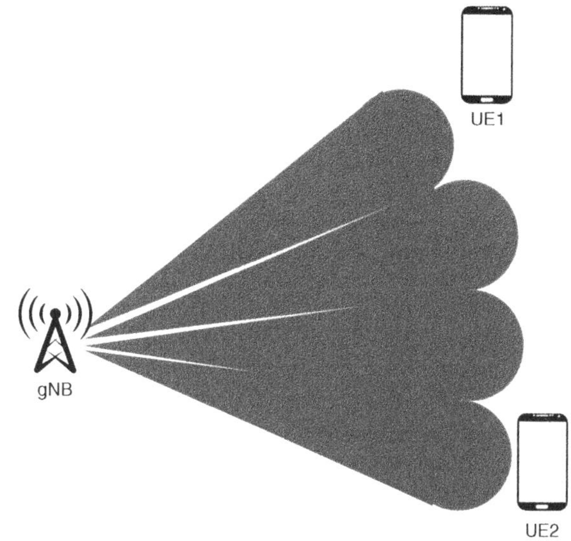

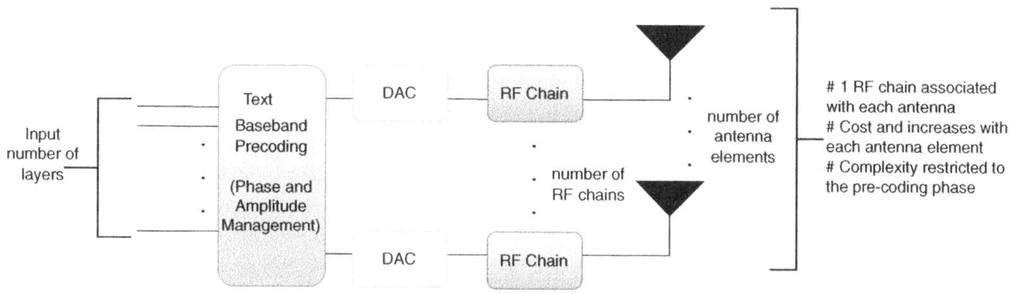

Figure I.2.3.2 Digital beamforming.

Multiple independent beams focused on specific directions can be supported by the digital beamforming processor.

Figure I.2.3.2 provides an illustration of digital beamforming. For digital beamforming, the signal is pre-coded (amplitude and phase modifications) in baseband processing before radio frequency (RF) transmission. Multiple beams targeting one user each can be formed simultaneously using the same set of antenna array elements, also called MU-MIMO in 4G LTE and 5G NR systems. Multiple transmit/receive chains, typically one per user, are required at the base station. Digital beamforming (MU-MIMO) is used in LTE advanced transmission modes 7, 8, and 9 and in all 5G NR. Traditionally, it is used in LTE/NR systems and is suitable for sub-6 FR1 deployments given the reduced number of antenna elements used for this frequency range.

Advantages of digital beamforming

- Very flexibility and scalable
- Dynamically accommodates the number of antennas, transmission modes, beams, or data streams
- Provides an easy method to implement MU-MIMO
- Better and faster control of amplitude and phase.

Challenges of digital beamforming

- Each antenna element is associated with its own RF chain. This impacts UE battery power consumption and incurs higher costs. This mechanism does not scale well beyond a certain number of antenna elements. Note that the digital-to-analog conversion (DAC) or analog-to-digital conversion (ADC) consumes most of the power in the RF chain.

I.2.3.2.2 Analog Beamforming

Analog beamforming is supported by having the signal phases of individual antenna signals adjusted in the RF domain. This allows for regulating the radiation pattern and gain of the individual antenna array elements and thus provides the required directionality to improve coverage. Unlike digital beamforming, only one beam per set of antenna elements is possible. A large number of antenna elements can be supported with analog beamforming, given the reduced complexity. mmWave requires high directionality, which can be achieved only with large antenna array elements; hence, the use of analog beamforming is a fundamental requirement for mmWave operation. Figure I.2.3.3 provides an illustration of analog beamforming.

Advantages of analog beamforming

- It allows for reduced power consumption and costs, given that a single RF chain supports all the antenna elements.
- It is far less complex than digital beamforming and, hence, easier to implement.

Challenges of analog beamforming

- It supports a single data stream well but does not scale well for multiple data streams.
- MU-MIMO requires multi-panel arrays, with each array supporting independent users.
- The phase shifter design can be complex.

I.2.3.2.3 Hybrid Beamforming

The hybrid beamforming structure optimally combines the functions of analog and digital beamforming systems to reduce hardware complexity while retaining the required flexibility. To support MU-MIMO and allow for multiple antenna elements to serve a given user in mmWave, hybrid beamforming realization is required. One suggested approach is to use analog beamforming for coarse beamforming and, inside the analog beam, use a digital beamforming scheme to enable MU-MIMO or SU-MIMO. The optimal combination will depend on RF band and hardware (HW)

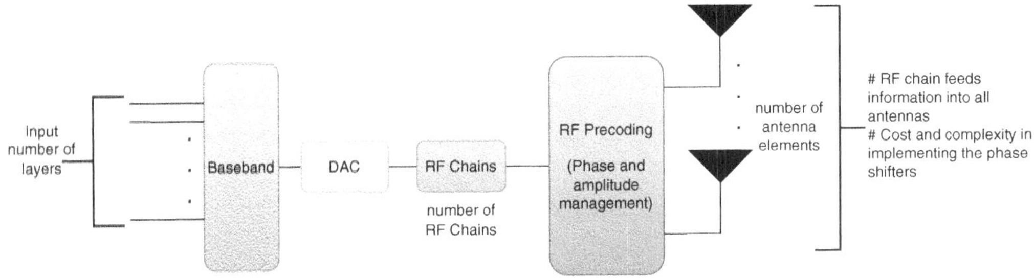

Figure I.2.3.3 Analog beamforming.

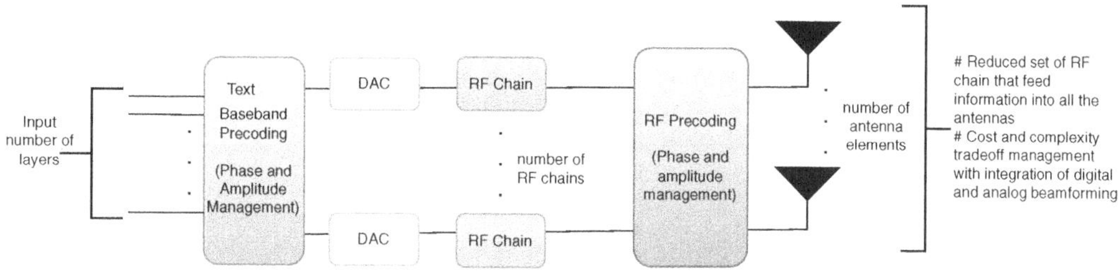

Figure I.2.3.4 Hybrid beamforming.

complexity, and an ideal mix of digital and analog beamforming types will be to utilize all the benefits while suppressing the disadvantages with the advantages of the other technique. Figure I.2.3.4 provides an illustration of hybrid beamforming leveraging the benefits of both digital and analog beamforming.

I.2.3.3 Beam Management

Beam management supports intra-cell beam transitions and mobility across cells while maintaining the optimum connection for radio link operation. Beam management aspects are important and are treated in an independent section.

5G NR supports various beam management methods to support optimal RF operations for both the network and the UE. As shown in Figure I.2.3.5, the beam management procedures are enabled by beam sweeping, beam refinement, and beam switching. In addition, there are beam failure and recovery procedures.

Beam sweeping allows the gNB to cover the entire cell area by sweeping beams over time. This mechanism is used only for common channels, which include broadcast, paging, and access channels.

Beam refinement allows the gNB to switch the UE from operating in a coarse, wider beam to a narrow beam focusing its energy on the UE location, which improves signal-to-noise ratio (SNR) and cell coverage. This mechanism is used for traffic beams to better serve the individual user while reducing the interference for the other users.

Beam switching is a fundamental mobility procedure and allows the gNB/UE to select the best beam as the user moves around.

I.2.3.4 Massive MIMO, Operation in UL and DL

M-MIMO (massive MIMO) operation is supported by large antenna arrays. By large, it is referring to arrays with more than eight antennas. M-MIMO is typically enabled with 32, 64, 128, or even 256 array elements. The large antenna array allows for fully digital steerable antennas, providing the flexibility to serve many users simultaneously. The beamforming types include azimuth and elevation beamforming, and the combination of the two is actively employed to target a beam to a given UE. The beam steering method is applied to both azimuth and elevation beamforming, also referred to as 3D beamforming. This is achieved by manipulating the antenna signals at the

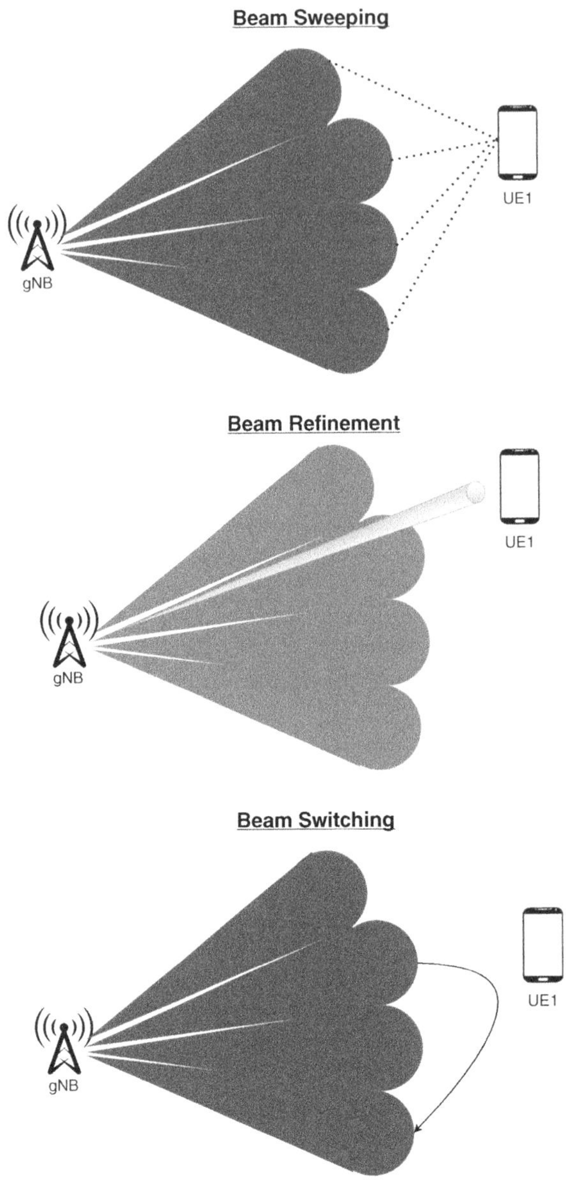

Figure I.2.3.5 Beam management.

physical layer. Figure I.2.3.6 shows a pictorial view of finer beamforming accounting for both azimuth and vertical elevation of the UE relative to the base station.

An alternative definition for M-MIMO is when the number of antennas exceeds the number of active users in the system, although this is a more colloquial reference.

Benefits of M-MIMO include greater coverage, throughput, and capacity. It helps to compensate for larger path loss at higher frequencies, which is where the 5G NR networks are deployed. The spatial reuse of the same physical resources in a cell significantly improves both the system capacity and the individual user throughput.

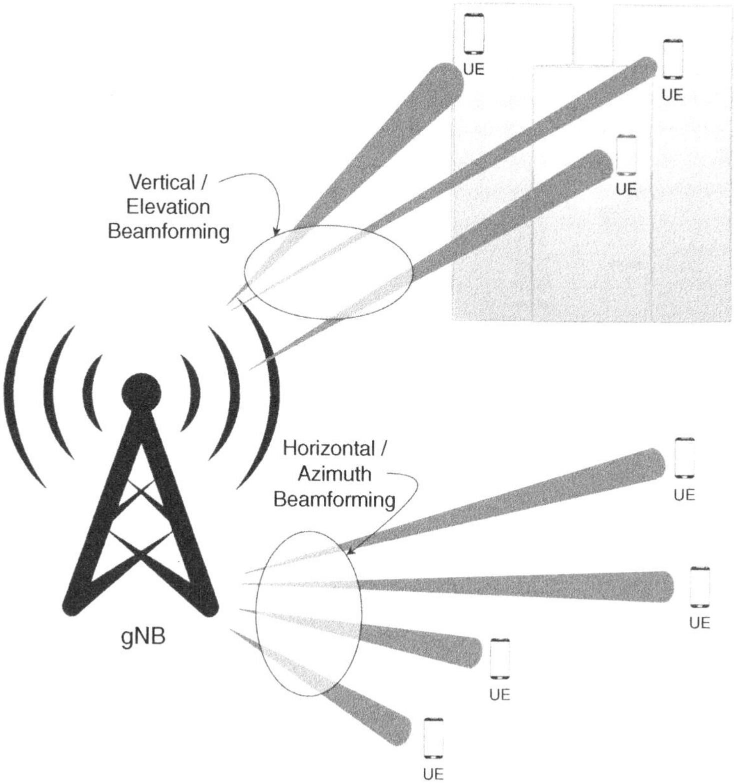

Figure I.2.3.6 Massive MIMO.

I.2.3.4.1 DL-MIMO Operation – Sub-6

A combination of digital or hybrid beamforming and digital precoding at baseband is used based on the number of antenna ports supported. Typically, a single panel array is used for both SU-MIMO (up to eight layers) and MU-MIMO (up to 12 layers from the network). Note that the UE typically supports 4 × 4 MIMO (rank 4) or a rank smaller than that. Some form of hybrid beamforming is required for MU-MIMO operation to be feasible in sub-6 FR1 spectrum. The precoding options in baseband can be based on precoding matric index (PMI) from channel state information (CSI)-RS measurement reports from the UE or on sounding reference signal (SRS)-based methods, where the UE transmits the SRS reference signals and the gNB interprets the information for closed-loop spatial multiplexing, uplink transmitting timing control, and reciprocity multiuser downlink precoding.

Figure I.2.3.7 shows the MIMO operations and the behaviors from the base station for both single-user-MIMO (SU-MIMO) and multiuser-MIMO (MU-MIMO). The complexity of realization of the MU-MIMO is largely on the base station side having received spatial relationship through CSI feedback and SRS reference signal transmissions from the UE. The base station needs to be ensure that the UE are sufficiently spatially separated for MU-MIMO realization by scheduling multiple UE using the same radio resources simultaneously.

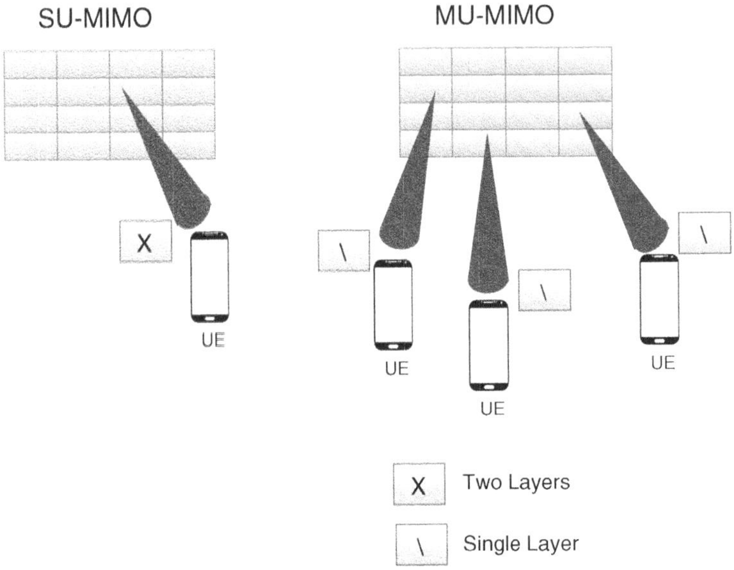

Figure I.2.3.7 Downlink MIMO.

I.2.3.4.2 Channel Reciprocity

With beamforming, apart from selecting the DL beam, the optimal UL beam also needs to be determined.

For time division duplex (TDD), given that the UE is operating on the same channel, the best beam on the DL tends to be the best beam to use on the UL and forms an implicit channel reciprocity. This implies that the SRS sent by the UE on the UL in the TDD spectrum can be used to determine the PMI for beamforming in the DL for the same TDD channel.

For frequency division duplex (FDD), however, given that the channels in the DL and UL are independent and can be far apart, the UE uses the best receive beam that it uses to receive the DL transmissions as its UL beam. Additionally, the UE explicitly reports the channel quality information (CQI)or PMI based on the CSI-RS DL reference signals so that the network can use that for beamforming on the DL. The UE will transmit the SRS on the UL, which is used by the gNB for UL scheduling operations. Figure I.2.3.8 provides the operations of FDD channels where the DL and UL channels are separated, and MIMO operations depends on the UE feedback and cannot rely on reciprocity. The figure also illustrates the operations on the TDD channels where the SRS reference signals and the CSI feedback information from the UE are together used to perform MIMO operations.

I.2.3.4.3 DL CSI Feedback

Given that M-MIMO fundamentally relies on forming finer beams, accurate CSI feedback is required for the proper functioning of the system.

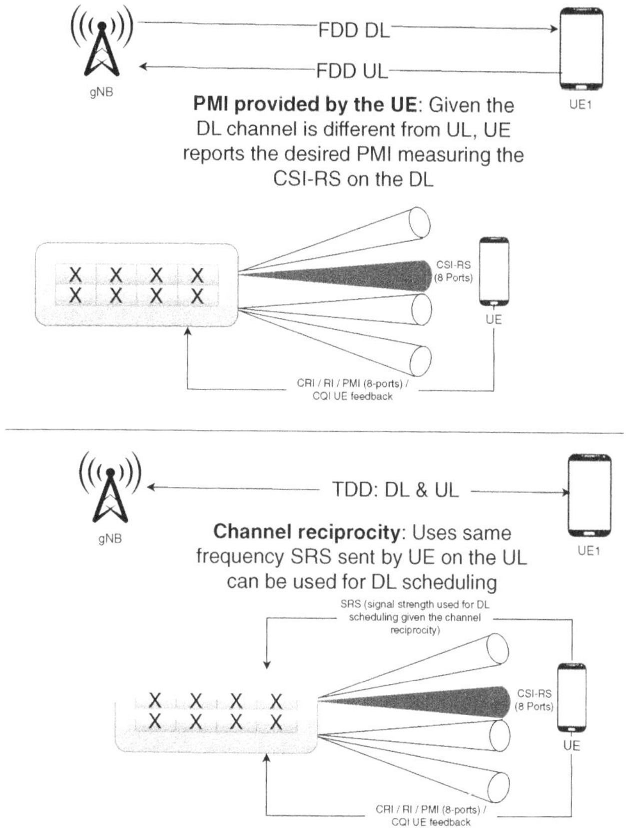

Figure I.2.3.8 Channel estimation with and without reciprocity.

5G NR defines two types of CSI feedback mechanisms to determine the channel conditions. The gNB configures the UE with the CSI feedback type to be used for DL CSI reporting.

CSI feedback type	Description
CSI feedback type 1	• *Single panel* ○ *N1 × N2 cross-polarized antenna elements* ○ *Supported the use of long-term frequency-independent and short-term frequency-dependent precoding matrices* • *Multipanel* ○ *Supported the use of a long-term, frequency-independent precoding matrix that can reflect the beam per panel* ○ *CSI with significantly higher spatial granularity* ○ *Target MU-MIMO*
CSI feedback type 2	• *CSI with significantly higher spatial granularity* • *Target MU-MIMO*

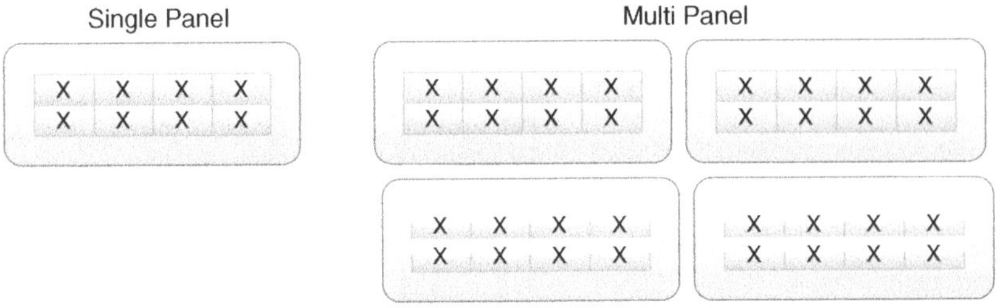

Figure I.2.3.9 Single and multiple panels.

Figure I.2.3.9 provides a basic illustration of operations based on single and multiple panels. Channel State Information (CSI) feedback in 5G NR is crucial for enabling the network to adapt to varying channel conditions, optimizing data transmission through techniques like beamforming, multiple input multiple output (MIMO), and link adaptation. CSI feedback can be categorized based on whether it involves a single antenna panel or multiple antenna panels. Here's an overview of CSI feedback using single-panel and multiple-panel operations in NR.

I.2.3.4.3.1 CSI Feedback in Single-Panel Operations

In single-panel operations, the user equipment (UE) uses a single antenna panel to receive and report CSI. This is typically simpler and involves lower complexity compared to multiple-panel operations.

- **Key Components**
  - **Single Antenna Panel:** The UE is equipped with one antenna panel, which may consist of multiple antenna elements.
  - **CSI Reporting Types**
    - **Channel State Information Reference Signal (CSI-RS):** The network transmits CSI-RS, and the UE measures the received signal to generate CSI feedback.
    - **Precoding Matrix Indicator (PMI):** Indicates the preferred precoding matrix based on the channel conditions.
    - **Channel Quality Indicator (CQI):** Reflects the overall channel quality, guiding the network on modulation and coding scheme (MCS) selection.
    - **Rank Indicator (RI):** Indicates the number of spatial layers the UE can support for optimal MIMO transmission.
  - **Operations**
    - The UE measures the CSI-RS transmitted by the network using its single antenna panel.
    - Based on these measurements, the UE generates and reports CSI, which includes PMI, CQI, and RI.
    - The network uses this feedback to optimize beamforming and MIMO operations, ensuring efficient use of the radio channel.
  - **Use Cases**
    - **Single User MIMO (SU-MIMO):** Optimized for scenarios where a single user utilizes all the available spatial layers.
    - **Beamforming:** The single antenna panel feedback helps in selecting the optimal beam for data transmission.

I.2.3.4.3.2 CSI Feedback in Multiple-Panel Operations

In multiple-panel operations, the UE is equipped with multiple antenna panels, each capable of receiving signals independently. This setup is more complex but offers significant benefits, especially in high-frequency bands (e.g., mmWave) where beamforming and spatial multiplexing are crucial.

- **Key Components**
  - **Multiple Antenna Panels:** The UE uses multiple antenna panels, often arranged to cover different spatial directions.
  - **Extended CSI Reporting**
    - **Panel-Specific CSI Reporting:** Each antenna panel can independently measure CSI-RS and report its own CSI.
    - **Combined CSI Reporting:** The UE can also combine measurements from multiple panels to provide an aggregated CSI report.
    - **Inter-Panel Measurements:** The UE may perform measurements considering the interaction between panels, optimizing the overall feedback.
  - **Operations**
    - The UE receives CSI-RS from the network using all its antenna panels.
    - It measures the channel quality, precoding matrix, and other parameters independently for each panel.
    - Depending on the configuration, the UE either reports panel-specific CSI or combines the measurements into a single, comprehensive CSI report.
    - The network uses this feedback to make informed decisions on beamforming, MIMO configurations, and other advanced transmission techniques, especially for scenarios involving multiuser MIMO (MU-MIMO).
  - **Use Cases**
    - **Multiuser MIMO (MU-MIMO):** Essential for scenarios where the network serves multiple users simultaneously, leveraging spatial diversity.
    - **Advanced Beamforming:** Multiple panels allow for more precise beamforming, particularly in dense urban environments or with mmWave deployments.

I.2.3.4.3.3 Comparison and Implications of Operations Based on Single and Multiple Panels

- **Complexity:** Multiple-panel operations are more complex due to the need to manage and combine feedback from multiple antenna panels. This complexity is justified by the performance gains in scenarios requiring advanced spatial multiplexing and beamforming.
- **Performance:** Multiple-panel operations offer significant advantages in terms of spatial diversity, allowing for better beamforming and MIMO performance, especially in high-frequency bands where line of sight is critical.
- **Use Cases:** Single-panel operations are sufficient for most low- to mid-band frequencies and simpler deployment scenarios, while multiple-panel operations are critical for high-frequency bands and scenarios requiring advanced multiuser support.

CSI feedback in NR using single-panel and multiple-panel operations caters to different deployment scenarios and performance requirements. Single-panel operations are simpler and suited for general use, while multiple-panel operations provide enhanced capabilities for scenarios demanding advanced spatial processing and high-frequency operations. The choice between these operations depends on factors like network deployment strategy, UE capabilities, and the specific needs of the radio environment.

I.2.3.4.4 DL Precoding – PMI versus SRS

The use of PMI and SRS depends on the spectrum and the availability of channel reciprocity. The table below captures the key aspects of the two approaches and their applicability.

Precoding methods	Description
PMI based	• *The codebook-based approach can be used for both FDD and TDD systems.* • *PMI is preferred when RI (Rank Indictor)> # SRS antennas (without SRS antenna switching) given that the SRS alone cannot be used to determine the required precoding.* • *Less granularity will implicitly restrict MU-MIMO operations.*
SRS based	• *SRS is the primary method used when channel reciprocity is possible, as in the TDD spectrum.* • *Easier to approach to accommodate antenna switching and usable only when the RI = <#SRS antennas.* • *More granularities will enable greater MU-MIMO support.*

I.2.3.4.5 UL M-MIMO Transmission Schemes

Radio resource control (RRC) signaling is used to select between codebook-based transmission and non-codebook-based transmission via information element (IE) "u/T×Config" = "Codebook" or "NonCodebook."

Tx scheme	Description
Tx scheme A	• *Codebook-based transmission (closed loop)* • *Frequency-selective precoding for CP-OFMD* • *TPMI is indicated for the UE*
Tx scheme B	• *Non-codebook-based transmission (closed loop)* • *Frequency-selective precoding for CP-OFDM* • *Indication of DL measurement RS is used by the UE to calculate the candidate precoder*

I.2.3.5 Summary

This section covers the basics of beamforming techniques. Beamforming is a tool used in NR systems to improve coverage and capacity. Beamforming is supported by three fundamental procedures: beam sweeping, beam refinement, and beam switching. Beam sweeping allows the gNB to cover the entire cell area by using narrow beams. Beam refinement allows for a more focused beam to be used to serve a given UE. Beam switching is used to support UE mobility. The mechanism of digital/analog/hybrid beamforming allows for compensating for RF path loss seen with the higher frequencies used in a 5G NR network. M-MIMO, with its antenna techniques, enables both SU-MIMO and MU-MIMO, allowing spatial reuse and serving many users using the same physical resources simultaneously.

Further Reading

1 3GPP R1-1700772, On forming wide beams, January 2017, Ericsson
2 Practical Hybrid Beamforming Schemes in Massive MIMO 5G NR Systems
3 G-NR Network Planning: Impact of Massive MIMO and Beamforming in Coverage Predictions
4 Hybrid Beamforming in 5G NR Networks Using Multi User Massive MIMO at FR2 Frequency Bands
5 Nokia Bell Labs, "Who will satisfy the desire to consume?" last accessed June 2020. [Online]. Available: http://www.iot.gen.tr/wp-content/uploads/2017/03 160531-Nokia Bell Labs Mobility Traffic Report.pdf
6 A. Fragoso, "Impact of Massive MIMO Antennas on High Capacity 5G-NR Networks," Master's thesis, Instituto Superior Te´cnico, 2019.
7 Yuan, Y. and Wang, X. (2017). 5G New Radio: Physical Layer Overview. *ZTE Communications* 1.
8 3GPP, "Study on new radio access technology: Radio access architecture and interfaces," 3rd Generation Partnership Project (3GPP), Technical Specification (TS) 38.801, 3 2017, version 14.0.0. [Online]. Available: https: //http://www.3gpp.org/ftp/Specs/archive/38 series/38.801/
9 Holma, H., Toskala, A., and Nakamura, T. (2020). *5G Technology: 3GPP New Radio*. Wiley.
10 GSMA, "5G Implementation Guide," July 2019, last accessed June 2020. [Online]. Available: https://www.gsma.com/futurenetworks/wp-content/uploads/2019/03/5G-Implementation-Guideline-v2.0-July-2019.pdf
11 Harrison J Son, last accessed April 2020. [Online]. Available: https://www.netmanias.com/en/post/oneshot/14488/5g/5g-nsa-option-3a-3x-generic-operation
12 Huawei Technologies Co. Ltd., "5G Spectrum - Public Policy Position." [Online]. Available: https: //http://www-file.huawei.com/-/media/CORPORATE/PDF/public-policy/public policy position 5g spectrum.pdf
13 Chilamkurti, N., Zeadally, S., and Chaouchi, H. (2013). *Next-Generation Wireless Technologies: 4G and Beyond*, Computer Communications and Networks. London: Springer.
14 R. Rios, "5G Network Planning and Optimization using Atoll," Master's thesis, Escola Te'cnica d'Enginyeria de Telecomunicacio´ de Barcelona, 2019.
15 GSMA, "5G Spectrum - Public Policy Position," March 2020, last accessed June 2020. [Online]. Available: https://www.gsma.com/spectrum/wp-content/uploads/2020/03/5G-Spectrum-Positions.pdf
16 D. Anzaldo, "LTE-Advanced Release-12 shapes new eNodeB transmitter Architecture: Part 1, Technology Evolution." [Online]. Available: https://www.maximintegrated.com/en/design/technical-documents/app-notes/6/6062.html
17 5G Americas, "Advanced antenna systems for 5G networks," Tech. Rep., 2019, last accessed June 2020. [Online]. Available: https://www.5gamericas.org/wp-content/uploads/2019/08/5G-Americas Advanced-Antenna-Systems-for-5G-White-Paper.pdf
18 Liu, L., Chen, R., Geirhofer, S. et al. (2012). Downlink MIMO in LTE-advanced: SU-MIMO vs. MU-MIMO. *IEEE Communications Magazine* 50 (2): 140–147.
19 Ericsson, "Advanced antenna systems for 5G networks," Tech. Rep., 2019, last accessed June 2020. [Online]. Available: https://www.ericsson.com/4a8a87/assets/local/reports-papers/white-papers/10201407 wp advanced antenna system nov18 181115.pdf
20 C. Shepard, H. Yu, N. Anand, E. Li, T. Marzetta, R. Yang, and L. Zhong, "Argos: practical many-antenna base stations," August 2012.

21 Hong, J.-K. (2018). Performance analysis of dual-polarized massive MIMO system with human-care IoT devices for cellular networks. *Journal of Sensors* 3604520. https://doi.org/10.1155/2018/3604520.

22 Flordelis, J., Rusek, F., Tufvesson, F. et al. (2018). Massive MIMO performance-TDD versus FDD: what do measurements say? *IEEE Transactions on Wireless Communications* 17 (4): 2247–2261.

23 S. Popoola, P. A. Atayero, N. Faruk, C. Calafate, O. Abiodun, and V. Matthews, "Standard Propagation Model Tuning for Path Loss Predictions in Built-Up Environments," 07 2017, pp. 363–375.

24 Nokia, "9955 RNP V7.4.0 Technical Reference Guide for Radio Networks," 2019, internal documentation.

I.2.4

NR Millimeter Wave

I.2.4.1 mmWave Introduction

The low-band and mid-band spectrum are already very congested, and with the wider bandwidths introduced in 5G, a larger spectrum space is required to leverage the full capability of 5G. It is intended that the mmWave can fulfill the demand for enhanced mobile broadband (eMBB) and novel 5G use cases that require more spectrum. There are several advantages and challenges with using higher frequencies. With higher frequencies, antenna size becomes very small, and a larger antenna array can be supported, allowing for higher gain. With more antennas, it supports directivity, enabling better beamforming. With higher path loss and the directivity supported by additional antennas, better spatial reuse becomes viable. Along similar lines, it does come with its set of challenges as well. Higher frequencies imply an inferior link budget, bringing with it significant deployment challenges. The higher spectrum is also used by satellites, and tighter coexistence requirements with incumbent satellite operations need to be addressed. 5G mmWave operation is defined to be between 24,250 MHz and 52,600 MHz. Given the short range of coverage provided by the mmWave spectrum, this spectrum is very suitable for private networks. The large available bandwidth and the fact that the signal does not penetrate far enable specific viable use cases that can be supported for enterprises without impacting neighboring enterprises. Table I.2.4.1 provides the currently defined set of mmWave bands per 3GPP standards specifications.

I.2.4.1.1 Impact of Environment on mmWave

The environmental impact of mmWave is significant due to the high-frequency range. mmWave propagation is affected by atmospheric gas attenuation, which includes water vapor absorption and oxygen absorption. It is also impacted by foliage (trees, plants, etc.) and rain (water droplets in the atmosphere). This causes scattering due to diffused and specular reflections, diffraction, and significant losses by buildings, which form major obstructions for mmWave.

mmWave has an extremely poor link budget and experiences significant losses even with line-of-sight and no obstructions. Some of these losses can be recovered by antenna gain techniques but still face significant limitations. Because of its coverage and line-of-sight (LOS) limitations, mmWave technology is better suited for dense urban deployment environments. Due to its poor link budget and, consequently, the range limitations, mmWave is not a practical choice for suburban and rural areas.

Mobile Communication Systems for Private Networks, First Edition. Srinivasan Balasubramanian.

Table I.2.4.1 Currently defined mmWave bands for NR operations.

Band	f (GHz)	Common name	Subset of band	Uplink/downlink (GHz)	Channel bandwidths (MHz)
n257	28	LMDS		26.50–29.50	50, 100, 200, 400
n258	26	K-band		24.25–27.50	50, 100, 200, 400
n259	41	V-band		39.50–43.50	50, 100, 200, 400
n260	39	Ka-band		37.00–40.00	50, 100, 200, 400
n261	28	Ka-band	n257	27.50–28.35	50, 100, 200, 400

Due to these reasons, mmWave is typically viable only for short-range communications. It is best suited for small cell deployments. Additionally, given the lack of reliability, mmWave will only be used to augment the capacity with the device connected to both sub-6 GHz and mmWave simultaneously. Non-stand-alone mode (NSA) or NR dual connectivity (NR-DC) mode with long-term evolution (LTE)/NR in sub-6 GHz and NR in mmWave is expected to be the deployment model. Of course, with the use of fixed wireless, customer premise equipment (CPE) can be deployed with mmWave, with the backhaul connected through mmWave and offering Wi-Fi connectivity to users in the proximity of the CPE.

I.2.4.2 Mitigative Techniques to Operate with mmWave

I.2.4.2.1 Antenna Arrays in mmWave

Beamforming and multiple antenna elements are used to overcome significant losses with mmWave. mmWave antennas require smaller wavelengths, have a smaller aperture, and experience lower received power. This brings in the need to make up lower received power and higher loss propagation. Antenna arrays and beamforming techniques are used to overcome these limitations. Massive multiple-input multiple-output (mMIMO), miniaturized antenna arrays, adaptable beamforming, and smart active repeaters are some of the techniques that can be used to overcome the issues of mmWave. A large number of antennas create a radiation pattern with narrow beamwidth while providing high gain. Large arrays fit into a small form factor at mmWave. Due to the smaller wavelength, large antenna arrays can be built into a small form factor, making it practical for implementation.

With the intent to create a radiation pattern with the required gain, antennas are designed to meet the criteria. Antennas are designed to support many antenna elements in horizontal and vertical directions with inter-element spacing. Each of these elements also needs to support a relative feed of current amplitude and phase to realize the beamforming.

Although mmWave, with its wide bandwidth, can provide high throughput, connecting these mmWave cells will require fiber backhaul connectivity, which in itself can become a challenge significantly raising the cost of deployment. Smart repeaters can be used to boost the mmWave signals, but these tend to reduce the cell capacity. Table I.2.4.2 provides a possible choice for mmWave antenna choices that can be employed at the radio base station along with the relevant criteria that can be used to make the preferred choices. Table I.2.4.3 provides the criteria and the arbitration to be used from the user equipment (UE) perspective.

Table I.2.4.2 mmWave base-station antenna choice criteria.

Criteria	Description
Gain/directivity	• Based on link budget and EIRP restrictions; highest gain with size constraint preferred • Number of elements per user and antenna size (base station and mobile)
Beamforming	• Base station below clutter (small cells, stadium showerhead antennas) – square grid antennas for elevation and azimuth beamforming • Base station above clutter (macro cells) → rectangular grid antennas for more azimuth beamforming
Polarization	• +45/−45 cross polarized elements • V/H polarized elements
Capacity	• Number of MU-MIMO users to be supported • Number of antenna elements required per user
Active antenna system	• One key aspect of mmWave propagation is to explore analog beamforming • Use an active antenna system (AAS) to facilitate beamforming and maximize its gain • Practical implementation to include PA and heat sink may change the actual dimensions

Table I.2.4.3 mmWave mobile antenna choice criteria.

Criteria	Description
Link budget	Achieve the target radiated power with high bandwidths at mmWave frequencies
Power consumption	Support multi-Gigabit throughput with high power efficiency
Mobility	Maintaining reliable mmWave connectivity with narrow beam widths can be quite challenging.
Device size restrictions	To achieve high antenna efficiency with multi-band support can be challenging, although mmWave tends to be supported as an independent RF path from the sub-6 GHz spectrum.
Thermal performance	Support high transmission power while maintaining thermal stability and avoiding localized hot spots
Regulatory compliance	Optimize transmission power and throughput while meeting regulatory requirements
UE transmit power – EIRP	Equivalent isotropic radiated power (EIRP). It represents the peak directional power transmitted from the antenna array relative to an isotropic transmission. With mmWave, support for antenna arrays with beamforming at the UE is required to achieve the necessary UL Tx Power. Antenna spacing is determined by the wavelength and the effective number of antennas in the array that can be utilized while remaining within the emission standards, which will determine the maximum EIPR that can be achieved (in real time).

(Continued)

Table I.2.4.3 (Continued)

Criteria	Description
Mobility challenges	High-gain directional antenna arrays • Analog beamforming with narrow beamwidth is required to close the link for mmWave. The narrow beams require more frequent beam transitions, both intra-cell and inter-cell. • The transmit and the receive beams may be different both in the UE and gNB. Although beam reciprocity can be used for mmWave, the beamwidth in the DL and UL can be different based on the antenna arrays used. Typically, better coverage can be achieved with DL than with UL. See sections I.2.3 and I.2.6 on MIMO and Beam Management and also NR Mobility, where the topics of beam switching, beam correspondence, beam tracking, etc., are covered.

I.2.4.2.2 Phase Noise Consideration

Components of phase lock loop (PLL) produce wideband and stationary parts of the phase noise, which are most detrimental. Temperature-Compensated Crystal Oscillators (TCXO) produces narrowband and non-stationary parts of the phase noise, which can be tracked through channel estimation. The impact is much more pronounced at mmWave frequencies and is a key issue that needs to be addressed. NR introduced a new Phase Tracking Reference Signal (PTRS) channel for uplink (UL) and downlink (DL) to track the phase. This function is required for both the UE and the gNB. This is done in addition to time/frequency synchronization.

I.2.4.3 Summary

The large bandwidths available with mmWave will help relieve growing network congestion in crowded urban areas, such as sports arenas, concert venues, and airports. However, there are many challenges with mmWave realization both in the UE and network sides. Mitigative techniques are available but will take significant investments, and maintenance is required to deploy and manage the networks. Beamforming to create narrower beams helps to close the link and get better coverage, but this implies that UE mobility needs to be managed, potentially jumping between coarser and narrower beams. Environmental challenges will exist that may not allow for easy workarounds other than overpopulating the mmWave to achieve the required coverage. The UE power consumption aspects need to be managed for mmWave to become viable in the market. mmWave can definitely be utilized where there is low to no mobility, addressing deployments such as CPE, manufacturing, etc.

References

1. 3GPP Standards

[1] 3GPP TS 38.101-1: NR; User equipment (UE) radio transmission and reception; Part 1: Range 1 Standalone: This document outlines the technical specifications for NR, including the frequency bands and performance requirements for mmWave.

[2] 3GPP TS 38.211: NR; Physical channels and modulation: This specifies the physical channels and modulation schemes used in NR, including the definitions relevant to mmWave operations.

[3] 3GPP TS 38.300: NR; Overall description; Stage 2: Provides an overall description of NR, including the high-frequency mmWave bands and their use cases.

2. Textbooks and Academic References

[4] Dahlman, E., Parkvall, S., Sköld, J. (2018). 5G NR: The Next Generation Wireless Access Technology. Academic Press. This book provides a comprehensive overview of 5G NR, including detailed sections on mmWave technology, its potential, and associated challenges.

[5] Rappaport, T. S., Heath, R. W., Daniels, R. C., Murdock, J. N. (2015). Millimeter Wave Wireless Communications. Prentice Hall. A foundational text that dives deep into mmWave communications, discussing its principles, channel models, and applications in 5G networks.

I.2.5

NR Unlicensed

I.2.5.1 Introduction

Apart from licensed spectrum, leveraging unlicensed spectrum will allow for a more comprehensive approach to wireless support. The notion of requiring licensed clean channels for cellular technology is not sufficient; enabling an alternative technology to be available for data connectivity in unlicensed spectrum, other than Wi-Fi, can be useful based on the requirements for services and their associated that need to be met. It should be noted that shared licenses for spectrum are being allocated quality of service (QoS) across the globe in individual countries for enterprise connectivity. Having a unified technology to support cellular technologies like long-term evolution (LTE) and new radio (NR) on the shared spectrum and opportunistically leveraging unlicensed access with just augmentation at the medium access control (MAC)/physical layer allows for seamless connectivity across licensed, shared licensed, and unlicensed spectrums. Another way of looking at it is to envision connectivity from diverse types of terrestrial and non-terrestrial networks that include cellular macro, small cells, high altitude platform systems (HAPS) with satellites (LEO, MEO, GEO), hot-air balloons, air-to-ground communication with airplanes, and unmanned arial vehicle (UAVs)/drones, each leveraging all available spectrum.

3GPP defined NR standards to allow this vision to be realized and defined different techniques such as the subcarrier spacing (SCS), flexible frame structures, etc. One such technique is self-contained time transmit interval (TTI), which allows for the unlicensed operations by contending for the channel in a single slot and completing the grant, data transmission, and acknowledgment within a single transmit interval. This primarily opened up the use of unlicensed channels for LTE/NR support.

Both licensed assisted access (LAA) with LTE and NR-U (NR operation on unlicensed spectrum) have yet to gain traction in the market. This chapter is structured to show the enabling technology aspects that support NR operations in unlicensed spectrum. A quick comparison of LAA and NR is presented in Table I.2.5.1.

Figure I.2.5.1 provides the set of connectivity options with NR-U. The expectation is that NR-U will typically not be used in isolation and will be connected with the licensed spectrum as the anchor. NR-U enables both uplink (UL) and downlink (DL) operations, supporting the 5G features, i.e., flexible numerologies, dynamic time-division duplex (TDD), beamforming, and dynamic scheduling/HARQ (hybrid automatic repeat request) timing, while also supporting

Mobile Communication Systems for Private Networks, First Edition. Srinivasan Balasubramanian.

Table I.2.5.1 Comparison of LAA and NR-U.

Modes of operation	NR-U	LAA
Operational bands	2.4, 3.5, 5, 6, 37, 60 GHz	5 GHz
Duplexing mode	FDD, semi-static TDD, dynamic TDD	FDD (LAA), semi-static TDD (eLAA)
Channel access scheme	LBT	LBT
Carrier sense	Omnidirectional, directional	Omnidirectional
Time-domain resource allocation granularity	1 OFDM symbol: 0.066, 0.033, 0.017, 0.008 ms	1 subframe: 1 ms
Frequency-domain resource-allocation granularity	1 resource block (RB): 180, 260, 720, 1,440 kHz (numerology dependent)	1 RB: 180 kHz

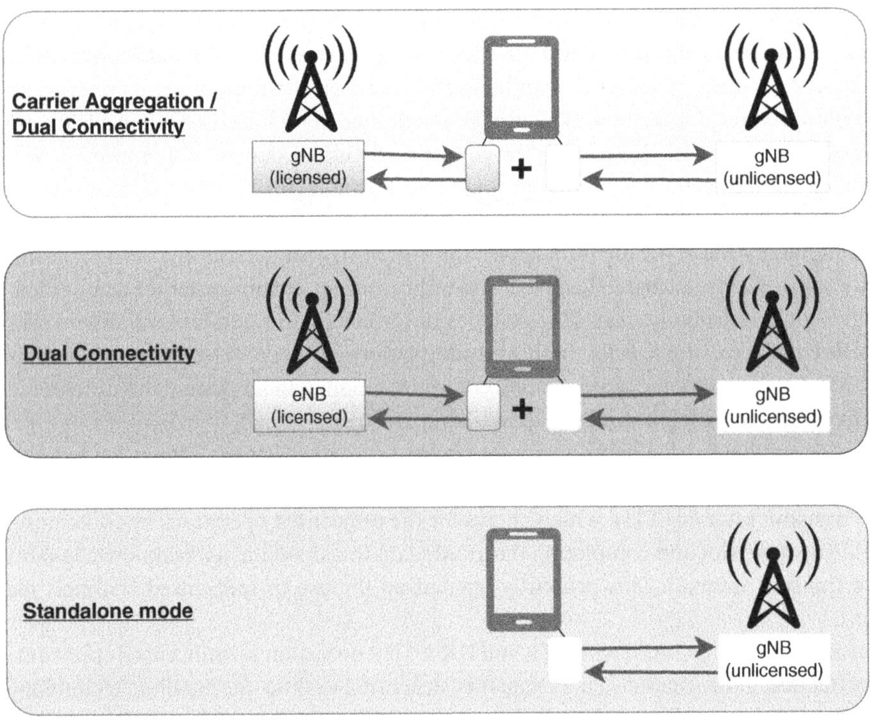

Figure I.2.5.1 NR-U connectivity scenarios.

the wider carrier bandwidths. With licensed anchor, it can be supported as dual connectivity (DC) with LTE as master cell group (MCG) and NR-U acting as secondary cell group (SCG). With NR, both DC and carrier aggregation (CA) are possible. The more complex behaviors with LTE and NR in licensed spectrum using DC and supporting NR-U as CA as part of SCG are also possible, but based on the market drive to advance to NR deployment, this is an unlikely scenario. NR-U as a standalone deployment is also possible if reliability can be relaxed for the use case.

I.2.5.2 Techniques Introduced in 3GPP to Aid NR-U

Refer to 3GPP TS 37.213 for details on physical layer procedures for shared spectrum channel access. The key concepts are captured in the sections below. NR-U is aided by the functions listed below.

- Multiple transitions between DL and UL in the frame structure of LBT to allow for better use of the available capacity for DL and UL operations.
- Support for scheduling multiple TTIs for PUSCH, which is required to reduce the amount of control information sent on the channel.
- Access priorities used for data multiplexing to ensure the appropriate QoS criteria are met for the individual flows.
- Support LBT in sub-bands within a wideband carrier. For wideband operations, channel contention-based access (CCA) is performed in units of 20 MHz to better manage the available spectrum in a modular way while still retaining the required flexibility.
- NR-U discovery reference signal (DRS) is used for channel detection and coherent operation.
- Block-interlaced transmission for PUCCH and PUSCH to improved operations on unlicensed channel.
- Support for multiple physical downlink shared channel (PDSCH) starting points to allow for a more flexible scheduling operation.

A *channel occupancy* refers to transmission(s) on channel(s) by evolution node B (eNB)/g node B (gNB)/user equipment (UE) after performing the corresponding channel-access procedures.

A *channel occupancy time* (COT) refers to the total time for which eNB/gNB/UE sharing the channel occupancy performs transmission(s) on a channel.

A *DL/UL/SL (sidelink) transmission burst* is defined as a set of transmissions from an eNB/gNB without any gaps greater than 16 μs. Transmissions from an eNB/gNB separated by a gap of more than 16 μs are considered separate DL/UL/SL transmission bursts. An eNB/gNB can transmit transmission(s) after a gap within a DL/UL/SL transmission burst without sensing the corresponding channel(s) for availability.

A *discovery burst* refers to a DL transmission burst that includes a set of signal(s) and/or channel(s) confined within a window and associated with a duty cycle. The *discovery burst* can be any of the following:

- Transmission(s) initiated by an eNB that include a primary synchronization signal (PSS), secondary synchronization signal (SSS), and cell-specific reference signal(s) (CRS) may also include nonzero power CSI reference signals (CSI-RS).
- Transmission(s) initiated by a gNB include at least an SS/physical broadcast channel (PBCH) block consisting of a PSS, SSS, PBCH with an associated demodulation reference signal (DM-RS), and may also include CORESET for physical downlink control channel (PDCCH) scheduling PDSCH with SIB1, and PDSCH carrying SIB1 and/or nonzero power CSI-RS.

I.2.5.2.1 Listen Before Talk (LBT)

NR-U channel access in both downlink and uplink relies on the listen-before-talk (LBT) feature. As with carrier sense multiple access (CSMA), a device wanting to use the channel first senses the channel to check for any ongoing transmissions and to see if the channel is free to be occupied before initiating transmissions. When a communication channel has a wide bandwidth of up to 100 MHz, channel sensing requires detecting the energy level on multiple sub-bands. The LBT parameters (such as type/duration and clear channel assessment parameters) are configured in a wireless device by the base station.

The new frame structure type 3 has been introduced for operations in the unlicensed communication channels. DL and UL operate on the same frequencies/channel as TDD operations. However, there are no rigid DL/UL identified slots, and both UEs and base stations will need to contend for the channel before transmitting. Figure I.2.5.2 provides an illustration of the listen-before-talk operation using the frame structure type 3. Table I.2.5.2 provides the LBT categories. Tables I.2.5.3 and I.2.5.4 provide the content-based channel access parameters for DL and UL.

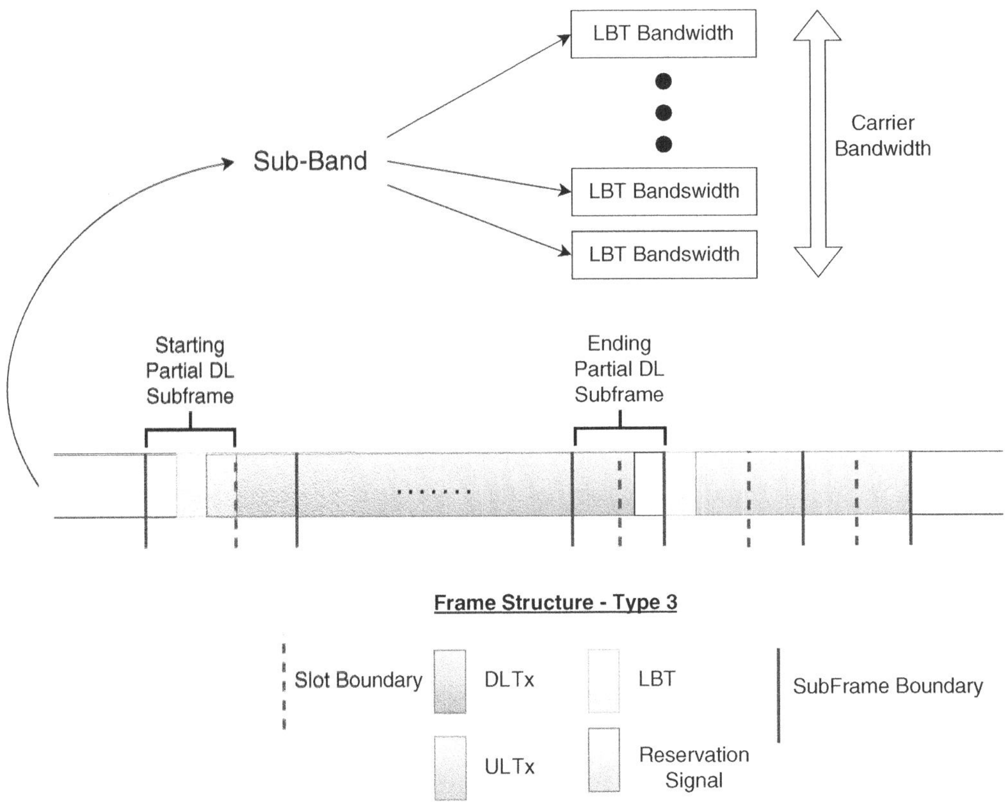

Figure I.2.5.2 LBT and operation with frame structure type 3.

Table I.2.5.2 LBT types.

LBT type	Description	Notes
Category-1	transmit immediately after 16 μs of idle time	Supports DL and UL transmission.
Category-2	transmit immediately after 23 μs of idle time	If the gap is less than 16 μs and the transmission duration is ≤584 μs, transmission can happen immediately.
Category-3	LBT with random back-off with fixed-size CW (contention window)	Not used in NR-U
Category-4	LBT with random back-off and varying CW based on channel conditions	Supports DL and UL transmission

Table I.2.5.3 Channel access priority class (CAPC) for DL.

Channel access priority class (p)	m_p	$CW_{min,p}$	$CW_{max,p}$	$T_{mcot,p}$	Allowed CW_p sizes
1	1	3	7	2 ms	{3,7}
2	1	7	15	3 ms	{7,15}
3	3	15	63	8 or 10 ms	{15,31,63}
4	7	15	1,023	8 or 10 ms	{15,31,63,127,255,511,1023}

Source: Reproduced from 3GPP TS 37.213 Table 4.1.1.1.

Table I.2.5.4 Channel access priority class for UL.

Channel access priority class (p)	m_p	$CW_{min,p}$	$CW_{max,p}$	$T_{ulmcot,p}$	Allowed CW_p sizes
1	2	3	7	2 ms	{3,7}
2	2	7	15	4 ms	{7,15}
3	3	15	1,023	6 ms or 10 ms	{15,31,63,127,255,511,1023}
4	7	15	1,023	6 ms or 10 ms	{15,31,63,127,255,511,1023}

[a] For $p = 3, 4$, $T_{ulmcot,p} = 10$ ms if the higher layer parameter absenceOfAnyOtherTechnology-r14 or absenceOfAnyOtherTechnology-r16 is provided, otherwise, $T_{ulmcot,p} = 6$ ms.
[b] When $T_{ulmcot,p} = 6$ ms, it may be increased to 8 *ms* by inserting one or more gaps. The minimum duration of a gap shall be 100 μs. The maximum duration before including any such gap shall be 6 ms.*Source:* Reproduced from 3GPP TS 37.213, table 4.2.1.1.

I.2.5.2.2 Contention Window Adaption

I.2.5.2.2.1 Contention Window Adaptation for DL

For eNB, the normal rule of 80% NACK in HARQ-ACK is applied to change the contention window (CW).

For gNB, there are two rules used. If transmission is successful, the CW will not be increased if at least one HARQ-ACK feedback is "ACK" for PDSCH(s) with transport block-based transmissions, or if at least 10% of HARQ-ACK feedback is "ACK" for PDSCH(s) with code block group-based transmissions.

I.2.5.2.2.2 Contention Window Adaptation for UL (LAA)

The UL transmission scheduled by the eNB and CW adaptation is provided here.

If no previous data transmission, if new data indicator (NDI) in HARQ is toggled on, or there is at least one ACK in previous HARQ-ACK, CW = CWmin; otherwise, increase CW.

If there was a previous data transmission using Cat 4 LBT, and if N or more subframes have elapsed and neither an UL grant nor an autonomous UL downlink feedback indication (AUL-DFI) was received, where N = max (*contentionWindowSizeTimer*, current transmission burst length + 1), increase CW; otherwise, CW remains unchanged.

If there is previous data transmission using Cat 4 LBT and N or more subframes have elapsed and the HARQ-ACK of the previous transmission is available, if there is at least one ACK in the previous HARQ-ACK, set CW = CWmin; otherwise, increase CW.

I.2.5.2.2.3 Contention Window Adaptation for UL (NR-U)

For UL transmissions scheduled by gNB, if the HARQ-ACK of the previous transmission is available, the CW is increased if at least one HARQ-ACK feedback is "ACK" for PDSCH(s) with transport block-based transmissions, or at least 10% of HARQ-ACK feedback is "ACK" for PDSCH(s) with code block group-based transmissions; otherwise, the CW remains unchanged.

If the current UL transmission includes retransmission or is transmitted after a set period Tw = max (Ta, current burst length + 1 ms) (where Ta = 5 ms if no other radio access technology, RAT, 10 ms otherwise), CW is increased, and otherwise, CW remains unchanged.

I.2.5.2.3 Channel Access Procedures

The CW may be maintained for each channel, or a single CW that is the large CW for all channels is used. Tables I.2.5.5 and I.2.5.6 provide the DL and UL multi-access channel procedures.

Table I.2.5.5 DL multichannel access procedures.

DL multichannel access type	Description
Type 1	Access procedures to be performed by an eNB/gNB, where the time duration spanned by the sensing slots that are sensed to be idle before a downlink transmission(s) is random.
Type 2A	An eNB/gNB may transmit a DL transmission immediately after sensing the channel to be idle for at least a sensing interval T_{short_dl} = 25 µs.Tshort_dl. The channel is considered to be idle for T_{short_dl} if both sensing slots of T_{short_dl} are sensed to be idle.
Type 2B	A gNB may transmit a DL transmission immediately after sensing the channel to be idle within a duration of T_f = 16 µs. The channel is considered to be idle within the duration T_f if the channel is sensed to be idle for a total of at least 5 µs, with at least 4 µs of sensing occurring in the sensing slot.
Type 2C	When a gNB follows the procedures in this clause for the transmission of a DL signal, the gNB does not sense the channel before the transmission of the DL signal. The duration of the corresponding DL transmission is at most 584 µs.

Table I.2.5.6 UL multichannel access procedures.

DL multichannel access type	Description
Type 1	Channel access procedures by a UE, where the time duration spanned by the sensing slots that are sensed to be idle before a UL transmission(s) is random.
Type 2A	The UE may transmit the transmission immediately after sensing the channel to be idle for at least a sensing interval $T_{\text{short\_ul}} = 25\,\mu s$. The channel is considered to be idle for $T_{\text{short\_ul}}$ if both sensing slots of $T_{\text{short\_ul}}$ are sensed to be idle.
Type 2B	The UE may transmit the transmission immediately after sensing the channel to be idle within a duration of T_f = 16 µs. The channel is considered to be idle within the duration T_f if the channel is sensed to be idle for a total of at least 5 μs, with at least 4 μs of sensing occurring in the sensing slot.
Type 2C	If a UE is indicated to perform Type 2C UL channel access procedures for a UL transmission, the UE does not sense the channel before the transmission. The duration of the corresponding UL transmission is at most 584 μs.

I.2.5.2.4 Channel Occupancy Time Structure

A wireless device determines when and where to transmit and receive based on the channel occupancy time (COT) structure. The COT comprises multiple slots, and each slot comprises downlink resources, uplink resources, or flexible resources. The COT structure provides some structure to the operations and helps reduce power consumption and channel access delay. Figure I.2.5.3 provides an illustration of channel occupancy time structures for the different DL and UL channels.

I.2.5.2.5 Interlace Resource Allocation

The NR-U system, unlike LTE, supports both contiguous and interlaced uplink resource allocations. With the use of interlaces, the resource allocation is performed in terms of "interlaces." Figure I.2.5.4 shows an example of interlaces with 20 MHz and 15 kHz SCS (specific patterns of the available 100 PRBs are identified as part of an interlace).

I.2.5.2.6 Multi-subframe Grant

In the eLAA system, a base station can allocate a maximum of four multiple consecutive subframes to a wireless device using the multi-subframe grants. Two new downlink control information (DCI) formats (i.e., format 0B and format 4B) allow the base station to transmit on the PDCCH to schedule resources for a wireless device in up to four consecutive subframes. Figure I.2.5.5 illustrates grants that are applied to multiple subframes.

I.2.5.2.7 Triggered Grant

In legacy LTE, a wireless device needs four subframes to process an uplink grant. The eLAA system enables fast resource allocation by specifying the triggered grants. The base station may first

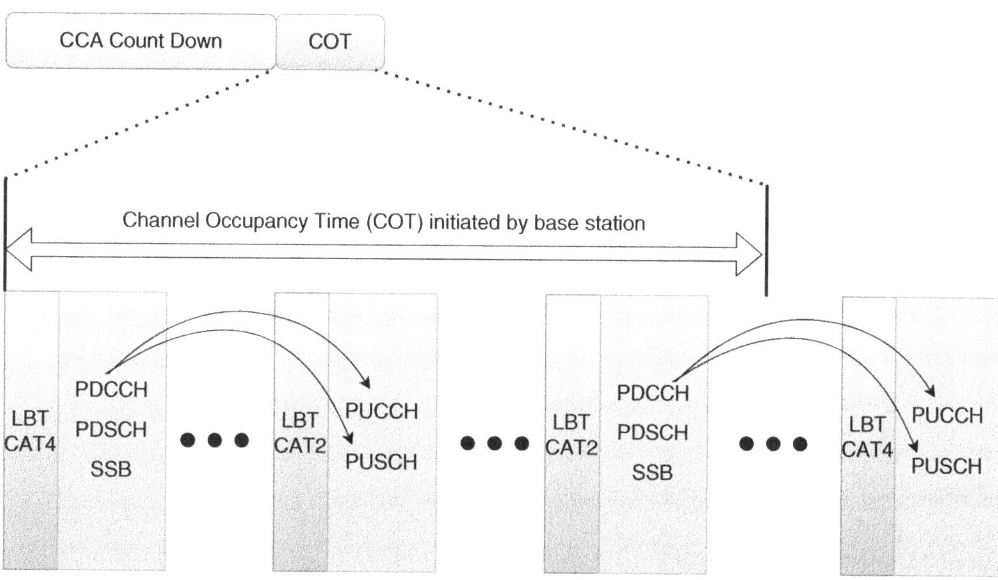

Figure I.2.5.3 Channel occupancy time.

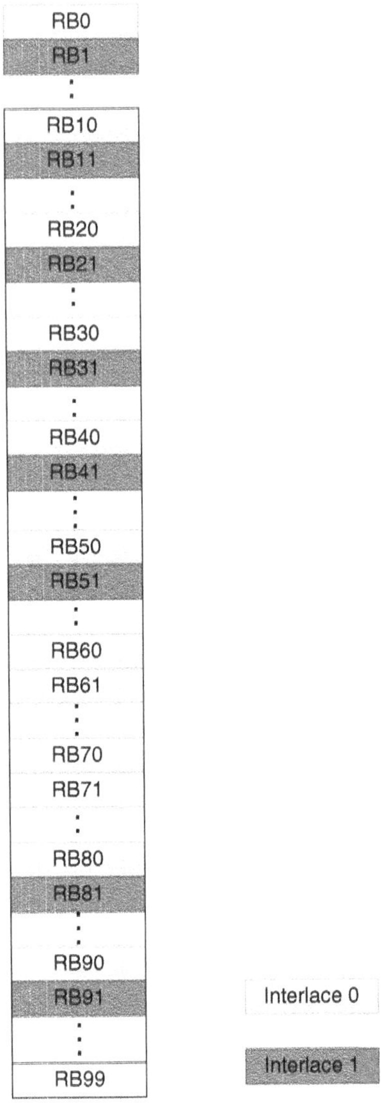

Figure I.2.5.4 Interlace resource allocation example.

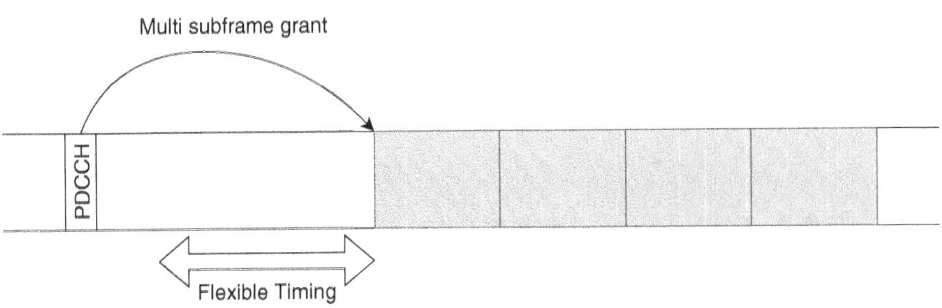

Figure I.2.5.5 Multi-subframe grant.

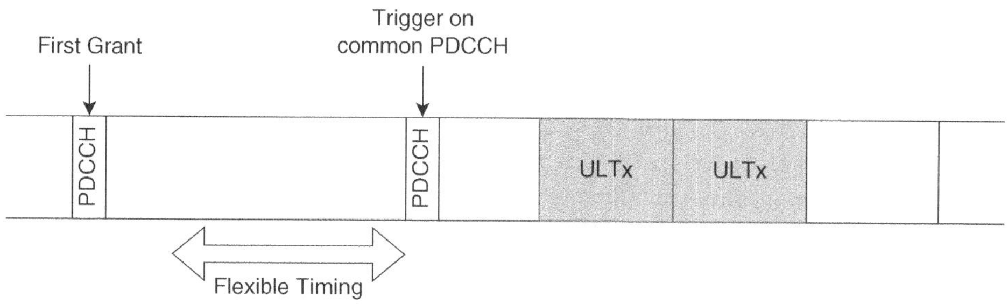

Figure I.2.5.6 Triggered grant.

transmit a resource allocation command to the wireless device and may later transmit a trigger, with a short processing time, to indicate to the wireless device the time for transmission. The timing between the resource allocation command and the trigger can be flexible. Figure I.2.5.6 provides a way to provide the grants with the resource allocation and separating the actual trigger to activate the grant with a shorter command to the UE.

I.2.5.3 Summary

This section provides the details of the unlicensed access procedures. The distinctive features introduced to accommodate channel acquisition and transmission on the unlicensed shared channel are described. LAA has not seen much traction in the market. NR-U is yet to see commercialization. However, NR-U, augmented with the lightly licensed shared spectrum usage, will enable the spectrum availability for private network deployments and could become a critical enabler for enterprise markets.

References

- 3GPP Standards
  - 3GPP TS 38.101-4: *NR; User equipment (UE) radio transmission and reception; Part 4: Performance requirements in unlicensed bands*: This document provides the technical specifications and performance requirements for NR operation in unlicensed bands.
  - 3GPP TS 38.300: *NR; Overall description; Stage 2*: Includes an overall description of NR, including aspects related to operation in unlicensed spectrum.
  - 3GPP TS 38.104: *NR; Base station (BS) radio transmission and reception*: Defines the requirements for NR base stations, including those operating in unlicensed bands.
  - 3GPP TR 38.889: *Study on NR-based access to unlicensed spectrum*: A technical report exploring the feasibility, challenges, and use cases of NR in unlicensed spectrum.
- Textbooks and Academic References
  - Dahlman, E., Parkvall, S., Sköld, J. (2021). *5G NR: The Next Generation Wireless Access Technology*. Academic Press. This book includes sections discussing the use of unlicensed spectrum in 5G, providing an overview of the technology and its applications.

- Research Papers and Journals
  - Hirzallah, M., et al. (2020). “5G New Radio Unlicensed: Challenges and Evaluation” in 5G New Radio Unlicensed: Challenges and Evaluation.
  - Kumbhar, A. S., et al. (2019). “A Survey on Legacy and Emerging Technologies for Public Safety Communications” in *IEEE Communications Surveys & Tutorials*. This survey includes a discussion on the use of unlicensed spectrum in 5G for public safety communications, covering NR-U.
  - Jiang, W., et al. (2019). “Machine Learning Paradigms for Next-Generation Wireless Networks” in *IEEE Wireless Communications*. This paper explores the application of machine learning to optimize NR-U, highlighting the unique challenges and solutions in unlicensed spectrum.
- Industry White Papers
  - Qualcomm (2018). “5G NR-U: Extending 5G to Unlicensed Spectrum.” This white paper from Qualcomm discusses the technical aspects and benefits of NR in unlicensed bands, including coexistence with other technologies like Wi-Fi.
  - Ericsson (2019). “Unlocking the Potential of Unlicensed Spectrum with 5G NR.” Ericsson’s white paper outlines the strategic importance of NR-U, detailing the technical challenges and potential use cases.
  - Nokia (2020). “5G NR-U: Enhancing 5G with Unlicensed Spectrum.” This document explains Nokia’s approach to NR-U, including deployment strategies and performance expectations.
- Conference Papers
  - Liu, G., et al. (2018). “5G New Radio Licensed-Assisted Access: Harmonious Coexistence with Wi-Fi in Unlicensed Spectrum” in *IEEE GLOBECOM*. Discusses coexistence strategies between NR-U and Wi-Fi, highlighting how NR-U can efficiently share the unlicensed spectrum with existing technologies.
  - Wang, Y., et al. (2018). “5G-NR Based Coexistence in Unlicensed Spectrum: Achievements and Challenges” in *IEEE ICC*. A conference paper that addresses the technical challenges of NR-U and presents solutions for successful deployment.

I.2.6

NR Mobility

I.2.6.1 Introduction

This section details the 5G NR idle mode, inactive mode, and connected mode mobility in stand-alone (SA) mode. Aspects of non-stand-alone (NSA) mode are also minimally captured to provide the reader with sufficient context to appreciate the aspects involved, given the lack of relevance of this mode of operation to private networks.

From a mobility perspective, the idle mode and inactive mode both behave the same way except for some signaling procedures that involve reading broadcast messages and access procedures. For all practical purposes, idle and inactive modes are equivalent, and only idle mode is referenced later. The exceptions as they apply to inactive mode are explicitly called out.

For connected mobility, the measurement event triggers related to mobility and the transitions are captured. The intra-NR mobility in NSA mode requires specific treatment and the associated procedures are captured. Inter-radio access technology (IRAT) in a private network setting, transitioning across NR and long-term evolution (LTE), is addressed for multimode campus deployments that support both LTE and NR.

The context of L3 mobility, together with the lower layer beam mobility and related procedures, is also addressed, along with a brief mention of the forward-looking concepts introduced in 3GPP Release-18 for mTRP (multi-transmission reception points) using LTM (L1/L2 triggered mobility).

I.2.6.1.1 NR Mobility Overview

The NR mobility follows similar procedures to LTE for mobility within NR. In fact, even the trigger event and required measurement reporting remain largely the same. The main difference lies in the search space and the signals the user equipment (UE) needs to report measurements for the serving and neighbor cells.

For non-access stratum (NAS) mode idle mobility, the UE is in idle mode only on LTE, and the NR is added to the radio resource control (RRC) connection only in connected mode as part of the dual connectivity (DC) procedures supporting both LTE as the master cell group (MCG) and NR as the secondary cell group (SCG). Given that, the idle mode mobility in NR in NSA mode is not relevant. The NSA connected mobility needs to support both NR mobility and LTE, with both performed together or independently. NR mobility SCG addition, release, and modification may be performed based on NR footprint change or when the LTE MCG changes due to LTE footprint/CC change, and the SCG NR is updated accordingly to be associated with the appropriate LTE MCG

Mobile Communication Systems for Private Networks, First Edition. Srinivasan Balasubramanian.

cell. IRAT mobility in NSA mode typically involves the UE transitioning to 3G/2G networks, and these procedures are executed from LTE per the existing procedures. Given that the private networks are deployed as 4G LTE and 5G NR, IRAT mobility from LTE to 3G/2G networks is not relevant. With NSA support, LTE to NR transitions are also not required, given that the MCG remains on LTE and NR is added or dropped in connected mode as SCG.

For SA mode, idle and inactive modes of operation with NR, transitions are executed using cell selection, cell reselection, and IRAT mobility into the LTE procedure. NR connected mobility across NR cells is performed using the measurement reports from the UE triggered on specific events that are based on the signal strengths of serving and neighbor cells. This includes both infra-frequency and inter-frequency NR transitions. IRAT mobility from NR to LTE is similarly handled using reselection/handover thresholds based on NR and LTE coverage. Typical configurations will support NR to be more preferred, and the UE will be required to look for LTE cells only when the UE is running out of NR coverage. Note that NR transitions to 3G/2G networks are not supported per the 3GPP specifications, and only IRAT transitions between NR and LTE are required. When the UE goes out of NR coverage and there is no LTE coverage, the UE goes out of service and runs a full scan to find 3G/2G based on the available coverage.

I.2.6.1.2 5G NR SA Mode Idle Mode Mobility

The NR SA mode initial power-up and idle mode mobility follow the same procedures as LTE. This includes system scans to find the preferred camping system and measurements of serving and neighbor cells for idle mode mobility.

Figure I.2.6.1 depicts the UE behavior of the power-up sequence. The steps involved address both the initial power-up and subsequent power cycles of the UE.

- UE Power On: If this is a power-up for the very first time, the UE will not have any archived information. For the subsequent power cycles, the UE will have archived information on the prior networks it has successfully camped on.

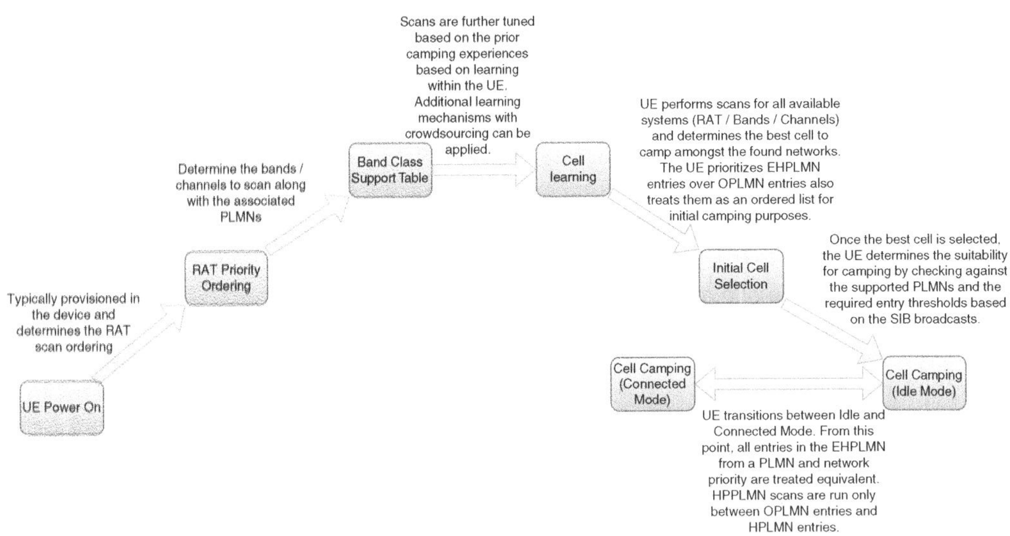

Figure I.2.6.1 NR UE initial power-up and system camping.

- Radio access technology (RAT) priority ordering: The UE is provisioned with a default RAT priority ordering. The UE uses this information to determine the scan sequence of the RATs supported by the device.
- Band class support table: The UE is provisioned with the information about the different supported bands, the channels within each band, and the supported public land mobile networks (PLMNs) associated with the bands/channels. The UE uses this ordering provided in this table to determine the band/channel scan order. This table is in addition to the PLMN tables provisioned along with the subscriber identity module (SIM) credentials that provide the equivalent home PLMN (EHPLMN) and operator PLMN (OPLMN), which are considered to be roaming partners.
- Cell learning: The UE learns about the bands, channels, PLMNs, and cell IDs of the cells where it has successfully camped. This information is used to further bias the scan ordering of the network that the device uses to perform system camping.
- Initial cell selection: The UE performs a full scan of all available networks and uses the EHPLMN list provisioned to determine the highest-priority network to camp on among the found networks. The priority ordering of the PLMNs in the EHPLMN is used only at the initial power-up, and subsequently, all the entries in the EHPLMN list are treated to be equivalent. The UE does not transition from one PLMN to another with the EHPLMN list through HPPLMN scan (higher-priority PLMN scans) and only relies on cell reselection procedures. However, when the UE is camped on an OPLMN network, it will continue to look for networks hosted by the PLMNs from the EHPLMN entries.
- Cell camping (idle mode): When the UE has found a preferred network that supports the PLMN listed in the SIM profile, the UE determines if the system is valid for camping by assessing the signal strength of the downlink (DL) reference signals. Additionally, the UE checks to ensure that there are no other mechanisms preventing the UE from camping on the cell. The UE then determines the access parameters and performs RACH (random access) to connect to the cell.
- Cell camping (connected mode): The UE supports traffic in this mode having established the connection through RRC procedures. The UE transitions between idle/inactive and connected modes based on the data traffic activity.

Figure I.2.6.2 depicts the UE behavior of idle mode mobility transitioning across beams both within and across cells.

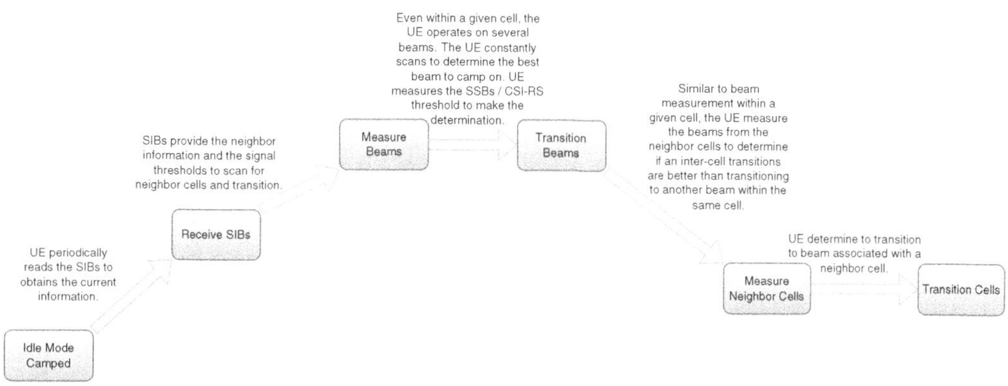

Figure I.2.6.2 NR UE idle/inactive mode mobility.

- Idle mode camped: The UE periodically reads the system information blocks (SIBs) to obtain the latest information. The network assumes a certain periodicity of UE reading the SIBs and the network assumes that in determining the UEs having refreshed the newer parameters provided in the broadcast messages.
- Receive SIBs: The SIBs provide the UE with the neighbor cell information apart from the required measurement event thresholds.
- Measure beams: From the UE perspective, all signals detected are beams, which include both intra-cell and inter-cell. The UE measures and reports on beams, and the network selects the most appropriate beam for the UE.
- Transition beams: The UE transitions beams, and based on the preferred target beam, the handover transition will be either intra-cell or inter-cell.
- Measure neighbor cells: The UE measures beams, and the network knows the beams associated with the neighbor cells. Once the UE transitions beams, it reads the SIBs to determine the target beam/cell-related details. The UE based on the SIB broadcasts determines the transition to be intra-cell or inter-cell.
- Transition cells: The UE associates with the target cell by acquiring the DL first and then the SIB broadcast parameters. If this transition results in the UE crossing tracking area (TA) boundaries, the UE initiates a RACH (random access) and informs the network that the UE is now operating in the newly entered TA.

I.2.6.1.3 5G NR Connected Mode Mobility

The connected mode mobility performs similar functions to LTE connected mode operations. Beam mobility and cell mobility are applicable for UE transitioning intra-cell and inter-cell in connected mode. The difference between idle mode and connected mode is that the neighbor cell information is obtained from the SIB broadcasts for idle mode, and the network provides the neighbors to measure for connected mode. Additionally, in idle mode, the UE transitions autonomously without the network implicitly knowing the UE beam/cell transitions unless the UE crosses specific TA boundaries. In connected mode, however, the network controls all transitions, and it is based on the UE providing measurement reports on the different beams it encounters to the network. The mobility procedures can be managed at the Layer 1/Layer 2 (physical layer (PHY); medium access control (MAC)) or at the Layer 3 (RRC) procedures.

I.2.6.1.3.1 Beam Mobility (Intra-cell)

The UE intra-cell beam mobility is controlled by MAC/PHY procedures. The UE reports the RSRP/RSRQ/SINR (reference signal received power / reference signal received quality / signal-to-interference and noise ratio) information associated with the DL beams that it sees and will include the beam identifier information along with the report. The UE transmits sounding reference signals (SRS) on the UL. The network determines the best DL beam and the best upperlink (UL) beam to serve the UE. For a time division duplex (TDD) spectrum, it is sufficient for the UE to report only the DL signal strength information and given that both the DL and UL operate on the same channel, beam reciprocity is used to implicitly select the UL beam associated with the selected DL beam. For a frequency division duplex (FDD) spectrum, explicit SRS reporting is required for the network to determine the best UL beam to use for the UE. Figure I.2.6.3 provides of view showing a given cell supporting multiple beams and the UE and the base station selecting the preferred beams on the DL and UL to communicate with each other.

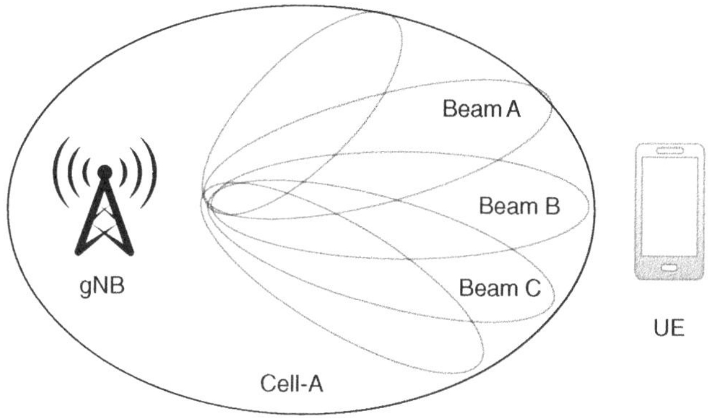

Figure I.2.6.3 NR intra-cell beam mobility.

The UE continues to report on the different beams, and the network constantly adapts the best beams to use to serve the UE. For more details on the beam-based measurement and reporting, see the chapter on beam management and multiple-input multiple-output (MIMO) (Chapter I.2.3)

I.2.6.1.3.2 Cell Mobility (Inter-cell)

For inter-cell mobility, the network provides the measurement object with the neighbor cell information for the UE to perform measurements. This is a Layer 3 (RRC) level procedure. The UE measures the synchronization signal block (SSB) of the neighbor cells and determines the RSRP, RSRQ, and SINR information. The signal strengths associated with the different neighbor cells are reported to the network by the UE, and the network determines the appropriate neighbor cell to hand over the UE to. The UE transitions to the target cell and acquires the DL beam and performs contention-free random access to associate the UE with the target cell. Figure I.2.6.4 illustrates that each cell may employ beamformed operations and the UE needs to scan for the individual beams from the neighboring cells and provide the measurement information of the individual beams to the network for mobility operations.

The handover transitions for inter-cell involve Layer 2 (RLC, PDCP, and MAC) context transfers, apart from Layer 3 (RRC/NAS, quality of service (QoS), data network, and transport layers) from the source cell to the target cell.

I.2.6.1.3.3 Connected Mode Mobility

The NR SA option 2 is the network architecture where the gNBs are connected to the 5GC core network. This is strictly a 5G NR-only network. Figure I.2.6.5 provides exemplary events that are

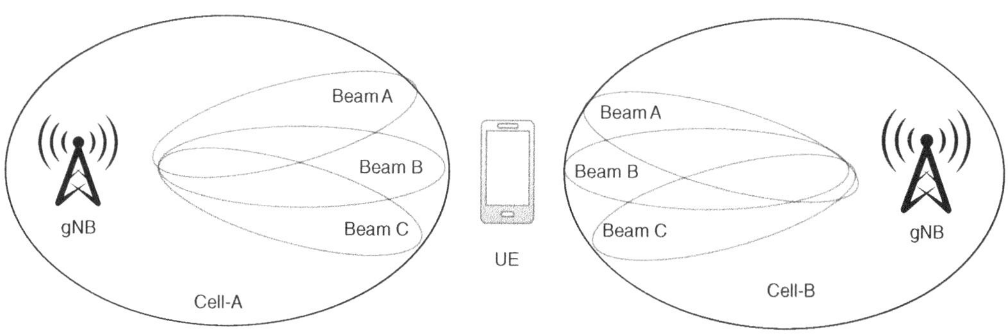

Figure I.2.6.4 NR inter-cell handover.

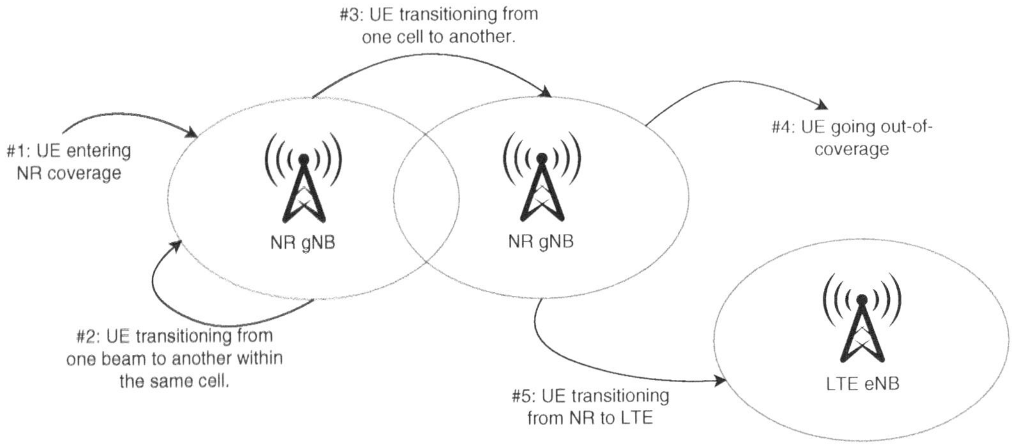

Figure I.2.6.5 NRSA mobility transition events.

typically performed in the NR network by the UE. The following is a brief description of these transitions:

1) Entering NR footprint: UE moves into NR coverage.
2) Intra-cell NR mobility: UE moves from one beam to another within an NR cell.
3) NR inter-cell handover: UE mobility within NR coverage from one cell to another (triggered by the A3 event).
4) UE leaves NR footprint: The UE moves out of NR coverage and does not have another RAT to transition to. The UE performs a full-band scan to find available networks.
5) UE transitioning from NR to LTE: The UE moves out of NR coverage and performs IRAT scans to find LTE networks. The UE may also find 2G/3G networks in a typical macro network. In an enterprise network, it will be only LTE and NR networks that are deployed.

The 3GPP-defined NR SA mobility event triggers are described in the next section. The network controls the UE actions for these transitions, and significant effort goes into optimizing the network by tuning these thresholds. The UE, based on these thresholds, performs measurements and reports those measurements to the network. The network, based on the UE-reported thresholds, determines the required transitions. In addition to these events that are governed by the network, there is UE-specific learning based on the encountered networks, and the UE takes proactive steps to report measurement events to the network.

I.2.6.1.3.4 SA Mobility – Measurement Events

List of measurement events and use cases for SA mobility are provided in Table I.2.6.1. The thresholds for these events are provided by the current serving cell in the broadcast messages SIB. Apart from the event threshold levels, the transition direction of the threshold is employed for executing the measurements and reporting to the network. The UE, based on the event type, uses a leading-edge transition going above the threshold or a trailing edge going below a threshold to perform the relevant actions. Note that the UE performs multiple measurements, typically three measurements spaced by 40 ms to determine a threshold. Based on the neighbor cell being measured, the network

Table I.2.6.1 NR SA mode transition events (reference from 3GPP TS 38.331).

		Use case in NSA targeting NR cells		
Event	**Trigger definition**	**Configured by**	**RAT of object**	**Purpose**
A1	Serving cell becomes better than an absolute threshold	gNB	NR	Serving cell in coverage indication
A2	Serving cell becomes worse than an absolute threshold	gNB	NR	Serving cell out of coverage indication
A3	The neighbor cell becomes offset better than Pell/PSCell	gNB	NR	Intra-frequency handover
A4	The neighbor cell becomes better than an absolute threshold	gNB	NR	Load balance handover
A5	Pell/PSCell becomes worse than absolute threshold1, and the neighbor becomes better than absolute threshold2	gNB	NR	Inter frequency handover
A6	The neighbor becomes an amount of offset better than SCell	gNB	NR	CA SCell mobility
B1	Neighbor RAT becomes better than absolute threshold	gNB	NR	IRAT to LTE
B2	PCell becomes worse than absolute threshold1 AND neighbor RAT becomes better than another absolute threshold2	gNB	NR	IRAT to LTE

needs to provide measurement gaps to the UE to transition frequencies to measure inter-frequency/inter-band neighbor cells.

I.2.6.1.4 Radio Link Failure Scenarios

The UE monitors specific DL reference signals (CSI-RS) to maintain link status. The network performs similar functions based on reference signal (SRS) transmissions from the UE. Apart from the L1 reference signals, L2 and L3 metrics are also measured to determine the proper functioning of the DL and UL for the UE.

RLF triggers	**Layer**
T310 expiry – measures the PDCCH BLER	L1
Unsuccessful beam failure recovery (BFR) procedure	L1
RACH failure	L2
RLC failure: AM DRB maximum retransmission exceeded	L2
T304 timer expiry: handover failure	L3
RRC reconfiguration failure	L3

Note that for a UE in DC (dual connectivity state), both the PCell (primary component carrier) as part of the Master Cell Group (MCG) and the PSCell or SCell associated with the SCG require radio link maintenance. When radio link failure (RLF) is declared on the PCell, it will trigger an RRC reestablishment procedure. RLF declared on the SCG will trigger a failure, and the connection continues with only the MCG until the SCG is reestablished.

I.2.6.2 Connected Mode Mobility – NSA Option 3 Family

Option 3 network architecture has the LTE as the MCG and NR as SCG as part of the DC operations. The anchor is always the LTE network in idle mode, and the UE typically enters the connected mode in LTE only. Then, based on the availability of the NR network, it adds the NR as SCG to the UE's RRC connection. This form of DC with LTE as the MCG and NR as SCG is called evolved UMTS terrestrial radio access (EUTRA) NR dual connectivity (EN-DC). EUTRA refers to the formal term used for LTE, and NR is the 5G new radio. The later versions of the 3GPP standards Release-17 and beyond allow for direct RRC connection establishment with both MCG and SCG, which was not supported in the earlier versions. The typical sequence for EN-DC operation is captured next. Note that this mode of operation was supported when the networks have large LTE footprints already rolled out and incremental NR cells are added to the network. See Table I.2.6.2 for the transition event for LTE+NR EN-DC NSA mode of operation along with the configuring node and the purpose for the these event triggers.

1) Establish LTE RRC connection: The UE establishes an RRC connection on LTE. The UE may or may not be in NR coverage, and the network triggers measurement of the IRAT NR to determine if NR can be added as SCG to the RRC connection.
2) NR addition as SCG: UE moves into NR coverage, meets the B1 NR trigger, and reports this to the network via LTE. The network adds the appropriate NR cell as SCG.
3) LTE mobility: The UE's mobility will result in the UE requiring changing the LTE anchor cell while retaining the same gNB as SCG (LTE events A3/A4/A5 are used to determine the LTE cell change required).
4) NR mobility: UE mobility may require the NR cell to be changed while retaining the same LTE anchor. These are captured by NR-based measurements, primarily NR A2 events and LTE B2 events.
5) SCG release: The UE may move out of NR coverage (NR event A2), or the throughput no longer requires the UE to keep the SCG active. The network releases the SCG under these conditions.
6) LTE and NR mobility: UE mobility can require both LTE and NR cells to be changed. This can be performed either by first transitioning to LTE-only operation and then adding NR to the target LTE cell, or by providing both LTE and NR target configurations and having the UE transition in EN-DC mode from source LTE + NR to target LTE + NR operation.

Note that for NR acquisition in EN-DC mode, explicit RACH procedures on NR are required to both synchronize with the NR network and determine proper DL and UL channel acquisition in connected mode, and the NR channel quality information (CQI) must be reported before the UE is scheduled for traffic on NR.

I.2.6.2.1 NSA Mobility – Measurement Events

Table I.2.6.2 LTE+NR EN-DC NSA mode transition events (reference from 3GPP TS 38.331).

		Use case in NSA targeting NR cells		
Event	**Trigger definition**	**Configured by**	**RAT of object**	**Purpose**
A1	The serving cell becomes better than an absolute threshold	Not typically used		
A2	The serving cell becomes worse than an absolute threshold	gNB	NR	NR cell removal
A3	The neighbor cell becomes offset better than Pell/PSCell	gNB	NR	NR cell change
A4	The neighbor cell becomes better than an absolute threshold	gNB	NR	Add NR SCell in CA
A5	Pell/PSCell becomes worse than absolute threshold1, and the neighbor becomes better than absolute threshold2	gNB	NR	NR PSCell change
A6	Neighbor becomes an amount of offset than SCell	gNB	NR	Change NR CA SCell
B1	Neighbor RAT becomes better than absolute threshold	eNB	NR	Add NR PSCell
B2	PCell becomes worse than absolute threshold1 AND neighbor RAT becomes better than another absolute threshold2	Not typically used		

I.2.6.3 Summary

- Idle mode mobility differs between NSA and SA modes because NSA relies on LTE idle procedures and in SA the procedures are based on NR RRC parameters.
- In connected mode mobility for option 3 (NSA), EN-DC addition, modification, and release require that the UE performs RACH to synchronize with the gNB.
- There are six intra-system measurement events – A1 through A6 – and two inter-system measurement events – B1 and B2 – in both NSA and SA modes.

References

1. 3GPP Standards

3GPP TS 38.300: NR; Overall description; Stage 2: This document provides an overall description of 5G NR, including the architecture, mobility procedures, and operational aspects. It is the key reference for understanding how mobility is managed in NR.

3GPP TS 38.331: NR; Radio resource control (RRC) protocol specification: This document specifies the RRC procedures for mobility management in NR, including connection setup, handover procedures, and cell reselection.

3GPP TS 38.304: NR; UE procedures in idle mode and connected mode: It defines the mobility procedures for UEs in both idle and connected modes, focusing on how the UE handles cell reselection, handover, and paging.

3GPP TS 38.133: NR; Requirements for support of radio resource management: This document outlines the requirements for mobility, including measurements, thresholds, and handover conditions.

3GPP TS 37.340: NR; Multi-connectivity; Stage 2: This document covers the mobility aspects related to dual connectivity, which involves UEs connected to both LTE and NR networks simultaneously, also known as EN-DC (E-UTRAN NR Dual Connectivity).

2. Textbooks and Academic References

Dahlman, E., Parkvall, S., and Sköld, J. (2021). *5G NR: The Next Generation Wireless Access Technology*. Academic Press. This comprehensive book provides insights into the fundamentals of NR, including a detailed discussion of mobility operations and handover procedures.

Rodriguez, J. (2015). *Fundamentals of 5G Mobile Networks*. Wiley. A textbook that includes chapters on mobility management in 5G, providing an overview of key mobility procedures and challenges.

Marsch, P., Bulakci, Ö., and Queseth, O. (2018). *5G System Design: Architectural and Functional Considerations and Long Term Research*. Wiley. This book delves into the 5G system architecture, including detailed discussions on NR mobility operations and multi-RAT (radio access technology) mobility.

3. Research Papers and Journals

Gómez, G., et al. (2020). "Mobility Enhancements in 5G New Radio: A Survey on Standards, Challenges, and Future Trends" in *IEEE Communications Surveys & Tutorials*. This paper surveys the mobility enhancements introduced in 5G NR, comparing them to LTE and highlighting future trends.

Zhou, Y., et al. (2019). "Handover and Mobility Management in 5G HetNets: A Comprehensive Survey" in *IEEE Communications Surveys & Tutorials*. This paper discusses handover strategies, mobility management in heterogeneous networks (HetNets), and the specific enhancements introduced in NR.

Jiang, W., et al. (2021). "Mobility Management in 5G and Beyond: Challenges and Solutions" in *IEEE Wireless Communications*. A detailed exploration of the challenges in 5G NR mobility and proposed solutions, focusing on handover optimization and cross-layer coordination.

4. Industry White Papers

Qualcomm (2020). "5G NR Mobility: Optimizing Seamless Mobility in 5G Networks." This white paper discusses the key innovations and optimizations in NR mobility, including handover procedures and improvements over LTE.

Ericsson (2019). "Mobility Management in 5G NR Networks." Ericsson's white paper explains how mobility management is handled in 5G NR, detailing various handover scenarios, measurement reporting, and multi-connectivity strategies.

Nokia (2021). "Handover and Mobility Solutions for 5G Networks." This white paper focuses on the handover and mobility strategies for 5G NR, providing insights into both stand-alone (SA) and non-stand-alone (NSA) deployment models.

5. Conference Papers

Mezzavilla, M., et al. (2018). "Mobility Management in 5G NR: Challenges and Opportunities" in *IEEE ICC*. This paper presents an in-depth discussion of the challenges associated with NR mobility and the opportunities for optimization, particularly in high-frequency (mmWave) deployments.

Lee, S., et al. (2020). "5G NR Handover Performance in Dense Urban Environments" in *IEEE VTC*. This paper analyzes the handover performance of NR in dense urban environments, focusing on challenges like interference and mobility robustness.

Martinez, I., et al. (2019). "Mobility Solutions for Ultra-Dense 5G Networks" in *IEEE Globecom*. This paper explores mobility strategies for ultra-dense 5G networks, including mobility management in small cells and mmWave networks.

6. Technical Reports

3GPP TR 38.913: Study on scenarios and requirements for next-generation access technologies: This report provides a broader context for 5G, including a discussion of the key scenarios and requirements for mobility in NR.

3GPP TR 37.801: Study on new radio (NR) to LTE interworking: This technical report explores how mobility is managed between NR and LTE networks, especially in the context of dual connectivity and handover scenarios.

I.2.7

NR Protocols

I.2.7.1 Introduction

The new radio (NR) protocol stack is very similar to the long-term evolution (LTE) protocol layers. To aid fast packet processing due to the shorter time intervals compared to LTE, some changes are introduced. Support is introduced to perform just-in-time packet forming, and due to the large payload sizes supported, packets are allowed to be processed as they are received without having to receive the full payload. Some functions are moved between the radio link control (RLC) and packet data convergence protocol (PDCP) layers to enable higher reliability. Also, another layer called the service data adaptation protocol (SDAP) layer is introduced for better handling of quality of service (QoS) flow by separating the radio access network (RAN) and core network functions, in addition to supporting quick QoS flow activation. The SDAP layer is applicable only when the user equipment (UE) is operating in 5G NR standalone (SA) mode.

The RAN network is associated with the core network with the evolved packet system (EPS)-bearer ID when connected to the evolved packet core (EPC) in non-stand-alone (NSA) mode and SDAP-config when connected to the 5GC core (SA mode). In the case of NSA, the bearer ID is unique within the UE, implying that the master cell group (MCG) data radio bearer (DRB) cannot use the same ID as a split DRB. Note that for a split DRB, the same ID is used for both the MCG and the secondary cell group (SCG). Figure I.2.7.1 illustrates the protocol layers supported in NR and the interactions involved between the NR protocols, as well as with the physical layer and the higher layer to exchange signaling and data packets.

The radio resource control (RRC) layer supports broadcast of system information, RRC connection control, inter-radio access technology (RAT) mobility, and measurement configuration and reporting. RRC connection control supports several functions, including paging, initial security activation, establishment/modification/suspension/resumption/release of RRC connection, RRC connection mobility, establishment/modification/release of resource block (RBs) carrying user data (DRBs), radio configuration control, and recovery from radio link failure.

Mobile Communication Systems for Private Networks, First Edition. Srinivasan Balasubramanian.

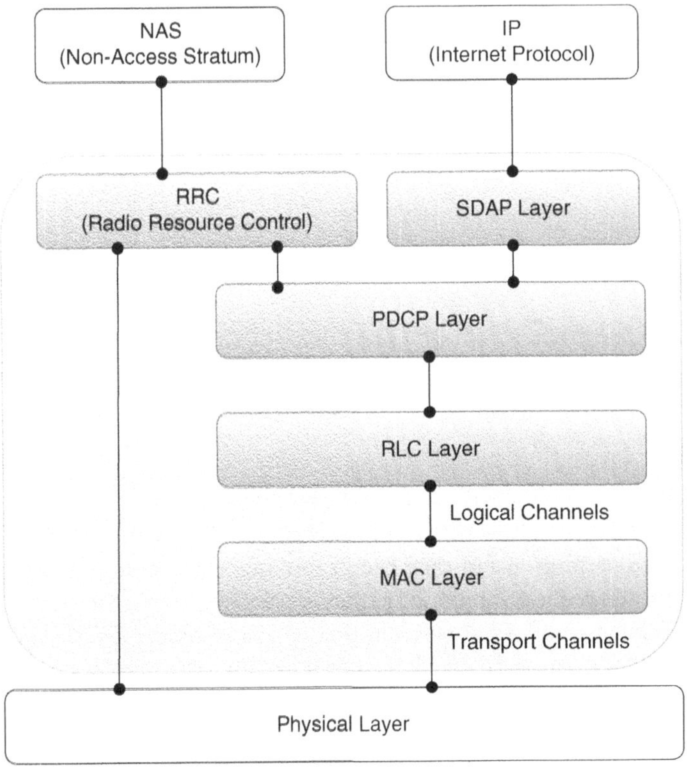

Figure I.2.7.1 NR protocols: high-level view.

I.2.7.2 NSA Option 3 Mode of Operation

Revisiting some of the terminology, clarifying the concepts of PCell, SCell, PSCell, and sPCell.

Dual connectivity terminology	Description
PCell	Primary cell: This applies for carrier aggregation (CA). One cell is used to initiate initial access. This cell is called the PCell. The PCell is the anchor cell in the MCG.
SCell	Secondary cell: This applies to CA. The PCell under the MCG and the SCell under the MCG are combined by using CA.
MCG	Master cell group: This applies to dual connectivity (DC) and the anchor RAT/node that is initially established before adding the SCG. The MCG itself can support multiple cells as CA.
SCG	Secondary cell group: This applies to DC and is added through interactions with MCG. The SCG itself can support multiple cells, such as CA.
PSCell	Primary cell in the SCG. This is the cell on which the SCG is initially established and acts as the anchor for the SCG. The PSCell and SCell under the SCG are also combined through CA.
sPCell	Special cell: This is more of a nomenclature for ease of representation. Since most signaling messages are sent only on the PCell and PSCell, the concept of sPCell is used to represent both together. sPCell = PCell + PSCell

In NSA option 3, the UE will not use the NR RRC connection setup procedure. In dual connectivity mode, LTE acts as the MCG and adds 5G NR as the SCG. The UE has dual connectivity with LTE and NR and supports mobility activities such as handover and primary and secondary cells (PSCell) changes. The UE camps on LTE cells, and for NR addition, the UE needs to search for and measure NR cells. The measurement report of an NR cell can be sent via the LTE signaling radio bearer (SRB). After NR is added, the SRB on directly NR can be supported to enable NR-level (SCG) mobility. This is referred to as signaling radio bearer 3 (SRB3). Note that SRB0, SRB1, and SRB2 are supported on LTE.

I.2.7.3 5G NR RRC States: SA Option 2

SA option 2, UE support the complete NR RRC state machine to operate only with NR in a self-contained manner without requiring the LTE anchor. It supports seamless mobility between NR and LTE using inter-RAT (IRAT) handovers in connected mode and reselection in idle and inactive modes. The RRC inactive state is introduced in 5G NR and LTE to support ultra-low latency applications that require quick reactivation into connected mode. Although introduced in LTE, the inactive mode is not supported commercially. Figure I.2.7.2 illustrates an overview of the UE RRC state machine and state transitions in NR. A UE can have only one RRC state in NR at a time. Figure I.2.7.3 illustrates an overview of the UE state machine and state transitions in NR, as well as the mobility procedures supported by combinations of NR and 5th generation core (5GC), evolved universal terrestrial radio access (E-UTRA) and evolved packet core (EPC), and E-UTRA and 5GC.

I.2.7.4 PDCP Duplication

PDCP PDUs can be duplicated for transmission over two RLC bearers. These RLC bearers can be on the PCell and SCell across the MCG and SCG component carriers (CC). This was introduced to address critical reliability and latency requirements for applications that require ultra reliable low

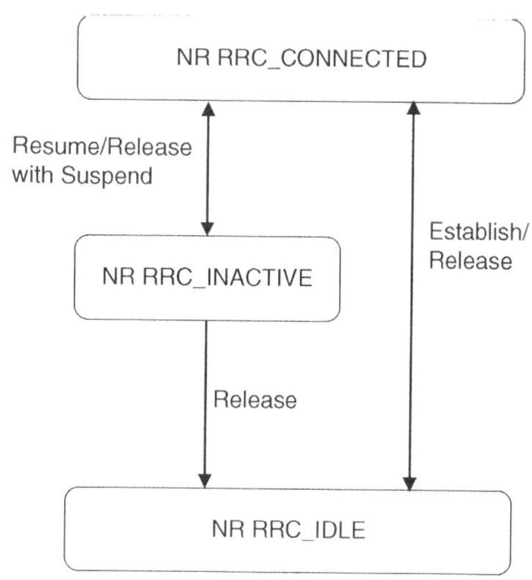

Figure I.2.7.2 UE state machine and state transitions in NR (from 3GPP TS 38.331, figure 4.2.1-1).

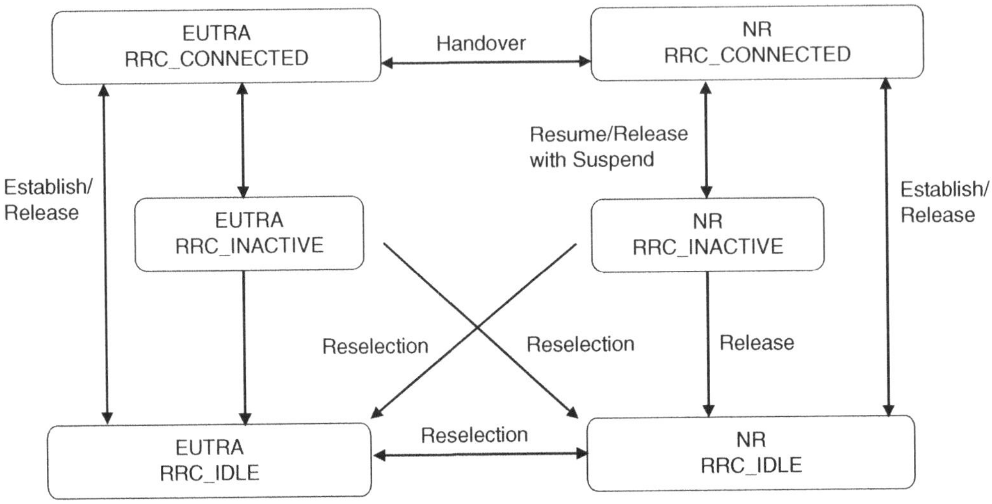

Figure I.2.7.3 UE state machine and state transitions between NR/5GC, E-UTRA/EPC, and E-UTRA/5GC (from 3GPP TS 38.331, figure 4.2.1-2).

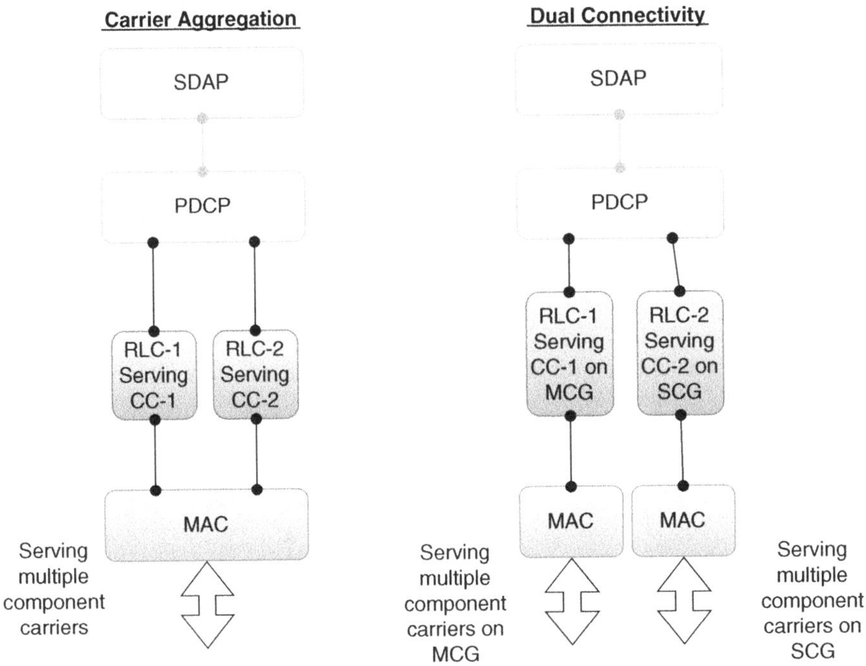

Figure I.2.7.4 PDCP duplication.

latency communication (URLLC) support. Note that the duplication may be selectively applied based on the active QoS flows and the real-time radio conditions. Figure I.2.7.4 illustrates protocol layer configurations where the PDCP packets can be duplicated. The first approach is supporting multiple RLC instances in a given component carrier (CC) and second approach is by sending the PDCP packets over independent CCs with each supporting its own RLC / MAC (medium access control) instances.

CA Case: The packets are duplicated, and user data at the MAC layer is transmitted via different CCs and is performed using a single MAC entity serving both the PCell and SCells.

Dual Connectivity Case: The RLC bearers are mapped to different cell groups (i.e. MCG and SCG). This case means that the MCG and SCG will be served by independent radio nodes, and the duplicated PDUs are transmitted via two separate MAC entities.

I.2.7.5 SDAP Layer

SDAP is configured by RRC to map QoS flows to DRBs when connected to 5GC and operating in NR-only mode (as in NR SA mode option 2). The major functions of SDAP include mapping between a QoS flow and a DRB for both downlink (DL) and upperlink (UL), and marking the QoS flow ID in both DL and UL packets. One of the key functions introduced is the reflective QoS flow to DRB mapping concept for the UL SDAP data PDUs, which allows for quick activation via the user plane without requiring control signaling exchange between the UE and the network. This assumes that the radio bearer is already established and only the packet filters to map to the flow of the established QoS bearer are supported from the SDAP layer. This addresses short bursts from the UE that require QoS support to be provided without the heavy lifting needed to establish the QoS flow. An SDAP protocol data unit (PDU) consists of an SDAP service data unit (SDU) (typically an IP packet), concatenated with SDAP header. The SDAP header consists of the following fields.

- SDAP Layer Configuration: The RRC protocol is responsible for configuring the SDAP layer, which has the flexibility to function with or without header information.
- Header Size: The SDAP layer's header is 1 byte in size.
- Header Inclusion: In the DL transmission through SDAP, the header information is incorporated when there is a reflective QoS provision. Conversely, if no reflective QoS is present, header information is not added.
- Header Addition Points: Adding header information can occur at the access stratum (AS) layer or the non-access stratum (NAS) layer, contingent on reflective QoS.

  One LU Packet Filter (Derived from the LD packet)
  QFI (QoS Flow Identifier)
  Precedence value (the order in which a QoS rule shall be evaluated):

- *RDI (Reflective QoS Flow to DRB Mapping Indication)*: This 1-bit information signals the UE to implement reflective QoS at the AS layer. When set to 1, it signifies that the QoS flow to DRB mapping has been updated by the UE.
- *RQI (Reflective QoS Indication)*: This 1-bit data instructs the UE to apply reflective QoS at the NAS layer. A value of one indicates that the UE has informed the NAS layer about updates in the service data flow (SDF) to QoS flow mapping rules.
- *QFI (QoS Flow Identifier)*: A 6-bit value that is integral to both RDI and RQI. It facilitates the comprehension of the mapping between QoS flows and DRBs.

The PDU session and QoS flow are identified by the gNB by a GTP-U header, which stands for general packet radio service (GPRS) tunneling protocol—user plane. In the gNB, the SDAP layer maps it into a specific DRB (Figure I.2.7.5). If the header is used for reflective QoS, the SDAP layer specifies the QoS flow associated with the packet. By using this information, the UE can decode the mapping between the QoS flow and DRB for uplink transmission. In the DL, the QoS flow under the PDU session is identified using an identity in the GTP-U header called the GTP-U tunnel end point identifier (TEID).

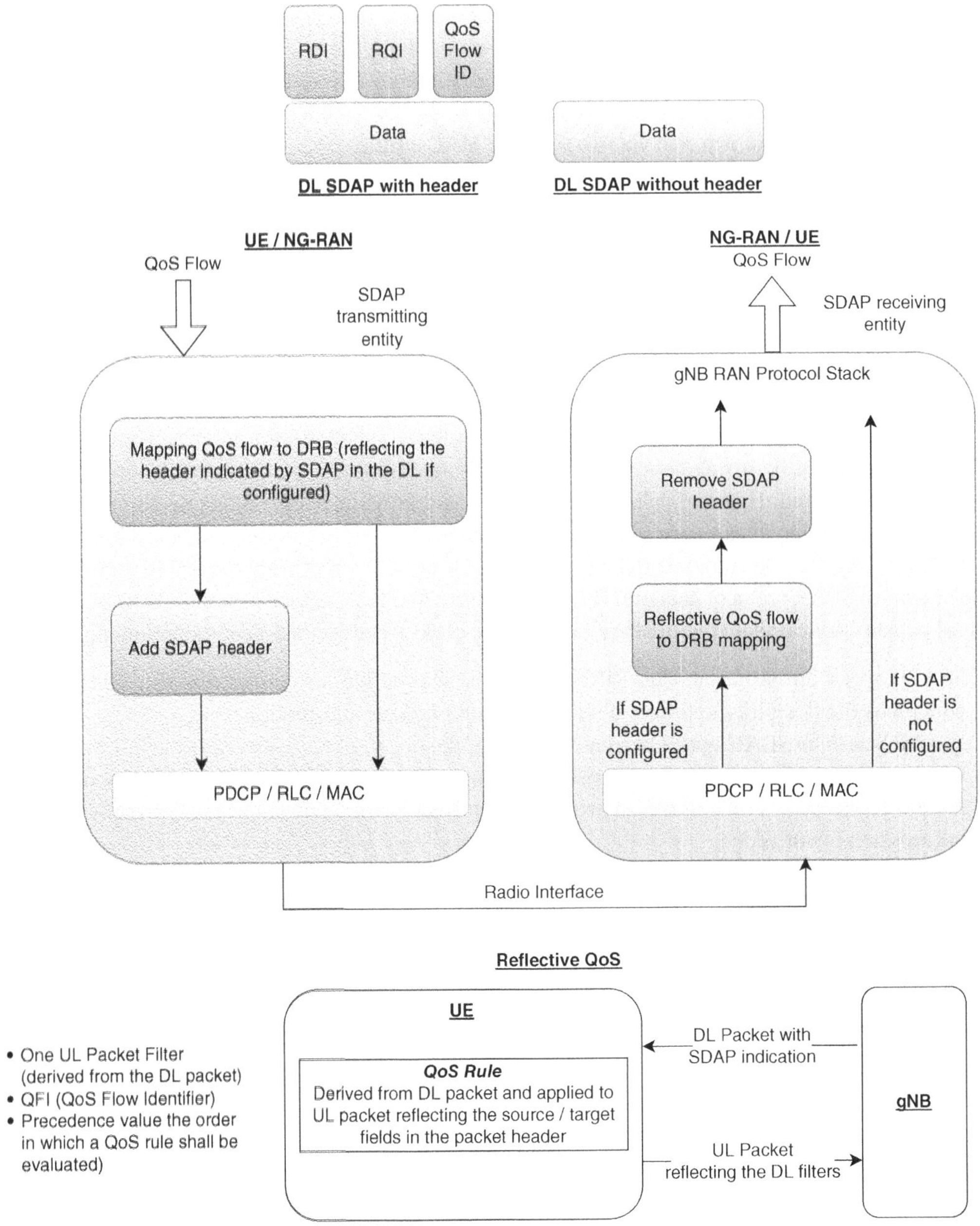

Figure I.2.7.5 NR SDAP layer.

Reflective QoS reduces signaling overhead during QoS setup. It occurs when the UE maps UL user plane traffic to QoS flows without QoS rules provided by the session management function (SMF). The UE indicates support for reflective QoS for every PDU session during the PDU session establishment procedure when establishing in 5GS or transferring from EPS without N26, and during the PDU session modification procedure when transferring from EPS with N26. The UE creates UE-derived QoS rules for the uplink traffic based on the received DL traffic. It is applied on a per-packet basis for IP or ethernet sessions.

I.2.7.6 PDCP Functions

The main services and functions of the PDCP are similar to LTE. Key new PDCP functions include PDCP split bearer functionality for NSA mode operations, reordering and duplicate detection, and PDCP PDU duplication. Figure I.2.7.6 provides the illustration from 3GPP specifications showing the breakdown and the sequence of the functional blocks within the PDCP layer from both the transmitter and receiver perspectives.

I.2.7.7 RLC Functions

5G NR RLC functions are similar to LTE. They include the transfer of upper layer PDUs, in accordance with three transmission modes: assured mode (AM), unassured mode (UM), and transparent mode (TM); error correction through automatic repeat request (ARQ) (AM data side transfer); (re) segmentation and reassembly of SDUs; and RLC reestablishment. There are a few modifications

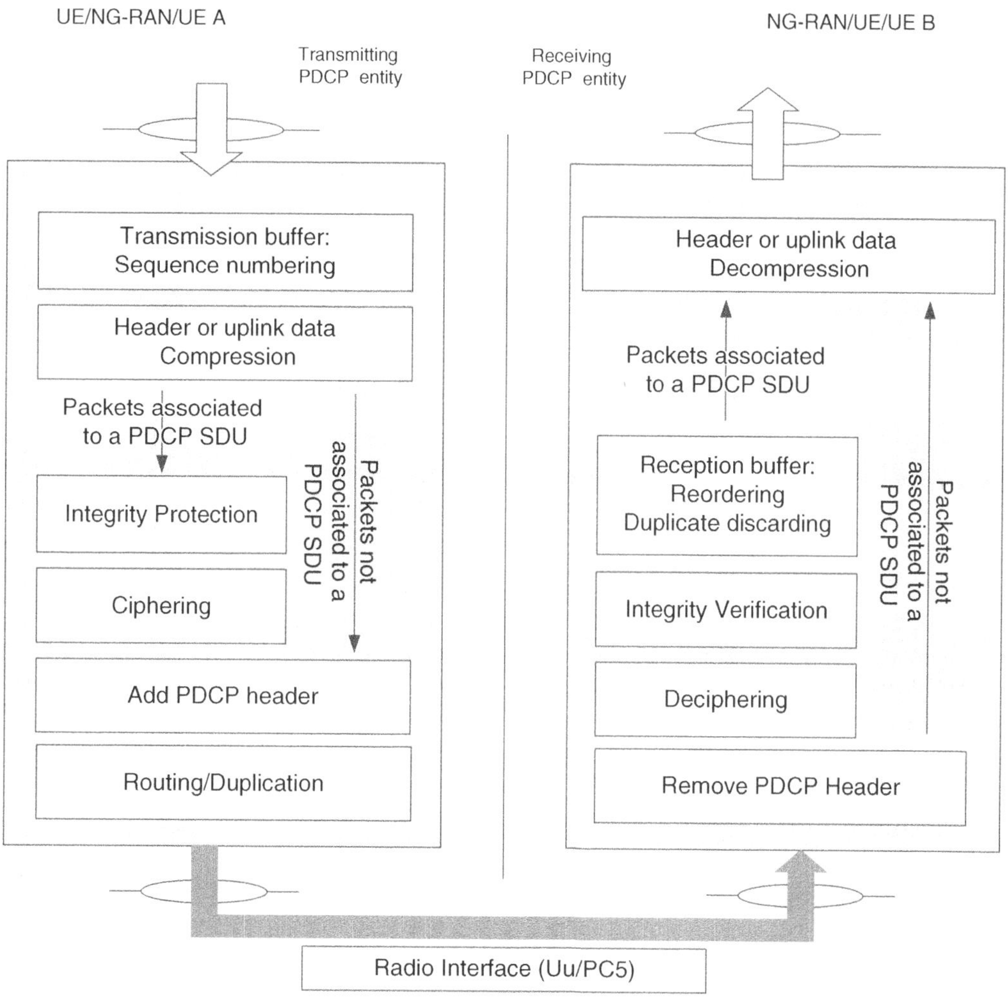

Figure I.2.7.6 PDCP layer functional view (from 3GPP TS 38.323, figure 4.2.2-1).

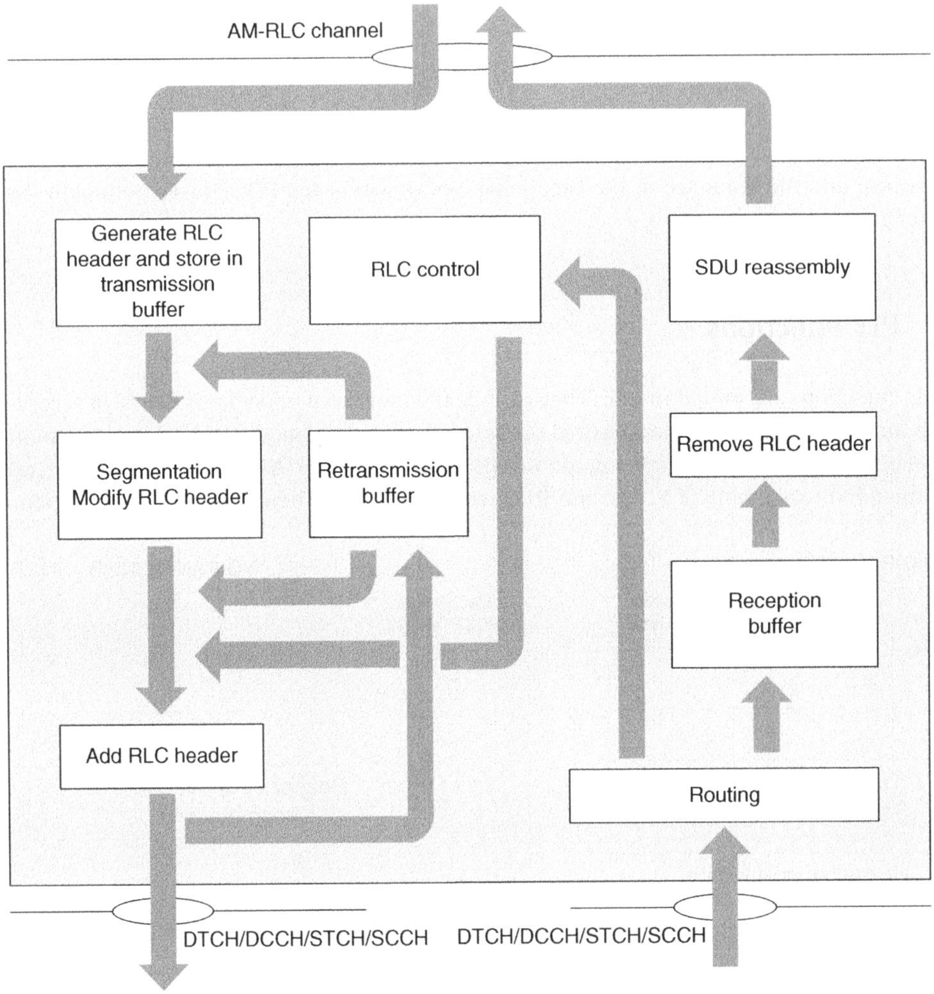

Figure I.2.7.7 Model of an acknowledged mode entity (from 3GPP TS 38.322, figure 4.2.1.3.1-1).

from the LTE RLC to support higher throughput, quicker packet formation for transmission, and improved processing at the receiver. New in 5G NR, RLC does not support SDU-level reordering and allows the PDCP layer to receive out-of-order packets. This allows for packet duplication at the PDCP layer and processes the packets as they are received, independent of the RLC instance over which a given PDCP sequence-numbered packet is received. NR RLC does not support concatenation (concatenation of RLC PDUs is performed in MAC). Like LTE, transparent, unacknowledged, and acknowledged modes are supported in NR as well. See Figures I.2.7.7–I.2.7.9.

I.2.7.8 MAC Layer

5G NR MAC functions, similar to LTE MAC layer, perform mapping between logical and transport channel operations. A new MAC PDU structure is introduced in 5G NR to improve latency.

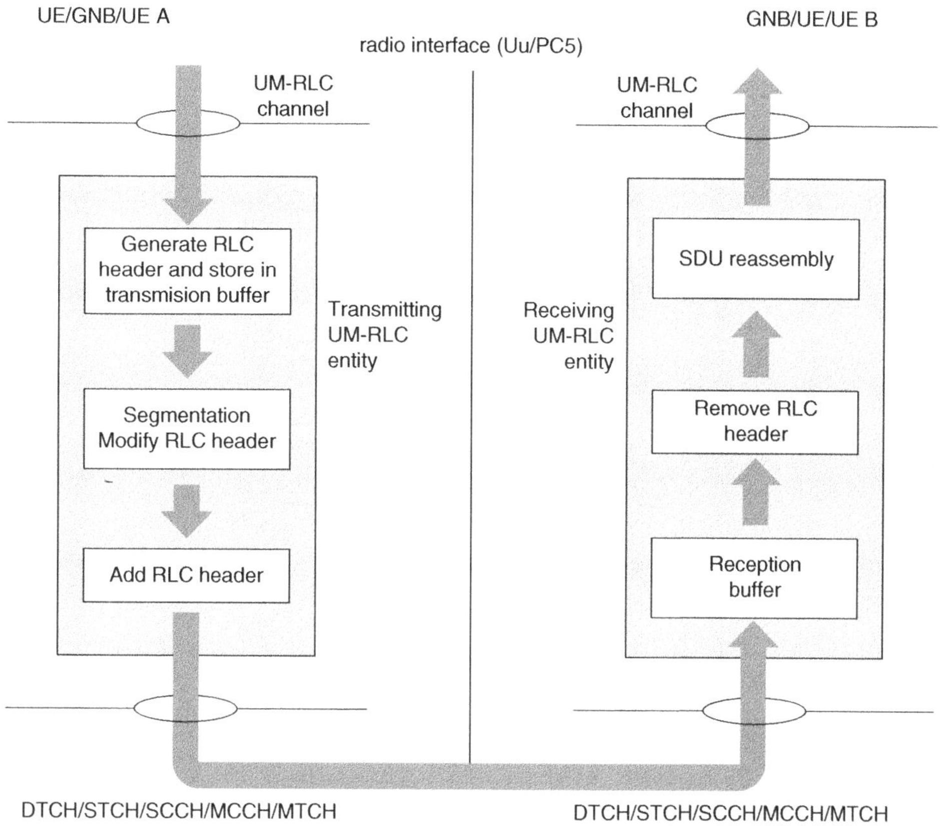

Figure I.2.7.8 Model of two unacknowledged mode peer entities (from 3GPP TS 38.322, figure 4.2.1.2.1-1).

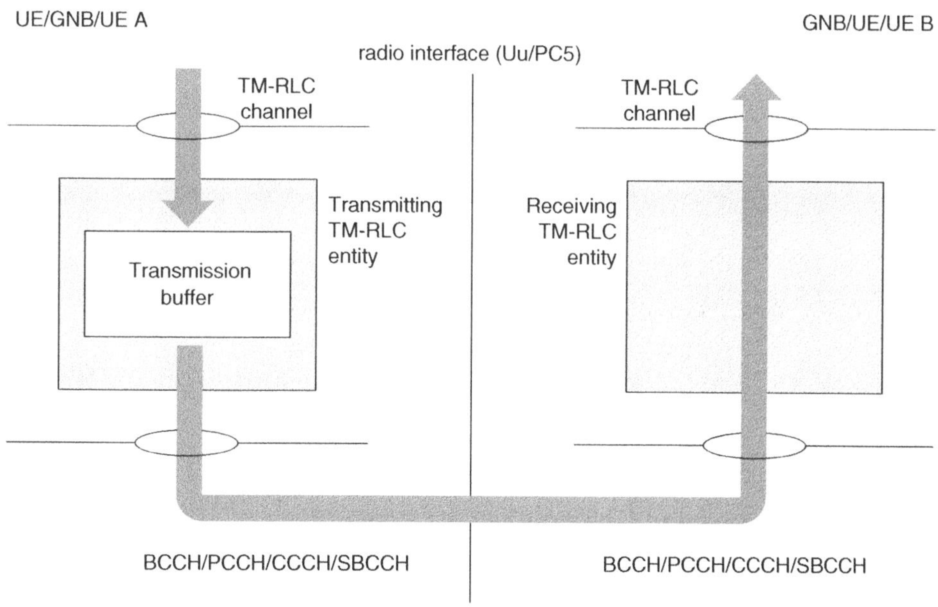

Figure I.2.7.9 Model of two transparent mode peer entities (from 3GPP TS 38.322, figure 4.2.1.1.1-1).

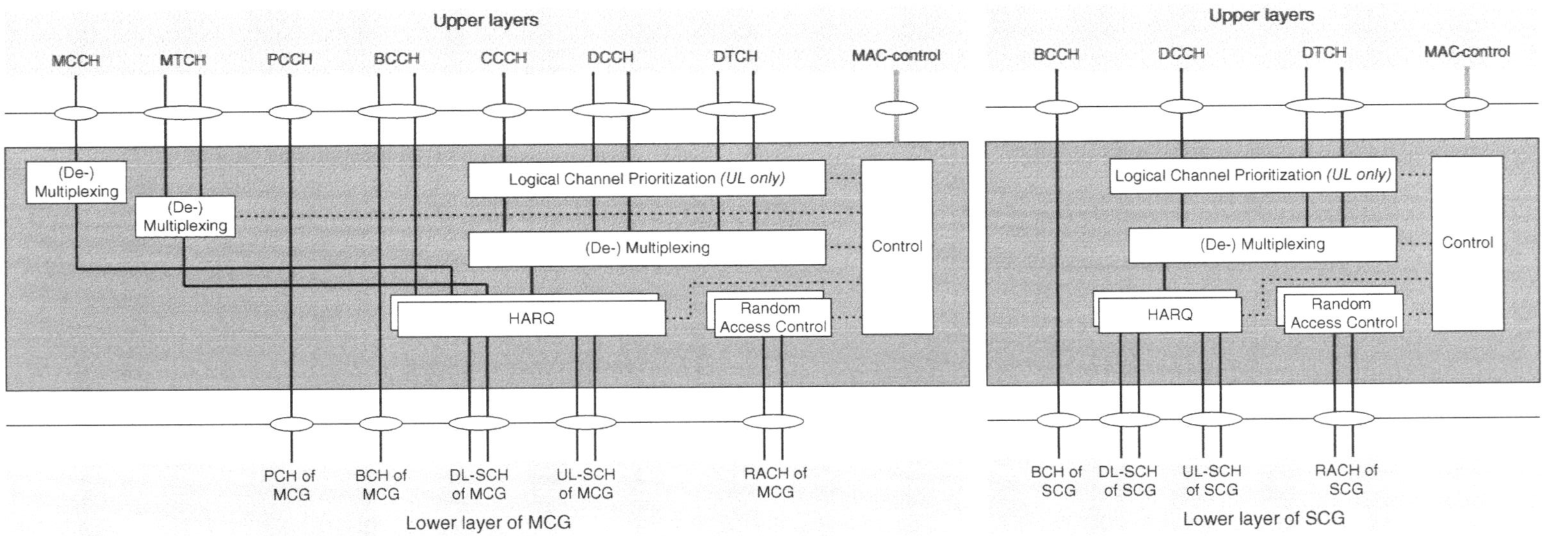

Figure I.2.7.10 MAC structure overview with two MAC entities (from 3GPP TS 38.321, figure 4.2.2-2).

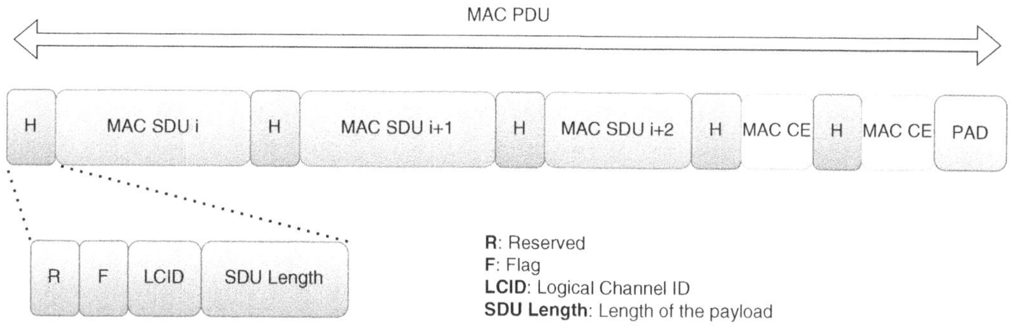

Figure I.2.7.11 MAC PDU.

5G NR MAC functions like LTE, including multiplexing of MAC SDUs, logical channel prioritization, scheduling, and hybrid ARQ (HARQ) procedures. The mux/demux functions are updated to support just-in-time packet forming, with the individual packet headers and payload grouped together, unlike in LTE. The HARQ procedures are updated to accommodate self-contained slots and the lack of HARQ feedback channels in the DL. See Figure I.2.7.11 for the structure of the MAC PDU.

New MAC functions include beam management and support for multiple numerologies. Although beams were supported in LTE, they are not defined with the sophistication in NR. Additionally, LTE supports only 15 KHz SubCarrier Spacing (SCS), while NR supports 15 KHz, 30 KHz, 60 KHz, 120 KHz, and 240 KHz, based on the spectrum and channel(s) of operation. See the NR physical layer section to see the logical channel to transport channel mapping.

Figure I.2.7.10 illustrates one structure for the MAC entities when MCG and SCG are configured.

MAC PDU structure: MAC subheaders are placed immediately in front of the corresponding MAC SDUs, MAC control elements (CEs), or padding. This allows the MAC layer to push each processed MAC SDU toward physical layer (PHY) prior to the completion of the whole MAC PDU. The MAC CEs are included toward the end to allow for the time required for computation to be performed for inclusion within the MAC PDU.

I.2.7.9 Summary

This chapter provides the details of the NR protocol layers, covering the L2 and L3 layers of the radio protocol stack. It includes both the control and user planes. The focus is on showing the key differences relative to the LTE protocol layers. Most of the changes are in the user plane to accommodate just-in-time packet forming, given the smaller slot sizes in NR compared to LTE.

References

1. Physical Layer Protocols

3GPP TS 38.211: NR; Physical channels and modulation: Defines the physical channels and their modulation schemes, including how data is carried over the physical layer.

3GPP TS 38.212: NR; Multiplexing and channel coding: Describes how different channels are multiplexed and encoded for error protection and data transmission.

3GPP TS 38.213: NR; Physical layer procedures for control: Specifies the physical layer procedures for control channels like physical downlink control channel (PDCCH).

3GPP TS 38.214: NR; Physical layer procedures for data: Describes how the physical layer handles data channels like physical downlink shared channel (PDSCH) and physical uplink shared channel (PUSCH).

3GPP TS 38.215: NR; Physical layer measurements: Defines the measurement procedures for the NR physical layer, which are critical for mobility, link adaptation, and scheduling decisions.

2. MAC Layer Protocol

3GPP TS 38.321: NR; Medium Access Control (MAC) protocol specification: Describes the MAC layer procedures, including scheduling, hybrid automatic repeat request (HARQ), and logical channel prioritization. It handles mapping between logical channels and transport channels and manages the access to physical resources.

3. RLC Layer Protocol

3GPP TS 38.322: NR; Radio Link Control (RLC) protocol specification: Defines the RLC procedures, including segmentation, reassembly, error correction through automatic repeat request (ARQ), and in-sequence delivery. It sits between the MAC and PDCP layers and ensures reliable data transfer.

4. PDCP Layer Protocol

3GPP TS 38.323: NR; Packet Data Convergence Protocol (PDCP) specification: Describes the PDCP functions such as header compression (ROHC), ciphering, integrity protection, and in-sequence delivery of data. PDCP plays a key role in ensuring secure and efficient data transfer.

5. SDAP Layer Protocol

3GPP TS 37.324: NR; Service Data Adaptation Protocol (SDAP) specification: SDAP is responsible for quality of service (QoS) mapping between QoS flows and data radio bearers. This layer is unique to 5G NR and ensures that QoS requirements are met for different services.

6. RRC Layer Protocol

3GPP TS 38.331: NR; Radio Resource Control (RRC) protocol specification: Defines the RRC layer, which is responsible for managing the connection states of the UE, including idle and connected modes. RRC handles mobility procedures, paging, and the setup of radio bearers and manages control signaling between the UE and the network.

7. NAS Protocol

3GPP TS 24.501: NR; Non-Access-Stratum (NAS) protocol for 5G: The NAS protocol operates between the UE and the 5G core network (5GC). It manages session establishment, authentication, security control, and mobility at a higher level than the RRC. It also handles registration, deregistration, and tracking area updates.

8. Core Network Protocols

3GPP TS 23.501: System Architecture for the 5G System (5GS): Provides an overview of the architecture of the 5G system, including its interfaces and protocol interactions.

3GPP TS 23.502: Procedures for the 5G System (5GS): Describes the network procedures, including mobility, session management, and interworking with LTE networks.

3GPP TS 23.503: Policy and Charging Control Framework for 5G: Outlines the framework for policy control and charging in the 5G system, including QoS and network slicing support.

9. 5G NR Dual Connectivity and Multi-RAT Protocols

3GPP TS 37.340: NR; Multi-connectivity; Stage 2: Specifies the protocol architecture for dual connectivity in 5G NR, which allows a UE to be connected to both LTE and NR (EN-DC) simultaneously.

3GPP TS 38.401: NR; NG-RAN; Architecture description: Defines the architecture of the NG-RAN, including how NR interacts with the core network and other radio access technologies.

10. Higher Layer Protocols and Network Slicing

3GPP TS 23.501: System Architecture for the 5G System: This standard introduces network slicing, allowing multiple virtual networks with different QoS requirements to be created on top of the same physical infrastructure.

3GPP TS 28.531: Management and orchestration; 5G Network Resource Model: Defines the management and orchestration aspects, including support for slicing, resource allocation, and monitoring.

11. Security Protocols

3GPP TS 33.501: Security architecture and procedures for 5G system: This document covers security protocols for 5G, including authentication, encryption, and integrity protection for both the access and core networks.

12. Transport Layer (NG and Xn Interfaces)

3GPP TS 38.420: NG-RAN; Xn interface; General aspects and principles: Defines the Xn interface used for communication between gNodeBs (gNBs), enabling inter-cell handovers and coordination.

3GPP TS 38.425: NG-RAN; NG interface; General aspects and principles: Defines the NG interface between the gNodeB and the 5G Core (NG-C and NG-U), handling control and user plane interactions.

I.3

Standards

This chapter captures a high-level view of the different standards bodies, their working group structures, and some of the relevant specifications that are employed to design, develop, and deploy enterprise private networks.

I.3.1 3GPP

Visit www.3gpp.org, where all the working group information, specifications, and other ongoing activities are captured. 3GPP covers the long-term evolution (LTE) and new radio (NR) specifications, the basis for 4G, 5G, and, moving forward, 6G definitions. Given that the LTE and NR realizations for the macro network are used directly for private networks, most, if not all, of the 3GPP specifications apply to private networks as well. The current private network deployments are based on Release 15 and employ definitions from all layers. Release 16 has provided definitions for non-public networks (NPN), which are currently being studied and awaiting market drivers for their use.

I.3.1.1 3GPP Working Groups

Figure I.3.1 provides the list of working groups in 3GPP along with the hierarchical relationships of these groups. 3GPP creates study and work items that are agreed upon, and once created, contributions are submitted against these study and work items.

I.3.1.2 LTE Specifications

Table I.3.1 provides a listing of the 3GPP LTE specifications that are relevant for private network design, development, and deployment.

I.3.1.3 NR Specifications

Table I.3.2 provides a listing of the 3GPP NR specifications that are relevant for private network design, development, and deployment.

Mobile Communication Systems for Private Networks, First Edition. Srinivasan Balasubramanian.

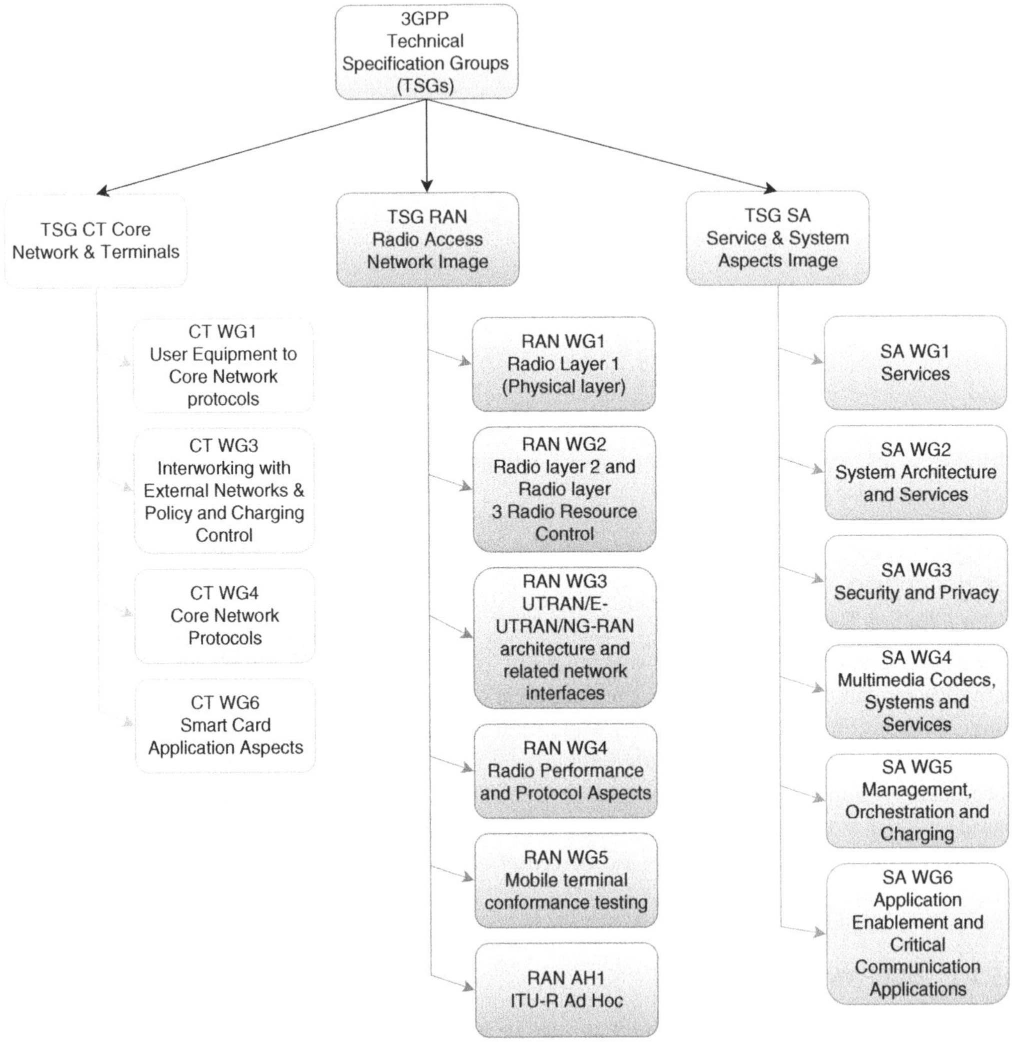

Figure I.3.1 3GPP working groups.

I.3.2 WinnForum Specifications for Shared Spectrum Usage

The primary focus at this time from this forum will be on the citizens broadband radio service (CBRS) working group for private network deployments, which includes the spectrum access system (SAS), environmental sensing capability (ESC), and eNB/gNB/CPE (where CPE stands for "customer premise equipment") rules for acquiring spectrum for its operations.

Wireless Innovation Forum (WinnForum) actively promotes and develops standards and specifications for shared spectrum access, particularly in the context of cognitive radio and dynamic spectrum access. It has published a set of specifications and documents to address various aspects of shared spectrum access. The key WinnForum specification areas include:

1) **SAS Specifications:** The SAS is a critical component in the shared spectrum access framework. WinnForum has worked on specifications related to SAS, which are used to manage the allocation and sharing of spectrum resources in the CBRS in the United States. These specifications

Table I.3.1 Some of the relevant 3GPP LTE specifications.

Specification number	Title
36.101	User equipment (UE) radio transmission and reception
36.104	Base station (BS) radio transmission and reception
36.106	FDD repeater radio transmission and reception
36.116	Relay radio transmission and reception
36.133	Requirements for the support of radio resource management
36.201	LTE physical layer; general description
36.211	Physical channels and modulation
36.212	Multiplexing and channel coding
36.213	Physical layer procedures
36.214	Physical layer measurements
36.216	Physical layer for relaying operation
36.300	Evolved universal terrestrial radio access (E-UTRA) and evolved universal terrestrial radio access network (E-UTRAN); overall description; stage 2
36.302	Services provided by the physical layer
36.304	UE procedures in idle mode
36.306	UE radio-access capabilities
36.321	Medium access control (MAC) protocol specification
36.322	Radio link control (RLC) protocol specification
36.323	Packet data convergence protocol (PDCP) specification
36.331	RRC protocol specification
36.401	E-UTRAN; architecture description
36.410	General aspects and principles of S1
36.411	S1 layer 1
36.412	S1 signaling transport
36.413	S1 application protocol (S1AP)
36.414	S1 data transport
36.420	X2 general aspects and principles
36.421	X2 layer 1
36.422	X2 signaling transport
36.423	X2 application protocol (X2AP)
36.424	X2 data transport
36.440	General aspects and principles for interfaces supporting multimedia broadcast multicast service (MBMS) within E-UTRAN
36.441	Layer 1 for interfaces supporting MBMS within E-UTRAN
36.442	Signaling transport for interfaces supporting MBMS within E-UTRAN
36.443	M2 application protocol (M2AP)
36.444	M3 application protocol (M3AP)
36.445	M1 data transport

(*Continued*)

Table I.3.1 (Continued)

Specification number	Title
36.446	M1 user plane protocol
23.002	Network architecture
23.003	Numbering, addressing, and identification
23.041	Technical realization of cell broadcast service (CBS)
23.122	Non-access-stratum (NAS) functions related to the mobile station (MS) in idle mode
23.203	Policy and charging control architecture
24.301	NAS protocol for evolved packet system (EPS); stage 3
29.118	Mobility management entity (MME) – visitor location register (VLR) SGs interface specification
29.272	EPS; MME; and serving GPRS support node (SGSN) related interfaces based on the diameter protocol
29.274	3GPP EPS; evolved general packet radio service (GPRS) tunneling protocol for control plane (GTPv2-C); stage 3
29.281	GPRS tunneling protocol user plane (GTPv1-U)
32.422	Telecommunication management; subscriber and equipment trace; trace control, and configuration management
37.320	Radio measurement collection for minimization of drive tests (MDT); overall description; stage 2

Table I.3.2 Some of the relevant 3GPP NR specifications.

Specification number	Title
38.101-1	NR; user equipment (UE) radio transmission and reception; part 1: range 1 stand-alone
38.101-2	NR; UE radio transmission and reception; part 2: range 2 stand-alone
38.101-3	NR; UE radio transmission and reception; part 3: range 1 and range 2 interworking operation with other radios
38.104	NR; base station (BS) radio transmission and reception
38.133	NR; requirements for support of radio resource management
38.211	NR; physical channels and modulation
38.212	NR; multiplexing and channel coding
38.213	NR; physical layer procedures for control
38.214	NR; physical layer procedures for data
38.215	R; physical layer measurements
38.300	NR; NR and NG-RAN overall description; stage 2
38.306	NR; UE radio access capabilities
38.321	NR; Medium Access Control (MAC) protocol specification

Table I.3.2 (Continued)

Specification number	Title
38.322	NR; Radio Link Control (RLC) protocol specification
38.323	NR; Packet Data Convergence Protocol (PDCP) specification
38.331	NR; Radio Resource Control (RRC); protocol specification
38.401	NG-RAN; architecture description
38.413	NG-RAN; NG application protocol (NGAP)
38.415	NG-RAN; PDU session user plane protocol
38.423	NG-RAN; Xn application protocol (XnAP)
38.425	NG-RAN; NR user plane protocol
38.463	NG-RAN; E1 application protocol (E1AP)
38.473	NG-RAN; F1 application protocol (F1AP)
37.340	NR; multi-connectivity; overall description; stage 2
37.324	Evolved universal terrestrial radio access (E-UTRA) and NR; service data adaptation protocol (SDAP) specification
24.501	Non-access-stratum (NAS) protocol for 5G system (5GS); stage 3
23.003	Numbering, addressing, and identification
23.501	System architecture for the 5G system (5GS)
23.502	Procedures for the 5G system (5GS)
29.500	5G system; technical realization of service based architecture; stage 3
29.502	5G system; session management services; stage 3
29.503	
29.510	
29.518	

define how SASs should operate and how they should interact with other components of the CBRS ecosystem.

2) **CBRS Rules and Procedures:** WinnForum has developed rules and procedures for the operation of CBRS, which is a prime example of shared spectrum access in the 3.5 GHz band. These rules and procedures include details on how spectrum access is coordinated, how interference is managed, and how priority access licenses (PALs) are granted.
3) **Spectrum Access System Interoperability Specification:** This specification outlines the requirements for interoperability between different SASs operating within the CBRS band. It ensures that SASs from different vendors can work together efficiently to manage spectrum resources.
4) **Environmental Sensing Capability Specifications:** The ESC is a component of the CBRS framework responsible for sensing and detecting the presence of federal radar systems in the 3.5 GHz band. WinnForum has developed specifications for ESCs to ensure accurate radar detection and to avoid harmful interference to incumbent users.
5) **Spectrum Management Databases:** WinnForum has been involved in the development of databases and database-to-database interface specifications. These databases help manage and coordinate spectrum access among different users in shared spectrum environments.

Table I.3.3 WinnForum – CBRS baseline standards for initial certification (Release 1).

WINNF-TS-0016Version 1.2.721 March 2022	SAS to CBSD technical specification
WINNF-TS-0022Version 1.5.017 November 2020	CBRS PKI certificate policy
WINNF-TS-0061Version 1.5.17 October 2019	WG4 SAS test and certification specification
WINNF-TS-0065Version 1.3.017 November 2020	CBRS communications security technical specification(also named WINNF-15-S-0065-V 2.0.0, 24 April 2017)
WINNF-TS-0071Version 1.0.026 July 2017	CBRS operational security technical specification(also named WINNF-15-S-0071-V 1.0.0, 21 June 2016)
WINNF-TS-0096Version 1.3.211 March 2020	SAS-SAS protocol technical specification
WINNF-TS-0112Version 1.9.113 March 2020	CBRS's operational and functional requirements
WINNF-TS-0122Version 1.0.2 25 November 2020	CBRS CBSD test specifications
WINNF-TS-0245Version 1.2.03 March 2021	Operations for citizens broadband radio service (CBRS)
WINNF-TS-0247Version 1.6.0 9 September 2022	CPI accreditation standard

6) **Certification and Testing Specifications:** WinnForum has established specifications for the certification of SAS and ESC devices to ensure that they meet the regulatory requirements for shared spectrum access. These specifications also address testing procedures and methodologies.

The CBRS Baseline Standards Release 1 was created by the Wireless Innovation Forum to address the requirements of 47 Code of Federal Regulations (CFR) Part 96 (https://www.ecfr.gov/cgi-bin/text-idx?mc=true&node=pt47.5.96&rgn=div5) and to develop an ecosystem of interoperable SAS and CBRS device technologies.

Additional emerging technologies can be considered in subsequent releases. Details can be found in the release plan at https://winnf.memberclicks.net/assets/CBRS/WINNF-SSC-0004.pdf. CBRS Baseline Standards (Release 1) can be found at https://cbrs.wirelessinnovation.org/release-1-standards-specifications. Tables I.3.3 and I.3.4 provide the relevant set of specifications for private network deployments.

I.3.3 OnGo Alliance

I.3.3.1 Purpose

Reproduced from https://ongoalliance.org

Support the common interests of members, implementers, and operators in the development, commercialization, and adoption of LTE and 5G NR solutions for the U.S. 3.5 GHz CBRS.

Table I.3.4 WinnForum – enhancements to CBRS baseline standards (Release 2).

WINNF-TS-1001Version 1.5.0 6 June 2023	CBRS Release 2 operational and functional requirements
WINNF-TS-3002Version 1.5.06 June 2023	Extensions to the SAS-CBSD interface technical specification (Release 2)
WINNF-TS-3003Version 1.3.0 6 June 2023	Extensions to the SAS-SAS interface technical specification (Release 2)
WINNF-TS-4003Version 1.0.03 May 2021	CBRS Release 2 test specification for SAS is UUT-approved
WINNF-TS-4004Version 1.1.014 September 2021	CBRS Release 2 test specification: CBSD DP as UUT
WINNF-TS-4005Version 1.1.027 June 2022	CBRS Release 2 self-testing policy
WINNF-TS-5006Version 1.2.023 August 2021	CBSD antenna pattern database
	Release 1 specification for Release 2 reference:
WINNF-TS-0247Version 1.6.0 9 September 2022	CPI accreditation standard

I.3.3.2 Mission

Reproduced from https://ongoalliance.org

- Evangelize LTE-based and 5G NR OnGo technology, use cases, and business opportunities
- Drive technological developments necessary to fulfill the mission, including multi-operator LTE and 5G NR capabilities
- Identify required advocacy steps (e.g. marketing, promotion, certification, branding, regulatory, etc.) and catalyze action in these areas
- Establish an effective product certification program for LTE and 5G NR equipment in the US 3.5 GHz band, ensuring multi-vendor interoperability

I.3.3.3 OnGo Alliance Working Group and Documentation

Figure I.3.2 provides the list of working groups in OnGo Alliance.

OnGo Alliance specifications are distributed only to their members. Memberships are offered at several levels, and even basic membership allows access to their specifications.

Visit https://ongoalliance.org/resource/, where the OnGo Alliance releases case studies, whitepapers, certification information, and more. The whitepapers are fairly detailed and provide a good understanding

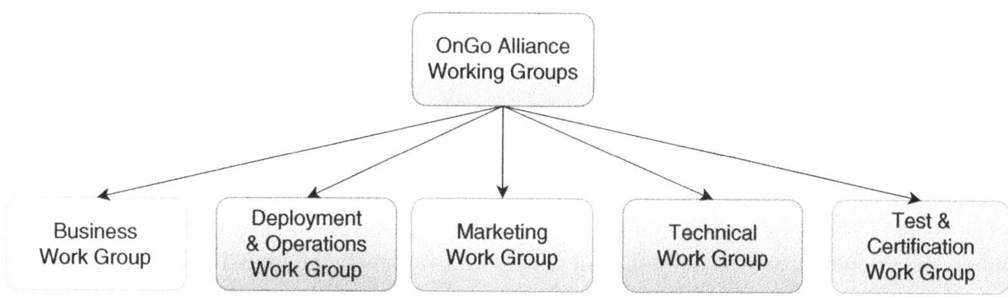

Figure I.3.2 OnGo Alliance – working groups.

of the technology, options, and deployment aspects. For example, they include the OnGo roaming whitepaper and the OnGo neutral host network (NHN) deployment guide.

The OnGo Alliance also allows network identifiers to be purchased for use in the CBRS band. Visit https://ongoalliance.org/ongo-identifiers/for details.

The current PAL spectrum allocations can be viewed on this map: https://ongoalliance.org/pal-map.

The OnGo Alliance provides the definitions for LTE and NR systems to be deployed in the CBRS that are primarily targeted toward private networks. The specifications address coexistence operation with PAL and general authorized access (GAA) operation, and network camping behavior, including geofencing and security procedures. It also addresses the different modes of UE operation, including the coexistence of LTE/NR systems with Wi-Fi.

I.3.4 Small Cell Forum

I.3.4.1 Who We Are

Reproduced from www.smallcellforum.org.

Small Cell Forum.

Small cell forum (SCF) is a global organization whose mission is to enable and accelerate the sustainable digital transformation of industry, enterprises, and communities. We do this by supporting a range of agile, cost-effective, scalable cellular infrastructure and solutions for established and emerging service providers and deployers.

We gather requirements from service providers and businesses, and, directed by our board, these inputs shape our work program. Our specifications, technical papers, and enterprise-focused outputs are made freely available to benefit the wider industry.

Today, our members are working on projects spanning split architectures, private networks, neutral host requirements, business model evolution, 5G small cell products, and policy and regulation.

The primary aspect is to track the network functional application platform interface (nFAPI). This corresponds to the radio access network (RAN) split option 6 (see Part II RAN section). This is one of the key architectures used for RAN nodes in private network deployments.

I.3.4.2 Work Program

Figure I.3.3 provides the set of working groups in Small Cell Forum.

I.3.4.3 Specifications

Table I.3.5 provides the set of specifications published by Small Cell Forum.

I.3.5 GSMA

I.3.5.1 What Is the GSMA's Role?

Reproduced from www.gsma.com.

The Global System for Mobile Communications (GSMA) is a global organization unifying the mobile ecosystem to discover, develop, and deliver innovations foundational to positive business environments and societal change. Our vision is to unlock the full power of connectivity so that people, industry, and society thrive.

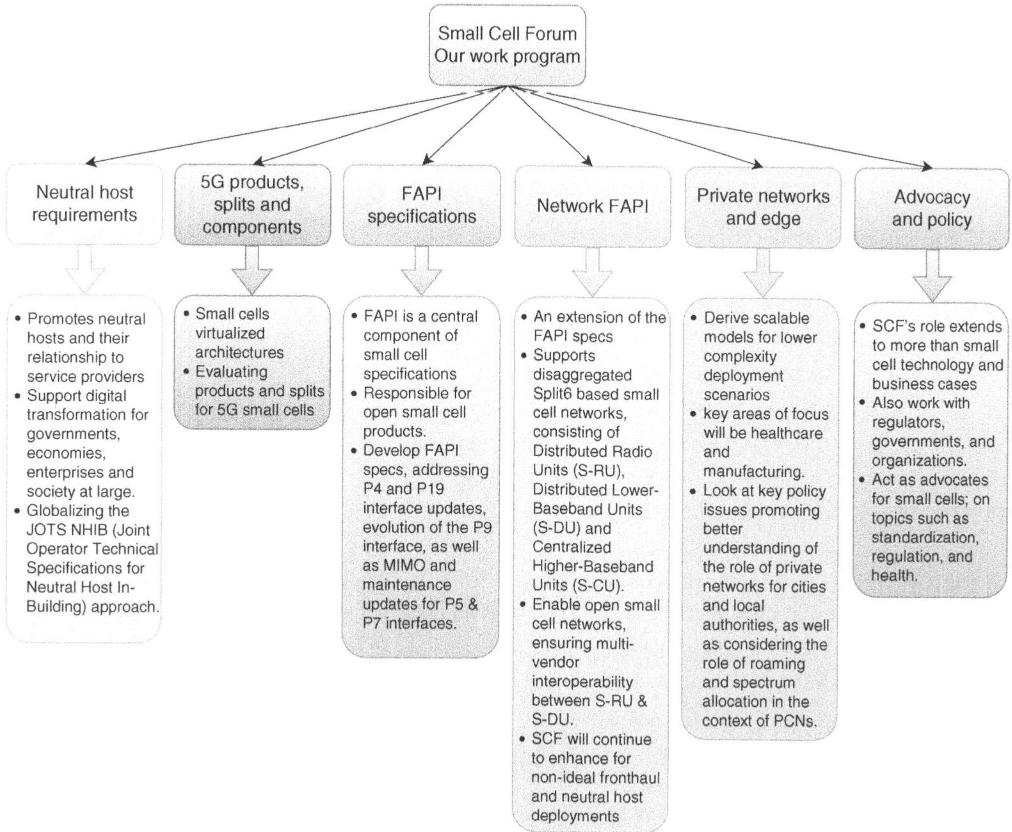

Figure I.3.3 Small Cell Forum – work program.

Representing mobile operators and organizations across the mobile ecosystem and adjacent industries, the GSMA delivers for its members across three broad pillars: connectivity for good, industry solutions, and events.

Connectivity for good engages members, governments, and civil society to advance positive policy and spectrum outcomes, facilitate digital innovation to reduce inequalities in our world, and tackle today's biggest societal challenges such as digital inclusion, climate change, and sustainability.

Industry solutions supports the technology and interoperability that make mobile work. For instance, we assist the industry's development in areas such as 5G, mobile IoT, fraud, and security through our projects, working groups, and other collaborative activities.

While our services offer data, resources and tools to help businesses in the ecosystem work together more effectively, leading to better customer experiences on mobile devices.

Our events provide successful ways of bringing the ecosystem and adjacent industries together to make strong business connections and drive a positive impact – from the world's largest and most influential connectivity event, Mobile World Congress (MWC), in Barcelona, Shanghai, Las Vegas, and Africa, to the growing M360 series that has a more regional focus.

The UE credential provisioning with remote subscriber identity module (SIM) provisioning (RSP) is the key definition leveraged from this forum for private networks. Further enhancements for private network credential distribution and management are being pursued to address specific use cases such as conference centers, including timed release of eSIM credentials.

Table I.3.5 Some of the relevant Small Cell Forum specifications.

Specification number	Title
SCF245	Neutral host requirements part 2: Hosted RAN high-level design http://scf.io/doc/245
SCF238	5G small-cell architecture and product definitions https://scf.io/en/documents/238_5G_Small_cell_architecture_and_product_definitions.php
SCF251	5G NR FR1 reference design https://scf.io/en/download.php?doc=251
SCF222	5G FAPI: PHY API specification https://scf.io/doc/222
SCF223	5G FAPI: P19 RF and digital frontend control API https://scf.io/doc/223
SCF225	5G nFAPI specifications https://scf.io/doc/225
SCF224	5G FAPI: network monitor mode API https://scf.io/en/documents/224_5G_FAPI_Network_Monitor_Mode_API.php
SCF229	5G FAPI operations, administration, and maintenance (OAM) protocol for inline high-PHY https://www.scf.io/doc/229
SCF228	S-RU and S-DU test support http://scf.io/doc/228
SCF225	5G nFAPI specifications https://scf.io/en/documents/225_5G_nFAPI_specifications.php
SCF228	S-RU and S-DU test support https://scf.io/en/documents/228_S-RU_and_S-DU_Test_Support.php
SCF226	About 5G nFAPI https://scf.io/en/documents/226_About_5G_nFAPI.php
SCF255	Private 5G network blueprints https://www.smallcellforum.org/private-network-blueprints
SCF235	Our latest publication: private cellular networks with small cells https://www.smallcellforum.org/private-networks
SCF234	Edge computing and small cell networks http://scf.io/doc/234

GSMA is also working on Telco Cloud definition, which deliberates on advancements to multi-access edge compute (MEC), which will become very relevant for stand-alone and neutral host private network deployments.

I.3.5.2 Specifications

Table I.3.6 provides the relevant set of specifications published by GSMA that are applicable to private network deployments.

Table I.3.6 Some of the relevant GSMA specifications.

Specification number	Title
SGP.22	SGP.22 technical specification v2.4 – eSIM – GSMA https://www.gsma.com/esim/resources/sgp-22-technical-specification-v2-4
IR.92	IR.92 IMS profile for voice and SMS v14.0 (current) https://www.gsma.com/newsroom/wp-content/uploads/IR.92-v15.0-2.pdf
IR.94	IR.94 IMS profile for conversational video service V14.0 – GSMA https://www.gsma.com/newsroom/all-documents/ir-94-ims-profile-for-conversational-video-service-v14-0
IR.88	IR.88 EPS roaming guidelines v25.0 (current) https://www.gsma.com/newsroom/wp-content/uploads/IR.88-v25.0-17.pdf
IR.51	IMS profile for voice, video, and SMS over untrusted Wi-Fi access. https://www.gsma.com/newsroom/wp-content/uploads/IR.51-v8.0.pdf

I.3.5.3 Telco Edge Cloud Forum

Reproduced from the white paper by GSMA on "Telco Edge Cloud Value & Achievements": https://www.gsma.com/futurenetworks/wp-content/uploads/2022/03/GSMA-TEC-Value-Whitepaper-v13.pdf

The Telco Edge Cloud (TEC) Forum is a body that monitors and guides the developments in TEC and associated services (IaaS, PaaS, CaaS, NaaS) and aims to promote compatibility, portability, and interconnection of parallel deployments.

The TEC Forum currently consists of 24 operators and platform providers and holds several in-person or virtual events scheduled around GSMA events throughout the year.

TEC aims to become a digital "one-stop-shop" that packages and offers MNOs' unique edge computing and network resources and capabilities for customers to deliver and end users to consume commercial edge services seamlessly across different networks.

The initiative has already delivered great results, showcasing edge applications like drone orchestration, cloud XR gaming, AR-based virtual human guides, holographic videoconferencing, and assisted driving (cellular vehicle-to-everything (C-V2X)) across multiple operators and countries. This has shown the feasibility and flexibility of the edge federation mechanisms defined by the GSMA. Figure I.3.4 provides a conceptual view of Telco Cloud as envisioned by GSMA.

The forum seeks to enable integration and seamless roaming behavior across MNOs while still capitalizing on available edge compute resources. It enhances MEC for ease of supporting different use cases. See the whitepaper for further details on the specific use cases and the approach taken to address the scenarios involved.

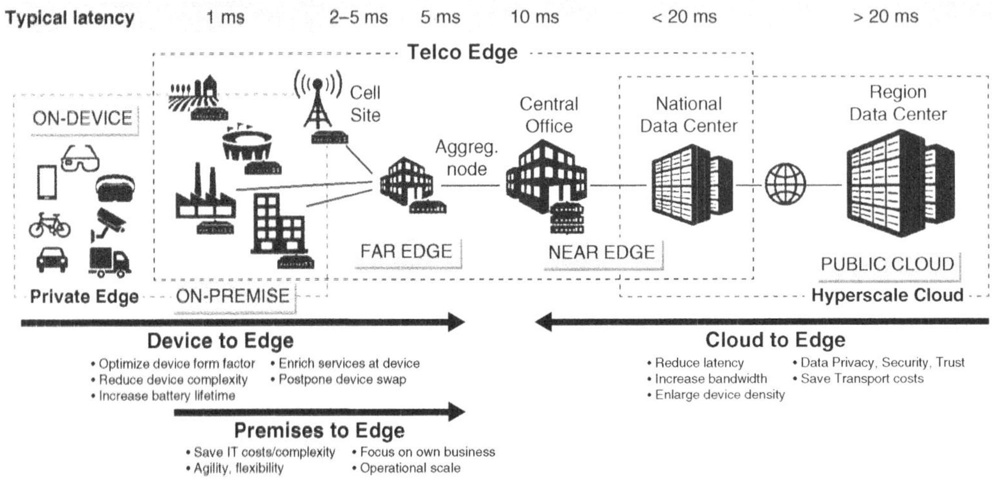

Figure I.3.4 Conceptual view of Telco Cloud as envisioned by GSMA. Reproduced from https://gsma.com (GSMA white paper on Telco Edge Cloud).

I.3.6 5G ACIA

Reproduced from https://5g-acia.org.

I.3.6.1 About Us

To make 5G a success for industrial applications, 5G-ACIA (Alliance for Connected Industries and Automation) brings together widely varying 5G stakeholders. These include organizations from the operational technology (OT) and information and communication technology (ICT) industries. OT companies include industrial automation enterprises, machine builders, and end users. ICT companies can be chip manufacturers, network infrastructure providers, or mobile network operators. The 5G-ACIA membership also includes academic institutions such as universities and research institutes, as well as other relevant entities such as government bodies and associations.

This is the key forum for industrial IoT (IIoT) definitions. It addresses key IIoT network architectures, including neutral hosts, quality of service (QoS), and end-to-end connectivity.

It also addresses integrating multiple disjoint networks, including open platform communications (OPC) UA and time-sensitive networks (TSN), for time-ordered critical operations.

I.3.6.2 Our Structure

The 5G-ACIA management team comprises three main groups: the 5G-ACIA Board, led by the general chair and general vice-chair; working groups, led by working group chairs and vice-chairs; and the 5G-ACIA office, led by the secretary. Figure I.3.5 provides the structure of the working groups in 5G ACIA.

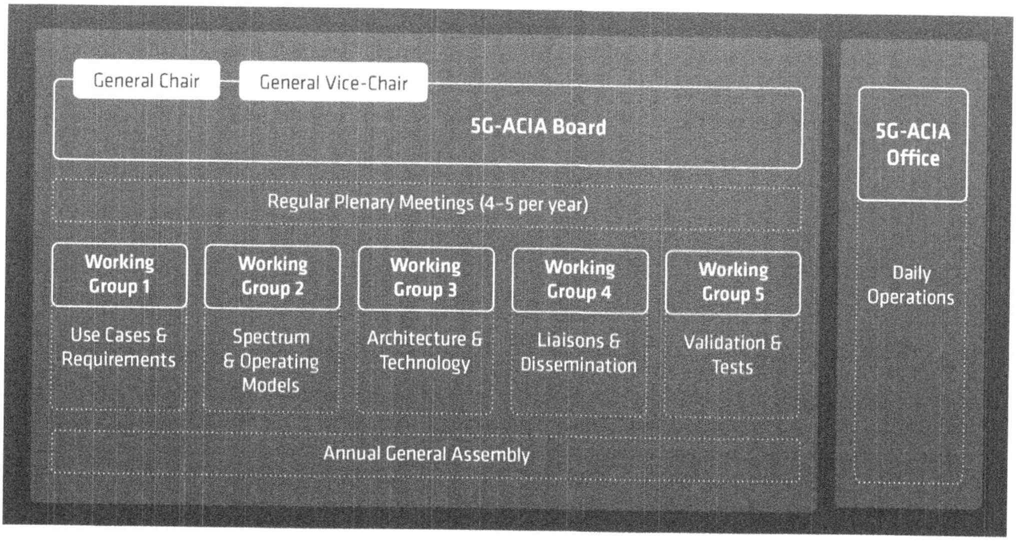

Figure I.3.5 5G ACIA working group structure (reproduced from https://5g-acia.org).

I.3.7 O-RAN Alliance

Reproduced from https://www.o-ran.org.

I.3.7.1 About O-RAN ALLIANCE

The O-RAN ALLIANCE was founded in February 2018 by AT&T, China Mobile, Deutsche Telekom, Nippon Telegraph and Telephone Corporation (NTT) DOCOMO, and Orange. It was established as a German entity in August 2018. Since then, the O-RAN ALLIANCE has become a worldwide community of mobile network operators, vendors, and research and academic institutions operating in the RAN industry.

O-RAN ALLIANCE's mission is to reshape the RAN industry toward more intelligent, open, virtualized, and fully interoperable mobile networks. O-RAN specifications enable a more competitive and vibrant RAN supplier ecosystem with faster innovation to improve user experience. O-RAN-based mobile networks improve the efficiency of RAN deployments as well as operations by the mobile operators.

O-RAN ALLIANCE operates in compliance with World Trade Organization (WTO) principles for the development of international standards, guides, and recommendations: transparency, openness, impartiality and consensus, effectiveness and relevance, coherence, and addressing the concerns of developing countries. Learn more in our white paper.

This forum provides the fundamental definitions of RAN split options architecture with the use of radio unit (RU), distributed unit (DU), and central unit (CU). This architecture is used for both private and public networks, leveraging the different RAN split options. The compute resources used and the viable architectures will vastly differ between the private and public networks.

This alliance expects to enable interworking across vendors with this architecture, which leaves the system integration across these vendors to be potentially managed by a single entity. This architecture is very flexible and useful even for RAN split option realizations, even for a single vendor, and has been absorbed into 3GPP definitions.

The O-RAN alliance also focuses on RAN intelligent controller (RIC), which allows for artificial intelligence (AI) and machine learning (ML) functions to be introduced. This allows for learnings that are specific to each enterprise private network to be supported while also applying the relevant learning across private networks.

I.3.7.2 What We Do

Figure I.3.6 provides the activities associated with the O-RAN Alliance.

I.3.7.3 Specifications

The link https://orandownloadsweb.azurewebsites.net/specifications has all the O-RAN specifications and allows for open access. The different working groups within the O-RAN alliance support a set of specifications, and they are the following:

- WG1: Use cases and overall architecture workgroup
- WG2: Non-real-time RIC and A1 interface workgroup
- WG3: Near-real-time RIC and E2 interface workgroup
- WG4: Open fronthaul interfaces workgroup
- WG5: Open F1/W1/E1/X2/Xn interface workgroup
- WG6: Cloudification and orchestration workgroup
- WG7: White-box hardware workgroup

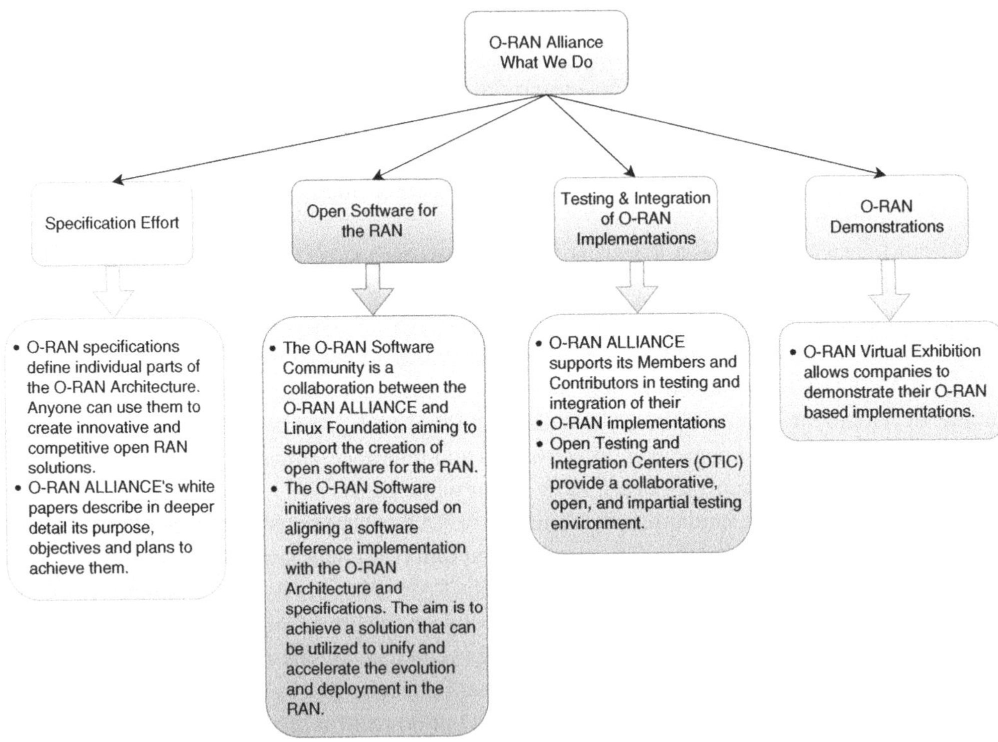

Figure I.3.6 O-RAN alliance: what we do.

- WG8: Stack reference design workgroup
- WG9: Open X-haul transport workgroup
- WG10: OAM for O-RAN
- TIFG: Test and integration focus group
- WG11: Security working group

I.3.8 National Spectrum Consortium

Reproduced from www.nationalspectrumconsortium.org.

National Spectrum Consortium (NSC) working groups serve as a unique collaborative platform between industry, academia, and the government. Started in 2021, this collaborative platform brings together the single largest pool of scientists and engineers who understand the technical details relating to spectrum and spectrum-dependent systems, and their relationship to new and emerging technology in the 5G and beyond ecosystem, across both commercial and military applications. The working group platform is intended to leverage that expertise to inform national policy and commercial standards in concrete and measurable ways to advance U.S. competitiveness.

This forum is currently deliberating on enabling the 3.1–3.45 GHz spectrum for fully licensed and shared license operations. Making this spectrum to be available for private networks will greatly enable sophisticated use cases to be supported in private networks with significant improvement in the throughput performance and the QoS guarantees that it can provide.

I.3.8.1 What the Working Groups Aim to Do

Figure I.3.7 provides the set of working groups in NSC. Each working group serves as an overarching umbrella for more narrowly scoped task groups that focus on a specific topics; each task group develops and delivers tangible outputs within a defined timeframe. Potential task group products include the following:

- Recommended practices, white papers, and/or study reports;
- High-quality, interoperable specifications and architectures for dynamic spectrum access, sensing, zero-trust architectures, etc.;
- Inputs to supranational standards bodies;
- Position papers, use cases, and/or architectural constructs for federal agencies, e.g. National Telecommunications and Information Administration (NTIA), Federal Communications Commission (FCC), and the Department of Defense.

The working group structure is intended to be flexible and iterative. NSC members are invited and encouraged to propose and help foster new working and/or task groups that address areas of interest or concern where NSC expertise can add value.

I.3.9 Summary

The standards bodies of 3GPP, WinnForum, OnGo Alliance, Small Cell Forum, GSMA, 5G-ACIA, and O-RAN Alliance are covered to provide the reader with some of the standards specifications that are employed for enterprise network design, development, and deployment. There are other

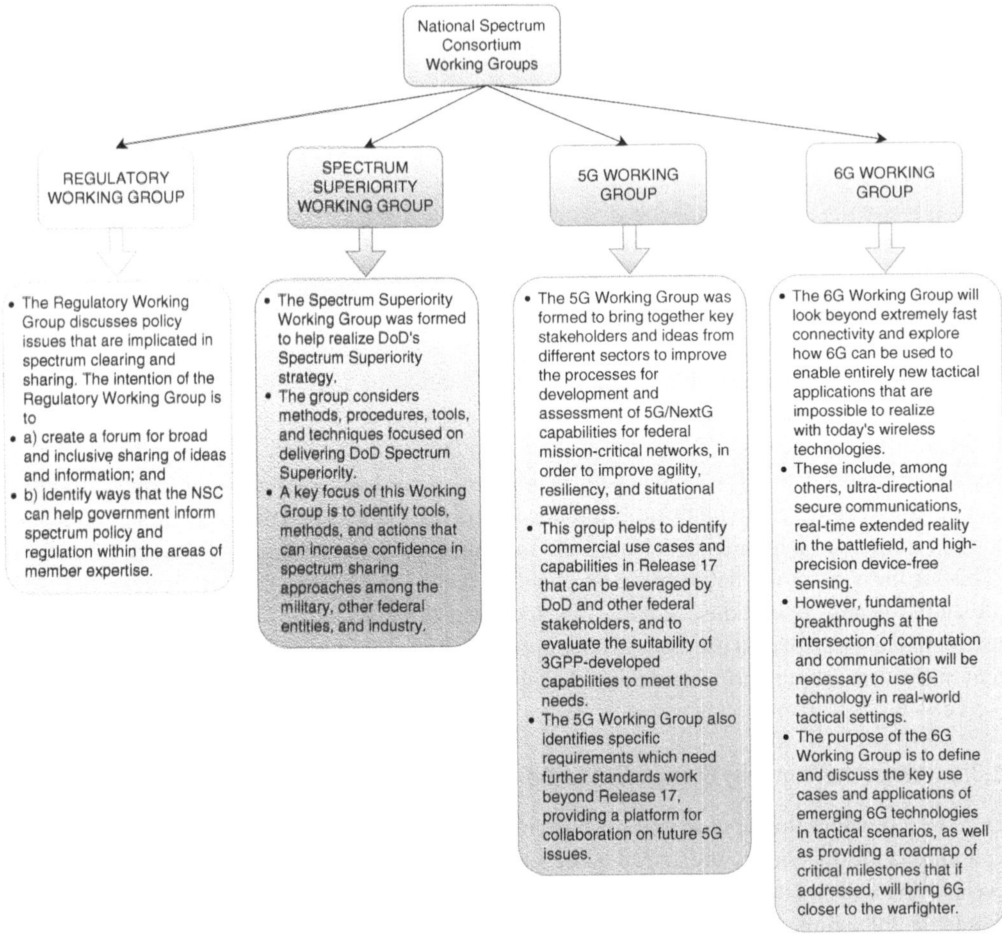

Figure I.3.7 NSC working groups.

standards specifications as well such as Internet Engineering Task Force (IETF), TM Forum, and MulteFire Alliance (MFA) that may apply as well. There is a wealth of information in each of the standards bodies, and the reader, based on the information desired, is encouraged to visit their websites to obtain it. There are several standards forums that require membership to obtain access to their specifications, and most of these are reasonably priced, particularly if only access to the specification is desired without active participation.

References

https://www.3gpp.org
https://www.wirelessinnovation.org
https://ongoalliance.org
https://www.smallcellforum.org
https://www.gsma.com
https://5g-acia.org
https://www.o-ran.org
https://www.nationalspectrumconsortium.org

Part II

Technological Framework

Part II.1

Radio Access Network Aspects

II.1.1

Global Private Spectrum Allocations

II.1.1.1 Introduction

Traditional spectrum allocations primarily assumed nationwide coverage requirements. Wireline telephony services were handled by large companies, and transitioning to wireless support led these companies to adopt wireless cellular technology. This required nationwide coverage, and spectrum policies were naturally driven to meet the needs of such large deployments. Spectrum allocation needed to be on a larger scale so that mobility could be easily supported. Even more importantly, band support capability in both the network and end-user devices needed to be built around a limited set of bands to keep costs manageable. Although the number of bands supported by devices has grown, aggregate operation across bands and the total bandwidth still remain limited. Over the wireless generations, the adoption of different spectrum regions has been enabled, starting with the low band below 3 GHz, moving into the mid-band spectrum between 3 GHz and 6 GHz, and further exploring the mmWave spectrum from 24 GHz to 51 GHz as the high band. 4G LTE was primarily deployed in the low band, with some deployments in the mid-band. 5G NR is primarily deployed in the mid-band, with some deployments in the low band as Long Term Evolution (LTE) deployments are reallocated to New Radio (NR). NR is also supported in the high-band, although this has not yet seen significant adoption in the market. Spectrum, even with a brief time period of wireless deployment, has become a very valuable commodity and auctioned at extremely high prices that can be purchased only by large carriers.

With the demand for reliable availability of spectrum for localized use in smaller footprints for enterprises to support cellular technologies for campus coverage, the concept of shared spectrum was born. The intent is to set aside some spectrum for shared use among the enterprises, with payment only for the spectrum used within campus footprints. This keeps the costs limited and allows for the deployment of cellular technologies that offer a better grade of service (GoS) compared to Wi-Fi. In the USA, the concept of shared spectrum was created with the citizens broadband radio service (CBRS), which supports dynamic spectrum allocation via a central arbiter while accommodating multiple tiers of users on the spectrum. See the chapter on CBRS for more details. This approach is innovative, adapting to real-time changes by dynamically adjusting the allocations to the different entities, accounting for the interference and priorities of users along with the location of the devices. Although this concept is not fully adopted for shared spectrum use in different countries, the need for shared spectrum to enable enterprise deployments has become noticeably

Mobile Communication Systems for Private Networks, First Edition. Srinivasan Balasubramanian.

clear, and several countries have already provided shared spectrum allocations or are in the process of approving them. Most countries require the enterprises to provide the location and the required coverage map and to apply for spectrum grants that are provided for a limited time, with the chance to renew them in the future. Table II.1.1.1 provides a list of countries where private network decisions have already been made or are in planning. Each country has a specific process for getting the allocations for spectrum. Given the preliminary stages of the shared spectrum allocation, closer follow-up will be required to understand the process involved in procuring the spectrum allocations in individual countries.

They include bands defined in the 3GPP for 5G-NR (see 3GPP TS 38.101-1, TS 38.101-2), the operation mode, bandwidth, and spectrum access model considered by administrations.

Figure II.1.1.1 provides a visual representation of the bands used in the different countries.

Figure II.1.1.2 provides a visual representation of the bandwidth available for private network deployments in the different countries. Although this is an aggregation of the bands supported for private networks in these countries, the aggregate bandwidth may not be usable depending on the network and end-user device capabilities.

The spectrum allocations are technology-agnostic and can support non-3GPP RATs as well. However, the focus is on LTE and NR-based deployments. The spectrum license provided can be exclusive or shared within the specified geographic region. Spectrum allocations may be obtained through several methods, including auctions, spectrum trading or sub-leasing (which may be allowed in specific countries), administrative procedures by applying for it, and through a common database broker.

For example, based on Ofcom's defined process in the UK, the *Shared Access license* provides access to four spectrum bands that support mobile technology: 1,800 MHz, 2,300 MHz, 3.8–4.2 GHz, and the lower 26 GHz band. The *Local Access license* allows other users to access spectrum that has already been licensed to the UK's mobile network operators (MNOs) in locations where an MNO is not using its spectrum. This is available for the 800, 900, 1,400, 1,800, 1,900, 2,100, 2,300, 2,600, and 3.4 GHz bands. Europe is working with Conference of Postal and Telecommunications Administrations (CEPT) to align all of the European Union (EU) to use 3.8–4.2 GHz, and this is being discussed within FM60 (regulatory framework – FM60_01) and European Consumer Centres Network (ECC) PT1 (sharing studies – PT1_47). Germany has already decided to allocate 100 MHz between 3.7 GHz and 3.8 GHz and manage the individual enterprise allocations through BnetzA, which is the Federal Network Agency (German: Bundesnetzagentur or BNetzA), a regulatory office for the electricity, gas, telecommunications, post, and railway markets.

In addition to locally licensing shared spectrum, it is possible for private networks to be deployed on existing, already-licensed spectrum. There are entities that help arbitrate the subleasing of the licensed spectrum by working with the entity that holds the license to make it available to the enterprises. In Europe, a two-tiered geolocation-database-based sharing framework called evolved licensed shared access (eLSA) has been developed; see European Telecommunications Standards Institute (ETSI) TS 103652. eLSA coordinates with the incumbents and National Regulatory Authorities (NRA), employing automatic tools to facilitate spectrum sharing.

Unlicensed spectrum is available in the 2.4 GHz, 5 GHz, and now also the 6 GHz regions. This is used primarily by Wi-Fi and Bluetooth®, although other technologies can be deployed using these unlicensed spectrums. LTE defined licensed assisted access (LAA), which was targeted to augment the DL capacity with the anchor supported by licensed spectrum. Similarly, NR has NR-U (NR Unlicensed), which supports Downlink (DL) and Uplink (UL) traffic but has not yet seen market adoption. In the USA, the Federal Communications Commission (FCC) authorized two different types of unlicensed operation: standard-power and indoor low-power operations in the 6 GHz

Table II.1.1.1 Global private network spectrum allocation.

Country	Spectrum (MHZ)	NR Band	Mode of operation	Bandwidth	Access model
Australia	3,700–4,200	n77	TDD	TBD	Local licensing
Belgium	3,800–4,200	n77	TDD	TBD	Under consideration
Brazil	3,700–3,800	n78	TDD	100 MHz	Local licensing
Canada	3,900–3,980	n78	TDD	80 MHz	Local licensing
Chile	3,750–3,800	n78	TDD	50 MHz	Local licensing
China	5,925–6,425	n96, n102	TDD	TBD	Licensing
Croatia	3,400–3,480	n78	TDD	80 MHz	Local licensing/leasing
Czech Republic	3,400–3,480	n78	TDD	2×20 MHz	Allocated to CSPs, leases available
Czech Republic	3,640–3,700	n78	TDD	2×20 MHz	Allocated to CSPs, leases available
Denmark	3,740–3,800	n78	TDD	60 MHz	Allocated to CSPs, leases available
Finland	2,300–2,320	n40	TDD	20 MHz TBD	Allocated to CSPs, leases available
Finland	3,410–3,800	n78	TDD	20 MHz TBD	Allocated to CSPs, leases available
France	2,575–2,615	n38	TDD	40 MHz	Allocated to CSPs, leases available
France	3,490–3,800	n78	TDD	4×50 MHz	Allocated to CSPs, leases available
France	3,800–4,200	n77	TDD	100 MHz	Allocated to CSPs, leases available
Germany	3,700–3,800	n78	TDD	100 MHz	Local licensing
Greece	3,410–3,800	n78	TDD	TBD	Allocated to CSPs, leases possible
Japan	2,575–2,595	n38	TDD	20 MHz	Local licensing
Japan	4,600–4,900	n79	TDD	300 MHz	Local licensing
Netherlands	2,300–2,400	n40	TDD	100 MHz	New Regs in 2023
Netherlands	3,410–3,450	n78	TDD	40 MHz	New Regs in 2023
Netherlands	3,750–3,800	n78	TDD	50 MHz	New Regs in 2023
New Zealand	2,575–2,620	n38	TDD	TBD	Local licensing
Norway	3,400–3,800	n78	TDD	TBD	Allocated to CSPs, leases available
Norway	3,800–4,200	n77	TDD	TBD	Local licensing
Poland	3,800–4,200	n77	TDD	100 MHz	Announced
Republic of Korea	4,720–4,820	n79	TDD	100 MHz	Local licensing
Sweden	3,720–3,800	n78	TDD	80 MHz	Local licensing
Taiwan	4,800–4,900	n79	TDD	100 MHz	Under consideration
United Kingdom	2,390–2,400	n40	FDD + TDD	10 MHz	Local licensing/shared spectrum
United Kingdom	3,800–4,200	n77	FDD + TDD	400 MHz	Local licensing/shared spectrum
USA	3,550–3,700	n48	TDD	<150 MHz	Sha

Figure II.1.1.1 Private network spectrum allocation bands.

Figure II.1.1.2 Private network spectrum allocation bandwidths.

band. Standard-power operations, which encompass standard-power access points and fixed client devices (collectively referred to as standard-power devices), are permitted in the 5.925–6.425 GHz and 6.525–6.875 GHz portions of the 6 GHz band. They must operate under the control of an automated frequency coordination (AFC) system to prevent harmful interference to fixed microwave links that operate in the band. It is likely that NR-U will be used in the 6 GHz spectrum if and when the market gains traction for NR deployment in the unlicensed spectrum.

The reference section provides the different sources used to identify the spectrum allocations for the different countries for private network operations. It also points to the different regulatory bodies and the policies applied towards localized spectrum allocation for private network operations. Spectrum is managed by the agencies of the individual countries or as a collective like in the European Union.

II.1.1.2 PATHSS

In the National Spectrum Consortium (NSC), under the Regulatory Working Group, a specific task force has been formed called Partnering on Advancing Trusted and Holistic Spectrum Solutions (PATHSS). It was formed to address the industry to collaborate with the Department of Defense (DoD) on sharing in 3.1–3.45 GHz.

This industry group will collaborate with the DoD to explore sharing solutions to make more mid-band spectrum available for commercial 5G, specifically in 3.1–3.45 GHz. The group will provide a forum for industry and the DoD to exchange sensitive and classified information on current and projected military and commercial requirements in these bands. Together, the group will identify and develop use cases based on a shared understanding of federal and commercial needs.

Partnering to Advance Trusted and Holistic Spectrum Solutions (PATTHS) discussions will be open to any NSC member or approved member of the U.S. government. A subset of the group, drawn from a wide range of stakeholders, will be given access to classified information to provide broad insight into DoD needs.

Currently, there are myriad organizations lobbying for more spectrum. The most immediate concern is the 3.1–3.45 GHz band. Some companies – namely, the big wireless carriers represented by the trade group Cellular Telephone Industries Association (CTIA) – want this spectrum auctioned for exclusive, licensed use, while other organizations prefer spectrum-sharing schemes such as what the FCC and DoD implemented for the CBRS spectrum.

There are federal incumbents in the 3.1–3.45 GHz, so the National Telecommunications and Information Administration (NTIA) is involved in discussions about the best use of this band. There are several outcomes from the ongoing discussions, including fully auctioning the spectrum for licensed use, allowing the full spectrum to be allocated for shared use like the CBRS, or applying parts of the spectrum to licensed use while making the rest available for sharing.

The nature of sharing, particularly with airborne incumbents, is being discussed, and applying the environment sensing capability (ESC), similar to CBRS, to the use of incumbent informing capability (IIC) is considered. In this approach, incumbents indicate dynamic use to a central server, which, in turn, is used to regulate the channel resources for users that have a lower priority.

For more information or to join the group, visit NSC's website: http://www.nationalspectrumconsortium.org/working-groups

II.1.1.3 Summary

The evolution of the concept of shared spectrum use is introduced. The innovative approach to CBRS adopted in the USA is discussed, which may have triggered the global process of shared spectrum allocations. Some examples of how the shared spectrum allocations are provided are described.

Most of the world is aligning toward the use of parts of the 3–4.2 GHz spectrum for private network operations. Decisions are made within individual countries. The EU is considering making a collective decision to enable uniform use of the spectrum for private networks in these countries. It is noted that each country will follow its own procedures for local spectrum allocations. Europe is coordinating for more harmonized allocations in the 3.8–4.2 GHz region.

The subleasing approach with licensed spectrum is briefly described to show that, beyond these shared spectrum allocations, it is possible to employ already licensed spectrum by working with the licensee for private network deployments within specific regions.

The use of unlicensed spectrum is briefly described, providing some context on AFC. A table showing the current set of spectrum allocations in the different countries and the visual representation of the bands and bandwidths available are provided.

Information on the ongoing effort by the NSC PATHSS task group is provided to track the approach used for enabling the 3.1–3.45 GHz band.

References

1 Ofcom: "Enabling wireless innovation through local licensing – Shared access to spectrum supporting mobile technology," July 2019
2 Ofcom: "Shared Access Licence – Guidance document," September 2022
3 Ofcom: "Local Access Licence – Guidance document"
4 ECC Work Item FM60_01 "Terrestrial wireless broadband systems providing local-area (i.e. low/medium power) network connectivity in 3.8-4.2 GHz (Task 2 of the EC mandate)"
5 ECC Work Item PT1_47 "Feasibility and sharing studies on the shared use of the 3.8-4.2 GHz frequency band by terrestrial wireless broadband systems providing local-area (i.e., low/medium power) network connectivity (Task 1 of the EC Mandate)"
6 Bundesnetzagentur "Nummern für Campusnetze"
7 The Society of Broadcast Engineers "Frequency Coordination"
8 Rijksinspectie Digitale Infrastructuur "Frequentieruimte boeken via LSA-boekingssysteem"
9 ETSI TS 103 154: "Reconfigurable Radio Systems (RRS); System requirements for operation of Mobile Broadband Systems in the 2 300 MHz - 2 400 MHz band under Licensed Shared Access (LSA)"
10 ETSI TS 103 235: Reconfigurable Radio Systems (RRS); System architecture and high-level procedures for operation of Licensed Shared Access (LSA) in the 2 300 MHz - 2 400 MHz band
11 ETSI TS 103 652-2: Reconfigurable Radio Systems (RRS); evolved Licensed Shared Access (eLSA); Part 2: System architecture and high-level procedures
12 FCC "3.5 GHz Band Overview"
13 FCC "FCC Requests 6 GHz Automated Frequency Coordination Proposals", October 2021
14 Intel "Spectrum Sharing Using Automated Frequency Coordination", December 2022

15 FCC "OET Announces Conditional Approval for 6 GHz Band AFC Systems"

16 Qualcomm "Global update on spectrum for 4G & 5G", December 2020

17 Ericsson White Paper "5G spectrum for local industrial networks", April 2023

18 3GPP TS 38.101-1: "NR; User Equipment (UE) radio transmission and reception; Part 1: Range 1 Standalone"

19 3GPP TS 38.101-2: "NR; User Equipment (UE) radio transmission and reception; Part 1: Range 2 Standalone"

II.1.2

CBRS Fundamentals

II.1.2.1 Concept of Shared Spectrum

A shared spectrum is a way of using radio frequencies that allows multiple network deployments (referred to as users to reference a generic entity wanting to use the shared spectrum) to access the same spectrum. If one were to stand at a location, look vertically up, and assess the activity across the full range of communication frequencies, it would reveal that only a fraction is utilized at any given time. Spectrum sharing suggests an approach to optimize the use of wireless communication channels by sharing across different users, potentially allowing for opportunistic use based on the real-time demands of those sharing the spectrum. The sparse availability of spectrum necessitates the sharing of wireless communications. See the article on "The Spectrum Crunch" [7] by National Institute of Standards and Technology (NIST).

3GPP has defined three main use cases: evolved mobile broadband (eMBB), massive internet of things (mIoT), and ultra-reliable low-latency communication (URLLC), with further evolution leading to additional use cases such as reduced capabilities (RedCap) as part of the 5G networks. 5G-Advanced will bring further use cases, with 6G already being contemplated by both the industry and standards bodies alike.

Even more importantly, the entities deploying and managing the networks are changing. Traditionally, wireless networks have been handled by macro network operators, which focus on outdoor and longer-range coverage, supporting services required by the public, such as internet connectivity and voice calling. Indoor and short-range communications relied on Wi-Fi-based connectivity using unlicensed spectrum. This does not meet the quality of experience (QoE) and reliability demands of enterprises. With increased awareness and savviness of individual users and evolving use cases, even the expectations of the residential users have significantly elevated regarding wireless operations. Improved short-range communications are now compelling and necessary and no longer considered a luxury.

Spectrum allocations are also nationwide, catering to larger operators, which is not a usable form for shorter-range operations, such as an enterprise that may be multi-sited, with each location requiring a smaller coverage footprint. There are also multistory buildings potentially supporting multiple enterprises on different floors, each requiring independent networks. A comparable situation arises for residential networks as well. Follow the FCC activities allows the reader to be immediately aware of the ongoing spectrum related discussions including regulatory discussions and decisions being made [3].

Mobile Communication Systems for Private Networks, First Edition. Srinivasan Balasubramanian.

Studies on the actual spectrum used in real-time across the full spectrum range, even with the currently utilized commercial spectrum, have shown that only a small percentage is used outside of peak times. The rigid allocations to different macro network operators, along with the changing dynamics of end-users that have subscribed to a given Macro Network Operator (MNO) at a given location, result in congestion for the users of the given MNO while leaving unused spectrum from other MNO allocations.

There are several benefits to shared spectrum usage. One benefit of shared spectrum is that the spectrum costs can be shared. This is because multiple users can share the same spectrum, reducing the need for each user to have their own. Sharing allows for improved efficiency in radio spectrum usage, as peak usage demands vary over time among the networks sharing the spectrum. Shared spectrum can also help improve the quality of service for radio users. This is because multiple users can share the same spectrum, which means that there is less need for each user to have their own spectrum.

Sharing spectrum across network deployments does increase the complexity both from a regulatory and operational perspective that requires careful management to ensure that interference is avoided or at least minimized. Citizen Broadband Radio Service (CBRS) is an innovative spectrum management approach that allows for localized allocation and operation by individual enterprises.

See [5] for National Telecommunications and Information Administration (NTIA) response on 3.5G GHz band specifying the regulatory framework for spectrum sharing, allowing for designating smaller zones for protection, supporting commercial operations, and mechanisms for incumbent protection for the CBRS band.

This section details the operations of the CBRS band, together with the regulatory aspects involved, to support dynamic allocation arbitrating across the different networks within a given locale. This is an early venture into spectrum management and a fantastic experiment that is proving to be successful based on the traction it is getting in the market. Globally, in other countries, the spectrum allocation is being handled in a more static manner, where individual enterprises submit the network operating parameters, along with information on the access points, power levels, and antenna directionality, to a government organization for allocation and authorization for spectrum use.

WInnForum standards body focuses on spectrum sharing mechanisms and addresses co-existence aspects of multiple disjoint networks with fair sharing of the spectrum resources. WinnForum focuses on spectrum sharing mechanisms for CBRS that are agnostic to the access technology [1]. There is another example of the 6 GHz band where automatic frequency coordination (AFC) enables unlicensed access to the 6 GHz band by coordinating shared spectrum between standard power access points (SP) and incumbent point-to-point microwave systems. This topic is treated briefly in an independent section. This AFC is, in part, similar to the spectrum access system (SAS), which is discussed further in this section.

Apart from spectrum sharing, there are other forms of network sharing, and the details of such sharing are discussed in the context of the neutral host.

In the USA, there are discussions ongoing to allow for sharing mechanisms to be supported in the soon-to-be-released 3.1–3.45 GHz spectrum from DoD control.

OnGo Alliance defines specifications and manages the certification program for operating LTE and NR networks on the CBRS band [2]. CBRS is a shared spectrum service with three tiers of users and strict priority ordering. The three tiers are incumbent access (IA), which is the highest priority; priority access license (PAL), which is second in the hierarchy; and general authorized access (GAA), which has the lowest priority and is intended for opportunistic use. CBRS as a band allows for supporting any radio technology, and coordination with the SAS is performed to ensure that access is regulated. The most common deployment is supported using the 3GPP technologies of 4th generation long-term evolution (LTE) and 5th generation new radio (NR), the underlying technology of an orthogonal frequency division multiplexing (OFDM)-based system with time division duplexing (TDD)-based operation. CBRS is a dynamic spectrum control scheme using short-term leases to enable services, with the granted resources periodically refreshed by the SAS to retain the spectrum/resource allocation.

The CBRS channel is technology neutral and allows for any technology to be operated on the channel and not restricted to 3GPP systems. Cambium networks is one such an example [4].

This section details the fundamentals of operating on a CBRS channel.

II.1.2.2 CBRS Overview

The rules for operating on the CBRS spectrum (3.55–3.7 GHz) are defined by the Federal Communications Commission (FCC) in Code of Federal Regulation (CFR) 47 part 96. Three tiers of users, in ranked order of priority, are the IA, PAL, and GAA. The incumbents using IA are federal radiolocation services, primarily focused on the Navy and on the coast of the USA to accommodate communications with naval transports, including ships. IA also supports wireless internet service providers (WISPs), which are fixed satellite service (FSS) providers and utilities that operate on the CBRS band. These IA entities have priority over all other entities by specifying interference protection and uninterrupted usage for these existing incumbent users from commercial usage.

On September 5, 2019, the FCC published the rulemaking (NPRM) regarding the PAL-based operations in the CBRS band. The PAL auctions were held subsequently, with the entities making purchases in individual counties nationwide, which raised ~$3.5 billion USD. The allocations are specific to individual counties, and the bidding process included regular macro network operators, cable network companies, and other individual organizations wanting to acquire local spectrum to serve their needs.

On September 18, 2019, the FCC allowed the use of the CBRS spectrum for GAA, which created the momentum toward enterprise private networks.

CBRS spectrum operates in the 3.55–3.7 GHz band and is also called the innovation band, given the novel approach to shared spectrum management. CBRS was envisioned to enable nontraditional wireless carriers to offer services or operate a locally owned network in smaller footprints without incurring large spectrum costs, making it suitable for enterprise private networks. It is intended to allow enhanced services to be enabled in these private networks and can be seen as an augmentation to the campus Wi-Fi networks. Citywide deployments are also planned by the traditional macro and cable network operators. FCC

The CBRS specifications support both indoor and outdoor deployments, although in a much smaller footprint compared to the macro networks. This is primarily regulated by specifying the maximum allowed power levels for the base stations supported on the CBRS band, which also depends on the height at which they are deployed.

CBRS is considered "lightly licensed" as opposed to unlicensed, which is typically used by Wi-Fi and Bluetooth networks, or "fully licensed," which is used exclusively by a given MNO that has purchased the spectrum. The spectrum usage is regulated by a set of central entities called the SAS, which enforces the rules for the users on the CBRS band. The CBRS band supports 150 MHz and is managed as 15 channels of 10 MHz each for allocation to the individual base stations. This includes the operations of the base stations with both PAL and GAA spectrum. PAL channels, although pre-allocated, can still be revoked by the IA. GAA users opportunistically use the available spectrum as long as it is not occupied by either the IA or PAL. The channel occupancy is determined by the SAS, which regulates the PAL and GAA use of a specific 10 MHz channel. The SAS also coordinates allocations across the base stations for GAA usage to help avoid interference with one another.

As it stands now, there are several enterprise verticals that are already deployed or being planned in the market. See Part II of the book for details on these industry verticals.

Figure II.1.2.1 provides a high-level architecture of a CBRS system. The SAS is the central entity that regulates the spectrum allocations across all the entities and individual nodes, enabling the effective functioning of the CBRS network. SASs either detect IA using environmental sensing capability (ESC) deployed along the coast or receive explicit input from the federal entities when access to the set of channels is desired. The SAS can regulate the power levels of operation as well, but it is mainly focused on channel allocations. The end-user or commercial premise equipment(CPE)that provides Wi-Fi connectivity with connectivity on the CBRS channel as backhaul operates on the CBRS network based on authorization by the network and does not require access approval from the SAS.

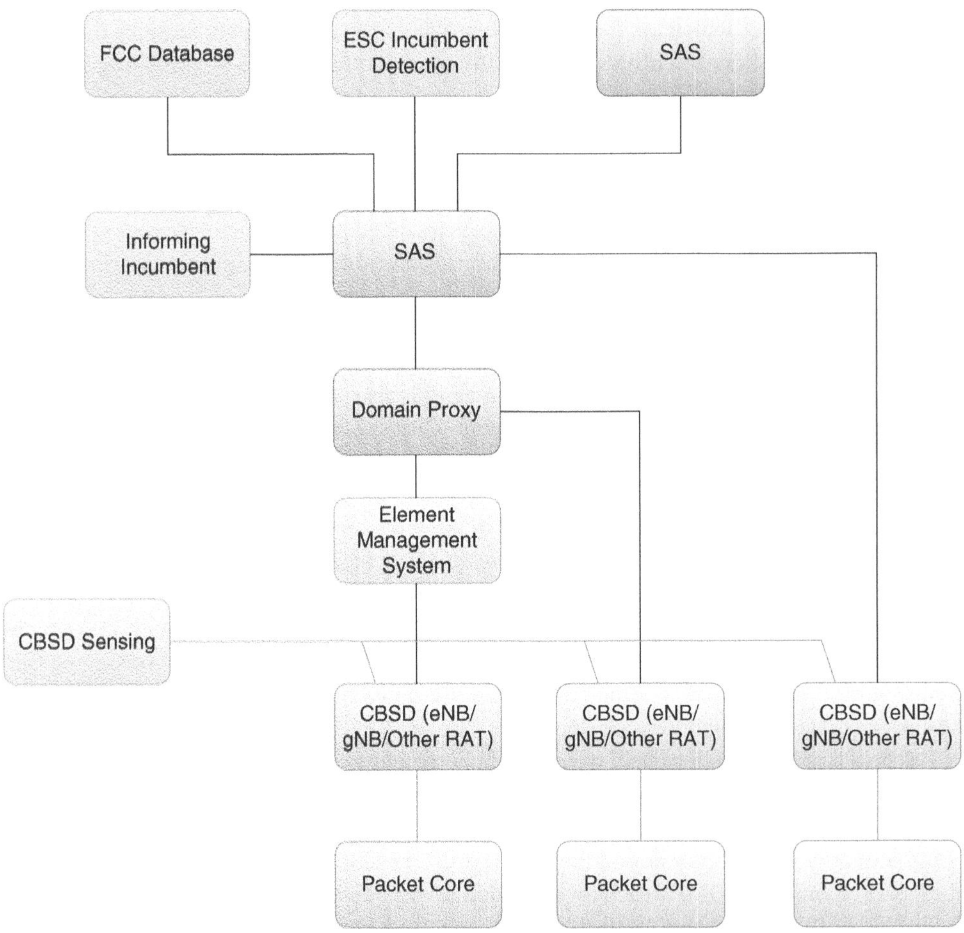

Figure II.1.2.1 CBRS reference architecture.

The CBRS band is defined as Band 48 for 4G LTE and n48 for 5G NR. This is essentially Bands 42 and 43 that have been combined, creating 150 MHz of spectrum allocation. The band requires a TDD mode of operation, supporting downlink (DL), uplink (UL), and switching slots based on the configuration. The smallest channel bandwidth allocation on CBRS is 5 MHz for LTE and 10 MHz for NR. However, in practice, only 10 MHz allocations are supported for both LTE and NR, given the complexity of managing the spectrum from the SAS.

CBRS networks are typically deployed using 3GPP-based 4G LTE or 5G NR wireless access technology that utilizes the LTE band 48/NR n48 band, which requires TDD wireless access. There are other proprietary technologies that use the CBRS band as well, for example Cambium Networks. The actual category of the end-user devices supported on the CBRS network depends on the radio access technology. For example, CBRS using LTE can support the regular categories, as well as supporting LTE Cat-M and LTE NB-IoT.

CBRS is an innovative technology that will be closely watched over worldwide. The use of shared spectrum for smaller footprint networks is becoming an industry norm and is being employed in many countries, with other countries investigating ways to enable it. CBRS is a very dynamic system, with spectrum allocations managed in real-time, adapting to the demands of the different users in the Radio Frequency (RF) proximity. This is where CBRS as a technology is poised to take on this challenge with ease.

This section covers the aspects required for operating a CBRS system, introducing the different nodes/functions and the role they play in the CBRS ecosystem.

CBRS will play a key role in the democratization of wireless spectrum for smaller footprint networks, enabling newer entrants into the market and supporting varying use cases. This certainly sets the stage to take the wireless operations to a completely different dimension. This is indeed an exciting time to be in wireless.

II.1.2.3 CBRS Spectrum

CBRS has 150 MHz of contiguous spectrum between 3.55 and 3.7 GHz and is intended for shared usage, with rules for usage specified.

Figure II.1.2.2 shows the CBRS spectrum and the three tiers of users that share the CBRS band. The tiered users have a ranked priority, with Tier 1 (IA) having priority over Tier 2 (PAL), and Tier 2 having priority over Tier 3 (GAA).

The CBRS band follows an International Telecommunication Union (ITU) LTE band plan, as indicated in Figure II.1.2.3, showing the 5 MHz channels. There is a maximum of 15 10 MHz (150 MHz) TDD channels in the CBRS band.

CBRS does allow for 5 MHz increments for LTE, as shown in Figure II.1.2.3, although for all practical purposes, the SASs provide only a 10 MHz allocation. This is aligned with the minimum supported bandwidth of 10 MHz for NR in the CBRS band.

The CBRS allocation scheme follows the equation below for a 10 MHz channel allocation to enable flexible allocations that support interference mitigation.

$$\left(3550+[n-1]\times 53\,550+n\times 5\right) \text{ where n is from 1 to 30.}$$

Figure II.1.2.4 provides the possible TDD configurations in LTE, where D is downlink, U is uplink, and S is a special subframe that is used for switching from DL to UL operations. In macro networks, TDD config #2 is used given the DL-centric traffic support needed. For enterprise private

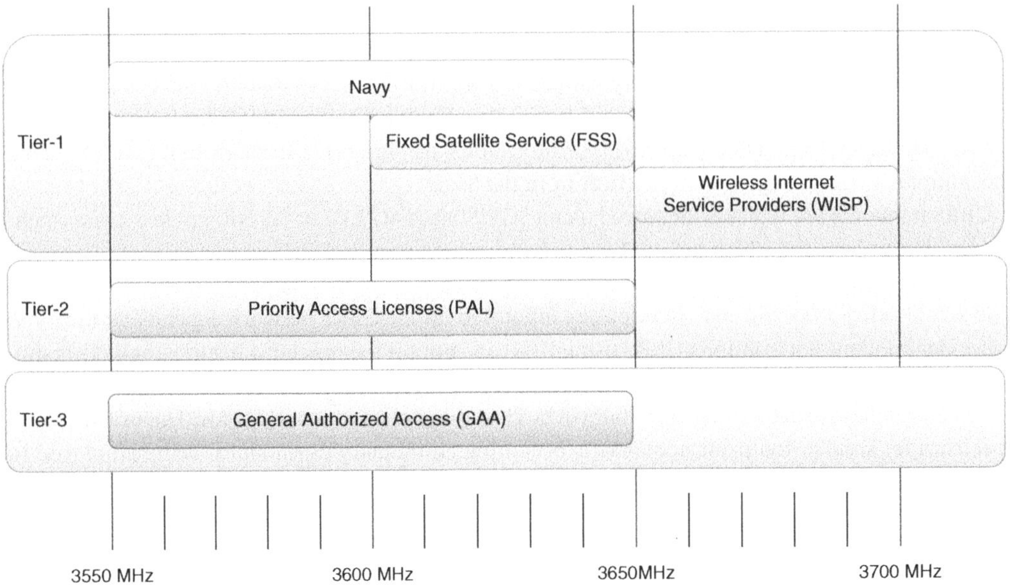

Figure II.1.2.2 CBRS spectrum.

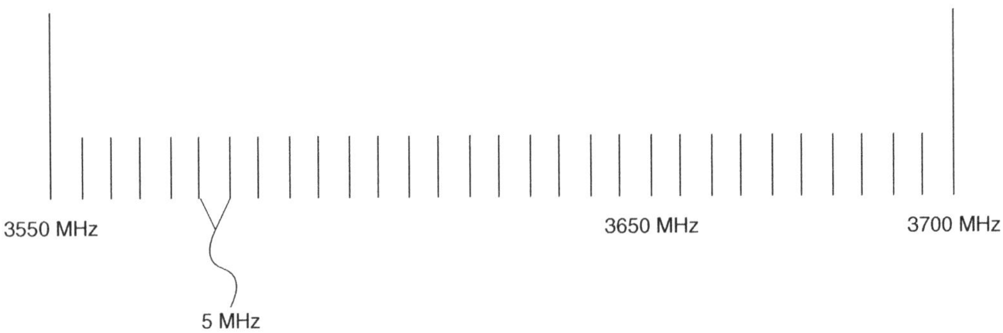

Figure II.1.2.3 CBRS channel (5 MHz increments).

TDD Config	Downlink to uplink switch point periodicity (ms)	Subframe number										Number of subframes/frame		
		0	1	2	3	4	5	6	7	8	9	D [DL]	U [UL]	S [SSF]
0	5	D	S	U	U	U	D	S	U	U	U	2	6	2
1	5	D	S	U	U	D	D	S	U	U	D	4	4	2

TDD Config	Downlink to uplink switch point periodicity (ms)	Subframe number										Number of subframes/frame		
		0	1	2	3	4	5	6	7	8	9	D [DL]	U [UL]	S [SSF]
2	5	D	S	U	D	D	D	S	U	D	D	6	2	2
3	10	D	S	U	U	U	D	D	D	D	D	6	3	1
4	10	D	S	U	U	D	D	D	D	D	D	7	2	1
5	10	D	S	U	D	D	D	D	D	D	D	8	1	1
6	5	D	S	U	U	U	D	S	U	U	D	3	5	2

Figure II.1.2.4 CBRS LTE TDD channel configuration options (from 3GPP TS 36.211 table 4.2-2).

networks, there are several use cases where more UL capacity is required, and the channel configuration is adjusted accordingly (e.g. use TDD config #1 or even #0 based on the capacity requirements in UL and DL). NR supported flexible TDD configurations with repeated patterns (see "NR Fundamentals" chapter). Handling a mix of configurations in a given deployment or across deployments is hard, and careful planning is required to avoid cross-link interference (DL traffic to a user equipment (UE) from a neighboring cell interfering with the UL transmission in the current cell).

TDD config	Downlink to uplink switch point periodicity (ms)	Subframe number										Number of subframes/frame		
		0	1	2	3	4	5	6	7	8	9	D (DL)	U (UL)	S (SSF)
0	5	D	S	U	U	U	D	S	U	U	U	2	6	2
1	5	D	S	U	U	D	D	S	U	U	D	4	4	2
2	5	D	S	U	D	D	D	S	U	D	D	6	2	2
3	10	D	S	U	U	U	D	D	D	D	D	6	3	1
4	10	D	S	U	U	D	D	D	D	D	D	7	2	1
5	10	D	S	U	D	D	D	D	D	D	D	8	1	1
6	**5**	**D**	**S**	**U**	**U**	**U**	**D**	**S**	**U**	**U**	**D**	**3**	**5**	**2**

II.1.2.4 CBRS User Categories

Figure II.1.2.5 provides an illustration of the tiers of users supported on the CBRS band. For channel allocations, IA can preempt and take over the channel use from PAL/GAA users, and PAL users can preempt GAA users within a given locale. The SAS initiates the preemption, and the reallocations are done based on the channel availability. This may result in reduced bandwidth allocations for the PAL and GAA users. It is possible that the SAS is unable to provide orthogonal

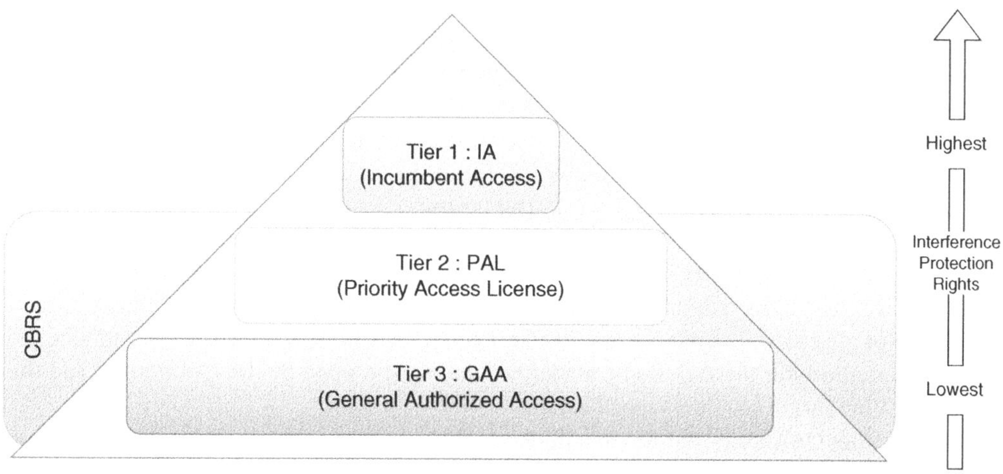

Figure II.1.2.5 User tiers in CBRS band.

allocation, and the Citizen Broadband Radio Service Devices (CBSDs) need to operate while accounting for the interference experienced. Note that PAL users are given sufficient separation to avoid interference from the GAA users. It is also noted that the PAL users may contend for GAA spectrum allocation like the generic GAA users on the channel and may operate on both the PAL and GAA channels. The SAS tries to provide some degree of fairness in the GAA channel allocations, acting as an arbiter. The decisions regarding channel allocation grants, revocation, and reallocations are based on the priority of the CBRS user and are coordinated by the SAS. The behaviors based on the three user tiers are described below.

II.1.2.4.1 Incumbent Access

IA has the highest priority and absolute priority over other types of allocation between 3,550 and 3,700 MHz and has unrestricted spectrum access. The SASs do not regulate their access, and the IA entities start using the channel by providing brief notice of the upcoming channel occupancy. The IA may occupy any part of the bottom 100 MHz of the CBRS channel. The SAS senses the IA signal and regulates the PAL and GAA users. IA entities are protected against PAL and GAA users. SASs declare a dynamic protection area (DPA) when an IA wants to use a segment of the channel in the CBRS band.

IA users include authorized federal users who can occupy the 100 MHz from 3,550 to 3,650 MHz in the CBRS band. The Navy radar has a 1.6 MHz transmission bandwidth affecting up to two 10 MHz channels, and the occupancy occurs dynamically based on the need from IA. FSS uses 3,600–3,650 MHz in the CBRS band for the space-to-Earth link and tends to be more fixed in nature; the channel availability is restricted for PAL and GAA within a certain perimeter around these ground stations. The third IA comprises wireless broadband licenses that operate in the 50 MHz between 3,650 and 3,700 MHz, and for a finite period, they are grandfathered in for spectrum use.

II.1.2.4.2 Priority Access License

The PAL auctions were held for up to 7 to 10 MHz channels in the 100 MHz region of 3,550–3,650 MHz. The PAL licenses are granted on a county basis across the USA. These licenses do not specify 10 MHz spectrum and leave that open, given that reallocations may be needed based on the IA demands. These licenses are granted for 10 years, with the option to renew them further. With the restriction of only 7 of these 10 MHz channels that can be licensed for PAL use, this limits it to a maximum of 70 MHz, leaving the rest for GAA use. Together with the upper 50 MHz, where PAL cannot be allocated, it allows for at least 80 MHz to be available for GAA use. As such, channels not used by IA or PAL are available for GAA use. There is also a restriction of a maximum of four 10 MHz channels (40 MHz) that a single entity can license.

Tier 2 PAL users receive interference protection from GAA users and are managed by the SAS. A PPA (PAL protection area) goes into effect when a CBSD authorized to use the PAL channel is radiating. The GAA users' grants on the PAL channels are estimated for possible interference, accounting for the county boundaries, and reallocated by the SAS. Specific models to estimate the possible interference for the PAL users are defined and agreed upon by the PAL entities and the FCC in the WInnForum standards specifications.

Similar to other GAA users, entities in addition to their PAL licenses can also contend for GAA channel allocations from the SAS. These GAA channel allocations to the PAL entities are treated with the same priority as the allocations for the other GAA users.

The PAL entities have interacted together with the SASs and have obtained specific channel allocations. Given that a given PAL licensee may have acquired multiple PAL licenses, it is desirable for these allocations to enable ease of base station implementation. With these PAL channel allocations, it does fragment the GAA channels, requiring techniques like carrier aggregation (CA) to use the spectrum allocation for a given CBSD.

PAL licensees can be subleased to another entity or even outright transfer their licenses. These are handled in the secondary market. Although it is viable, the FCC process to handle these subleases is not fully established and is an activity that is being pursued.

The buildout requirements for PAL CBSDs are defined in CFR 47 part 96, along with the other PAL license rules.

Note that even when PAL licenses are purchased, other CBSD users can still operate on the channel if the PAL licensee does not have deployments in the region that require protection in the PAL Protection Area (PPA). Note as well that the PAL entity is protected only within the county where the license has been purchased, and the PPA terminates at the county boundary. It is possible for a given PAL entity to have purchased PAL licenses across adjoining counties, but the computation for PPA assessment is done within each county.

The PAL auction was closed on August 25, 2020. The FCC database publishes the list of PAL licensees. Licenses are valid for 10 years. PAL licensees can use their PAL licenses with any SAS, starting on the date indicated in the CBRS status summary.

II.1.2.5 PAL Channel Allocation

SAS administrators coordinated to develop a methodology for PAL channel allocation in accordance with the CBRS functional and operational requirements developed in WInnForum. The methodology was developed by receiving the input from each operator on their channel preferences for their auctioned logical PAL channels.

All PAL licensees received information on the PAL Channel Assignment Procedure in December 2020. If you did not get the email about the PAL channel assignment procedure, or if you want to know more about the assignment procedure, send an email to the SAS administrators at cbrs_pal_channels@outlook.com.

II.1.2.6 Secondary Market

The PAL licensees can sell or sublicense their PALs to other operators for all or part of the licensed area. Sublicense agreements can be recorded by Google SAS in the FCC Universal Licensing System (ULS) database. To verify a licensee's claim of a PAL or sublicensed PAL, SAS checks the FCC ULS database.

II.1.2.6.1 General Authorized Access

GAA is intended to be opportunistic. GAA users can access the entire 150 MHz of the CBRS band between 3,550 and 3,700 MHz if IA and PAL users do not restrict its use. GAA channel allocations are done in 10 MHz bandwidth increments from the SAS. All GAA channel allocations are treated equally, and fairness is maintained by the SAS across the GAA allocations. GAA channel allocations can be preempted by IA and PAL users, and the CBSD needs to support switching from the current operating channel to the new allocations provided by the SAS. This change in allocation may be temporary and could result in reduced bandwidth, including complete non-availability of channels for GAA use.

A given deployment will typically support multiple CBSDs. The SAS provides the set of channels available to each CBSD. The self-organizing network (SON) within the deployment accounts for the allowed set of channels for each CBSD and tries to orthogonalize the channels used by each CBSD.

The use of neighboring network channels is determined by channel sensing. Based on the location of individual CBSDs and accounting for neighboring deployments using GAA channels, the GAA channel allocation to each CBSD is determined by the SON, avoiding interference with neighboring networks as well as with cells deployed within the same network.

With the PAL allocations in a county at a maximum of 70 MHz, the minimum available spectrum for GAA is 80 MHz. If there are fewer PAL allocations, more of it is available for GAA use.

With GAA and light licensing, while adhering to the rules of the channel usage, including the interactions with the SAS for authorization, LTE and NR deployments for enterprises become viable, similar to Wi-Fi. This GAA channel usage is a primary driver for the growth of private networks.

II.1.2.7 CBRS Architecture

CBRS is an LTE/NR TDD system that supports a dynamic spectrum allocation (DSA) scheme and is managed by a SAS. The SAS regulates the spectrum allocations/grants to the individual CBSDs. Once the spectrum assignment to the CBSD is complete, the CBSD operates as a regular eNB/gNB. The use of the spectrum is continually checked with the SAS through heartbeats to maintain the grants.

CBRS uses LTE/NR networks with some additional components to support CBRS operations. A CBRS network itself can be a private network integrated with the macro network or cable operator network. A private network can be configured to support neutral host networks (see Part II chapter on "NHN"), and the macro network can be configured to support PNI-NPN (see Part II chapter on "Non-public Networks").

Figure II.1.2.6 provides the key components associated with a CBRS-based network. The additional components needed for CBRS operations, including domain proxy (DP), SAS, and ESC functions, are also shown. It also includes the FCC database and a method to inform SAS of planned or active incumbent use through an Application Programming Interface (API) interface. CBSDs are LTE eNB or NR gNB and retain the functions as defined per 3GPP definitions.

The SAS provides grants to CBSD to use spectrum resources. The SAS enables a three-tiered priority access scheme, protecting higher-tier users from lower-tier users on a county basis. This approach enables many industry verticals to share spectrum with incumbent federal and non-federal users of the CBRS band while ensuring fairness. Apart from its operating parameters, the CBSD also reports on the radio environment seen on all 15 channels in the CBRS band and even the adjoining C-band in the 3.7 GHz and 3.45–3.55 GHz bands. Note that the transmission on one 10 MHz channel in the CBRS band has some interference seen up to 40 MHz around the 10 MHz, even with the low-power transmissions allowed in this band (1 W – category A; 50 W – category B). The neighboring bands to CBRS can transmit at ~3,500 W, a magnitude significantly higher than what is allowed in the CBRS band. The cells deployed in the CBRS band may conduct network planning to place the cell using the frequencies closer to the adjoining band, further away from the macro network cells as much as possible (e.g. indoors where the macro signal penetration will be significantly weaker).

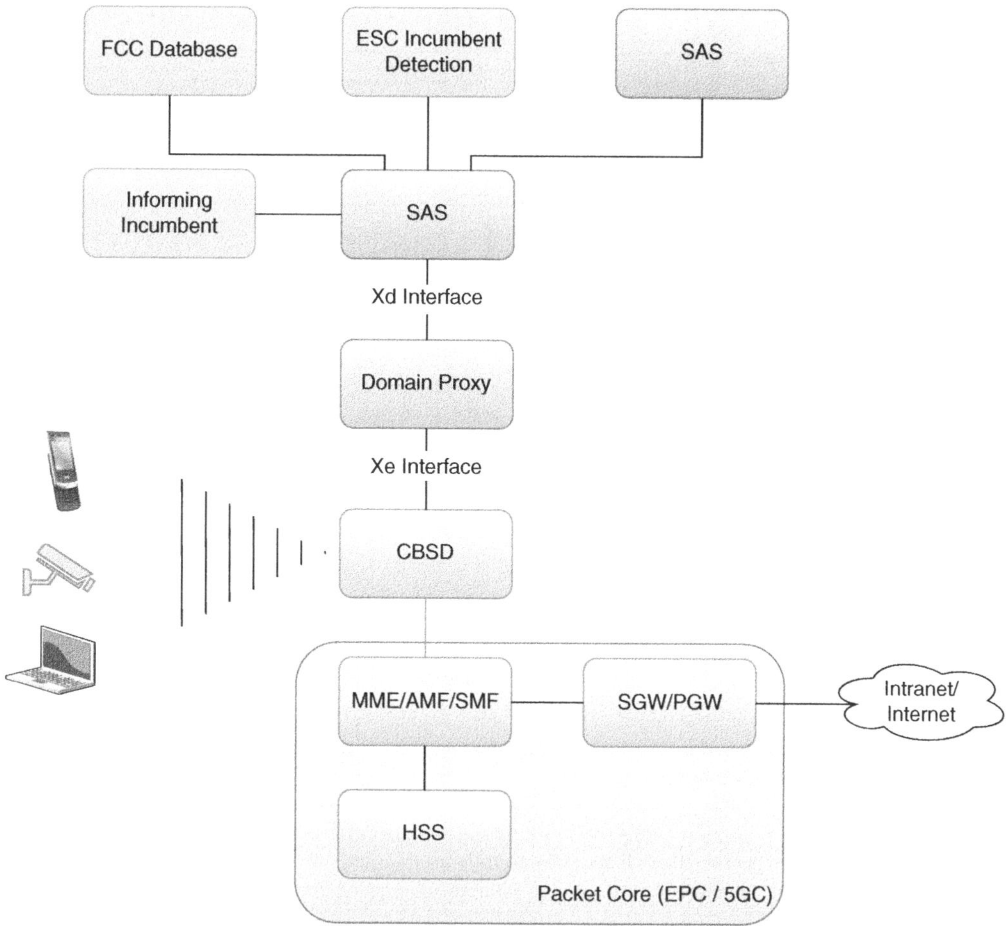

Figure II.1.2.6 CBRS network high-level architecture.

When managing the operations in the CBRS band, the SASs must also address interference complaints from FSS licensees. These, along with any other issues across deployments, need to be raised by the network operators to the SASs to address the concerns. It is extremely difficult to detect such occurrences from the SASs even if the different network deployments are willing to actively share their radio environment reports.

The SAS itself does not need to be a central entity and allows for multiple SAS vendors. The only requirement is that the SASs exchange "sufficient" information without disclosing the network operators to the other SASs so that effective coordination of the spectrum allocations can be performed. There are over 3,200 counties in the USA, and the SASs need to coordinate spectrum allocation in each of the counties. This is both a daunting technical undertaking and a huge computational complexity, with the expectation that this coordination is done on a daily basis, typically done during the night. Currently, there are several approved SAS vendors in the market, and the individual deployments choose to work with a specific SAS vendor. It may also depend on the network vendor supporting the CBSD and DP, which may have performed the certification only with specific vendors.

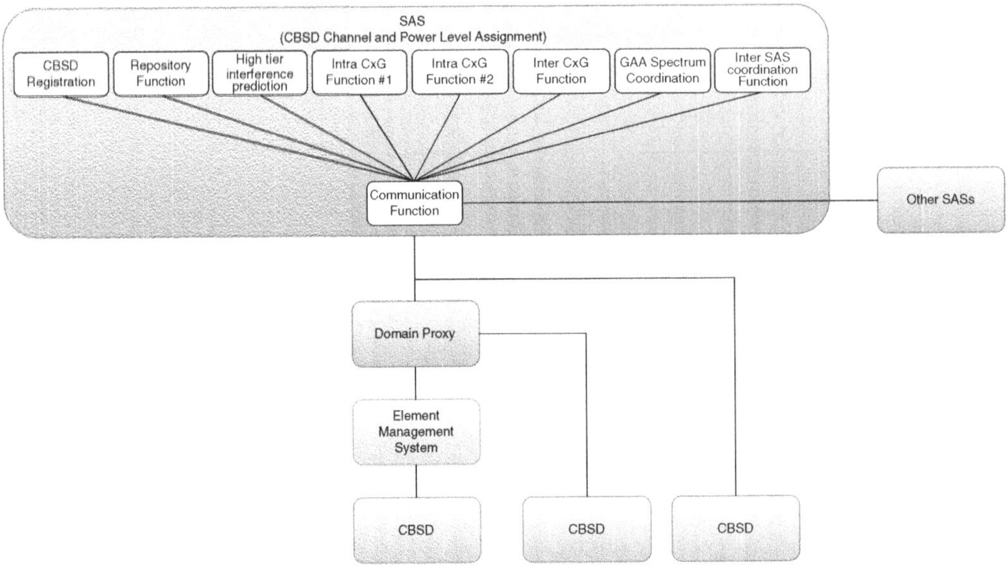

Figure II.1.2.7 SAS functional depiction.

A depiction of the key SAS function is shown in Figure II.1.2.7. The association with the CBSD/DP is shown.

SAS function	Description
CBSD registration function	Support CBSD registrations and deregistrations. It assigns the user ID and grant. IDs that are subsequently used for referencing the allocations provided to a CBSD.
Repository function	Stores data records and datasets for SAS to access through APIs. This includes all information about the CBSDs organized by county and ESC-related information.
Higher-tier protection function	Interface to receive information from the ESC and CBSDs regarding interferences observed. This information is used to determine the enforcement needed to protect the higher-tier users.
Intra-CxG coordination function	Support coexistence functions using a logical grouping of CBSDs. The grouping information is provided to the SAS as part of the registration, and the SAS ignores the interferences these CBSDs may cause to each other in doing the computations for channel assignment.
Inter-CxG coordination function	It is a functional block that coordinates spectrum allocations between CBSDs belonging to different CxGs. SAS supports the process by identifying potential interference relationships between CBSDs and aids by providing resolutions to address the interferences caused.
GAA spectrum coordination (GSC) function	Coordinates the GAA resource allocations across CxGs to minimize interference. Note that the interference associated with the CBSDs in each CxG is managed by that CxG. With GAA, groups of CBSDs are often on the same channel, and this grouping information is defined by the following group types: • Coexistence groups (CxG): The GSC performs the inter-CxG interference coordination for GAA spectrum users. CBSDs are configured as a particular CxG.

SAS function	Description
	• Interference coordination groups (ICG): A CxG can be part of one or more ICGs. What is important is that CSBDs in an ICG group are capable of managing interference among themselves. • Common channel groups (CCG): A CBSD can be part of a CCG, which is a subset of the CBSDs for an ICG. In the CCG, all CBSDs use the same channel assignment issued from the CxM. GSC assumes a single TDD configuration in coordinating spectrum allocation for both Inter- and Intra-CxG and is operating in a synchronous manner. Time drifts can happen when using different clock sources, and these need to be detected in the field and the defaulting network address to the timing distribution issue.

II.1.2.8 Environmental Sensing Capability

The ESC is a collection of sensors deployed along the coast of the USA to detect Navy radars, identifying incumbent usage and alert the SAS. Once the alerts are received, the SAS clears parts of the CBRS band for the IA users. The ESC sensors can also be located inland to support other functions.

ESCs can and will detect any IA frequency use in and adjacent to the CBRS frequency band and make this information available to the SASs in real time. Based on the ESC information provided, the SAS can provide reallocations to the PAL and GAA users.

A SAS can use an independent ESC or have its own ESC deployed. Like the SAS, there can be multiple ESC vendors deployed, potentially in the same region. Given the receive sensitivity of the ESC, a region around the ESC is marked as having lower power usage requirements by the CBSDs. Such subdued operations are required to allow the ESC to reliably detect the Navy radars.

II.1.2.9 Domain Proxy

The DP is an intermediary that is used to consolidate a set of CBSDs deployed on a given campus or potentially even across campuses to interact with the SAS. This helps avoid the need for individual CBSDs to establish communication channels with the SAS. The DP can aggregate messages from several CBSDs to the SAS and can receive aggregated messages from the SAS to be distributed to the CBSDs. The DP can also house the function of SON or coexistence coordination for interference migration for CBSDs using GAA with a deployment.

Figure II.1.2.8 shows functional blocks that comprise the DP.

II.1.2.10 Citizens Broadband Radio Service Device (CBSD) - eNB/gNB

A CBSD is the radio base station for a CBRS network – eNB/gNB. The radio access network (RAN) architecture can range from a “fat-AP” with all the features built into a single box to supporting different split architectures (see Part I, “NR fundamentals” chapter) and is realized using O-RAN functional separation with Radio Unit (RU), Distributed Unit (DU), and Central Unit (CU) (see Part II, “RIC” chapter). Figure II.1.2.9 is a depiction of the functional blocks of a typical CBSD.

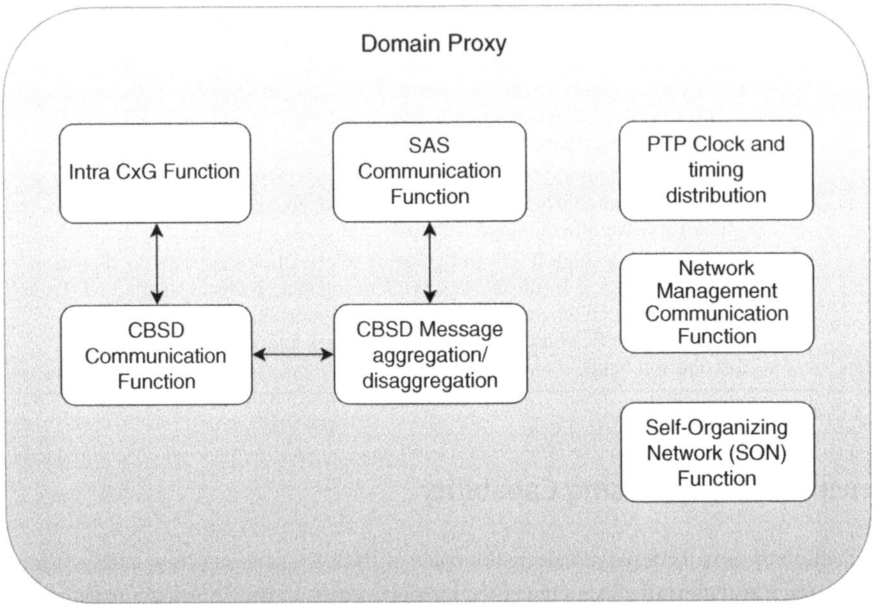

Figure II.1.2.8 Domain proxy functional blocks.

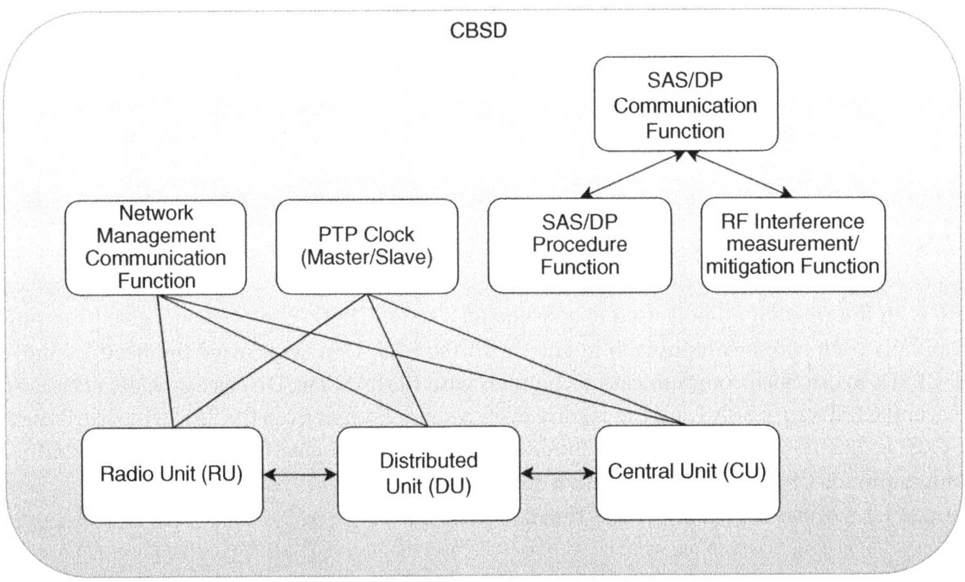

Figure II.1.2.9 CBSD functional blocks.

The PAL/GAA channel allocations are provided to these nodes for operations in the CBRS band.

The CBSD may optionally support measurements to determine RF interference in the 15 CBRS channels. This may be essential for GAA operations.

CBSDs can be either category A or category B devices. Category A device can operate both indoors and outdoors and supports a lower antenna gain compared to category B. Category B

Table II.1.2.1 CBSD categories.

Category	A	B
EIRP (per 10 MHz)	30 dBm	47 dBm
Location	Indoor/outdoor <6 m AGL	Outdoor
Certified (professional install)	No	Yes

devices are required to operate outdoors only with higher effective isotropic radiated power (EIRP) or antenna gain.

Table II.1.2.1 provides the operating parameters for CBSD categories A and B. These categories are independent of PAL or GAA modes of operation.

Note that with CBRS, relays or repeaters are not allowed, which includes mesh networks on the CBRS band as specified by FCC guidelines.

II.1.2.11 CBRS Identifiers

CBRS leverages the LTE/NR identifiers as is. In addition, there is a set of identifiers that support the operations on CBRS. The CBRS-specific identifiers, userId and grantId, are used to recognize specific users and devices operating in the CBRS band. The userId identifies to the SAS who the CBSD network owner is, while the grantId identifies the specific spectrum grant or lease given by the SAS, which the DP implements. Aside from this, additional identifiers are specified for coexistence between PAL and GAA operations defined to allow for appropriate use of the shared spectrum.

There is a set of LTE and NR identifiers that define system camping and mobility within systems deployed on the CBRS band, which share the identifier address spaces. Given that, the values a given user in the CBRS band is allowed to use are regulated and issued by the OnGo Alliance.

Refer to Part I "LTE Fundamentals" and "NR Fundamentals" on the different identifiers that help the User Equipment (UE) camp and operate on various networks. The CBRS-specific applicability of the relevant identifiers is captured below. Visit the OnGo Alliance web pages (see [6]) to purchase the identifiers. These can be purchased by both members and non-members of the CBRS Alliance. Refer to the OnGo Alliance website for purchasing details.

The identifiers related to LTE/NR for CBRS are:

Identifier	Description
PLMN ID	Broadcast by the eNB/gNB and used by the UE to find valid networks to camp on, based on the provisioning of the Public Land Mobile Network (PLMN) list in the UE. OnGo Alliance, through the Alliance for Telecommunications Industry Solutions (ATIS) organization, requested and obtained the allocation of the 315-010 PLMN-ID for use on the CBRS band, which can be shared by any entity wanting to operate on the CBRS band. Note that this identifier, 315-010, is restricted to use only on the CBRS band and cannot be used on any other band. OnGo refers to this identifier as the home network identifier (HNI), given that this PLMN will be used in smaller footprint networks, including enterprises. The international mobile subscriber identifiers (IMSIs) and other network identifiers, like the E-UTRAN Cell Global Identifier (ECGI)/tracking area identifier (TAI), are issued against this PLMN-ID and managed by the OnGo Alliance. When the numbers are exhausted, the OnGo Alliance can get other PLMN-ID/HNI allocations (Figure II.1.2.10).

(*Continued*)

Identifier	Description
	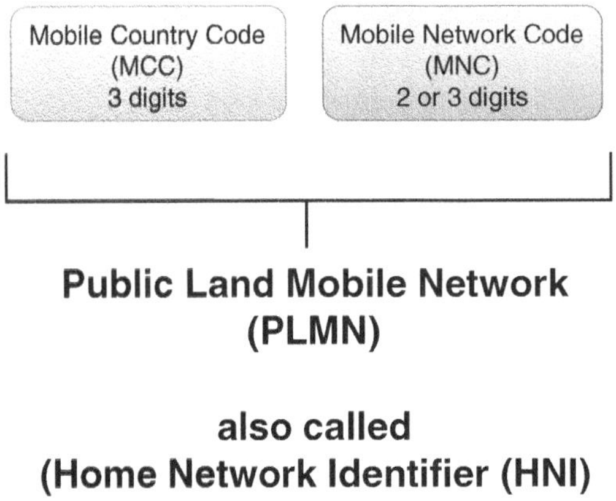 **Figure II.1.2.10** PLMN-ID.
Network ID	This can be broadcast by the network, and the UE uses it to find such networks (see chapter on "Non-public Networks"). This may be used as an identifier to recognize the credentials in the UE and is associated with a geofence for an enterprise network provisioned by the device provisioning platforms. The network ID for CBRS is called the CBRS-NID. The CBRS-NID is a CSG-ID (closed subscriber group ID) in LTE/NID (network identifier in NR). This network identifier is used to distinguish one private network from another, given that the PLMN-ID may be shared among private networks. The OnGo Alliance has obtained a PLMN-ID of 315-010, which is available to any private network that wants to use it. Even when the network does not broadcast the NID, it can be associated with the credential provisioned on the device, and the device provisioning platform provisions the geofence information associated with the NID. The NID allocations are received by a network vendor, and based on the private network deployed and the regions of use, the NID itself may be reused as long as there is no likelihood of geographic overlap of the network or the possibility of the end-users going into the footprint of the wrong network. This can easily be regulated by provisioning the relevant geofence(s) of the valid private network in the individual devices. The CBRS-NID is assigned by the CBRS Alliance for setup and annual maintenance fees and can be purchased by both members and non-members of the CBRS Alliance.
IMSI	The IMSI recognizes the identity of the subscribed credential stored in the device. The format of an IMSI is shown in Figure II.1.2.11. With an IMSI, the Mobile Country Code (MCC) and Mobile Network Code (MNC), as the HNI, are used to identify a shared CBRS HNI. The shared HNI for CBRS is 315-010. There are 10 K IBN numbers available, and within each IMSI Block Number (IBN), there can be 100 K unique numbers. However, there are a few IBNs that are already defined. Currently, two IBNs have been set aside. • 0000 – Unassignable • 9999 – Test purposes Associated with each IBN purchase, 10K IMSIs are made available, derived from the assigned IBN.

Identifier	Description
	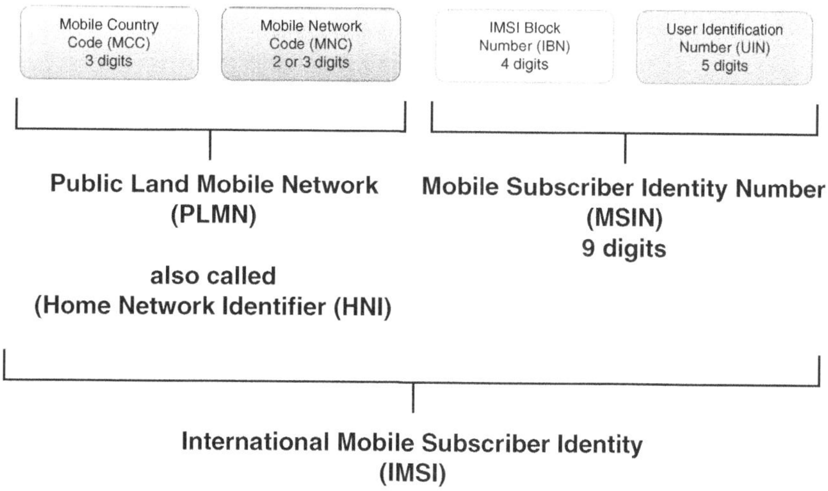 **Figure II.1.2.11** IMSI.
MME ID/ AMF ID	This network identifies the Mobility Management Entity (MME) and Access and Mobility Management Function (AMF) supporting mobility across networks. This may not be relevant until roaming and mobility across private networks are supported. In an LTE network, the MME is part of the authentication and mobility process. Each MME in an LTE network has four identities that define it. • MME code (MMEC) • MME group identity (MMEGI) • MME identifier • Globally unique MME identifier (GUMMEI) Figure II.1.2.12 shows the relationship between the PLMN-ID and the MMEI for creating the GUMMEI. The GUMMEI is assigned by the OnGo Alliance. 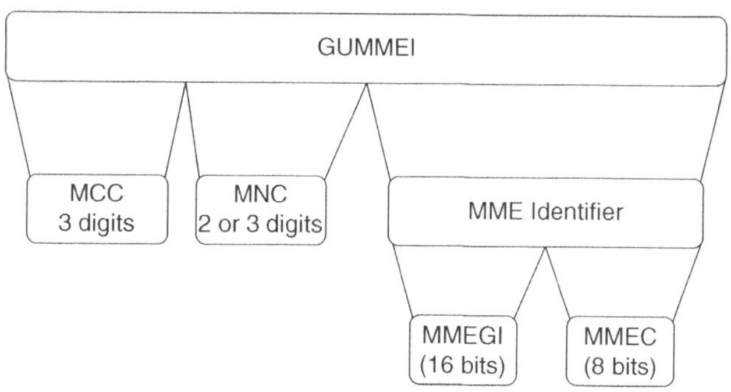 **Figure II.1.2.12** GUMMEI.

(Continued)

Identifier	Description
ECGI	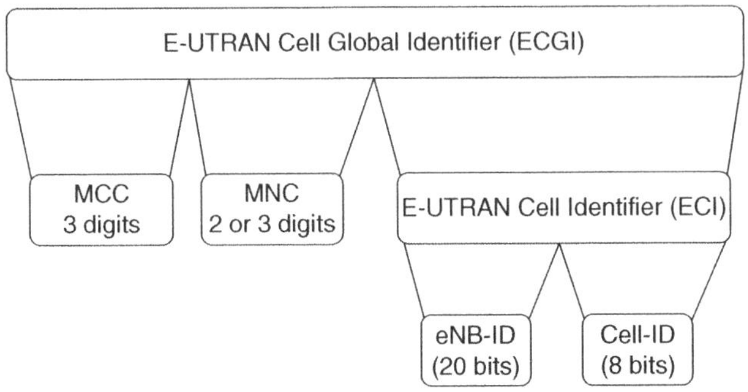 **Figure II.1.2.13** ECGI. It is the global cell identifier for each eNB/gNB that is deployed. The ECGI is how you identify an LTE/NR cell or sector, and it is made up of three unique identifiers. The ECGI is a globally unique ID and is composed of HNI (PLMN-ID), E-UTRAN cell identity (cell ID), and the eNB ID. The macro eNB ID is 20 bits, while the small-cell ID is 28 bits. For NR, the size of the macro gNB ID is flexible, with the cell ID occupying 36 bits. The cell ID (a smaller address space used for UE reporting for mobility), which typically ranges in value from 0 to 503, is unique and is used to distinguish the LTE cell from its surrounding neighbors. NR supports double the number of cell IDs, ranging from 0 to 1007. The cell IDs can be reused, but with sufficient separation in the deployment, the UE will not see two eNBs/gNBs that have the same cell ID (Figure II.1.2.13). EGCIs need to be explicitly purchased by the network vendor or deployment entity.
TAI	The tracking area code (TAC) identifies a tracking area within a particular network, identifying paging zones, and the UE informs the network when it transitions between TAC regions. TAI is globally unique, as shown in Figure II.1.2.14. As part of the purchase of the IBN, OnGo Alliance allows for six TAIs to be available to the CBRS user. The TAI is derived as (IBN, IBN + 10 K, IBN + 20 K, IBN + 30 K, IBN + 40 K, IBN + 50 K). The number of IBNs available is 10 K. A CBRS user can purchase one or more IBNs. There are no restrictions in terms of the IMSIs derived from the IBNs used for a deployment and the TAIs used for a given campus if they are from the same CBRS user. With 10 K IBNs and 6 TAIs per IBN, 60 K TAIs are possible. This leaves 5535 TAIs ([2^16 = 64 K] – 60 K) to be available. OnGo Alliance allows for these TAIs to be purchased on a county basis and is managed independently of the IBN purchases. For NR TAI, both 16 bits and 24 bits are supported. Apart from these 16-bit TAI, OnGo Alliance makes available a set of six allocations from the higher-order byte, supporting up to 240 24-bit TAIs associated with a given IBN purchase. The 5535 16-bit TAIs, along with the extensions to the higher-order byte from the 24-bit TAI, are available for purchase from OnGo Alliance on a county basis. 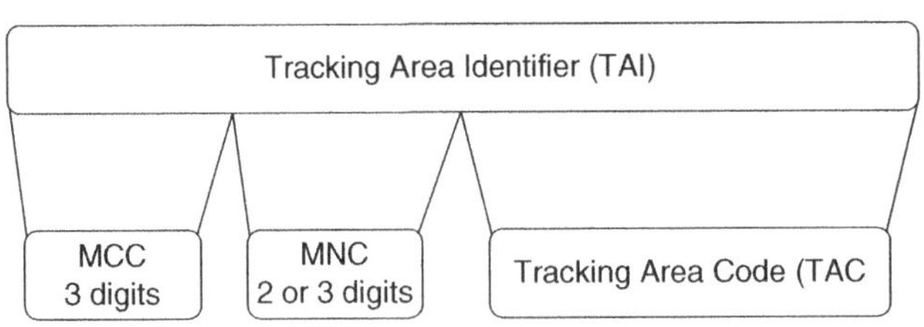 **Figure II.1.2.14** TAI.

II.1.2.12 CBSD Interactions with the SAS

The CBSD operations on the CBRS band are regulated by the SAS. This section details some of the key procedures used by the CBSD to interact with the SAS to acquire channel allocations and to operate.

Figure II.1.2.15 shows the CBSD interactions with the SAS via the DP. The sequence of activities taken by the CBSD is described in Table II.1.2.2 with the identified steps below. Each deployment is configured with a preferred SAS vendor and the associated Fully Qualified Domain Name (FQDN)/IP address for interaction.

1) Registration of the CBSD
2) Spectrum inquiries
3) Grants (temporary spectrum leases)
4) Heartbeat
5) Relinquishments – surrendering of the RF channels
6) Deregistration of the CBSD

A brief description of each of the major processes is provided below.

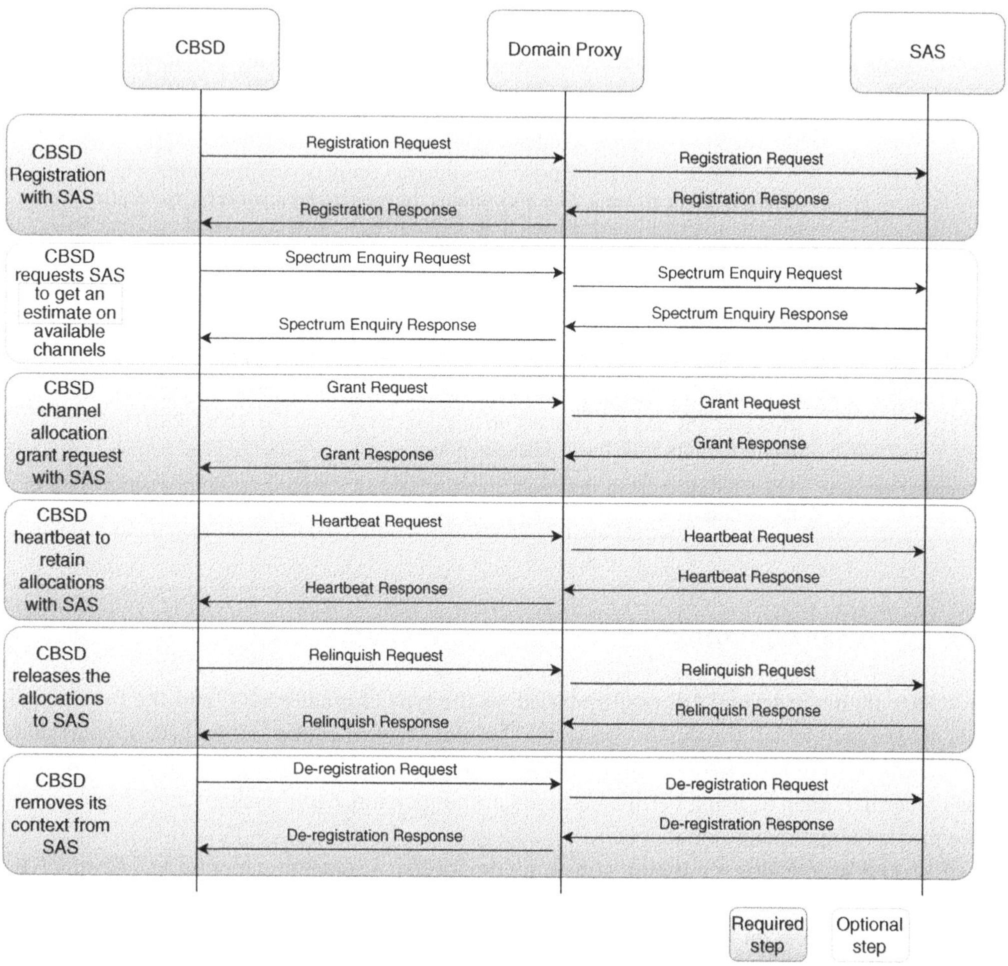

Figure II.1.2.15 CBSD and SAS interactions.

Table II.1.2.2 CBSD – SAS interactions.

Procedure	Description
Registration	All CBSDs must register with the SAS to be allowed to operate on the CBRS spectrum. Registration is typically done via a domain proxy (DP). The CBSD provides its geolocation, category A/category B operations, elevation, and the antenna parameters to register with the SAS. Typical deployments abstract the connectivity procedures to the SAS via a DP, with the CBSD interacting with the DP to perform the registration on its behalf. The SAS returns a CBSD-ID upon completing the registration, and this identifier is used for subsequent communications.
Spectrum inquiry	The spectrum inquiry allows the CBSDs to assess the possible set of channels that the SAS may make available to them. This allows for planning across the CBSDs in a deployment before requesting an actual grant for spectrum from the SAS.
Grant request/ response	The Grant Request is the explicit request for spectrum allocation. This step may or may not use the spectrum inquiry information. SAS provides the grants and associates them with the CBSD-ID. The grant information includes the time of the grant, the allocated channels, and the power level to be used for operations. The CBSD, having received the grant allocations, still needs to go through one heartbeat cycle/procedure prior to using the allocations provided.
Heartbeat request/ response	The heartbeat request message is used to retain the spectrum allocations provided. The heartbeat request has the cbsdID as well as the grantID. The periodicity of the message ensures that the grants do not expire. SAS can use the response to indicate the suspension and/or termination of the grants provided to the CBSD. It is possible that an enterprise loses internet connectivity, preventing it from sending the heartbeats. The SAS retains the context for a period of time, after which, upon not hearing back from CBSD/DP, the grants are revoked. The CBSD can free-loop until the keep-alive timer expires, after which it needs to stop radiating.
Relinquish	The relinquishment process begins with the CBSD and occurs when the CBSD decides it no longer requires the spectrum allocations. The cbsdID and grantID are provided to the SAS to relinquish the grant. The CBSD needs to stop radiating after relinquishing the grant. These channels can be reallocated to other CBSDs. However, the SAS does not act on this proactively, and the other CBSDs need to request grants to receive additional grants.
DeRegistration	The CBSD can deregister itself from the SAS. This is typically done when a CBSD is decommissioned.

II.1.2.13 User Equipment

With CBRS, there are several UE profiles based on the type of credential(s) and the private and public networks to which the device connects. The more typical configuration is to support dual SIMs: private and public network credentials. It is also possible for the device to support non-SIM-based credentials such as using certificate-based authentication. See the chapter on security and device provisioning for additional details.

A CBRS end-user device is a typical consumer device like a smartphone or an IoT device, NB-IoT, or category for machine-type communication (MTC) (Cat-M).

The end-user devices on a CBRS network allow a maximum EIRP of 200 mW, similar to regular cellular handsets used on commercial wireless licensed frequency bands.

The number of CBRS-capable devices is growing constantly. The URL http://www.cbrsalliance.org/certification/provides a view into the current ecosystem of UE devices supporting CBRS. One can largely assume that all devices currently available in the market are certified and support operation on the CBRS spectrum.

II.1.2.14 Summary

CBRS is finally here. CBRS is a shared spectrum service with three tiers of users, as defined by the FCC in CFR 47 part 96. The three tiers, in ranked order of priority, are the IA, PAL, and GAA. The incumbents using IA are federal radiolocation services (radar) and WISPs, who have priority over everyone else. On September 18, 2019, the FCC green-lighted the use of the CBRS spectrum for GAA.

CBRS spectrum is in the 3.5 GHz band, also called the innovation band. CBRS can be deployed using any wireless technology. Private networks are planned to support 3GPP LTE and NR systems. The CBRS consists of Environmental Sensing Capability (ESC), SAS, DP, and CBSD. The function of the SAS is to provide dynamic policy control for CBRS spectrum usage by granting temporary leases for CBSDs to use. The DP manages the local CBSDs by providing some dynamic spectrum control primarily for GAA users. CBSDs are the cell sites that use the CBRS band for short-term leases.

Both PAL and GAA grants for the channel are coordinated with the SAS. The SAS, however, for GAA does not coordinate access among GAA users at any given location. These issues need to be addressed locally (see Part II chapter on "SON").

Although the GAA spectrum availability can be a concern, it is expected to be reliable once deployed and spectrum allocations verified, given that the network deployment in the neighborhood will be reasonably stable. The GAA spectrum availability, particularly for in-building applications—which is the typical use case for a private network—should be ample.

CBRS enables non-traditional wireless carriers to potentially offer services at significantly lower costs than cellular carriers. CBRS also allows private wireless systems to be built, supporting campus and in-building applications. The entry of nontraditional wireless carriers and private networks fosters innovations that have been hampered due to recurring access fees. CBRS is important because it can unleash the true potential of IoT in the Industrial, medical, building automation, and hospitality industries, among others.

References

1 www.wirelessinnovation.org WInnForum focuses on spectrum sharing mechanisms for CBRS that are agnostic to the access technology
2 https://ongoalliance.org OnGo Alliance defines specifications and manages the certification program for operating LTE and NR networks on the CBRS band.
3 www.fcc.gov The FCC is also a reliable source of information, especially regarding rules and regulations for this frequency band.
4 https://www.cambiumnetworks.com
5 https://ntia.gov/fcc-filing/ntia-letter-fcc-commercial-operations-3550-3650-mhz-band
6 https://ongoalliance.org/resource/ongo-identifier-whitepaper/
7 https://www.nist.gov/advanced-communications/spectrum-crunch

II.1.3

RAN Scheduler

II.1.3.1 Introduction

This section addresses the aspects of a typical radio access network (RAN) scheduler implementation. It also suggests the knobs that should be made available, along with the scheduler properties that they invoke and the performance implications.

II.1.3.2 Background

The RAN schedulers have become fairly sophisticated of late and customized to specific services the quality of services (QoS) demands. A good balance is between meeting the QoS requirement of the individual flows associated with the user equipment (UE) and managing the UE's power consumption needs while optimizing the system capacity. With limited spectrum availability, the efficiency of the scheduler catering to the enterprise specific service needs becomes even more heightened. Meeting the demands of the enterprise is an extremely sensitive topic that must be considered in the inherent design of the enterprise network. Although the scheduler aspects cannot be directly discussed with the enterprises—where the focus will be on the actual service experience—this topic becomes front and center of every discussion. The radio frequency (RF) design, the number of base stations deployed, the location of the base stations, together with the RF planning, QoS requirements of different enterprise applications, system capacity scaling allowing room for future growth, and definitions and agreements signed with the service-level agreements (SLA) based on the defined service-level objectives (SLOs) are, in some form, directly or indirectly impacted by the choices made in the scheduler.

The base station RAN scheduler models of using Max-C/I, where the fairness across UEs is ignored to maximize cell throughput, to the other extreme of absolute fairness across UEs with the round-robin approach accommodate the throughput ignoring the cell capacity exist. The proportional-fair scheduler is defined to balance the two aspects of maintaining high cell throughput while still guaranteeing some fairness for all the UEs in the cell. This is done by assigning each data flow a data rate or scheduling priority that is directly proportional to the signal strength of the UE and inversely proportional to the already severed throughput for the UE, which translates to managing the UEs' anticipated resource consumption. Proportional fairness can be applied for best-effort flows; however, this does not directly address the QoS requirements for the individual flows. Special considerations need to be provided for meeting the packet delay budget (PDB) of the individual flows associated with the UE. Additionally, the

Mobile Communication Systems for Private Networks, First Edition. Srinivasan Balasubramanian.

UE sleep cycles of connected mode discontinuous reception (C-DRX) need to be supported to allow the UE to sleep between points of exchanging traffic on the downlink (DL) and uplink (UL) to enable power-saving for the UE.

The UE is scheduled at a slot level using physical resource blocks (PRB). For DL, the network knows the accumulated traffic and uses that to determine the UEs that need to be scheduled. For the UL, the UE needs to report the current buffer status information to the network, which the network uses to provide the appropriate UL grants to the UE. Refer to the "RAN Fundamental" and "NR Fundamentals" sections in the book, where these details are captured.

RAN scheduler ranges from Max-C/I, which is completely biased toward scheduling UEs with the strongest signal strength and ignores fairness, all the way to round-robin, which ensures fairness but ignores signal strength, thereby impacting system capacity and potentially QoS demands of the individual flows. The more typical choice is to use a Proportional-fair scheduler (PFS), where the scheduling function is directly proportional to the signal strength of the UEs and inversely proportional to the data throughput already served to the UE in the immediate past. This approach works for best-effort type of flows such as web browsing and email traffic. Specializations are needed to support specialized services like Voice over IP (VoIP), conversational video, which has real-time, throughput, and delay constraints.

This chapter covers details that are an inherent part of RAN scheduler design and implementation. It discusses the different attributes that typically drive the RAN scheduler. A description of the different attributes with the tradeoffs involved are covered along with potential parameters that can be employed.

II.1.3.3 Typical Goals of a RAN Scheduler

Table II.1.3.1 discusses the different attributes and goals associated with a typical RAN scheduler. The RAN metrics and key performance indicator (KPIs) to measure scheduler performance are described in Table II.1.3.2.

Table II.1.3.1 RAN scheduler goals.

Scheduler Metric	Description
Accessibility	How easy it is for the user to obtain a requested service within the specified tolerances and other given conditions. Session setup time and call success rate are the examples of accessibility KPIs.
Retainability	The network's ability to continuously provide the requested service under specified conditions over the desired period. An example of a KPIs in this context is the session abnormal rate, which indicates poor retainability of the network.
Integrity	The degree to which the service is provided without excessive impairments, such as uplink/downlink throughput, latency, and packet drops.
Mobility	When the user moves from one cell to another, the handover performance and other mobility-related performance are measured in mobility KPIs.
Availability	The percentage of the time is considered available. In some cases, although the cell may seem to be up and running, it can be sleeping or in an outage condition due to some anomaly or may be disabled manually because of the operator's maintenance procedures. In such case, poor network availability or complete outage can occur.
Utilization	The simultaneous use of network resources without affecting the end-user experience.
CPU limitations	Only a few UEs can be scheduled in each slot for scheduling due to CPU limitations.
Fairness criteria	The choice of fairness and priority calculation is made to avoid floating-point calculations and reduce computational impacts.
Metrics/KPI monitoring	To monitor and optimize or assess the scheduler to provide better performance.

Table II.1.3.2 RAN metrics/KPIs to measure scheduler performance.

Metrics/KPIs	Requirement
Throughput	Collect the downlink and uplink throughput over certain slot for scheduling to understand the behavior of the scheduler under a specific configuration setup.
Latency	The time it takes to schedule the first packet on the air interface.
Packet drop or packet drop	The rate of congestion-related packet losses (for example, packets dropped due to active queue management)
Handover procedure time	Observe the events of intra- and inter-frequency handover times.
Handover success rate	Observe the events of intra- and inter-frequency success rates.
Service interruption time in ms	Observe the events of intra- and inter-frequency service interruption times.
Service accessibility (%) and completed session ratio (%)	Calculate the accessibility of application services or data services, such as FTRAFFIC-PRIORITY and HTTRAFFIC-PRIORITY.
Accessibility	1) RRC connection establishment 2) Random access 3) Initial E-RAB establishment success rate 4) RRC connection establishment counters S1 signaling connection establishment
Retainability	1) Mobility Management Entity (MME)-initiated session and UE context release UE session time
Integrity	1) Throughput KPIs 2) Latency KPIs Packet loss KPIs
Mobility	1) X2 handover-based preparation and execution 2) Intra-frequency handover preparation and execution 3) Inter-frequency handover preparation and execution S1-based handover preparation and execution
Availability	Partial cell availability
Utilization	Measure the utilization of the network to determine whether the network capacity has reached its resources.

II.1.3.4 Scheduler Configurations

Parameter setting	Default setting	Description
Scheduler weights for GBR bearers	Guaranteed bit rate (GBR) bearer {1,2,3,4} = assigned weights {8,6,7,5}	A higher weight is used for GBR bearers with higher priority.
Scheduler weight for QCI-5	QoS class identifier (QCI) {5} = assigned weight {9}	Support signaling radio bearer (SRB) and session initiation protocol (SIP), which need to be treated with the highest priority.
Scheduler weights for low latency bearer	Low latency bearer {80} = assigned weights {11}	Low latency bearers need to be treated with urgency and are more prioritized than the signaling and the GBR bearers, which can handle some amount of latency.

(Continued)

Parameter setting	Default setting	Description
Scheduler weights for delay critical bearers	Non-GBR bearer {82,83,84,85,86,87,88,89,90} = assigned weight {10}	The delay critical GBR requires the data traffic to be supported up to a certain throughput level, and any generated traffic above that limit is specified to be handled with low priority. These are typically used in industrial settings where control systems are established and require tight timing to manage the manufacturing processes. The priority of this traffic needs to be handled above that of regular GBR bearers and the signaling bearer.
Scheduler weights for GBR bearers	Non-GBR bearer {6,7,8,9} = assigned weights {4,3,2,1}	Non-GBR bearers have a lower priority than other bearers, however, they maintain a relative priority among themselves.
Fairness factor	0	A bias that can be applied to the fairness that can be maintained across users' flows.
Traffic-priority-weight	QCI-based weight bias	In addition to the strict priority of handling the different flows, this bias can be used to further adapt the extent to which it is applied. This approach can be implement a non-linear bias in managing the different traffic types.
W_{PDB}	0	The extent of bias that can be applied when the packets in the queue are getting closer to the PDB value. This approach will allow for elevating the priority of the queue that has packets coming close to the PDB while there is still traffic in the higher-priority queues.
Maximum number of UEs schedulable in a slot for scheduling	N-users-per-slot for scheduling	There is a central processing unit (CPU) limit on the number of UEs that can be scheduled in each slot for scheduling. This number for small cells typically tends to be ≤ 5.
Scheduler refresh window	~500 ms	This scheduler window is used to ensure that different UEs get the requisite grants within this window while still allowing some flexibility in the scheduler to handle the different users to accommodate better system throughput. A very small window implies that the scheduler has extremely low flexibility, while a very large window will imply that there is starvation of specific flows which may result in not meeting the QoS requirements.

II.1.3.5 Per Flow Input Parameters

PFS selects candidate for scheduling based on the following parameters associated with the individual flows:

Input parameter	Description
QCI weight (QCI_{Weight})	Weight associated with a specific flow activated in the UE. The value will depend on the bearer type of low latency, delay critical, signaling, GBR, maximum bit rate (MBR), aggregate maximum bit rate (UE-AMBR).
Fairness window	Proportionality applied on the scheduler refresh window based on the serviced data throughput within that interval.
Traffic-priority-weight (traffic-priority)	This indicates the weight associated with the real-time channel conditions of the UE. The CQI/SRS/PER value reported by UE is used to determine the the selected entry of the TBS-tables used. The weight is determined based on the the selected entry of the TBS-tables used to schedule a given UE.
Packet delay budget weight (W_{PDB})	This is applicable for the DL only and looks at the delays incurred by the enqueued packets yet to be serviced by the scheduler and provides the weights subject to the PDB limits specified for the flow.

II.1.3.6 UE Scheduler Fairness Time-Period Window

Each time a UE is connected to the cell, the first scheduling event for the UE starts the clock for the initial fairness time-period window. This happens when the UE connects to a cell, enters connected mode from idle mode, or is handed over from another cell into this cell. Each UE will follow its own fairness time-period window. To avoid spikes in CPU, a maximum of N UEs are aligned to a specific slot (see Figure II.1.3.1).

This fairness time-period window is currently a fixed interval. At the expiration of this timer, all the scheduler metrics used for the given UE are reset and restarted at every refresh cycle.

During this fairness time-period window, the UE's scheduling priorities are computed for the individual flows, subject to the real-time context of the serviced data throughput, UE's channel conditions, and queue buildup.

II.1.3.7 Fairness Factor

Fairness factor (F_{Factor}) tries to maintain the same average throughputs for all UEs within each fairness time-period window. This F_{Factor} is applied as an overarching outer-loop function and is handled independently of the instantaneous metrics applied toward each schedulable event (typically a single time slot – see "Part I: long term evolution (LTE) Fundamentals and NR Fundamentals" for the definition of a slot), where queue/data from specific UEs and flows associated with the UE are scheduled. The F_{Factor} ensures the different UEs and the flows within each UE are served with the required fairness over the longer time interval. This allows for short optimizations to be performed independently of the longer-term averaging needed to maintain the fairness in the system.

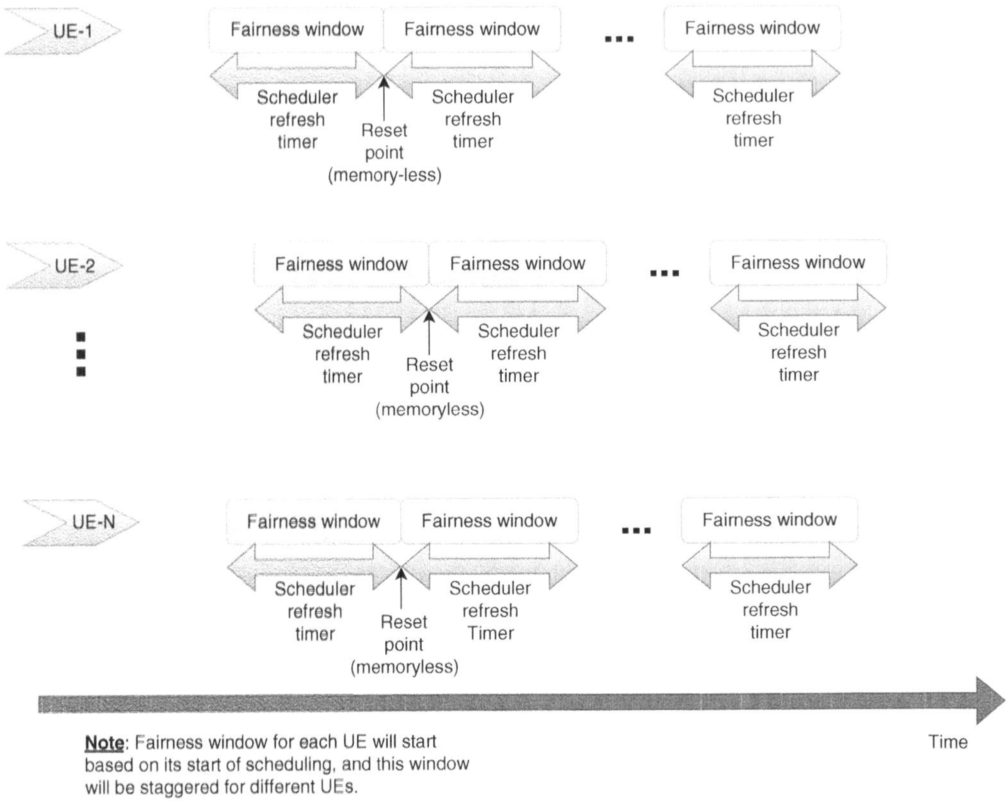

Figure II.1.3.1 RAN scheduler refresh window.

The choice of the fairness time window size determines the experience seen with the different services in the network. A larger time window will allow for better adaptability for the individual schedulable events but will increase burstiness/jitter in the individual UE/UE flows. A smaller time window will ensure a more uniform service experience for the individual UE/UE flows but reduced flexibility for each schedulable event and hence can impact overall system capacity. An optimal choice needs to be made considering the trade-offs and the real-time enterprise service experience, with parameters tuned accordingly.

A fairness coefficient can be used to better manage the bias as well, for example, UE/UE flows; the throughput metric calculation for a given UE can be managed as a sliding window to avoid such discreetness in the enforcement caused by the fairness window.

Fairness is calculated for the individual UE and the flows associated with the UEs.

II.1.3.8 CQI Bias (W_{CQI})

The channel quality indicator (CQI) bias gives higher priority to UEs with better CQI, which helps improve spectral efficiency and cell throughput.

A CQI bias coefficient can additionally be used to control how much weight is to be applied to the CQI bias in the PFS priority calculation. The scheduler realization can be done by specifying a set of scheduler parameters and grouping them in transport block tables (TBS-tables). A specific entry from the TBS-tables is selected, and the scheduler operations are guided by the parameter choices specified as part of this TBS-tables entry. The selected entry of the TBS-tables used value that is maintained as part of the scheduler definition, and each index provides a variation to the weight's realization associated with the different QCIs. The TBS-tables entry can be changed in real time, subject to the active adaptation needed, such as congestion levels in the network or the types of QoS flows that require priority based on the time of day or day of the week. This allows for learning of the traffic and usage patterns from the enterprise, enabling an appropriate choice of the scheduler parameters by selecting the TBS-tables entry.

II.1.3.9 Packet Delay Budget Weight (W_{PDB})

Delay is one of the primary metrics in delivering QoS for both GBR and non-GBR traffic. GBR flows are used to support services like VoIP, conversational video, and so on, with flows that have both minimum throughput guarantees and delay constraints that need to be met in real time. Non-GBR flows are typically best-effort flows like web browsing and email downloads. From a scheduler perspective, managing the packet delays of the enqueued packets is a fundamental metric used to define the scheduler function. The maximum supportable delay in the scheduler queue is typically specified for GBR bearers. The packet delay budget weight (W_{PDB}) is used to increase the priority of candidate UEs/individual flows that have older packets or service data unit (SDU) in the queue. Packet delay is calculated based on the timestamp of the oldest packet in logical channel queue at the scheduler. The delay budget is typically established when the QoS flow is created for the UE, and the same value is typically applied to all UEs with the QoS flows with specific LTE QCI or 5G QoS identifier (5QI) values. For more details on QoS, see "Part II: Slices" chapter in the book.

Although the scheduler typically treats that flow based on the priorities which are derived from the QCI/5CI associated with the flows, when treating the packets across UEs for a given QCI, the PDB tends to dominate the UE/UE flow selected to be scheduled. Specific scheduler realizations are possible where only the PDB is used as the scheduler function, based on the enterprise campus and the types of services that need to be supported for that enterprise.

II.1.3.10 Per Flow Instantaneous Scheduling Priority

The scheduling priority of the individual flows is determined in real time by looking across UEs for identifying the flows/UEs that need to be scheduled in each schedulable event (typically a slot).

Proportional-fair scheduler priority is used for prioritizing and resource allocation within the same service type. The QCI weight is used to prioritize the flows before applying the PFS across UEs with the same QCI/QCI weight. This is typically managed within a refresh window that allows for the scheduler to be memoryless in its realization without carrying the weight of significant history. This determined PFS priority is used to select the UE and the UE flows to be scheduled. The PFS priority is computed for each scheduling event, adjusting based on the UE/UE flows that have already been served.

II.1.3.10.1 DL (Downlink) Flow Scheduling Priority Determination

The priority for scheduling the individual DL flows for a given slot for scheduling, and hence the UEs scheduled in the slot for scheduling is determined based on the following information:

PFS priority ($P_{pfs}-_{DL}$) for a QCI flow associated with the UE in the DL is calculated as

$$P_{pfs-DL} = W_{QCI} * F_{Fairness} * W_{PDB}$$

where

- (W_{QCI}) is the weight associated with the QoS that is determined by the QCI/5QI value assigned to the flow.
- ($F_{Fairness}$) is a fairness factor is determined in real time based on the serviced data within the fairness time-period window.
- (W_{PDB}) is the packet delay budget weight and is determined in real time based on the time remaining for the packet that has remained longest in the queue.

II.1.3.10.2 UL (Uplink) Flow Scheduling Priority Determination

The priority for scheduling the individual UL flows for a given slot, and hence the UEs scheduled in the slot are determined based on the following information. Given that the base station (eNB/gNB) provides grants to the UE, these grants are provided for a logical channel rather than specific flows. A given logical channel can support multiple flows in the UL. The UE requests for grants as an overall buffer buildup or on a logical channel basis, depending on the data within the flows associated with the individual logical channels. The UE, based on the UL grants provided from the eNB/gNB, transmits the packets based on the flow priority and other metrics, including PDB.

The PFS priority of a logical channel ($P_{pfs} - _{UL}$) for QCI flows associated in the logical channel with the UE in the UL is calculated as follows:

$$P_{pfs-UL} = W_{QCI} * F_{Fairness} * W_{PDB}$$

where,

- (W_{QCI}) is the weight associated with the QoS that is determined by the QCI/5QI value assigned to the flow.
- ($F_{Fairness}$) is a fairness factor determined in real time based on the serviced data within the fairness time-period window.
- (W_{PDB}) is the packet delay budget weight and is determined in real time based on the time remaining for the packet that has remained longest in the queue.

II.1.3.11 PFS Implementation

The input queues to the scheduler are one per service type associated with each UE. Priority among the different service types within a given UE is absolute; that is, the scheduler always selects candidates from the higher-priority service type queue. Only when all candidates in the higher-priority queue are served does it move to the next/lower-priority queues to look for candidates.

II.1.3.11.1 DL PFS

In DL, the schedulable entity is QoS flow, which can be GBR or non-GBR. The priority of the individual flows is computed every slot for scheduling. The flows with the highest computed priorities $P_{pfs} - _{DL}$ are selected to be scheduled in each slot. This also implicitly selects the UEs that need to be scheduled. Given the computation limits at the eNB/gNB, with the scheduler decisions having to run through the queues for each scheduling slot, the number of UEs that can be accommodated will be limited. This limitation is a key factor for small cells used for private networks. The eNB/gNB not only has to prepare the data packets for transmission on the physical downlink shared channel (PDSCH) but also prepare the physical downlink control channel (PDCCH) control information to be provided on the DL, identifying the UEs being scheduled. Once a UE is selected, typically all traffic from that UE is accommodated, including the lower-priority ones. The scheduler limits the number of UEs for each schedulable event to a fixed number, which may result in some wasted resources if there is not enough traffic to occupy the full slot based on the UEs selected for scheduling.

The scheduler follows the sequence illustrated in Figure II.1.3.2.

Across the identified UEs for scheduling, and for flows within a UE for a given slot for scheduling, the queues for scheduling are selected based on the ordering indicated below. The priority queue list based on service/resource type is as follows, from high to low:

- Radio resource control (RRC) and non-access stratum (NAS) signaling traffic carried on the SRB
- GBR flows supported up to the minimum throughput guarantees
- GBR flows proportionally accommodating up to the MBR associated with the GBR flows
- Non-GBR bearers to opportunistically occupy the remaining available resources, subject to the aggregate maximum bit restrictions for the individual UEs.

The signaling flow is accommodated first. The hybrid ARQ (HARQ) retransmissions are scheduled after the signaling queues. Then the data queues for the identified UEs are processed. The GBR flows are scheduled. Once the GBR bit rate is met for all GBR flow, the bit rate of (MBR-GBR) data is processed. Subsequent to that, the queues from the non-GBR bearers are processed and are subject to the limitations of the UE-AMBR.

II.1.3.11.2 UL PFS

In UL, the schedulable unit is a logical channel group (LCG). The priority of the individual flows is computed every slot for scheduling. The flows with the highest computed priorities are selected to the scheduled in each slot for scheduling. This also implicitly selects the UEs that need to be scheduled. The scheduler limits the number of UEs scheduled to maximum number of UEs it can handle in a slot for scheduling.

The scheduler follows the sequence illustrated in Figure II.1.3.3.

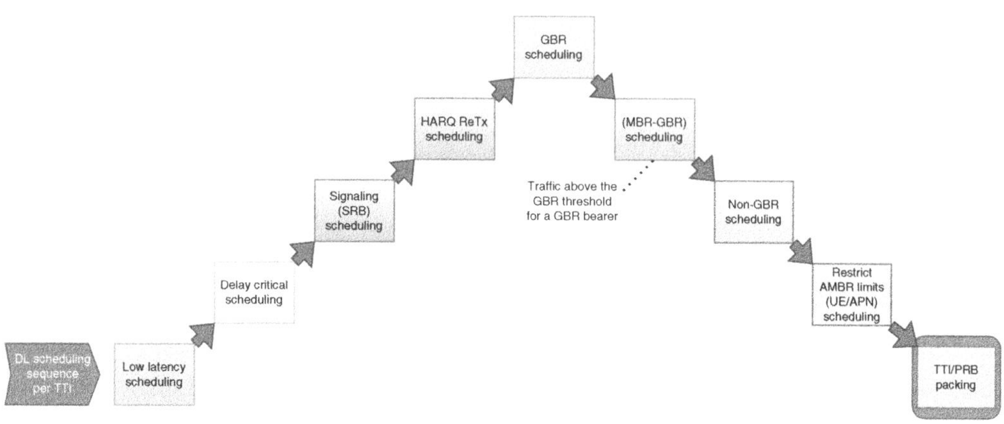

Figure II.1.3.2 RAN DL scheduling sequence per slot for scheduling.

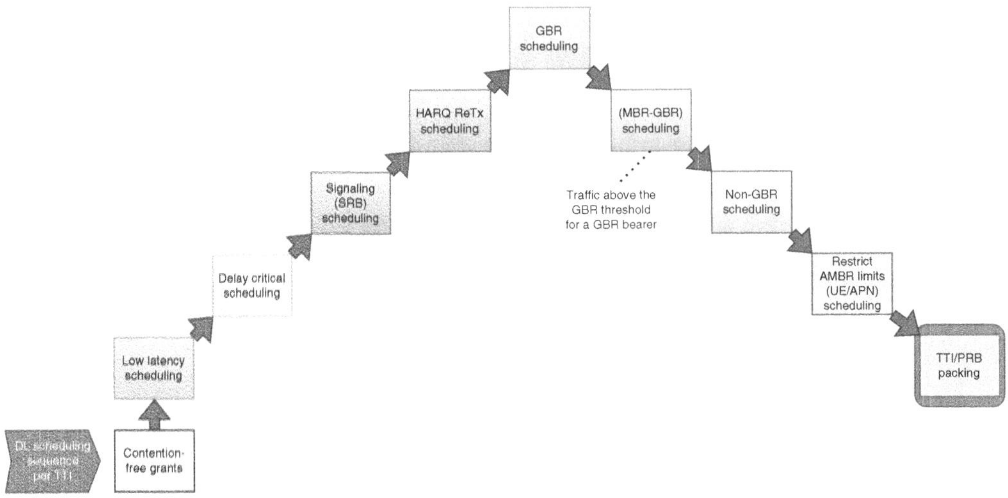

Figure II.1.3.3 RAN UL scheduling sequence per slot for scheduling.

Across the identified UEs for scheduling, and for flows within a UE for a given slot for scheduling, the queues for scheduling are selected based on the ordering indicated here. The priority queue list based on service/resource type is as follows, from high to low:

- Random access resources (RACH), both contention-based and contention-free
- RRC and NAS signaling traffic carried on the SRB
- GBR flows supported up to the minimum throughput guarantees
- GBR flows proportionally accommodating up to the MBR associated with the GBR flows
- Non-GBR bearers are to opportunistically occupy the remaining available resources, subject to the aggregate maximum bit restrictions for the individual UEs.

The contention-free grants, signaling flows, and scheduling request (SR) requests are accommodated first. The HARQ retransmissions are scheduled after the signaling queues. Then the data queues for the identified UEs are processed. The GBR flows are scheduled. Once the GBR bit rate is met for all GBR flows, the bit rate of (MBR-GBR) data is processed. Subsequent to that, the queues from the non-GBR bearers are processed and are subject to the limitations of the UE-AMBR.

II.1.3.11.3 Slot for Scheduling PRB Packing

Once the UEs/flows are selected for scheduling, the packets need to be prepared for transmission by packing them into the payload. For a given user, both on the DL and UL, data from multiple flows is included, and the medium access control (MAC) SDU is packed to prepare the MAC protocol data unit (PDU). The PRBs are determined for transmitting these packets. For DL, the network prepares these packets for transmission on the PDSCH. The UE is provided with the DL scheduling information on PDCCH, and the UE monitors the identified PDSCH resource to receive the packet. For UL, PDCCH commands for physical uplink shared channel (PUSCH) grants are provided to the UE, and UE performs the required packing to deliver the payload using the provided grant resource.

II.1.3.12 Summary

This section addresses the aspects of a typical RAN scheduler implementation. It also suggests a potential set of knobs that would be beneficial to be made available, along with the scheduler properties they invoke and the performance implications. The typical limitations of the compute resources in a small cell that is used for private network deployments, which justify the scheduler realization choices made, are highlighted.

Further Reading

1 Capozzi, F., Piro, G., Grieco, L.A. et al. (2012). *Downlink Packet Scheduling in LTE Cellular Networks: Key Design Issues and a Survey. IEEE Communications Surveys & Tutorials* This paper provides an extensive survey of different downlink packet scheduling algorithms for LTE. It examines fairness, resource allocation, and QoS metrics under varying conditions.

2 Kawser, M., Farid, H., Hasin, A. et al. (2012). *Performance Comparison Between Round Robin and Proportional Fair Scheduling Methods for LTE. International Journal of Information and Electronics Engineering*. This study compares two widely used LTE schedulers—Round Robin and Proportional Fair—highlighting trade-offs in throughput and fairness.

3 Pedersen, K.I., Niparko, M., Steiner, J. et al. (2016). *System Level Analysis of Dynamic User-Centric Scheduling for a Flexible 5G Design. IEEE GLOBECOM*. Focuses on flexible scheduling strategies in 5G and the dynamic management of resources based on user location and service requirements.

4 Panno, D. and Riolo, S. (2018). *A New Joint Scheduling Scheme for GBR and Non-GBR Services in 5G RAN. IEEE CAMAD*. Discusses a scheduling method that prioritizes both Guaranteed Bit Rate (GBR) and non-GBR services in 5G networks to optimize resource utilization and service quality.

5 Oliveira, A. and Vazão, T. (2021).RAN Slice Scheduler Simulator. *Zenodo*. This study explores scheduling methods in the context of 5G RAN slicing, focusing on service differentiation and resource allocation.

II.1.4

RAN Intelligent Controller (RIC)

II.1.4.1 Introduction

Artificial Intelligence (AI)/Machine Learning (ML) is actively being employed to address optimizations in many fields, and it is an active area of research ongoing in several wireless standards forums, including 3GPP and O-RAN. The landscape of the current happenings in 3GPP regarding AI/ML is captured in Figure II.1.4.1 for context. At a broad level, there are improvements being done to the NG air interface (physical layer/MAC layer) and other more generic optimizations classified under NG radio access network (RAN). These are more far-reaching, with some planned in 3GPP Release 18 (considered 5G Advanced) and most of it falling under 3GPP Release-19 (which falls more under sixth generation [6G]). Although these aspects don't immediately apply to private networks, watching this actively evolving space will be important.

Outside of the standards bodies, both user equipment (UE) and network vendors are enabling optimizations that support the learning functions (both localized and crowdsourced) and activate the currently supported standards features based on specific conditions being met. For example UE mobility handover failures are predicted, and proactive measurements and handovers are triggered in the system. Such techniques are applied in both macro networks and, equally so, private networks.

Private networks more so lend themselves to predictable patterns of behavior on services used, including the time of day and day of the week, that are custom to the individual enterprises and even localized to specific locations of a given enterprise. Private networks and the types of verticals are numerous, and tuning them individually will not allow for a scalable solution. Employing AI/ML potentially for both the Radio Access Network (RAN) and even some aspects of the core networks becomes essential.

The RAN intelligent controller (RIC) is a framework that can be employed, and the learnings across the private network verticals, with typical models developed through learnings potentially across participating network and UE vendors, will allow for significantly improved private network operations. These learnings can potentially be applied to macro networks as well, including transitions across macro and private networks. With the distributed antenna solutions (DAS) used for in-building deployment of private networks using licensed spectrum by the managed service provider (MSP, which many of the current Macro Operator Network (MNOs) are taking up in this function), the learnings for such solutions, together with operations using shared spectrum, will provide ample room for optimizations using AI/ML.

Mobile Communication Systems for Private Networks, First Edition. Srinivasan Balasubramanian.

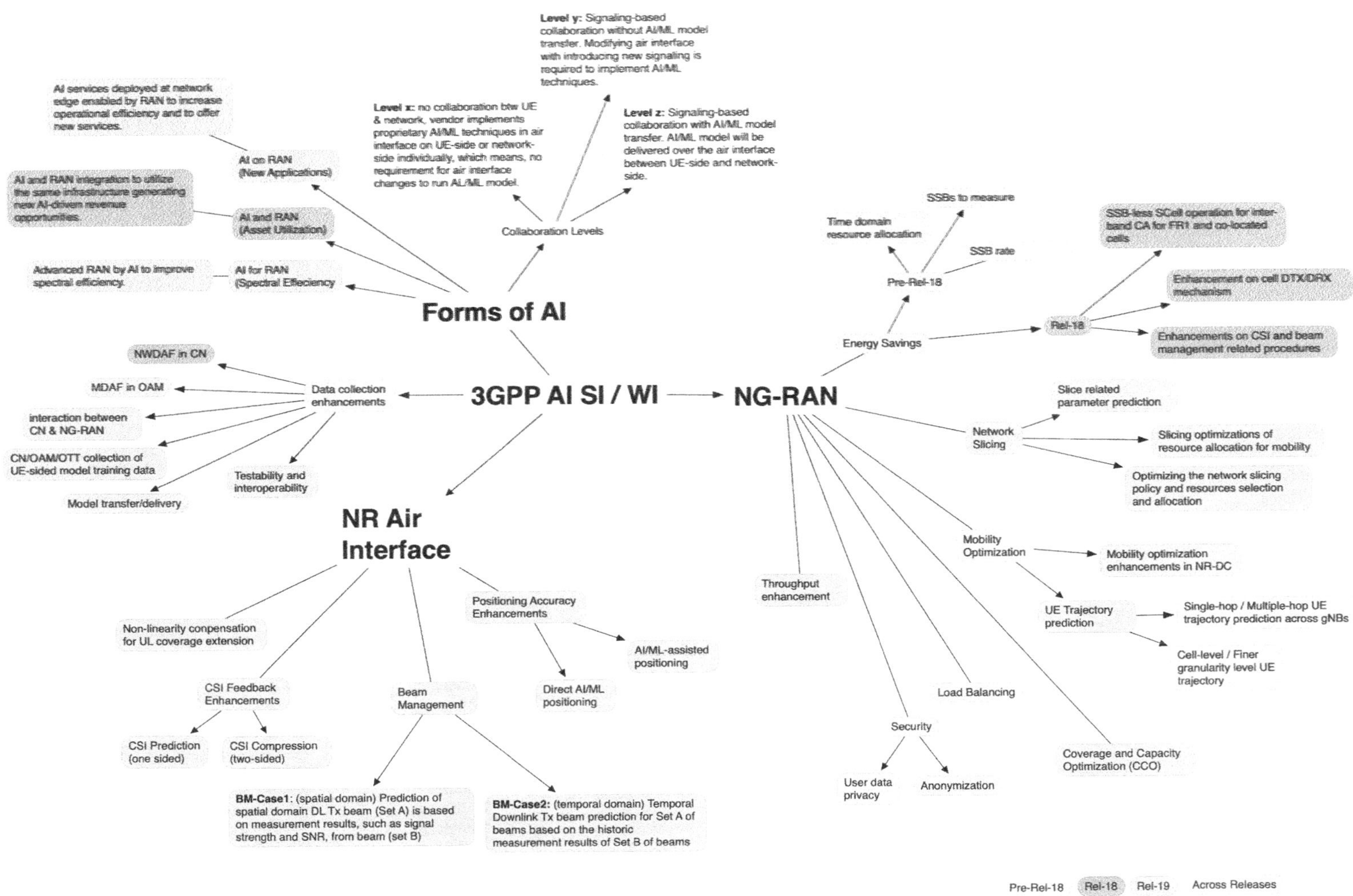

Figure II.1.4.1 3GPP AI/ML landscape.

The metrics collection with the network data analytics function (NWDAF) (5G network data analytics function) and the integration of the RIC operations with the metrics collected from both the UE reports and network nodes are illustrated.

This chapter's main focus is to introduce the RIC architecture and motivate the reader to employ such techniques for AI/ML realization for enterprise campuses. Some additional details on the current happenings in the 3GPP are presented to provide a longer-term view for the reader to appreciate the need to focus on AI/ML aspects for private networks as well.

II.1.4.2 AI/ML for 5G in 3GPP

3GPP's progress on #AI/#ML for 5G started with Release 15 – a new network function, #NWDAF, which was introduced and continuously enhanced in Releases 16 and 17.

In the OA&M aspect, 3GPP introduced the management data analytics function (#MDAF) by using AI/ML techniques for data analytics.

- In Release 17, 3GPP started a study item on AI/ML for NG-RAN with three use cases:
  - Network Energy Saving: The conventional energy-saving schemes may cause potential issues such as
    - (1) inaccurate cell load prediction,
    - (2) conflict between performance and energy efficiency, and
    - (3) energy-saving parameters are configured by traditional operations rather than in a smart way.
    - With AI/ML techniques, optimizing cell activation or deactivation decisions based on predictive traffic load to balance performance and energy savings.
  - Load Balancing: Load balancing should consider future cell load status, or it may cause ping-pong handover or cell overload; thus, quality of service (QoS) may degrade.
    - Improving load-balancing performance by introducing AI/ML techniques to guarantee the service performance after performing the action of load balancing. (Load balancing: distributed among cells, transferring part of the traffic from congested cells, or offloading users from a cell.)
  - Mobility Optimization: Guarantee the service continuity during the mobility by minimizing the call drops, RLFs, unnecessary handovers, and ping-pong effects by leveraging AI/ML techniques.
- Release 18, as the first release of #5G Advanced, 3GPP has studied AI/ML for the air interface with 3 use cases:
  - Channel State Information (CSI) feedback enhancement
    - Sub-use case: Spatial-frequency domain CSI compression:
      - UE generates CSI data by measuring downlink reference signal (RS) and provides a CSI report to the gNB for better downlink transmission. In massive Multiple Input Multiple Output (MIMO), a large number of antennas results in a huge CSI dimension with substantial CSI feedback overhead.
      - Leveraging AI/ML techniques to improve the technical limitations in massive MIMO deployment is a goal.
      - AI/ML-based CSI feedback enables compressed CSI feedback data from the UE through the encoder model and reconstructed CSI feedback data by the decoder model from the gNB intelligently to reduce CSI feedback overhead.

      - The different AI-based encoder/decoder from multiple vendors leads to challenges in interoperability and compatibility.
    - Sub-use case: Time domain CSI prediction
      - The CSI report (gNB network received from UE) becomes outdated, especially in massive MIMO and when UE speed is higher. Therefore, another sub-use case in AI/ML-based CSI feedback enhancement is to improve the CSI prediction using a UE-side AI model.
  - Beam management: The goal is to reduce reporting overhead and minimize latency.
    - Spatial domain: Reuse of measurements made on one beam applied to operating on a neighboring beam
    - Time domain: Predictions for channel state information based on past measurements for current and future slots
  - Positioning accuracy enhancement: Improve positioning accuracy, and the mechanisms below are being studied (see further details in the Release-19 descriptions later in this section)
    - Direct AI/ML positioning
    - AI/ML-assisted positioning
- The security aspect of AI/ML for 5G is also under investigation, and 3GPP points out that the importance of user data privacy and anonymization should be respected during AI/ML operations.
  - Source: TR 33.877.
  - Key issue #1: User privacy of the RAN AI/ML framework. No agreed-upon solutions address this key issue; therefore, no normative work is pursued.
  - Key issue #2: Robustness of the RAN AI/ML framework against data positioning attacks. No agreed-upon solutions address this key issue; therefore, no normative work is pursued.
  - Key issue #3: Security of information transfer between RAN AI/ML framework nodes. Information transfer security in the AI/ML framework RAN nodes can be supported within the existing security mechanisms; therefore, no normative work is pursued.

#R19 workshop took place in the RAN#100 meeting (Release-19 workshop – June 2023)

The RAN1/2/3 work package in #R19 was decided upon and approved in the RAN#102 meeting in December 2023. Three topics are relevant to #AI/#ML in Release 19:

- AI/ML – #AirInterface: normative work item (led by RAN1)
  - (1) Provide specifications: AI/ML-based beam management and AI/ML-based positioning accuracy enhancement
  - (2) Continue to study: AI/ML-based CSI feedback enhancement (continued studies from Release-18 – see details above in this section)
- AI/ML for air interface (mobility): new study item (led by RAN2)
  - The detailed document can be found in RP-234039, RP-233088, and RP-233087.
  - Beam management: Optimizing Downlink (DL) Tx beam prediction in the spatial and time domains for data transmission, reducing measurement overhead and latency.
    - BM-Case 1: (spatial domain) Prediction of the spatial domain DL Tx beam (set A) is based on measurement results, such as signal strength and Signal to Noise Ratio (SNR), from the beam (set B)
    - BM-Case 2: (temporal domain) temporal downlink Tx beam prediction for set A of beams based on the historic measurement results of set B of beams
  - Positioning enhancements
    - Direct AI/ML positioning: RP-233087 – UE location (e.g. fingerprinting based on channel observation as the input for the AI/ML model).

  - Case 1: UE-based positioning with a UE-side model >> (second priority) Case 2b: UE-assisted/ Location Management Function (LMF)-based positioning with an LMF-side model >> (first priority) Case 3b: NG-RAN node-assisted positioning with an LMF-side model.
  - AI/ML-assisted positioning: RP-233087 – New measurement and/or enhancement of existing measurements (e.g. Line of Sight (LOS)/ Non Line of sight (NLOS) identification, timing and/or angle of measurement, likelihood of measurement).
  - Case 2a: UE-assisted/LMF-based positioning with UE-side model >> (first priority) Case 3a: NG-RAN node-assisted positioning with gNB-side model.
- AI/ML for **#NGRAN**: study item followed by a work item (led by RAN3)
  - AI/ML-based coverage and capacity optimization (CCO)
    - RP-233133: Potential study direction
    - RP-233428: Cell capacity and coverage prediction to take actions in advance
    - RP-233428: Prediction information and CCO strategy exchange between NG-RAN nodes
  - AI/ML-based network slicing
    - RP-233133: Potential study direction
    - RP-233428: Slice-related parameter prediction
    - RP-232889: Optimizing the network slicing policy and resource selection and allocation
    - RP-233084: AI/ML slicing optimizations of resource allocation for mobile

II.1.4.3 RIC High-Level Architecture

II.1.4.3.1 End-to-End Open RAN Architecture

Figure II.1.4.2 shows the high level Open RAN architecture with interfaces. A given distributed unit (DU) supports one or more radio units (RUs). A given DU can have an integrated RU and may additionally support multiple RUs. The 5G network functional application platform interface (nFAPI) 1.0 adds a network transport wrapper around the 5G FAPI PHY API to create the split option-6 interface between RU and DU network nodes. The interface between the DU and RU is supported using the nFAPI interface. Control messages (P5) move PHY through a state machine. Per Slot/Transmit Time Interval (TTI) messages (P7) define what is transmitted and received over the air every subframe. Figure II.1.4.3 shows the nFAPI P5 protocol stack and Figure II.1.4.4 shows the nFAPI P7 protocol stack.

A single Central Unit (CU) controls multiple DUs. The combination of a single DU together with its CU is considered a gNB. A CU, together with multiple DUs, constitutes multiple gNBs. The interface between the CU and DU is supported using the F1 interface (F1-C and F1-U). Figure II.1.4.5 shows the interface protocol structure for the control plane F1-C. Figure II.1.4.6 show the interface protocol structure for F1-U.

II.1.4.4 RIC Architecture

The RIC consists of a non-real-time controller (supporting tasks that require >1 s latency) and a near-real-time controller (latency of 10–100 ms). Non-real-time (non-RT) functions include service and policy management, RAN analytics, and model training for the near-RT RAN.

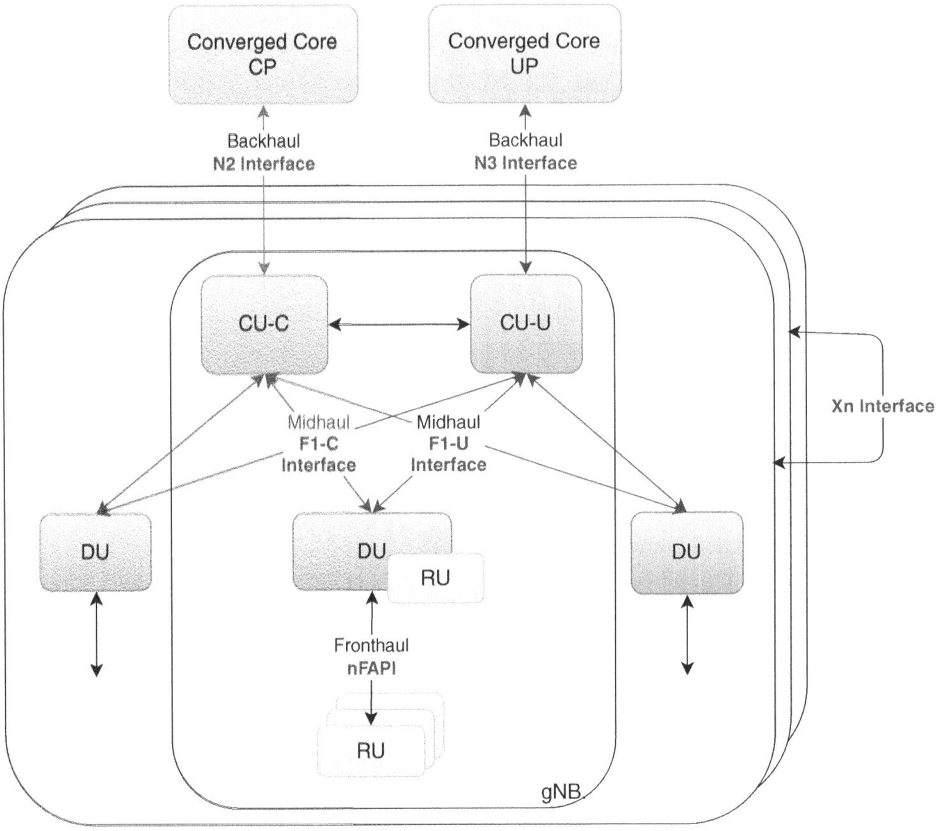

Figure II.1.4.2 Open RAN architecture with interfaces.

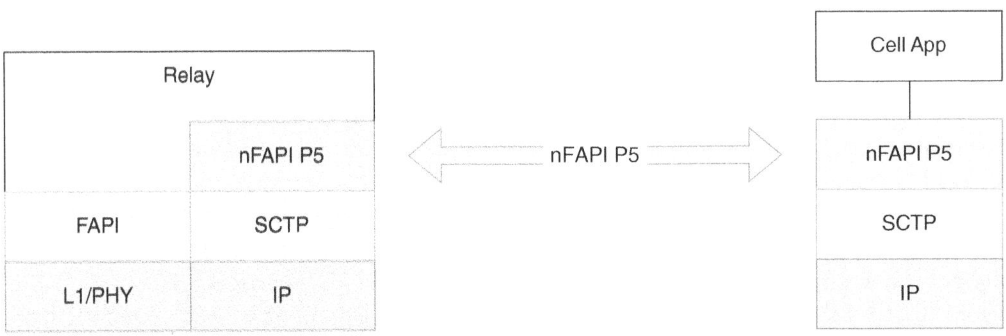

Figure II.1.4.3 nFAPI P5 protocol stack.

Figure II.1.4.7 RIC high-level architecture provides a high-level view of the RIC realization. The gNBs report metrics information to the near-RT RIC via the E2 interface. The non-RIC interacts with the near-RT RIC by providing policy-based guidance and configuration information for it to optimize the RAN network operation. The separation of functionalities on southbound and northbound interfaces enables more efficient and cost-effective radio resource management for real-time and non-real-time functionalities as the RIC customizes network

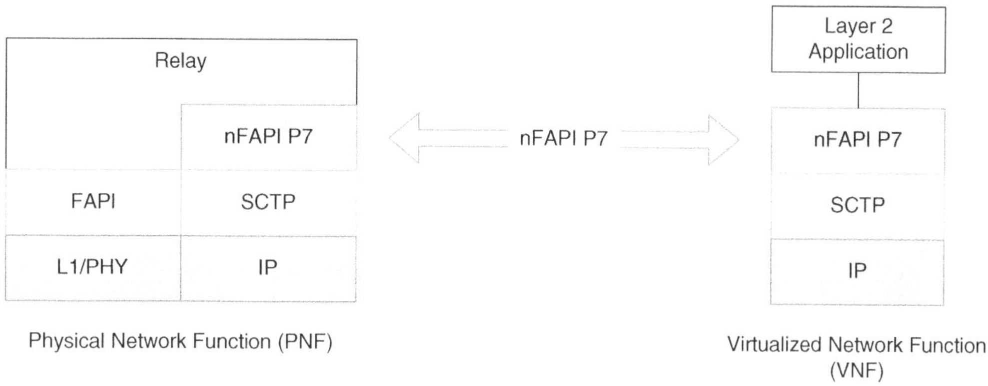

Figure II.1.4.4 nFAPI P7 protocol stack.

optimization for each network environment and use case. RIC provides advanced control functionality, which delivers increased efficiency and better radio resource management. These control functionalities leverage analytics and data-driven approaches, including advanced ML/AI tools, to improve resource management capabilities. It enables the use cases of network intelligence through features like policy enforcement and handover optimizations, resource assurance through features like radio link management and improved SON, and resource control through features like load balancing and slicing policies.

Figure II.1.4.8 RIC modules integrated with the O-RAN architecture presents a representation suggesting the compute nodes where the RIC modules are located. Based on the functionality expected from the near-RT RIC and the information that needs to be obtained from the RAN node(s) to make the determination, as well as the required turnaround time, the near-RT RIC functions are placed appropriately. Note that all near-RT RIC functions don't need to be collocated in the same compute resource and can be supported in a distributed manner. Non-real-time (non-RT) RIC also follows a similar structure; however, it is more based on the required need for exposure to the orchestration layer versus handling it internally with the converged core. It is subject to the sensitive nature of the information being exposed outside of the enterprise 4G/5G deployments and the required control from the orchestration layers that need to be exercised by enterprise IT, the network vendor, and potentially third-party entities like MSPs, who need to exercise control over the deployed network.

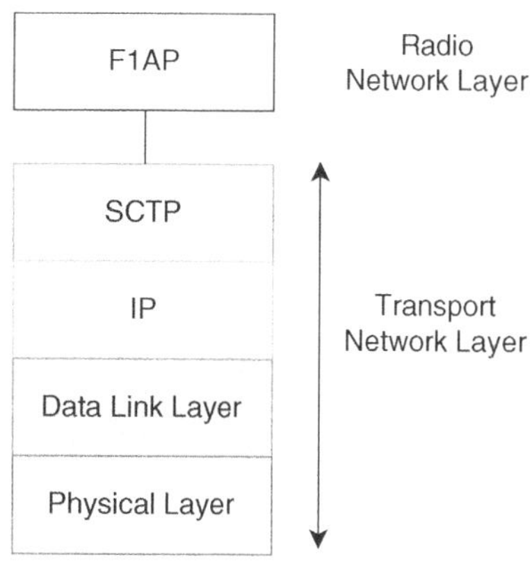

Figure II.1.4.5 Interface protocol structure for the control plane F1-C.

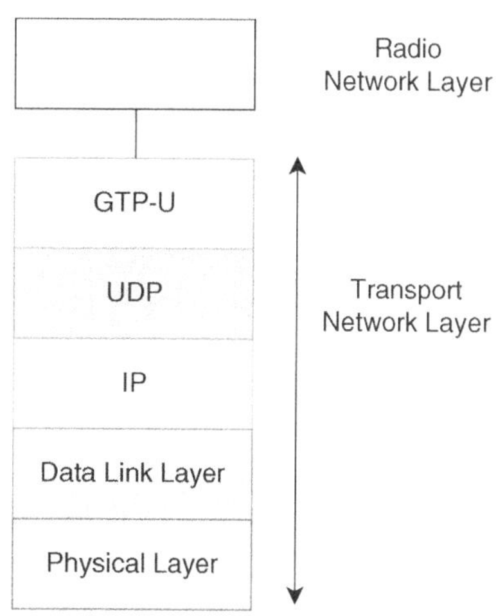

Figure II.1.4.6 Interface protocol structure for F1-U.

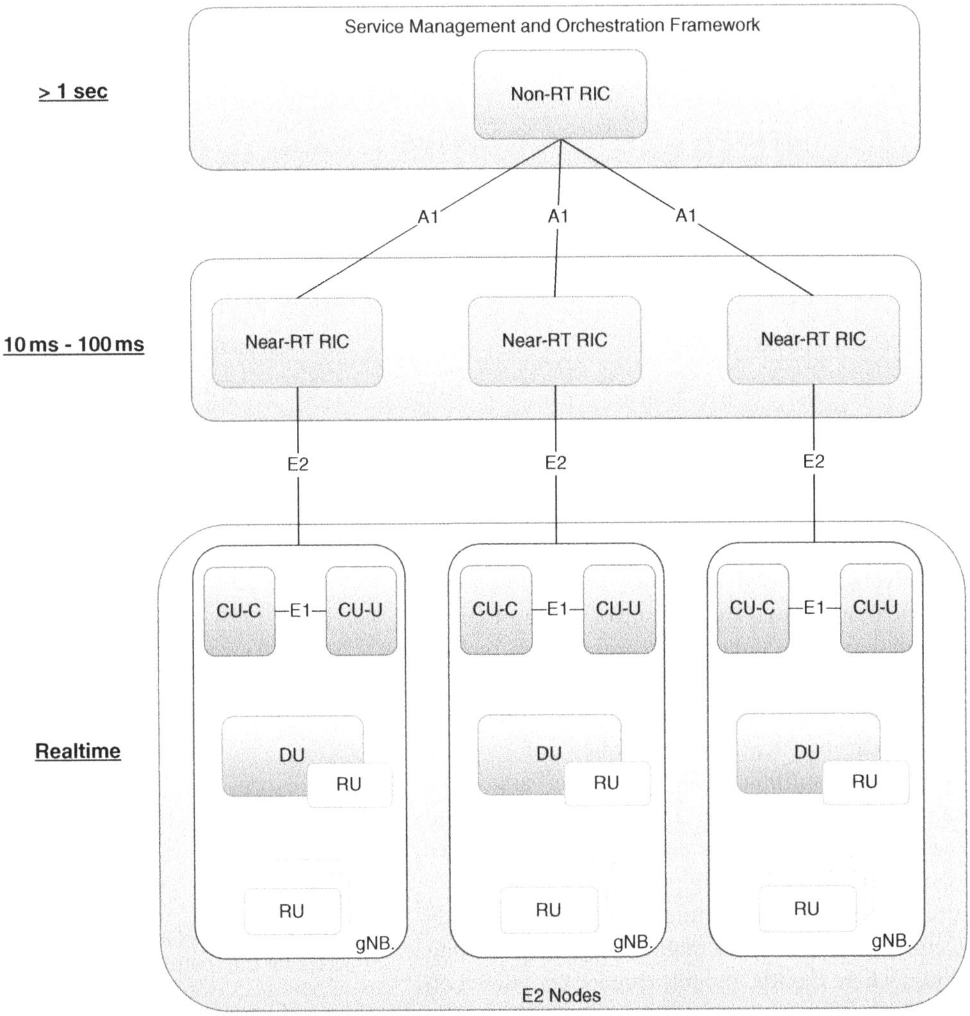

Figure II.1.4.7 RIC high-level architecture.

II.1.4.4.1 Near Real-time RAN Intelligent Controller

Near-RT RIC (see Figure II.1.4.9) is a near-real-time, micro-service-based software platform for hosting applications called xApps. The xApps work together with the data analytics and AI functions they run on the near-RT RIC platform. xApps use the E2 interface to collect information for both individual UEs and cell-wide data.

This provides a cloud-based infrastructure for controlling a distributed collection of RAN infrastructure nodes (eNB, gNB, CU, DU) via the E2 – a southbound interface. Northbound interfaces A1 and O1 are exposed from the near-RT RIC for it to receive management control and policy information.

Examples of xApps include microslicing, mobility, Radio Resource Manager (RRM), admission control, interference coordination, and channel Bandwidth (BW) allocation-related optimizations.

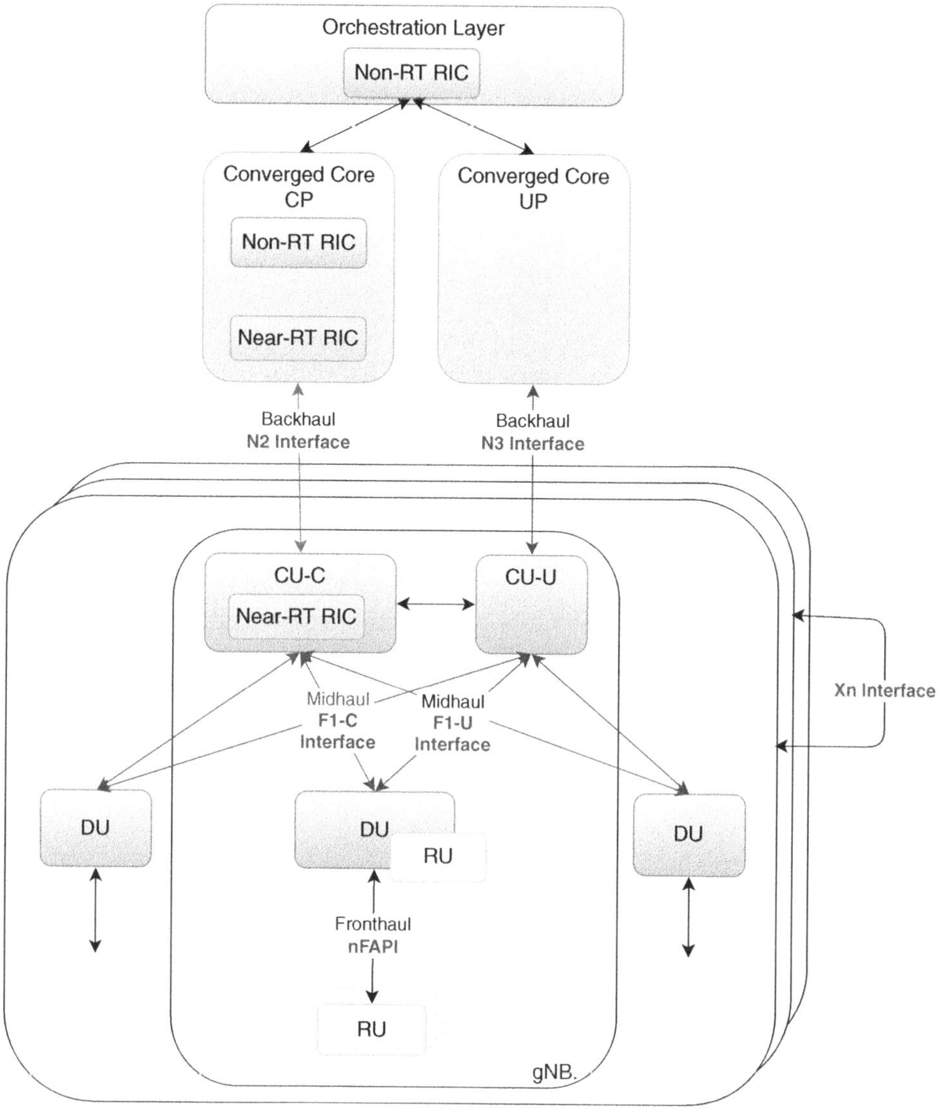

Figure II.1.4.8 RIC modules are integrated with the O-RAN architecture.

RAN functional partitioning between the near-RT RIC and the E2 node is managed on a feature basis based on the extent of AI control that is supported in the near-RT RIC and the E2 node's capabilities. The near-RT RIC can monitor, suspend/stop, override, or control the E2 node based on the non-RT RIC-defined policies.

The RIC xApps can be broadly classified into two categories: static configuration type and dynamic real-time control type. Examples of static configuration-type xApps include RAN slicing, Radio Frequency (RF) configuration that covers aspects of Self-Organizing Networks (SON) and cell neighbor list management, and persistent resource allocation to specific applications in the form of QoS guarantees or resource block (RB) allocation, BW and channel allocation, and Time Division Duplex (TDD) configuration settings. These static configurations

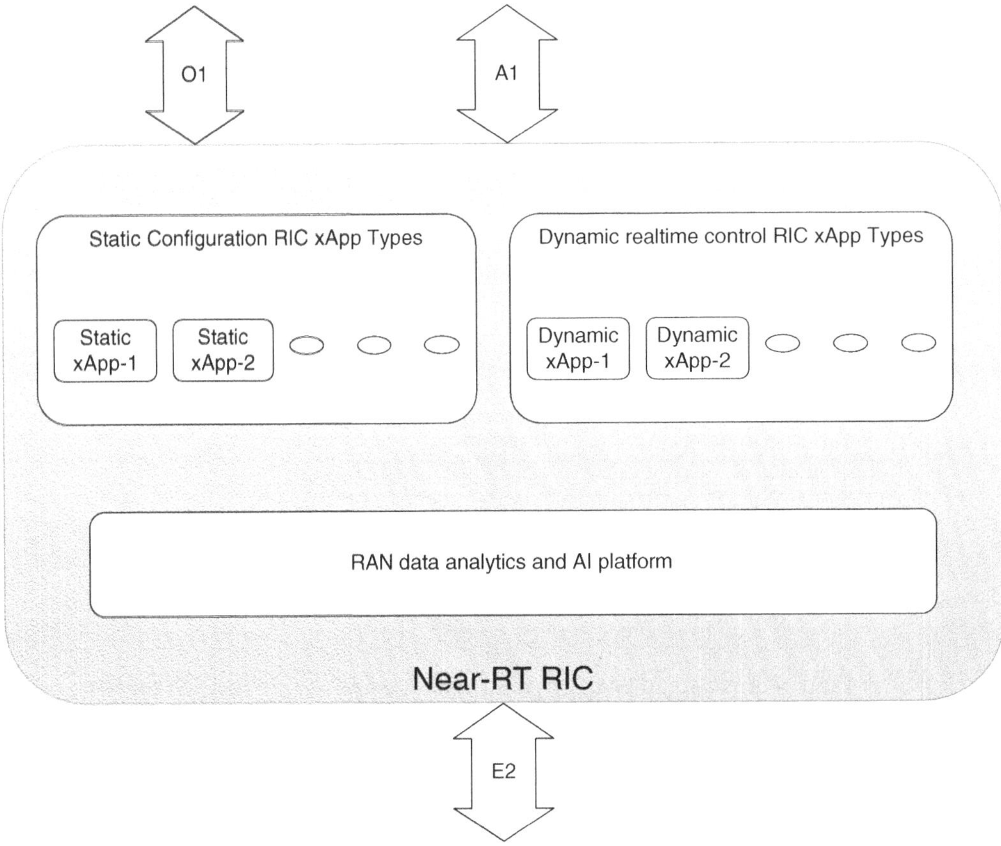

Figure II.1.4.9 Near-RT RIC.

change very infrequently and have system-wide implications, potentially involving interactions with external entities like the Spectrum Access System (SAS). Examples of dynamic real-time control-type xApps include carrier aggregation, interference management, admission and congestion control with load balancing across cells and RATs (radio access technologies of New Radio (NR), Long Term Evolution (LTE), and Wi-Fi) and across RF bands, mobility management, and QoS flow-based scheduling techniques. These algorithms run at the granularity of a minimum schedulable RB to a few 10s of milliseconds, managing specific UEs and the gNB system capacity. Both the static configuration and dynamic control support UE-specific and cell-level operations.

The RIC platform that hosts the near-RT RIC supports a radio network information base (R-NIB) database that captures the near real-time state of the underlying network and feeds RAN data to train the AI/ML models, which are then fed to the near-RT RIC to facilitate radio resource management for subscribers.

The near-RT RIC can be deployed in a centralized or distributed model, depending on network topology.

Independent of the near-RT RIC functioning state, the E2 node is defined to be self-sufficient and continues to function, potentially subject to some suboptimal behaviors.

II.1.4.4.2 Non-real-time RAN Intelligent Controller

Non-RT RIC primarily aids near-RT RIC by providing the operating parameters that both aid localized eNB/gNB level and end-to-end system-wide optimal operations. It allows for monitoring longer-term trends and provides adaptations. Non-RT RIC supports optimizations to configuration, device, fault, performance, and lifecycle management for all network elements in the network. Non-RT RIC provides optimization for network parameters for individual service operations that meet the Service Level Agreement (SLA) agreements made with the different enterprises. This includes defining network slices, RAN slices, and network slices, along with the associated QoS parameters for optimal operation of the services on the enterprise campuses.

The non-RT RIC acts as the outer loop, while the near-RT RIC acts as the inner loop in managing the RAN functions. The setpoints based on longer-term trends are provided by the non-RT RIC to the near-RT RIC. The near-RT RIC closely monitors the RAN functions and optimizes the behaviors to the setpoints provided. The two control loops run independently and in parallel. Trained feedforward models and control functions produced in the non-RT RIC are distributed to the near-RT RIC for runtime execution. Network slicing, security, role-based access control, and RAN sharing are key aspects that are enabled by the combined controller functions—real-time and non-real-time—across the network.

II.1.4.4.3 RIC Enabling Interfaces: A1 and E2

In an enterprise deployment setting, it is typical to see a specific vendor deploying gNB that includes the support of the CU, DU, and RU. There may be a mix of vendors for gNB that need to be integrated with a converged core. This converged core, in turn, needs to be configured and controlled by the enterprise Informational Technology (IT) functions and requires integration with an orchestration platform. O-RAN working group 1 looks after overall use cases and architecture across not only the architecture itself but also all of the working groups.

It is possible for all three pieces of the puzzle to be delivered by a single vendor. However, to enable potential interworking with third-party entities, the bridges across the gNB and the converged core, as well as the converged core to the orchestration layer, need to follow well-defined interfaces for RIC functions to be vertically integrated. There are two key interfaces that support this from the RIC open RAN definition: A1 and E2. The O-RAN working group 5 defines the open F1/W1/E1/X2/Xn interfaces to provide fully operable multi-vendor profile specifications that are compliant with 3GPP specifications. These F1/W1/E1/X2/Xn interfaces may not play a key role, particularly from an RIC functional enablement perspective, and are not discussed here.

II.1.4.4.3.1 A1 Interface

The **A1** interface connects the orchestration platform with the converged core. The orchestration layer will house the non-RT RIC functions apart from the overall network configuration and management aspects and allow for measuring the extent of SLAs delivered to the customer while maintaining the optimal operating conditions of the network and the individual user. The required parameter settings and trained feedforward mechanisms are provided to the converged core, which supports the near-RT RIC. O-RAN working group 2 is responsible for the non-real-time RAN intelligent controller and A1 interface definition, with the primary goal that the non-RT RIC supports non-real-time intelligent radio resource management, higher-layer procedure optimization, policy optimization in RAN, and providing AI/ML models to the near-RT RIC. See [7] O-RAN WG2 specification, which specifies A1 interface general aspects and principles and specifies A1 interface application protocols.

II.1.4.4.3.2 E2 Interface

The **E2** interface defines the interactions between the near-RT RIC and the E2 nodes, which are the underlying RAN elements. O-RAN working group 3 is responsible for the near-real-time RIC and E2 interfaces, with a focus on defining an architecture based on the rear-real-time radio intelligent controller (RIC), which enables near-real-time control and optimization of RAN elements and resources via fine-grained data collection and actions over the E2 interface. See [7] O-RAN-WG3. E2GAP, which specifies general aspects and principles of the E2 interface. See [7] O-RAN-WG3. E2AP, which specifies application protocols for the E2 interface.

To E2, APIs are defined to allow for a disparate set of RAN elements to be managed and used as a "service model"-based abstraction to support their operations. Each RAN element announces a service identifying the RAN functions it is able to support. The near-RT RIC uses the operations below to access/control the individual RAN services. Each RAN element, through its published service, defines the relevant set of functions that can be activated, the variables that can be reported, and the policies that can be set.

Subscription: RIC requests the RAN element to report a function-specific value setting.

Control: RIC instructs the RAN element to activate a control/user-plane function.

Guidance: RIC sets a policy parameter on one of the activated functions.

In Figure II.1.4.10, near real-time RIC interfacing with the E2 node shows high-level interactions between the RIC platform and the RAN E2 node, which is the gNB/eNB. This interface is used by the RAN node to provide the metrics information, which could include raw or digested/aggregated

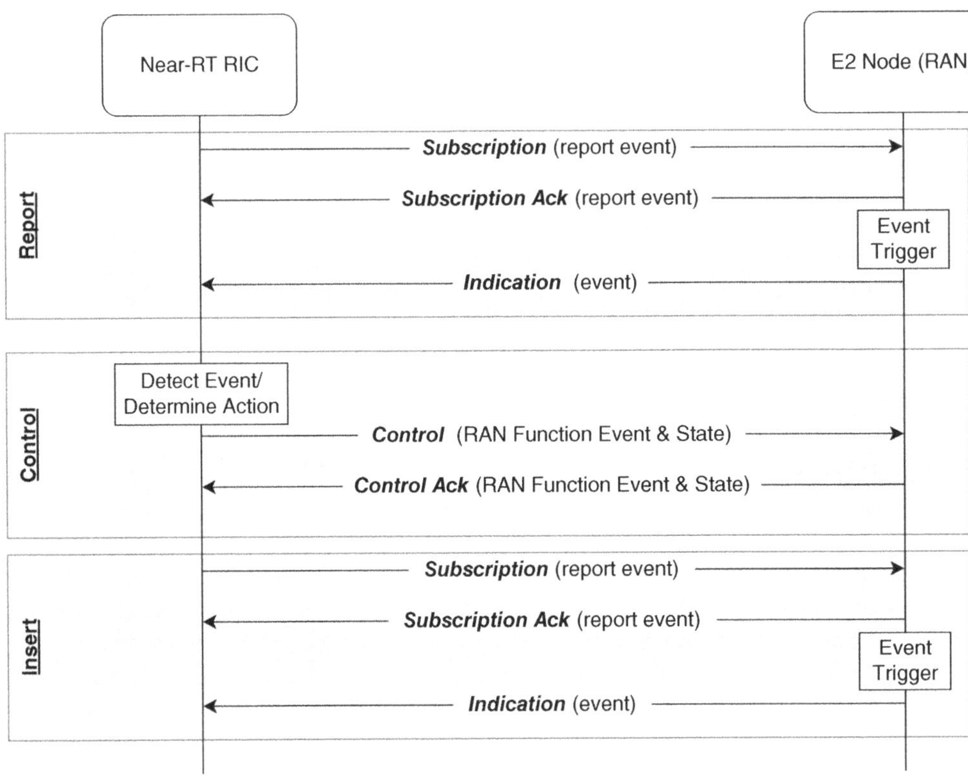

Figure II.1.4.10 Near real-time RIC interfacing with the E2 node.

information, and the near-RT RIC processes the metrics and exercises specific control based on the APIs exposed by the E2 node.

The O-RAN standard has defined generic framework APIs without defining concrete parameterized metric reporting or specific RAN control functions. There are specific behaviors and expectations that are evolving in the market; however, the interactions are tied to the RAN and near-RT RIC implementations, which are typically supported by the same vendor. The non-RT RIC is evolving as an "intent"-based approach, where the APIs from the RAN and core networks are defined to meet specific goals, and the non-RT RIC functions are implemented, making some basic assumptions about the deployed enterprise network behavior.

II.1.4.4.3.3 End-to-End RIC Operations

Figure II.1.4.11 presents the RIC framework and the interacting pieces. The RAN E2 nodes host an E2 agent that bridges the near-RT RIC with the individual RAN functions.

The near-RT RIC does the heavy lifting to enable RIC operations. It "Subscribes" for "Reports" from the RAN E2 node. The RAN E2 node sends "Indications" carrying "Reports" on event triggers. The near-RT RIC sends "Control" messages to manage the control and user-plane functions in the RAN E2 node. It also provides "Guidance" on an activated function in the E2 node.

The non-RT RIC interacts with the near-RT RIC using the rApps via REST APIs to instruct specific xApps with policy, parameter settings, or learned feedforward mechanisms. The A1 interface supports "Policy" setup, update, and delete procedures. The non-RT RIC also accesses the information collected by the near-RT RIC in the R-NIB for data mining to determine custom behaviors for specific enterprises.

The growth will come from non-RT RIC to enable the enterprise-deployed 5G LAN to be employed as NaaS. This allows developers to focus on the business logic and deliver the key value of enterprise use cases using the standard interfaces to integrate with logging, authentication, certificate management, and data movement. Developers who are experienced in cloud-native development, including microservices, can reuse the industry-standard information along with open RAN knowledge to push the boundaries of automation.

Near-RT RIC is very tied to the RAN and requires custom and specialized expertise to enhance support for it. This tends to be a hidden layer and tends not to be an open interface for generic evolution by external entities that are outside the system integration process.

Focus on the service management and orchestration (SMO) interfaces for openness: O1, O2, A1, and rApp enablement:

- network evolution
- network deployment
- network optimization
- network healing

It should view it as a self-organizing neighborhoods (SONg) rather than SON. The paper talks about centralized SON (C-SON), which is not relevant to us.

The described stages of rApp development provide a good perspective. Enabling rApps through Software Development Kit (SDK) releases is important.

xApp needs to be tied closely to our platform. The generic and extensible parts need to be realized through rApp, including third-party solutions.

Load balancing across frequencies is the key problem to solve.

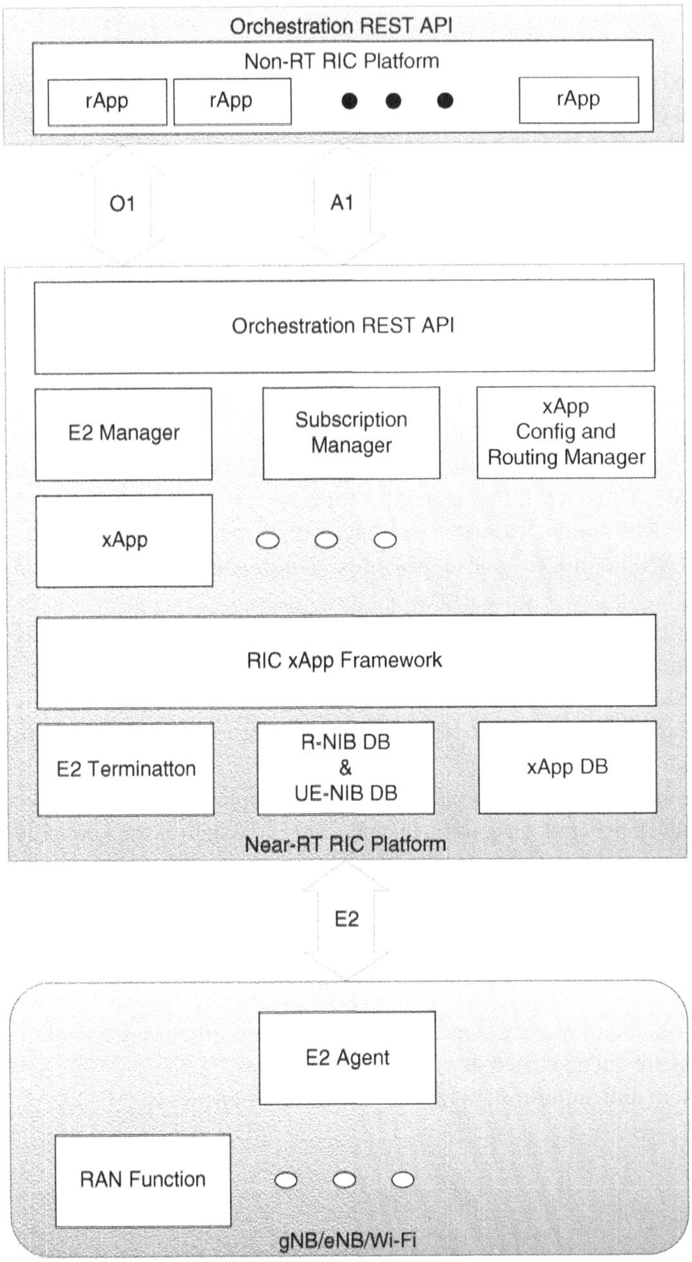

Figure II.1.4.11 RIC framework.

Figure II.1.4.12 provides a high-level view of the control loops running between the non-RT RIC, near-RT RIC, and RAN algorithms.

The A1 interface supports the outer loop, while the E2 interface supports the inner loop. Each of these aids the parameter settings provided to the RAN algorithms implemented in the DU, which include the real-time RAN functions like the scheduler, mobility management, and resource management. The functional distribution across the non-RT RIC, near-RT RIC, and RT RAN algorithms is dependent on the specific realization needed. Based on the available compute resources, the AI functions for learning for near-RT will likely be implemented at the enterprise site for tighter coupling for localized learning. The non-RT RIC learning will likely be in the cloud platform, allowing for learning across multiple enterprise sites and potentially across enterprises to develop more centralized policies.

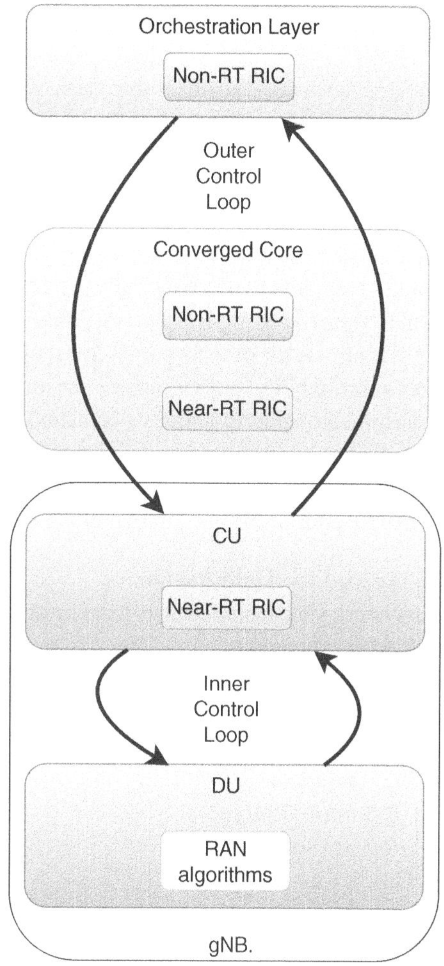

Figure II.1.4.12 Non-RT RIC, near-RT RIC, and RAN algorithms control loops.

II.1.4.5 A1 and E2 Compliance

A1 is a REST API-based interface.

For the E2 interface

- Protobuf instead of XML (we can use Neural Autonomic Transport System (NATS)/ Google Remote Procedure Calls (GRPC) as methods of communication)
- Method is pub-sub
- Framework interfaces can be supported using
  - GRPC (preferred – real-time reporting)
  - NATS (pub-sub) (slow and okay for configuration)
- Language is C++ (real-time feedback), Python (models), Go (interfaces, network communications)
- RIC functional procedures
  - Subscribe
  - Indication
  - Control
  - Service update
- E2AP global procedure (framework parts)
  - Setting up E2
  - Resetting the E2
  - Load management
  - Report of general error scenarios

The near-RT RIC should be located on-premises. Based on the architecture of the RU/DU/CU/converged core, the near-RT RIC should be supported on the equipment closest to the edge of the on-premises setup. The near-RT RIC will typically be located on the Celona edge or on the CU node of the RAN.

This provides a framework for operating RAN, near-RT RIC, and non-RT RIC. With this framework in place, the feedback from the RAN nodes can be extended based on the XApps being developed. Both the RAN metrics that are published and the individual XApps that are developed evolve based on the individual enterprise campus needs.

II.1.4.6 Integration with NWDAF

NWDAF leverages the pub-sub-model, with the network functions (NFs) requesting specific types of metrics/events to be delivered to them upon request. The information requested can be UE/UE group-specific, UE application-specific, or applicable across UEs and targeted to a specific NF, slice, or other variants. The information exchange is supported by directly accessing the data or managed through the data collection coordination function (DCCF) and supported through a messaging framework adapter function (MFAF). The NWDAF itself can host analytics logical functions (AnLF) and model training logical functions (MTLF), which can be used to provide processed data to the requesting NF. The information provided can be instantaneous, batched, or historical data. It allows for observed service experience (MOS), NF metrics, loading/congestion analytics, QoS sustainability, among others. Dispersion-based information collection is also suggested to determine hotspots of activity associated with UE and application-type behaviors. Figure II.1.4.13 shows the basic functional blocks for data collection architecture using data collection coordination.

The types of observed events include the following:

- Slice load-level information;
- Network slice instance load-level information;
- Service experience;
- NF load;
- Network performance;
- Abnormal behavior;
- UE mobility;
- UE communication;
- User data congestion;

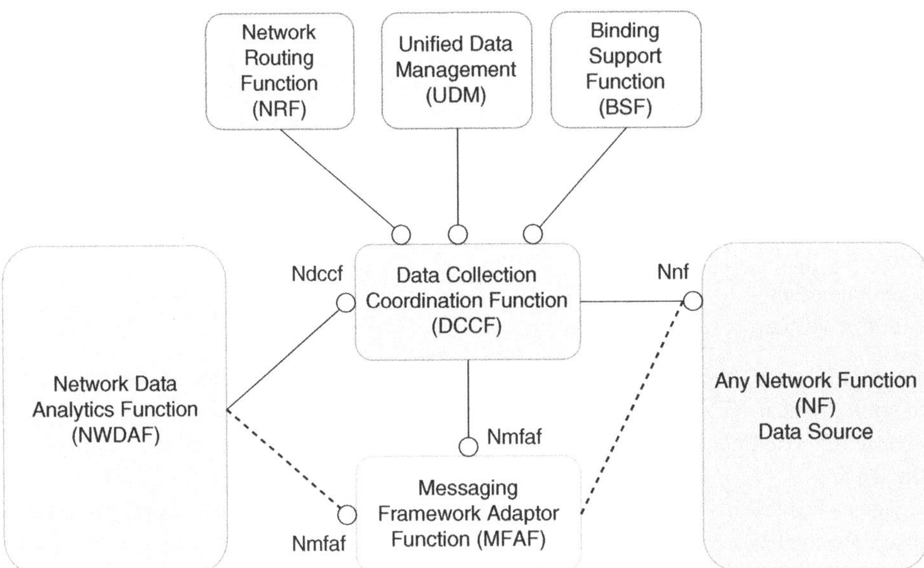

Figure II.1.4.13 Data collection architecture using data collection coordination.

- QoS sustainability;
- Service Management (SM) congestion control experience;
- Dispersion;
- Redundant transmission experience;
- Wireless Local Area Network (WLAN) performance; and
- Data Network (DN) performance.

Table II.1.4.1: Analytics information provided by NWDAF gives a list of standards-defined analytics IDs that reference a type of data to be collected.

Table II.1.4.1 Analytics information is provided by NWDAF.

Analytics information	Request description	Response description
Slice load-level information	Analytics ID: load-level information	Load level provided as the number of UE registrations and the number of Protocol Data Unit (PDU) sessions for a network slice and network slice instances, as well as resource utilization for network slice instances.
Observed service experience information	Analytics ID: service experience	Observed service experience statistics or predictions may be provided for a network slice or an application. They may be derived from an individual UE, a group of UEs, or any UE. For slice service experience, they may be derived from an application, a set of applications, or all applications on the network slice.
NF load information	Analytics ID: NF load information	Load statistics or prediction information for specific NF(s).
Network performance information	Analytics ID: network performance	Statistics or predictions on the load in an area of interest; in addition, statistics or predictions on the number of UEs that are located in that area of interest.
UE mobility information	Analytics ID: UE mobility	Statistics or predictions on UE mobility. When the visited Area of Interest AOI(s) is included in the analytics filter information, only statistics on UE mobility can be provided.
UE communication information	Analytics ID: UE communication	Statistics or predictions on UE communication.
Expected UE behavioral parameters	Analytics ID: UE mobility and/or UE communication	Analytics on UE mobility and/or UE communication.
UE abnormal behavior information	Analytics ID: abnormal behavior	List of observed or expected exceptions, including exception ID, exception level, and other information, depending on the observed or expected exceptions.
User data congestion information	Analytics ID: user data congestion	Statistics or predictions on user data congestion for transfer over the user plane, for transfer over the control plane, or for both.
QoS sustainability	Analytics ID: QoS sustainability	For statistics, the information on the location and the time of the QoS change and the threshold(s) that were crossed; or, for predictions, the information on the location and the time when a potential QoS change may occur and which threshold(s) may be crossed.

(*Continued*)

Table II.1.4.1 (Continued)

Analytics information	Request description	Response description
Session management, congestion control experience	Analytics ID: session management congestion control experience	Statistics on session management and congestion control experience for specific Data Network Name (DNN) and/or S-NSSAI.
Redundant transmission experience	Analytics ID: redundant transmission experience	Statistics or predictions aimed at supporting redundant transmission decisions for Ultra Reliable Low Latency Communications (URLLC) services.
WLAN performance	Analytics ID: WLAN performance	Statistics or predictions on the WLAN performance on UE.
Dispersion	Analytics ID: UE dispersion	Statistics or predictions that identify the location (i.e. areas of interest) or network slice(s) where a UE or a group of UEs disperses their data volume, mobility, session management transactions, or both.
DN performance	Analytics ID: DN performance	Statistics or predictions on user-plane performance for a specific edge computing application.

II.1.4.7 Summary

The context of AI/ML happenings in 3GPP is provided to motivate this fast and upcoming topic and the need to actively watch in this space to absorb the relevant concepts for private networks.

The enterprise deployments vary from the regular macro networks and require specific considerations for a financially and functionally viable solution. From a RAN split architecture, options 2 and 6 are seen to be viable approaches to take. To enable this architecture choice, the 3GPP-defined F1 interface is used between the converged core and the gNB, while the small cell forum-defined nFAPI interface is also utilized. Integrating RIC into this architecture, which supports the non-RT RIC, near-RT RIC, and RAN algorithms, is facilitated by the A1 and E2 interfaces defined by O-RAN. The use of the A1 and E2 interfaces allows for mixing vendors across the orchestration platform, converged core, and gNBs.

RIC itself has many individual functions that can be enabled and will evolve as data analysis, and AI functions reveal aspects of optimizations that can be introduced into the product line.

Develop the RIC framework for supporting RAN functions and xApps. Create APIs that allow for rApps to be developed independently, treating the 5G LAN network as NaaS. The O-RAN provides standardized interfaces for integrating E2 nodes with near-RT RIC, and the RIC frame with rAPPs. 3GPP NWDAF provides the typical set of metrics that need to be collected for non-RT RIC operation. Combining O-RIC and 3GPP standards allows for realization that can significantly enhance the availability and use of enterprise-deployed networks for enterprise-specific optimizations.

References

1 3GPP TS 23.288 Architecture enhancements for 5G System (5GS) to support network data analytics services
2 3GPP TS 29.520 5G System; Network Data Analytics Services
3 3GPP TS 38.470 version 15.2.0 Release 15 5G; NG-RAN; F1 general aspects and principles
4 About 5G nFAPI: Network

5 SCF Document 225.2.0 5G nFAPI specifications
6 The O-RAN Alliance WIKI page
7 https://www.o-ran.org/specification-access
8 RIC as project of the O-RAN software community (https://o-ran-sc.org) has formally started in June 2019
9 Candidate seed code: https://gerrit.o-ran-sc.org/r/admin/repos
10 RSAC contribution archive: https://wiki.o-ran-sc.org/display/RSAC/Contributions
11 https://resources.questex.com/l/open-ran-summit
12 https://resources.questex.com/l/open-ran-summit?industry=ericsson
13 https://resources.questex.com/l/open-ran-summit?industry=parallel-wireless
14 https://resources.questex.com/l/open-ran-summit?industry=anritsu
15 https://resources.questex.com/l/open-ran-summit?industry=cisco-systems

II.1.5

Enterprise RAN Slice

II.1.5.1 Introduction

Effective management of radio resources is the key aspect that differentiates the various network solutions. Functionally, this is realized by the radio access network (RAN) scheduler implementation, which addresses the quality of service (QoS) requirements, fairness, and system capacity aspects, and handled by sufficiently parameterizing the scheduler function. Even within the macro networks, there are different grades of users (e.g. gold, silver, bronze) that require the RAN resources to be prioritized based on the user group. This is typically managed by applying different weights to the scheduling function of the individual groups.

However, with different entities establishing contracts, there is a notion of reserving a finite amount of resources availability to be guaranteed. This aspect will be required for macro network connectivity provided to both enterprise users and the macro network users (see Part II, "Non-public Network" chapter covering public network integrated non-public network (PNI-NPN)) who are getting connectivity from the enterprise networks (see Part II, "Neutral Host Networks" chapter).

This chapter suggests the aspects involved in regulating the RAN resources, the criteria that need to be considered to retain fairness while optimally using these resources, and an implementation that can achieve these goals. This approach can be used in both the macro network and private networks. I am sure there are other ways to implement this, one of which is varying applications of weight and iterative ways to arrive at the optimal function for each scheduling event. The suggested approach aims to achieve this as a single-pass scheduler employing inner and outer loops as stabilization functions while minimizing the compute cost, which is a fundamental criterion for enterprise networks to keep the costs as low as possible. Enterprises face constrained budgets, viewing the 4G/5G wireless network as a "nice to have" rather than "a necessity," at least until the tangible benefits can be perceived.

Looking at business relationships, it is possible for two high-level models to exist. One is macro network operator core network (MNO) networks obtaining resources from the enterprise neutral host networks (NHN). The other is the enterprise obtaining resources from the macro network, potentially operating as a PNI-NPN. Both of these models can leverage some fundamental slicing behaviors and adjust dynamically based on the user equipment (UE) population in different locations, but they are viewed as an aggregate set of resources managed across the sites where access is allowed.

Mobile Communication Systems for Private Networks, First Edition. Srinivasan Balasubramanian.

II.1.5.1.1 RAN Slice and Core Network Slice

RAN-level slices as physical resource block (PRBs) are determined and specified for each eNB/gNB:

- Applied as an instantaneous metric on a slot-by-slot basis and handled as use-it-or-lose-it basis.
- Address changing time division duplex (TDD) configurations based on time of day and predicted downlink (DL) and uplink (UL) traffic.

Core-level slices are managed as allowed peak bitrates:

- For neutral host, all traffic will flow through the MOCN GW and into the MNO core. However, it is possible that local-traffic-offload (LTO) to allow access to the enterprise core may be supported.

The PRB allocation at the RAN is proportionally allocated based on the weights of the enterprise and the different MNO-x entities.

II.1.5.1.2 RAN Slice and Core Network Slice Realization

Any RAN slice realization will need to account for the behavior illustrated in Figure II.1.5.1. There will be limitations in terms of the number of users that can be served in a single scheduling instance (e.g. slot), and equipartitioning the resources in every scheduling occasion will not be possible. However, guarantees of service need to be supported across a larger time scale to prevent starvation. Given that priority and the scheduling need to be handled to accommodate both

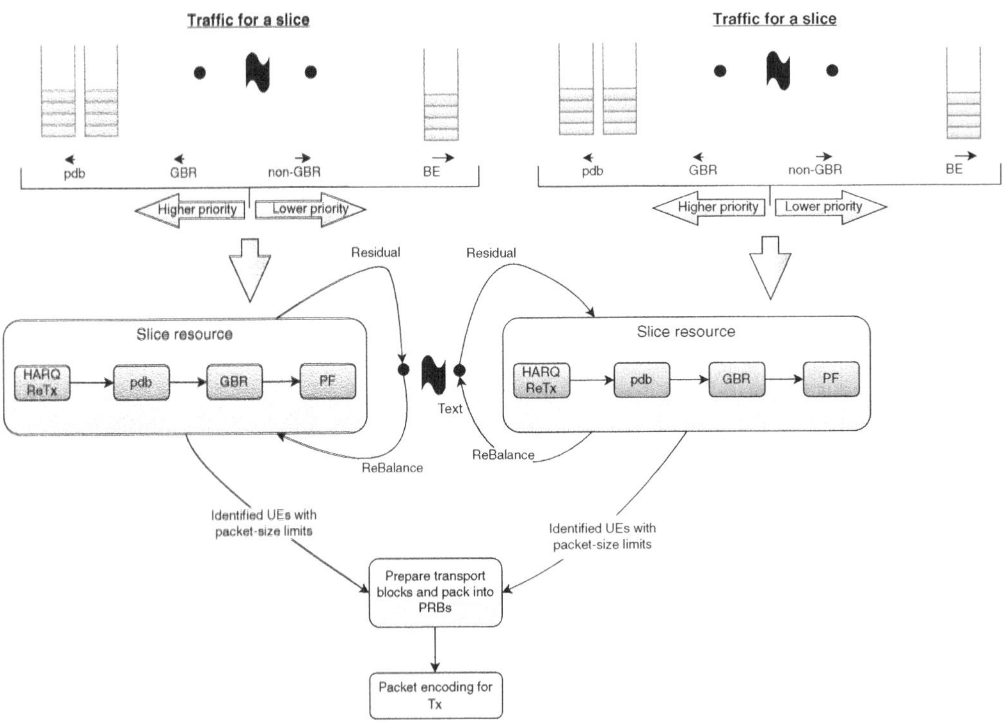

Figure II.1.5.1 Generic RAN slice implementation.

the QoS of the individual flows and the extent of resources that is allowed for a given RAN slice, the underlying assumption for the scheduler implementation is that there are admission and congestion control algorithms in place to avoid over-accommodating users of a given slice while preventing access to the system from users of other slices. As such, without loss of generality, enterprise private users in an NHN are treated as slice, and the macro network in a PNI-NPN similarly isolates resources for enterprise users from the other users in the network. Note as well that there should be no wastage of RAN resources, and capacity should always be fully utilized at all times.

A realization of the two models: MNO user on NHN and enterprise users on MNO networks, including PNI-NPN networks. See Figure II.1.5.1 for an illustration of a Generic RAN Slice Implementation.

- For each slice:
  - Assume a limit on the number of UEs that can be supported for this slice.
  - Determine hybrid automatic repeat request (HARQ) reTx requirement four slots before. Identify the available "space."
    - This can be done four slots prior.
  - Use the predetermined implicit priority ordering of the queues for each slice based on the QoS parameters when visiting queues.
  - Apply the following prioritization in the suggested order sequentially:
    - pdb → GBR → PF (applied to non-GBR and best effort [BE] traffic).
    - The pdb and guaranteed bit rate (GBR) functions can potentially be run right after the new data indicator (NDI) requirements are determined. The proportional-fair (PF) can also be run, assuming prior channel quality information (CQI), and the procedures can be rerun only when the CQI information changes significantly.
      - Note 1: The network knows when the next periodic CQI for a given UE will be received based on the previous slot where the previous report was received.
      - Note 2: The periodic CQI is only a subband report and may not capture the information associated with the PRBs being scheduled.
    - Each of these prioritization functions is treated as plug-ins that can be replaced, potentially employing different functions based on varying scenarios
- For each slice:
  - When specific queues (along with the associated UEs) have close prioritization results, increase the priority for UEs that have other traffic as well that can be scheduled together.
  - Subject it to UE-AMBR, APN-AMBR, and slice resource limits.
  - Start from the highest priority and identify the UEs that can be accommodated in the slot for this slice.
  - Identify the residual leftover "space."
  - Also, identify the traffic not scheduled and that can occupy the channel. This can apply to the UEs that are already scheduled in the slot as well.
- Use the residual from each slice, both space and UEs that can be accommodated in the slot.
  - Distribute the residual resources proportional to each slice's subscription.
  - Run through the slice-level steps to allocate the appropriate traffic.
- Provide the identified UEs, the traffic flows, and the buffer limits that should be scheduled to the L2 and L1 layers for framing and packing into PRBs for transmissions.
- Receive feedback on what was transmitted and adjust the subsequent computations accordingly.

- Need to determine the extent of parallelism that can be achieved based on the target platform. Accounting for compute resource requirement across slots including performing pre-computation in preparing the packets and required real-time computation. The scheduling prioritization functions and commands are given to the L2/L1 layers based on priorities associated with the different data queues for the individual user that belong to a given slice.

II.1.5.1.3 Fairness Models

There are several fairness enforcement models. Two such indices are suggested next. Of course, fairness can be ensured by measuring specific set of QoS parameters and determining the distance to the required QoS metric as well. See https://en.wikipedia.org/wiki/Fairness_measure for more details.

II.1.5.1.4 Jain's Fairness Index

$$F\left(x_1, x_2, \ldots, x_n\right) = \frac{\left(\sum_{i-1}^{n} x_i\right)^2}{n * \sum_{i-1}^{n} x_i^2} = \frac{\overline{x}^2}{\overline{x^2}} = \frac{1}{1 + \widehat{C_v}^2}$$

Rates the fairness of a set of values where there are n users, x_i is the throughput for the ith connection, and C_v is the samplecoefficient of variation. The result ranges from $\frac{1}{n}$ (worst case) to 1 (best case), and it is maximum when all users receive the same allocation. This index is $\frac{k}{n}$ when k users equally share the resource, and the other $(n-k)$ users receive zero allocation. This metric identifies underutilized channels and is not unduly sensitive to atypical network flow patterns.

To achieve a given fairness level F, one approximate method is to let $x_k = A * k^{\propto}$, where

$$\propto = \frac{1 - F + \sqrt{1 - F}}{F}$$

and A is an arbitrary factor, typically used for normalization. This gives an allocation with a fairness close to F, and the allocation can then be refined to get even closer. Note this also allows for a prioritization of allocation, as the x_k will be sorted.

Applying this fairness technique, determine this index for the full site, within each cell, and within each slice. Explore how this can be evolved to include QoS metrics and proportional fairness. Consider fairness in terms of opportunistic and non-opportunistic traffic when determining if fairness is met.

II.1.5.1.4.1 G's and Bossaer's Fairness Index

The G's fairness index is primarily used by telecom operators in the context of bandwidth allocation. G's k^{th} order fairness index scales the fractions of the product-based fairness index by a powered sine transformation

$$f(x) = \sin\left(\frac{x\pi}{2}\right)^{\frac{1}{k}}$$

$$G_k(x) = \prod_{i=1}^{n} \sin\left(\frac{\pi x_i}{2 * \max(x)}\right)^{\frac{1}{k}}$$

where $k \epsilon R^{+}$. The first quadrant of the sine wave is used as a mapping function to inflate fractions. As such, the sensitivity of the product-based fairness is decreased for values close to max(x), while the index still outputs a value between 0 and 1.

G's fairness index: Compared to Jain's fairness index, G's fairness index yields smaller values, is more sensitive to potential unfair bandwidth distribution, and can go to zero.

Bossaer's fairness index: Whereas G's fairness index inflates the fractions closer to max(x), the Bossaer's fairness index inflates the fractions closer to 0. Bossaer's k^{th} order transformation function $f(x) = x^{\frac{1}{k}}$ yields the fairness index:

$$B_k(x) = \prod_{i=1}^{n} \left(\frac{x_i}{\max(x)} \right)^{\frac{1}{k}}$$

II.1.5.2 MNO Users Obtaining Resources from NHN Deployments

II.1.5.2.1 Goals with RAN Slice Scheduling

The following set of goals is suggested for RAN resource sharing with the different MNOs and enterprise entities:

- Allow for clear representation of how the shared resources from an enterprise deployment will be managed across MNOs and private enterprise users.
- MNOs are provided SLOs/SLAs, viewed as capacity allocations and QoS guarantees provided to the MNO UEs that camp on the enterprise network.
- The enterprise network is managed by a specific MNO.
- When an MNO signs up for neutral host connectivity support with an enterprise campus, it also makes available the MNO-x dedicated spectrum (e.g. licensed spectrum enabled for use within an enterprise campus while still supporting shared spectrum usage with all MNOs, such as priority access licenses (PAL) allocation in citizen broadband radio service (CBRS) spectrum) that the MNO has purchased for the enterprise campus use.
- It is possible for multiple MNOs to have neutral host agreements with a given enterprise campus, each providing its MNO-x dedicated spectrum for use within the enterprise campus.
- When specific spectrum needs to be isolated for allocation to an MNO, this is supported using explicit hardware (at the RF layers). An alternative approach is to allow the MNO to support their system identifiers in the enterprise network and enable roaming for other MNO devices to camp on the deployed network.

II.1.5.2.2 Assumptions

Some fundamental assumptions are suggested that will apply to all deployments. These can form a basis for solution proposals that are viable for the different deployment models.

- It is better to provide service level objective (SLAs) that are aggregated across the enterprise campus to manage capacity allocations for a given MNO.
- Admission control
  - Admission control for idle system camping needs to be regulated based on proportional capacity allocation requirement for a given MNO.

    - If there is capacity available, UEs are admitted independent of the MNOs. It is possible to reserve resources so that when other MNO UEs enter the system, it does not result in immediate preemption for an MNO that has exceeded its capacity allocation. This will be similar to reserving resources for mobility support to receive UEs transitioning into a given access point (AP) from neighboring APs in the enterprise network.
  - Admission control for connected mode operations will need to be accommodated, given that the idle camping system is regulated. Under heavy congestion, the UEs need to be redirected to the macro frequency.
    - Emergency; wireless priority service (WPS)
  - Admit flows based on GBR bearer-based operations must ensure that capacity occupancy is within what is allocated to the MNO on a given AP.
- Congestion control
  - The QoS requirements for GBR bearers are handled based on the needs of the individual flows.
    - The handling of the additional throughput to scale up to maximum bit rate (MBR) rates will scale proportionally to the capacity allocated to the MNO.
    - The GBR allocated to the flow will also be subject to the allocated capacity to the MNO and managed during admission control. It is possible that a flow does not get admitted, and a service is blocked for the user or is admitted with a subdued GBR.
  - For the non-GBR bearers, the throughput is managed through proportional capacity allocation; minimum throughput guarantees are required.
- Preemption is handled based on the proportional resource allocation for each MNO.
  - No preemption is done until the resource limits of a given cell are reached. This is dependent on the capacity allocated to a given MNO and the amount utilized by that MNO's UEs.
  - An ordering of priority for users and services within each MNO is maintained for preemption when the limits are reached. If arbitration is required among equal priority users, a random user is selected for preemption.
  - MNO users can use any available capacity from the cell. Only when the enterprise user or other MNO users require the capacity based on the capacity partitioning does the MNO usage beyond the allocated capacity require preemption.
- Proportionality is handled based on the bearer type, the MNO-x dedicated allocations provided for in-campus operations, or other arrangements based on specific business agreements between the MNO and enterprise, and the population of the UEs (individual MNOs and enterprise UEs) subject to the peak support agreement established with the campus.

II.1.5.2.3 Token Bucket Definition

The use of token bucket is suggested to realize the RAN slice implementation. The RAN scheduler pulls tokens from each MNO-x token bucket and schedules traffic for the individual users within each MNO-x based on the number of available tokens. The preferred approach will be to complete the scheduling process for each slot with a single pass through all the users' queues, accounting for the required QoS prioritization of the packets. Multiple passes will allow for optimal selection and packing, which requires additional compute resources that are typically not possible with small cells. See Figure II.1.5.2 showing a Token Bucket for RAN Slice PRB management implementation.

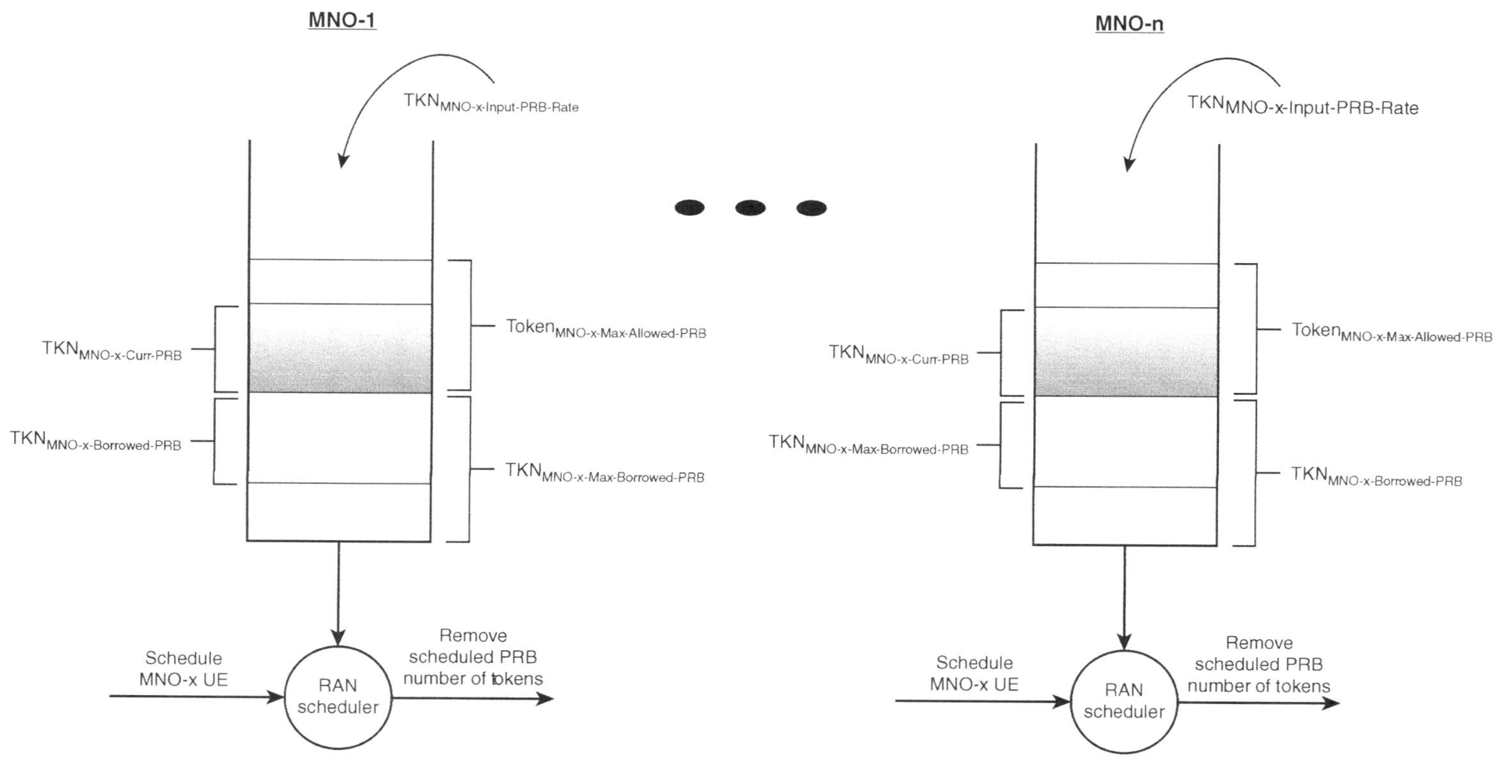

Figure II.1.5.2 Token bucket for RAN slice PRB management.

Token bucket parameter	Description
$TKN_{MNO\text{-}x\text{-}Input\text{-}PRB\text{-}Rate}$	Tokens are refreshed at a rate proportional to the RAN slice capacity allocation. The token refresh rate can be done at every slot or at periodic intervals, potentially even once every refresh interval. It is derived from $TKN\text{-}DL\text{-}PRB_{MNO\text{-}x\text{-}Allocation}$ and $TKN\text{-}UL\text{-}PRB_{MNO\text{-}x\text{-}Allocation}$ and adjusted to the $T_{MNO\text{-}x\text{-}TKNRefresh}$, the token refresh time period. • $DL\text{-}TKN_{Input\text{-}PRB\text{-}Rate} = TKN\text{-}DL\text{-}PRB_{MNO\text{-}x\text{-}Allocated} * T_{MNO\text{-}x\text{-}TKNRefresh}/$ Scheduler-Refresh-Time. • $UL\text{-}Token_{Input\text{-}PRB\text{-}Rate} = TKN\text{-}UL\text{-}PRB_{Allocated\text{-}MNO\text{-}x} * T_{MNO\text{-}x\text{-}TKNRefresh}/$ Scheduler-Refresh-Time.
$TKN_{MNO\text{-}x\text{-}Curr\text{-}PRB}$	Indicates the current number of tokens in the bucket.
$TKN_{MNO\text{-}x\text{-}Borrowed\text{-}PRB}$	These are tokens borrowed for scheduling a given MNO's UEs. These many tokens are more than what is available tokens in the bucket, but borrowed against the future token refreshes. As tokens are replenished, the value is decremented until it reaches 0. Any further token added are accumulated in the $Token_{MNO\text{-}x\text{-}Curr\text{-}PRB}$.
$Token_{MNO\text{-}x\text{-}Max\text{-}Allowed\text{-}PRB}$	To prevent over allocation of tokens to a given MNO, the tokens allowed in the bucket are capped at a certain level. • Defaulted to tokens for up to one refresh intervals. • This value determines the extent of starvation that can be caused by the other MNOs.
$TKN_{MNO\text{-}x\text{-}Max\text{-}Borrowed\text{-}PRB}$	To prevent penalizing an MNO for borrowing tokens based on its usage, which may arise from a lack of traffic from other MNOs, the tokens borrowed in the bucket are capped at a certain level. • Defaulted to tokens for up to one refresh intervals. • This value determines the extent of starvation that can be caused by a given MNO.

Note: All the aforementioned parameters can be provisioned on a per-MNO basis.

Assuming a single-pass scheduler, some practical options are suggested here. Static resource partitioning tends to be restrictive but allows for the simplicity of management and communication of the available resources to a two MNOs for SLO/SLA establishment. However, static resource partitioning comes with the disadvantage of not being able to use the resources when the traffic for a given MNO is low, which implies that these resources go wasted. A dynamic resource allocation allows for better utilization of the available RAN resources, but it does come with increased complexity. Additionally, communicating the available capacity to an MNO can be tricky and requires a certain level of sophistication to establish SLO/SLAs, accounting for lean traffic and peak traffic periods with variable compositions of the different MNO devices/users operating in the enterprise campus. The two-pass scheduler is also described, providing relevant context in case this becomes viable in the future.

II.1.5.2.4 Static Partition with One-Pass Scheduling

The resource allocation for the individual MNOs and the enterprise devices is provisioned in the eNB/gNB. The paging and access capacity are shared across all MNOs and enterprise UEs.

II.1.5.2.4.1 Fixed RAN Resource Allocations for each MNO

The resources will be statically allocated across all eNB/gNB independent of the composition of the UEs in the cell. The value is specified in units of PRBs for a refresh interval time period – $TKN\text{-}DL\text{-}PRB_{MNO\text{-}x\text{-}Allocated}$ and $TKN\text{-}UL\text{-}PRB_{MNO\text{-}x\text{-}Allocated}$. The available PRBs are identified as a percentage of the total capacity of the AP, and the PRBs available to an MNO on an AP are determined based on the bandwidth (BW) allocated to the AP by the self organizing network (SON) algorithm.

Any leftover capacity is allocated to enterprise devices – TKN-UL-$PRB_{Enterprise}$ and TKN-DL-$PRB_{Enterprise}$. The enterprise is treated like another MNO from this point onward in terms of RAN slice resource management.

II.1.5.2.4.2 RAN Slice Scheduling Procedure

- UEs are selected for scheduling according to the existing prioritization.
- The contention resolution list, HARQ retransmissions, signal list SRB + SR request, and GBR list are handled using the existing procedures.
  - The token from the MNO-x bucket is removed based on the PRBs used to serve the UEs.
- If there are UEs from different MNOs that have GBR traffic, UEs associated with MNO-x are selected based on the MNO-x that has the largest number of tokens.
  - This is done to ensure that when the MBR/AMBR traffic is scheduled, the selected UEs have sufficient tokens to be scheduled, thus providing fairness across MNOs for scheduling traffic.
  - It is possible for different MNOs to have different RAN capacity allocations; in such scenarios, an inverse proportionality is applied to the number of available tokens used for comparison.

Additionally, for the MBR list and AMBR list, the following steps are followed:

- An MNO-UE is scheduled only when $TKN_{MNO\text{-}x\text{-}Curr\text{-}PRB} > 0$.
- If there are UEs from different MNOs that have AMBR traffic, UEs associated with MNO-x are selected based on the MNO-x that has the largest number of tokens.
- When there are no other UEs with traffic, the UEs that do have traffic are chosen, including those belonging to MNOs that have $TKN_{MNO\text{-}x\text{-}Curr\text{-}PRB} < 0$.
- When there are not enough tokens, tokens are borrowed to allow the UE to be scheduled.
  - Borrowing is allowed even when $TKN_{MNO\text{-}x\text{-}Borrowed\text{-}PRB} = Token_{MNO\text{-}x\text{-}Max\text{-}Allowed\text{-}PRB}$.
  - This is used to accommodate the limitations on the number of UEs that can be scheduled in a slot and to address the scenario where other MNOs may not have enough traffic that needs to be scheduled.

II.1.5.2.5 Dynamic Rebalancing of MNO-x Slice Resource

The procedure remains the same as the previous option described but with the added function of rebalancing the resource allocations across the APs for each MNO. This is treated as an aggregate campus-wide resource allocation for a given MNO.

The aggregate campus-wide capacity is determined based on the sum of capacity allocated to the individual APs in terms of PRBs. Note that this capacity adapts based on changes to the APs and the BW allocations to the individual APs as determined by the SON algorithm.

The capacity allocated to each MNO is determined by the following procedure. Any rebalancing of resources across the APs maintains this total capacity allocation for each MNO.

$$Total\ Capacity_{MNOx} = \sum_{APs} PRB_{AP} * Percentage_{MONx}$$

II.1.5.2.5.1 AP's Request for Rebalancing of Resource Allocations

Each AP determines if rebalancing of resources is needed. This is determined by looking at the offered load and comparing it with the capacity allocated to each MNO. All reports are sent to a central entity, the MNO capacity rebalancer (MCR).

- If (OfferedLoadMNO-x < 80% CapacityMNO-x), then it sends a notification to the MCR indicating the capacity the AP is willing to relinquish for that MNO-x.

- If (80% CapacityMNO-x < OfferedLoadMNO-x < 120% CapacityMNO-x), then it sends a notification to the MCR indicating that it has optimal capacity allocation for MNO-x.
- If (OfferedLoadMNO-x > 120% CapacityMNO-x), then it sends a notification to the MCR indicating the capacity the AP wants an increased allocation for MNO-x.

The capacity requests from the AP to the MCR are sent either as a percentage of the AP capacity or in terms of the PRBs.

II.1.5.2.5.2 MCR Operations

The MCR looks at the input received from each AP and determines if the resources can and need to be moved from one to another based on the requests received. It ensures the finding of the combination that allows optimal use of the network capacity while retaining the overall capacity allocation for each MNO for the site. The capacity is rebalanced as percentage of the AP capacity or sent in terms of the PRBs.

The available rebalancing of resources for the APs is determined based on the following conditions. The resource allocation includes BW allocation to each AP and the amount of resources allocated to each MNO within each AP.

- When an AP requests less capacity for all MNOs, then the AP is a candidate for BW reduction.
- An AP is a candidate for rebalancing only when the request from that AP includes an MNO that requests more resources and another MNO from the same AP that requests a reduction in the capacity allocation.
- When the request from the AP is for all MNOs and includes either a requirement to retain the current capacity allocation or a request for more resource allocation, then rebalancing with the current BW allocation will not be possible. Such APs are candidates for BW expansion.

In a scenario with only one MNO, which can just be the enterprise users alone, this reduces to a trigger from the citizen broadband radio service device (CBSD) requesting a BW change in allocation. It can be to increase or willing to support a reduced BW. This information can be used in a central manner as part of the SON algorithm to allow rebalancing the BW allocations, including ways to support frequency reuse of one along with PRB usage separation across the APs.

II.1.5.2.6 Static Partition with Two-Pass Scheduling

The resource allocation for the individual MNOs and the enterprise devices is provisioned in the eNB/gNB.

II.1.5.2.7 Fixed RAN Resource Allocations for Each MNO

The resources will be statically allocated across all eNB/gNB, independent of the composition of the UEs in the cell. The scheduler will go through the individual MNO UEs and utilize the capacity allocated to that MNO. The enterprise private users' connectivity is treated like that of an MNO in terms of resource allocation.

A second pass is made to redistribute the unused capacity from the individual MNOs and enterprise resource allocations to other UEs. Fairness in handling the remaining capacity is achieved by distributing it in a round-robin manner.

II.1.5.2.8 Dynamic Rebalancing of MNO-x Slice Resource

This is the same as the previous proposal, with the additional feature of rebalancing the allocations to the individual MNOs, as suggested in the single-pass approach with a dynamic rebalancing option.

II.1.5.2.9 Support a Weighted-Fair-Share Scheduler

A completely independent approach is suggested using a weighted fair share (WFS)–based scheduler realization.

II.1.5.2.9.1 Weights Determination

Weights are determined statically and provided to the RAN scheduler for each UE:

- $\mathbf{W_{Enterprise} = 1}$
  - This is the weight that applies to a UE operating with an enterprise subscription.
- $\mathbf{W_{MNO\text{-}x} = 1 + (NumberOfMNO\text{-}x\text{-}DedicatedChannels_{MNO\text{-}x}/15)}$, where NumberOfMNO-x-DedicatedChannels$_{MNO\text{-}x}$ is the number of MNO-x dedicated channels provided by MNO for enterprise-level operation.
  - This is the weight that applies to a UE operating with an MNO-x subscription.
  - It is computed for each MNO that supports a neutral host on the enterprise campus.

II.1.5.2.9.2 Application of the Weights

- Admission control
  - To prioritize admitting UEs into the system.
  - To admit specific flows for a given UE into the system.
  - To determine the allowed GBR and MBR values for a given GBR bearer.
  - To specify the non-GBR QCI value.
    - QCI = 9,8,7,6; where the priority levels are applied as QCI = 6 > QCI = 7 > QCI = 8 > QCI = 9
- Congestion control
  - For a GBR bearer, the scaling of the traffic above the GBR bit rate up to MBR bit rate is proportionally adjusted based on the weights of the individual flows;
  - Handling non-GBR bearers
    - Approach 1: For non-GBR bearer, the scheduling algorithm (e.g. proportional fair) is further biased by the weight associated with the flow.
    - Approach 2: The non-GBR bearers are associated with specific QoS class identifier (QCI) values from 6 to 9. The weights for these QCIs are assigned based on the weight determined for the enterprise and MNO-x per the logic described earlier.
- Preemption
  - Preempting of GBR bearers/UE is further biased based on the weights associated with the UE.

II.1.5.2.10 RAN Slice Scheduler Metrics

This section describes the typical set of metrics that need to be collected to determine the RAN performance. This information is used to identify the deviations from the QoS metrics that need to be met for the individual flows. It is also used to assess the fairness across the different users within and across MNOs

- The scheduler metrics are aggregated and reset every refresh interval.
- The capacity, in terms of the PRBs allocated to the individual UEs, is collected within the refresh interval – DL-PRB$_{MNO\text{-}x\text{-}UE}$ and UL-PRB$_{MNO\text{-}x\text{-}UE}$. This counter is also reset at the start of the next refresh interval.
- The sum of the DL-PRBs allocated to all the UEs associated with a given MNO is determined in every DL slot – DL-PRB$_{MNO\text{-}x}$ = $\Sigma_{MNO\text{-}x}$ DL-PRB$_{MNO\text{-}x\text{-}UE}$.
- The sum of the UL-PRBs allocated to all the UEs associated with a given MNO is determined in every UL slot – UL-PRB$_{MNO\text{-}x}$ = $\Sigma_{MNO\text{-}x}$ UL-PRB$_{MNO\text{-}x\text{-}UE}$.

- The refresh internal starting slots are selected by spreading the UEs of a given MNO across slots to avoid having them all fall on the same slot.

II.1.5.2.11 Evolving the Scheduler Behavior Based on Real-Time Metrics

II.1.5.2.11.1 Use of Sigmoid Function for Priority Determination

As the schedule evolves, more metrics-based prioritization will be required. This process will go beyond using the GBR/MBR/AMBR-based scheduling.

When such an approach is utilized, normalization across different independent metrics used for scheduling the various flows is required. The following proposal suggests the use of a sigmoid function that is determined for each QoS flow type and each metric assessed to determine if the SLO/SLA is met for the associated flow, as well as the relative prioritization across UEs and QoS flows used to determine the UEs/QoS flows that need to be scheduled.

- The metrics used for prioritization are based on filtered values. The filter constants can be adjusted based on the individual metric. An exponential filter should be sufficient.
- For pdb = packet delay in the scheduler.
- For GBR = R_avg – R_gbr
- For non-GBR/BE = R_inst – R_avg – R_gbr; removing non-opportunistic traffic from the computation.
- All priority are computed in the range of [0, 1] = [low, high].
- A higher computed metric will result in a value closer to 1.
- As more resources are granted to the traffic flow/UE, it is less likely to receive additional resources in the future.
- This behavior makes the system implicitly nonlinear.
- The steepness of the curve can be adjusted based on the metric, controlling the aggressiveness of the throttling.
- This approach allows for normalizing all scheduler metrics on a single scale.

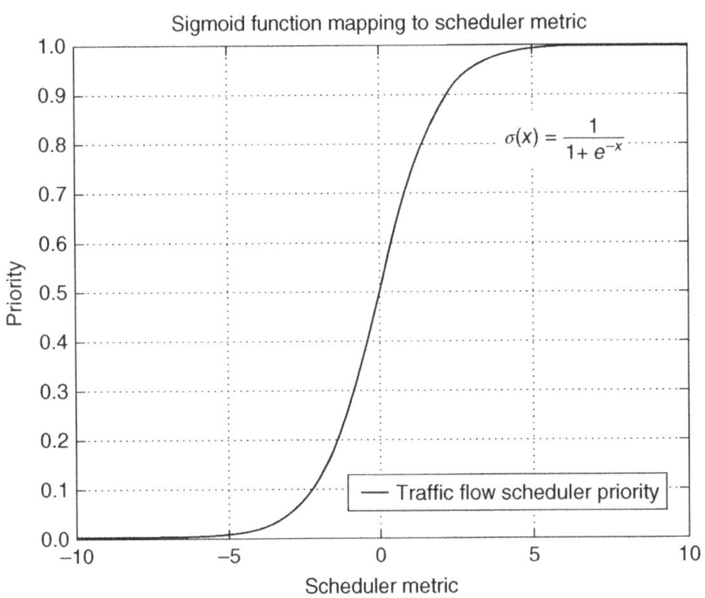

II.1.5.3 Enterprise Slice RAN Resource Management Concept Proposal for PNI-NPN

II.1.5.3.1 Background

A typical approach to RAN resource allocation employed in the market now is provided as a background here.

The RAN resources are partitioned to a specific percentage (of PRBs) across all cells in the country. The resource utilization on the individual cells for the enterprise slice is limited to this predetermined amount. The restrictions on RAN resource usage may be applied in a filtered manner (e.g. 100 ms) rather than as an instantaneous limit for enterprise slice resource partitioning currently employed in the market.

Infra networks have two or three radio resource partitioning schemes. Detailed implementation may vary:

- Different cells serve different slices.
- Fixed reservation/hard reservation: PRB are allocated at a fixed percentage; unused or unassigned PRBs may be shared, with no preemption across reservations.
- Shared partitioning, priority scheduling per QoS, with preemption potentially taking effect.

II.1.5.3.2 Goals for Enterprise Slice on a PNI-NPN Network

II.1.5.3.2.1 Enterprise Requesting for Slice Resources

- A typical enterprise is either
  - located in a specific location spread across a few buildings within a city or
  - located across multiple cities with specific locations/buildings within each city.
- A given enterprise will typically be interested in providing the enterprise slice access when within a certain set of locales.
  - This locale can be restricted to the physical footprint of the enterprise or extend to the full county/city/adjoining cities.
  - The decision for required coverage for the enterprise slice is made on a location basis.
- The enterprise obtains required resources within each location, subject to the application/service support needed and the enterprise employee population in the location.
  - The enterprise may negotiate for an extension of location-specific resource limits and may require country-wide limits.
- Control from the enterprise will be fundamental to the success of the enterprise slice deployment.
- The enterprise will want to regulate the operations of the device either through
  - the backend of the MNO network through APIs or
  - provision of the devices with mobile device management (MDM) policies.
- Currently, most resource partitioning is static in nature, with less flexibility for enterprises to control resource allocation among their consumers.
- This results in wastage of resources, as the resource usage could vary across different sites, and there is no mechanism for the reuse of the unused resources.
- There is no technical mechanism for an end-to-end guarantee where an enterprise can share the unused resources from a site that is underutilizing the resources with an overloaded side.
- There is no technical solution for the enterprise to control the admission control of its users.

II.1.5.3.2.2 Limitations Seen with the Approaches Used Currently in the Market

The limit on the RAN resources is applied independently of the number of enterprise users within a given cell. The resource usage for the enterprise slice, when there is extra capacity available on the cell, may result in wasted resources with this restriction enforced.

Both the leftover resources from the enterprise slice and the available extra unused resources from the cell can be utilized by enterprise slice users.

II.1.5.3.3 Proposed Solution

II.1.5.3.3.1 Proposed Enhancement to RAN Resource Allocation

- SLA for the enterprise slice:
  - $M_{E\text{-}Max\text{-}Users}$: Support for maximum number of users across the entire enterprise slice.
  - $M_{EC\text{-}Max\text{-}Users}$: Support for the maximum number of users in each cell.
  - Authorized QoS flow/metrics/user types supported.
  - Authorized tunneling into the enterprise core network/IP domain/VLAN/DN.
  - $M_{E\text{-}Max\text{-}GBR}$: Total GBR limits across the entire enterprise slice.
  - $M_{EC\text{-}Max\text{-}GBR}$: Total GBR limits in each cell for the enterprise slice users.
- Approach to RAN resource allocation:
  - Users are admitted to a cell as long as the following conditions are met:
  The total number of enterprise users in the system is below $M_{E\text{-}Max\text{-}Users}$.
  The total number of enterprise users in the cell is below $M_{EC\text{-}Max\text{-}Users}$.
  - QoS flows are admitted into the system as long as the following conditions are met:
  The sum total of the GBR assigned to all enterprise users in the system is below $M_{E\text{-}Max\text{-}GBR}$.
  The sum total of the GBR assigned to all enterprise users in the cell is below $M_{EC\text{-}Max\text{-}GBR}$.

II.1.5.3.3.2 RAN Scheduler Realization

- A typical RAN scheduler implements a strict priority ordering while processing the different data queues across and within a given user, while supporting a WFS within each priority.
- For each scheduling event:
  - Walk through the queues in the following order: control signaling – DL/UL, broadcast/paging – DL, RACH – UL, HARQ reTx, GBR QoS priority, non-GBR QoS priority.
- While ensuring the resource allocations for the users within an enterprise slice:
  - (Slice A, Slice B, . . . , eMBB)
  - Treat eMBB users as belonging to a single slice, even though an explicit slice may not be established.
- Instantaneously, when there is no traffic available for certain other flows, the flows with active traffic in the buffer occupy the channel without wasting any radio resources.
  - When additional resources are allocated to a given slice, the averaging the serviced data across a larger time window allows for rebalancing of the resource allocation among other users or slices within a given cell.
  - A certain forgetting factor or finite tail in the resource allocation is used to avoid longer-term impacts on given slices or users.
- When there is saturation of the number of users associated with the individual slices, the users within each slice will be limited to the percentage of resource allocation that is provided.
- Additionally,, there may be subjective details or limitations on the number of users allocated within a given scheduling event. This limitation is also addressed by longer-term (~100 ms) filtering, applying the WFS within a given priority level both within and across slices.

II.1.5.3.3.3 Admission and Congestion Control

- The logic, as specified before, boils it down to allocating the RAN resources associated with the enterprise slice for a given cell.
- The resource allocation is adjusted proportionally to the number of users and the QoS flows associated with the enterprise users currently camped on the cell.
  - The admission control is performed subject to the $M_{E\text{-}Max\text{-}Users}$, $M_{EC\text{-}Max\text{-}Users}$, $M_{E\text{-}Max\text{-}GBR}$, and $M_{EC\text{-}Max\text{-}GBR}$, as described earlier across the full network.
  - This implies that the resources allocated to a given enterprise slice are dynamically managed based on the number of user and QoS flows associated with the enterprise currently camped on the cell.
  - Additionally, based on the user priority within the enterprise, some users or QoS flows may be preempted to accommodate other users or QoS flows within a given cell and across cells within the network.
- The network and region where this logic is applied can be as narrow as a cell or as wide as the entire network, including anything in between (e.g. cells within a given tracking area code [TAC], city, and so on).
- Users and QoS flows blocked or preempted due to admission or congestion control will be blocked, with indications provided in the report to the enterprise.
  - The enterprise can consider this and determine if more resources need to be purchased from the MNO.
  - It is possible for the UE or QoS flow to be admitted as part of the general pool when resources are available, if the enterprise supports overage charges when crossing the negotiated limits.
  - Access traffic steering-switching-splitting (ATSSS) policies can be defined to allow the UE to react to the blocks in service, leaving the enterprise slice and requesting service from the general pool. The MNO may treat this like roaming behavior and apply roaming charges, with the roaming flag indicator highlighted in the UE. This may be enterprise's or user's preference to transition to such roaming camping.

II.1.5.3.3.4 UE Behavior to Assist Admission/Congestion Control in the Network

- When the UE's radio resource control (RRC) connection or QoS flow is blocked, the network provides an indication in the reject message to inform the UE that the resource allocation is denied due to slice resource constraints.
  - This may include a back-off timer; the UE will retry after the timer has expired.
  - In such scenarios, based on provisioned policies, the UE may attempt to transition to using regular resources instead of the slice-based resources.
- The policies can be captured as part of ATSSS.
  - The services and QoS available during such operation may be diminished, given that the enterprise UE is operating outside of the enterprise slice.
  - It is left up to the network to manage such policies and behaviors.
  - The provisioned policies can also indicate to the UE when to reattempt using the enterprise slice.
  - Re-registration procedures can be initiated from the UE, and network can either reject the UE's transitions to the enterprise slice or allow the UE to move into the enterprise slice.
  - This transition request can be initiated either by the UE based on specific conditions, including back-off timer expiry, or by the network asking the UE to initiate a re-registration into the enterprise slice.

- As the UE moves into the enterprise slice from the default operation, the triggers for QoS flow(s) establishment are handled from the network, recognizing the active flows in the system.
- If there is an internet protocol (IP) address change during the transition, the active services are terminated and reestablished.
- The indication that there will be an IP address change is provided in the policies to the UE, allowing it to decide on the appropriate time to initiate the transition.
- Supporting application-level transitions through REINVITE procedures can be used to transition the active services to the new IP address, using the security context of the session established with the IP address assigned to the UE prior to the transition.
- If the IP address can be retained across the transition, service continuity can be directly accommodated.

Outer Control Loop – Enterprise Slice

Figure II.1.5.3 illustrates the Outer control loopto manage the resources allocated to anenterprise slice.

RAN Enterprise Slice Scheduler

Figure II.1.5.4 shows a RAN enterprise slice scheduler.

Figure II.1.5.5 provides an illustration of a static and dynamic RAN resource scheduling behaviors. The dynamic scheduler provides for a more flexible RAN resource management.

II.1.5.3.3.5 Mechanisms for Enterprise to Control the Load

Passive Slice Load Management Mechanism

A mechanism to provide cell-level slice load indicators to the device is suggested. Slice cell-level load indicators can be utilized by the UE to take the following actions:

- Self-regulate the GBR/MBR of applications using the loaded slice (e.g.: decrease the resolution of a very low-latency video for an enterprise to admit other users from the enterprise.)
- Device and slice-level policy provisioning, which can be provisioned via MDM by the enterprise. Slice policy manager on iOS will control the regulation.

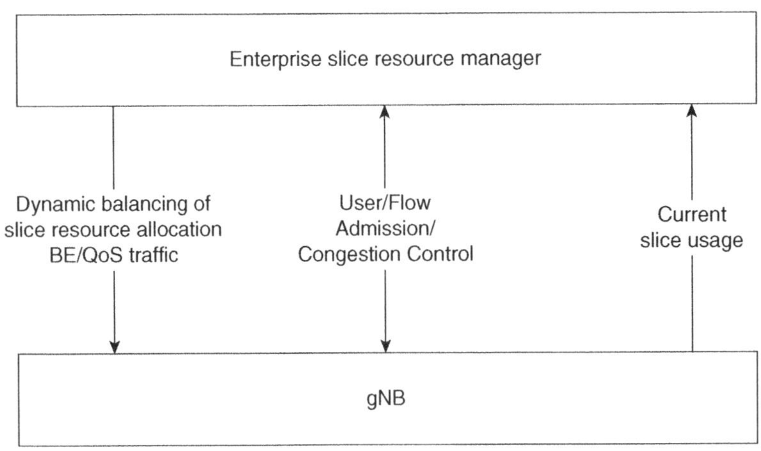

Figure II.1.5.3 Outer control loop – enterprise slice.

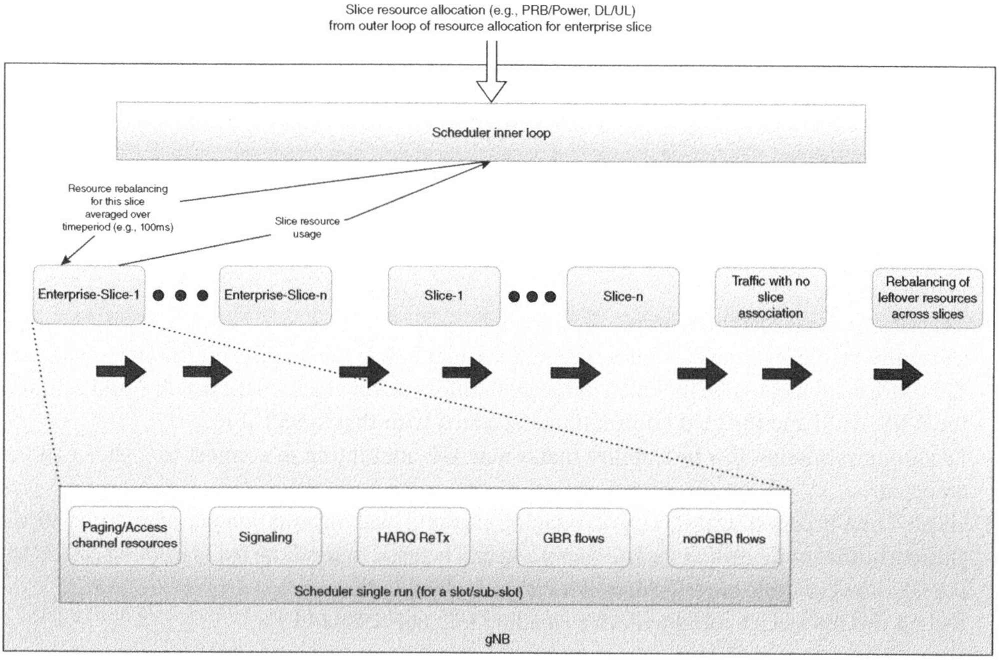

Figure II.1.5.4 RAN enterprise slice scheduler.

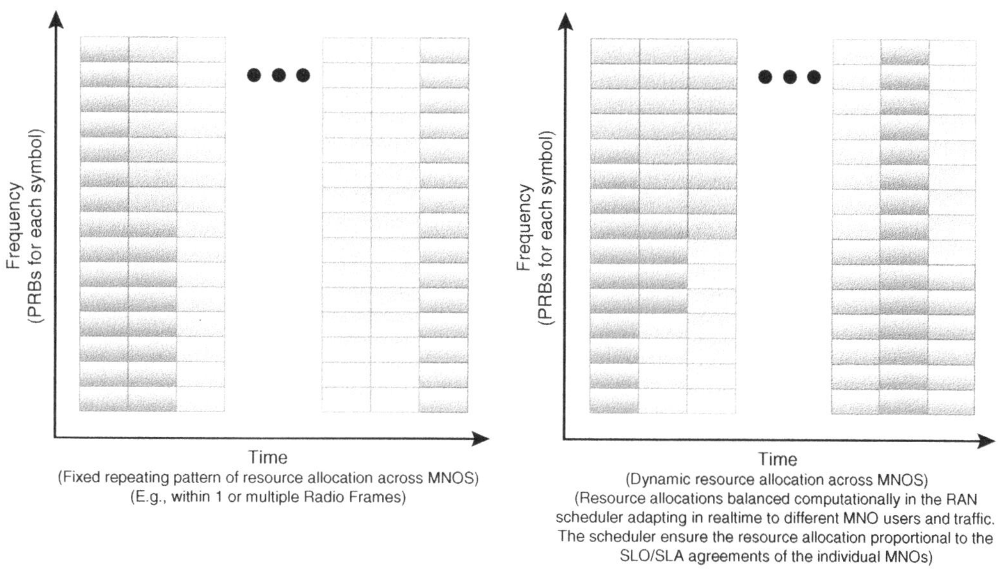

Figure II.1.5.5 Static and dynamic RAN resource scheduling.

- Adapting the back-off algorithms (restarting the UE NAS-level timer *T3526 – "S-NSSAI not available due to maximum number of UEs reached"*) for a particular slice (rejected network slice selection assistance information (NSSAI) list) when the UE receives an admission control reject for that slice.

Intelligent decisions on slice selection when the UE has access to multiple slices (multiple entries in the allowed NSSAI list). For example, if the enterprise slice is loaded, the UE can fall back to the general slice for UE traffic.

Two delivery mechanisms for load feedback to UEs are:

- Broadcast slice-level load indicators
  - Currently, cell-level broadcast information does not include the loading information per slice.
  - This information could be included in a system information block (SIB), which could contain the S-NSSAI Id and the load information associated with that S-NSSAI Id.
  - Loading information is a probability that a new UE attempting to connect to a slice will be accepted.
- Dedicated non-access stratum (NAS) messaging carrying load information per configured slice.
  - Currently, the *configuration update command* can be used to send the list of *allowed NSSAI* to the UE; however, this message does not carry any load indicators.
  - Extend this interface to send to devices loading info per NSSAI Id.

Figure II.1.5.6 provides a depiction of passive slice load information on dedicated and broadcast messages.

The load indicator from SIB can be used to throttle the attempts made to request the slice. Additionally, on a preconfigured threshold from the policy manager, application traffic can be switched to the default slice to access the network.

It is possible that already registered users may need to be moved out if there are higher-priority users that need to be accommodated. In such scenarios, dedicated NAS messages can be used to communicate the information to the UE, with the UE taking subsequent actions.

After a UE is admitted to a slice and applications are actively using the slice, there may be an increased load detected. In response to this, the session management function (SMF) will send a

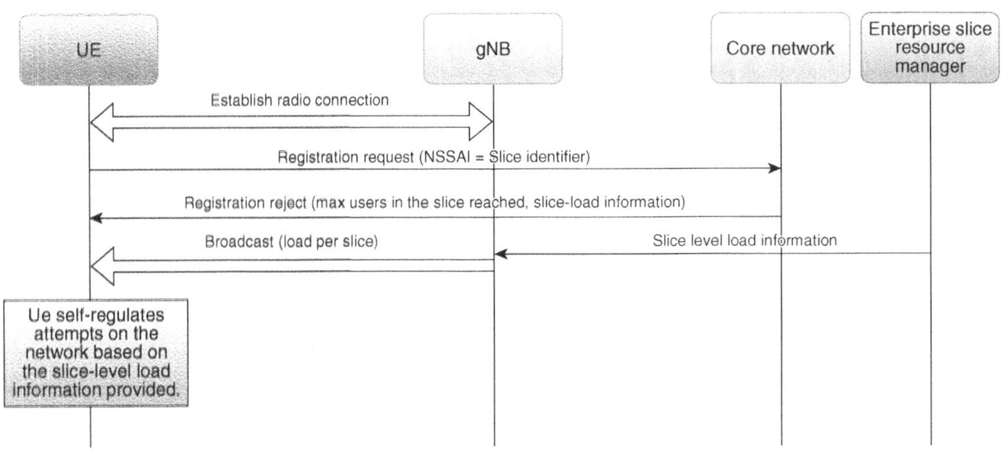

Figure II.1.5.6 Passive slice load information on dedicated and broadcast messages.

dedicated message via a configuration update command with the load per S-NSSAI. The slice-specific load is reported to the UE slice controller, which, in conjunction with the UE slice policy manager, reacts to throttle the GBR for applications.

II.1.5.3.3.6 Active Slice Load Management Mechanism

In addition to passive measures of providing load indicators to UEs and then expecting UEs of a particular slice to self-regulate, two new mechanisms are claimed to actively throttle the slice load.

QoS flow-level blocking is based on load thresholds at the gNB. The SMF can trigger a *PDU session modification command* to block certain QoS flows associated with a protocol data unit (PDU) session corresponding to a particular slice (S-NSSAI). This is achieved using the *operation code to delete the existing QoS flow description*. A particular application may meet a subset of QoS demands while the other flows rely on best-effort delivery. For example, preempt the QoS flow for video while retaining the audio QoS flow. The SMF can update the session-AMBR for a particular QoS flow using the PDU session modification command to throttling a certain QoS flow. For example, a particular application that is mapped to a QoS flow can be downgraded by reducing the QoS grant provided, which forces the application to reduce its resolution.

II.1.5.3.3.7 Summary Thoughts on the Suggested Approach

The proposed solution allows for the flexibility of the enterprise to request and manage the slice resources. The enterprise can either regulate the operations of the device through the backend of the MNO network through APIs, dynamically adjusting the policies in real-time, and/or provision the devices with MDM policies, enabling the devices to self-regulate with specific overall control information related to the enterprise slice from the network. This allows the enterprise to control the resources that are allocated to its enterprise slice.

The benefit of the approach allows for dynamic RAN resource allocation and the ability to move dynamically with the population/concentration of the enterprise users across the network. Hopefully, this is seen as a cleaner and more viable market realization with optimal network resource utilization of the enterprise slice allocation. It supports a more scalable enterprise slice implementation in the market, allowing for improved revenues for the MNOs. It accommodates dynamic clustering of UEs of a given enterprise with proportional resource allocation within a given cell and can be seen as an improved way for an MNO to request resources from the enterprises.

It avoids static resource allocation for a given enterprise slice across the full network and allows for support multiple slices and scales seamlessly for both GBR and non-GBR traffic. Additionally, wastage of radio resources is prevented with dynamic resource allocation, and the RAN scheduler optimally occupies the channel with active flows that have data in the buffer that need to be transmitted.

This is a scalable approach to managing the resource allocation associated with a given enterprise slice, potentially managing the behavior within a defined region, with the region itself being adaptably specified.

II.1.5.4 Summary

Both business models of an MNO user camping on the NHN network deployed by the enterprise and the enterprise user camping on MNO networks (including PNI-NPN-based solutions) are addressed. These are intended to be leading suggestions on approaches to take and even establish viable and scalable deployment models in the market. Enabling ease of deployment and establishing seamless transitions across macro, PNI-NPN, enterprise, and NHN networks make connectivity available to the user primary, and any approach that supports this should be embraced.

References

1 *Proportional Fair Scheduling in LTE*. This study analyzes PF scheduling in LTE downlink, showing how it improves fairness while maintaining good spectral efficiency by prioritizing users with better instantaneous channel conditions. Available on IEEE Xplore.

2 *Cell-Throughput Analysis of the Proportional Fair Scheduler*. This paper offers an analysis of PF scheduling in MIMO systems, focusing on maximizing cell throughput and fairness. Available on IEEE Xplore.

3 Yongzhou, C., Ruihao, Y., and Haitham H. (2023). Radhika Mittal Channel-Aware 5G RAN Slicing with Customizable Schedulers. *20th USENIX Symposium on Networked Systems Design and Implementation (NSDI)*. This paper introduces RadioSaber, a channel-aware scheduling mechanism that dynamically allocates resources across different RAN slices. The design improves throughput and fairness across slices by breaking the cyclic dependencies between inter-slice and intra-slice schedulers.

4 Machine Learning-Driven RAN Schedulers: Overview and Performance Analysis. *IEEE Communications Magazine*. This paper discusses how machine learning can be applied to optimize RAN scheduling in virtualized and software-defined environments. The paper analyzes different ML-driven algorithms to improve spectral efficiency, reduce latency, and adapt to changing network conditions in real time.

5 *A QoS Improving Downlink Scheduling Scheme for Slicing in 5G RAN*. This paper discusses a downlink scheduling scheme that enhances QoS by efficiently allocating radio resources in network slices, particularly in 5G environments. It focuses on how to support stringent QoS for diverse services. ResearchGate link

6 *An Enhanced Joint Scheduling Scheme for GBR and non-GBR Services in 5G RAN*. The paper presents a joint scheduling approach to manage both Guaranteed Bit Rate (GBR) and non-GBR traffic in 5G, improving QoS and balancing service fairness. Link available on Springer (SpringerLink).

II.1.6

Self-organizing Networks (SON)

II.1.6.1 Graph Theory Application for Self-Organizing Networks

II.1.6.1.1 Why Is Graph Theory Covered Here?

Enterprise private networks are supported using small cells that have very low output power and limited computing resources. The power is typically 1 W for indoor cells and 50 to 75 W for outdoor cells. This implies that the coverage footprint of these cells is approximately 50 m for indoor cells and about 150–300 m with outdoor cells. To cover the enterprise campus, several nodes (~10 to 50) need to be deployed to provide the requisite service unlike a macro cell that can cover several kilometers with an output power that is greater than 3,500 W. Given the large size of the macro cells, the UE is typically within the footprint of a stronger cell and can be served by that one cell without causing interference to the neighboring cells, even when using the same frequency allocation. When using small cells (both indoor and outdoor), employing the same frequency for neighboring cells in close proximity makes inter-cell interference unavoidable. Additionally, given the low computing resources available on these small cells, even if all the interfering signals are identified, running interference cancellation (IC) becomes an almost impossible task. Due to these limitations, a decision is made to orthogonalize the channel allocations to the small cells that are close to each other to prevent interference. This implies the need to detect cells that can interfere with each other. Additionally, given that the private network spectrum is often limited, and wider allocations of up to 100 MHz are possible for 5G NR (while LTE supports up to 20 MHz), spectrum reuse must be employed but only on cells that do not interfere with each other. If spectrum becomes limited and spectrum reuse in a region is required despite interference, fractional reuse techniques can be employed (see II.1.7 Fractional Frequency Reuse (FFR) Techniques).

Based on the deployment of the small cells determined by the coverage required in the enterprise campus, the frequency allocations for individual cells must be planned as part of the self-organizing network (SON) function. This is best addressed using connected graphs.

The key graph theory concepts required to run the SON function are described. The application of SON is discussed together with the description of the concepts. For a more detailed treatment of graph theory, please refer to a dedicated book on that subject.

Mobile Communication Systems for Private Networks, First Edition. Srinivasan Balasubramanian.

II.1.6.1.2 The Optimization Problem

The criteria are used to provide frequency and bandwidth allocation to the individual small cells in a deployment:

- Using the available spectrum, which may vary based on the location of the small cell, accounting for nodes both within the same deployment and across neighboring deployments;
- Providing the maximum bandwidth allocation to each individual small cell;
- Using the knowledge of the type of spectrum used (e.g. dedicated to that network user/deployment; shared access across deployments);
- Causing minimal interference to both cells within the same deployment and across deployments, achieved by orthogonalizing the channel allocations across the small cells;
- Account for the individual small cell capabilities regarding bandwidth limits and carrier aggregation;
- Account for use cases that need to be addressed for a given site (DL-centric versus UL-centric). Note that this criterion may change with the day of the week/time of day and may require dynamic spectrum management for the individual cells;
- Employing the knowledge of the directionality of the antennas;
- Determining the footprint of the individual cells based on the maximum allowed power used (indoor versus outdoor);
- Allowing for adjusting the maximum power under constrained scenarios to get authorization for large bandwidth used from the central authorizing entity (e.g. SAS);
- Address effective mobility transitions for the UE jumping across the nodes, requiring service continuity, implying some uniform approach to spectrum/resource allocation for the individual nodes;
- The spectrum/resource allocation needs to be adapted in near real time to accommodate the concentration of the users in different locations on the campus. Typical deployments, however, employ static spectrum allocation to avoid the increased complexity involved, particularly with debugging the network performance issues.

II.1.6.1.3 Introduction to Graph Theory

Discrete mathematics is a branch of mathematics that deals with countable, distinct, and separate objects or structures. It is concerned with mathematical structures and concepts that are fundamentally distinct from continuous mathematics, which deals with real numbers, real variables, and continuous functions. Discrete mathematics focuses on topics such as set theory, logic, number theory, combinatorics, discrete structures, algorithms, complexity theory, and graph theory.

Set theory is the foundation of discrete mathematics and deals with sets, elements, unions, intersections, and other set operations. Logic is used to reason about propositions and includes propositional logic and predicate logic, which are fundamental to computer science and artificial intelligence. Number theory explores the properties of integers, prime numbers, divisibility, and modular arithmetic, which are typically used for security and cryptography. Combinatorics is the study of counting, arrangements, and combinations of objects. It plays a crucial role in solving problems related to permutations, combinations, and probability. Discrete structures include topics like trees, sequences, and relations, which are essential in computer science and discrete mathematics. Discrete mathematics is the foundation for analyzing the efficiency and complexity of algorithms. The study of algorithms often involves discrete structures and combinatorial analysis.

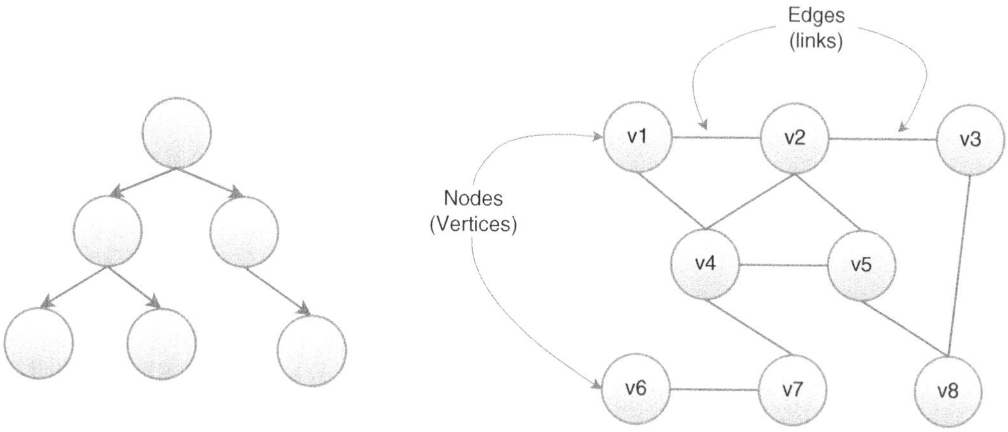

Figure II.1.6.1 Trees and graphs.

Graph theory, the focus of this section, deals with networks and the relationships between objects. Graphs consist of vertices and edges and are used to model various real-world problems such as social networks and transportation systems. Trees are a subset of graphs and have specific rules that are adhered to (e.g. everything starts from one root node and flows in only one direction; a binary tree has only two branches per node). Graphs are more generic and can accommodate any structure without restrictions. Additionally, graphs do not have a root node. Figure II.1.6.1 illustrates the trees and graphs.

A singleton graph is a graph with a single node. This is relevant for deployments with single nodes such as in a home network, where these single nodes will still be sitting next to other neighboring networks. The behaviors for such nodes, as part of the SON algorithm, need to be addressed. Most deployments will support multiple nodes, requiring both intra- and inter-deployment aspects to be considered. When the graph has multiple "nodes" (sometimes referred to as vertices), they can be interconnected through links called "edges" (sometimes referred to as links).

Edges can connect nodes in any way possible! The different types of edges are important when it comes to recognizing and defining graphs. Graphs can have two types of edges: an edge that has a direction or flow (directed edges) and an edge that has no direction or flow (undirected/bidirectional edges). In a directed edge, two nodes are connected in a very specific way/direction. Note that two nodes can be connected by two unidirectional edges pointing in opposite directions, with each edge with a different type of property. For SON algorithm, this key property is leveraged to determine the spectrum allocation. The interference caused by cell A to cell B is different from the interference caused by cell B on cell A.

At a broad level, graphs can be classified as directed graphs and undirected graphs. It is possible to envision both types of edges being supported in a single graph. However, this increases the complexity and is a lot cleaner to support bidirectional edges as two unidirectional edges with reversed flow direction. Figure II.1.6.2 shows the directed and undirected edge for graphs.

The study of graphs is referred to as graph theory. Graph theory is used to solve many types of problems. The suggestion here is to employ it to address SON. Graphs are a way to formally represent a network, which is just a collection of base stations that are supported in a deployment. Graph data structures are used to realize graph implementations in simulation modeling, and the terms used to describe the details are directly leveraged from graph theory (e.g. ordered pairs).

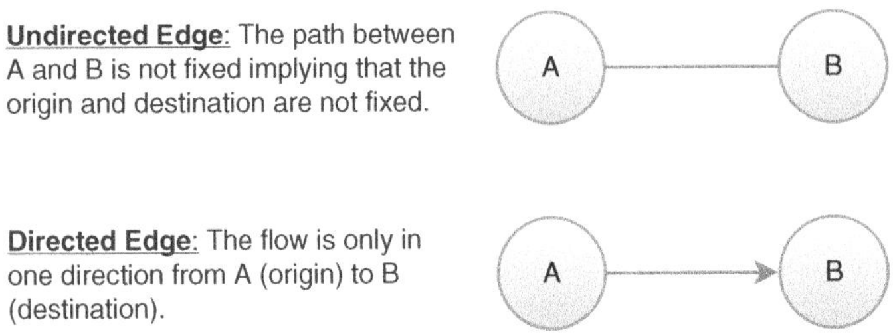

Figure II.1.6.2 Directed and undirected edge for graphs.

A graph is defined as G = (V, E), where V is the set of vertices and E is the set of edges. From Figure II.1.6.1, we can see the set V = {v1, v2, v3, v4, v5, v6, v7, v8} is an unordered set of nodes and the set E = {{v1, v2}, {v1, v4}, {v2, v3}, {v2, v4}, {v2, v5}, {v3, v8}, {v4, v7}, {v4, v5}, {v5, v8}, {v6, v7}} is the set of unordered pairs. However, for our purposes, the ordering matters, and the set E of edges needs to be defined as a set or ordered pairs, where the sequence in which the pairs are listed matters. As recognized before, the ordering matters for the SON algorithm, as the location, signal strength, and antenna directionality define the influence that one node (cell) has on another node (cell).

II.1.6.1.3.1 The Adjacency Matrix (A)

A weighted graph has weights on the edges. In an unweighted graph, all edges have weight of 1. The adjacency matrix for a graph is n X n, and each element contains 0 for non-neighbors and the edge weight for neighbors. The adjacency matrix is symmetric ($A = A^{T}$). Additionally, for a simple graph with no self-edges, elements on main diagonal are 0. This typical configuration will be used for deployments, given that a cell causing interference to itself is not relevant. There could be scenarios where there are different sectorized antennas at a single site that can interfere with each other. However, these can be modeled as independent cells, and given the nature of the sectorized antenna, they can be tuned to avoid interfering with each other.

Figure II.1.6.3 shows an adjacency matrix (A) for a directed graph. Figure II.1.6.4 shows an adjacency matrix (A) for an undirected graph. A directed graph with an adjacency matrix based on nodes that have directional interactions is usually not symmetric. A weighted adjacency matrix for a directed graph (see Figure II.1.6.5) allows for specifying the intensity of the influence of one node on another. For the SON algorithm, an outdoor higher-powered cell that is much stronger can have a significantly greater influence on the indoor lower-powered cell. Similarly, a much higher-powered

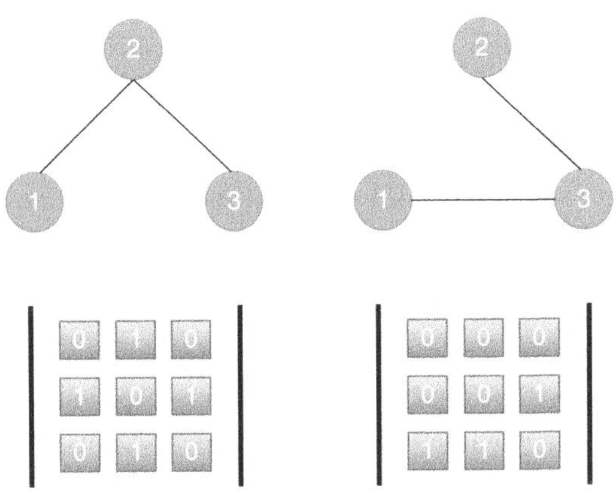

Figure II.1.6.3 Adjacency matrix (A) for a directed graph.

macro base station can have a substantial influence on an enterprise cell deployed, based on the directionality and the proximity involved.

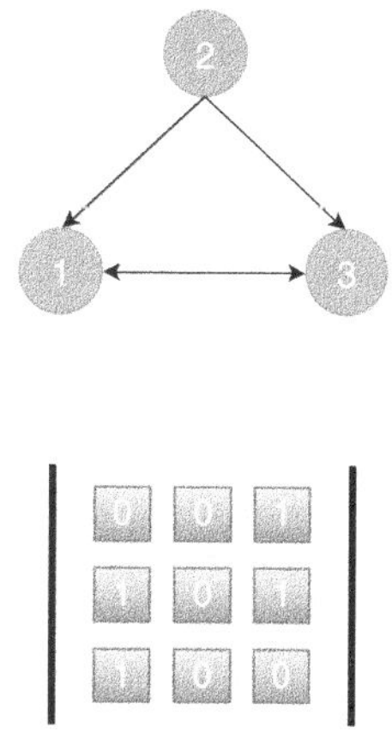

Figure II.1.6.4 Adjacency matrix (A) for an undirected graph.

II.1.6.1.3.2 Degree of a Vertex

The degree of a vertex is the number of edges connected to it. In a directed graph, there are both in-degrees (incoming edges) and out-degrees (outgoing edges). This becomes especially useful to determine the cells influenced by a given node; hence, the node with the highest degree can be used as a starting for the SON algorithm to orthogonalize the spectrum allocations.

II.1.6.1.3.3 Path and Cycle

A path is a sequence of vertices in which each adjacent pair is connected by an edge. A simple path has no repeated vertices or edges.

A cycle is a path that starts and ends at the same vertex, with no repeated edges or vertices (except for the starting and ending vertex). In terms of communication networks, this specifies redundancy and can be useful as alternative routes for the wired interconnection of the base stations. Alternate routes could be used to get between any pair of nodes, and a single break in wired connection will allow continued operations.

Although not directly useful for SON algorithm, it can be used to determine the possible wireline outages that can happen in the network and can be used for both detection and recovery methods.

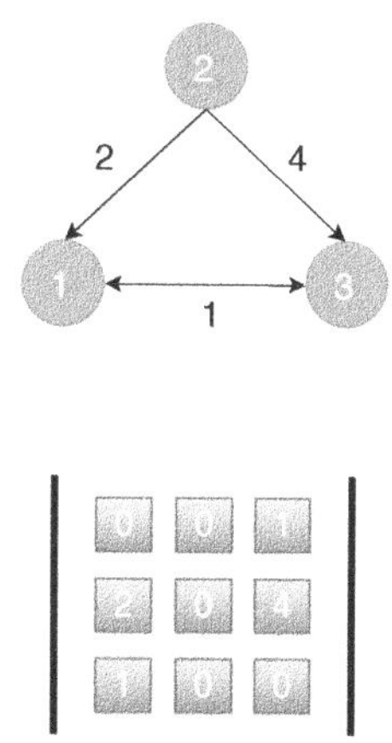

Figure II.1.6.5 Weighted adjacency matrix (A) for a directed graph.

II.1.6.1.3.4 Hypergraphs and Bipartite Graphs

Hypergraphs are a generalization of the concept of graphs, where edges can connect more than two vertices. In a traditional graph, edges connect pairs of vertices, but in a hypergraph, an edge can connect any number of vertices. This extended structure allows for more complex and versatile representations of relationships and dependencies among elements. The nodes/vertex remains the same as regular graphs. The hyperedge, however, is a set of vertices where each hyperedge can connect any number of vertices (including just one or more than two). The number of vertices contained within a hyperedge is known as its hyperedge cardinality.

A bipartite graph is a specific type of graph in which the set of vertices can be divided into two distinct and non-overlapping subsets, often referred to as "partite sets," typically denoted as U (the left or top set) and V (the right or bottom set). All edges in a bipartite graph connect vertices from set U to vertices from set V. There are no edges that connect vertices within the same set. In other words, there are no edges between vertices in U or between vertices in V. Bipartite graphs are used to represent relationships or connections between two diverse types of entities.

A brief description is included here only for completeness, and although a SON algorithm can use this sophistication, it is sufficient to rely on regular graphs.

II.1.6.2 SON Algorithm Definition

Figure II.1.6.6 provides an illustration of the sample network deployment. It includes a typical building with both indoor and outdoor deployment covering the campus. Also illustrated are cells detected from neighboring deployments that share the same spectrum or have interference caused by base stations deployed in adjacent licensed spectrum used on the enterprise campus. The outdoor cells typically have a higher power of >50 W. Indoor cells typically use a power level of ~1 W. Licensed spectrum usage cells will use a power level of >3,500 W, and due to such high power and potential lack of guard bands, they can cause interference in adjoining bands. For example, C-band licensed spectrum (3.7 GHz) can interfere with the Citizens Broadband Radio Service (CBRS) band (3.55–3.7 GHz). The tree foliage impacts the propagation and those shown as well, and depending on the sophistication of the SON algorithm, these aspects can be included in the computations as well.

The focus here is on small cells, not on distributed antenna solutions (DAS) deployments, where a single spectrum is used across the entire deployment to address both indoor and outdoor coverage.

The typical deployment starts with designing a network by analyzing the campus environment to understand the radio frequency (RF) propagation aspects involved and the level of QoS that needs to be delivered. This requires understanding of the building structure and materials involved. For example, there will be metal barriers preventing RF penetration, and building with energy-efficient glass can block signals from outside antenna. The antennas are placed in appropriate

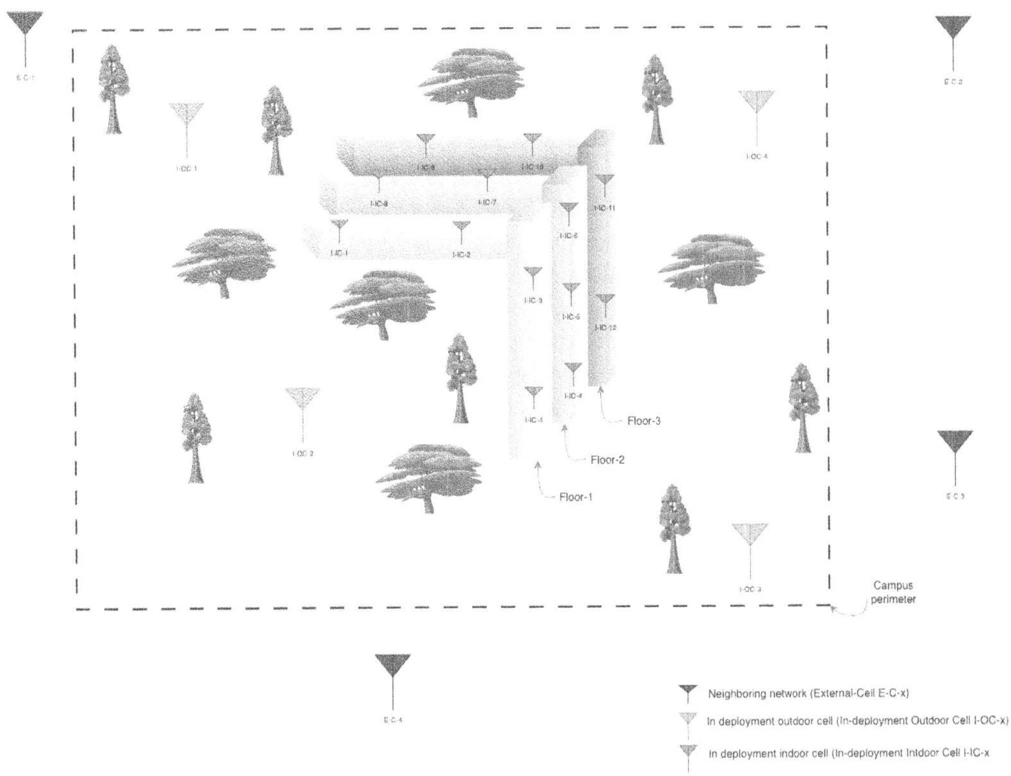

Figure II.1.6.6 Sample network deployment.

locations, taking these aspects into consideration, and the campus coverage is ascertained. Site-map tools are available from several vendors (e.g. Google) that can be used to place antennas and allow for visualizing the propagation on campus. For instance, putting the antenna on specific rooftops allows visualization of the propagation, including the impact of foliage, to see the coverage that can be achieved.

There will be some errors in this and can only be corrected on-site by doing a walk-through once the base stations are installed. Moving the cells after installation is extremely hard and the approach when coverage holes are discovered is to add cells in strategic locations. This step may be required when there are a lot of handover failures that occur when the UE moves across the different cells on campus.

With the cell plan in place, the next step will be to determine the actual spectrum allocations for the different cells. The spectrum used for determining the allocation will depend on the region and can include both dedicated and shared spectrum use across neighboring deployments. See the section on spectrum for details of types of spectrum allocations for enterprise deployments.

The matrix of the associations across the different cells deployed on campus is defined, along with the associated weights proportional to the interference caused to the adjacent nodes. The SON algorithm needs to be run to maximize the orthogonality of the spectrum allocation, accounting for the optimization criteria specified earlier in the section. Typical algorithm steps will start with the node that has the highest degree and work their way down to the lower-degree nodes, given that a choice of spectrum for the node with the higher degree will impact several other nodes. Figure II.1.6.7 shows a way to visualize the cell footprints for a camp deployment, accounting for outdoor cells, indoor cells, and external interferers. Note that although the cells are shown with an omni configuration (360° coverage), it is likely that at least the outdoor cells will use directional antennas (90° or 120°). The extent of down-tilting will also dictate the footprint and its influence on other neighboring cells. The outdoor cell will have a higher power and a weighting different from that of an indoor cell in terms of influence and required orthogonality. Using this information, the matrix of the interacting cells is prepared, and the SON algorithm is run to determine the orthogonal spectrum allocations. It is also necessary to account for vertical impact by considering the interference caused across floors rather than looking at a horizontal layout.

Once the spectrum allocation for a given node is determined by the SON algorithm, if it includes shared spectrum, the node needs to reach out to a central arbiter (e.g. domain proxy for CBRS spectrum allocation) to obtain grants before using the spectrum. It is possible that, based on the physical location of the node, it may not be allowed to use specific parts while other nodes in the same deployment may be allowed.

The SON algorithm may need to iterate with the subsequent information on the allowed and disallowed spectrum for the individual nodes, influencing the orthogonalization algorithm accordingly.

These algorithm realizations tend to be very customized and may not require all the optimization criteria, and potentially different nodes in the deployment may require different behaviors (e.g. a cell servicing a security camera will require higher UL capacity). Due to the limited availability of spectrum, complete orthogonalization may not be possible.

It is possible to alter the power level to minimize the interference and may allow for the central entity managing the shared spectrum allocation to provide a higher bandwidth and improve orthogonalization within a deployment. However, such methods are not preferred, given that they will change the campus footprint and are not a desirable alternative.

Deployments may decide to manually tune the network on-site; although it is not scalable, it is a viable option.

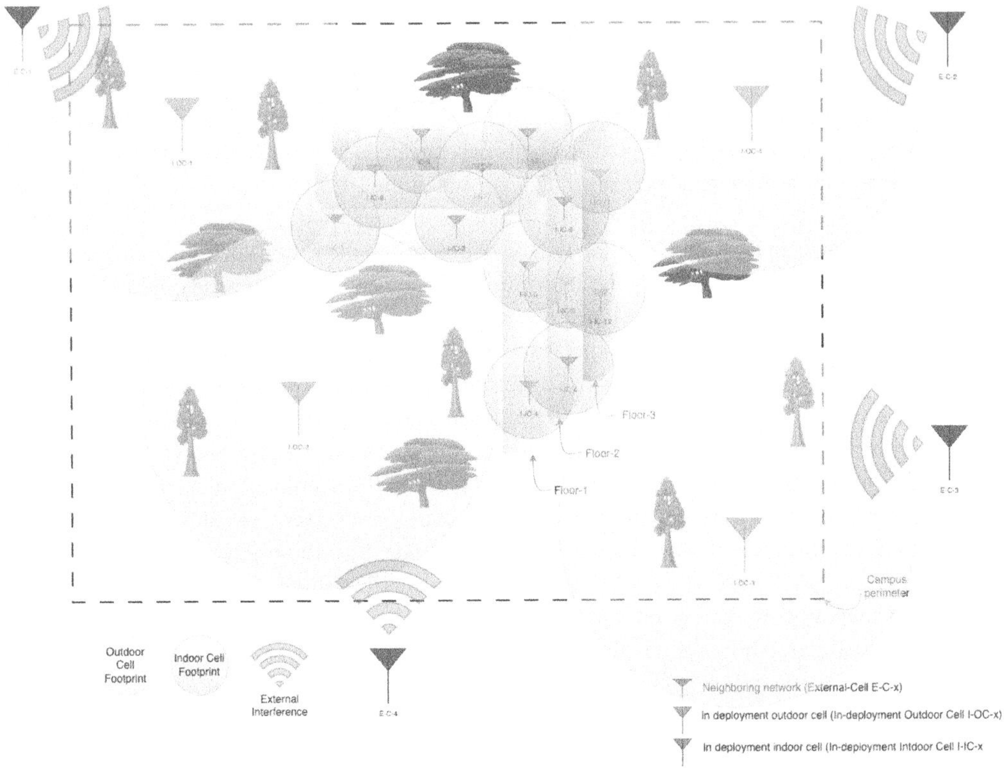

Figure II.1.6.7 Sample network deployment with cell footprints illustrated.

This suggested graph-theoretic approach is employed by the central entity to arbitrate across deployments and choose the spectrum allocation to minimize interference.

II.1.6.3 SAS Functions

II.1.6.3.1 WInnForum

The WInnForum, formerly known as the "Wireless Innovation Forum," is an organization that focuses on advancing and promoting the development and use of wireless communication technologies, particularly in the field of software-defined radio (SDR) and cognitive radio (CR). WInnForum standards serve several essential functions within this context:

1) Interoperability: WInnForum standards help ensure that different wireless devices and systems can work together effectively. They define common interfaces and protocols, which can be especially important in environments with diverse and heterogeneous radio systems.
2) Spectrum Efficiency: One of the primary goals of WinnForum is to improve the efficient use of the radio spectrum. Standards developed by WinnForum can include mechanisms for dynamic spectrum access (DSA), which allows wireless devices to use available spectrum bands more effectively.

3) Regulatory Compliance: WInnForum standards can help wireless technologies comply with relevant regulations and requirements, particularly in terms of spectrum management and RF emissions. This is especially important in scenarios where CRs adapt their behavior based on real-time spectrum conditions.
4) Innovation: The WInnForum encourages innovation in the field of wireless communications, and its standards can help promote the development of new, more flexible, and adaptable wireless technologies, particularly in the SDR and CR domains.
5) Research and Development: Standards developed by WInnForum are often the result of collaboration among industry experts, researchers, and practitioners. They provide a common framework for research, development, and testing in SDR and CR.
6) Spectrum Sharing: WInnForum standards can address challenges related to spectrum sharing, enabling multiple users and systems to share spectrum resources efficiently while minimizing interference.
7) Security: Standards may include security provisions and protocols to ensure that SDR and CR technologies can operate securely in a variety of settings.
8) Certification: The organization may establish certification programs to ensure that devices and systems meet their standards, promoting quality and consistency in the market.
9) Education and Advocacy: The WInnForum also plays a role in educating stakeholders, advocating for favorable regulatory policies, and promoting the benefits of SDR and CR technologies.

Overall, WInnForum standards play a vital role in advancing the field of software-defined and CR and in addressing the technical, regulatory, and business challenges associated with wireless communication technologies. The CBRS spectrum definition and its use are done in a dynamic, real-time management of the RF nodes operating across the USA. A revolutionary idea of spectrum sharing is being adopted in some form in individual countries. The dynamic spectrum management across multiple tiers of users requires a central server/service to determine the RF conditions and provide the appropriate allocations. The spectrum access system (SAS) is defined for this purpose.

II.1.6.3.2 Spectrum Sharing

Spectrum sharing refers to the practice of allowing multiple wireless communication systems or users to share the same frequency spectrum for their operations. It is a key concept in modern telecommunications and is crucial for efficient and dynamic spectrum management. Spectrum sharing can be implemented in several ways, depending on the specific use case and regulatory framework. Here are some details and methods of spectrum sharing:

1) **Dynamic Spectrum Sharing:** This approach allows different users to access the same spectrum dynamically based on real-time demand and availability. CR systems are an example of dynamic spectrum-sharing technology. CR devices can sense the spectrum and opportunistically use available frequencies without causing harmful interference to primary users.
2) **Licensed Shared Access (LSA):** In LSA, secondary users are granted access to spectrum that is primarily licensed to other users (e.g. government agencies or incumbent operators) on a shared and controlled basis. The primary users retain priority, and secondary users must avoid interfering with them.
3) **Priority Access:** In this model, certain users (e.g. public safety agencies) have priority access to the spectrum, while others may access it if the primary users do not require it. This approach ensures that critical communications take precedence.

4) **Geographical Spectrum Sharing:** Spectrum usage can vary by location. In some areas, the spectrum may be heavily utilized, while in others, it remains underutilized. Geographical spectrum sharing allows users to access spectrum where it is available, reducing interference and optimizing spectrum use.
5) **Frequency Bands:** Spectrum sharing can take place in various frequency bands, including licensed bands (e.g. cellular networks), unlicensed bands (e.g. Wi-Fi), and shared bands. Shared bands often involve multiple users accessing the same spectrum, subject to certain regulatory and interference management rules.
6) **Database-Driven Approaches:** DSA databases, like the SAS used in the CBRS in the United States, maintain records of available spectrum and coordinate access for various users. These databases ensure that users do not interfere with one another or with incumbent users.
7) **Regulatory Frameworks:** Spectrum sharing is governed by regulatory authorities. Regulations define how various types of spectrum sharing can occur, set rules for interference management, and address issues related to licensing, registration, and compliance.
8) **Interference Mitigation:** To prevent harmful interference, spectrum-sharing systems often use technologies like sensing, power control, and CR techniques to adapt their transmission parameters based on the real-time spectrum environment.
9) **Coexistence and Compatibility:** Spectrum-sharing technologies and devices must be designed to coexist and be compatible with other users, particularly in cases of shared and unlicensed bands.
10) **Enforcement and Compliance:** Regulatory agencies enforce spectrum-sharing rules and standards, ensuring that users adhere to the agreed-upon protocols and do not disrupt other users' services.

Spectrum sharing is a key strategy to address the growing demand for wireless connectivity and the limited availability of spectrum resources. It allows for more efficient use of the radio spectrum by enabling multiple services, technologies, and users to coexist in the same frequency bands while minimizing interference and maximizing spectrum utilization. Effective spectrum sharing is essential for the deployment of 5G networks, the Internet of Things (IoT), and various other wireless services.

II.1.6.3.3 Shared Spectrum Priority Levels

Shared spectrum priority levels refer to the different tiers of access or priority granted to various users in a shared or dynamic spectrum allocation system (SAS). These priority levels are established to manage and regulate spectrum usage, ensuring that certain critical users or services receive preferential treatment while others may access the spectrum on a secondary or opportunistic basis. The specific priority levels and their definitions can vary depending on the regulatory framework and the nature of the shared spectrum environment. Here are some common shared spectrum priority levels:

1) **Primary Users (Incumbents):** Primary users are the original or licensed holders of spectrum in a particular frequency band. They have the highest priority and exclusivity for spectrum access. Primary users are typically entities such as government agencies, licensed cellular operators, and public safety organizations.
2) **Secondary Users (Licensed or Authorized):** Secondary users are authorized to access the spectrum under certain conditions and with specified limitations. They have priority access but must yield to primary users when necessary. These users often include entities with special rights such as LSA or priority access license (PAL) holders.

3) **Protected Users:** Certain users or services may be designated as "protected" due to their critical nature. For example, public safety and emergency services are often considered protected users, and they have priority access to the spectrum to ensure they can maintain communication during emergencies.
4) **General Authorized Users:** General authorized users include numerous services and applications permitted to access the spectrum, subject to regulatory guidelines. They may operate under standard licensing conditions and share the spectrum with secondary users.
5) **Unlicensed or Opportunistic Users:** Unlicensed or opportunistic users do not hold a dedicated spectrum license. Instead, they access the spectrum opportunistically, following rules and protocols set by regulatory authorities to ensure they do not cause harmful interference to primary or secondary users. Examples of unlicensed users include Wi-Fi devices operating in the industrial, scientific, and medical (ISM) bands.
6) **Dynamic Spectrum Access Users:** In DSA systems, such as CR networks, DSA users are those who employ technology to sense the spectrum in real time and access available frequencies opportunistically without causing harmful interference to higher-priority users. DSA users adapt their operations based on the spectrum environment and the presence of primary and secondary users.
7) **Interference Protection Levels:** Some shared spectrum frameworks define various levels of interference protection based on the type of service. For example, a low-priority service may have lower interference protection requirements, while a critical service might require strong protection from interference.

These shared spectrum priority levels help ensure the efficient and fair utilization of spectrum resources. See Figure II.1.6.8 illustrating the three-tiered spectrum access system (SAS). Regulatory authorities establish and enforce these priority levels to manage coexistence, mitigate interference, and protect essential services. In practice, these priority levels are often implemented through technologies such as DSA databases, interference management algorithms, and communication protocols that enable different users to access the spectrum in accordance with their designated priority.

II.1.6.3.4 SAS Functions

Figure II.1.6.9 shows the spectrum access system (SAS) architecture. The SAS makes the advanced three-tier spectrum-sharing framework adopted by the FCC for CBRS possible. Given that the spectrum was already being used, an incumbent tier as the highest level is established. Auctions were held by the FCC to sell up to a maximum of 70 MHz in the individual counties creating the second tier, while retaining 80 MHz for general authorized access (GAA) use, identified as the third tier. The novel three-tier sharing framework coordinates spectrum access among the incumbent military radars, satellite earth stations, and new commercial users.

The three tiers of users are incumbent, PAL, and GAA. The SAS is an advanced, highly automated radio spectrum coordinator within the CBRS 3.55–3.7 GHz band and ensures the protection of the higher-tier users from lower-tier users while optimizing the spectrum allocations to the individual nodes with effective reuse. The SAS maintains a database of all CBRS radio base stations (CBRD), including their tier status associated with the 15 10 MHz segments of the band, the associated geographical location, including the county where they are deployed, and the relevant RF parameters, including the transmit power assignments. The information associated with the incumbent detected in real time by the environment sensing capability (ESC), from the citizen

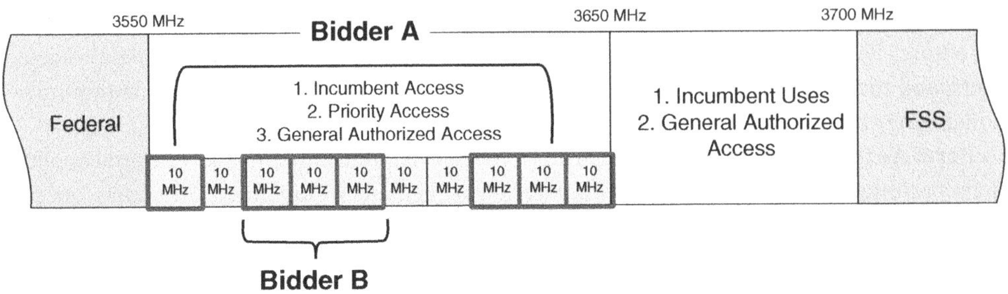

Figure II.1.6.8 The three-tiered spectrum access system (SAS).

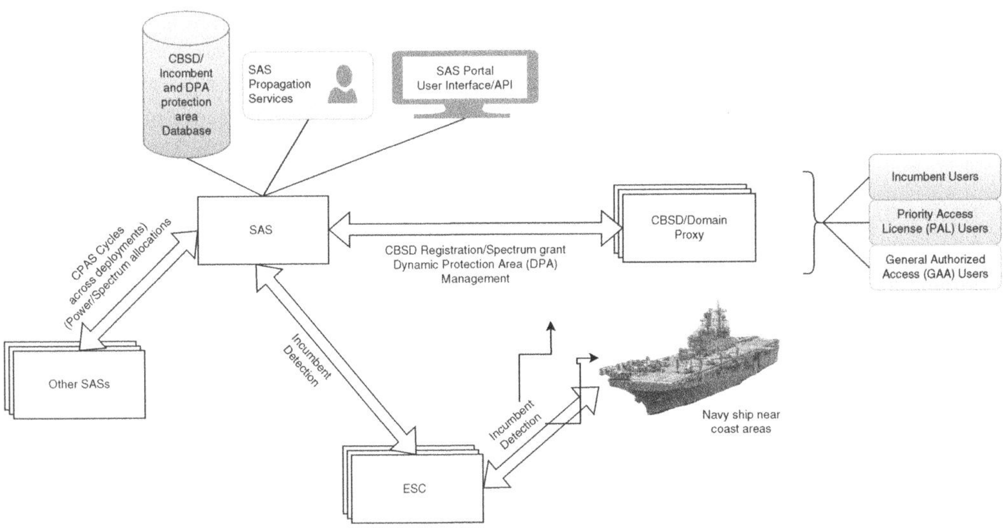

Figure II.1.6.9 Spectrum access system (SAS) architecture.

broadband radio service devices (CBSDs) with PAL only, PAL + GAA, and GAA-only associations, is used to monitor and protect the CBSDs and the incumbent from potential interference. Given that there are several SAS vendors and not just one central entity and given that the individual CBSDs may choose to work with specific SAS vendors, the SASs must coordinate with each other for the spectrum allocations. The SAS uses the information from the CBSDs that are registered with it, the information about the other CBSDs in the neighborhood, accounting for the dynamic protection area (DPA) of the PAL CBSDs within the county where the PAL purchases are made, and the landscape of buildings and trees to map the RF propagation and required protection associated with the individual CBSDs. This propagation of information is determined across the whole country, one county at a time. Using graph models similar to those described for the SON algorithm, which is run within a single deployment, it extends to a much larger scale to apply it across the USA. This consumes a lot of computing resources, and the expectation is that the deployed CBSDs do not change very often. The information exchange between the SASs happens once a day (e.g. at midnight) and typically takes a few hours to complete. This updated information received from the other SASs is used by the individual SAS to perform the required recomputes and adjust the spectrum allocations to the CBSDs accordingly.

As discussed above, per FCC rules, at least 80 MHz of spectrum will be available for GAA. Additionally, when higher-priority incumbents and the PAL users are not using the channel (even when the PAL channel has been purchased), it is available for use as GAA. The SAS models the RF propagation to ensure that FCC rules are always enforced. The SAS retains the authority to revoke or reassign spectrum to individual CBSDs, and this will happen dynamically based on several factors, including the arrival of a higher-priority user on a channel, which may require the other CBSD users to vacate the channel. This enforces protection of the top-tier incumbent users, which is especially important for federal users. Additionally, when a new PAL node is deployed, it will require the GAA users to be reassigned to other channels. When additional GAA nodes arrive, this will require the SAS to balance the spectrum resources and fairly share the allocations across the GAAs, accounting for the existing or newer ones in the neighborhood.

Federal use of the CBRS band is expected to be rare, but it is important to allow access when required. Even when the incumbent wants to use the channel, it typically occupies only parts of the band for a short period of time (like a few hours). To detect the federal incumbents, such as naval ships, the SAS is notified by the environmental sensing capability (ESC), which supports the sensors to detect signal initiated by the incumbents. Given that these incumbents are naval ships, the ESC sensors are deployed along the U.S. coastline for signal detection and to protect the incumbents from any interference by shared spectrum users. The ESC sensors reliably detect a steady signal for a finite time period to ensure the incumbent is indeed trying to use the channel and inform the SAS of the impacted channels in the CBRS band. The SAS works to reallocate shared spectrum users, which include both PAL and GAA channels, to other available channels within the 3.5 GHz spectrum band.

There are no costs associated with using the spectrum as a GAA user, apart from interacting with the SAS and operating with the spectrum allocations provided by the SAS. This is prime mid-band spectrum, and the low costs of operating a network on that band make it extremely attractive, particularly for enterprise private network entities. Figure II.1.6.10 show the environmental sensing

Figure II.1.6.10 Environmental sensing capability (ESC) detects and informs incumbent activity.

capability (ESC) deployed in a coastal region that helps detecting incumbent activity and informs SAS about it.

The SAS also includes incumbent protections for fixed satellite systems and other grandfathered wireless internet service providers through exclusion zones (EZs) and the utilization of aggregate interference data. Note that this CBRS spectrum does not dictate a specific radio access technology (RAT) to be deployed and is not restricted to 3GPP-defined 4G LTE and 5G NR systems (e.g. cambium network uses this spectrum to deploy its proprietary technology solution). The SAS supports hierarchical spectrum-sharing procedures and determines the available spectrum that can be allocated to the individual nodes. Fairness is maintained and managed through software implementation employing system modeling, which supports the allocations programmatically without requiring manual intervention.

II.1.6.3.5 The ESC Processes

The ESC process is an integral part of the CBRS framework in the USA. It is designed to protect incumbent users of the 3.5 GHz band, particularly federal radar systems, by detecting their presence and ensuring that CBRS devices operating in the band do not cause harmful interference.

Software interface-based approaches are being considered for incumbents to report their time of use, potentially both offline and in real time. However, there are a lot of legacy devices that do not easily accommodate such reporting, which implies that an external detector, like the ESC, needs to be deployed.

Here is an overview of the ESC process:

1) **Spectrum Sharing in the 3.5 GHz Band:** The 3.5 GHz band is designated as a shared spectrum in the USA. This means multiple users and services, including federal radar systems and CBRS devices, can use the same frequency range. To prevent interference with federal radar systems, the CBRS framework employs an ESC to detect the presence of these radar systems.
2) **ESC Deployment:** ESCs are specialized sensors or networks of sensors strategically deployed in geographic areas where CBRS operation is allowed. These sensors are designed to continuously monitor the 3.5 GHz band for signals from federal radar systems.
3) **Radar Detection:** The primary role of the ESC is to detect the transmissions from federal radar systems. These radar systems operate in the 3.5 GHz band for various purposes, including weather monitoring, defense applications, and aviation safety. The ESC sensors are equipped with the capability to identify radar signals and distinguish them from CBRS transmissions.
4) **Protection Levels:** The ESC system categorizes the detected radar signals into different protection levels based on their characteristics. Higher protection levels are assigned to radar systems with the greatest priority such as those used in critical safety applications.
5) **Database Communication:** The ESC communicates with the SAS in the CBRS framework. When radar signals are detected, the ESC sends information to the SAS to inform it about the presence and location of the radar systems.
6) **SAS Coordination:** The SAS uses the information provided by the ESC to make real-time decisions about spectrum access for CBRS devices. When radar signals are detected in a specific area, the SAS may dynamically adjust the frequency bands available for CBRS operation in that area to avoid interference with the radar systems.
7) **Dynamic Spectrum Access:** CBRS devices access the 3.5 GHz band through the SAS, which ensures that they do not operate in frequencies that may interfere with the radar systems. When radar signals are detected in a particular area, the SAS will dynamically manage CBRS device access in that area to protect the radar operations.

8) **Interference Mitigation:** By continuously monitoring the spectrum and coordinating with the SAS, the ESC helps prevent harmful interference to radar systems while enabling efficient DSA for CBRS devices. This approach allows for coexistence and shared spectrum use.

The ESC process is a crucial component of the CBRS ecosystem, ensuring that shared spectrum access in the 3.5 GHz band does not disrupt the operation of incumbent federal radar systems, which are essential for safety and security applications.

Figure II.1.6.11 shows the basic geometry of the reciprocal-propagation monitoring approach (Source: NTIA). The incumbents in the CBRS band are typically navy ship that want to grab the channel when new the coast. There are specific regions inland as well where the incumbents is required and in these regions, the channel used by the incumbents are typically permanently blocked for PAL and GAA users. Figure II.1.6.12 shows the coastline along the continental USA is segmented in a designated DPA (Source: NTIA).

II.1.6.3.6 SAS Spectrum Allocation Process

The spectrum allocation system (SAS) is a principal component of the CBRS framework in the USA. It plays a critical role in managing and allocating spectrum resources in the 3.5 GHz band, which is shared by various users and services. The SAS spectrum allocation process ensures that CBRS devices operate without causing harmful interference to incumbent users such as federal radar systems. Here is an overview of the SAS spectrum allocation process:

1) **Database-Driven Spectrum Management:** The SAS is a database-driven system that maintains records of available spectrum in the 3.5 GHz band. It keeps track of both the available spectrum for typical use and the protected spectrum areas where CBRS devices must avoid interfering with incumbent users.
2) **CBRS Device Registration:** Before operating in the CBRS band, CBRS devices, including small cells, access points, and end-user devices, must register with a certified SAS. This registration includes information about the device's location, characteristics, and intended operation.
3) **Database Query:** When a CBRS device is powered on or moved to a new location, it queries the SAS to determine which frequencies are available for operation at its specific location. The SAS provides the device with a list of available frequency channels.
4) **Protection for Incumbent Users:** The SAS is responsible for protecting incumbent users such as federal radar systems. It continuously receives information from ESC sensors that detect the presence of radar signals. The SAS uses this data to protect the radar systems by avoiding interference from CBRS devices.

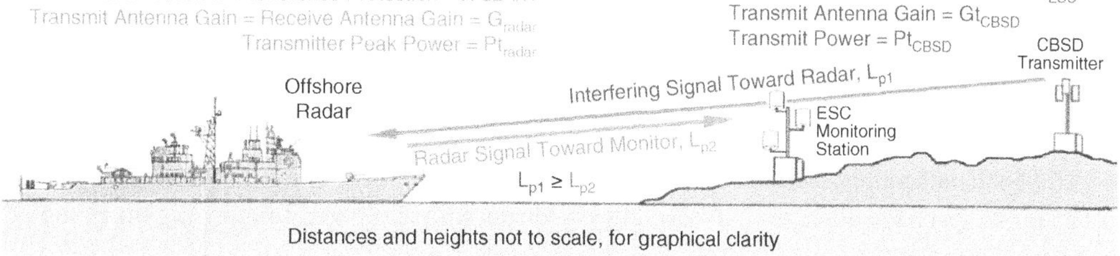

Figure II.1.6.11 Basic geometry of the reciprocal-propagation monitoring approach (*Source:* NTIA).

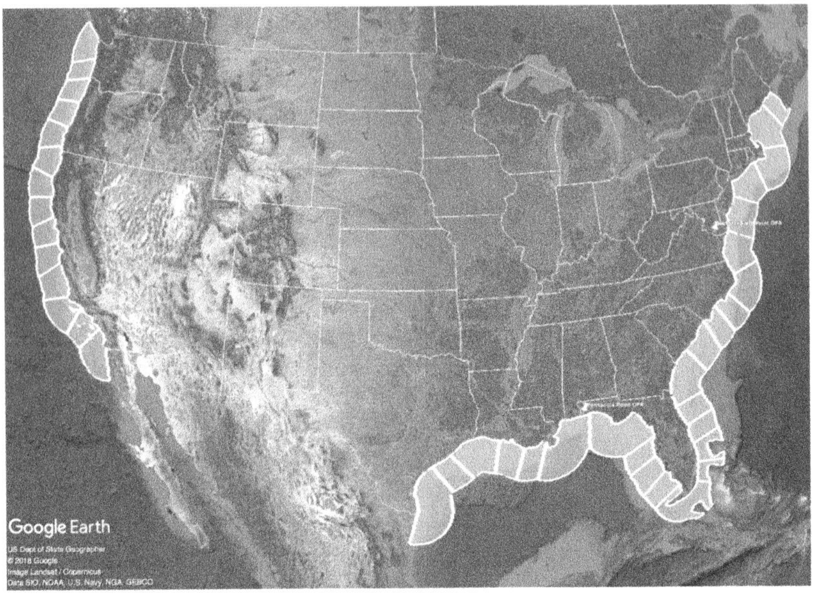

Figure II.1.6.12 The coastline along the continental USA is segmented in a designated DPA (*Source:* NTIA).

5) **Spectrum Assignment:** The SAS assigns specific frequencies or channels to CBRS devices based on their registration information, location, and the current spectrum availability. It ensures that CBRS devices do not operate on frequencies that could cause harmful interference to incumbent users, especially in areas where radar systems are active.
6) **Dynamic Spectrum Access:** The SAS employs DSA techniques, meaning that it can dynamically allocate and de-allocate spectrum resources as needed. This allows for efficient spectrum use and coexistence with incumbent users.
7) **Coordinated Operation:** CBRS devices operate under the coordination of the SAS, which manages their access to the shared spectrum. If there is a change in the spectrum environment or if incumbent users become active, the SAS may instruct CBRS devices to adjust their operations to avoid interference.
8) **Database Updates:** The SAS continuously updates its database with real-time information on CBRS device registrations, ESC data, and the availability of spectrum. This ensures that the most accurate and up-to-date information is used for spectrum allocation.
9) **Interference Management:** The SAS helps mitigate interference by ensuring that CBRS devices operate within power limits, on assigned frequencies, and with protocols that prevent harmful interference to other users.
10) **Spectrum Monitoring and Enforcement:** The SAS monitors CBRS devices to ensure compliance with regulations. If a device operates outside its authorized parameters, the SAS can stop or mitigate interference.

The SAS spectrum allocation process is designed to enable efficient and responsible sharing of the 3.5 GHz bands among various users while protecting incumbent users. It allows for dynamic and adaptive spectrum allocation, maximizing spectrum utilization and minimizing the potential for harmful interference.

II.1.6.3.6.1 CPAS Cycles

[Text derived from WInnForum standards specification WINNF-SSC-0008-V1.0.0]

Spectrum Sharing Committee Policy and Procedure: Coordinated Periodic Activities Policy

Coordinated Periodic Activities Policy

According to WInnForum requirements, SASs shall collaborate to determine CBSD power allocation in a substantially similar fashion. To achieve synchronous power allocation among all SASs, a procedure called cooperative periodic activities among SASs (CPAS) is defined. CPAS is a periodic process performed by all SAS administrators synchronously.

CPAS is defined as the following process:

Every 24 hours, starting at time T_1, all SASs perform the following functions synchronously:

1) T1: Each SAS creates a full dump record (all data should be "the state as of T1"), including
   a) All CBSDs with at least one active grant.
   b) All existing active grants, that is, all grants that should be used in IAP.
   c) All PPAs.
   d) Location, antenna characteristics, and protection levels of all ESC sensors.
2) At time T_2
   a) Each SAS pulls the full dump record from all other SASs.
   b) Each SAS synchronizes with all external databases (FCC and WInnForum).
3) Upon completion of step 2, each SAS performs Pre-IAP filtering activities in the following order:
   a) Determine conflict grants, that is, CBSDs having approved grants from multiple SASs simultaneously, and remove those grants from the rest of the process.
   b) Apply EZ protections; CBSDs within the EZ, with the grants associated to the EZ, are removed from the rest of the process for the EZ corresponding channels.
      - PPA,
      - GWPZ,
      - Part 90 subpart Z (GWBL stations within 150 km of FSS operating within 3,650–3,700 MHz),
      - All inlands federal radars protected by EZ.
   c) Calculate FSS Purge List for all FSS stations with TT&C = ON. The purged CBSDs are removed from the rest of the process.
4) Upon completion of step 3, using the exchanged records, all SASs perform the following activities independently:
   a) Using *maxEirp* (within *requestedOperationParam* for CBSDs managed by other SASs if provided, otherwise within *operationParam*), run the IAP algorithm to protect all non-federal higher-tier protection entities (GWPZ, FSS Cochannel, FSS blocking, PPAs, and ESC sensors).
   b) Using *maxEirp* (within *requestedOperationParam* for CBSDs managed by other SASs if provided; otherwise within *operationParam*), perform DPA move list calculation for all offshore and inland DPAs.
5) At time T3: Each SAS responds to all CBSDs that it manages and requires power decrease (termination through *heartbeatResponse*).
6) At time T3 + 240 sec: Each SAS may respond to all CBSDs that it manages, allowing a power increase, and responds to new grant CBSD's requested approved *maxEIRP*.

The values of T_1, T_2, and T_3 are determined and agreed upon by all SAS administrators.

II.1.6.3.7 CBSD Registration Process with the SAS to Obtain Spectrum Allocations

The process of CBSD registration and spectrum allocation from the SAS in the CBRS framework involves several steps to ensure efficient and interference-free operation. Here is an overview of this process:

CBSD Registration

1) **CBSD Initialization:** When a CBSD is powered on or deployed in a new location, it initiates the registration process with the SAS.
2) **Location Determination:** The CBSD determines its geographic location using various methods, including GPS, and provides this location information as part of the registration process.
3) **Environmental Sensing Capability (ESC) Information:** The CBSD may also provide information about its ESC sensor, which is used to detect radar signals in the area and share this information with the SAS.
4) **Registration Request:** The CBSD sends a registration request to a SAS, which includes the device's identity, location, and ESC information, among other details.

SAS Verification and Spectrum Allocation

5) **SAS Verification:** The SAS receives the registration request from the CBSD and verifies the information provided, including the device's location and ESC sensor data.
6) **Database Query:** The SAS consults its database, which contains information about available spectrum and protected incumbent users. It checks for spectrum availability at the CBSD's specific location.
7) **Protection of Incumbent Users:** The SAS ensures that the CBSD's intended operation does not interfere with incumbent users such as federal radar systems. It uses information from the ESC to protect these radar systems.
8) **Spectrum Allocation:** If spectrum is available and does not interfere with incumbent users, the SAS assigns a set of specific frequencies or channels to the CBSD for its operation. These assigned frequencies are chosen based on the CBSD's location and the current spectrum availability.
9) **Dynamic Spectrum Access:** The SAS uses DSA techniques to ensure efficient use of the shared spectrum. If there is a change in the spectrum environment or the presence of incumbent users in the area, the SAS may instruct the CBSD to adjust its operation to avoid interference.
10) **SAS Response:** The SAS sends a response to the CBSD, indicating whether the registration was successful and providing details of the allocated frequencies and operating parameters. If registration is denied, the SAS specifies the reason for the denial.
11) **Operational Parameters:** The SAS may also specify various operational parameters, including transmit power levels and operating bandwidth, to ensure that the CBSD operates within regulatory and interference limits.
12) **CBSD Operation:** The CBSD configures itself based on the information received from the SAS, ensuring that it operates within the allocated spectrum and follows the prescribed parameters.
13) **Continuous Monitoring:** The SAS continuously monitors the operation of CBSDs to ensure compliance with regulatory requirements. It also remains prepared to manage any changes in spectrum allocation and interference management.

This registration and spectrum allocation process is critical for managing shared spectrum access in the CBRS framework, as it allows CBSDs to operate within the 3.5 GHz band while preventing harmful interference to incumbent users. It ensures that the shared spectrum is used efficiently and that coexistence between different services and technologies is achieved.

II.1.6.3.8 Domain Proxy Functions

A domain proxy, in the context of the CBRS and DSA, serves several essential functions in managing shared spectrum access and ensuring interference-free operation. See Figure II.1.6.13 illustrating the domain proxy interactions with SAS for spectrum allocations. It is a key component within the CBRS ecosystem and plays a critical role in coordinating and regulating spectrum use. Figure II.1.6.14 shows the state machine of the CBSD SAS registration status and the involved transitions. Figure II.1.6.15 show the CBSD SAS registration/grant sequence for obtaining spectrum allocations from the SAS before turning on service on the individual cells.

Here are the functions of a domain proxy:

1) **CBSD Registration and Coordination:** The domain proxy is responsible for overseeing the registration and coordination of CBSDs within a specific geographic area, known as a "domain." CBSDs include small cells, access points, and end-user devices that operate in the CBRS band.
2) **Protection of Incumbent Users:** It ensures that the operation of CBSDs does not interfere with incumbent users, especially federal radar systems. The domain proxy uses information from ESC sensors to protect incumbent users by avoiding interference.
3) **Domain Management:** Each domain proxy manages the allocation of available spectrum resources within its designated domain. It ensures that the CBSDs within its domain operate in a manner that complies with regulatory requirements and does not cause interference.
4) **ESC Interaction:** The domain proxy communicates with ESC sensors within its domain to receive real-time data about the presence of radar signals and other incumbent user activities.

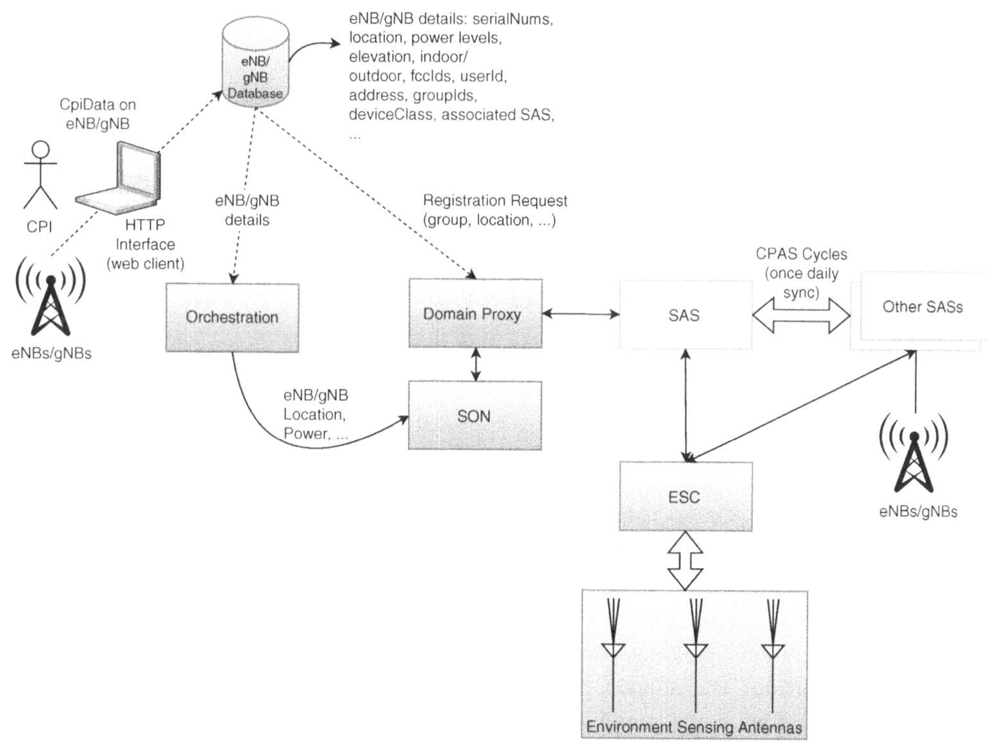

Figure II.1.6.13 Domain proxy interactions with SAS for spectrum allocations.

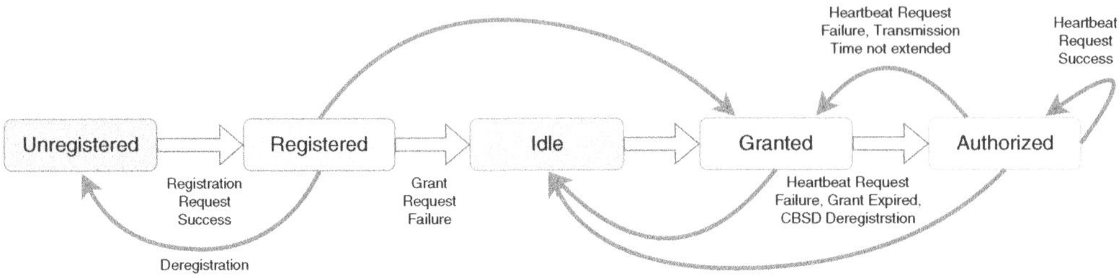

Figure II.1.6.14 CBSD SAS registration status.

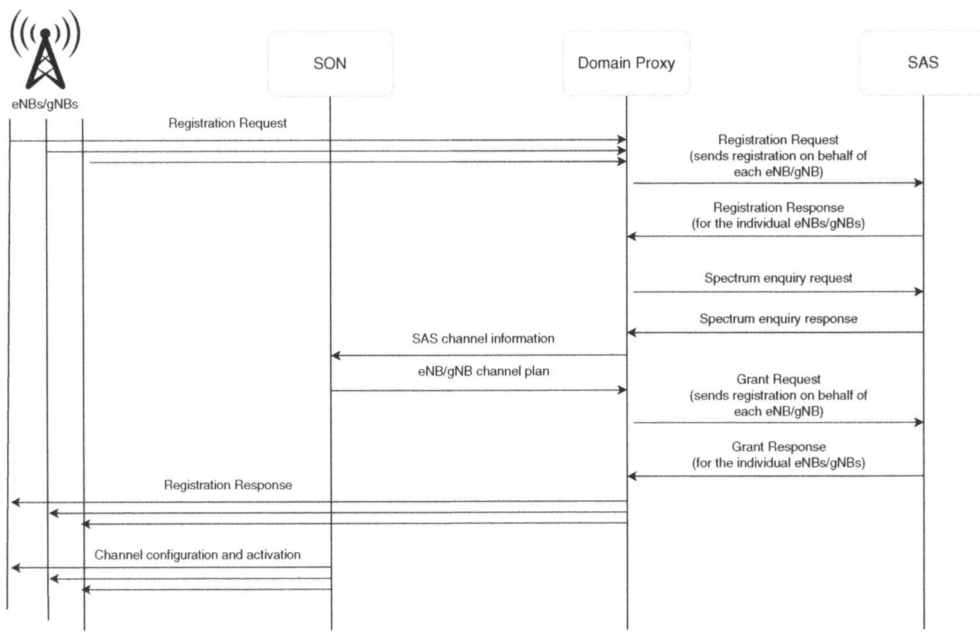

Figure II.1.6.15 CBSD SAS registration/grant sequence.

It uses this information to make informed decisions about spectrum allocation and interference protection.

5) **Database Query and Updates:** It queries the SAS and the CBRS database to access information about available spectrum and registered CBSDs. The domain proxy also updates the SAS and database with information about the CBSDs in its domain.
6) **Dynamic Spectrum Management:** The domain proxy manages spectrum allocation dynamically, considering the current spectrum environment, the presence of incumbent users, and the requirements of CBSDs. It can adjust spectrum assignments and operational parameters as needed to minimize interference.
7) **Interference Mitigation:** In the event of interference concerns or changes in the spectrum environment, the domain proxy takes actions to mitigate interference such as instructing CBSDs to adjust their operational parameters or move to different frequencies.
8) **CBSD Authorization:** The domain proxy authorizes CBSDs to operate within its domain based on their registration and compliance with regulatory and technical requirements. It can grant or revoke authorization, as necessary.

9) **SAS Coordination:** The domain proxy works with the SAS to ensure efficient and interference-free spectrum use. It communicates with the SAS to obtain spectrum allocation information and updates, ensuring that CBSDs in its domain operate within the allocated spectrum.
10) **Enforcement and Compliance:** The domain proxy enforces regulatory compliance and manages the behavior of CBSDs within its domain. It ensures that CBSDs adhere to the rules and standards set by regulatory authorities and the SAS.
11) **Real-Time Monitoring:** The domain proxy continuously monitors the operation of CBSDs and the spectrum environment within its domain to respond to changes and ensure interference-free operation.

In summary, a domain proxy is a critical component in the CBRS framework, serving as a local coordinator of CBSDs within a specific geographic area or domain. It plays a vital role in managing shared spectrum access, protecting incumbent users, and ensuring that CBSDs operate efficiently and responsibly.

II.1.6.4 Summary

A graphic-theoretic approach is described. The use of graph theory to build a map of the eNBs/gNBs deployed on campus is suggested with the power levels of the cells to determine the proximity and isolate the channel allocations for the individual cells, which is captured as the SON algorithm. The SON algorithm also includes the detected cells from the neighboring networks as part of the plan, avoiding conflicting channels for orthogonal channel allocations to avoid interference. The aspects of ESC networks for sensing for the high priority incumbents have been described. The SAS functions of managing three priority levels of users—incumbents, PAL users, and GAA users—and the architecture and the procedures involved with the eNB/gNB communicating with the SAS via the domain proxy have also been discussed. The SASs interact with the other SASs every night to exchange information about the eNB/gNB that each of the SASs manage, providing a comprehensive view of all the deployments to assist the SASs form a channel plan. The registration and channel grant procedures of the individual eNB/gNB from the SAS have also been described.

References

Books and Standards

1 Seppo Hämäläinen, Henning Sanneck, and Cinzia Sartori (). *Self-Organizing Networks (SON): Self-Planning, Self-Optimization and Self-Healing for GSM, UMTS and LTE*. It was published by Wiley in 2014.
This book provides a comprehensive overview of SON principles and applications across different network generations. It discusses SON functions, algorithms, and use cases across 3G, 4G, and 5G networks.
3GPP Standards: 3GPP has published specifications on SON functions, which are integrated into LTE and NR standards. Key documents include:

2 *3GPP TS 32.500: Telecommunication management; Self-organizing networks (SON) for Radio Access Network (RAN).*
3GPP TR 36.902: A technical report that outlines use cases and solutions for SON in LTE.

Key Research Papers

3 Sanneck, H. et al. (2010). *Self-Organizing Networks (SON) in 3GPP LTE. IEEE Vehicular Technology Conference.*
This paper outlines the concepts and challenges of SON in LTE, with a focus on practical aspects like configuration, optimization, and self-healing in real-world deployments.

4 Giambene, R., Marabissi, F. et al. (2018). A Survey on Self-Organizing Networks in LTE Systems. *IEEE Communications Surveys & Tutorials.*
This survey paper provides an overview of SON functionalities in LTE and LTE-Advanced networks. It covers SON's impact on network performance and explores different SON algorithms for load balancing, handover optimization, and energy savings.

5 Challita, U., Saad, W., and Bettstetter, C. (2019). Machine Learning-Based Self-Organizing Networks for 5G. *IEEE Transactions on Wireless Communications..*
This paper discusses SON applications in 5G, emphasizing machine learning and artificial intelligence. It explores the potential of ML-based SON for real-time optimization and interference management.

6 Vasilakos, K. et al. (2017). Self-Healing in Future Cellular Networks: A Survey and Real-World Case Study. *IEEE Communications Magazine..*
This paper provides a survey on self-healing techniques within SON frameworks, highlighting approaches used in LTE and future networks like 5G. It includes a case study on real-world network issues and SON's role in resolving them.

Industry Reports

7 Nokia Bell Labs. Self-Organizing Networks in LTE: Challenges and Benefits.
This report by Nokia Bell Labs explores the benefits and challenges of implementing SON in LTE networks. It also discusses how SON can evolve to meet the demands of 5G and beyond.

II.1.7

Fractional Frequency Reuse (FFR) Techniques

II.1.7.1 Introduction

This chapter covers the concept of fractional frequency reuse (FFR). There are several network configurations where FFR can be used, although it initially started with sharing the spectrum across a macro cell and a set of small cells within the same footprint and was even considered between two macro cells. With the sparsity of shared spectrum use for private networks and load shifting across small cells, the dynamic rebalancing of resources can play a key role in meeting the Service Level Objective (SLO)/ Service Level Agreement (SLA) requirements for a given enterprise.

The concept of inter-cell interference cancellation (ICIC) is introduced. This chapter introduces the different variants of FFR. With Citizen Broadband Radio Service (CBRS) spectrum and tiered user levels, the rebalancing of resources when a higher-tier user has claimed the spectrum and the need to leverage FFR are discussed. A scheduler-based approach to handle FFR is proposed.

II.1.7.2 Introduction of ICIC Features

II.1.7.2.1 Inter-cell Interference Coordination (ICIC)

- Coordinates inter-cell interference in frequency and power
- Manages radio resources, notably the physical resource blocks (PRBs), so that multiple cells coordinate the use of frequency-domain resources
- Defines coordination between cells that belong to two different eNBs
- **The X2AP message,** Load Information**, carries the information required for the purpose of *ICIC*.**
  - For **uplink (UL) ICIC** (see Figure II.1.7.1), two IEs, *overload indication* (OI) and *high interference indication* (HII), are used.
    - The *UL interference OI* IE received in the Load Information message indicates the interference level experienced by the indicated cell across all resource blocks, per PRB. For each PRB, one of three levels of interference—high, medium, or low—is indicated. The receiving eNB would take this OI information into account when setting its scheduling policy to help improve the interference situation for the eNB that sent this OI.

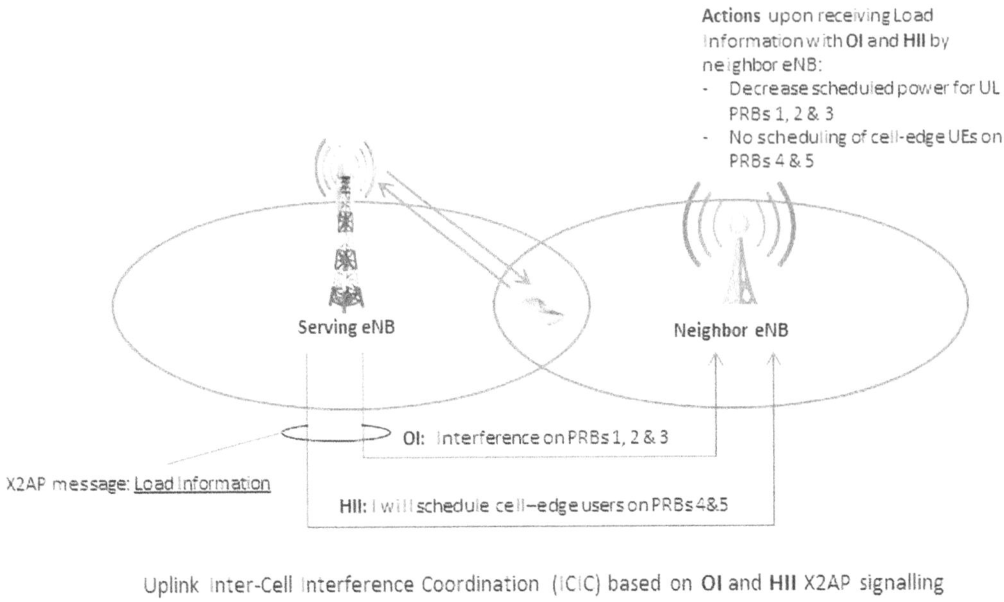

Figure II.1.7.1 UL ICIC.

- *The UL* HII IE received in the LOAD INFORMATION message indicates, per PRB, a potential high sensitivity to interference as observed by the sending eNB. The receiving eNB should try to avoid scheduling cell-edge user equipment (UE) in its own cells for the affected PRBs. This reduces UL interference for cell-edge transmissions in both its own cells and in the cells of the eNB from which the HII was received. The *target cell ID* IE, received within the HII IE, indicates the cell for which the corresponding UL HII is intended.

- For **downlink (DL) ICIC** (see Figure II.1.7.2) purposes, the Information Element (IE) *relative narrowband Tx power* (RNTP)
  - RNTP indicates, per PRB, whether DL transmission power is lower than the value indicated by the RNTP threshold IE; that is, the sending eNB indicates if DL Tx power is higher or lower than a set threshold value. As shown in Figure II.1.7.2 DL ICIC, the receiving eNB may take such information into account in scheduling its own cell-edge terminals and try not to schedule on the same PRBs to avoid interference.

II.1.7.2.2 Enhanced Inter-cell Interference Coordination (eICIC)

Figure II.1.7.3 provides an illustration of the a small cell deployed within the footprint of a macro cell and the time division resource allocations to the small cell when to macro cell only transmits reference signals.

- Coordinates inter-cell interference in the time domain.
- Time domain ICIC is realized through almost blank subframes (ABS). ABSs are subframes with reduced transmit power (including no transmission) on some physical channels and/or reduced activity. ABSs do not carry any data (PDSCH), and thus there is no corresponding control information (Physical Downlink Control Channel (PDCCH), Enhanced PDCCH (EPDCCH), Physical Control Format Indicator Channel (PCFICH), and Physical channel HybridARQ Indicator Channel (PHICH)).

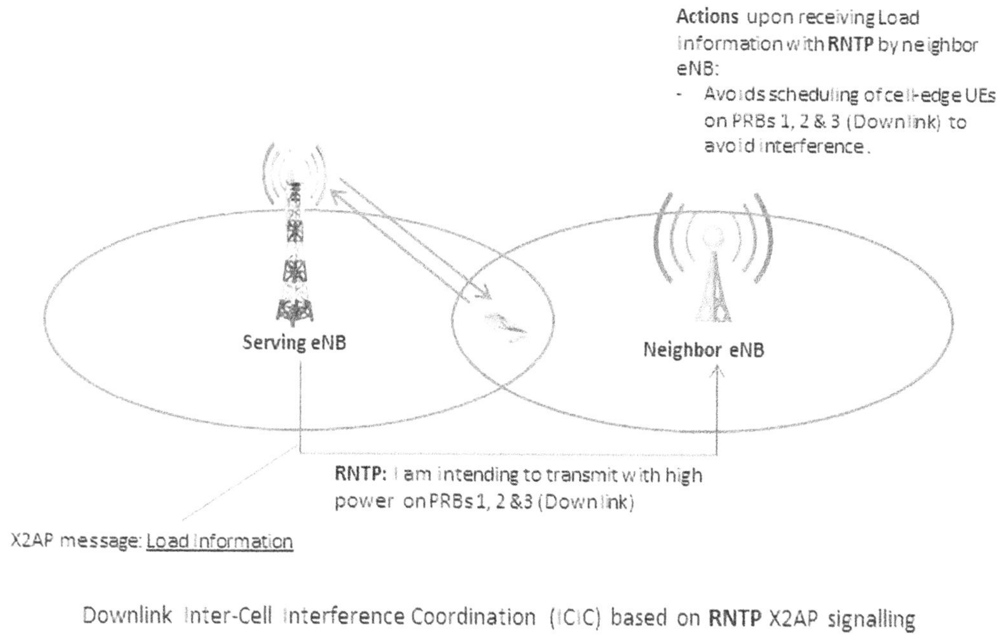

Figure II.1.7.2 DL ICIC.

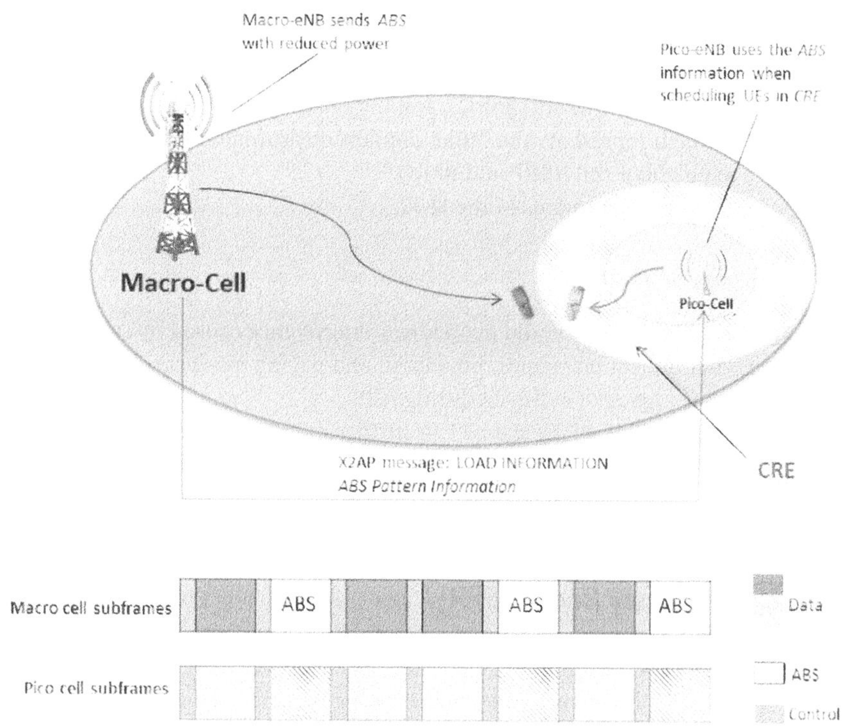

Figure II.1.7.3 eICIC.

- ABS contains the necessary signals with low power. These signals include cell specific reference signals (CRS), synchronization signals (Primary synchronization Signal (PSS)/ Secondary Synchronization Signal (SSS)), broadcast information (SIB1), and paging messages.
- The illustration is shown as macro and pico for coverage extension (CRE). However, the same can also be applied to two small cells.
- The X2AP message LOAD INFORMATION is used.
- ABS pattern info is a 40-bit string, with each bit indicating a subframe, where the value "1" indicates ABS and "0" indicates a normal subframe. This pattern repeats every 40 subframes in the case of Frequency Division Duplex (FDD), whereas for Time Division Duplex (TDD), the periodicity depends on the UL/DL configuration.
- The source eNB also includes the IE measurement subset in ABS information. The eNB of the target cell may use the measurement subset information to configure specific measurements for its UEs. This is a 40-bit string indicating a subset of the ABS pattern explained earlier. This subset is a recommendation from the source cell to the target cell for configuring measurement resource restrictions for Radio Resource Manager (RRM)/ Radio Link Monitoring (RLM)/ Channel State Information (CSI) measurements toward a UE.
- The interference experienced by a UE connected to the victim cell in the CRE region may vary significantly between protected (aggressor cell's ABS) and non-protected subframes. A UE may add measurements from the protected subframes to those from the non-protected subframes for averaging purposes. Therefore, it is important to restrict the UE's measurements to specific subframes, which are called measurement resource restrictions.
- UE should support feature group indicator (FGI) #115.
- There are three distinct kinds of measurement-restriction patterns:
  - IE measSubframePatternPCell (40-bit pattern) represents the "time domain measurement resource restriction pattern for the PCell measurements (Reference Signal Received Power (RSRP), Reference Signal Received Quality (RSRQ), and the radio link monitoring)."
  - IE measSubframePatternNeigh represents the "time domain measurement resource restriction pattern applicable to neighbor cell RSRP and RSRQ."
  - Resource restrictions for CSI measurements of the Pcell.

II.1.7.2.3 Further Enhanced ICIC (FeICIC)

- The eICIC scheme introduced in Release-10 did not address interference caused by cell specific reference signals (CRS), synchronization signals, broadcast, and paging messages, as these signals are still transmitted by the aggressor cell even during ABS.
- ICIC and eICIC evolved from LTE 3GPP Release-11 to further enhanced ICIC (FeICIC). The focus here is on interference handling by the UE through inter-cell interference cancellation for control signals.

II.1.7.3 Fractional Frequency Reuse (FFR)

FFR is an interference management technique well suited to Orthogonal Frequency-Division Multiplexing (OFDMA)-based cellular networks, in which cells are partitioned into spatial regions with different frequency reuse factors. Two of the possible variant for FFR are illustrated in Figure II.1.7.4 and Figure II.1.7.5.

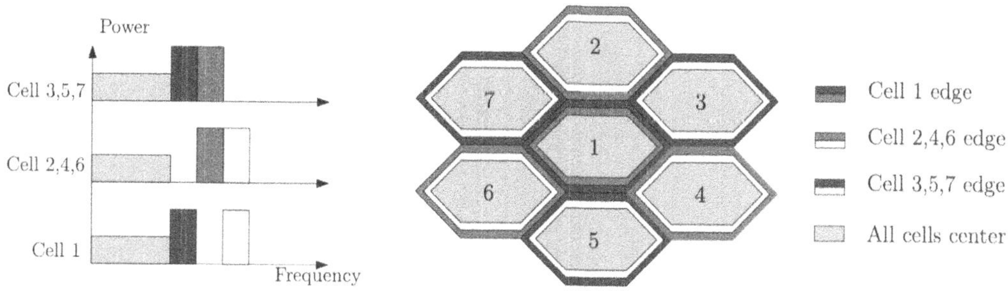

Figure II.1.7.4 FFR for edge cell users: 1.5.

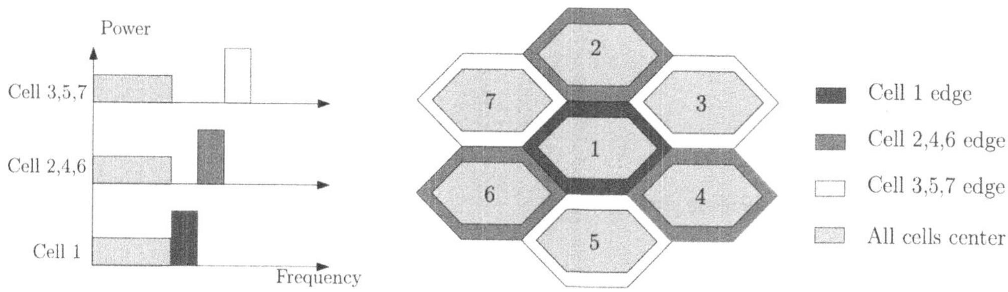

Figure II.1.7.5 FFR for edge cell users: 3.

II.1.7.3.1 Frequency Reuse Schemes

II.1.7.3.1.1 No-frequency Reuse Scheme

It is like a full-frequency reuse scheme; that is, there is no partition between the eNBs of the same core network. It has a frequency reuse factor of one. See Figure II.1.7.6 for an illustration of no-frequency reuse scheme. All the eNBs make use of the entire system bandwidth, and the signals are transmitted with uniform power over all radio base stations. This technique helps in achieving a very high peak data rate, but due to the huge level of interference from nearby or neighboring cells, edge cell users' performance is highly limited. It is the simplest of all other algorithms and is installed by default on eNBs.

II.1.7.3.1.2 Hard Frequency Reuse Scheme

This reuse scheme or algorithm improves the reduction of interference from neighboring cells and reduces ICI. See Figure II.1.7.7 illustrating hard frequency reuse scheme. The entire system bandwidth is divided into a small number of disjoint sub-bands, typically 3, 4, or 7. All the ENBs of these cells are allotted different sub-bands of frequencies. The frequency reuse factors will be equal to the number of sub-bands. It improves the cell users' performance by reducing ICI at the cell edge. The disadvantage of this scheme is that the peak data rate level can also be a limiting factor.

II.1.7.3.1.3 Strict Frequency Reuse Scheme

This frequency reuse scheme, or algorithm, combines both full and hard frequency reuse schemes. See Figure II.1.7.8 illustrating strict frequency reuse scheme.

The full system bandwidth is split into two parts with different frequency reuse factors.

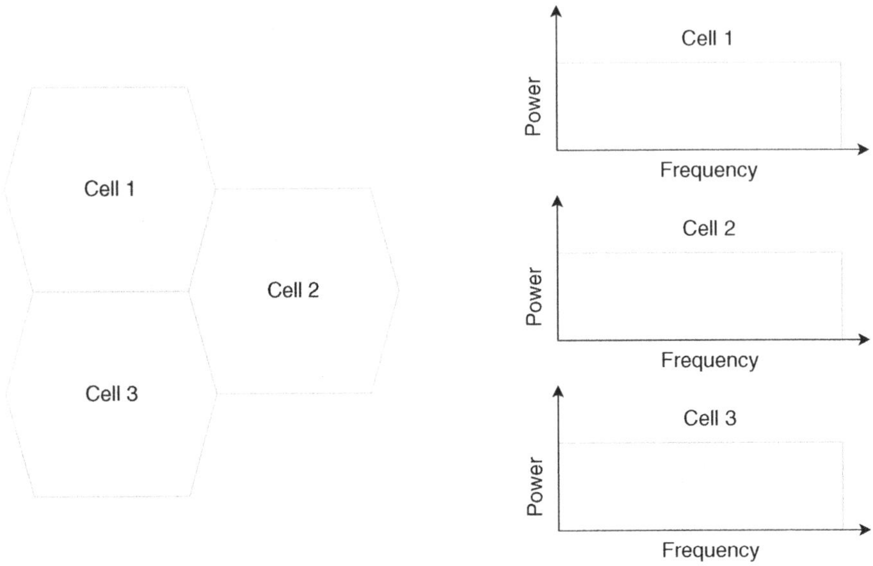

Figure II.1.7.6 No-frequency reuse scheme.

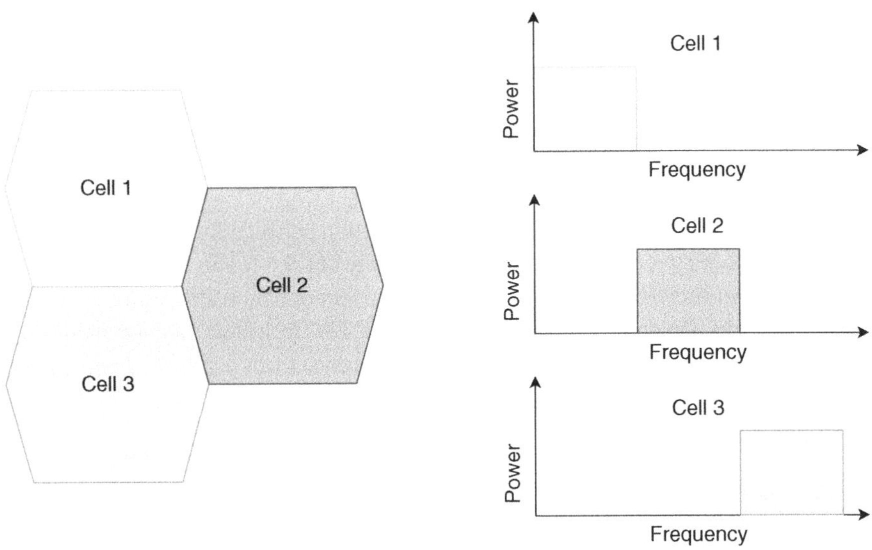

Figure II.1.7.7 Hard frequency reuse scheme.

A single sub-band frequency of the system bandwidth is allotted to each interior of the cell, having a frequency reuse factor of 1, and the remaining bandwidth is distributed among the nearby eNbs, similar to what we have in hard frequency reuse (having a reuse factor of N), which creates one sub-band providing a very low level of ICI within every sector. UEs inside the center region are allocated the fully reused frequencies, while the edge cell UEs are allocated orthogonal frequencies. This means that interior UEs will not have spectrum interference with edge UEs from neighboring cells. This will reduce the interference for both.

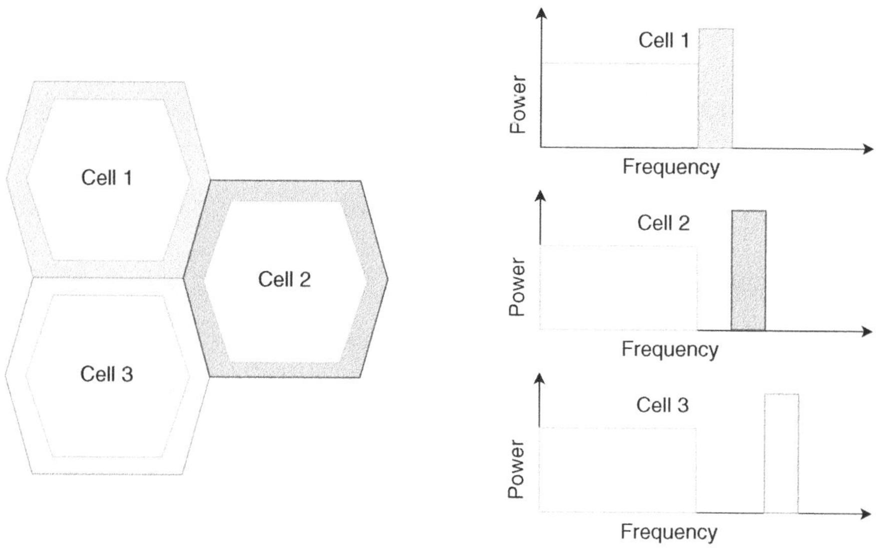

Figure II.1.7.8 Strict frequency reuse scheme.

The strict frequency reuse (SFR) scheme needs a total of N + 1 sub-bands and also helps to manage the frequency reuse factor in the range of 1 to 3.

II.1.7.3.1.4 Soft Frequency Reuse Scheme

In the soft frequency reuse scheme or algorithm, each eNB utilizes the entire system bandwidth for transmission. Inside the cell, there will be two sub-band frequencies within UEs that are supplied with different power levels. The UEs at the cell center share the entire bandwidth with the neighboring cells by transmitting less power at the center than the edge cell users. The soft frequency bandwidth scheme is more bandwidth-efficient compared to SFR, as it makes use of the full system bandwidth. The drawback of this scheme is that it produces much more interference with edge users as well as the cell interior.

There are two different available versions of the soft frequency reuse scheme.

SFR Version 1 In this first version, the available sub-band of small frequency is given over to the cell-edge UEs and can be allocated to center UEs residing in the cell, but only at a lower power level, provided they are not engaged by the edge cell UEs. The sub-band allotted to the cell center is accessible only for UE at the center. Figure II.1.7.9 illustrates the soft frequency reuse scheme version 1.

SFR Version 2 In this second version, the small frequency band that was given over to cell center UE cannot be allocated for cell-edge UE. Hence, all the cells can make use of the full system bandwidth along with reduced neighboring cell interference.

A lower level of ICI for the cell edge can be acquired at the expense of lesser spectrum utilization.

The Figure II.1.7.10 the power and frequency plans for SFR version 2. As shown, the soft frequency reuse algorithm manages two maps.

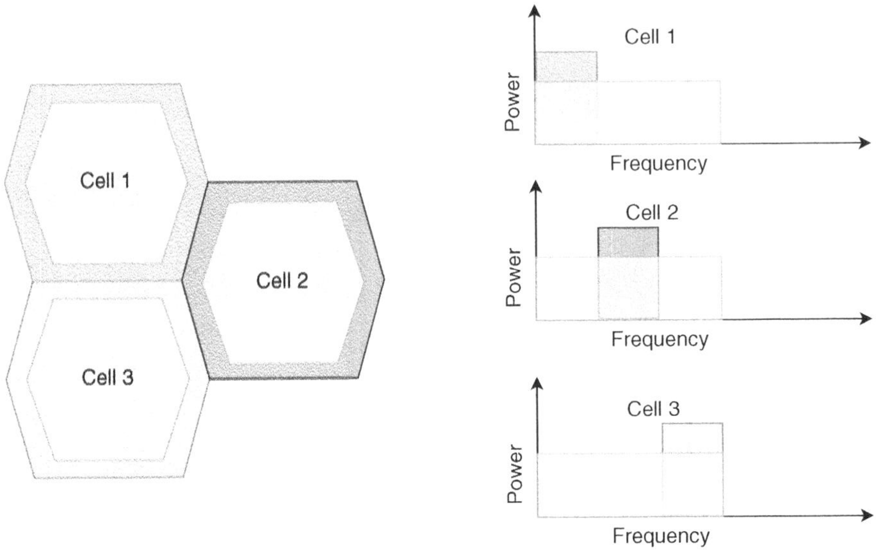

Figure II.1.7.9 Soft frequency reuse scheme version 1.

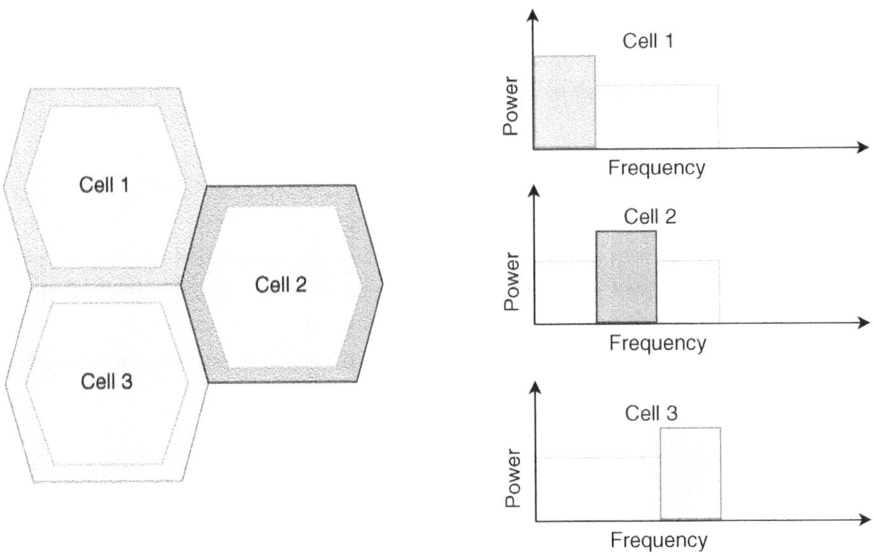

Figure II.1.7.10 Soft frequency reuse scheme version 2.

To determine the level of transmission power, the UE should also provide the SFR algorithm, which helps in handling the measurements related to UE, after which those are compared with the threshold value. The quality of the signal threshold obtained for the inner as well as the outer area can be configured by system attributes.

II.1.7.3.1.5 Soft fractional Frequency Reuse Scheme

The soft fractional frequency reuse (SFFR) scheme is a composite of the SFR and soft frequency reuse schemes. SFR makes use of different sub-bands for the outer regions in neighboring cells.

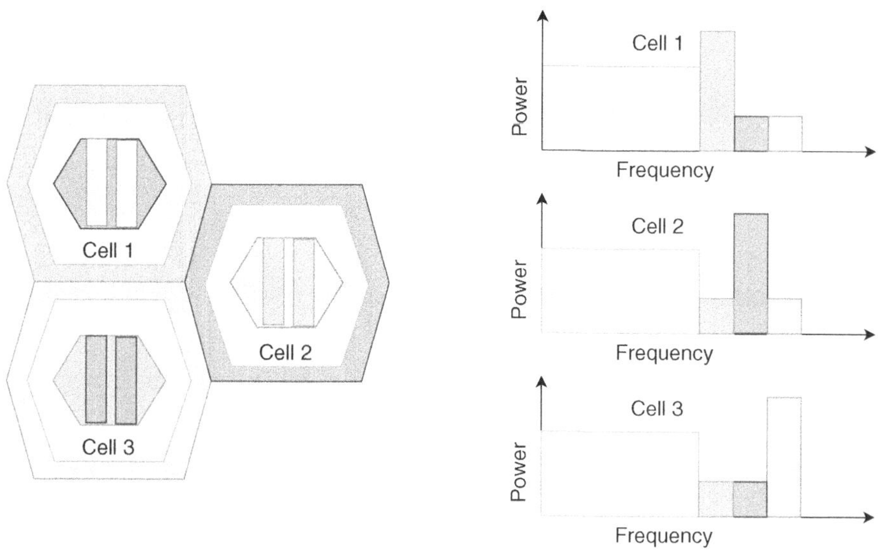

Figure II.1.7.11 Soft fractional frequency reuse scheme.

The inner cell's transmitting power uses soft FFR with less transmitting power. Thus, under these circumstances, SFFR uses the sub-band with both greater and lower transmitting power levels, similar to SFR. Figure II.1.7.11 illustrate the soft fractional frequency reuse scheme.

The soft FFR helps increase the throughput of the inner cell UEs.

II.1.7.3.1.6 Enhanced Fractional Frequency Reuse Scheme

Enhanced fractional frequency reuse (EFFR) describes three cell types to the directly adjacent cells in the given cellular system. Figure II.1.7.12 illustrates the enhanced fractional frequency reuse scheme. This reserves for each cell type a part of the entire frequency band, tagged as the primary segment. This will be one of the different types of cells, and they must also be orthogonal among themselves. Hence, the reuse on the secondary segment by each cell must follow two rules:

1) Monitor the segment's use in advance
2) Resource reuse depending on Signal-to-Interference-plus-Noise Ratio (SINR) evaluation

Every cell takes notice of each secondary sub-channel every time. Also, it makes SINR estimation before choosing the secondary sub-channel reported by the gathered channel quality information (CQI). Accordingly, it will choose the best-estimated values for reuse.

The scheduling process consists of three steps and two scheduling policies.

1) Reuse with factor 1 subchannels can only be used with users present at the cell center.
2) Reuse with factor 3 subchannels can also be used by the users residing at the cell edges but only on the condition of no edge user.
3) The transmission for the users present in the cell center will be provided by reusing three subchannels.

The figure below shows the EFFR scheme representing the power and frequency plan.

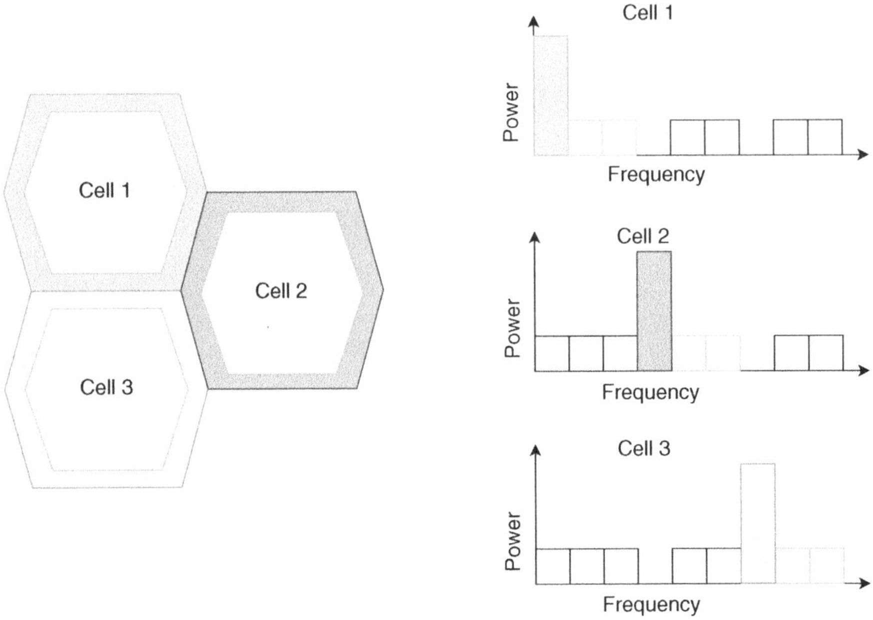

Figure II.1.7.12 Enhanced fractional frequency reuse scheme.

II.1.7.3.1.7 Distributed Fractional Frequency Reuse Scheme

This distributed fractional frequency reuse (DFFR) algorithm accordingly improves, focusing especially on the distribution of received power levels. See Figure II.1.7.13 showing the steps involved in the distributed fractional frequency reuse sequence. The DFFR algorithm adaptively selects RBs for the cell-edge sub-band based on coordination information from adjacent cells. This will be notified at the base stations that belong to the adjacent cells, indicating which RBs are preferred for use in the edge sub-band. Each cell base station makes use of the information received. The basic equation used for the calculation of the cell-edge band metric A_k for each radio base station Resource Block (RB) is given by

$$A_k = \sum_{j \in J} \omega_j X_{j,k}$$

where J → neighbor cell set

$X_j,k = \{0, 1\}$ → RNTP from the jth neighboring cell.

It is set to 1, when the kth RB in the jth neighboring cell w_j → weight with respect to neighboring cell j.

If the value of received power is high, it means that the ith cell experiences very high interference from the jth cell. If the RB is low, it means the ith cell has lower interference levels from another neighboring cell. The serving cell has to select a number of eRBs, as the cell-edge sub-band is configured in ascending order of Ak. At last, those RBs are chosen in which a smaller number of edge cell UE receives large level of interference due to neighboring cells. The updated value of RNTP is directed to all adjacent cells.

- In strict frequency reuse (SFR), the cell area is divided into two regions: a central region where the entire frequency band is available and a cell-edge area where only a small fraction of the

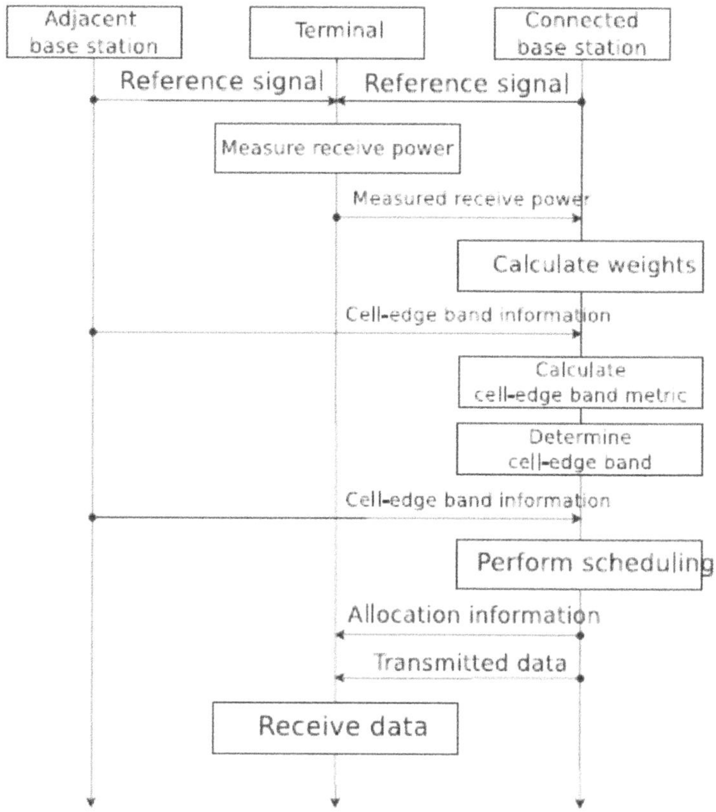

Figure II.1.7.13 Distributed fractional frequency reuse sequence.

spectrum is available. The spectrum dedicated to the cell edge may also be used in the central region if it is not being utilized at the cell edge. The lack of spectrum at the cell edge may result in a significantly reduced Shannon capacity for that region. This is addressed by allocating high-power carriers to the users in this region, thus improving the SINR and the Shannon capacity.

- SFFR scheme is a composite of SFR and soft frequency reuse scheme. SFR makes use of different sub-bands for the outer region in neighboring cells. The inner cell transmitting power uses soft FFR with lower transmitting power.

II.1.7.4 FFR for CBRS

With CBRS networks and tiered user levels, it is possible for a higher-tier user to take away spectrum resources from lower-tier users (incumbent taking away resources from PAL [priority access license] and GAA [general authorized access] users, and PAL taking away resources from GAA users; see chapter on "CBRS" for details). The incumbent taking away resources from PAL and GAA typically occurs due to a dynamic protection area (DPA) event. A PAL user deploying a new cell may take away resources from GAA users based on the criteria defined by the Federal Communications Commission (FCC) for interference computation done by the spectrum access system (SAS).

When DPA and channel suspension occur, the SAS informs the individual Citizens Broadband Radio Service Device (CBSD) (via the domain proxy) of the channels being revoked and the allowed set of channels, which may be a completely new set of assignments. The Self Organizing Network (SON) algorithm needs to be run again to rebalance the spectrum allocations across the cell in the private network deployment. Note that there will be an impact on the neighboring private network deployments as well, and there may be changes in the interference observed from the neighboring networks based on the spectrum reallocations made in those networks. The assessment is performed for each CBSD running through the 15 10 MHz channels based on the associated information on availability indicated by the SAS. The logic below is suggested.

- Each CBSD or sector makes the assessment:
  - If channel is suspended
    - Perform a spectrum inquiry
    - For each of the 15 channels that are available for use
    - For the channels not used by any CBSDs on the site
      - mark the priority for the channel as "HIGH"
    - For the channels used by other CBSDs on the site
      - If the channel has not been suspended for any CBSD or sector,
        - mark the priority for the channel to be "MEDIUM"
      - Else if the channel has been suspended for any CBSD or sector
        - mark the priority for the channel to be "LOW"
      - Else if the channel has been suspended for any CBSD or sector
        - mark the priority of the channel as "UNAVAILABLE"
  - If channel is not suspended
    - No action is required. Co-channel allocation and PRB sharing may be required to support other CBSDs or sectors.
- The PRB loading information for each CBSD or sector is made available.
- For each CBSD or sector, determine the channel reallocation based on the following logic:
  - Process the channels in the priority order of "HIGH," "MEDIUM," and "LOW." Ignore the "UNAVAILABLE" channels.
  - Request for the grant of channels with "HIGH."
    - If granted, use this channel for CBSD or sector; otherwise, move to the next step.
  - Request for the grant of channels with "MEDIUM." Order the requested channels based on the CBSD or sectors that use the channel but do not have a connected edge above those that have a connected edge.
    - If granted, use this channel for CBSD or sector; otherwise, proceed to the next step.
  - Request for grant of channels with "LOW." Order the requested channels based on the CBSD or sectors that use the channel but do not have a connected edge, placing these above those that have a connected edge.
    - If granted, use this channel for the CBSD or sector.
    - Otherwise, move to the next step.
  - If this results in required channel sharing with CBSDs or sectors with connected edge or the same CBSD, prepare for the next step of PRB sharing.
    - Alternatively, consider allocating 10 MHz for each CBSD or sector instead of dynamic PRB rebalancing across the CBSDs or sectors.
- For co-channel operational scenarios, employ the ICIC approach for PRB sharing suggested in the attached document. The proposal is detailed toward the end of the document – you can ignore the initial descriptions of ICIC and FFR.
- Continue to perform the spectrum inquiry to see if the DPA has been removed and revert to the channel allocations prior to the DPA.

II.1.7.5 Proposal for Implementation FFR

This section describes an approach to managing the operations across cells when the SON algorithm is unable to orthogonalize the channel allocations due to limitations in spectrum availability. With Long Term Evolution (LTE), the maximum allowed bandwidth is 20 MHz per component carrier. Based on the available spectrum, it is possible to achieve orthogonal allocations. With NR, a single component carrier can support up to 100 MHz. It is exceedingly difficult to support orthogonal channel allocations with such a wide bandwidth. To capitalize on a wider bandwidth allocation for the individual cells and achieve the required orthogonalization across the cells while also accommodating load balancing is suggested in the following section.

II.1.7.5.1 The Proposal

Share the PRB allocations among the APs sharing a common spectrum and having an overlapping footprint.

Assumption: special subframes will not be used for scheduling. Appropriate sharing needs to be defined if the special subframe DL and UL symbols are used for scheduling (both control and data). One approach could be to predetermine the symbols that can be used for sharing and specify them statically, rather than coordinating this dynamically.

II.1.7.5.2 Schedulable Resource

One PRB spans 12 subcarriers, which, with the 15-kHz subcarrier spacing, corresponds to 180 kHz. When full-PRB transmission is used, the smallest time-frequency resource that can be scheduled to a device is one PRB pair mapped over two slots, which, for the normal Cyclic Prefix (CP) length case (with seven OFDM symbols per slot), corresponds to 12 subcarriers over 14 OFDM symbols. Figure II.1.7.14 shows the LTE subframe structure and Figure II.1.7.15 shows the LTE slot, PRB,

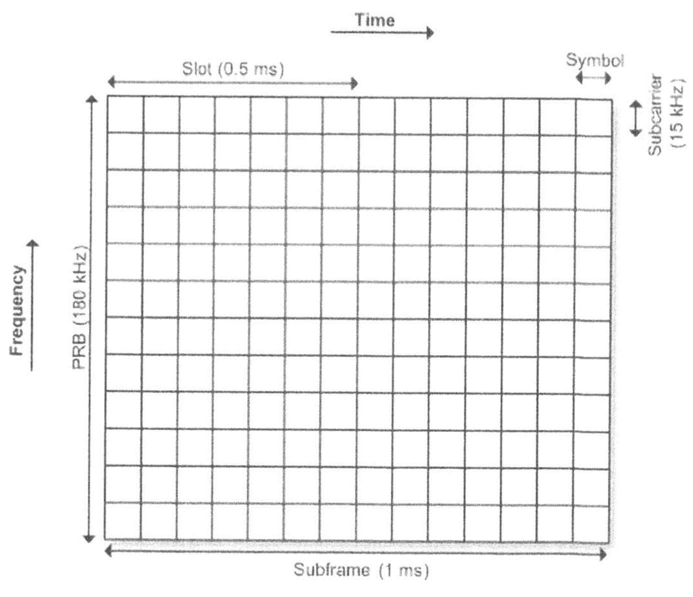

Figure II.1.7.14 LTE subframe.

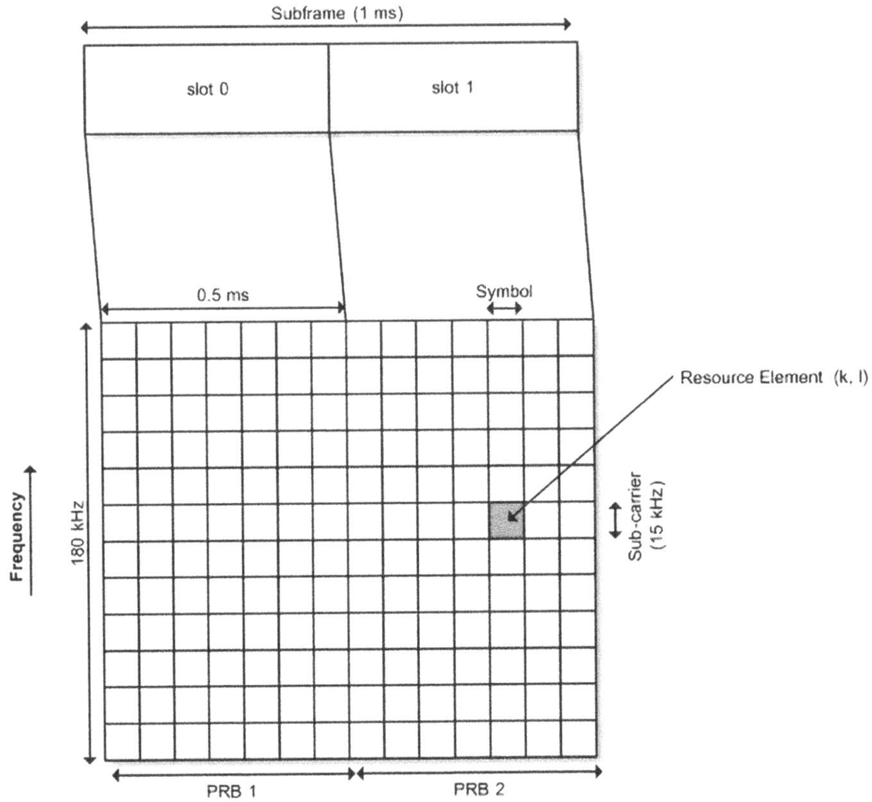

Figure II.1.7.15 LTE slot, PRB, and schedulable unit.

and schedulable unit. Table II.1.7.1 the number of PRB computed for the different scenarios based on carrier bandwidth and the TDD configurations used.

When the spectrum is shared across the APs, the schedulable units highlighted in the table above, based on the Bandwidth (BW) and TDD configuration, need to be partitioned based on the loading on each of the cells. A centralized algorithm decides on the extent of the number of schedulable resources allocated to each AP.

II.1.7.5.3 PRB Allocation Logic

- Use the logic below to determine the resource allocation for a given AP:
  - Compute the PRB usage on each Access Point (AP) relative to the allocated capacity
    - Filtered over a To Be Determined (TBD) time period.
    - The trade-off will be to adapt to the rate of change of traffic patterns versus creating a steady state for Transmission Control Protocol (TCP)/ Quick UDP Internet Connections (QUIC) window buildup.
    - Typical rebalancing of capacity will be only for non-GBR-type traffic.
  - AP and offload/onload capacity
    - Allocated PRB utilization <60%: capacity can be offloaded to the neighboring cells.
    - Allocated PRB utilization is between 60% and 80%: optimal allocation and no change required.
    - Allocated PRB utilization >80%: request for additional capacity allocation.

Table II.1.7.1 PRB computation for different scenarios.

	20 MHz	10 MHz
Number of PRBs	100	50
TDD Config #2		
Number of DL PRBs for TDD configuration 2 in a frame	100×2×6 = 1,200	50×2×6 = 600
Number of DL schedulable units in a frame	1,200/2 = 600	600/2 = 300
Number of UL PRBs for TDD configuration 2 in a frame	100×2×2 = 400	50×2×2 = 200
Number of UL schedulable units in a frame	400/2 = 200	200/2 = 100
TDD Config #1		
Number of DL PRBs for TDD configuration 1 in a frame	100×2×4 = 800	50×2×4 = 400
Number of DL schedulable units in a frame	800/2 = 400	400/2 = 200
Number of UL PRBs for TDD configuration 1 in a frame	100×2×4 = 800	50×2×4 = 400
Number of UL schedulable units in a frame	800/2 = 400	400/2 = 200

- Guaranteed Bitrate (GBR) flow considerations
  - GBR flows also have variability, and recognizing sustained diminished throughput across the flows can be used to offload capacity as well.
  - When new GBR flows are admitted, they are allowed if there is residual capacity available on the cell, subject to the PRB limits allocated to the AP.
  - Active rebalancing of resources can be considered when the GBR demand goes above the current PRB resource allocation to the AP, and the AP can support additional flows with additional resource allocation.

II.1.7.5.4 Design Considerations

- When driving the PRBs across APs, it is preferable to distribute the allocation for each slot/subframe.
  - This will allow for addressing the limitation on the number of UEs that can be scheduled per slot/subframe and address Packet Delay Budget (PDB) constraints that may arise in handling the different QoS flows.
  - Given that power management is on a slot basis, it will allow for better regulation within and across the APs for a given slot/subframe.
- The loading conditions can be used to rebalance the BW allocations to the different APs, apart from the PRB isolation.
- The DL algorithm needs to be treated independently of the UL realization.

II.1.7.6 Summary

This chapter goes over the concepts of ICIC and FFR. Practical ways to handle the dynamic spectrum reallocations in the context of shared spectrum use with CBRS are described. A scheduler-based approach to separate PRBs for FFR reuse realizations is described, which supports the dynamic rebalancing of resources across cells without having to change the spectrum used for operating the individual cells.

The mechanisms suggested can be applied within a single private network deployment or can be implemented cooperatively across neighboring private networks and potentially with the macro network operators that are deploying networks using the shared spectrum.

References

1 Guillaume de la Roche, Andreia Cattoni, and Jens Zander (2011). *LTE-Advanced and Next Generation Wireless Networks: Channel Modelling and Propagation* .

2 Erik Dahlman, Stefan Parkvall, and Johan Skold (). *5G NR: The Next Generation Wireless Access Technology*.

Part II.2

Cellular Core Network

II.2.1

Converged Core

II.2.1.1 Introduction

Traditionally, the core network (CN) refers to the functions that are not part of the radio network. With the advent of cloud computing, edge computing, multi-access edge computing (MEC), and the more recent evolution of the Telco cloud and open RAN, the functions supported in a core platform have a wide range of varying configurations. Like the RAN functions, the separation of control and user plane (UP) functions applies to the CN as well. The available compute nodes, including specialized hardware, are rapidly evolving, and the demands of the enterprise network are met by deploying these functions on the enterprise premises, in a metro cloud in a localized region closer to the enterprise, in a demilitarized zone (DMZ) centrally located across all the given enterprise locations, in a public cloud with one of the hyperscalers, or in a public operator's CN. There are specific RAN functions that need to be closely located with the transmission points, such as the RAN scheduler, hybrid automatic repeat request (HARQ), precoding, MIMO/beamforming, and power control, which typically constitute the lower Medium Access Control (MAC) layer/physical layer functions. Aside from these, the higher MAC and layer 2 functions can potentially be hosted along with the other traditional core functions based on the demands of the enterprise verticals/applications. This concept of architecting the higher-layer RAN function, core function, and service/vertical/application functions into the appropriate compute nodes, accounting for control user plane separation (CUPS) architecture, and managing the compute costs involved while delivering the required QoS or QoE for the enterprise is referred to as "converged core."

In this section, the details of the converged core's functional constitution and a view into the architectural variants are provided. The evolution from 4G networks to 5G networks is illustrated with consideration of the functional grouping involved. Some of the key concepts such as slices, QoS, traffic detection function (TDF), framed routes, and other related topics are explicitly treated. The core–RAN interconnect is fundamental to the nature of traffic management, with enterprise deployments supporting LTE-only, NR-only, and LTE + NR systems that support the non-standalone (NSA) mode and SA mode of operation.

Why go through the rigors of understanding all the functions defined to be part of the CN that apply to a macro network and when an enterprise network requires basic authentication, connectivity to the enterprise core, and some QoS support for specific enterprise applications? Two key reasons.

Not all enterprises are cut the same way. Their demands and needs can be sophisticated, sometimes much more so than those required from public macro network operations. Understanding the core functions defined in 3GPP allows for assessing the enterprise requirements and selectively leveraging solutions already defined in 3GPP that have gone through extensive deliberations.

Mobile Communication Systems for Private Networks, First Edition. Srinivasan Balasubramanian.

The second and equally important reason is to identify the scenarios not addressed in the standards and contribute back to the standards forums, elevating the currently subdued focus on the growing demand for private networks for enterprise deployments. With more users spending most of the day indoors, either at home or at work, shopping, or entertainment centers—including sports arenas—private and small networks require a lot more energy directed toward them and will be the key growth area for 4G, 5G, and even 6G networks. With spectrum scarcity, the use of mmWave spectrum is becoming essential. With extremely high path loss for mmWave-based operations and the support of short-range communications, its use for enterprise private networks seems like a natural fit and should be capitalized on.

Some of the architecture charts briefly introduced in Part I, "LTE Fundamentals and NR Fundamentals," are for both completeness and to provide additional details connecting the different pieces and illustrating the evolutionary path toward realizing a converged LTE evolved packet core (EPC) and NR 5GC CN functions.

II.2.1.2 LTE and NR End-to-End Architecture

This section covers the network architecture details, illustrating the functional nodes and the interconnecting interfaces involved. The basic in-home (not roaming) operations are shown. This will be the typical configuration of the 4G/5G enterprise networks that will be deployed. Roaming between private enterprise networks, private networks, and public networks will be treated explicitly in an independent section of the book. The 4G LTE and 5G NR architectures are treated independently in this section. Subsequent sections will cover the combined operations of the LTE and NR networks, leading toward a converged core.

II.2.1.2.1 LTE Network Architecture

Figure II.2.1.1 provides the LTE end-to-end network architecture representing the RAN and core network nodes.

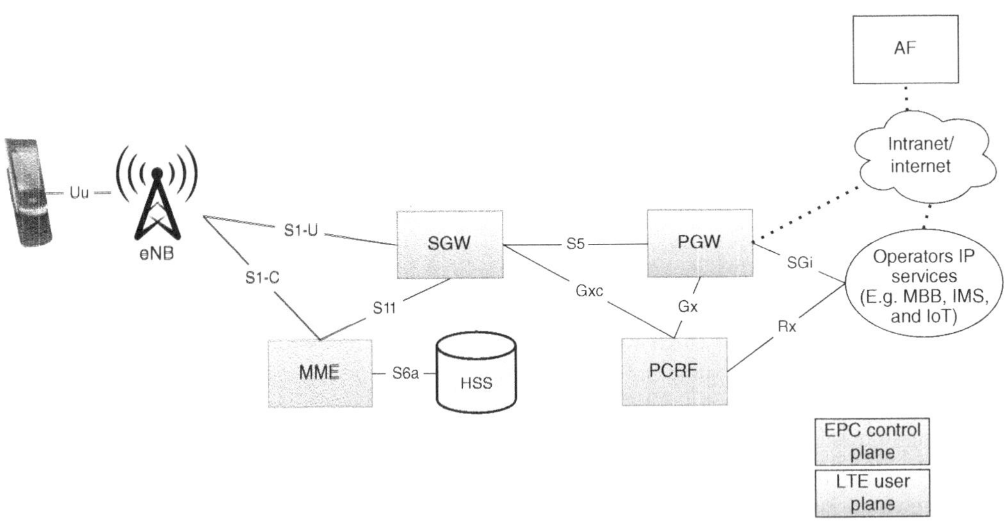

Figure II.2.1.1 Converged core – LTE end-to-end network architecture.

In the sections below, a more detailed description of the LTE functional nodes and the interfaces between these LTE core functional nodes is provided.

II.2.1.2.1.1 LTE Network Functions

LTE network function	Description
MME	*Mobility management entity*. The MME is at the edge of the LTE EPC, between the core and radio networks. The MME is responsible for handling signals between active user equipment (UEs) and the network within the LTE EPC architecture. It is also responsible for signaling between eNodeBs and the CN. For continuous functionality, the MME authenticates UEs by communicating with the home subscriber service (HSS), and the mobility function allows the UE to access the network and keeps track of its location and state.
SWG	*Serving gateway*. A serving gateway node handles user data traffic but is not responsible for the signaling data used. It transports Internet Protocol (IP) data from UEs to the LTE CN. The SGW also routes incoming and outgoing IP packets for better system collaboration and serves as an anchor for the UE when it moves from one eNodeB to another.
PGW	Packet data gateway. PGW is the network node that connects the EPC to external IP networks. What PGW does is that it routes packets to and from external IP networks. Beyond that, it also allocates an IP address to all UEs and enforces different policies regarding IP user traffic such as packet filtering.
PRCF	Policy and charging rules function. The PCRF node specifies the service policy and the QoS information. This node guarantees that the users will receive services according to the contract, meaning that services are charged accordingly. It also ensures that the charging system is defined.
HSS	Home subscriber server. The HSS is the central database that contains all relevant details about a subscriber's information and user authentication. The HSS also provides information for call and IP session setup. This server makes it easier for service providers to manage their subscribers' information in real time. A regular mobile network needs only one HSS, but there can be more than one. If there are two or more, they need to communicate with each other and have their databases updated because the servers need to have a synchronized database to function properly.

II.2.1.2.1.2 LTE Interfaces

LTE interface	Description
S1-MME	Interface for the control plane (CP) protocol between the evolved UMTS terrestrial radio access network (E-UTRAN) and the MME.
S1-U	Reference point between E-UTRAN and serving Gateway (GW) for the per-bearer UP tunneling and inter-eNodeB path switching during handover.
S3	It enables user and bearer information exchange for inter-3GPP access network (AN) mobility in idle and/or active states.
S4	It provides related control and mobility support between the General Packet Radio Service (GPRS) core and the 3GPP anchor function of the serving GW. In addition, if the direct tunnel is not established, it provides UP tunneling.
S5	It provides UP tunneling and tunnel management between serving GW and PDN GW. It is used for serving GW relocation due to UE mobility and when the serving GW needs to connect to a non-collocated PDN GW for the required PDN connectivity.

(Continued)

LTE interface	Description
S6a	It enables the transfer of subscription and authentication data for authenticating/authorizing user access to the evolved system (AAA interface) between the MME and HSS.
Gx	It provides the transfer of (QoS) policy and charging rules from the PCRF to the policy and charging enforcement function (PCEF) in the PDN GW.
S8	Inter-PLMN reference point providing UPs and CPs between the serving GW in the VPLMN and the PDN GW in the HPLMN. S8 is the inter-PLMN variant of S5.
S9	It provides the transfer of (QoS) policy and charging control information between the home PCRF and the visited PCRF to support the local breakout function.
S10	Reference point between MMEs for MME relocation and MME-to-MME information transfer.

II.2.1.2.2 NR Network Architecture

At a high level, similar to the previous generations of wireless networks, the 5G system network architecture consists of the AN and the CN that interacts with the UE.

The 5G system is architected to support data connectivity and verticals/services that are enabled by deployments that use techniques such as network function virtualization (NFV) and software-defined networking (SDN). The 5G system architecture leverages service-based interactions between CP network functions (NFs). Some of the key enabling concepts include the following:

- CUPS-based architecture where the UP functions are realized independently, allowing for independent scalability, evolution, and flexible deployments based on the available compute platforms in the enterprise, local, metro, DMZ, and centralized cloud environments. Examples of these include centralized locations or distributed (remote) locations.
- Modularize functional design to allow for effective slice-based implementation for end-to-end operations that include IP address allocation, IP domain management, QoS realizations across the different hops in the network, and over-the-air accounting for both downlink (DL) and uplink (UL) operations.
- Support NFs and their network functional services (NFS) communicate directly or indirectly via the service communication proxy (SCP), together with the discovery mechanisms using network routing functions (NRF).
- Sufficient isolation of the CN functions and services from the AN to avoid changes in one impacting the other. Minimize dependencies between the AN and the CN.

This architecture is enabled via a converged core implementation that brings together the different access technologies and allows for evolution through the multiple generations of access and CN feature introductions into the individual technologies. Effective prioritization and use of the appropriate access and CN technologies are based on the UE capability, the available coverage in the current UE location, and the required quality/grade of service that needs to be actively delivered to the UE, with such determinations made in real time.

The network functions (NF) and NF services are able to communicate directly and are referred to as direct communication or indirectly via the SCP, which is referred to as indirect communication.

Note that only the key functions and interfaces are shown, and these are typically the functions implemented for an enterprise private network realization. It should provide a sufficient understanding of the aspects involved in the network implementation. For more detailed information, it is best to refer to the 3GPP standards specifications directly.

5G core architecture models, as specified in 3GPP, provide both versions of reference point system architecture and service-based system architecture. The reference point representation shows the interaction between network functional elements as a point-to-point interface definition. These interface definitions provide the functional partitioning across the functional nodes, the information flow between the functions, and hence the information ownership associated with each node. The NG-C, NG-U, N4, N6, N9, and N11 are examples of such interfaces as shown in Figure II.2.1.2.

A service-based representation, where NFs within the CP, enables other authorized NFs to access their services. This representation also includes point-to-point reference points between functional nodes where necessary. In the service-based system architecture, as shown in Figure II.2.1.3, each NF is connected to a bus and connection labeled as Namf, Nsmf, Npcf, etc.

Figure II.2.1.4 provides a view of the 5GC core platform with all the point-to-point interfaces shown. It also shows the N26 interface, which is used for UE transitions across LTE and NR radio

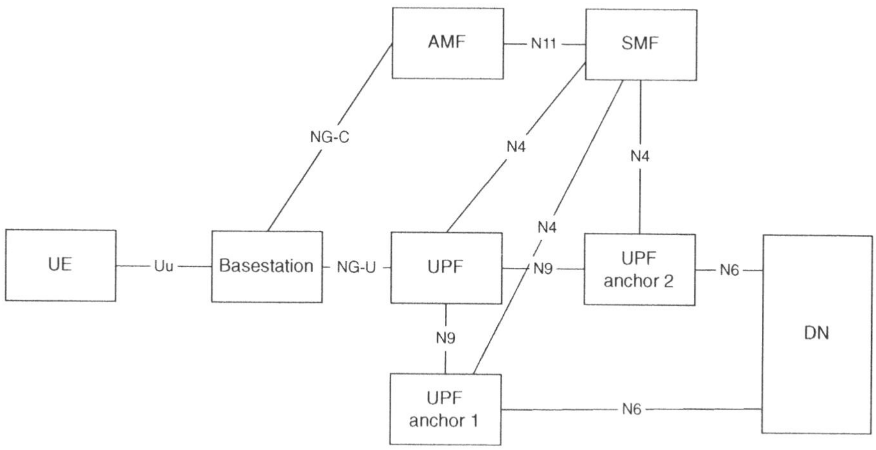

Figure II.2.1.2 Converged core – 5GC core functions reference-point-based model.

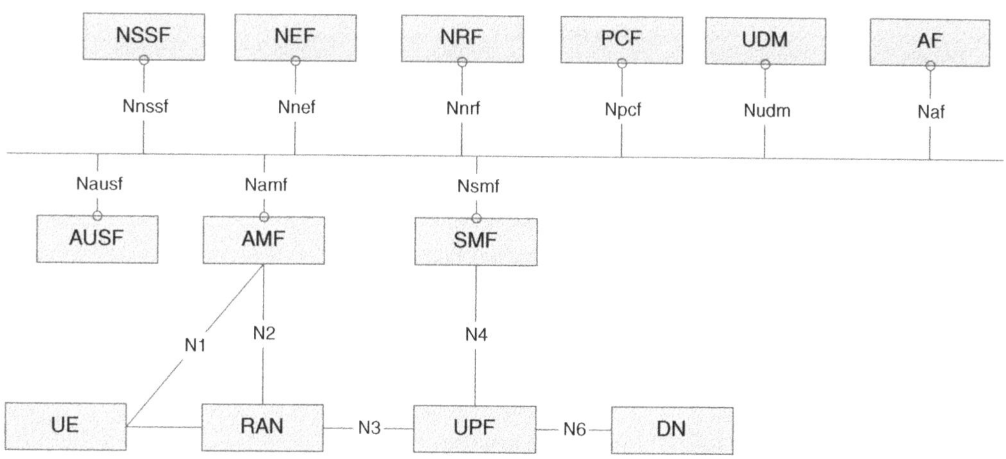

Figure II.2.1.3 Converged core – 5G core network architecture service-based model.

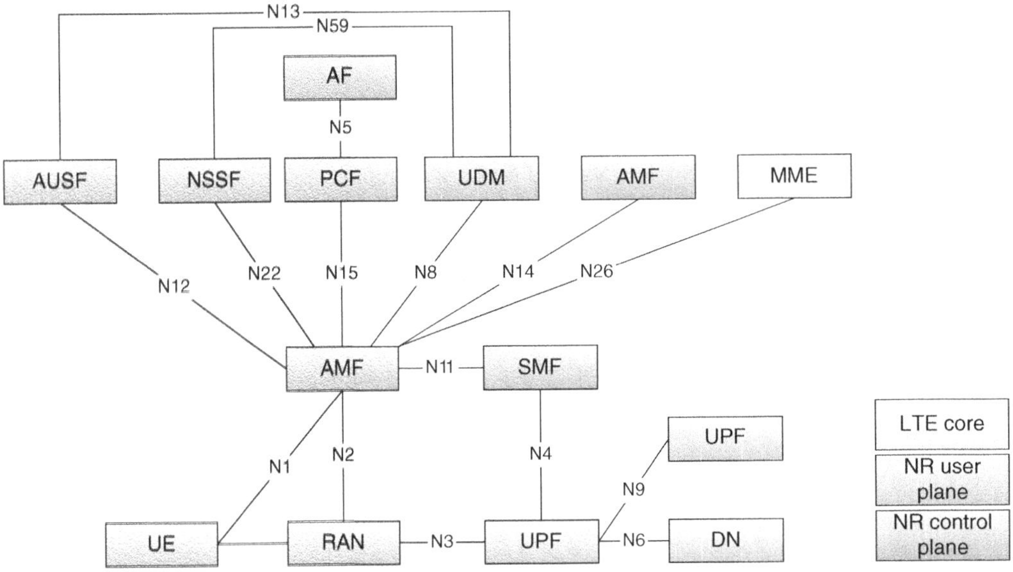

Figure II.2.1.4 Converged core – 5GC network interfaces.

access technologies (RATs), with the 5GC interacting with the MME in the LTE CN to enable such transitions. The control and UP functions are also represented.

In the sections below, a more detailed description of the NR functional nodes and the interfaces between these 5GC core functional nodes is provided.

II.2.1.2.2.1 NR Network Functions

NR network function	Description
AUSF	Authentication server function
AMF	Access and mobility management function
DN	Data network
UDSF	Unstructured data storage function
NEF	Network exposure function
NRF	Network repository function
NSSAAF	Network slice-specific authentication and authorization function
NSSF	Network slice selection function
PCF	Policy control function
SMF	Session management function
UDM	Unified data management
UDR	Unified data repository
UPF	User plane function
AF	Application function

NR network function	Description
UE	User equipment
RAN	Radio access network
SCP	Service communication proxy
5G-EIR	5G-equipment identity register
NWDAF	Network data analytics function
CHF	Charging function
SCP	Service communication proxy

II.2.1.2.2.2 NR Interfaces

An exhaustive list of NR interfaces defined in 3GPP is shown below.

NR interface	Description
N1	Reference point between the UE and the AMF.
N2	Reference point between the (R)AN and the AMF.
N3	Reference point between the (R)AN and the UPF.
N4	Reference point between the SMF and the UPF.
N5	Reference point between the PCF and an AF.
N6	Reference point between the UPF and a data network.
N7	Reference point between the SMF and the PCF.
N8	Reference point between the UDM and the AMF.
N9	Reference point between two UPFs.
N10	Reference point between the UDM and the SMF.
N11	Reference point between the AMF and the SMF.
N12	Reference point between AMF and AUSF.
N13	Reference point between the UDM and the authentication server is the AUSF.
N14	Reference point between two AMFs.
N15	Reference point between the PCF and the AMF.
N16	Reference point between two SMFs.
N16a	Reference point between SMF and I-SMF.
N17	Reference point between AMF and 5G-EIR.
N18	Reference point between any NF and UDSF.
N19	Reference point between two PSA UPFs for 5G LAN-type services.
N22	Reference point between AMF and NSSF.
N23	Reference point between PCF and NWDAF.
N24	Reference point between the PCF in the visited network and the PCF in the home network.
N26	Reference point between AMF and MME
N27	Reference point between NRF in the visited network and the NRF in the home network.
N28	Reference point between PCF and CHF.
N29	Reference point between NEF and SMF.

(*Continued*)

NR interface	Description
N30	Reference point between PCF and NEF.
N31	Reference point between the NSSF in the visited network and the NSSF in the home network.
N32	Reference point between the security edge protection proxy (SEPP) in the visited network and the SEPP in the home network.
N33	Reference point between NEF and AF.
N34	Reference point between NSSF and NWDAF.
N35	Reference point between UDM and UDR.
N36	Reference point between PCF and UDR.
N37	Reference point between NEF and UDR.
N38	Reference point between I-SMFs.
N40	Reference point between SMF and the CHF.
N50	Reference point between AMF and the Cell Broadcast Centre Function (CBCF).
N51	Reference point between AMF and NEF.
N52	Reference point between NEF and UDM.
N55	Reference point between AMF and the UE Capability Management Function (UCMF).
N56	Reference point between NEF and the UCMF.
N57	Reference point between AF and the UCMF.
N58	Reference point between AMF and the NSSAAF.
N59	Reference point between UDM and the NSSAAF.

II.2.1.3 LTE and NR Evolution Toward a Converged Core

The previous sections covered the details of the LTE EPC and NR 5GC CNs, showing the functional nodes and the interconnecting interfaces involved. Enterprise campus deployments currently support either an LTE network or an NR network, meeting specific needs for the enterprise.

There are many features introduced into the 5G standards that really have not seen practical realization in the market. Several market verticals are evolving with ubiquitous connectivity required for eMBB, energy-efficient communication with IoT, reliable and low-latency communication for IIoT, high throughput Uplink (UL) and DL communications for eXtended Reality (XR) applications, automotive including D2D functions, effective use of multicast/broadcast services, macro network and enterprise-centric connectivity addressing outdoor and indoor coverage, together with public and private network transitions, zero trust realization, and building quantum resistance,, with each requiring a different type of UE modem and network optimizations for effective vertical realization. Effective use of all available spectrum, together with multi-technology integration, including 3GPP and non-3GPP technologies, terrestrial and non-terrestrial networks, and stationary, ground-based, and airborne device operation, will be critical to be successful in the rapidly evolving marketplace. Given this context, moving forward with disparate solution requirements for different verticals/services for a given enterprise campus—from very low cost/low complexity devices needed for IoT, which typically will require an LTE solution, all the way to the other end of the spectrum of high-cost/high-complexity devices needed for IIoT, which typically will require an NR solution—and also adapting to the evolution of the Wi-Fi solutions, a converged solution will be required for any enterprise deployment.

Figure II.2.1.5 Converged core – LTE and NR evolution.

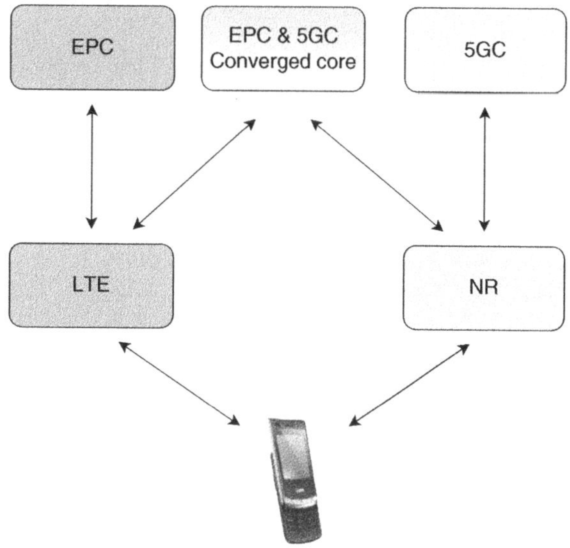

The subsequent section addresses the details involved in a multimode campus deployment that supports LTE and NR solutions. The coexistence with Wi-Fi will be discussed independently later in the book. Figure II.2.1.5 provides a very high-level view of the different UEs and their association with the LTE-only, NR-only, and LTE and NR multimode deployments.

In general, it can be assumed that the UE cannot support both LTE and NR in the same band due to the complex filter requirements. Currently, there is limited spectrum allocated for private network operations, and typically only a single band is available. Given this, for multimode LTE and NR deployments in each enterprise campus, it will require that the LTE and NR networks be supported independently from a radio operating in different parts of the same band, and the UE camps either on the LTE network or the NR at a given time, subject to the UE's capabilities. The UE operates either in LTE-only mode or NR-only mode. The CNs for LTE and NR can, however, be integrated and implemented as a converged core supporting the service-based architecture (SBA), CUPS, and providing QoS and IP domain operations based on the devices, independent of the RAT on which the UE is currently camped.

II.2.1.3.1 LTE and NR Operating Configurations

There are additional bands that are currently in discussions with the government bodies in individual countries, and it is possible for other combinations of LTE and NR operations with UEs simultaneously connected and exchanging traffic on both RATs at a given time. At that point, different configurations illustrated in Figure II.2.1.6 show converged core – LTE and NR connectivity with EPC and 5GC, with LTE or NR being the master and the other Radio Access Technology (RAT) acting as a slave. These configurations are collectively called "dual connectivity," referencing the UE's operation over LTE and NR simultaneously. The radio signaling and data paths over LTE and NR are illustrated.

It should be noted that among the options shown, configurations #1 and #2 are prevalent in enterprise private networks across the world. The options for supporting LTE and NR together will be predicated on the shared spectrum availability across multiple bands to allow for the UE to operate the individual RATs on independent bands.

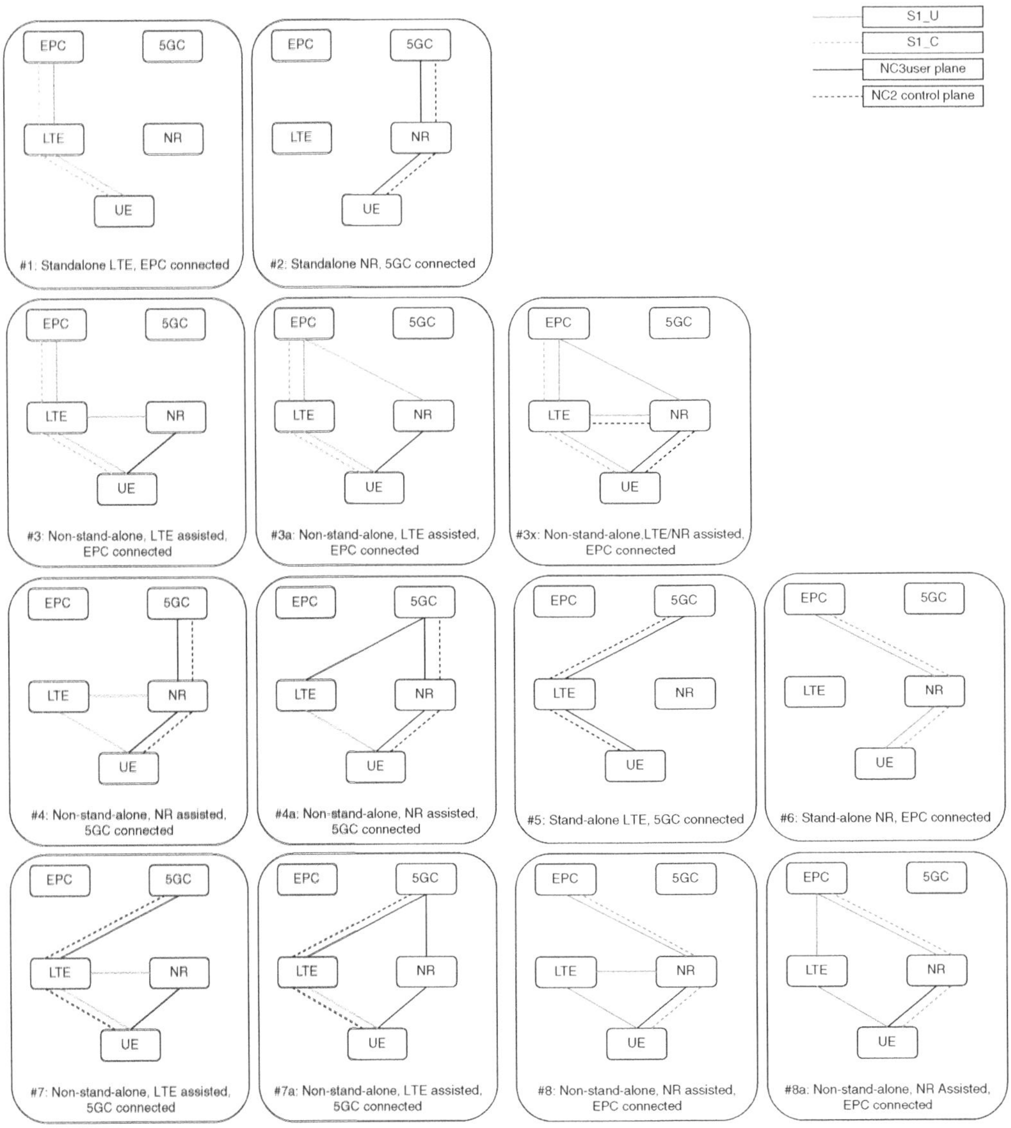

Figure II.2.1.6 Converged core – LTE and NR connectivity with EPC and 5G core.

With macro networks, one of the variants of configuration #3, #3a, and #3x is what is employed, retaining LTE as the master while introducing 5G NR in the markets as a slave and retaining the EPC CN as an anchor. The macro networks are slowly evolving toward configuration #2 to support 5G NR in the stand-alone mode with the 5GC. There are still hurdles in moving to NR stand-alone mode that depend on power-optimized operations of VoIP-over-NR (VoNR) and video-over-NR (ViNR) that lag behind what can be achieved with LTE, given the asynchronous nature of the HARQ procedures supported over both DL and UL for NR, with LTE supporting asynchronous HARQ on the DL and synchronous HARQ on the UL. NR does come with the additional complexity of not supporting pilots in the central frequency, requiring the UE to scan to find the pilots, making the mobility procedures, together with beamforming, more difficult to achieve. Some of the details will be covered in the LTE and NR radio access descriptions of the book.

LTE and NR operating mode	Description
#1	Stand-alone LTE, EPC-connected. Here, the UE is camped on an LTE-only network and associated with the EPC CN.
#2	Stand-alone NR, 5GC connected. Here, the UE is camped on an NR-only network and is associated with the 5GC CN.
#3	Non-stand-alone, LTE-assisted, EPC-connected. The UE is associated with LTE and NR simultaneously, with LTE as the master and NR as the slave. The authentication and IP context are established with the EPC core. All NR over-the-air traffic is routed via the LTE eNB to the NR gNB.
#3a	Non-stand-alone, LTE-assisted, EPC-connected. The UE is associated with LTE and NR simultaneously, with LTE as the master and NR as the slave. The authentication and IP context are established with the EPC core. With this option, the LTE traffic from the EPC is routed to the eNB, and the NR traffic from the EPC is directly routed to the gNB.
#3x	Non-stand-alone, LTE-assisted, EPC-connected. The UE is associated with LTE and NR simultaneously, with LTE as the master and NR as the slave. The authentication and IP context are established with the EPC core. With this option, the LTE traffic from the EPC is routed to the eNB, and NR traffic is directly routed to the gNB. Additionally, the X2 interface between the LTE eNB and NR gNB is supported to allow for undelivered traffic on one RAT to be transferred to the other RAT when either is in poorer or no coverage while there is good coverage available from the other RAT.
#4	Non-stand-alone, NR-assisted, 5GC-connected. The UE is simultaneously associated with LTE and NR, with NR as the master and LTE as the slave. The authentication and IP context are established with the 5GC core. All NR over-the-air traffic is routed via the NR gNB to the LTE eNB.
#4a	Non-stand-alone, NR-assisted, 5GC-connected. The UE is associated with LTE and NR simultaneously, with NR as the master and LTE as the slave. The authentication and IP context are established with the 5GC core. With this option, LTE traffic is routed directly from the 5GC to the eNB, and NR traffic is routed directly from the 5GC to the gNB.
#5	Stand-alone LTE, 5GC connected. In this case, the UE is camped on an LTE-only network and associated with the 5GC CN. This configuration is also referred to as eLTE.
#6	Stand-alone NR, EPC-connected. Here, the UE is camped on an NR-only network and is associated with the EPC CN.
#7	Non-stand-alone, LTE-assisted, 5GC-connected. The UE is associated with LTE and NR simultaneously, with LTE as the master and NR as the slave. The authentication and IP context are established with the EPC core. All NR over-the-air traffic is routed via the LTE eNB to the NR gNB.
#7a	Non-stand-alone, LTE-assisted, 5GC-connected. The UE is associated with both LTE and NR simultaneously, with LTE as the master and NR as the slave. The authentication and IP context are established with the EPC core. With this option, LTE traffic from the EPC is routed to the eNB, while NR traffic from the EPC is directly routed to the gNB.
#8	Non-stand-alone, NR-assisted, EPC-connected. The UE is associated with both LTE and NR simultaneously, with NR as the master and LTE as the slave. The authentication and IP context are established with the EPC core. All LTE over-the-air traffic is routed via the NR gNB to the LTE eNB.
#3a	Non-stand-alone, NR-assisted, EPC-connected. The UE is associated with LTE and NR simultaneously, with NR as the master and LTE as the slave. The authentication and IP context are established with the EPC core. With this option, LTE traffic from the EPC is directly routed to the eNB, and NR traffic from the EPC is directly routed to the gNB.

II.2.1.3.2 Converged Core Functions

The SBA and CUPS were discussed during the later stages of the LTE/EPC 3GPP standardization process. With the legacy architecture already in place, it was difficult to evolve the LTE/EPC networks to incorporate this concept. With the 5G NR/5GC 3GPP definitions, these concepts were included as part of the base design assumptions. The emergence of enterprise private networks that support both LTE and NR allowed for the SBA and CUPS architectural approaches to be supported even with LTE/EPC and additionally integrated with the NR/5GC functions for a converged core realization.

This section discusses the functional groupings typically considered part of the converged core. With an enterprise focus, in addition to the typical wireless CN functions, additional functions such as shared spectrum management, integration with the enterprise network, and enterprise applications, as well as exposure functions to support network as a service (NaaS), are also discussed. Figure II.2.1.7 provides a visual breakdown of the functional components of the converged core. This section further describes the individual functional groups involved.

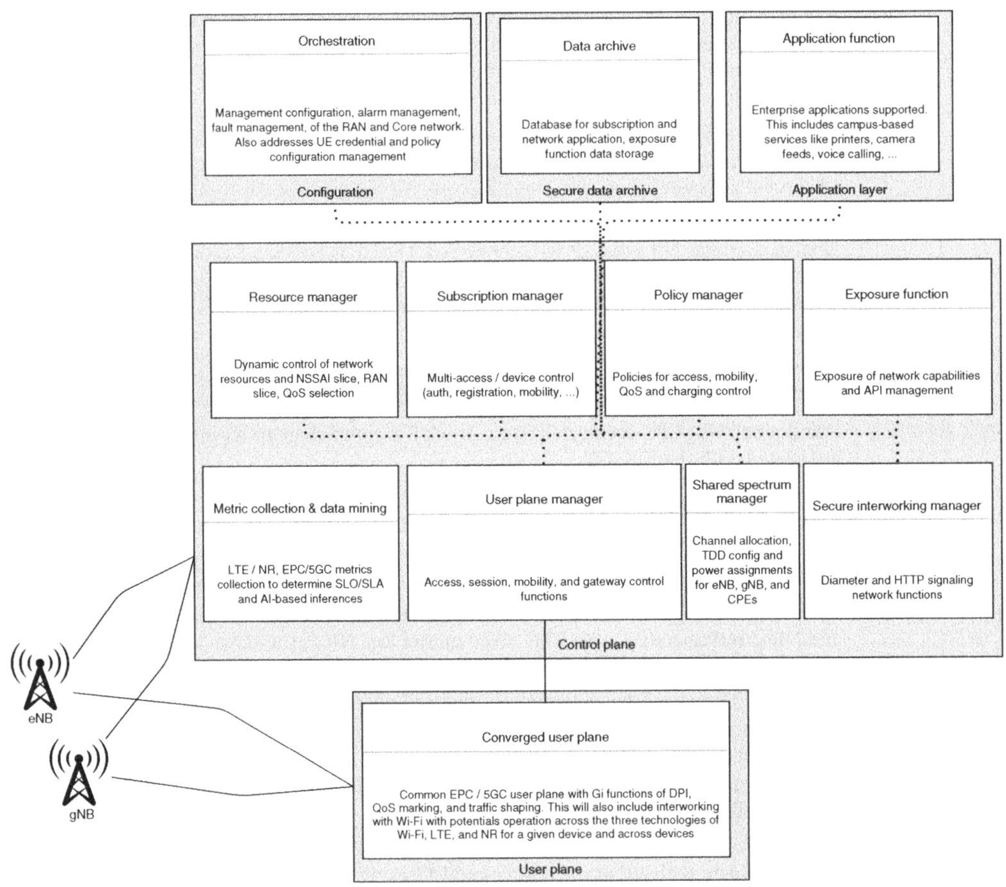

Figure II.2.1.7 Converged core – EPC and 5GC converged core modular functions.

The SBA architecture is fundamentally enabled by the NRF, which provides NF service registration and discovery, enabling NFs to identify appropriate services in one another. All CN services/functions are identified as NFs, run on specific compute resources, and the NRF assists in interconnecting these NFs. A completely new protocol, HTTP/2, is employed as compared to diameter to communicate between various NFs. EPC functions are regrouped in 5GC for better organization and division of roles, which allows for improved scalability and compute resource management. Example of the MME in EPC separated as access mobility function (AMF) and session management function (SMF) to delineate the AMFs from the core IP domain connectivity aspects. 5G also introduced specific signaling functions that include SCP, binding support function (BSF), and security edge protection proxy (SEPP). 5GC also supports a separate authentication server and other new functions such as the network slice selection function (NSSF) and NEF to allow for NaaS and external manipulation of the deployed CN through exposed application programming interfaces (APIs). Table II.2.1.1 below defines some key terms providing a brief description for each.

Table II.2.1.1 Key terms for Converged Core

Term	Description
NG-RAN	A RAN that supports one or more of the following options, with the common characteristic that it connects to 5GC: Stand-alone new radio New radio is the anchor with E-UTRA extensions. Stand-alone E-UTRA E-UTRA is the anchor with new radio extensions.
MEC	Multi-access edge compute. An ETSI standards body describes the approach for application developers and content providers to deploy networks at the edge. Refer to https://www.etsi.org/technologies/multi-access-edge-computing for the detailed specifications.
Hyperscaler	Refers to hyperscale computing, which allows for the processing of data and functions through a software architecture that scales based on the system's demands. Examples of hyperscalers include Amazon Web Services (AWS), Microsoft Azure, and Google Cloud (GCP).
CUPS	Control and user plane separation. This concept has been discussed since the later stages of 4G networks and has become an integral part of 5G network standardization. Both 4G and 5G networks can be deployed using this concept, which is the preferred approach.
NSA mode	Non-stand-alone mode. This refers to a deployment where both LTE and NR are deployed, with one of the technologies—LTE or NR—acting as the master and the other acting as a slave. This is defined to address the evolution from 4G LTE networks to allow for the introduction of 5G NR networks and to gain improved performance by having the device connect to both RATs simultaneously.
SA mode	Stand-alone mode. In this mode, NR-only is deployed. LTE-only network deployments are supported, although it is not called SA mode due to the legacy nature of 4G networks.
EPC	Evolved packet core. It is the 4G packet core of LTE and LTE + NR NSA modes. It consists of multiple nodes that include MME, SGW, PGW, HSS, and PCRF. It supports functionality such as mobility management, device authentication, session management, and establishing quality of service (QoS) bearers based on the defined policies.
5GC	5G core network. It is the 5G packet CN of eLTE, NR, NR+LTE, and NR+NR SA modes. It consists of multiple nodes that include AMF, SMF, UPF, AUSF, UDM, and PCF. Like LTE, it supports functionality such as mobility management, device authentication, session management, and establishing QoS bearers based on the defined policies. Architecturally, it is enabled as a service-based architecture (SBA).

II.2.1.3.2.1 Orchestration

LTE and NR networks can be complex, and any simplification achieved to make the enterprise deployment easier should be considered. There are several aspects of configuration on the eNB, gNB, EPC, and 5GC that are required, and creating typical configuration types based on the industry verticals as baseline configurations to start off with will be essential for making minor tweaks for enterprise-specific issues as needed. UE provisioning is a major detail in terms of both managing the supply chain with preconfigured information and effective credential distribution, minimizing the work involved as part of the mobile device management (MDM) procedures, which significantly ease the pressures on the enterprise IT. The ease of network configuration and provisioning to support the required user groups, QoS management, slice management, and application/service-specific support must meet the enterprise-specific service-level objectives (SLOs) and service-level agreements (SLAs), while also addressing dynamic changes that adapt to evolving enterprise needs. Alarm and fault management, and raising them at the appropriate level, become essential to both ensuring proper attention is provided to the aspects that matter and allowing the IT enterprise to ignore those that do not require their coordination.

II.2.1.3.2.2 Application Function

Each enterprise has a specific set of application functions that need to be supported. These applications typically are already supported over wired or Wi-Fi connectivity. Effectively transitioning these applications to operate over private LTE/NR, while understanding the application QoS needs, will be essential to allowing these services to be supported over private LTE/NR. It is likely that the operations over LTE/NR need to be shown to be more reliable and have a better QoS rendering. This will enable the enterprise entity to consider deploying private LTE/NR networks.

II.2.1.3.2.3 Shared Spectrum Manager

A lot of the private LTE/NR networks are enabled using the shared spectrum that is lightly licensed, like Citizen Broadband Radio Service (CBRS) in the US, or unlicensed spectrum in 2.4 GHz, 5 GHz, and 6 GHz, as utilized by the current Wi-Fi networks that can also support LTE/NR RATs. An independent arbitrating entity like the SAS or automatic frequency control (AFC) system is accessed by the individual deployed nodes to obtain a spectrum allocation for use. This shared spectrum use has become the most critical enabler for private networks, allowing for improved indoor and outdoor connectivity within the enterprise campuses. The CBRS aspects are discussed in an independent section of the book.

II.2.1.3.2.4 Converged User Plane

The converged UP provides a common UP function with UPF, PGW-U, SGW-U, and other Gi functions integrated into it. It delivers advanced and highly efficient processing of data payloads, including support for distributed deployment. It further supports tight interworking between 5GC and EPC to ensure that the NF implementations are reused across the two realizations for LTE and NR connectivity.

With scalable software architecture, the UP and CP scale independently to accommodate a range of services and associated traffic profiles. These NFs are deployed across the enterprise local compute, metro cloud within a certain locale, such as a county or city, DMZ centrally located across sites for an enterprise, or a public cloud. UP functions are typically supported locally within the enterprise to address low-latency applications and better regulate the traffic on campus.

It supports high throughput, advanced payload processing, and value-added traffic management functions based on intelligent traffic steering, employing traffic detection functions in combination with service chaining and integration with the UPF as one managed solution.

Examples of traffic detection functions include five-tuple (source/target IP address/port number and Differentiated Services Code Point (DSCP) marking) deep packet inspection, content insertion such as header enrichment, content optimization, and transmission control protocol (TCP) optimization, comparable to an external TCP optimizer.

Such scalability allows for ease in introducing new services, adjusting the network capacity to support the required grade of service while maintaining the QoS for the existing enterprise services.

II.2.1.3.2.5 User Plane Manager

The UP manager establishes the UE's access to the network, provides the IP context connectivity to the appropriate IP domain, and supports mobility across the RAN nodes within the enterprise campus. This is supported by the AMF and SMF for 5GC, and the mobility management entity (MME) for EPC. The UP manager, together with the converged UP, allows for a clean realization of the CUPS architecture. The NRF allows the NFs to be discoverable to each other, enabling ease of scaling. The UP manager additionally performs load balancing and appropriately establishes connectivity with the UP compute resources to meet the QoS for each application/vertical. The services are dynamically moved across compute resources to ensure that compute costs are minimized while maintaining the SLO/SLA.

Such an architecture allows for different enterprise network configurations, including LTE-only, NR-only, and both LTE & NR, to be supported on a single campus. Additionally, it allows for network evolution to progress from an LTE-only deployment to an LTE and NR deployment and, at some potential future point when LTE is no longer required, to transition the campus to an NR-only configuration. Given the integrated nature of the EPC and 5GC functions, common platforms can support integrating similar functions, for example subscription information. This further allows for cleaner integration with the existing enterprise functions like the remote authentication dial-in user service (RADIUS) server and other enterprise metric collection for a single pane of glass for enterprise IT management. This greatly aids in the total cost of ownership (TCO), offering maximum flexibility for an enterprise deployment and management.

II.2.1.3.2.6 Secure Interworking Manager

The secure interworking manager supports identifying and connecting the different NFs in the converged core and provides access to external entities that treat the private LTE/NR NaaS. Internal registry services are supported for NFs to announce their availability and the compute node location(s) that the other NFs can query to establish connectivity. The secure interworking manager also supports the required security protocols to allow these NFs to be accessed in a secure manner, with the requisite permissions and restrictions applied as needed. Explicit functions are defined for NF access within the CN and when exposed to external entities, supported through an independent function to avoid any security breaches, establishing a "front door" for entry. The complexity of transitioning the different firewalls needs to be addressed by taking special considerations into account regarding the currently deployed infrastructure in the enterprise campus.

II.2.1.3.2.7 Resource Manager

There are several resources that need to be managed in the LTE/NR private networks. There are radio-specific resources, CN resources, and enterprise application resources. For usability for a given user, end-to-end resource allocations are required in each of the entities.

Radio resources are managed by specifying the supportable bit rates, packet error rates, packet delay budgets, a time after which the packets are discarded, and relative priority across services. The RAN scheduler realization will support the different QoS flows that are accommodated by the admission and congestion control mechanisms. The typical set of radio resources that need to be shared includes physical resource blocks (PRB), power, MIMO, and beamforming abilities to schedule the different users' QoS flows. The RAN scheduler function is discussed in an independent section in the book.

From a CN perspective, it is typically supported as slices, recognizing the required IP domain isolation, regulating the hop-to-hop delays involved, and reacting to real-time detection of traffic types for QoS flow establishment. Dynamic scaling of the CN resources based on the required throughput will be a fundamental part of managing these resources. The concept of slices will be discussed in an independent section in the book.

The resources required by the enterprise applications are typically managed by the enterprise IT and not in the purview of the private LTE/NR deployments, given that this spans across wired and Wi-Fi connectivity as well.

II.2.1.3.2.8 Subscription Manager

Subscription manager integrates the 4G HSS and 5G unified data management (UDM). It also supports the key derivation and authentication functions, segregating these functions between the serving network for the UE and the authenticating home network. It also supports the equipment registry function to detect stolen devices.

II.2.1.3.2.9 Policy Manager

Policy manager supports the policy charging and rules function (PCRF) in EPC and the Policy Control Function (PCF) in 5GC. The integrated policy manager supports a centralized policy function that can be accessed by the LTE and NR networks for regulating the user camping function, QoS grants based on the application and user credentials, and supports the addition and removal of users from the system. It also supports integration with the enterprise RADIUS server to allow the enterprise IT to support a single pane of glass for managing all users, including LTE, NR, Wi-Fi, and wired connectivity.

II.2.1.3.2.10 Exposure Function

The exposure function is realized as the service capability exposure function (SCEF) in EPC and a similar NEF in 5GC within the converged platform. It aggregates the APIs via the SCEF and NEF to enable the private LTE/NR networks as NaaS. The APIs are typically customized, and specific interfaces are exposed based on enterprise needs. Most enterprises typically have closed walls, and explicit care needs to be taken to ensure that only the required functions are exposed. It is possible that these exposure interfaces are available only to well-trusted parties who are allowed access through established secure connectivity.

II.2.1.3.2.11 Data Archive

The data archive supports the unified data repository (UDR) and unstructured data storage function (UDSF) and is defined as part of the 5GC core. These data stores are used for information archiving by the individual NFs and are accessed by the other NFs to make more informed decisions. Although they are defined as part of the 5GC, these data stores can equally be used as part of the EPC realizations.

II.2.1.3.3 Converged Core Integrated High-level View

Figure II.2.1.8 provides the LTE and NR end-to-end architecture nodes including the RAN and core network nodes / functions.

II.2.1.3.4 Converged Core Functional Breakdown

Figure II.2.1.9 provides a view of the individual functions of the converged CN, along with the grouping of these functions into functional groups. This section discusses the description of the functional groups and the specific roles played by the individual functions.

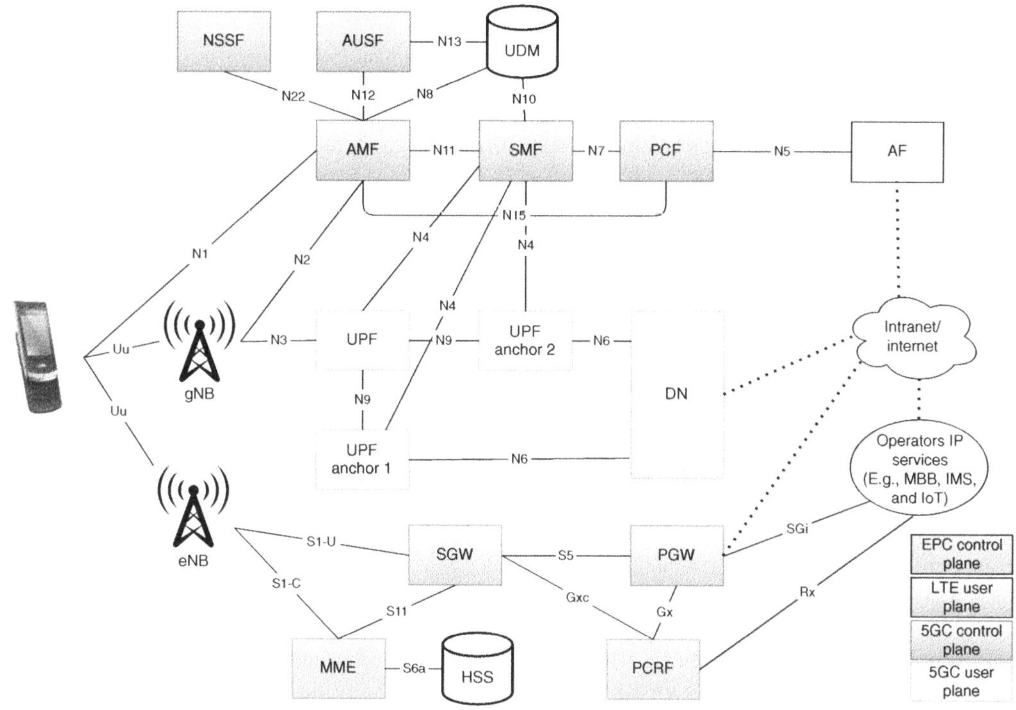

Figure II.2.1.8 Converged core – LTE and NR end-to-end architecture.

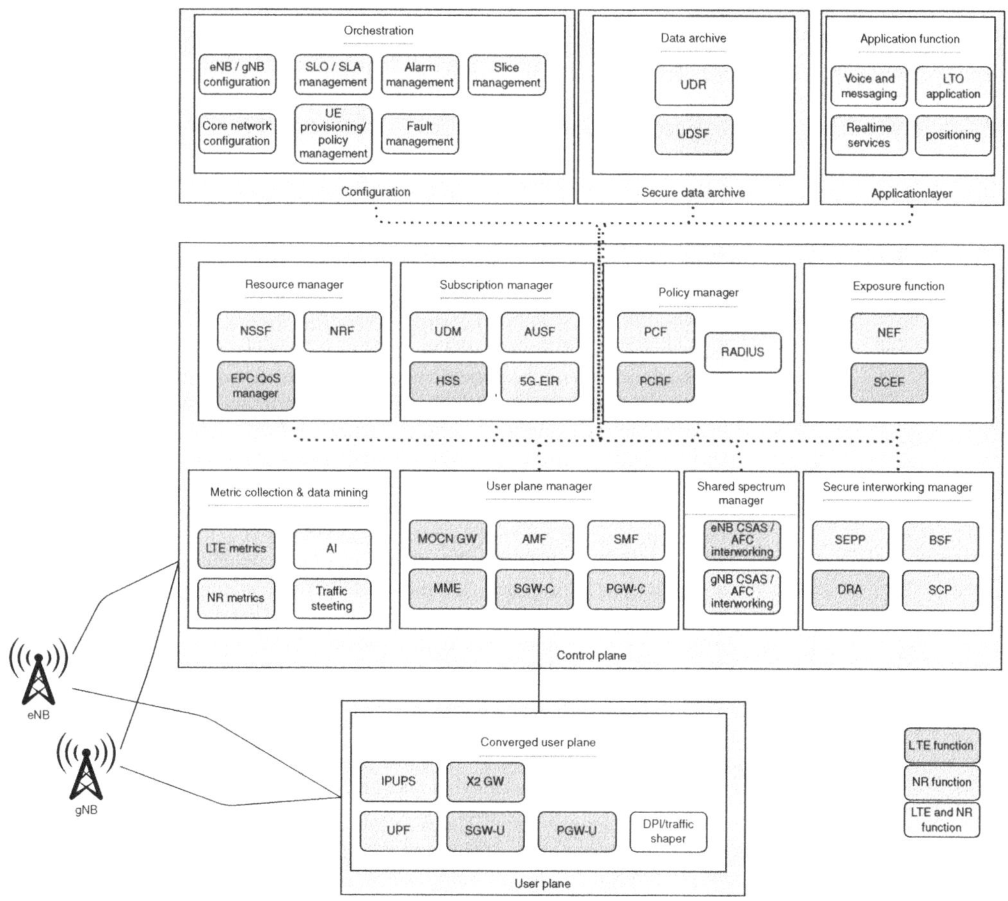

Figure II.2.1.9 Converged core – EPC and 5GC converged core modular components.

II.2.1.3.4.1 Functional Group – Orchestration

This section addresses the functions involved in configuring, operating, and monitoring the network to manage it effectively.

Function	Description
eNB/gNB configuration	Managing the eNB connectivity and over-the-air operational parameters based on the enterprise campus and the type of devices. Also manages the software/firmware upgrades of the eNB.
SLO/SLA management	Management of the definition of SLO/SLA, report generation, and system capacity assessment of replanning needs for the network.
CN configuration	CN orchestration for CP and UP operations includes on-premises and cloud functional separation, as well as capacity management. It also involves integration with existing Wi-Fi networks and connectivity to MNOs.
UE provisioning/policy management	UE enterprise credential request and policy for multi-RAT operation provisioning.
Slice management	Support the different slices on 4G and 5G platforms, allowing for: • RAN slices, which will typically be based on PLMN-based separation of resources. This topic is treated in an independent section as part of the RAN discussions in the book. • Network slice selection assistance information (NSSAI). This is used to identify the IP domain association for specific functions executed from the UE. From an enterprise perspective, it is treated as VLAN/VxLAN separation based on the UE type, credentials, and applications accessed by the UE. Typically, for enterprise-centric devices, there is only one application/function associated with a UE, and the segregation of user access and traffic is done by the user identity or the network slice access preferences indicated by the UE. The topic of slices is discussed in an independent section and treated together with QoS functions to provide an end-to-end view. • Radio bearer and radio access bearer management refer to the end-to-end QoS based on the active application flows. A detailed description of this is provided as part of the slice discussions in this book. This will include the static and dynamic management of slice definition and activation/deactivation behaviors. • Integration with SLO for QoS support required for the specific enterprise is considered, and the associated SLA is defined based on the SLO. The QoS realizations may not be possible with rigid parameter definitions for all congestion levels in the network. Given that a primary or preferred QoS metric is defined, and under higher congestion levels, an acceptable secondary QoS context is also considered practicable rather than blocking the service under resource-constrained scenarios. It is wholly possible that a given application requires a fixed set of parameters for operation (e.g. IIoT applications), and only a primary QoS metric is defined for such scenarios. For applications like video telephony, some degradation is acceptable, as a secondary QoS metric can be defined for operation in congested scenarios. The primary and secondary QoS metric applications may also depend on the user type in the enterprise, with some users or user groups treated with a higher priority than others.
Alarm management	Panel for alarm management and escalation. The alarms represented will have some generic aspects that apply to all enterprise private networks, along with enterprise-specific customizations as needed based on the enterprise's preferences regarding aspects that take precedence.
Fault management	Panel for fault management. The fault information represented will have some generic aspects that apply to all enterprise private networks and enterprise-specific customizations as needed based on the enterprise's preferences regarding aspects that take precedence.

II.2.1.3.4.2 Functional Group – UP Manager

Function	Description
MOCN GW	This is a generic NF used to realize a neutral host network and is used by both LTE and NR-based networks deployed as neutral hosts. The LTE/NR RAN networks are deployed on the enterprise campuses. The MOCN GW acts as EPC-MME/5GC-AMF to the eNB/gNB deployed on the enterprise campus for CP message exchanges. The MOCN GW acts as EPC-SWG/5GC-UPF to the eNB/gNB deployed on the enterprise campus for UP message exchanges. Correspondingly, the MOCN GW acts as an eNB/gNB when connecting to the macro network operator CN. All interconnects are protected with IPSec; tunnel endpoints will need to be established for EPC and 5GC independently. The interacting functions will also need to be adapted based on EPC and 5GC functions within the MOCN GW. See the section on neutral host operations in this book that addresses the details of neutral host operations.
AMF	A 5GC NF, access and mobility management function (AMF) addresses all access camping and mobility aspects. Some of the key functions of the AMF include • UE registration allows the UE to camp on the network • UE access authentication and access authorization interacting with the UDM • UE reachability from the UDM to ensure UE is reachable and provides UE activity information • Radio connection management • Mobility management across the radio access nodes • Non-access stratum (NAS) ciphering and integrity protection algorithms • Acts as a conduit for the session management messages between the SMF and UE • Supports connectivity to lawful intercept (LI) systems
SMF	Session management function includes the following functionalities: • UE session establishment, modification, and release • UE IP address allocation and management based on the UE credentials, associating the UE with the appropriate VLAN/VxLAN IP domain • DHCPv4 (server and client) and DHCPv6 (server and client) functions to reserve the IP address in the identified IP domain • Selection of the UPF and establishment of the data path tunnel between the UPF and gNB • Support the DL data notification to page the UE to get the UE into connected mode if it is in idle or inactive modes • Assist in identifying the application function nodes based on the enterprise network policies and UE identifiers
MME	An EPC NF, MME supports NAS signaling with the UE. The MME supports the functions listed below. • UE attach procedures for UE camping on the network • Authentication of the UE interacting with the HSS • Initiating paging when DL data arrives while the UE is in idle mode, tracking the location of the UE within a tracking area code (TAC) • IP session in the appropriate VLAN/VxLAN IP domain interacts with the packet data gateway (PGW) • QoS establishment based on triggers from the PCRF • Establishes UE data path connectivity between the SGW and eNB • Mobility management across the radio access nodes • Connective with the 2G/3G network for circuit-switched services
PGW-C	An EPC NF, packet data gateway CP (PGW-C) supports the control signaling to establish the IP and QoS flow contexts.
SGW-C	An EPC NF, SGW-C supports the establishment of a data traffic tunnel to the current serving eNB. It receives its control information from the MME and sits between the eNB and the PGW.

II.2.1.3.4.3 Functional Group – Converged UP

Function	Description
IPUPS	A 5GC NF, inter-PLMN UP security (IPUPS) functionality at the border of their network protects their network from interacting with home-routed networks when the UE is roaming onto the given network. The UPFs supporting the IPUPS functionality in the visited PLMN (VPLMN) and the home PLMN (HPLMN) are controlled by the visited SMF (V-SMF) and the home SMF (H-SMF) of that protocol data unit (PDU) session, respectively. The SMF can activate the IPUPS functionality together with other UP functionalities in the same UPF or insert a separate UPF for the IPUPS functionality in the UP path (which e.g. may be dedicated to being used for IPUPS functionality). Typically, secure tunnels are established between the visited and home networks via the SEPP, and the interface between the visited-SEPP (vSEPP) and home-SEPP (hSEPP) is termed the N32 interface.
UPF	A 5GC NF, UP function (UPF) supports the data path connectivity between the data network (DN) and the gNB, establishing connectivity for each UE and potentially multiple QoS flows for a given UE. It performs packet routing and forwarding, packet inspection, and QoS handling and acts as an anchor point for intra- and inter-RAT mobility. Defined as part of the CUPS architecture, the UPF supports the UP packet process and traffic aggregation functions and enables the converged core. UPF supports the interfaces below with the other NF in the 5GC. • N3: interface between RAN (gNodeB) and the (initial) UPF • N6: interface between the DN and UPF • N4: interface between the SMF and the UPF • N9: interface between two UPFs (intermediate I-UPF and UPF session anchor) UPF supports the key functions below: • External PDU session point interconnects with the DN • Anchor points for intra-RAT and inter-RAT mobility (where applicable) • Packet routing and data forwarding • QoS management for the UP • Traffic usage reporting • UL traffic verification • Transport-level packet marking in UL and DL • DL packet buffering and triggering DL data notifications
X2GW	X2 gateway (X2GW) is the node that interacts with eNB and acts as a hub. For an enterprise campus, the inter-eNB connectivity can potentially be supported directly without requiring X2GW, given the small number of interacting nodes. However, when X2 interconnections between the eNBs are not supported, the X2GW can be leveraged to perform this function when introduced between the CN and the RAN networks. Note as well that when X2 interconnect is not supported between eNBs, the S1 interface connection with the CN can be used to serve the same purpose, supporting UE transitions from one eNB to another eNB within the enterprise campus.
SGW-U	An EPC NF, serving gateway user plane (SGW-U) is a data plane path that sits between the serving eNB and the packet data gateway (PGW). User traffic in the DL is flooded to the SGW-U, and it performs flow control to deliver the requisite amount of data to the servicing eNB to avoid starvation of the radio resource while still minimizing the amount of traffic that needs to be resent to the target eNB when the UE moves from one serving eNB to anther target eNB.

Function	Description
PGW-U	An EPC NF, packet data gateway user plane (PGW-U) is the data plan anchor associated with an IP domain. It provides IP address allocation to the UE and supports end-to-end QoS flows when established by the MME/PCRF.
DPI/traffic shaper	Deep packet inspection (DPI) is an NF used by EPC and 5GC. In 5GC, the function is defined under the name TDF. It uses the Domain Name Server (DNS) queries, traffic patterns that include packet sizes and the periodicity of packet arrivals, transport protocol detection (TCP/UDP/RTP/RTCP), and other techniques to identify the ongoing traffic and trigger-specific traffic treatment, including QoS flow establishment and traffic shaping, to achieve the network-level SLA/SLO.

II.2.1.3.4.4 Functional Group – Data Archive

With an increased focus on user identity protection and information collection, explicit functions are defined within 5GC that support the storage and retrieval of information for authorized entities. Some of the data/information is stored and/or shared for internal enterprise use, while other specific information is exposed to third-party entities.

Function	Description
UDR	The 5GC UDR function offers a unified database for storing application, subscription, authentication, service authorization, policy data, session binding, and application state information. UDR provides an HTTP2-based RESTful interface for other NFs and provisioning clients to access the stored data. The UDR supports the following key functionalities: • Storage and retrieval of UE subscription data by the UDM. • Storage and retrieval of policy data by the PCF. • Storage and retrieval of data for the NEF. • Application data includes enterprise-specific applications including packet flow descriptions (PFDs) for application detection and AF request information for multiple UEs by the NEF.
UDSF	The UDSF is intended for the storage and retrieval of unstructured data by a suitable NF. Unstructured data refers to customized data structures used by the individual deployments not defined in the 3GPP specifications. It is introduced to store dynamic state data, for example UE-related data; context can be stored in a central UDSF, and one or more AMFs access the stored information. It is used to handle seamless continuity of services to address individual AMF outages. Other NFs may have their own UDSF, or it can be integrated into a common platform. There are several levels of NF realizations based on the extent of UE-related state information that is retained in the NF and the associated access involved with the UDSF. The list below provides some approaches for the NFs. • No state: no UE state information is stored in the NF (e.g. UDM front-end). • Transactional state: UE state information is pulled by the NF from the UDSF for the duration of the transaction only (e.g. PCF). This approach is useful when there are typically a few message exchanges with the UE, and once the transaction is completed, the UE information is no longer required in the NF.

(*Continued*)

Function	Description
	• State efficient: UE state information is pulled by the NF from the UDSF and kept there during periods of high UE activity (the UE is in a connected state on the radio interface), cached for a few seconds or minutes, with the stable UE state information stored by the NF in the UDSF at the end of a certain procedure (e.g. AMF or SMF). This approach provides an optimal solution to avoid repeatedly accessing the UDSF and will address scenarios when the UE is actively using the network. • Stateful: the UE state information is stored permanently in the NF (e.g. UDR). This should be done very selectively, given that there will be duplication of information stored between the NF and UDSF, requiring periodic synchronization to ensure consistency. 3GPP TS 23.501, Annex C, provides guidelines on compute-storage separation in terms of managing UDSF. UDSF itself can be used as either primary or secondary storage based on the NF realization and the repeated access to the UDSF data required by the NF. With UDSF as primary storage, the NF is typically stateless or has minimal state. With the UDSF as secondary storage, the NF tends to be stateful and retains a lot of the transitional UE state information; the UDSF is typically used only to commit stable data storage information and is treated as backup storage. It should be noted that 3GPP does not standardize triggers for storing unstructured data but recommends that the transfer be performed once the state information is stable. As with any data store, implementation-dependent measures should be taken to handle race conditions, particularly when multiple writers and readers are involved (i.e. when multiple NFs attempt access simultaneously).
UDC	User data convergence (UDC) is an optional concept to ensure data consistency and simplify the creation of new services by providing easy access to user data, as well as ensuring the consistency of storage and data models and minimizing the impact on traffic mechanisms, reference points, and protocols of network elements. Refer to 3GPP TS 23.335: "User Data Convergence (UDC)"; "Technical Realization and Information Flows"; and Stage 2 for more details. 3GPP does not define the UD interface between the front-end and the UDR – see figure 4.1-1 in 3GPP TS 23.335.

II.2.1.3.4.5 Functional Group – Subscription Manager

Function	Description
UDM	Unified data management (UDM) is the 5GC equivalent to the HSS in EPC architecture. It supports the concept of UDC, which separates the UDR storing and managing subscriber information from the front-end processing of subscriber information. See section 6.2.7 in 3GPP TS 23.501. The UDM includes support for the following functionality: • Generation of 3GPP aka authentication credentials. • User identification handling (e.g. storage and management of Subscription Permanent Identifier (SUPI) for each subscriber in the 5G system). • Access authorization based on subscription data (e.g. roaming restrictions). • UE's serving NF registration management (e.g. storing serving AMF for UE, storing serving SMF for the UE's PDU session). • Support for service/session continuity (e.g. by keeping the SMF/DNN assignment of ongoing sessions). • MT-SMS delivery support. • Lawful intercept functionality (especially in the outbound roaming case where the UDM is the only point of contact for LI).

Function	Description
	• Subscription management. • SMS management. To provide this functionality, the UDM uses subscription data (including authentication data) that may be stored in the UDR, in which case a UDM implements the application logic and does not require an internal user data storage; therefore, several different UDMs may serve the same user in different transactions. The interaction between UDM and HSS is not addressed in 3GPP and is left up to the implementation. Also, the UDM is in the HPLMN of the subscribers it serves and supports access to the information in the UDR located in the same PLMN.
AUSF	The authentication server function is responsible for handling authentication requests for both 3GPP access (LTE/NR) and trusted and untrusted non-3GPP access (Wi-Fi). See section 6.2.8 of 3GPP TS 23.501 for more details on the functionality of AUSF.
HSS	An EPC NF, HSS diameter interfaces with packet DNs and applications for interworking. This NF stores the user credential information and assists in the authentication of the UE.
5G-EIR	5G system: EIR is defined in 3GPP TS 29.511. N5G-EIR is a service-based interface that is an optional NF supporting the following functionality: • Check the status of the equipment's identity (e.g. to verify that it has not been blacklisted). This is used to detect the usage of stolen devices in the market. The database of stolen devices is shared across the macro network and enterprise network operators and has federal implications when a stolen device is detected. During any procedure establishing a signaling connection with the UE, the network may optionally perform an ME identity check with 5G-EIR via the N5G-EIR equipment identity check service exhibited by 5G-EIR.

II.2.1.3.4.6 Functional Group – Policy Manager

Function	Description
PCF	A 5GC NF, PCF is the replacement for the corresponding EPC function, PCRF. Section 6.2.4 in 3GPP TS 23.501. "The Policy Control Function (PCF)" • provides support for a unified policy framework to govern network behavior. • provides policy rules to CP functions to enforce them. • accesses subscription information relevant for policy decisions in a UDR. • regulates the bit rates, QoS grants, and camping behaviors based on user subscriptions and enterprise network policies. These are mostly configured rules that are specified well ahead of time for enforcement; however, it is possible for the enterprises to enforce real-time policies that are ad hoc or specified as behaviors to be performed at specific times of the day, on specific days of the week, during congestion experienced in the network, or any other mandates governing the enterprise network. User-related policies are stored in the PCF associated with the home PLMN (HPLMN). When the UE is operating in a roaming network, the local PCF may additionally enforce policies associated with the visited enterprise network. The details of the PCF functionality are defined in clause 6.2.1 of 3GPP TS 23.503.

(Continued)

Function	Description
PCRF	EPC policy and charging rules function manages the service policy and sends QoS setting information for each user session and accounting rule information. Similar functions to support for 5GC PCF are supported for EPC PCRF with the caveat of managing the network based on the 4G LTE/EPC capabilities. These include IP domain connectivity and QoS grants, among other items, allowing or rejecting the media request and checking the allocation of added resources against the maximum authorized. PCRF allows for operator-defined charging rules applicable to each service data flow (SDF). The relevant charging rules are determined based on information provided by the P-CSCF such as the application identifier, type of stream (audio, video, etc.), and application data rate.
RADIUS	Remote authentication dial-in user service, which is often referred to as an AAA server, stands for "Authentication, Authorization, and Accounting." The RADIUS server gets its AAA name based on the functions that it performs. It uses an authentication protocol that grants or denies users access to a range of services, including Wi-Fi, VPN, and applications. The RADIUS server uses a directory of user/device information (also called an identity provider or IDP) for reference. This NF is focused on the existing connectivity, using both wired and Wi-Fi-based connections, and also supports access through a VPN tunnel into the enterprise campus from an external network. It supports the relevant user-based policies, including regulating the bit rate and allowing or revoking user connectivity, for example as enterprise users join or leave the company. In a converged core, the IT enterprise would like to have a single pane of glass to regulate all users across the wired/Wi-Fi and private LTE/NR connectivity. Such an integration is also typically achieved by having the private LTE/NR users identified in the RADIUS server and regulating the EPC PCRF and 5GC PCF policies from the RADIUS server.

II.2.1.3.4.7 Functional Group – Resource Manager

Function	Description
NSSF	The network slice selection function is viewed as a logical end-to-end network that can be dynamically created. A given UE may access multiple slices over the same AN (e.g. over the same radio interface). Each slice may serve a particular service type with an agreed-upon SLA. A network slice is defined within a PLMN and includes the CN CP and UP NFs, as well as the 5G AN. The 5G access network may be • a next generation (NG) RAN described in 3GPP TS 38.300 or • a non-3GPP AN where the terminal may use any non-3GPP access to reach the 5G CN via a secured IPSec/IKE tunnel terminated on the evolved packet data gateway (ePDG) EPC-based or a non-3GPP interworking function (N3IWF) that is 5GC-based. Note that the N3IWF only offers a more aesthetically improved structure for connecting to the CN from untrusted access compared to ePDG and is currently not supported by the network vendors. The ePDG-based solution supported with EPC is still relied upon even for 5GC connectivity. Network function is a 3GPP-adopted or 3GPP-defined processing function in a network, which has defined functional behavior and 3GPP-defined interfaces. (Note: A NF can be implemented either as a network element on a dedicated hardware, as a software instance running on a dedicated hardware, or as a virtualized function instantiated on an appropriate platform, e.g. on a cloud infrastructure.) Network slice is a logical network that provides specific network capabilities and characteristics. See the slices section of this book for a more detailed treatment of this topic.

Function	Description
NRF	The NRF is one of the main key components of the 5G SBA. The NRF maintains an updated repository of all the 5G elements available in the operator's network, along with the services provided by each of the elements in the 5G core that are expected to be instantiated, scaled, and terminated with minimal or no manual intervention. The NRF supports discovery mechanisms that allow 5G elements to discover each other and get the updated status of the desired elements. Some of the key functions of the NRF include the following: • Maintains the profiles of the available NF instances and their supported services in the 5G CN • Allows consumer NF instances to discover other providers' NF instances in the 5G CN • Allows NF instances to track the status of other NF instances • Interacts with every other element in the 5G CN, and it supports the aforementioned functions through the following services: – Management services – Discovery services
EPC slice manager	This function mainly provides access to specific IP domain(s) and QoS flow establishment procedures. This function, when integrated with the 5GC converged core, will need to be coordinated with the NSSF realization.
Slice and policies manager	This entity stores the information associated with the slices defined for a given enterprise and has recognized patterns of slices used across the enterprise's campuses globally that will allow for reuse across campuses.

II.2.1.3.4.8 Functional Group – Enterprise Application Function

Individual enterprises have specific needs and custom applications developed. Many of these applications are currently operational over a wired connection or via Wi-Fi. With the introduction of LTE and NR into private networks, this allows for better QoS control and operation even under congested scenarios. Given the proprietary nature of these applications, it will be difficult to capture them here. Some specific functions are called out as examples. See the section on enterprise industry verticals in the book for applications that are considered for support.

Function	Description
Voice and messaging services	IP multimedia services are very much MNO-based and support voice/video calling, SMS, etc. This service is currently not envisioned to be supported in an enterprise setting. Having said that, there are enterprise PBX-based services that exist, and messaging has become a fundamental need, with applications like Slack® being used for internal information exchange. There are varying applications of messaging, including reaching specific enterprise services, such as emergency events that are handled as alarms and notifications to specific individuals. These will take shape within an enterprise and may also include voice services such as PPT (push-to-talk over cellular).
Real-time service	There are several real-time services that are required on campus. These are mostly supported by existing application functions, for example video camera feeds and OTT voice. IP Multimedia Subsystem (IMS)-based services may become relevant in the future, and support will be considered at that point.
LTO application	There are several applications that require the enterprise network's specific services/applications that need to be reached. These services/applications may be isolated from the basic connectivity and will require explicit local traffic offload (LTO) functions to enable access to them, for example printer access.

(Continued)

Function	Description
Positioning	Indoor and outdoor positioning services will be critical to addressing specific requirements for enterprise campuses, and the effective enablement of location services with the required degree of accuracy will become a fundamental enabler using the different RATs (LTE, NR, Wi-Fi, Bluetooth® [BT], and other low-power wide area [LPWA] systems). Supporting both horizontal and vertical positioning will be essential for several commercial applications and will also be used for emergency services.

II.2.1.3.4.9 Functional Group – Exposure Function

Function	Description
NEF	A 5GC NF, NEF supports the exposure of NF capabilities in the 5G system to external NFs, including enterprise IT, third-party entities, and specific application functions. External exposure can be categorized into policy/charging capability, monitoring capability, provisioning capability, and analytics reporting capability. The policy/charging capability is for handling QoS and charging policy for the UE based on requests from external parties. The monitoring capability is for monitoring specific events for the UE in the 5G system and making information about such monitoring events available for external exposure via the NEF. The provisioning capability is for allowing external parties to provision information that can be used for the UE in the 5G system. The analytics reporting capability is for allowing an external party to fetch or subscribe/unsubscribe to analytics information generated by the 5G system and can include UE-specific information collected in the UDM. Third-party applications are typically seen as untrusted, and sufficient care needs to be taken with the APIs exposed through NEF for such interfaces. NEF in 5GC supports functions similar to those of the SCEF in EPC. Section 6.2.5 of 3GPP TS 23.501, "The Network Exposure Function (NEF)," supports the following exposure functions to NFs via NEF and may be regulated based on the interacting NFs, including third-party entities, application functions, enterprise IT, along with the User Interface (UI) representations: • Exposed capabilities available. • Exposed events from the 5G network. • Store and retrieval of structured data from UDR is typically available only from the same PLMN. • Establishment of the secure interfaces as needed based on the interacting entity for NEF communication. • Digested internal information that is transformed/obfuscated for external communication. User-specific data is carefully hidden to ensure that individual users are not tracked by entities that should not have such information. • NEF receives information from NFs and aids in archiving the information in the UDR as structured data (based on the exposed capabilities of other NFs). The stored information can be accessed and "re-exposed" by the NEF to other NFs and application functions and can be used for other purposes, such as analytics. • A NEF may also support a PFD function. The PFD function in the NEF may store and retrieve PFD(s) in the UDR and provide PFD(s) to the SMF. This can be based on a request from the SMF (pull mode) or on a request from the NEF for PFD management (push mode), as described in 3GPP TS 23.503. A specific NEF instance may support one or more of the functionalities described above; consequently, an individual NEF may support a subset of the APIs specified for capability exposure. Additionally, the supported functions exposed by NEF will depend on the application functions, including enterprise internal and third-party external application functions.

Function	Description
SCEF	SCEF is an EPC function that securely exposes the servers and capabilities provided by 3GPP network interfaces. The SCEF supports the following exposure functions to NFs via SCEF and may be regulated based on the interacting NF, including third-party entities, application functions, enterprise IT, along with the User Interface (UI) representations. • Non-IP data delivery (NIDD) for low-power devices • Monitoring a device's state • Device triggering performs application-specific actions, including communication with the service capability server (SCS) • Enhanced coverage restriction control

II.2.1.3.4.10 Functional Group – Shared Spectrum Manager

Function	Description
SAS/AFC interworking	The spectrum access system (SAS) allows for managing the spectrum allocation to the individual eNB/gNB for operation. SAS functions will include the environmental sensing capability (ESC), a network of sensors used to detect federal frequency use in the 3.55–3.65 MHz band in protection zones where U.S. Navy radar systems can operate. AFC is a spectrum-use coordination system designed to mitigate interference in the 6 GHz band between unlicensed NR-U/Wi-Fi 6E and seven devices and the licensed users already occupying that band. It resembles similar systems in place, such as the one supporting CBRS wireless operation. NR-U is 5G NR unlicensed operation, and Wi-Fi 6E is the standard that defines 6 GHz use. Varying portions of the 6 GHz band for unlicensed use have been allocated by the individual countries. Vendors will align the SAS and AFC functions into a single platform for commercial deployments.

II.2.1.3.4.11 Functional Group – Secure Interworking Manager

Function	Description
SEPP	Security Edge Protection Proxy The SEPP is part of the roaming security architecture. The N32 interface is used between the SEPPs of a VPLMN and an HPLMN in roaming scenarios. This interface will also be used to interconnect NFs across CNs, including isolated functions within an operation and across operators.
BSF	The 5G BSF is comparable to the session binding function on the diameter routing agent (DRA) used in 4G. It becomes a mandatory requirement when multiple PCF systems are deployed in the network. Because the BSF enables the correlation of sessions across multiple policy servers, it provides operators with the ability to scale the network. The core function of the BSF is to track sessions located anywhere in the network but sharing common criteria such as subscriber identifiers. The BSF is a function that can be deployed stand-alone or can be the functionality provided by other NFs such as the PCF, UDR, NRF, and SMF. The BSF is specified in 3GPP TS 23.502, 3GPP TS 23.503, and TS 29.513 for key functions such as the following: • Finding the binding information (e.g. the address information of the selected PCF) • Allowing systems (e.g. PCF) to register, update, and remove the binding information • Allowing systems (e.g. AF, NEF) to discover the binding information (e.g. the address information of the selected PCF)

(Continued)

Function	Description
DRA	A DRA is a functional element in the LTE network that provides real-time routing capabilities to ensure that messages are routed among the correct elements in the network. The DRA was introduced by the 3GPP to address the increased diameter signaling traffic and the growing complexity of 4G LTE networks.
SCP	The SCP is a decentralized solution composed of a CP and a data plane. This solution is deployed alongside 5G NFs to provide routing control, resiliency, and observability to the CN. The SCP has a CP and a data plane. The SCP solution is deployed either as a default outbound proxy to NF instances or as a router model, where SCP is configured as an http2 outbound proxy at each NF in cloud-native environments. SCP provides the following benefits to the 5G CN architecture: • Improved load balancing • Routing control • Message priority assignment/override • Circuit breaking and outlier detection • Overload control • Observability

II.2.1.3.4.12 Functional Group – Metric Collection and Data Mining

With the advent of artificial intelligence (AI), applying machine learning concepts toward wireless network deployments is a natural step to take. The data can be collected from the network nodes and retrieved from the UE. See 3GPP TS 37.320 radio measurement collection for minimization of drive tests (MDT); overall description; stage 2, which describes the method of configuring the UE to accumulate specific types of information and allows for this information to be reported to the network.

See the section on O-RAN RAN intelligent controller (RIC) for an architectural description of the metrics collection and the employment of Artificial Intelligence (AI) to control the RAN network operations. Like the RAN, metrics can also be collected from the CN nodes, and based on the needs of the enterprise, specific AI applications can be developed.

There are many commonalities among enterprise private networks, and information collected from several networks can be used to train algorithms for application across campuses. This can be referred to as "crowdsourcing" across enterprise campuses. There are enterprise-specific behaviors that are required, and such customized learning becomes imperative for effective implementation. This can be termed "unit sourcing," where the learned information is applied only to a specific enterprise and potentially to a specific site within an enterprise.

Function	Description
NR metrics	This includes NR RAN gNB and 5GC CN metrics.
LTE metrics	This includes LTE RAN eNB and EPC CN metrics.
AI	AI employs numerous machine learning techniques, including: • History-based information (e.g. when handover transitions across specific cells repeatedly fail in a certain direction, it can be learned, and early triggering of handover can be initiated, or the parameters can be adjusted to mitigate such failures). • Training on various network operational parameters. • Application detection and collection of performance metrics specific to a given application.

Function	Description
	• Anomaly detection allows for recognizing patterns in the network and API usage and flags any usage that deviates from the identified normal patterns. One application of this approach is in security, where it is extremely critical to ensure the network is not used for illegal purposes. • Inferences are a more advanced use of the information collected. This goes beyond basic regression, classification, and deep learning algorithms, allowing for the prediction of potential events even before they occur.
Traffic steering	With the UE associated with multiple access technologies, it needs to determine the percentage of traffic being routed to the appropriate RAT, assuming the same IP is supported on the RATs. See 3GPP TS 24.193 "5G System"; "Access Traffic Steering, Switching and Splitting (ATSSS)"; and "Stage 3," which describes UE provisioning methods from the network to control the RAT transitions and usage by the UE. See the section on LTE/NR and Wi-Fi coexistence for more details.

Figure II.2.1.10 provides the recommended set of functions that need to be supported as part of a private enterprise converged CN.

Figure II.2.1.11 provides the recommended set of functions that need to be implemented in the converged core part of neutral host realization. Although the neutral host topic is discussed in an independent section, it is presented here so that the reader has continuity and a complete view represented. The reader can return to this section when reviewing the neutral host topic to further reinforce their understanding.

Table II.2.1.2 presents a summary of the individual NFs and the recommended support for enterprise private networks and neutral host networks.

II.2.1.4 Converged Core EPC to 5GC

This section discusses the functional evolution from EPC to 5GC. Some of the functions from EPC directly translate to 5GC, potentially regrouped to better address the SBA and CUPS architecture.

With the converged core, even the EPC functions can be realized as SBA + CUPS. Figure II.2.1.12 illustrates the traditional EPC architecture that was the model used in the legacy and most of the currently deployed macro network operator networks. With the enterprise campus private networks being greenfield deployments, the EPC can be deployed using the CUPS architecture. The EPC realization with CUPS is shown in Figure II.2.1.13.

The integration of the control and UP functions for an EPC and 5GC converged core realization is illustrated in Figure II.2.1.14. The MME and PGW-C functions from EPC are redistributed into the AMF and SMF functions in 5GC. The UP function of PGW-U from EPC is supported using the UPF in 5GC. The SGW function, both control and UP, from EPC is no longer needed for 5GC, given the distributed architecture of the UPF, which supports the intermediate-UPF and anchor-UPF, allowing for a scalable deployment with 5GC. The user credentials supported in HSS in EPC are supported by UDM in 5GC. Apart from the secure storage of the credentials, 5GC supports a stronger key hierarchy definition and management, including support for concealed identification as part of the over-the-air authentication. The security-related details are captured in an independent section of the book.

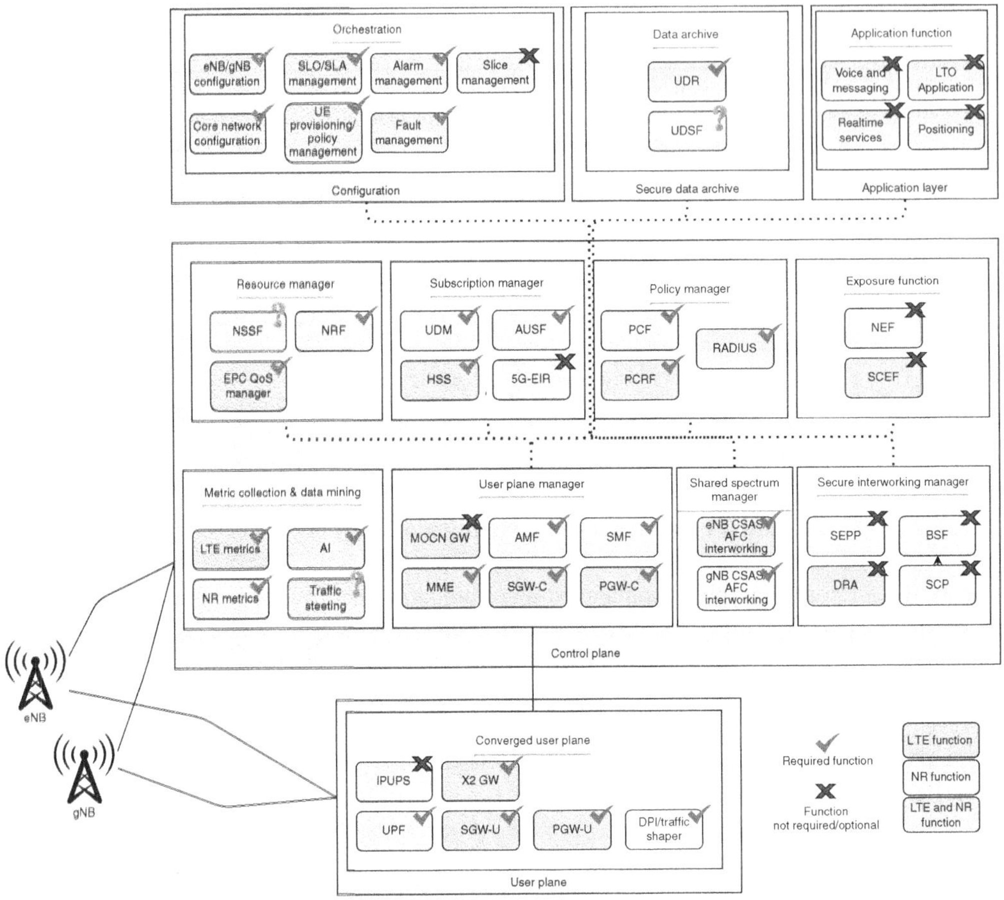

Figure II.2.1.10 Converged core – EPC and 5GC converged core for a private network.

Figure II.2.1.15 provides a pictorial view of the NF transitions from EPC to 5GC. The functional responsibilities of the individual nodes in EPC are called out, and the transitions of these functions to the 5GC are identified.

The EPC-MME functions of system camping, UE authentication, and mobility across the radio access nodes are captured by the AMF in 5GC. The session management aspects of the EPC-MME are handled by the 5GC SMF, and the AMF simply acts as a pass-through between the UE and SMF. The AMF, similar to the MME, performs UE authentication, NAS ciphering, and integrity protection algorithms. This precedes the UE authorization process, in which the 5G core SBA UDM function supersedes the HSS. This is performed over the N8 reference interface and, therefore, employs the HTTP/2 service-based interface (SBI) message bus. The AMF also connects with the LI systems and provides the plug-ins required to tap into the network for detection.

Based on the size and the geographic distribution of the enterprise network, it is possible that there are several AMF instances, with each AMF instance identified using a globally unique AMF identifier (GUAMI). The UE uses this identifier in the first NAS message it sends, which is routed to the required AMF by the RAN. This GUAMI can be used for both 3GPP and non-3GPP access. The GUAMI also ensures that messages from a UE registered through both ANs are forwarded to

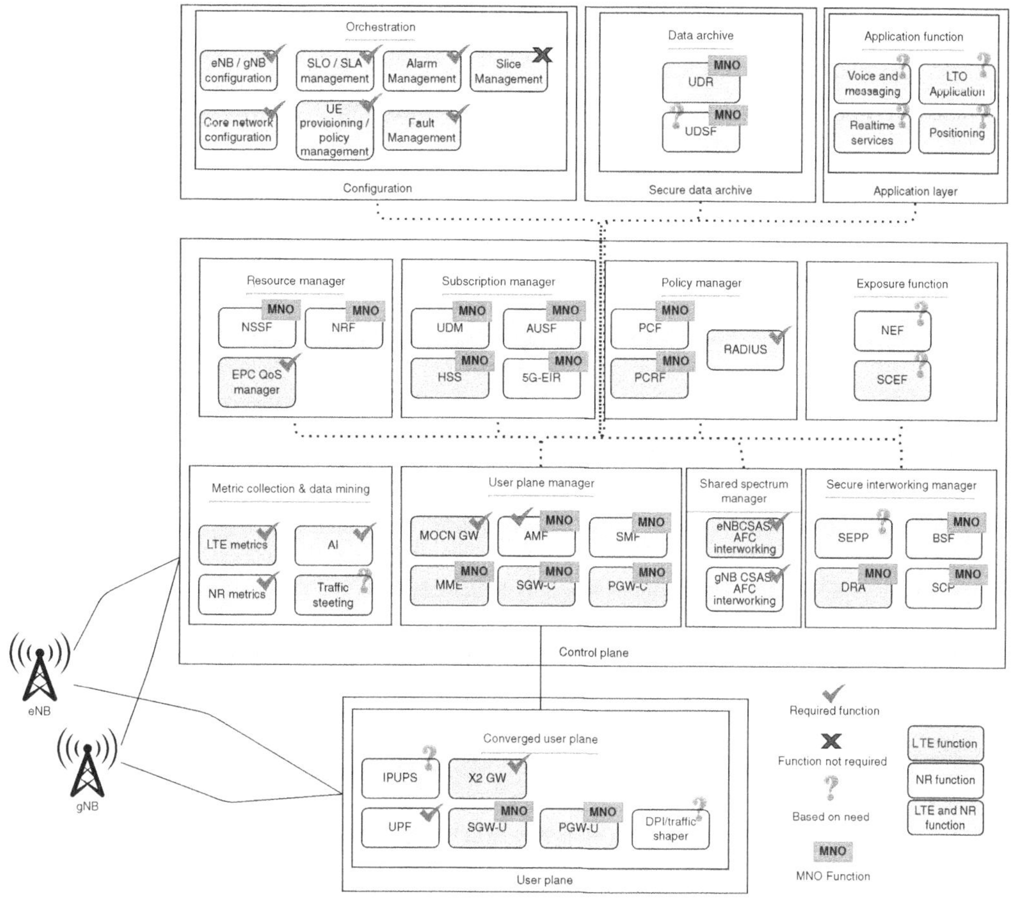

Figure II.2.1.11 Converged core – EPC and 5GC converged core for a neutral host network.

the same AMF. The non-3GPP interworking function (N3IWF) is responsible for routing messages for untrusted network access.

AMF supports inter-NR gNB handovers over the Xn interface (supported between gNBs) or over the N2/N3 interface (using AMF to reflect the messaging between gNBs). Handovers between LTE eNBs are supported over the X2 interface (supported between gNBs) or over the S1-C/S1-U interface (using MME to reflect the messaging between eNBs). The NR-updated reference interface application protocol (XnAP) employed between gNB base stations is defined in 3GPP TS 38.423.

The signal quality and the packet error rate performance are continuously monitored on the UL by the gNB/eNB, and the DL channel quality information is reported from the UE to the gNB/eNB. When the source node detects that a handover is required, it connects with the target gNB/eNB to commence the switching process. Once the tunnels have been moved across to the target gNB/eNB, the UE performs a handover and connects to that same target node. A path switch request is made from the target gNB/eNB to the AMF/MME, and once acknowledged, the data can flow from the UE through that target node and onto the prescribed UPF/SWG and PGW.

Figure II.2.1.16 provides the nodes and functions associated with UE authentication in EPC and 5GC. 5GC supports deeper key derivation and ephemeral transition keys that further protect the UE and network from being hacked.

Table II.2.1.2 Summary recommendations for 5GC modular components and functional support requirements.

Module	Functions	Support for private network	Support for neutral host
Orchestration	eNB/gNB configuration	Required	Required
	SLO/SLA management	Required	Required
	CN configuration	Required	N/A
	UE provisioning/policy management	Required	Partial
	Slice management	Required	Required
	Alarm management	Required	Required
	Fault management	Required	Required
Information archive	UDR	Required	Required
	UDSF	Optional	In MNO core
	UDC	Not required	In MNO core
	MicroSlice and policies manager	Required	Required
Enterprise application function	SMSF	Not required	Not required
	Real-time service	Supported by campus-based services	Not required
Resource manager	NSSF	Required	Required
	NRF	Required	Required
	EPC microslice manager	Required	Required
Subscription manager	UDM	Required	In MNO core
	AUSF	Required	In MNO core
	HSS	Required	In MNO core
	5G-EIR	Optional	In MNO core
Policy controller	PCF	Required	In MNO core
	PCRF	Required	In MNO core
Exposure function	NEF	TBD	TBD
	SCEF	TBD	TBD
Metric collection/data mining	NR metrics	Required	Required
	LTE metrics	Required	Required
	AI	Required	Required
	Traffic steering	Not immediate requirement	TBD
User plane manager	MOCN GW	Not required	Required
	AMF	Required	In MNO core
	SMF	Required	In MNO core
	MME	Required	In MNO core
	PGW-C	Required	In MNO core
	SGW-C	Required	In MNO core

Table II.2.1.2 (Continued)

Module	Functions	Support for private network	Support for neutral host
Domain proxy	eNB CSAS interworking	Required	Required
	gNB CSAS interworking	Required	Required
Secure interworking manager	SEPP	Not required	Maybe, based on the inter-PLMN roaming requirements
	BSF	Not required	Up to MNO core implementation
	DRA	Required	Required
	SCP	Not required	Up to MNO core implementation
Unified user plane	IPUPS	Not required	Depends on the choice of roaming architecture
	UPF	Required	Required
	X2GW	Required	Required
	SGW-U	Required	In MNO core
	PGW-U	Required	In MNO core
	DPI/traffic shaper	TBD	Required

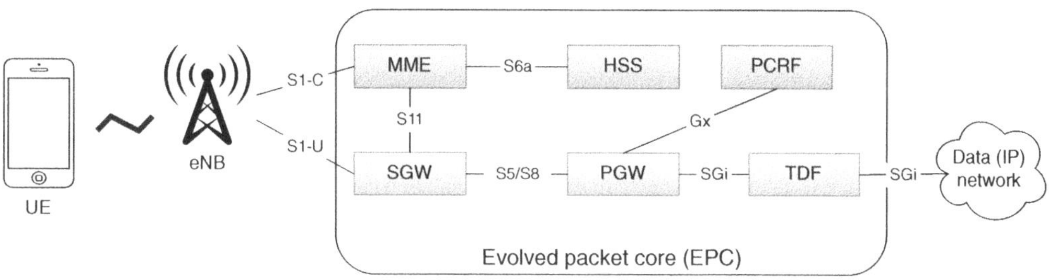

Figure II.2.1.12 Converged core – EPC before CUPS.

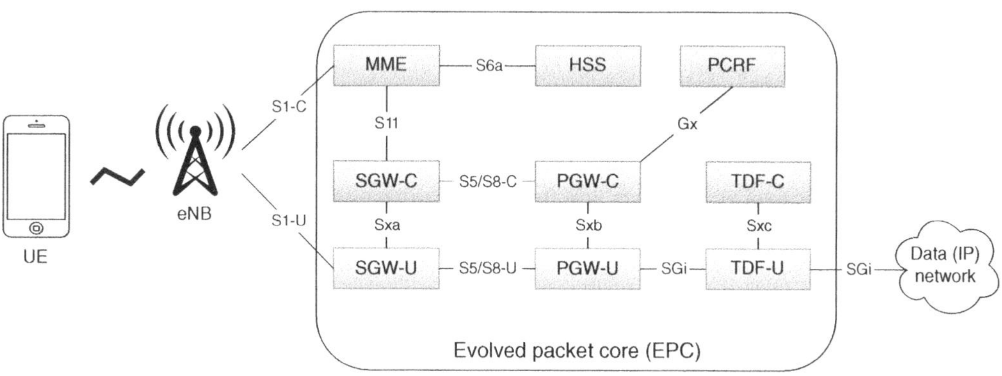

Figure II.2.1.13 Converged core – EPC after CUPS.

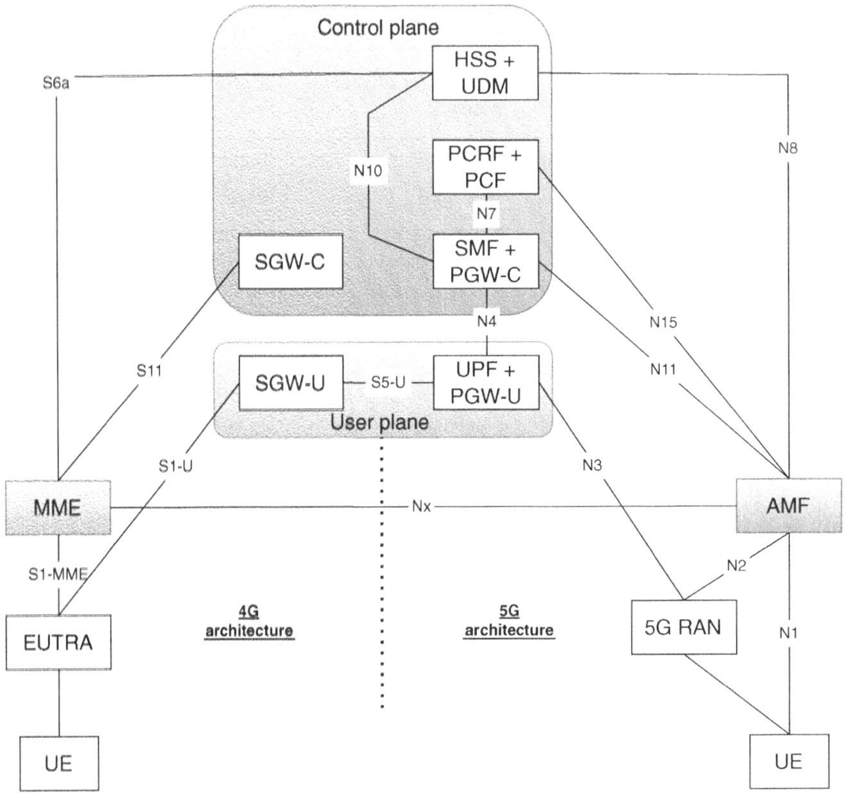

Figure II.2.1.14 Converged core – CUPS evolution to 5G architecture.

Figure II.2.1.17 provides an illustration of a network slice implementation with two network slices involved. The UE accesses the network through a common AMF. The UE is subscribed to one or more network slices and indicates that to the network. Each network slice is typically supported in an independent IP domain. With the session management supported by the SMF and the UPF associated with the IP domain of operation, these functions are independently supported in the individual network slice instance. The associated NFs of the DN, which provide the IP address assignment, the NRF to interconnect the slice-specific NFs, and the slice-specific policies supported by the PCF are also supported independently in each slice instance.

Figure II.2.1.18 provides that the policy functions are deployed in 5GC. The figure shows the EPC and 5GC functions, with the PCRF in EPC and PCF in 5GC integrated into a single functional node. In EPC, the PGW-C interfaces with the PCRF to determine the policies to be supported. In 5GC, the policy functions are handled by the CP entities by both the AMF and SMF functions. The Access Network Discovery and Selection Policy (ANDSP) supports the provisioning of the UE to provide information on applications and flows that can transition across 3GPP (LTE/NR) and non-3GPP (Wi-Fi) access technologies.

II.2.1.4.1 Packet Forwarding with N4 Interface

The N4 interface between the SMF and UPF in the 5GC supports the packet forwarding control protocol (PFCP). The SMF manages the packet forwarding rules by adding, modifying, or deleting

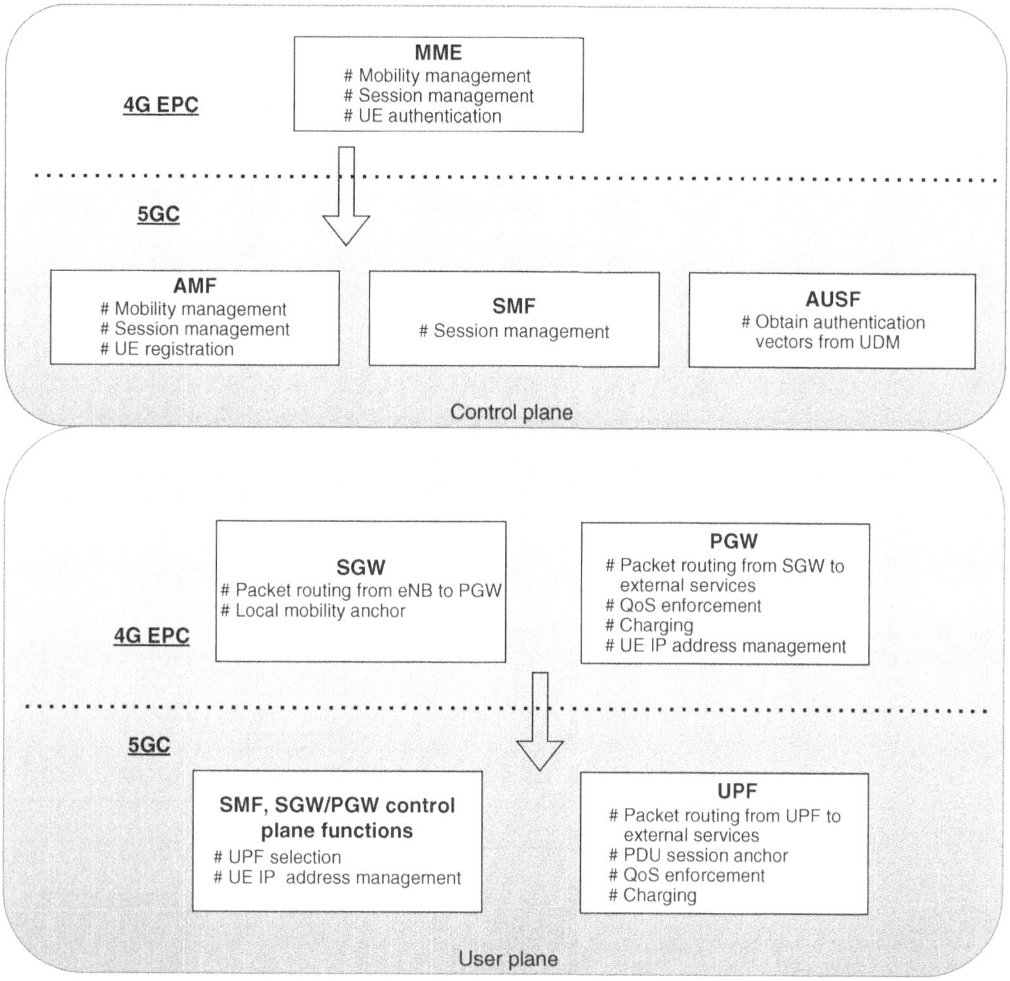

Figure II.2.1.15 Converged core – the evolution of control and user plane functions from EPC to 5GC.

Packet Detection Rule (PDRs), Forwarding Action Rules (FARs), QoS Enforcement Rules (QERs), Usage Reporting Rules (URRs), Buffering Action Rules (BARs), and/or multi-access rules (MARs), and by activating or deactivating predefined PDRs, FARs, QERs, and URRs.

Figure II.2.1.19 provides an illustration of the breakdown of the function involved in the packet forwarding on N4 interface. The Table II.2.1.3 captures a description of the functions involved in the packet forwarding management on the N4 interface.

II.2.1.5 Summary

This section introduces the network architecture of LTE/EPC. The concept of SBA and CUPS is introduced, and with that, the evolution and structure of the 5G NR/5GC are presented. The radio interworking and simultaneous operation of LTE and NR, along with the associated stand-alone, NSA, and dual-connectivity options, are covered. Additionally, the need for convergence with the EPC and 5GC is discussed, particularly regarding greenfield deployments

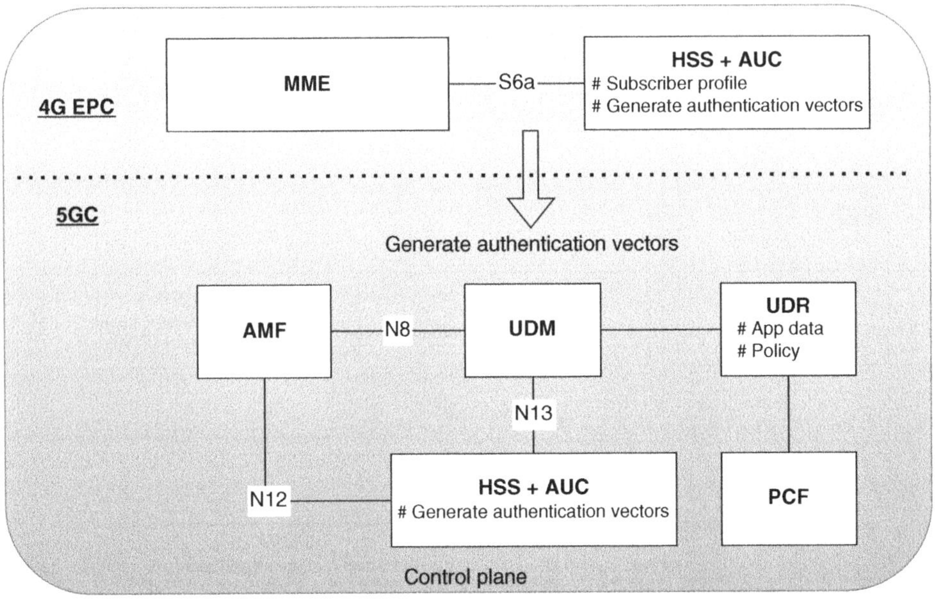

Figure II.2.1.16 Converged core – EPC to 5GC authentication.

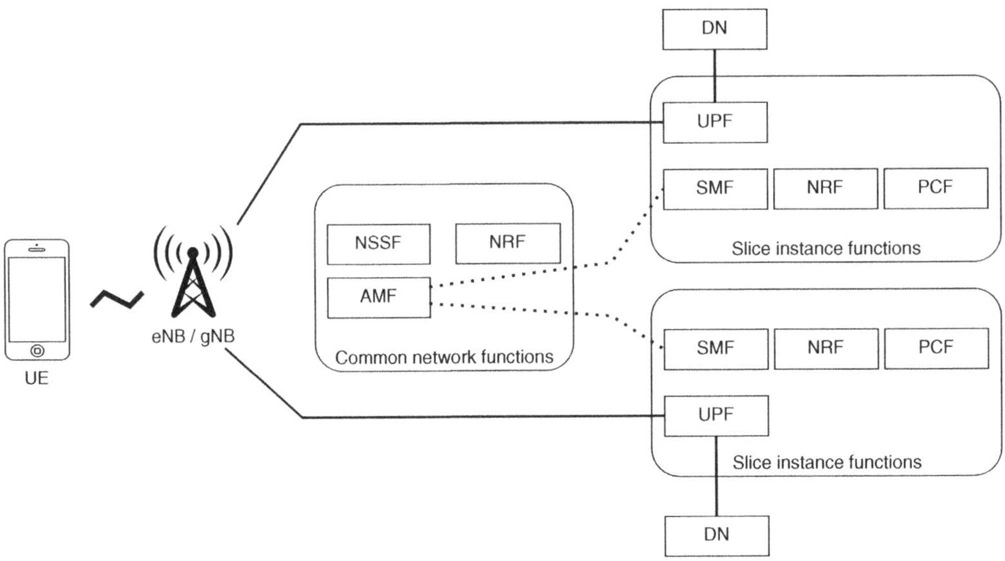

Figure II.2.1.17 Converged core – 5GC network slice.

with enterprise private networks using LTE and NR. The typical function needed for a converged core is discussed, identifying the functional groups involved. The NFs from EPC and 5GC associated with each converged core functional grouping are discussed, introducing the individual NFs. The typical/recommended set of NFs needed for a private enterprise network is presented. Along similar lines, the NFs required for a neutral host are also discussed. The

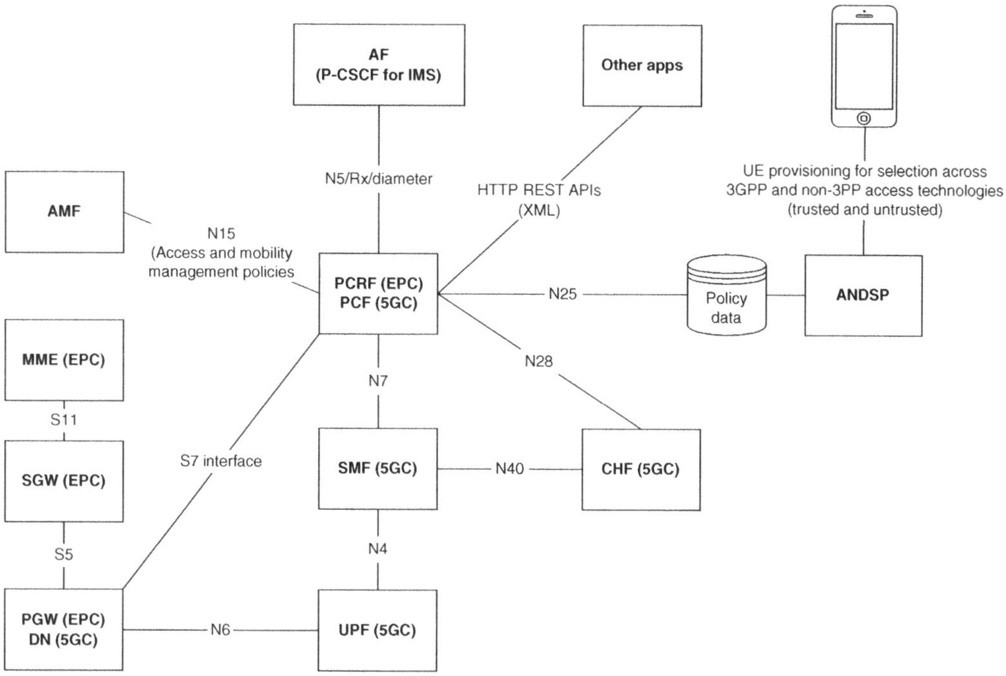

Figure II.2.1.18 Converged core – EPC to 5GC policy management.

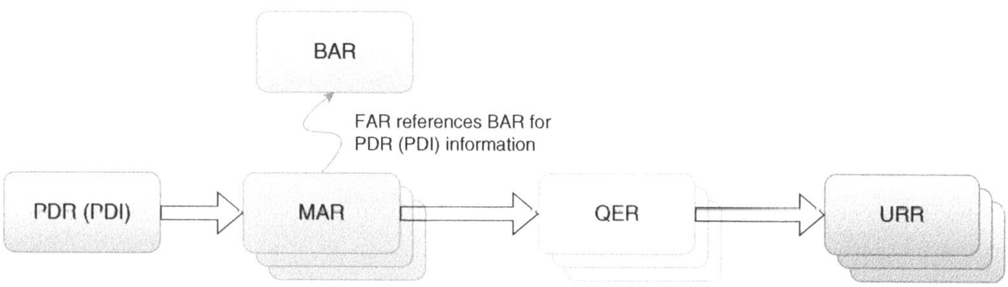

Figure II.2.1.19 Packet forwarding on N4.

typical EPC NFs are considered, and the evolution of these functions, along with the groups and roles of the 5GC NFs, is discussed.

With this, the reader should have a reasonable grasp of the EPC and 5GC CN functions involved and the aspects that need to be considered for a converged CN design, development, and deployment.

Table II.2.1.3 Packet forwarding management on the N4 interface.

PFCP function	Description
Multi-access rule (MAR)	Zero, one, or more MAR (ATSSS) (access traffic steering, switching, splitting) • Intended for multi-technology access • Not required for now • Software architecture needs to be accommodated for the longer term
Forwarding Action Rule (FAR)	One or more FARs • (forward, duplicate, drop, or buffer the packet) • (with or without notifying the CP) • Reference BAR • (Apply action)
Buffering Action Rule (BAR)	Zero, one, or more BAR • Provisioned at the PFCP session level and referenced by the FAR • Requires UP to support the feature UL/DL Buffering Control (UDBC) • UPF notifies the SMF when it receives the first DL packet for a given FAR identifying the packet detection rules (PDRs) with the packet detection information (PDI) – Allows paging policy differentiation from the SMF by setting the paging policy indicator (PPI)
QoS Enforcement Rule (QER)	Zero, one, or more QER • QoS Enforcement Rule Correlation ID → assigned to QERs • Reflective QoS marking • We will need to support this feature – for EPC: ○ at the session level (APN-AMBR, TDF session UL and DL bit rates, or UL and DL packet rate of a PDN connection) ○ at the bearer level (GBR, MBR for GBR bearers) ○ at the SDF or application level – for 5GC: ○ at the session level (session-AMBR or UL and DL packet rate of a PDU session) ○ at the QoS flow level ○ at the SDF or application level – Functions include ○ creating PDR(s) ▪ service data flow ▪ application ▪ QoS flow (for 5GC) ▪ bearer or session ○ creating QERs at the SDF/application level ○ creating QERs as an aggregate of SDFs with the same GBR QCI ○ creating QERs as an aggregate of SDFs with the same GBR QFI (for 5GC) ○ associating QER with PDRs ○ associating SDF or application QER with PDRs ○ associating the QER of the aggregate of SDFs with the PDRs associated with SDFs or applications that share the QER
Usage Reporting Rule (URR)	Zero, one, or more URR • measure the network resources usage in terms of traffic data volume, duration (i.e. time), and/or events, according to the provisioned measurement method • reports are sent to CP-based on thresholds, periodically, or immediately.

References

Standards and Specifications from 3GPP:

[1] *3GPP TS 23.501: System Architecture for the 5G System (5GS).*

Description: This standard outlines the architecture of the 5G Core (5GC) network, including the key principles of convergence with 4G networks. It describes how both the EPC and 5GC can interoperate, enabling backward compatibility and efficient resource usage.
Key Topics: Dual Connectivity (4G and 5G), non-standalone (NSA) operation, standalone (SA) operation, Service-Based Architecture (SBA).
Version: Continuously updated with new releases.
Access: 3GPP Website

[2] *3GPP TS 23.502: Procedures for the 5G System.*

Description: This specification defines the procedures and workflows for services in the 5G Core (5GC) network, including interactions with the EPC. It covers mobility management, session management, and QoS control between the two core networks.
Key Topics: Mobility management, interworking with EPC, service continuity, and multi-access edge computing (MEC).
Access: 3GPP Website

[3] *3GPP TR 23.700-20: Study on Architecture Enhancements for 5G System to Support Converged 5G Core Network.*

Description: This study focuses on the evolution of the converged core, covering new use cases and services enabled by combining 5GC and EPC functionalities. It discusses enhancements to optimize the network for a variety of devices and access technologies.
Key Topics: Converged core enhancements, use case-driven architecture changes, multi-access technologies.
Access: 3GPP Website

Research Papers on 3GPP Converged Core Network:

[4] Harri Holma, Antti Toskala, Klaus I. Pedersen (2019). Towards a Converged 5G Core Network: Challenges and Opportunities. *IEEE Communications Standards Magazine.*

Summary: This paper discusses the technical and operational challenges in developing a converged 5G core network. It covers dual connectivity, non-standalone architecture, and the Service-Based Architecture (SBA) that allows for a flexible, modular design.
Key Topics: Converged core architecture, SBA, dual connectivity.
Link: IEEE Xplore

[5] Shaolin Xu, Qiang Liu, Yi Luo (2020). 5G Core Network: Design Considerations and Deployment Challenges. *IEEE Network.*

Summary: The authors focus on the design and deployment issues of the 5G core network and how it interacts with the 4G EPC. The paper details challenges such as interworking, backward compatibility, and resource optimization in a converged environment.
Key Topics: 5GC design, EPC interworking, backward compatibility.
Link: IEEE Xplore

[6] R. Li, X. Zhao, Y. Gao, et al. (2020). Converged Core for Multi-Access Edge Computing in 5G Networks. *IEEE Access.*

Summary: This paper presents a framework for integrating the 5GC with MEC platforms, enabling low-latency services at the edge of the network. It discusses the interaction between MEC and the converged core to support real-time applications.
Key Topics: Multi-Access Edge Computing (MEC), converged core, low-latency services.
Link: IEEEXplore

[7] Khaled Salah, Elhadj Benkhelifa, et al. (2021). EPC and 5GC Interworking in 5G Networks: Architecture and Performance. *IEEE Transactions on Network and Service Management.*

Summary: This paper studies the interworking mechanisms between the EPC and the 5GC, focusing on the transition from 4G to 5G networks. It evaluates performance metrics such as latency, throughput, and signaling overhead.
Key Topics: EPC-5GC interworking, performance metrics, signaling overhead.
Link: IEEEXplore

[8] Tao Chen, Xiaoming Fu, Riccardo Trivisonno, et al. (2021). 5G and Beyond: A Survey on Converged Core Architectures and Technologies. *IEEE Communications Surveys & Tutorials.*

Summary: This paper provides a detailed survey of converged core network architectures, examining how different access technologies (4G, 5G, Wi-Fi) can be integrated into a single core. It reviews technological enablers such as NFV, SDN, and network slicing.
Key Topics: Converged core architectures, SDN, NFV, network slicing.
Link: IEEEXplore

[9] Susana Sargento, Javier Ramos, et al. (2020). Deployment Models for 5G Converged Core Networks: Challenges and Opportunities. *IEEE Communications Magazine.*

Summary: This paper explores deployment strategies for converged core networks, examining centralized, distributed, and hybrid models. It discusses the pros and cons of each model in terms of scalability, flexibility, and latency.
Key Topics: Deployment models, centralized vs. distributed architecture, scalability.
Link: IEEEXplore

Additional Resources:

[10] *NGMN 5G White Papers: The Next Generation Mobile Networks (NGMN) Alliance* publishes white papers and reports that often discuss the convergence of 4G and 5G core networks, especially from a practical deployment perspective. NGMN Resources.

[11] *ETSI Reports on NFV: The European Telecommunications Standards Institute (ETSI)* focuses heavily on Network Function Virtualization (NFV), which is a critical enabler of the 3GPP converged core. ETSI NFV Resources.

II.2.2

Network Interfaces

II.2.2.1 Introduction

This section discusses the network interfaces between the different functions, including the Radio Access Network (RAN) nodes and evolved packet core (EPC) and 5G core (5GC). These are 3GPP standards-defined interfaces. From an enterprise private network realization perspective, these interfaces typically follow the guidelines provided in the standards, subject to modifications and customization for ease of deployments in the enterprise networks.

The LTE/EPC and 5G NR/5GC are discussed independently. However, as described in the "Converged Core" section, the network functions (NFs) and interfaces are integrated for a combined implementation while retaining the integrity of the individual interfaces. A brief description of the interfaces is also presented in the "Converged Core" section. This section focuses on the protocol stack used for information exchange across the interfaces.

II.2.2.2 LTE Network Interfaces

The RAN node in Long Term Evolution (LTE) is the evolved node-B (eNB). The eNBs connect with the EPC, which includes the NF MME, Home Subscriber Server (HSS), Serving Gateway (SGW), and Packet Gateway (PGW). For a more detailed description, refer to the 3GPP TS 23.401 specification.

The eNB interacts with the EPC core, communicating with the two nodes MME and SGW. In Figure II.2.2.1, S1-C and S1-U interfaces provide the connections between the eNB and the EPC core network.

S1-C is the control interface between the eNB and MME. The S1 application protocol (S1-AP) is the application layer protocol between the eNodeB and MME. The stream control transmission protocol (SCTP) provides reliable delivery of signaling messages between the MME and eNodeB (S1). SCTP is defined in IETF RFC 4960. SCTP inherently offers improved performance over Transmission Control Protocol (TCP), which suffers from head-of-line blocking, lacks multihoming support for reliability, and is prone to denial of service (DoS) attacks, for example Synchronize (SYN) flooding. SCTP supports multiple logical streams and allows for message ordering within each stream, making it a better protocol to use for telecommunications inter-node communication in the network. SCTP supports a four-way handshake to prevent DoS attacks, supports message framing to prevent fragmentation of messages, supports reliable message delivery, allows for

Mobile Communication Systems for Private Networks, First Edition. Srinivasan Balasubramanian.

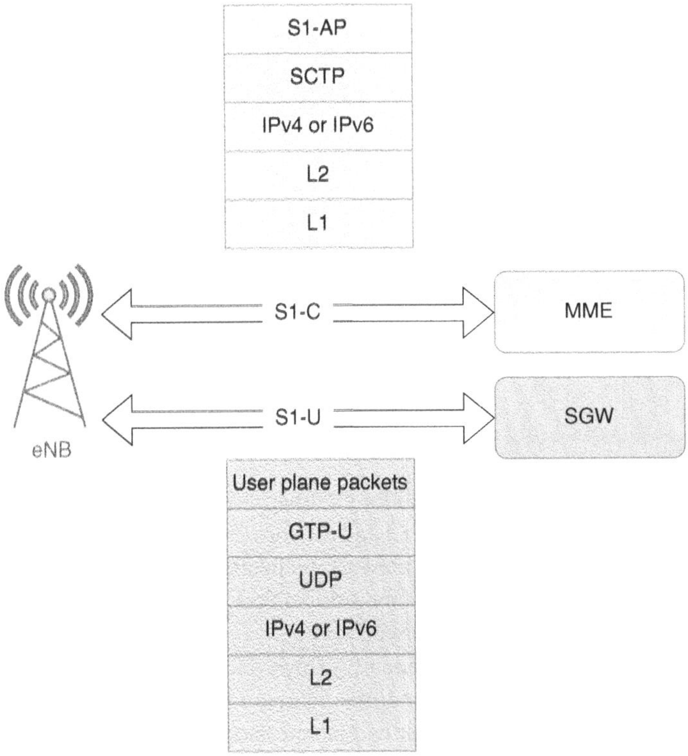

Figure II.2.2.1 S1-C and S1-U interfaces.

out-of-order delivery for better prioritization, and enables graceful shutdown that avoids half-closed connections.

S1-U is the user plane (UP) interface between the eNB and SGW. The GTP-U is used for carrying user data between the radio access network and the core network. The user data is transported using user datagram protocol (UDP) and can be carried in IPv4, IPv6, or Point to Point Protocol (PPP) formats. The UPs are prioritized by the routers based on the differentiated services code point (DSCP) marking, which, in turn, depends on the end-to-end quality of service (QoS) prioritization of the different IP flows.

In Figure II.2.2.2, signaling radio bearer (SRB) connectivity between RAN and EPC depicts the association that is established to carry radio signaling traffic. The SRB carries the Radio Resource Control (RRC) and non-access stratum (NAS) signaling messages over the air. These signaling messages must be treated with higher priority regarding reliability and latency. Associated with each user equipment (UE), there are explicit bearer and association identifiers that are created when the UE connects with the network. The signaling packets at the MME for a given UE are identified with the MME UE S1AP identifier and mapped to a corresponding identifier at the eNB with the eNB UE S1AP identifier. Once established, the signaling packets are exchanged between the eNB and MME using these identifiers and are used at the RAN to provide the appropriate scheduler treatment and to identify the UE association at the MME.

Figure II.2.2.3 shows the S11 interface between the MME and SGW, which is a control interface reference point between the MME and serving Gateway (GW). GTP-C is the protocol that tunnels signaling messages between the MME and SGW. UDP is used to transfer signaling messages

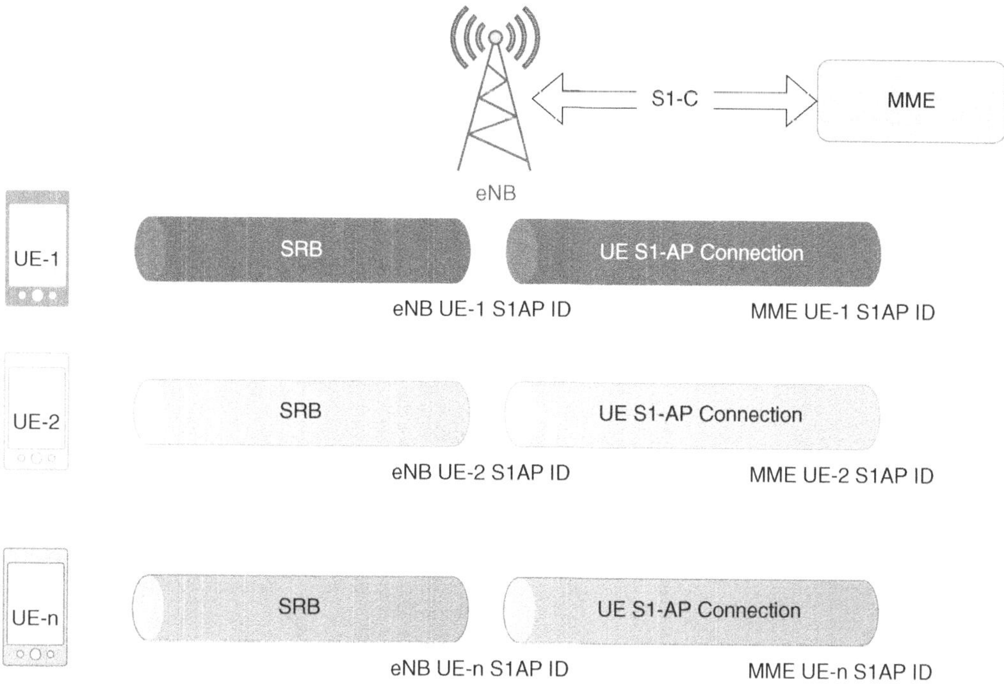

Figure II.2.2.2 Signaling radio bearer (SRB) connectivity between the RAN and the EPC.

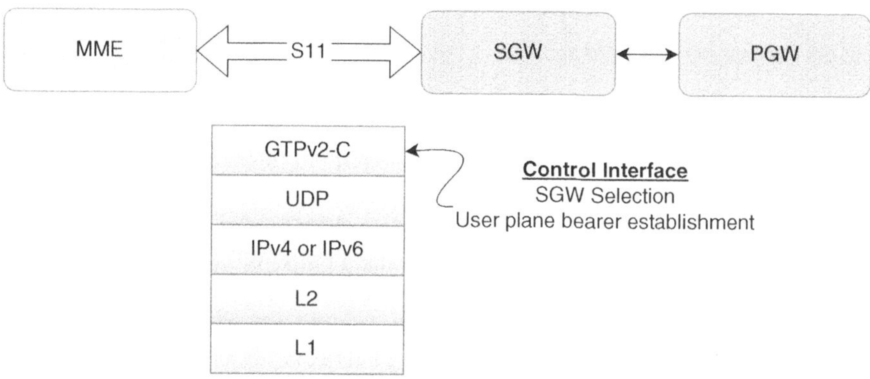

Figure II.2.2.3 S11 interface between MME and SGW.

between the MME and SGW, as defined in RFC 768. UDP itself is an unreliable protocol that allows for avoiding any latency in communication between the nodes. GPRS tunneling protocol (GTP) is used to provide the required reliability in the information exchange between the nodes.

In Figure II.2.2.4, the S5/S8 interface between the SGW and PGW is the user data exchange interface. The IP address is anchored at the PGW. The downlink (DL) packets are forwarded to the serving gateway (SGW), which is a node closer to the eNB and supports flow control functions to deliver adequate packets to the eNB, accommodating the UE's mobility across the eNBs.

The S5 interface provides UP tunneling and tunnel management between the SGW and PGW. This interface is used to associate with the appropriate SGW based on the UE's current eNB

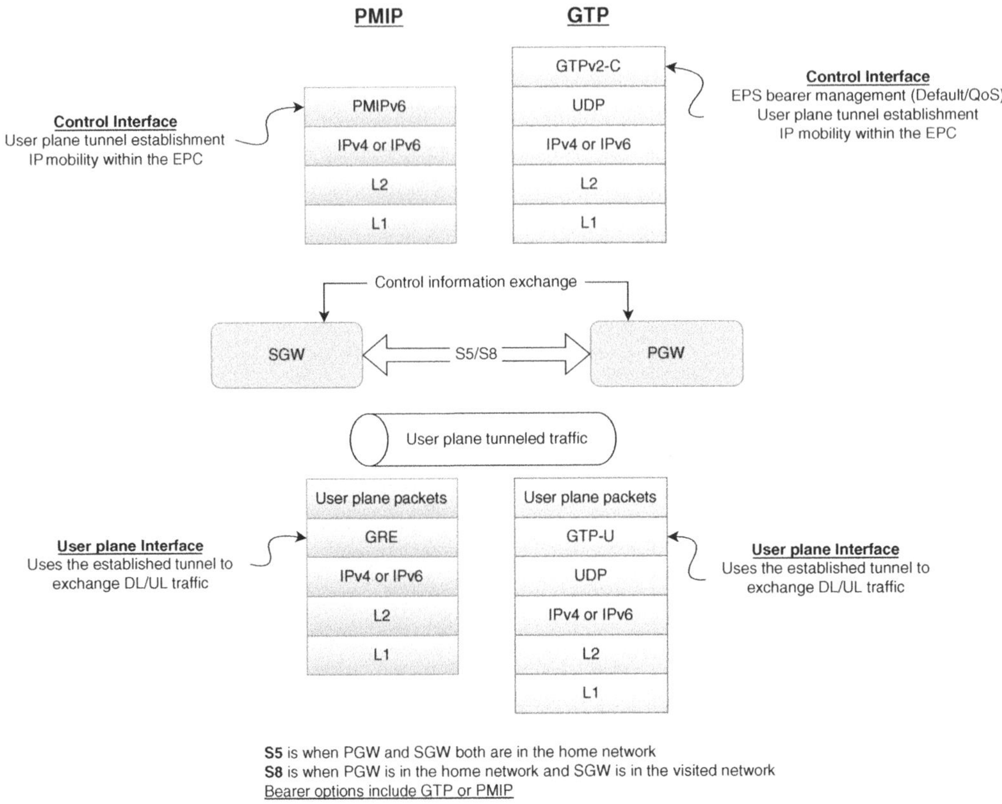

Figure II.2.2.4 S5/S8 interface between SGW and PGW.

association and to transition the SGW based on the UE's mobility in the network. Note that the PGW is typically not collocated with the SGW.

The S8 serves the same purpose as S5, except that it is an inter-PLMN reference point providing user and control plane functions between the SGW in the visited PLMN (VPLMN) and the PGW in the home PLMN (HPLMN). Although it was intended for inter-PLMN roaming scenarios, with more than one enterprise potentially using the same Public Land Mobile Network (PLMN), the S8 interface is used when the IP anchor (PGW) is in a different network from the currently serving network of the UE. For example the user may be visiting an enterprise while their subscription belongs to another enterprise.

Both the proxy mobile IP (PMIP) and GTP versions of the protocol stacks are illustrated. GTP is defined by 3GPP specifications. Only one of the two is employed at a time. The enterprise network deployment mainly uses GTP, given the size of the enterprises being small compared to the country-wide large macro networks. The GTP-C protocol tunnels signaling messages between the SGW and PGW. UDP transfers signaling messages between the SGW and PGW. UDP is defined in IETF RFC 768. There are differences in the capabilities of the two protocols. GTP supports bearer tunnel management, IP mobility management (MM), QoS signaling, and UP forwarding through tunneling. PMIP supports IP MM and packet forwarding through generic route encapsulation (GRE) but does not support QoS signaling. GRE is defined by the Internet Engineering Task Force (IETF). One key difference between GTP and GRE is that GTP uses individual bearers for each

Evolved Packet System (EPS) bearer (end-to-end QoS bearer that includes dedicated radio bearer [DRB] and IP QoS flow(s) in the packet core network), while GRE uses a single tunnel for all EPS bearers. Note that there is UE-based IP mobility based on dual-stack mobile IPv6 (DSMIPv6) and client mobile IP (CMIP) supported in the 3GPP standards. This has not gained traction with the 3GPP deployments, and one of the network-based solutions, either PMIP or GTP, is employed, given that this provides the required control in the network for supporting IP mobility, improves performance for the UE, and avoids fragmentation of solutions in the market, with different UEs having differing capabilities.

Note that tunneling is employed to allow traffic to be routed through specific processing gateways and to allow for specific nodes where traffic monitoring can be performed.

In Figure II.2.2.5, S6a interface between MME and HSS is a control signaling interface used to access the user credential information for user access verification. It enables the transfer of subscription and authentication data for authenticating and authorizing user access to the evolved system (Authentication Authorization and Accounting (AAA) interface) between MME and HSS. The diameter protocol supports the transfer of subscription and authentication data for authenticating and authorizing user access to the evolved system between MME and HSS (S6a). Diameter is defined in RFC 3588. The SCTP allows for reliable transfer of signaling messages. SCTP is defined in RFC 4960. Note that DIAMETER is an evolution of the remote authentication dial-in user service (RADIUS) protocol and supports several enhancements over the RADIUS protocol. RADIUS is actively used in enterprise networks to authenticate users for wireline and Wi-Fi connectivity. The LTE (and NR) system is designed to use the DIAMETER protocol, which offers additional protection compared to the RADIUS protocol. DIAMETER supports flexible options for interconnectivity and routing, supports four types of agents—relay, proxy, redirect, or translation—allows for further extensions for future compatibility, and supports improved roaming across operator/enterprise networks. For any coexistence between the LTE/NR and Wi-Fi networks, some form of integration between the HSS/UDM and enterprise RADIUS service is needed.

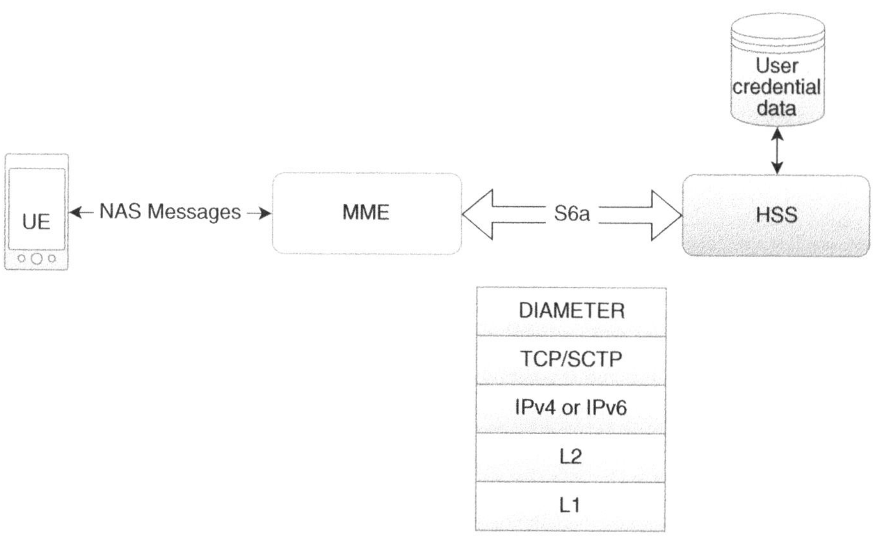

Figure II.2.2.5 S6a interface between MME and HSS.

In Figure II.2.2.6, the LTE interface signaling information exchange provides a summary view of the interfaces and the associated protocol stacks for exchanging signaling information across the eNB and EPC nodes.

In Figure II.2.2.7 the LTE interface UP data exchange provides a summary view of the interfaces and the associated protocol stacks for exchanging UP traffic across the eNB and EPC nodes.

In Figure II.2.2.8 the S13 interface between the Mobility Management Entity (MME) and Equipment Identity Register (EIR) enables device identification and is used to detect stolen and illicit devices and prevent access to the enterprise network. The diameter protocol supports the UE identity check procedure between the MME and EIR. Diameter is defined in RFC 3588. SCTP provides reliable transfer of signaling messages. SCTP is defined in RFC 4960.

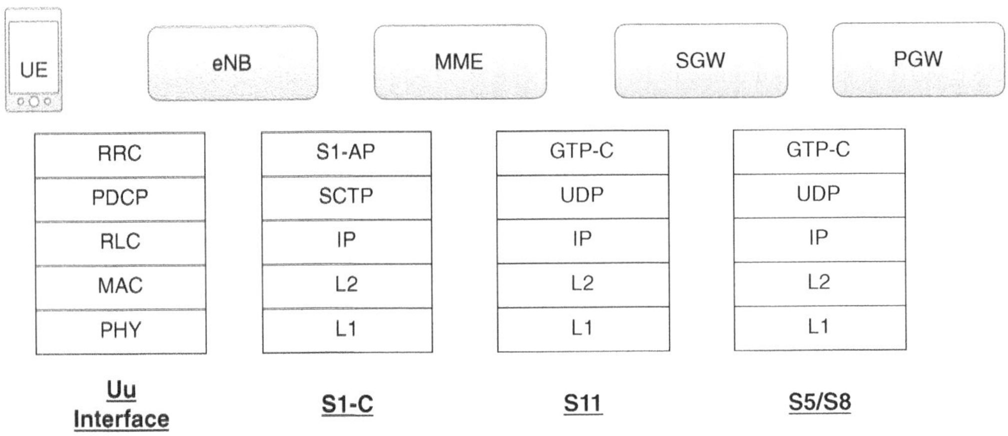

Figure II.2.2.6 Summary view of the LTE interface signaling information exchange.

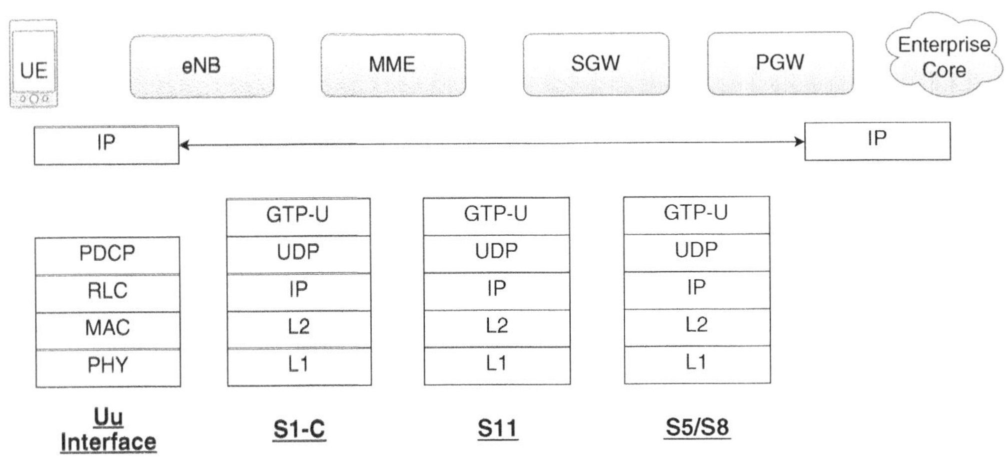

Figure II.2.2.7 Summary view of the LTE interface user plane (UP) data exchange.

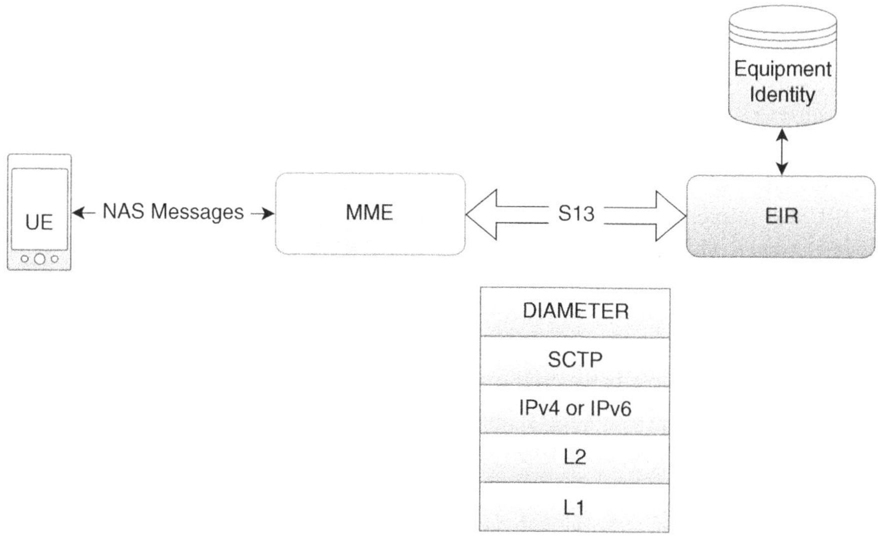

Figure II.2.2.8 S13 interface between the MME and the EIR.

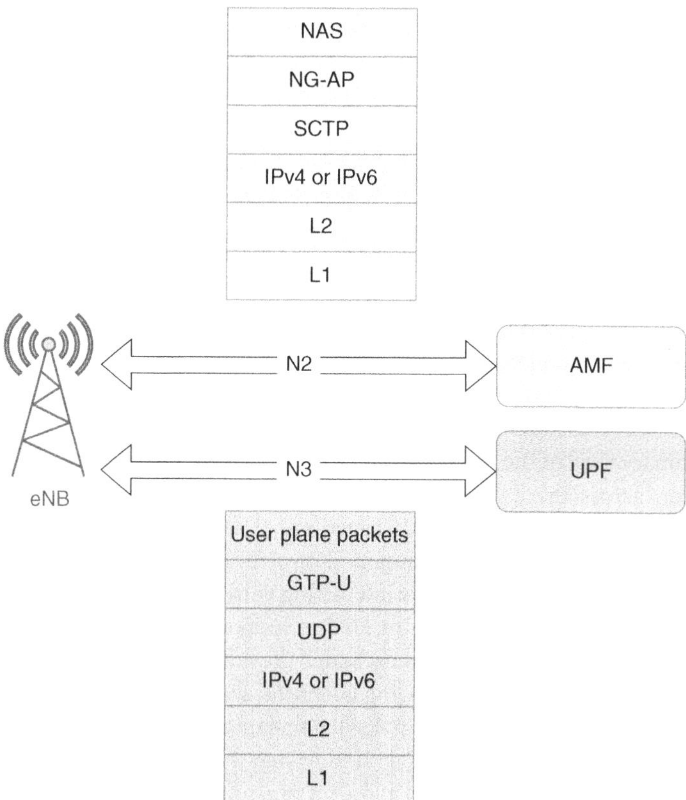

Figure II.2.2.9 N2 and N3 interfaces.

II.2.2.3 5G Protocol Stack

The 5G system, as a service-based architecture (SBA), includes a set of NFs providing services as defined in 3GPP standards. Although the SBA methodology was proposed and defined for the later stages of the LTE/EPC standardization effort, given that these network deployments were fairly entrenched and established in the market, these concepts did not gain market traction and had to wait for the 5G NR/5GC implementations. With the advent of enterprise private networks, even LTE/EPC deployments were greenfield, and similar techniques were used for both LTE/EPC and 5G NR/5GC deployment. In fact this approach allowed for an simple realization of a converged core.

The gNB interacts with the 5G core, talking to the two nodes, Access and Mobility Management Function (AMF) and User Plane Function (UPF). In Figure II.2.2.8 the S13 interface between the MME and EIR provides the interfaces between the gNB and the 5GC core network.

N2 is the control interface between the gNB and AMF. Next-generation application protocol (NG-AP) is the application layer protocol between the gNodeB and AMF. SCTP provides reliable delivery of signaling messages between the AMF and gNodeB on the N2 interface. SCTP is defined in IETF RFC 4960. The NAS protocol for MM capability in the AMF supports registration management (RM) capability, connection management (CM) capability, and UP connection activation and deactivation, apart from supporting ciphering and integrity protection of the NAS signaling message exchanges with the UE.

N3 is the UP interface between the gNB and UPF (Figure II.2.2.9). The GTP-U is used for carrying user data between the radio access network and the core network. The user data is transported as UDP and can be carried over IPv4 or IPv6. The UP packets are prioritized by the routers based on the DSCP marking, which in turn depends on the end-to-end QoS prioritization of the different IP flows.

In Figure II.2.2.10, SRB connectivity between RAN and 5GC depicts the association that is established to carry radio signaling traffic. The SRB carries the RRC and NAS signaling messages over the air. These signaling messages must be treated with higher priority regarding reliability and latency. Associated with each UE, there are explicit bearer and association identifiers that are created when the UE connects with the network. The signaling packets at the AMF for a given UE are identified by the AMF UE NGAP identifier and mapped to a corresponding identifier at the gNB with the gNB UE NGAP identifier. Once established, the signaling packets are exchanged between the gNB and AMF using these identifiers and are used at the RAN to provide the appropriate scheduling treatment and to identify the UE association at the AMF.

Figure II.2.2.11 provides a summary view of the interfaces and the associated protocol stacks for exchanging signaling information across the eNB and EPC nodes. The Session Management Function (SMF) supports the session management (SM) functions. The message exchanges between the SMF and UE are routed via the AMF. The SM function involves the creation of the IP/ethernet context with the UE, establishing the QoS/IP flows interacting with the policy and charging function (PCF), and creating the relevant context with the UPF to support the UP traffic.

In Figure II.2.2.12, the New Radio (NR) interface UP data exchange provides a summary view of the interfaces and the associated protocol stacks for exchanging UP traffic across the eNB and EPC nodes. The main difference between LTE and NR is the service data adaptation protocol (SDAP) layer. In LTE, there is a one-to-one mapping between the QoS IP flow and the DRB in the eNB. In NR, this mapping function has been made more flexible to allow for one or more QoS flows to be mapped to a DRB in the gNB. The SDAP is responsible for mapping a QoS flow from the 5G core network and a data radio bearer, as well as marking the QoS flow identifier (QFI) in uplink and downlink packets. The SDAP layer also supports a new functionality of reflective QoS, which is used

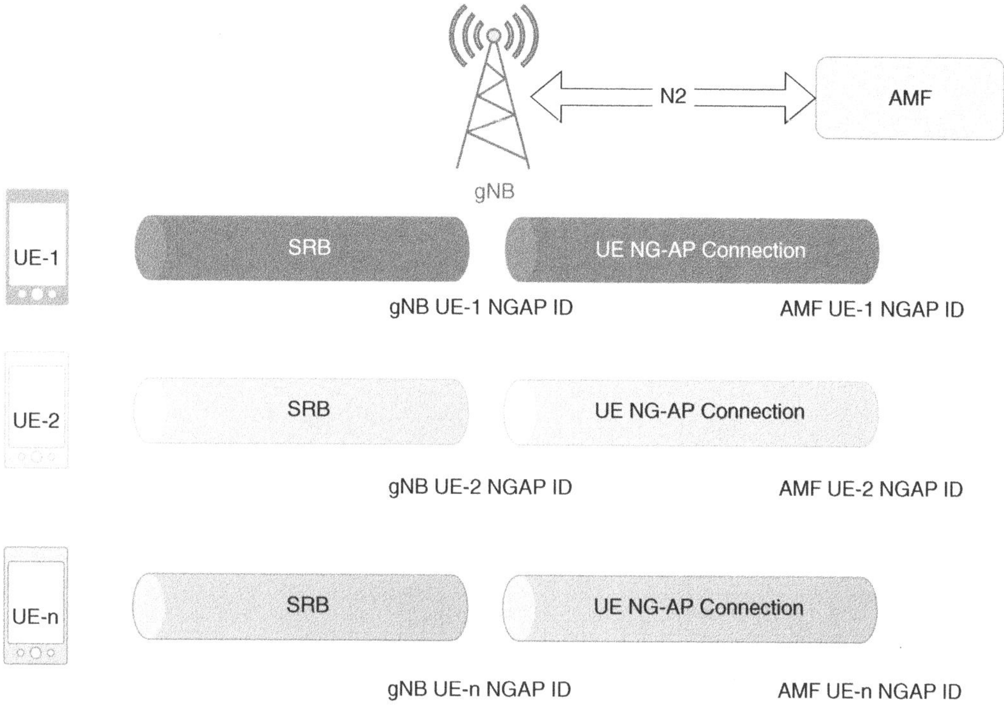

Figure II.2.2.10 SRB connectivity between the RAN and 5GC.

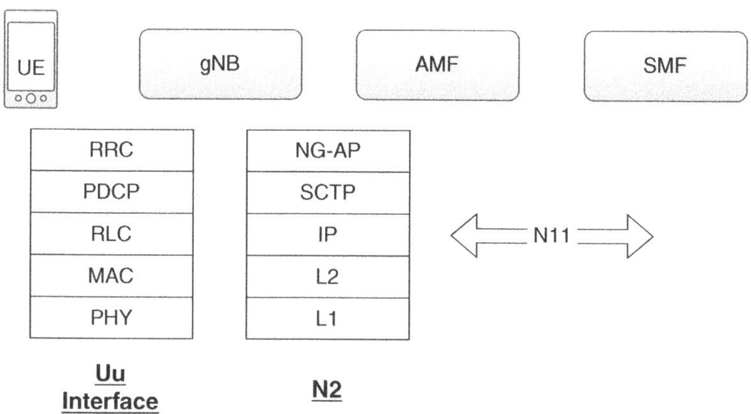

Figure II.2.2.11 Summary view of the NR interface signaling information exchange.

to map QoS flows to already established DRBs, avoiding the overhead of signaling to establish the QoS context in the UE and allowing for short bursts of traffic to be provided with the requisite QoS.

Apart from this, the UP routing functions are made more flexible by allowing an anchor UPF and an intermediary UPF (I-UPF). A 5G UP encapsulation is defined to carry traffic between the anchor UPF and I-UPF. Such a split allows for the realization of local breakout functions via the I-UPF, enabling enterprise network connectivity while still supporting traffic through the anchor UPF for other generic connectivity traffic. Concepts of multihoming functions enabled through IPv6 can be leveraged with such an architecture, allowing multiple prefixes to be assigned to a

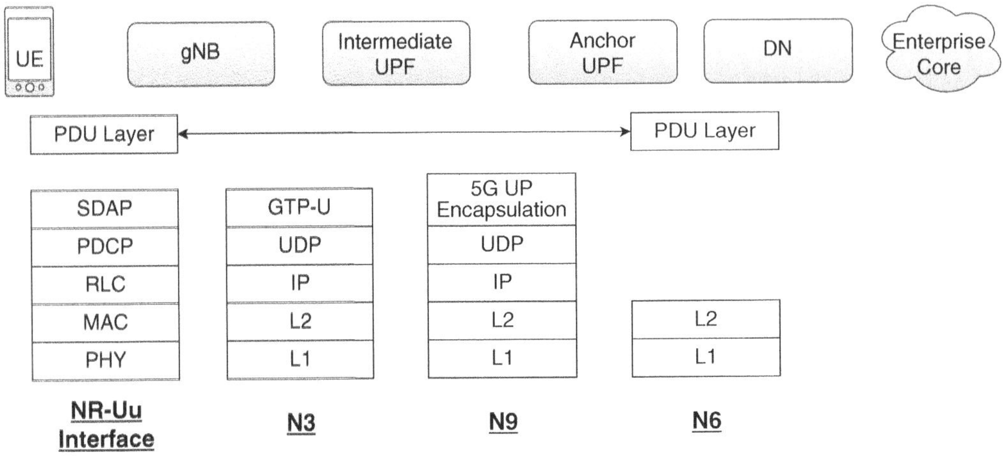

Figure II.2.2.12 Summary view of the NR interface UP data exchange.

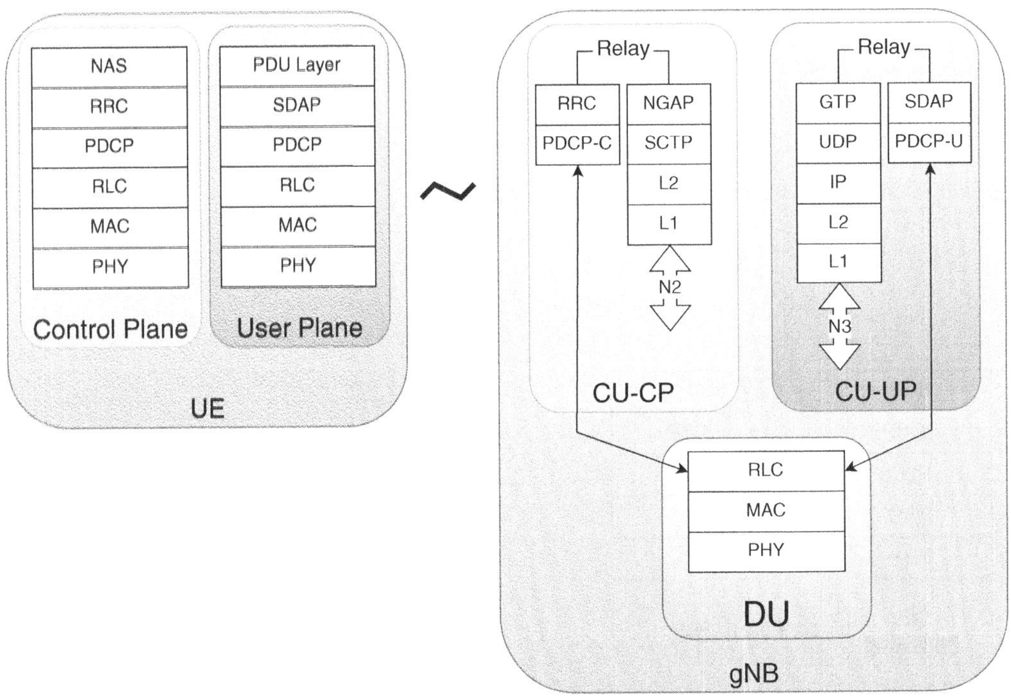

Figure II.2.2.13 UE–gNB protocol stack with O-RAN architecture.

given Protocol Data Unit (PDU) connection established with the UE. Separate PDU sessions are supported on the N9 and also handle the required QoS across the data traffic exchange between the anchor UPF and I-UPF. The uplink classifier (UL CL) is used to identify the traffic that is routed to the local domain via the I-UPF and packets that are routed to the anchor UPF. Note that the N9 interface can be either intra-PLMN or inter-PLMN/intra-enterprise or inter-enterprise domains.

In Figure II.2.2.13, the UE–gNB protocol stack with O-RAN architecture provides a view of the control and UP traffic exchanged between the UE and the gNB, along with the functional breakdown of the gNB into the central unit (CU) and distributed unit (DU), including the associated functional partitions involved. The CU itself is divided into the CU control plane (CU-CP) and CU UP (CU-UP). The CU-CP communicates with the AMF in the 5GC via the N2 interface. The CU-UP communicates with the UPF in the 5GC via the N3 interface. The DU supports both the control and UP traffic via established DRBs. The DU is typically deployed very closely with the radio unit (RU), which is the transmission and reception point (TRP). The CU is supported on a platform based on the QoS requirements of the flows it supports and can be closer to the DU or potentially integrated into the 5GC compute resources.

In Figure II.2.2.14 UE communicating with the 5GC entities via the N1 interface depicts the UE communicating with 5GC functions. Over the air, the previously described communication between the UE and AMF is leveraged.

The N1 NAS signaling connection is used for each received entry to which the UE is attached. The N1 endpoint is established in the AMF. N1 NAS signaling connections are used for both RM and CM, as well as for SM message exchanges with the UE.

The NAS protocol on N1 includes the NAS MM and NAS SM components. The N1 interface also supports UE policy exchanges and location-based services (LCS), among other functions. The AMF transports these messages and forwards them to the appropriate entity in the 5GC to implement the required specific functions, for example UE policy management and determining UE position. The security of the information exchange is supported in the AMF for the interactions with the UE, and the other functions in the 5GC use this established security context for information exchange with the UE.

See the converged core section for the other 5GC functional nodes. Apart from the above-described interfaces for 5G NR/5GC, the 5GC leverages an SBA and relies on the HyperText Transfer Protocol (HTTP)/2 protocol with JavaScript object notation (JSON) as the application layer serialization protocol.

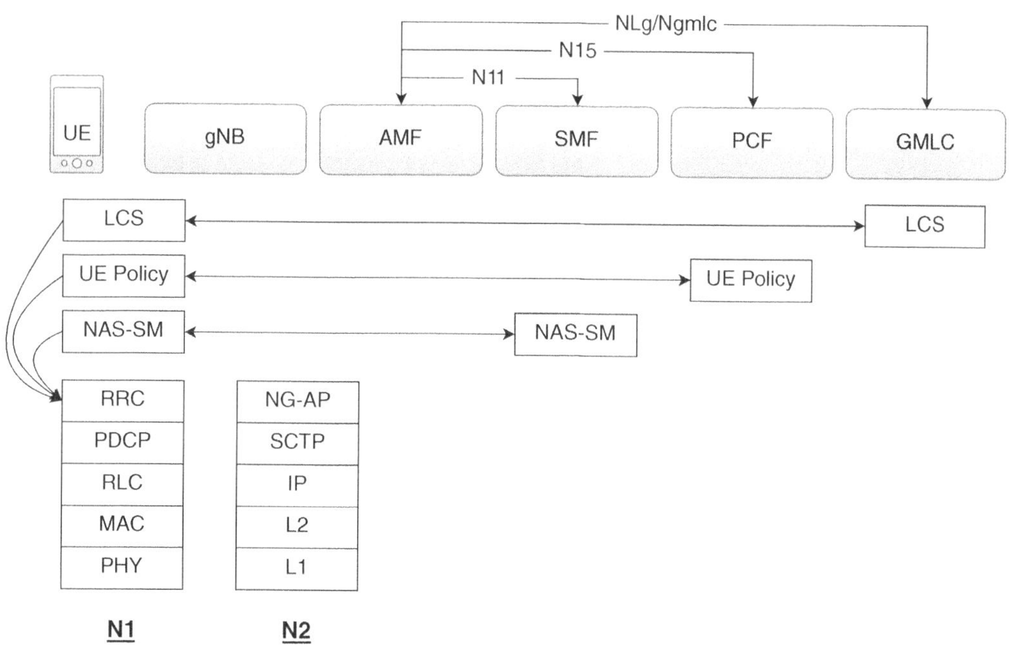

Figure II.2.2.14 UE is communicating with the 5GC entities via the N1 interface.

II.2.2.4 Summary

This section covers the protocol stacks used for the different interfaces for both LTE/EPC and 5G NR/5GC networks. The connectivity between the radio nodes eNB/gNB and the packet core network is described. The individual interfaces between the nodes within the packet core networks are presented, providing justifications for the protocols used where relevant. The end-to-end information exchange for signaling and UP traffic is shown for completeness. The 5G NR/5GC network is presented, assuming the context introduced for LTE/EPC, and the evolution of the 5G NR/5GC networks is provided, offering the reasoning behind the choices being made. The 5GC inter-function information exchange is significantly simplified, given that HTTP/2 is used as a generic definition for protocol structure, with the information exchange performed using JSON, making the interactions among these nodes generic, and allowing for significant reuse in the implementations.

References

S1 Interface:

Purpose: Connects the eNodeB (LTE base station) to the EPC (Evolved Packet Core), specifically to the MME (Mobility Management Entity) and the SGW (Serving Gateway).

Specification:

1 3GPP TS 36.412: "E-UTRA; S1 Layer 1 General Aspects and Principles"
2 3GPP TS 36.413: "E-UTRA; S1 Application Protocol (S1AP)"

X2 Interface:

Purpose: Enables communication between eNodeBs, allowing for functions like inter-eNodeB handovers and load balancing.

Specification:

3 3GPP TS 36.423: "E-UTRA; X2 Application Protocol (X2AP)"
4 3GPP TS 36.420 to TS 36.424: Cover different layers and procedures of X2.

S5/S8 Interfaces:

Purpose: Connects the SGW to the PGW (Packet Data Network Gateway). S5 is used within the same network (trusted network environment), and S8 is used when SGW and PGW are in different networks.

Specification:

5 3GPP TS 29.274: "3GPP Evolved Packet System (EPS); Evolved General Packet Radio Service (GPRS) Tunnelling Protocol for Control plane (GTPv2-C); Stage 3"

S10 Interface:

Purpose: Connects MMEs for UE handover and context transfer across MMEs.

Specification:

6 3GPP TS 23.401: "General Packet Radio Service (GPRS) enhancements for Evolved Universal Terrestrial Radio Access Network (E-UTRAN) access"

S6a Interface:

Purpose: Connects MME to HSS (Home Subscriber Server) for authentication, authorization, and subscriber information retrieval.

Specification:

7 3GPP TS 29.272: "Evolved Packet System (EPS); Mobile Application Part (MAP) between MME and HSS"

5G NR (New Radio) Network Interfaces

NG Interface (NG-C and NG-U):

Purpose: Connects the gNodeB (5G base station) to the 5G Core (NG-C for control plane signaling and NG-U for user data).

Specification:

8 3GPP TS 38.410: "NG-RAN; NG Layer 1"
9 3GPP TS 38.413: "NG-RAN; NG Application Protocol (NGAP)"

Xn Interface:

Purpose: Connects gNodeBs to support handovers, load management, and coordination in NR networks.

Specification:

10 3GPP TS 38.423: "NG-RAN; Xn Application Protocol (XnAP)"

N2 and N3 Interfaces:

Purpose: N2 connects the Access and Mobility Management Function (AMF) to the gNodeB for control plane, while N3 connects the gNodeB to the User Plane Function (UPF) for user data.

Specification:

11 3GPP TS 23.502: "Procedures for the 5G System (5GS)"
12 3GPP TS 29.244: "5G System; Interface between the Control Plane and User Plane"

N26 Interface:

Purpose: Connects the 5G Core (5GC) to the LTE EPC for interworking and mobility between 4G and 5G.

Specification:

13 3GPP TS 23.502: Detailed procedures for N26 in interworking scenarios.

E1 Interface:

Purpose: Connects the Central Unit (CU) and Distributed Unit (DU) within the 5G gNodeB, specifically for control and user planes.

Specification:

14 3GPP TS 38.470 to 38.474: Cover the E1 Application Protocol and the CU-DU split architecture.

II.2.3

Security

II.2.3.1 Introduction

Connectivity with public macro network operator (MNO) networks requires high security to ensure that the users are authenticated and authorized for connectivity. Typical access with the MNO connectivity tends to be to the public internet, and when enterprise network connectivity is required, virtual private network (VPN) tunnels are established over the MNO packet connections. For enterprise private network connectivity, both the user credential authentication and the access to the enterprise network need to be protected, and a lot of care is needed to avoid any breaches with the introduction of 4G/5G networks. From an enterprise core, the 4G/5G connection must be treated like a Wi-Fi connectivity, and given the increased attack surface of exposure, additional protections are needed to avoid exposure.

There are different deployment models supporting enterprise network connectivity. The private network can be deployed with the radio access network (RAN) and core network, including the authenticating modules supported within the enterprise campus – a self-contained architecture. There are other models where the RAN network and the user plane functions are housed in the enterprise campus, while the control plane modules are deployed in the cloud. For both models, the private network can be deployed by a network vendor or done through a managed service provider (MSP).

For the self-contained architecture, the home subscriber server (HSS)/unified data management (UDM) is within the enterprise campus; it is sufficient to support only the primary authentication to allow access to the enterprise core. This primary authentication procedure is employed as part of the long term evolution (LTE) attach/NR registration procedures. The credential distribution management and ensuring the validity of the credentials are under the control of the IT enterprise.

With the HSS deployed in the cloud platform outside of the enterprise campus, additional control may be needed to ensure access to the enterprise core. The credential distribution may be managed by the MSP as well, without direct control from the enterprise IT. Apart from the primary authentication with the EPC/5GC HSS/UDM modules in the cloud outside of the enterprise campus, the enterprise employs a second level of authentication. This second level of authentication can be a secondary authentication with the device authenticated as part of the PDN/PDU establishment procedures prior to providing IP address assignment to the user equipment (UE). An approach to support independent authentication outside of the 3GPP-defined procedures can be

Mobile Communication Systems for Private Networks, First Edition. Srinivasan Balasubramanian.

used too. This second level of authentication typically employs EAP-TLS procedures, with the server and client certificates provisioned and managed by the enterprise IT. The supplicant performs the second level of authentication with the authenticator deployed within the enterprise campus.

For credential management, integration with the RADIUS server is very desirable to allow the IT enterprise to regulate the user access from a single pane of glass for both LTE/NR and Wi-Fi.

This chapter provides a guide to bringing enterprise IT and cellular communications onto a common platform or infrastructure. Like Wi-Fi, which uses unlicensed spectrum, the enterprise private 4G/5G networks are also deployed on a shared spectrum, although there are explicit authorizations provided to use a certain bandwidth in the identified location(s). With shared spectrum, the typical MNO networks do not encounter full licensed spectrum use; therefore, better over-the-air protection needs to be enforced.

The fundamental tenets of zero trust architecture (ZTA) are discussed, and how it is realized with 4G/5G networks is illustrated. The details of mobile security and network access control are discussed, along with the cloud architectures and network resource allocation for the different functions. Some comparisons with Wi-Fi are provided. Effective integration of the two domains of operation is required for viable longer-term operations for an enterprise.

See the chapter on device credential management for details of device provisioning.

See chapters on citizens broadband radio service (CBRS) and private network spectrum for information on shared spectrum use for enterprise private networks.

See Part II, "Device Provisioning" chapter, for the credential distribution techniques, including credentials for primary and second layers of authentication for access to the private networks.

II.2.3.1.1 Seven Tenets of the NIST Zero Trust Architecture

Reproduced from NIST Special Publication 800-207 "Zero Trust Architecture." This publication is available free of charge at: https://doi.org/10.6028/NIST.SP.800-207

- All data sources and computing services are considered resources.
- All communication is secured, regardless of network location.
- Access to individual enterprise resources is granted on a per-session basis.
- Access to resources is determined by dynamic policy and may include other behavioral and environmental attributes.
- The enterprise monitors and measures the integrity and security posture of all owned and associated assets.
- All resource authentication and authorization are dynamic and strictly enforced before access is allowed.
- The enterprise collects as much information as possible about the current state of assets, network infrastructure, and communications and uses it to improve its security posture.

II.2.3.2 Zero Trust

Zero trust is a security model that requires strict identity verification (including authentication and authorization) for every person and device trying to access the individual resources on an enterprise private network, regardless of whether they are inside or outside of the network perimeter and the access technology used to establish the connectivity.

Figure II.2.3.1 provides a set of key concepts associated with ZTA and suggests some guidelines on how to evolve the current network implementation to enable zero trust (ZT). Greenfield deployments will be rare, so leveraging the current security measures and evolving them to achieve a ZT platform are required. "Rip and replace" is generally not an option; gradual evolution will provide the comfort needed by the enterprises to believe in the process of reaching ZT, while allowing time for network vendors to understand the needs of a given enterprise and focus on the immediate threat vectors, while moving the other aspects to mid- to long-term protective measures. Network as a service (NaaS) is an eventual goal for both the network vendor and enterprise IT, supporting the required abstraction of managing the deployment without manipulating the finer operational knobs necessary for the daily operation of the connectivity aspects of the individual radio access technologies (RATs).

Figure II.2.3.2 provides some practical measures to realize the ZT concepts of API support and the ZT guidelines from the key concepts suggested before.

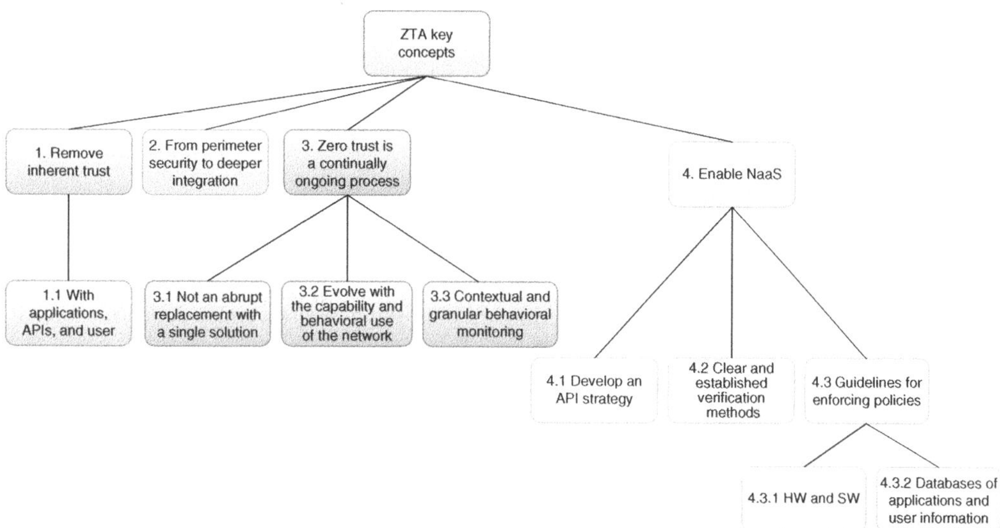

Figure II.2.3.1 ZTA key concepts.

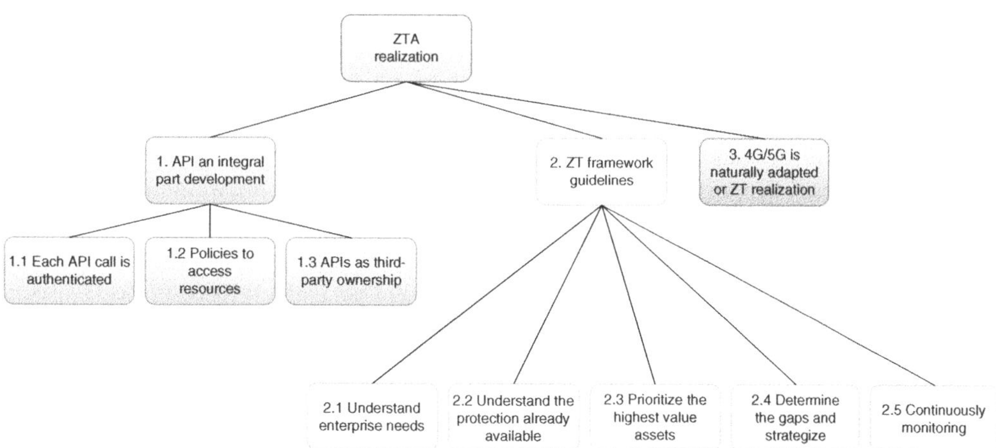

Figure II.2.3.2 ZTA realization.

Treating the 4G/5G-based connectivity supported as NaaS is fundamental to the process, and exposing the relevant APIs in a secure manner will allow for effective integration into the enterprise core. Supporting diverse types of enterprise users who access and manage the network functions – by both internal (enterprise IT, different internal players supporting enterprise applications, etc.) and external parties (network vendors, interacting enterprises, external macro network operators, external application functions, etc.) – through professionally managed exposed APIs will be necessary for both usability and scalability. Tracking usage and detecting anomalies in API usage will subsequently need to be supported to ensure proper use of the exposed APIs and effective functioning of the network without requiring manual monitoring and interventions.

Although the ZT framework provides general guidelines for it to become viable, it must primarily cater to the enterprise where the network is being deployed. It starts by first studying the existing functions and security procedures, identifying the high-value assets, identifying the gaps where relevant, and then suggesting secure procedural augmentations and wrappers to reduce the vulnerabilities involved. This process will not be a one of effort, but rather a continuous ongoing activity by both the enterprise entities and network vendors involved.

II.2.3.3 Security Aspects of 4G/5G Networks

II.2.3.3.1 Key Security Challenges and Mitigative Steps

This section provides a high-level view of the key challenges faced in the deployment and management of the enterprise 4G/5G networks. Steps to address those challenges are briefly introduced. The rest of the chapter details the behaviors that aid both the network vendor deployments and enterprise IT management in effectively handling these challenges.

Mitigative steps will need to be taken early in the process to avoid unnecessary exposure and create new threat vectors. Carefully choosing wireless technology (RAT) and dealing with performance, reliability, and security issues will be required. Not every campus environment requires all the sophistication of the different attributes of the 3GPP technologies defined, including determining the need for 4G LTE or 5G NR networks for a given enterprise. Enterprises face a distinct set of challenges compared to the macro networks, and specific security aspects may need to be further supported to allow for the basic protection needed. 4G/5G networks are inherently complex, given that they are designed to support macro network connectivity globally. Combining conventional wireless local area network (LANs) with advanced LTE/5G NR technology to supporting seamless wireless connectivity is like fitting a square peg into a round hole; appropriate trimming and alignment through functional addition will be required to enable the necessary simplicity of integration with the enterprise networks. Supporting an overlay atop existing enterprise networks that are fully integrated, including the existing enterprise framework that includes indoor and outdoor 4G/5G small cell access points, will be essential to the process. These access points connect via the 4G/5G integrated core networks, and both control and user plane integration will be handled explicitly. An easy-to-use alternative to traditional Wi-Fi wireless systems that are cost-effective and flexible, catering to vastly differing enterprise networks, will be required, with plug-and-play explicit security procedures put in place that can be mixed and matched, allowing for a scalable realization apart from transferring knowledge across enterprises.

As with any security procedures, the use of known and well-vetted security postures and procedures will be essential to avoid reinventing the wheel and discovering gaps later in the process.

The need for ZT-based considerations to be analyzed ahead of the deployments is essential to the process. The threat vectors remain the same: network, users, email, applications (web or cloud), remote access nodes, mobile devices, data in motion and at rest (enterprise data). Adding 4G/5G wireless networks to the enterprise does not change that. However, the addition of 4G/5G networks creates additional exposures that must be studied further to avoid unnecessary risks. This includes multiple technologies with different security levels, multi-access edge compute (MEC), the disaggregated nature of 4G/5G with service-based architecture (SBA), newer services enabled through 4G LTE/5G NR, and network exposure functions (NEFs) and interfaces that create a larger attack surface. However, 4G/5G network may also offer additional protection, and these aspects are discussed later in the chapter.

Table II.2.3.1 provides some of the key challenges faced in enterprise deployments and discusses some of the possible mitigative steps that can be undertaken.

Table II.2.3.1 Security key challenges.

Key challenge	Description
Spectrum management	Shared spectrum allows for easy spoofing from end-user devices but more so from the network side. A single cell at the entrance to the enterprise campus can trap devices, cause denial of service, and lead to other more severe issues. Networks need to be authenticated by the device as much as the device needs to be authenticated by the network. A form of mutual authentication best addresses what is needed.
Coverage deficiencies/ mobility across deployments	With smaller footprints and the likelihood of adjoining networks being encountered by the end-user device, care needs to be taken to prevent the devices from jumping between these networks. Additionally, the end-user device will encounter many smaller networks during mobility, and repeated attempts on these networks can and will occur. Even though these attempts do not result in connectivity, the device/user identities are exchanged with the visited network, allowing for device traceability. Explicit network identifiers for the networks, apart from geofencing of the valid/ allowed networks provisioned on the device, greatly aid in preventing such issues.
Quality of service	Quality of service (QoS), even the basic guarantees provided to the user, consumes network resources. Care needs to be taken to ensure that the QoS flow is authorized for use. Additionally, the extent of QoS guarantees provided can be time-of-day or day-of-the-week dependent, and policy enforcement rules (PER) positioned at the appropriate policy enforcement points (PEP) are required for effective functioning of the network. The policies will depend on service types, roaming agreements between the visited and roaming networks, user subscription, and potentially other aspects. The policies may come from within the camped network's wireless core network, from enterprise applications running within the campus, provided by the UE's subscription home network to the visited network, or from a third-party application leveraging the 4G/5G connectivity as a service over which the application is supported. Secure management of the PERs with the PEPs will require the interworking functions in the network to establish secure pipes between these entities. When transitioning across established security boundaries, secure connectivity may be established using VPN certificates. 3GPP specifies the Security Edge Protection Proxy (SEPP) function to allow for such connectivity to be supported.

(Continued)

Table II.2.3.1 (Continued)

Key challenge	Description
Data security	Protecting user's traffic is typically handled end to end between the application server and the end-user application. However, this is just the content of the information carried and there are several other exposure surfaces that need to be addressed. The packet headers, the typical usage time periods, usage location, the services accessed, and other aspects all have implications. Recognizing these patterns has become much easier with the use of Artificial Intelligence (AI) techniques. Over-the-air sniffers, in addition to wireline taps, are readily available, and methods are needed to protect the user and the enterprise organization from being hacked. Effective support of HyperText Transfer Protocol (HTTP) proxy allows for spoofing. Over-the-air encryption (3GPP supports 256-bit encryption, although only 128-bit encryption is supported in the market) provides some protection. Randomization of the radio resources used prevents denial of service issues from repeated attacks. Quantum computing, although not yet in commonplace usage, is likely to become available not too far in the future. This will imply that any of the encrypted traffic can potentially be decrypted with the master key by just performing exhaustive searches. Discussions in Rivest–Shamir–Adleman (RSA) forums are recommending that 2048-bit encryption be used to make it harder, even with quantum compute, to decrypt the packets.
Device onboarding	There are several types of users, each with a certain level of access to the enterprise core that is allowed. The types of users include enterprise employees and visitors. Even among employees and visitors, there will be multiple categorizations involved, potentially isolating regions within the enterprise campuses where access is allowed. Scalable credential management with eSIM technology, supporting the required customizations for individual credentials, allowing for the enterprise IT to manage them, will be required. See the chapter on credential management. Additionally, integration with other RATs like Wi-Fi and Bluetooth(R) (BT) will be required for both ease of management and avoiding discrepancies in the operations across the accesses for a given user.

II.2.3.3.2 4G/5G Security High-Level Architecture

4G/5G networks enforce strong device authentication through support of known, fixed endpoint device identification, with authentication for asset management. Mutual authentication is supported between endpoint devices and 4G/5G networks, including support for infrastructure functions and components to authenticate one another. Apart from relying on end-to-end application-level security, hop-to-hop security is supported over the air, through the 4G LTE/5G NR core network, enterprise LAN, and to any private or public cloud, including enterprise applications and connectivity to the intranet and internet.

Figure II.2.3.3 illustrates the 4G/5G wireless infrastructure that includes strong mutual authentication and encryption along the full data path across wireless and wired interconnects. As such, the protections offered are hop-to-hop and the functional realizations through micro services running in established trust zones. The resource allocations for the different users, QoS flows, including the control and user plane, are handled as segments over the air and through public and private networks. Guarantee availability and SLAs for critical applications based on their allowed QoS parameterization are supported by allocating the resource segments along the individual hops in

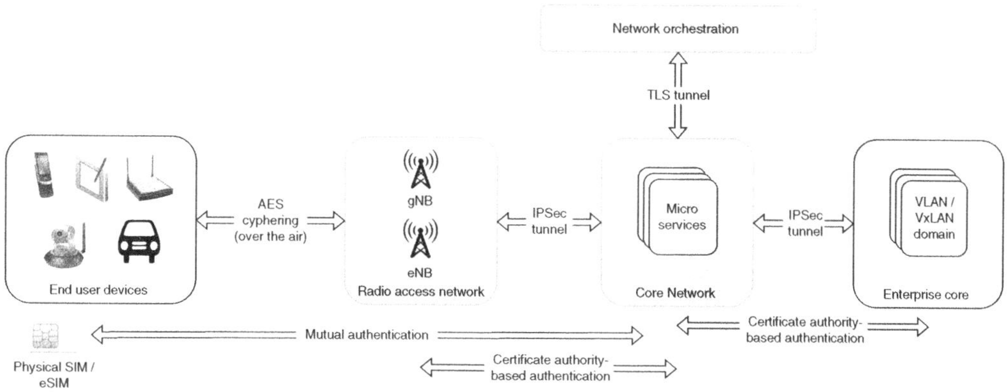

Figure II.2.3.3 4G 5G security high-level architecture.

the network and over the air to the end-user devices. Extensible architecture is supported through native microservice-based platform with APIs for extensibility and integrations.

Data privacy is maintained by managing the data and control paths for privacy and compliance based on the enterprise policies. Enterprise data remains 100% under enterprise IT/applications management control, alleviating privacy concerns of public 5G and private solutions from MNOs. Enterprises inherently do not want information exposure, especially with extremely sensitive data, and explicit protections need to be in place to ensure that unauthorized users or entities never have access to data payloads and cannot sell, share, or monetize any client or meta data. The same will apply to neutral host network (NHN) deployments, where MNO traffic and private enterprise network traffic must be segregated and secured from public connections right at the access point itself. This segregation can be supported at a hop immediately next to the access point, such as central unit (CU) instead of the distributed unit (DU), based on the RAN architecture employed.

Figure II.2.3.4 provides a view of the integrated core network deployment with the 4G EPC and the 5GC where the functions are deployed in the cloud platforms. The eNBs and gNBs (access points) are deployed as part of the RAN and are connected to the integrated core network platforms to reach the EPC/5GC function and enterprise services. The enterprise services are typically deployed in servers that are accessible through specific VLANs/VxLANs in the enterprise core network. The EPC, 5GC, and enterprise applications can be supported in the local enterprise's private cloud, locally within a region (e.g. city) in a metro cloud, in the enterprise global cloud in a de-militarized zone (DMZ), or in a public cloud platform (e.g. Amazon Web Services (AWS), Google Cloud Platform (GCP), Microsoft Azure Cloud Services). The compute resources for the functions may be dynamically augmented or relocated based on the real-time compute and interconnect needs, and care must be taken to ensure that the required security level is maintained across the function compute resource transitions. A single compute resource can and will house multiple EPC, 5GC, enterprise applications. Given that the security needs to be managed on a hop-to-hop basis, secure connections need to be established across the hops and may potentially require explicit authentication of connectivity based on the functions running on either side of the hop.

Figure II.2.3.5 illustrates the 4G/5G architecture employing control and user plane separation (CUPS). The compute resources for the control plane functions are vastly different from the user plane functions. Also, the control and user plane functions are implemented to be stateless in which the context information is retained in specific storage locations allowing for the functions to

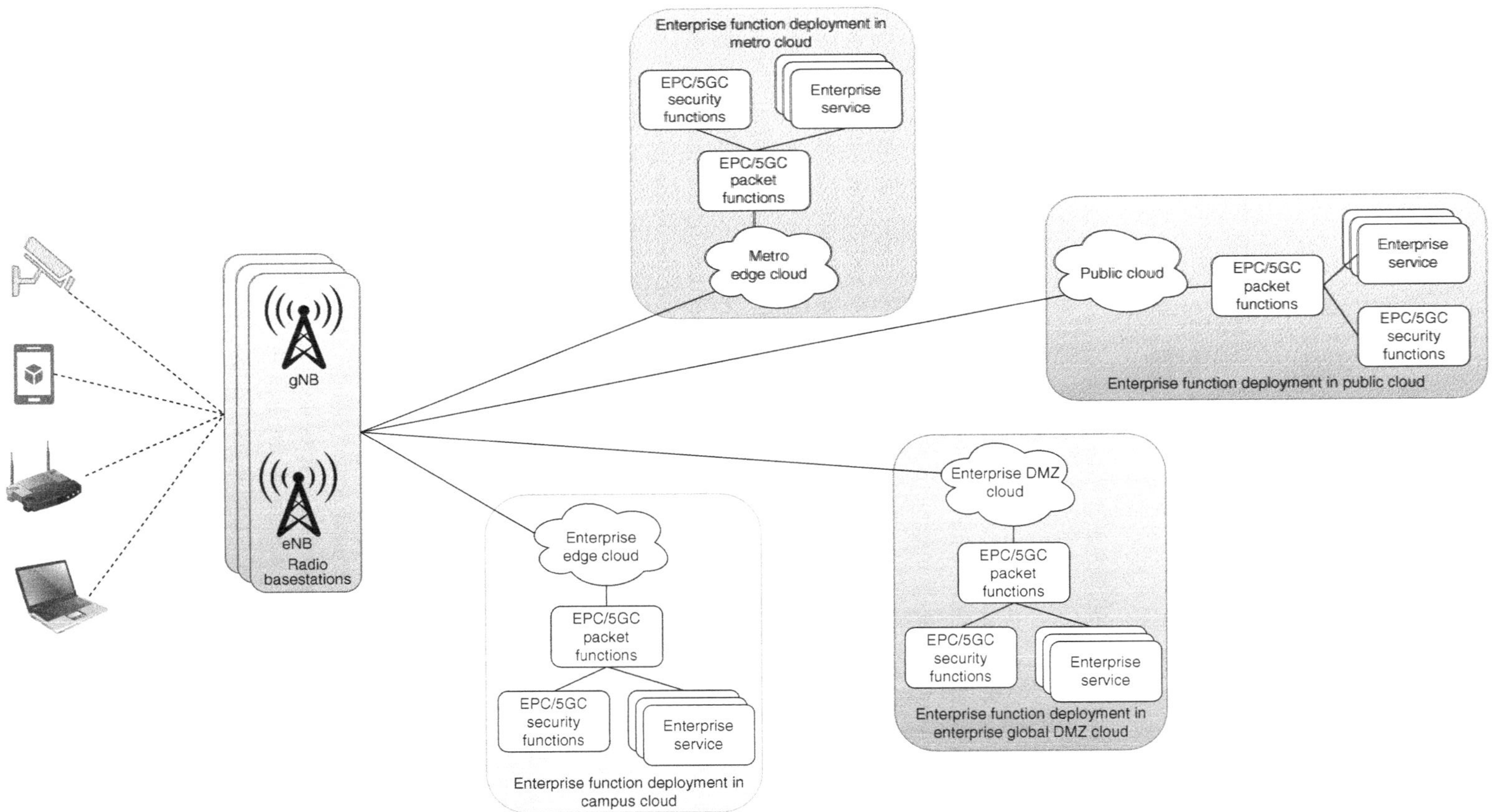

Figure II.2.3.4 ZT with SBA use in 4G EPC and 5GC.

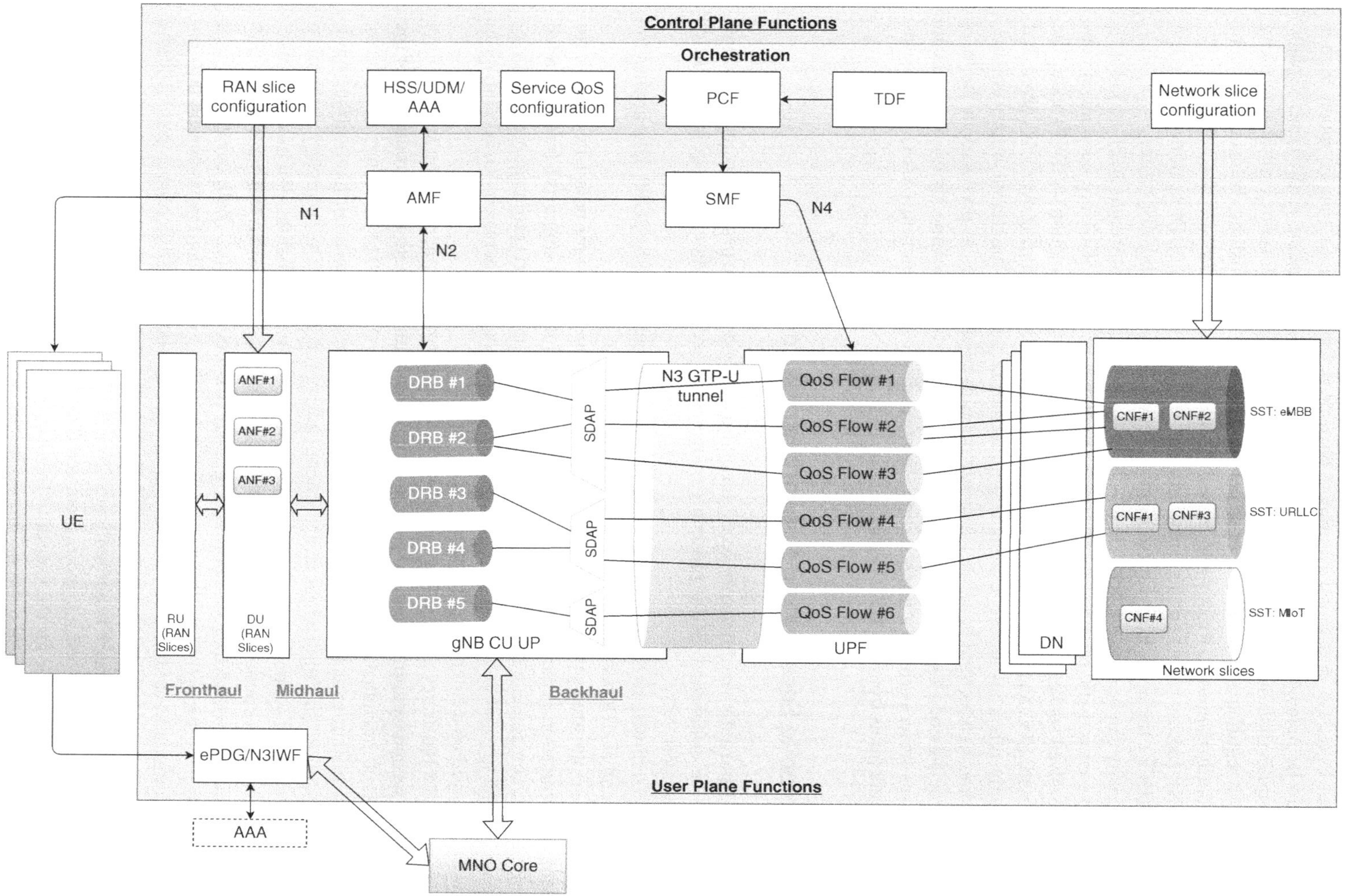

Figure II.2.3.5 ZT with CUPS.

be easily relocated, recovered from failure, and so on. This prevents security breaches that can be mimicked based on compute node crashes with user information and connectivity context separated from the EPC/5GC functional running. The user plane functions require much higher throughputs to be managed and cannot afford the same-level encryption as the control plane nodes. This implies that the control plane nodes manage the resource allocations for the user plane by ensuring the required authorizations to be performed prior to establishing the user plane context and constantly monitored for any aberration/abuse of use.

The eNB/gNB (access point) connectivity with the MNO core is for NHN operations. See the chapter on NHN for the procedures for establishing connectivity with the MNO core.

The connectivity can be over the 4G LTE, 5G NR radio interface, and through 3GPP access (primarily Wi-Fi) connectivity. For an end-user device to access the EPC/5GC core network, it connects via the evolved packet data gateway (ePDG) or N3 inter working function (N3IWF) node. The ePDG is used with EPC, and this connectivity is retained even when operating over 5GC, given that the N3IWF only offers an aesthetic architectural variation without functional improvements. N3IWF has some architectural benefits, which are not immediately seen as necessary in the market now. The ePDG node establishes an IKEv2 tunnel (similar to VPN connectivity), authenticating the end-user device with the authentication, authorization and accounting (AAA), which uses the derived credentials from the HSS/UDM.

II.2.3.4 Mobile Security and Network Access Control

Authenticated and authorized network access for end-user devices is the primary security function that needs to be established. 3GPP procedures adequately accommodate the required security functions to support a ZTA.

Figure II.2.3.6 illustrates the high-level security procedure employed by 3GPP. This applies for both 4G LTE and 5G NR networks.

Figure II.2.3.7 illustrates the primary authentication procedures used for both LTE and NR for mutual authentication as part of the attach/registration procedures. NR supports a more extended set of methods compared to LTE. Extensions have been added to support certificate-based authentication like Wi-Fi to allow for integrating authentication procedures between 4G/5G and Wi-Fi network deployed on a enterprise campus.

Figure II.2.3.8 illustrates a secondary authentication mechanism supported. The support for a basic form of secondary authentication is already supported with LTE with the introduction of the authentication of individual PDN connections using PAP/CHAP/EAP-TLS challenge procedures. This has been further extended with 5G NR by supporting network slice authentication, third-party authentication, and application-level authentication procedures. The secondary authentication procedures when supported are run in addition to the primary authentication mechanisms.

The end-user devices access the 4G/5G networks at different entry points. Although all the traffic is routed via the eNB/gNB (access points), core network-related traffic – both control and user plane – acts as pass-through from the access points, requiring independent protection in the core networks. Additionally, control plane and user plane traffic, due to the differences in the volume of data exchanged, need to be handled independently. Figure II.2.3.9 shows the key derivations used during and after the user is authenticated in the EPC/5GC, eNB/gNB functional nodes to ensure that the information exchanged is protected. The 4G key derivation is very rigid and, once established, does not change for the user until the user is re-authenticated. Also, the 4G networks do not allow for authentication to be performed by the home network and rely on the roaming

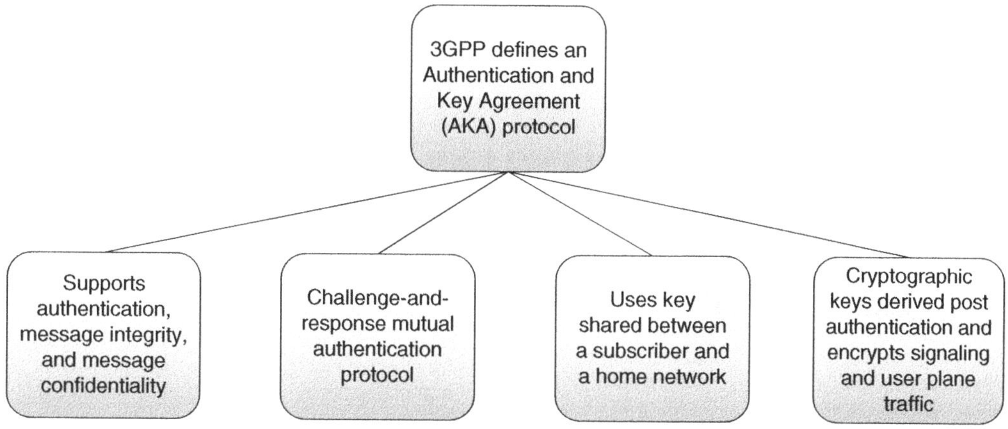

Figure II.2.3.6 3GPP authentication protocol.

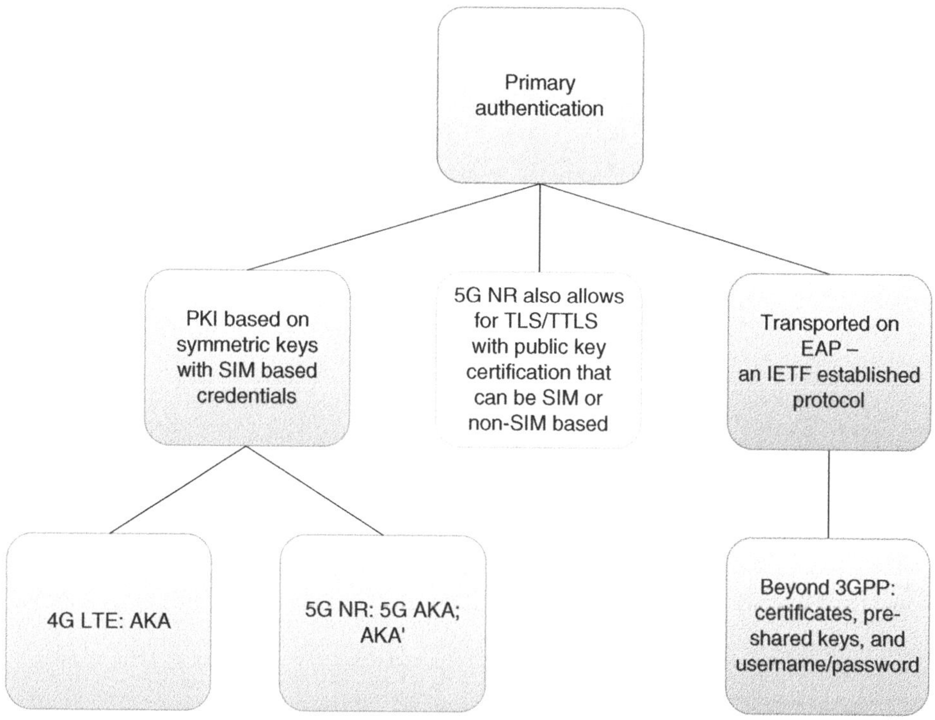

Figure II.2.3.7 3GPP authentication protocol – primary user authentication.

partner to support the required authentication (at the mobility management entity [MME]). With the 5G NR networks, a deeper key hierarchy is supported, allowing the home network to authenticate the end-user device and provide only ephemeral keys to the roaming network for real-time operations. The 5G authentication process allows the end-user device to be authenticated using SUbscription Concealed Identifier (SUCI) instead of using the SUbscription Permanent Identifier (SUPI). This offers further protection from the roaming networks against tracking the device

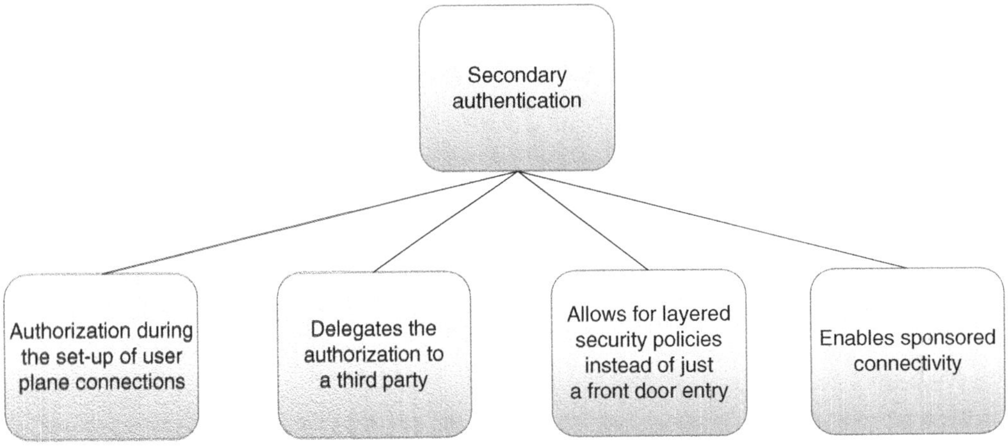

Figure II.2.3.8 3GPP authentication protocol – secondary user authentication.

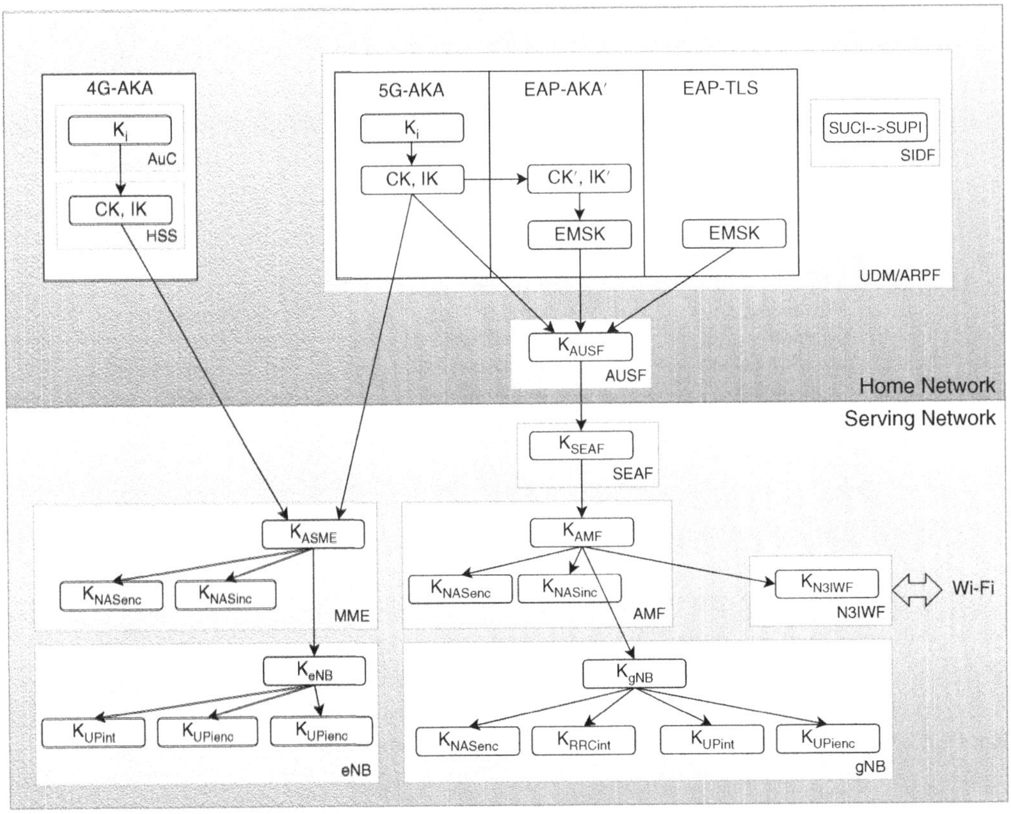

Figure II.2.3.9 3GPP authentication protocol – security framework – 4G/5G.

mobility across the networks, given that even basic access attempts can be used to track devices. The mutual authentication method used by the 4G and 5G procedures are also shown.

Figure II.2.3.10 illustrates the various aspects where improvements are introduced in 5G over the 4G networks. When fully employed, the 5G authentication procedures take it much further toward ZT realization.

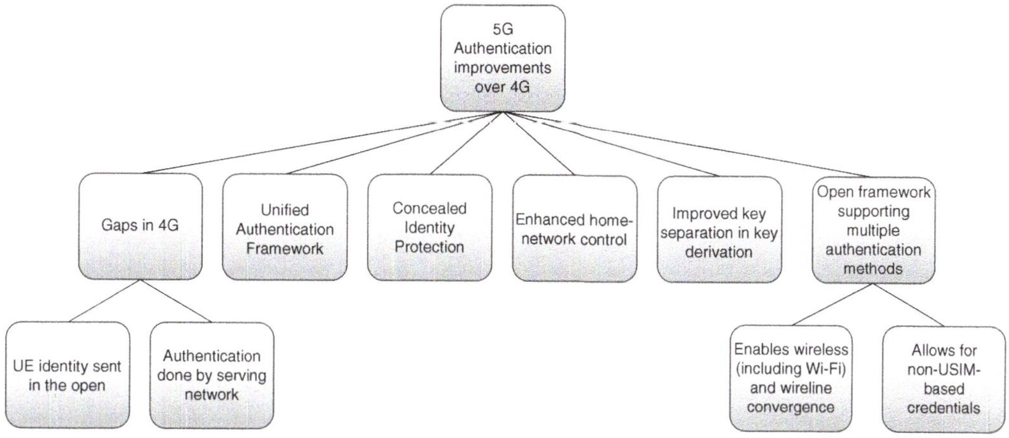

Figure II.2.3.10 5G authentication improvements over 4G.

Figure II.2.3.11 (with a more concise and current view) and Figure II.2.3.12 (with a more extended view) provide an illustration of the Wi-Fi authentication procedures used for the reader to compare with the 4G/5G procedures.

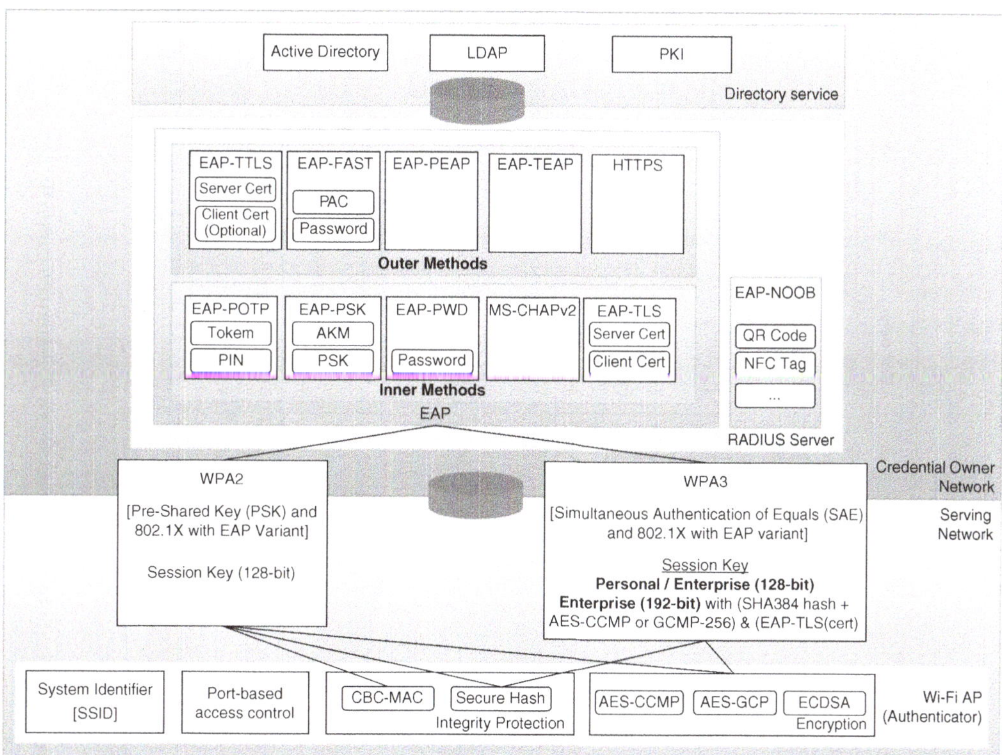

Figure II.2.3.11 Security framework – Wi-Fi (current context).

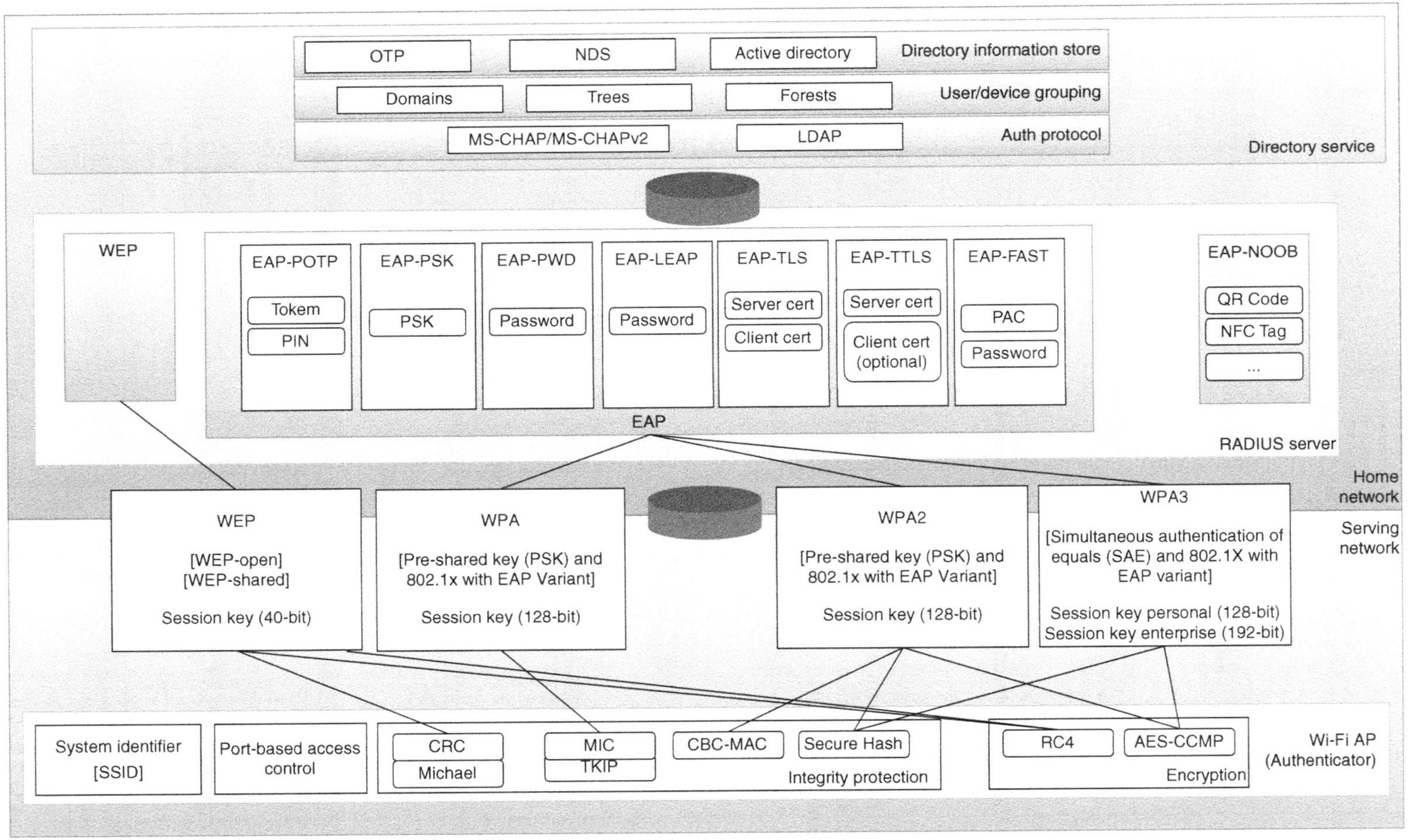

Figure II.2.3.12 Security framework – Wi-Fi (extended context).

II.2.3.5 4G and 5G Authentication Summary View

Table II.2.3.1: Summary view of the authentication method supported in 4G and 5G systems and the associated nodes

		Entities located in			Message Format		Trust model	UE Identity		SN Identity	Authentication vector generated by	Authentication of UE decided by	HN informaed of UE authentication	Anchor key heirarchy
		UE (User Equipment)	SN (Serving Network)	HN (Home Network)	UE <--> SN	SN <--> HN		UE --> SN	SN --> HN					
4G Authentication	EPS-AKA	USIM	MME	HSS	NAS	Diameter	Shared symmetric key	IMSI/ GUTI	IMSI	SN Id (MCC/ MNC)	HSS	MME	No	K_i -> CK+IK -> K_{ASME}
5G Authentication	5G-AKA'	USIM	SEAF	AUSF/UDM /ARPF/ SIDF	NAS	HTTP based web APIs	Shared symmetric key	SUCI/5G-GUTI	SUCI/ SUPI	SN Name (5G: MCC/MNC)	UDM/ARPF	SEAF & AUSF	Yes	K_i -> CK+IK -> K_{ASME} -> K_{SEAF}
	EAP-AKA'	USIM	SEAF	AUSF/UDM /ARPF/ SIDF	NASIEAP	HTTP based web APIs	Shared symmetric key	SUCI/5G-GUTI	SUCI/ SUPI	SN Name (5G: MCC/MNC)	UDM/ARPF	AUSF	Yes	K_i -> CK+IK -> CK'+IK' -> EMSK -> K_{SEAF}
	EAP-TLS	USIM/Non-USIM	SEAF	AUSF/UDM /ARPF/ SIDF	NASIEAP	HTTP based web APIs	Public key certificate	SUCI/5G-GUTI	SUCI/ SUPI	SN Name (5G: MCC/MNC)	N/A	AUSF	Yes	EMSK -> K_{AUSF} -> K_{SEAF}

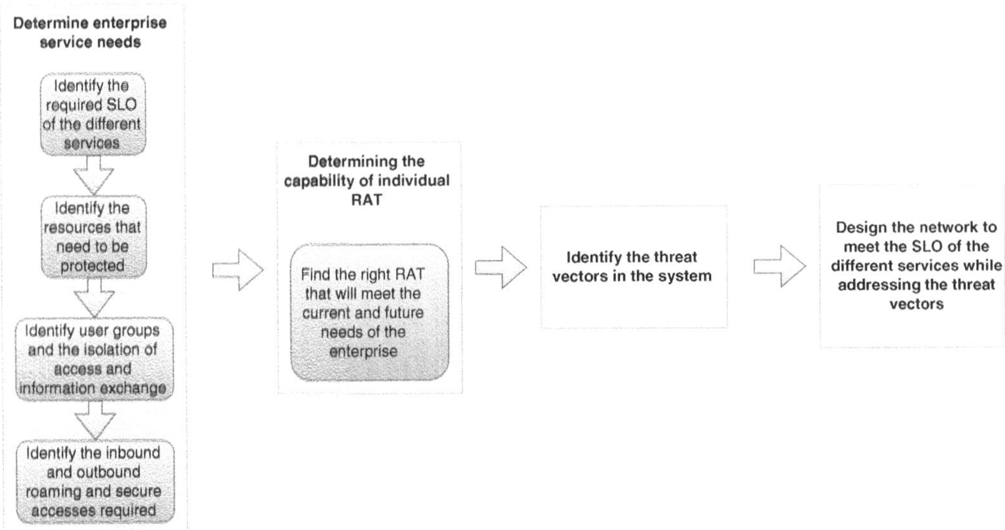

Figure II.2.3.13 Applying the information to design enterprise campus security.

Table II.2.3.1 provides a summary view of the authentication method supported in 4G and 5G systems.

Figure II.2.3.13 provides a high-level set of steps to employ in applying the information to design the enterprise campus-level security procedures when deploying 4G/5G private networks.

II.2.3.6 4G/5G and Wi-Fi Security Comparisons

4G and 5G offer sufficient sophistication for an improved ZT realization. They bring strong device identification and authentication, as well as network availability and QoS functions that require individual device authentication and authorization to support more critical applications that are not possible with Wi-Fi solutions. The RAN and core network resources can be better managed with improved segmentation, and hop-to-hop operations with 4G/5G from the enterprise core, the evolved packet core (EPC)/5G core (5GC), access points, and the end-user devices, with privacy enforced through strong key derivations. The required level of security enforcement is easily exposed for management by enterprise IT and enterprise application services, providing improved visibility into the active operations of the 4G/5G networks, including route management across the LAN/bridges/routers/NATs in the enterprise network.

Wi-Fi suffers from MitM and evil twin attacks, with potentially rogue AP broadcasting (spoofing) a legitimate service set identifier (SSID) as a honeypot, positioning itself between end-user devices and other resources. This attack is usually combined with spoofed de-authentication to coax clients to the honeypot. Such attacks are not possible with 4G/5G networks due to the support of mutual authentication.

As with any radio frequency (RF) medium, Wi-Fi is susceptible to layer 1 attacks, including jamming. Wi-Fi is also susceptible to layer 2 jamming attacks by malicious endpoints that use CTS/RTS packets to consume all airtime resources. 4G/5G networks are susceptible to layer 1 jamming attacks but not layer 2.

With in-built ZT functions, 4G/5G networks avoid additional overlay functions to be deployed to enforce security. Enabling secure monitored APIs in the network allows for easy operational behaviors to be supported that are well regulated to meet the compliance needs of the enterprises.

Security function	4G/5G	Wi-Fi
Device identification, authentication, and authorization	Unique immutable device identifiers are provided in the SIM/eSIM. Supporting SUCI allows for hiding the user identity in the visited network, while using SUPI explicitly identifies the user to the home network. Root key (certificate)-based mutual authentication is supported. Authorization supported through RAN, core, and application-level policies through well-defined interfaces.	Mainly based on medium access control (MAC) addresses. This is made harder with MAC randomization support to enhance user privacy. Allows for username/password or certificate (PKI) authentication. Requires user/cert directory connected to RADIUS. Authorization is an overlay function that is typically customized for each enterprise.
Device credential provisioning	Handled through a sophisticated platform used globally by MNOs	Relies on enterprise IT management platforms that are typically localized and supported using mobile device management (MDM).
Resource partitioning	Resource allocation is supported for users/QoS flows in the individual nodes (RAN, EPC/5GC, and enterprise core interconnect) and is interlinked to support the requisite QoS.	No explicit resource allocations supported. It can be supported as an overlay function through VLAN separation with specific data tunneling on the interconnects and access points.
Control signaling protections	4G/5G networks support different signaling radio bearers (SRBs). SRB0 supports basic accesses between UE and eNB/gNB for radio resource control (RRC) connection establishment using common channels. SRB1 is used with dedicated channels in acknowledged mode with encryption when the device is connected on an exclusive link (C-RNTI), which is used to authenticate the device. SRB2 is used after user authentication to transport messages between UE and EPC/5G core network.	Such protections are not available on Wi-Fi.
User plane traffic protections	Data encryption is supported in the individual hops from the eNB/gNB to the SGW&PGW/UPF function using derived keys based on the individual user's authentication credentials.	Over-the-air encryption is optionally configured via SSIDs with 802.1X and/or passphrase (PSK)-based networks; encryption over wired infrastructure is optional and requires a vendor-specific controller or tunnel termination appliance.

II.2.3.7 Summary

This chapter described the aspects involved in a ZTA. The choices made with 4G/5G security procedures clearly show that security is not an afterthought and is inherently built into the workings and interactions of the system. The nature of integration with the enterprise core network is shown, allowing for the mimicking of Wi-Fi connectivity, which provides improved credential management through the use of eUICCs. The 4G/5G network also provides further sophistication for packet data connectivity, supporting additional isolation where it may be desired through the use of QoS, network, and RAN slice functions. Some comparisons between cellular technologies and Wi-Fi are presented. The need to integrate with existing procedures for user management is discussed, allowing for a single pane of glass to regulate users' access to the enterprise network independent of the technology used for connectivity. An approach to integrating the 4G/5G networks with the RADIUS service is suggested to address this.

Further Reading

NIST

1 https://doi.org/10.6028/NIST.SP.800-207

IEFT References

2 Internet Engineering Task Force, "Improved Extensible Authentication Protocol Method for 3rd Generation Authentication and Key Agreement (EAP-AKA')," Request for Comments (RFC) 5448 (May 2009).
3 Internet Engineering Task Force, "Extensible Authentication Protocol (EAP)," Request for Comments (RFC) 3748 (June 2004).
4 Internet Engineering Task Force, "The EAP-TLS Authentication Protocol," Request for Comments (RFC) 5216 (March 2008).

3GPP Specification References

5 3GPP, "3GPP System Architecture Evolution (SAE) – Security Architecture" (Release 15), technical specification (TS) 33.401, v15.2.0 (September 2018).
6 3GPP, "Security Architecture and Procedures for 5G System" (Release 15), technical specification (TS) 33.501, v15.5.0 (September 2018).
7 3rd Generation Partnership Project; Technical Specification Group Services and System Aspects; Procedures for the 5G System (5GS); Stage 2.
8 5G;NR; Radio Resource Control (RRC); Protocol specification (3GPP TS 38.331 version 16.3.1 Release 16).
9 Universal Mobile Telecommunications System (UMTS); LTE; Characteristics of the Universal Subscriber Identity Module (USIM) application (3GPP TS 31.102 version 15.1.0 Release 15).
10 Digital cellular telecommunications system (Phase 2+) (GSM); Universal Mobile Telecommunications System (UMTS); LTE; Characteristics of the IP Multimedia Services Identity Module (ISIM) application (3GPP TS 31.103).

11 TR 33.899 3rd Generation Partnership Project; Technical Specification Group Services and System Aspects; Study on the security aspects of the next generation system.
12 TR 31.890 3rd Generation Partnership Project; Technical Specification Group Core Network and Terminals; CT WG6 aspects of 5G System Phase 1.

GSMA References

13 eSIM: The What and How of Remote SIM Provisioning, GSMA paper. https://www.gsma.com/solutions-and-impact/technologies/esim/wp-content/uploads/2018/12/esim-whitepaper.pdf
14 ISO/IEC 7816 smart card standard. https://en.wikipedia.org/wiki/ISO/IEC_7816#:~:text=ISO%2FIEC%207816%20is%20an,International%20Electrotechnical%20Commission%20(IEC)
15 SGP.21 V2.2 RSP Architecture. https://www.gsma.com
16 SPG.22 V2.2.2 SGP.22 Technical Specification. https://www.gsma.com

Conference Paper References

17 Zhenhua Li, Weiwei Wang, Christo Wilson, Jian Chen, Chen Qian, Taeho Jung, Lan Zhang, Kebin Liu, Xiangyang Li, and Yunhao Liu, "FBS-Radar: Uncovering Fake Base Stations at Scale in the Wild," Proceedings of the Internet Society Symposium on Network and Distributed System Security (NDSS) (February 2017).
18 Altaf Shaik, Ravishankar Borgaonkar, N. Asokan, Valtteri Niemi, and Jean-Pierre Seifert, "Practical Attacks Against Privacy and Availability in 4G/LTE Mobile Communication Systems," Proceedings of the Internet Society Symposium on Network and Distributed System Security (NDSS) (February 2016).
19 Byeongdo Hong, Sangwook Bae, and Yongdae Kim, "GUTI Reallocation Demystified: Cellular Location Tracking with Changing Temporary Identifier," Proceedings of the Internet Society Symposium on Network and Distributed System Security (NDSS) (February 2018).
20 David Basin, Jannik Dreier, Lucca Hirschi, Saša Radomirovic, Ralf Sasse, and Vincent Stettler, "A Formal Analysis of 5G Authentication," Proceedings of the 2018 ACM SIGSAC Conference on Computer and Communications Security (CCS '18) (October 2018).

II.2.4

Network Slices

Key Network Slice Acronyms

Term	Description
DN	Data Network
DNN	Data Network Name
NSI ID	Network Slice Instance Identifier
NSSAA	Network Slice-Specific Authentication and Authorization
NSSAI	Network Slice Selection Assistance Information
NSSF	Network Slice Selection Function
NSSP	Network Slice Selection Policy
PSA	PDU Session Anchor
RFSP	RAT Frequency Selection Priority
SD	Slice Differentiator

II.2.4.1 Introduction

User equipment (UEs), when connected to the network, support diverse types of traffic based on the enterprise application demands. At the application level, they are typically described as real time, near-real time, non-real time, conversational, streaming, gaming, IoT, IIoT, and potentially other classifications. From a 3GPP perspective, for 4G Long Term Evolution (LTE), the supported quality of service (QoS) types are guaranteed bit rate (GBR), non-guaranteed bit rate (non-GBR), and in 5G New Radio (NR), an additional type of delay-critical GBR is supported as well.

At a high level, network slices are nothing but resource allocation into the appropriate Internet Protocol (IP) domain, at the different hops in the network from the enterprise core to the radio nodes, and including the over-the-air traffic scheduling for each admitted UE data flow to meet their QoS guarantees. The definition and resource allocation are more focused on the core network

Mobile Communication Systems for Private Networks, First Edition. Srinivasan Balasubramanian.

(CN) and do not directly involve the radio access network (RAN). The RAN is impacted indirectly based on the QoS flow and its associated QCIs that need to be supported within the network slice. The realization of these network slices is the subject addressed in this section. A brief introduction to the QoS mechanisms defined in 3GPP is discussed, and the concept of network slices is addressed as an extension of the QoS realization to support packet prioritization and isolation in the different hops of the private network.

The actual realization of the QoS guarantees is typically implementation specific and has requirements that need to be met at both the RAN, EPC/5GC, enterprise core, and the node interconnects, including the routers/bridges and interface cards supporting the transportation of packets between the UE and the far-end service, including the enterprise application servers. The individual sections of the RAN and CN in the book provide suggestive approaches that should sufficiently point the reader in the right direction, apart from motivating aspects that need to be considered as part of the realization.

Network slices provide a way to manage CN resources, detect and configure the required QoS flows, and ensure the isolation of different traffic types to reach different parts of the enterprise IP core. 3GPP-defined network slices also support explicit access to subscribed users, along with authentication. Although mainly targeted toward macro network deployments, these techniques are highly applicable to private networks, given the sensitive connectivity demands of the enterprise applications.

A lot of private network deployments use the QoS constructs from 3GPP and user subscription types to determine the isolation (directed to specific VLAN/VxLAN) without explicitly using the network slices suggested in 3GPP. However, the use of network slices allows for improved controls that can be supported. Network slices have not yet found clear use cases in the macro network. Based on the enterprise and the extent of isolation of different user groups within the enterprise (e.g. executive, middle management, other employees, or users working on specific projects), ensuring resource availability for specific slices definitely opens up use cases that can be supported in an enterprise network. Together with the traffic detection function (TDF) and network exposure APIs for specific applications to request QoS flows to be established, this chapter describes the end-to-end connectivity that is established to illustrate the approach taken to meet the SLA demands from a given enterprise.

The chapter also ties together the components of QoS, network slicing, RAN slicing, and VLAN association to enable enterprise applications, users, and QoS flow within a private network. The references provided towards the end of the chapter include references to 3GPP specifications, IEEE papers / tutorials, and industry papers covering the network slice concept and uses.

II.2.4.2 QoS Handling in LTE and NR

The network retains the control over allocating the requisite QoS to the different data flows. The triggers for the QoS can be initiated either by the UE or by network nodes such as the policy and charging rules function (PCRF) (EPC), policy control function (PCF) (5GC), TDF, or applications (e.g. video services).

There are enterprise users who always seek a better user experience on their 4G LTE devices. In particular, the idea of deploying a private 4G/5G network is to achieve better network quality relative to Wi-Fi connectivity. These enterprises are installing 4G/5G private networks, potentially as an addition to their Wi-Fi networks, to support higher bandwidth and improved access for their devices. Not only subscribers but also some services themselves (e.g. VoIP call) require better priority handling in the network. QoS plays a critical role in this. Additionally, better regulation of network usage is possible, even during congestion, by accommodating different classes of users and services supported on the enterprise campus.

II.2.4.2.1 QoS Parameters for LTE/NR Private Networks

This section details the set of QoS parameters through which the QoS guarantees associated with individual QoS flows for LTE and NR are met via network implementation realizations.

Flow type	Description	Non-GBR	GBR		LTE/NR
Resource type for QoS parameters	An identifier for QoS characteristics that influence scheduling weights, admission thresholds, queue management thresholds, link-layer protocol configuration, etc.	Non-GBR	GBR	Delay-critical GBR	
5G QoS identifier (5QI)/QoS class identifier (QCI)	An index value that maps to a set of values associated with the QoS parameters.	M	M	M	LTE & NR
QoS flow Identifier (ID) (QFI)	The QoS flow identifier is used to index the QoS flows assigned to a UE.	M	M	M	LTE & NR
Allocation and retention priority (ARP)	Information about priority level (PL), preemption capability (can preempt resources assigned to other QoS flows), and preemption vulnerability (can be preempted by other QoS flows).	M	M	M	LTE & NR
Guaranteed bit rate (GBR)	Provides the value for the guaranteed minimum application-layer bit rate for the QoS flow.		M	M	LTE
Maximum bit rate (MBR)	Provides the value for the allowed application-layer maximum bit rate.		M	M	LTE
Reflective QoS attribute (RQA)	Optional parameter: certain traffic on this flow may use reflective QoS.	O			NR
Guaranteed flow bit rate (GFBR)	Measured over the averaging time window, it is set to the minimum application-layer bit rate for the QoS flow.		M	M	NR
Maximum flow bit rate (MFBR)	Set to the maximum application-layer bit rate allowed for the QoS flow.		M	M	NR
QoS notification control (QNC)	Configures NG-RAN to notify Session Management Function (SMF) if GFBR cannot be met. This is useful if the application can adapt to changing conditions. If alternative QoS profiles are configured, NG-RAN indicates if one of these matches the currently fulfilled performance metrics.		O	O	NR

(Continued)

Flow type	Description	Non-GBR	GBR		LTE/NR
Maximum packet loss rate (MPLR)	In Release 16, this is limited to voice media.		O	O	LTE & NR
Session/access point name (APN) – aggregate maximum bit rate (AMBR)	Provides the value for the aggregated bit rate allowed for a packet session connection across all QoS flows.	M			LTE & NR
UE-AMBR	Provides the value for the aggregated bit rate allowed across all packet session connections and QoS flows.	M			LTE & NR
PDB	The packet delay budget provides the time period that the packet can be enqueued above the RAN scheduler layer, and when the delay exceeds that timer value, the packet is dropped.	M	M	M	LTE & NR
PER	Allowed packet error rate for the application to function correctly.	M	M	M	LTE & NR
Averaging window	The QoS parameters for both downlink (DL) and uplink (UL) are measured within an averaging window.	M	M	M	LTE & NR
Maximum data burst volume (MDBV)	It is the allowed MDBV for a delay-critical GBR, and if the application generates bit rates higher than that, it will be supported with best-effort quality.			M	LTE & NR

II.2.4.2.2 LTE QoS

In LTE, network QoS is implemented between the UE and the packet data network (PDN) gateway (PGW), considered as end-to-end, and defined as a set of bearers. "Bearer" is a virtual concept supporting resource allocation across the nodes in the network and is a set of network configurations to provide special treatment to a set of traffic. For example, voice-over IP (VoIP) and video-telephone (VT) packets are prioritized by the network compared to other services that can be accommodated as best-effort traffic such as email and web browsing.

In LTE, the QoS support from UE to PGW is referred to as the radio access bearer. The radio access bearer itself is realized as hop-to-hop QoS across the nodes as the radio bearer (over-the-air QoS based on the RAN scheduler), S1 bearer (connectivity between the EPC core and the RAN), and S5/S8 bearer (connectivity between the EPC core and the enterprise IP domain). This is collectively referred to as the Evolved Packet System (EPS) bearer as shown in Figure II.2.4.1.

To best understand the concept of QoS, an understanding of the bearer types is required. See Figure II.2.4.2. At a high level, there are two types of bearers: default bearer and dedicated bearer. When a PDN connection is established, the default bearer is always established. This implies that

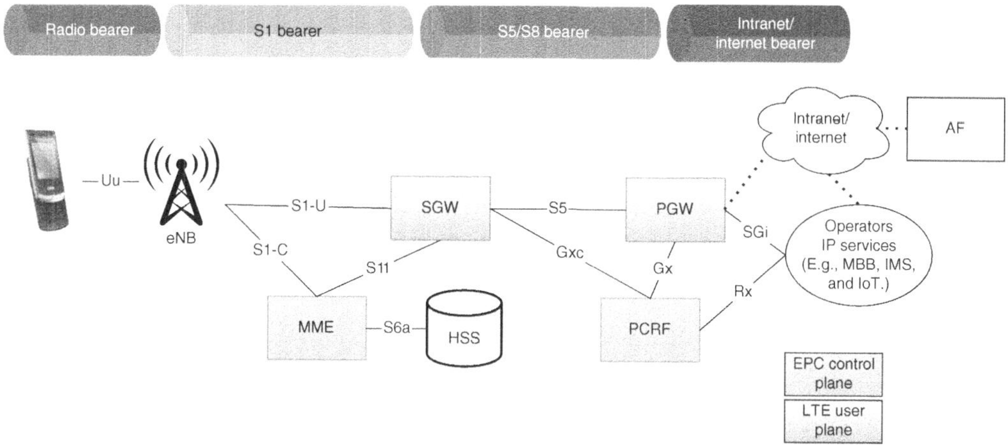

Figure II.2.4.1 LTE QoS bearer.

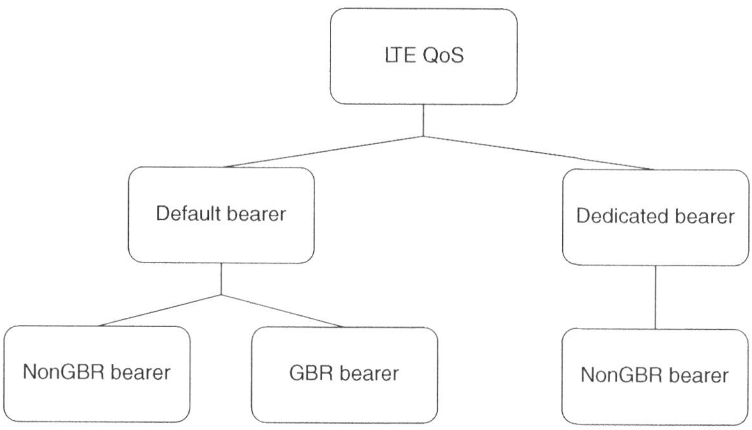

Figure II.2.4.2 LTE bearer types.

at least one default bearer is established when the UE attaches to the LTE network. One or more dedicated bearers can be established right at the beginning, like the default bearer, or, more typically, these dedicated bearers are established on demand based on the activation of specific services that require specific QoS flows based on the five-tuple (source/target IP address/port number, DiffServ code point [DSCP] markings).

Default bearers typically do not provide any guarantees, and based on the network congestion, they can experience variable performances. These default bearers are associated with non-GBR QoS configuration, and inter-UE traffic prioritization and intra-UE flow prioritization can be done. The non-GBR QCI associated with UE/flows within the UE is regulated based on the weights associated with the individual non-GBR QoS.

Table II.2.4.1 LTE standardized QCI values (copied from table 6.1.7-A, "Standardized QCI characteristics" [3GPP TS 23.203]).

QCI	Resource type	Priority level	Packet delay budget (NOTE 13)	Packet error loss Rate (NOTE 2)	Example services
1 (NOTE 3)	GBR	2	100 ms (NOTE 1, NOTE 11)	10^{-2}	Conversational voice
2 (NOTE 3)		4	150 ms (NOTE 1, NOTE 11)	10^{-3}	Conversational video (live streaming)
3 (NOTE 3, NOTE 14)		3	50 ms (NOTE 1, NOTE 11)	10^{-3}	Real-time gaming, V2X messages Electricity distribution – medium voltage (e.g. clause 7.2.2 of TS 22.261) Process automation – monitoring (e.g. clause 7.2.2 of TS 22.261)
4 (NOTE 3)		5	300 ms (NOTE 1, NOTE 11)	10^{-6}	Non-conversational video (buffered streaming)
65 (NOTE 3, NOTE 9, NOTE 12)		0.7	75 ms (NOTE 7, NOTE 8)	10^{-2}	Mission-critical user plane push-to-talk voice (e.g. MC-PTT)
66 (NOTE 3, NOTE 12)		2	100 ms (NOTE 1, NOTE 10)	10^{-2}	Non-mission-critical user plane push-to-talk voice
67 (NOTE 3, NOTE 12)		1.5	100 ms (NOTE 1, NOTE 10)	10^{-3}	Mission-critical video user plane
75 (NOTE 14)		2.5	50 ms (NOTE 1)	10^{-2}	V2X messages
71		5.6	150 ms (NOTE 1, NOTE 16)	10^{-6}	"Live" uplink streaming (e.g. TS 26.238)
72		5.6	300 ms (NOTE 1, NOTE 16)	10^{-4}	"Live" uplink streaming (e.g. TS 26.238)
73		5.6	300 ms (NOTE 1, NOTE 16)	10^{-8}	"Live" uplink streaming (e.g. TS 26.238)
74		5.6	500 ms (NOTE 1, NOTE 16)	10^{-8}	"Live" uplink streaming (e.g. TS 26.238)
76		5.6	500 ms (NOTE 1, NOTE 16)	10^{-4}	"Live" uplink streaming (e.g. TS 26.238)
5 (NOTE 3)	Non-GBR	1	100 ms (NOTE 1, NOTE 10)	10^{-6}	IMS signaling
6 (NOTE 4)		6	300 ms (NOTE 1, NOTE 10)	10^{-6}	Video (buffered streaming) TCP-based (e.g. www, email, chat, ftp, p2p file sharing, progressive video, etc.)
7 (NOTE 3)		7	100 ms (NOTE 1, NOTE 10)	10^{-3}	Voice, video (live streaming)Interactive gaming
8 (NOTE 5)		8	300 ms (NOTE 1)	10^{-6}	Video (buffered streaming) TCP-based (e.g. www, email, chat, ftp, p2p file sharing, progressive video, etc.)
9 (NOTE 6)		9			
10		9	1100 ms (NOTE 1, NOTE 17)	10^{-6}	Video (buffered streaming) TCP-based (e.g. www, email, chat, ftp, p2p file sharing, progressive video, etc.) and any service that can be used over satellite access with these characteristics
69 (NOTE 3, NOTE 9, NOTE 12)		0.5	60 ms (NOTE 7, NOTE 8)	10^{-6}	Mission-critical, delay-sensitive signaling (e.g., MC-PTT signaling, MC video signaling)

70 (NOTE 4, NOTE 12)	5.5	200 ms (NOTE 7, NOTE 10)	10^{-6}	Mission-critical data (e.g. example services are the same as QCI 6/8/9)
79 (NOTE 14)	6.5	50 ms (NOTE 1, NOTE 10)	10^{-2}	V2X messages
80 (NOTE 3)	6.8	10 ms (NOTE 10, NOTE 15)	10^{-6}	Low-latency eMBB applications (TCP/UDP-based); augmented reality

NOTE 1: A delay of 20 ms for the delay between a PCEF and a radio base station should be subtracted from a given Packet Delay Budget (PDB) to derive the packet delay budget that applies to the radio interface. This delay is the average between the case where the PCEF is located "close" to the radio base station (roughly 10 ms) and the case where the PCEF is located "far" from the radio base station, e.g. in case of roaming with home routed traffic (the one-way packet delay between Europe and the US west coast is roughly 50 ms). The average takes into account that roaming is a less typical scenario. It is expected that subtracting this average delay of 20 ms from a given PDB will lead to desired end-to-end performance in most typical cases. Also, note that the PDB defines an upper bound. Actual packet delays - in particular for GBR traffic - should typically be lower than the PDB specified for a QCI as long as the UE has sufficient radio channel quality.

NOTE 2: The rate of non congestion related packet losses that may occur between a radio base station and a PCEF should be regarded to be negligible. A PELR value specified for a standardized QCI therefore applies completely to the radio interface between a UE and radio base station.

NOTE 3: This QCI is typically associated with an operator controlled service, i.e., a service where the SDF aggregate's uplink / downlink packet filters are known at the point in time when the SDF aggregate is authorized. In case of E-UTRAN this is the point in time when a corresponding dedicated EPS bearer is established / modified.

NOTE 4: If the network supports Multimedia Priority Services (MPS) then this QCI could be used for the prioritization of non real-time data (i.e. most typically TCP-based services/applications) of MPS subscribers.

NOTE 5: This QCI could be used for a dedicated "premium bearer" (e.g. associated with premium content) for any subscriber / subscriber group. Also in this case, the SDF aggregate's uplink / downlink packet filters are known at the point in time when the SDF aggregate is authorized. Alternatively, this QCI could be used for the default bearer of a UE/PDN for "premium subscribers".

NOTE 6: This QCI is typically used for the default bearer of a UE/PDN for non privileged subscribers. Note that AMBR can be used as a "tool" to provide subscriber differentiation between subscriber groups connected to the same PDN with the same QCI on the default bearer.

NOTE 7: For Mission Critical services, it may be assumed that the PCEF is located "close" to the radio base station (roughly 10 ms) and is not normally used in a long distance, home routed roaming situation. Hence delay of 10 ms for the delay between a PCEF and a radio base station should be subtracted from this PDB to derive the packet delay budget that applies to the radio interface.

NOTE 8: In both RRC Idle and RRC Connected mode, the PDB requirement for these QCIs can be relaxed (but not to a value greater than 320 ms) for the first packet(s) in a downlink data or signalling burst in order to permit reasonable battery saving (DRX) techniques.

NOTE 9: It is expected that QCI-65 and QCI-69 are used together to provide Mission Critical Push to Talk service (e.g., QCI-5 is not used for signalling for the bearer that utilizes QCI-65 as user plane bearer). It is expected that the amount of traffic per UE will be similar or less compared to the IP Multimedia Subsystem (IMS) signalling.

NOTE 10: In both RRC Idle and RRC Connected mode, the PDB requirement for these QCIs can be relaxed for the first packet(s) in a downlink data or signalling burst in order to permit battery saving (DRX) techniques.

NOTE 11: In RRC Idle mode, the PDB requirement for these QCIs can be relaxed for the first packet(s) in a downlink data or signalling burst in order to permit battery saving (DRX) techniques.

NOTE 12: This QCI value can only be assigned upon request from the network side. The UE and any application running on the UE is not allowed to request this QCI value.

NOTE 13: Packet delay budget is not applicable on NB-IoT or when Enhanced Coverage is used for WB-E-UTRAN (see TS 36.300 [19]).

NOTE 14: This QCI could be used for transmission of V2X messages as defined in TS 23.285 [48].

NOTE 15: A delay of 2 ms for the delay between a PCEF and a radio base station should be subtracted from the given PDB to derive the packet delay budget that applies to the radio interface.

NOTE 16: For "live" uplink streaming (see TS 26.238), guidelines for PDB values of the different QCIs correspond to the latency configurations defined in TR 26.939 [54]. In order to support higher latency reliable streaming services (above 500ms PDB), if different PDB and PELR combinations are needed these configurations will have to use non-standardised QCIs.

NOTE 17: The worst case one way propagation delay for GEO satellite is expected to be ~270 ms, ~ 21 ms for LEO at 1200 km, and ~13 ms for LEO at 600 km. The UL scheduling delay that needs to be added is also typically a two way propagation delay e.g. ~540 ms for GEO, ~42 ms for LEO at 1200 km, and ~26 ms for LEO at 600 km. Based on that, the access network Packet delay budget is not applicable for QCIs that require access network PDB lower than the sum of these values when the specific types of satellite access are used (see TS 36.300 [19]). QCI-10 can accommodate the worst case PDB for GEO satellite type.

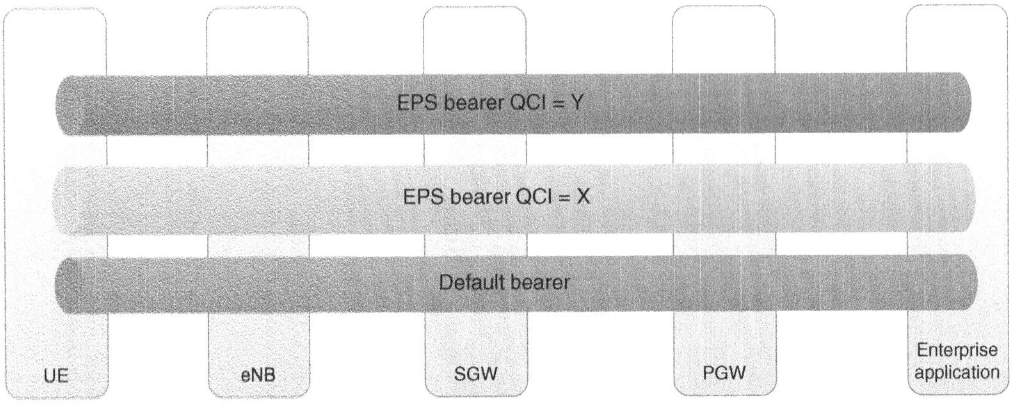

Figure II.2.4.3 LTE EPS bearers.

Dedicated bearers are the additional or secondary bearers created on top of the existing default bearer. The dedicated bearers share the IP address previously established by the default bearer as part of the PDN connection establishment and do not require an independent IP context to be established for the UE. Dedicated bearers are typically used as GBR services, although they can also be a non-GBR service.

Figure II.2.4.3 illustrates the EPS bearer and, in particular, shows that there is a one-to-one relationship between the CN and radio bearers and that a given QoS flow is established end-to-end with this rigid relationship.

The use of GBR or non-GBR bearers for the individual services based on the QoS demands and the policy of the enterprise will depend on the anticipated traffic load versus the dimensioned capacity. Assuming sufficiently dimensioned capacity is available, any service—real time, near real time, and non-real time—can be realized based on a non-GBR bearer.

The QoS is established and triggered from either the UE or one of the network functions (NFs). The allowed QoS and the supported parameters are regulated by the PCRF. The PCRF indicates the packet gateway (PWG), which in turn informs the Mobility Management Entity (MME) to establish the QoS flow. The MME interacts using signaling messages to establish the DL and UL QoS flows and also establishes the bearers at the eNB, SGW, and PGW, along with the required interconnections across the nodes. Once established, the QoS criteria are maintained by the compute resources in the PWG/SWG, the routers, the bridges across the hops, and the RAN scheduler function.

See table 6.1.7-A, standardized QCI characteristics in 3GPP TS 23.203, for the different standards defining the QCI value for LTE QoS operations, along with the associated parameters. The table is reproduced below for ease of readability for the user. The values for the QoS parameters associated with LTE QoS flows are defined, along with the type of service that will use the associated QCI and, hence, the QoS setting.

II.2.4.2.3 NR QoS

5QI (5G QoS identifier) is a pointer to a set of QoS characteristics such as priority level, packet delay, or packet error rate (see the snapshot). These QoS characteristics can either be standardized or nonstandardized. So, if you look at the table below, you can see different standardized

Table II.2.4.2 LTE standardized QCI values (copied from table 6.1.7-B, "Standardized QCI characteristics" [3GPP TS 23.203]).

QCI	Resource type	Priority level	Packet delay budget (NOTE B1)	Packet error loss Rate (NOTE B2)	Maximum data burst volume (NOTE B1)	Data rate averaging window	Example services
82 (NOTE B6)	GBR	1.9	10 ms (NOTE B4)	10^{-4} (NOTE B3)	255 bytes	2,000 ms	Discrete automation (TS 22.278, clause 8, bullet g, and TS 22.261, table 7.2.2-1, "Small packets")
83 (NOTE B6)		2.2	10 ms (NOTE B4)	10^{-4} (NOTE B3)	1354 bytes (NOTE B5)	2,000 ms	Discrete automation (TS 22.278, clause 8, bullet g, and TS 22.261, table 7.2.2-1, "Big packets")
84 (NOTE B6)		2.4	30 ms (NOTE B7)	10^{-5} (NOTE B3)	1354 bytes (NOTE B5)	2,000 ms	Intelligent transport systems (TS 22.278, clause 8, bullet h, and TS 22.261, table 7.2.2)
85 (NOTE B6)		2.1	5 ms (NOTE B8)	10^{-5} (NOTE B3)	255 bytes	2,000 ms	Electricity distribution – high voltage (TS 22.278, clause 8, bullet i, and TS 22.261, table 7.2.2, and Annex D, clause D.4.2)

NOTE B1: The PDB applies to bursts that are not greater than Maximum Data Burst Volume.
NOTE B2: This Packet Error Loss Rate includes packets that are not successfully delivered over the access network plus those packets that comply with the Maximum Data Burst Volume and GBR requirements but which are not delivered within the Packet Delay Budget.
NOTE B3: Data rates above the GBR, or, bursts larger than the Maximum Data Burst Volume, are treated as best effort, and, in order to serve other packets and meet the PELR, this can lead to them being discarded.
NOTE B4: A delay of 1 ms for the delay between a PCEF and a radio base station should be subtracted from a given PDB to derive the packet delay budget that applies to the radio interface.
NOTE B5: This Maximum Data Burst Volume value is set to 1354 bytes to avoid IP fragmentation on an IPv6 based, IPSec protected GTP tunnel to the eNB (the value is calculated as in Annex C of TS 23.060 [12] and further reduced by 4 bytes to allow for the usage of a GTP-U extension header).
NOTE B6: This QCI is typically associated with a dedicated EPS bearer.
NOTE B7: A delay of 5 ms for the delay between a PCEF and a radio base station should be subtracted from a given PDB to derive the packet delay budget that applies to the radio interface.
NOTE B8: A delay of 2 ms for the delay between a PCEF and a radio base station should be subtracted from a given PDB to derive the packet delay budget that applies to the radio interface.

5QI values for different QoS flow types such as GBR, non-GBR, and delay-critical GBR flows, while 5QI values from 128 to 254 are nonstandardized and can be used for operator-specific configurations.

The difference is that 5QI applies to a flow carried at some point in a bearer, while QCI applies to a bearer within which certain types of flows are expected. Additionally, you should note that the 5QI values are, as far as possible, aligned with the EPS standardized QCI characteristics defined in 3GPP TS 23.203, which makes the mapping of QoS easier, for example during mobility between 5GS and EPS.

Figure II.2.4.4 shows the mechanism of handling QoS in NR. In LTE, the QoS is established as a single end-to-end context from the application layer to the radio layers via the core. In NR, these are handled in a modular way. The application traffic generated reaches the IP domain as part of the Protocol Data Unit (PDU) session. The application traffic is segregated and recognized as IP flows in the user plane function (UPF). One or more of these IP flows is indicated to be carried over an established radio bearer. One or more of the radio bearers are established, with each IP flow mapped to a specific radio bearer. This architecture allows for a very flexible approach to managing the resources in the different parts of the networks independently, allowing for ease of scaling and integration.

- Each application interaction requires an end-to-end packet flow, which is called a service data flow (SDF) operating within a PDU session.
- Each SDF can be associated with a 5G QoS flow that has a specific QoS definition that can be assigned.
- One or more SDFs with the same QoS characteristics are grouped together in a 5G QoS flow.
- The 5G QoS flow is the most granular measure of QoS in the 5G network and the level at which QoS is enforced.
- If an SDF requires a different set of QoS characteristics, then another 5G QoS flow is defined to meet the requirements.
- Each QoS flow is identified by a QoS flow identifier (QFI), which lets the network elements know which flow to map to the SDF.
- Each QoS flow is defined by a QoS profile.
- The QoS profile identifies the 5G QoS characteristics with a 5G QoS identifier (5QI) and ARP parameters, which define a PL and whether the QoS flow can preempt another flow or if it can be preempted.
- The ARP can be used for admission control. The ARP values determine which flow takes precedence.
- Like 4G, 5G QoS provides a non-GBR and GBR classification.
  - In 5G, GBR and non-GBR classifications are at the QoS flow level and are part of the QoS profile.
  - For non-GBR flows, there is an AMBR that limits the overall usage across all SDFs within that QoS flow.
  - For GBR flows, there is a GFBR, an MFBR, and an MPLR.
- SMF functions
  - The SMF manages the PDU session and, hence, the related QoS flows, assigning a QFI and QoS profile to the flow based on information provided by the PCF.
  - The SMF then provides the UPF with the packet detection rules (PDRs) for mapping SDFs to the QoS flows.
  - The SMF sends the QoS profile to the next-generation node B (i.e. gNB) via the Access Management Function (AMF).
- The gNB can map the 5G QoS flow to a specific data radio bearer (DRB) on the radio interface.
- The AMF conveys the QoS rules to the UE to aid in mapping SDF flows to a 5G QoS flow and the correct DRB.

Table II.2.4.3 Standardized 5QI to QoS characteristics mapping (copied from table 5.7.4-1, "Standardized 5QI to QoS characteristics mapping" [3GPP TS 23.501]).

5QI value	Resource type	Default priority level	Packet delay budget (NOTE 3)	Packet error rate	Default maximum data burst volume (NOTE 2)	Default averaging window	Example services
1	GBR	20	100 ms (NOTE 11, NOTE 13)	10^{-2}	N/A	2,000 ms	Conversational voice
2		40	150 ms (NOTE 11, NOTE 13)	10^{-3}	N/A	2,000 ms	Conversational video (live streaming)
3		30	50 ms (NOTE 11, NOTE 13)	10^{-3}	N/A	2,000 ms	Real-time gaming, V2X messages (see TS 23.287). Electricity distribution – medium voltage, process automation monitoring
4		50	300 ms (NOTE 11, NOTE 13)	10^{-6}	N/A	2,000 ms	Non-conversational video (buffered streaming)
65 (NOTE 9, NOTE 12)		7	75 ms (NOTE 7, NOTE 8)	10^{-2}	N/A	2,000 ms	Mission-critical user plane push-to-talk voice (e.g. MC-PTT)
66 (NOTE 12)		20	100 ms (NOTE 10, NOTE 13)	10^{-2}	N/A	2,000 ms	Non-mission-critical user plane push-to-talk voice
67 (NOTE 12)		15	100 ms (NOTE 10, NOTE 13)	10^{-3}	N/A	2,000 ms	Mission-critical video user plane
75 (NOTE 14)							
71		56	150 ms (NOTE 11, NOTE 13, NOTE 15)	10^{-6}	N/A	2,000 ms	"Live" uplink streaming (e.g. TS 26.238 [76])
72		56	300 ms (NOTE 11, NOTE 13, NOTE 15)	10^{-4}	N/A	2,000 ms	"Live" uplink streaming (e.g. TS 26.238 [76])
73		56	300 ms (NOTE 11, NOTE 13, NOTE 15)	10^{-8}	N/A	2,000 ms	"Live" uplink streaming (e.g. TS 26.238 [76])
74		56	500 ms (NOTE 11, NOTE 15)	10^{-8}	N/A	2,000 ms	"Live" uplink streaming (e.g. TS 26.238 [76])
76		56	500 ms (NOTE 11, NOTE 13, NOTE 15)	10^{-4}	N/A	2,000 ms	"Live" uplink streaming (e.g. TS 26.238 [76])
5	Non-GBR	10	100 ms (NOTE 10, NOTE 13)	10^{-6}	N/A	N/A	IMS signaling
6		60	300 ms (NOTE 10, NOTE 13)	10^{-6}	N/A	N/A	Video (buffered streaming) TCP-based (e.g. www, email, chat, ftp, p2p file sharing, progressive video, etc.)

(Continued)

Table II.2.4.3 (Continued)

5QI value	Resource type	Default priority level	Packet delay budget (NOTE 3)	Packet error rate	Default maximum data burst volume (NOTE 2)	Default averaging window	Example services
7		70	100 ms (NOTE 10, NOTE 13)	10^{-3}	N/A	N/A	Voice, video (live streaming) Interactive gaming
8		80	300 ms (NOTE 13)	10^{-6}	N/A	N/A	Video (buffered streaming) TCP-based (e.g. www, email, chat, ftp, p2p file sharing, progressive video, etc.)
9		90					
10		90	1100 ms (NOTE 13, NOTE 17)	10^{-6}	N/A	N/A	Video (buffered streaming) TCP-based (e.g. www, email, chat, ftp, p2p file sharing, progressive video, etc.) and any service that can be used over satellite access types with these characteristics
69 (NOTE 9, NOTE 12)		5	60 ms (NOTE 7, NOTE 8)	10^{-6}	N/A	N/A	Mission-critical delay-sensitive signaling (e.g. MC-PTT signaling)
70 (NOTE 12)		55	200 ms (NOTE 7, NOTE 10)	10^{-6}	N/A	N/A	Mission-critical data (e.g. example services are the same as 5QI 6/8/9)
79		65	50 ms (NOTE 10, NOTE 13)	10^{-2}	N/A	N/A	V2X messages (see TS 23.287)
80		68	10 ms (NOTE 5, NOTE 10)	10^{-6}	N/A	N/A	Low-latency eMBB applications and augmented reality
82	Delay-critical GBR	19	10 ms (NOTE 4)	10^{-4}	255 bytes	2,000 ms	Discrete automation (see TS 22.261)
83		22	10 ms (NOTE 4)	10^{-4}	1,354 bytes (NOTE 3)	2,000 ms	Discrete automation (see TS 22.261); V2X messages (UE – RSU platooning, advanced driving: cooperative lane change with low LoA. see TS 22.186, TS 23.287)
84		24	30 ms (NOTE 6)	10^{-5}	1,354 bytes (NOTE 3)	2,000 ms	Intelligent transport systems (see TS 22.261)
85		21	5 ms (NOTE 5)	10^{-5}	255 bytes	2,000 ms	Electricity distribution – high voltage (see TS 22.261). V2X messages (remote driving. See TS 22.186, NOTE 16, see TS 23.287)
86		18	5 ms (NOTE 5)	10^{-4}	1,354 bytes	2,000 ms	V2X messages (advanced driving: collision avoidance, platooning with high LoA; see TS 22.186, TS 23.287)
87		25	5 ms (NOTE 4)	10^{-3}	500 bytes	2,000 ms	Interactive service – motion tracking data, (see TS 22.261)

88	25	10 ms (NOTE 4)	10^{-3}	1,125 bytes	2,000 ms	Interactive service – motion tracking data, (see TS 22.261)
89	25	15 ms (NOTE 4)	10^{-4}	17,000 bytes	2,000 ms	Visual content for cloud/edge/split rendering (see TS 22.261)
90	25	20 ms (NOTE 4)	10^{-4}	63,000 bytes	2,000 ms	Visual content for cloud/edge/split rendering (see TS 22.261)

NOTE 1: A packet which is delayed more than PDB is not counted as lost, thus not included in the PER.
NOTE 2: It is required that default MDBV is supported by a PLMN supporting the related 5QIs.
NOTE 3: The Maximum Transfer Unit (MTU) size considerations in clause 9.3 and Annex C of TS 23.060 [56] are also applicable. IP fragmentation may have impacts to CN PDB, and details are provided in clause 5.6.10.
NOTE 4: A static value for the CN PDB of 1 ms for the delay between a UPF terminating N6 and a 5G-AN should be subtracted from a given PDB to derive the packet delay budget that applies to the radio interface. When a dynamic CN PDB is used, see clause 5.7.3.4.
NOTE 5: A static value for the CN PDB of 2 ms for the delay between a UPF terminating N6 and a 5G-AN should be subtracted from a given PDB to derive the packet delay budget that applies to the radio interface. When a dynamic CN PDB is used, see clause 5.7.3.4.
NOTE 6: A static value for the CN PDB of 5 ms for the delay between a UPF terminating N6 and a 5G-AN should be subtracted from a given PDB to derive the packet delay budget that applies to the radio interface. When a dynamic CN PDB is used, see clause 5.7.3.4.
NOTE 7: For Mission Critical services, it may be assumed that the UPF terminating N6 is located "close" to the 5G_AN (roughly 10 ms) and is not normally used in a long distance, home routed roaming situation. Hence a static value for the CN PDB of 10 ms for the delay between a UPF terminating N6 and a 5G_AN should be subtracted from this PDB to derive the packet delay budget that applies to the radio interface.
NOTE 8: In RRC_IDLE, RRC_INACTIVE and RRC_CONNECTED mode, the PDB requirement for these 5QIs can be relaxed (but not to a value greater than 320 ms) for the first packet(s) in a downlink data or signalling burst in order to permit reasonable battery saving (DRX) techniques.
NOTE 9: It is expected that 5QI-65 and 5QI-69 are used together to provide Mission Critical Push to Talk service (e.g. 5QI-5 is not used for signalling). It is expected that the amount of traffic per UE will be similar or less compared to the IMS signalling.
NOTE 10: In RRC_IDLE, RRC_INACTIVE and RRC_CONNECTED mode, the PDB requirement for these 5QIs can be relaxed for the first packet(s) in a downlink data or signalling burst in order to permit battery saving (DRX) techniques.
NOTE 11: In RRC_IDLE mode, the PDB requirement for these 5QIs can be relaxed for the first packet(s) in a downlink data or signalling burst in order to permit battery saving (DRX) techniques.
NOTE 12: This 5QI value can only be assigned upon request from the network side. The UE and any application running on the UE is not allowed to request this 5QI value.
NOTE 13: A static value for the CN PDB of 20 ms for the delay between a UPF terminating N6 and a 5G-AN should be subtracted from a given PDB to derive the packet delay budget that applies to the radio interface.
NOTE 14: This 5QI is only used for transmission of V2X messages as defined in TS 23.287 and transmission of A2X messages as defined in TS 23.256 [136].
NOTE 15: For "live" uplink streaming (see TS 26.238 [76]), guidelines for PDB values of the different 5QIs correspond to the latency configurations defined in TR 26.939 [77]. In order to support higher latency reliable streaming services (above 500ms PDB), if different PDB and PER combinations are needed these configurations will have to use non-standardised 5QIs.
NOTE 16: These services are expected to need much larger MDBV values to be signalled to the RAN. Support for such larger MDBV values with low latency and high reliability is likely to require a suitable RAN configuration, for which, the simulation scenarios in TR 38.824 [112] may contain some guidance.
NOTE 17: The worst case one way propagation delay for GEO satellite is expected to be ~270ms, ,~ 21 ms for LEO at 1200km, and 13 ms for LEO at 600km. The UL scheduling delay that needs to be added is also typically two way propagation delay e.g. ~540ms for GEO, ~42ms for LEO at 1200km, and ~26 ms for LEO at 600km. Based on that, the 5G-AN Packet delay budget is not applicable for 5QIs that require 5G-AN PDB lower than the sum of these values when the specific types of satellite access are used (see TS 38.300 [27]). 5QI-10 can accommodate the worst case PDB for GEO satellite type.

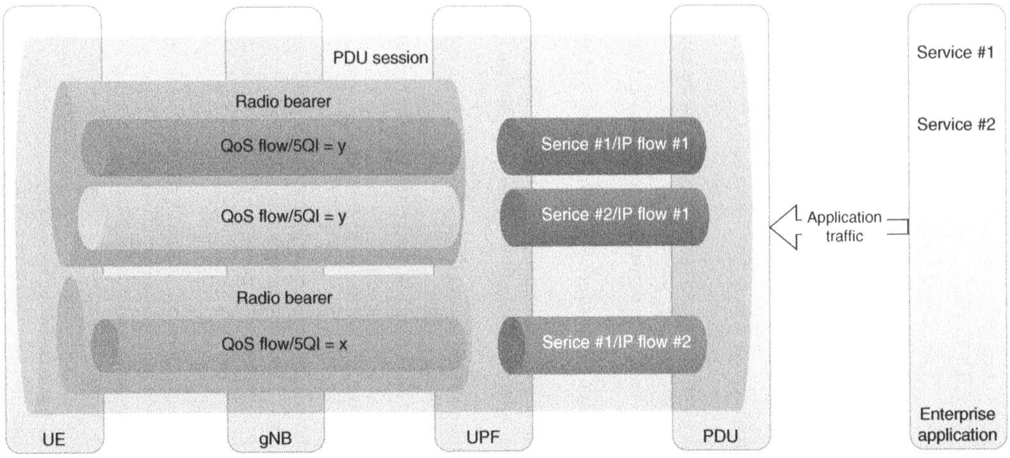

Figure II.2.4.4 NR QoS flows and IP flows.

II.2.4.3 NR Slices

The previous sections introduce the concept of QoS architecture and end-to-end behaviors for both LTE and NR. The network slice as a concept was introduced with the first NR release of the 3GPP standard (Release 15). This and the following sections provide a description of the network slices in NR, associating the network slices with different IP domains within the enterprise network and further providing the context of how QoS flows are embedded into the network slices framework. This concept is extended to LTE for a converged core realization. Further RAN slices are introduced to allow for segregating and managing the radio resources. Integrating all these pieces and establishing a generic concept of "slices" for an end-to-end representation are presented and hopefully provide the reader with a holistic view.

For a broad understanding, recognize the resources in the network nodes and hops, dynamically tie the required resources, and associate them with a set of UEs/QoS flows, treating each sliver as a slice that allows for the SLO/SLAs to be met for the individual UE/QoS flow.

II.2.4.3.1 Network Slices

Network slice is a dynamically created logical network that provides specific network capabilities and network characteristics. NSSAI is a collection of up to a maximum of 8 S-NSSAI. A max of 8 S-NSSAIs can be included in the allowed and requested NSSAIs. Allowed NSSAI is the set of NSSAIs that the network authorizes the UE to use during the UE's current association with the network. The requested NSSAIs sent by the UE can be a larger set compared to the allowed NSSAIs by the network for the UE. A network slice instance is a set of network function instances and the required resources (e.g. compute, storage, and networking resources in the 5GC core) that form a deployed network slice. A network slice instance can be associated with one or more S-NSSAIs, where several S-NSSAIs are associated with a common set of network resources. Additionally, an S-NSSAI can be associated with one or more network slice instances; based on the UE/subscription, the resource allocation in the network can be guided appropriately.

An S-NSSAI, as part of its definition, comprises an SST, which refers to the expected network slice behavior in terms of features and services – a slice differentiator (SD), which is optional information that complements the SSTs to differentiate among multiple network slices of the same SST. An

S-NSSAI can have 3GPP standard-defined S-NSSAI network-specific values: eMBB, URLLC, MioT, or it can be a nonstandard (not defined in the 3GPP standards) S-NSSAI with an SST and an SD, or a nonstandard S-NSSA with only an SST without a standardized SST value and no SD.

SST	Slice/Service Type It defines the behavior of the network slice in terms of specific features and services and has end-to-end realization expectations.
Network slice	A dynamically created logical network that provides specific network capabilities and characteristics. • Network Slice Selection Assistance (NSSAI) is a collection of a max 8 S-NSSAI. A max of 8 S-NSSAIs can be included in the allowed and requested NSSAIs.
Network slice instance	It is a set of network function instances and the required resources (e.g. compute, storage, and networking resources) that form a deployed network slice. • A network slice instance can be associated with one or more S-NSSAIs, and an S-NSSAI can be associated with one or more network slice instances.
An S-NSSAI comprises	• A Slice/Service type (SST), which refers to the expected Network Slice behavior in terms of features and services, • A Slice Differentiator (SD) is optional information that complements the Slice/Service type(s) to differentiate among multiple Network Slices of the same SST. – Standard S-NSSAI network-specific values: eMBB, URLLC, MioT, or – Nonstandard S-NSSAI, an SST, and an SD, or • Nonstandard S-NSSA with only an SST without a standardized SST value and no SD.

II.2.4.3.2 S-NSSAI Types

This section describes the set of S-NSSAI types as defined in the 3GPP standards.

S-NSSAI types	Description
Subscribed	• UE is provisioned with a set of S-NSSAIs stored in the Unified Data Management (UDM). • 5GC uses UDM-stored information as a default when the UE does not provide a requested NSSAI.
Configured	• May either be configured by a serving PLMN and apply to the serving PLMN or may be a default-configured NSSAI set by the Home Public Land Mobile Network (HPLMN) that applies to any PLMNs for which no specific configured NSSAI has been provided to the UE. • There is at most one configured NSSAI per PLMN. • Could be the same as the subscribed S-NSSAIs.
Allowed	• 5GC provides the list of S-NSSAIs that the UE can operate during the registration procedure. • Valid in a registration area or the PLMN over a given access type.
Requested	• UE requests a subset of the configured or allowed S-NSSAIs when registering with the network. • The UE sends this in both Radio Resource Control (RRC) and Non-Access Stratum (NAS) signaling as part of registration. • RAN uses this for AMF selection and provisioning handling before being allowed NSSAI. • 5GC uses this for slice selection, validation, etc., and returns the allowed NSSAI.
Rejected	• Set of S-NSSAIs disallowed by the network for the UE from the requested S-NSSAIs. • Can be rejected in the registration area (or) for the entire PLMN. • The UE should not attempt this NSSAI again in that Registration Area (RA) or in the PLMN.

II.2.4.3.3 Slice Usage

This section describes the process of a UE requesting specific slices and provides a high-level description of the steps in the 5GC CN to establish network slice connectivity for the UE. Note that a given UE may be associated with one or more network slices within a given network.

Figure II.2.4.5 provides a pictorial view of the nodes and interconnections involved in establishing and operating a network slice.

- The network may serve a single UE with one or more network slice instances simultaneously via a 5G-AN, regardless of the access type(s) over which the UE is registered (i.e. 3GPP access and/or non-3GPP [N3GPP] access).
- UE connects
  - Max 8 slices in parallel
  - Common AMF for a single UE across all slices
- Different slices for different service types
  - Committed services – slice types
  - Dedicated customers
- May comprise
  - 5G CN (control plane [CP] and user plane [UP])
  - 5G RAN
  - Interworking functions to non-3GPP access networks
- The UE sets up a PDU session to the data network (DN), where all communication with the DN takes place.
- See 3GPP TS 23.501, section 5.15.
- Traffic segregation is a fundamental function for realizing the network slice implementation. The network slice definition allows for traffic segregation based on the PLMN of UE association with the network, the S-NSSAI that the UE requested and was authorized by the network, and is further classified by the Slice Differentiator (SD) if explicitly identified. Within the defined network slice, the traffic needs to be further segregated based on the IP and QoS flows associated with the 5QI. Hence, $Traffic\ segregation = Function\ (PLMN, S-NSSAI(SD), 5QI)$.
- To support the different types of services, the network resources, all the way from the RAN to internet access, will require the ability to have end-to-end "slices," each with its own performance characteristics, isolated from the other slices.
- Each slice will have a requirement for a different QoS, security considerations, latency characteristics, in-line services, etc. For example, the network characteristics for a best-effort IoT slice will differ significantly from those of a high-end enterprise slice (consider throughput, latency, always-on versus intermittent connection, data volume, voice versus data-only).
- The network slicing functionality contains access network slices, CN slices, and a selection function that connects these slices into a complete network slice comprised of both the access network and the CN.
- The selection function routes communications to an appropriate CN slice that is tailored to provide specific services.
- The criteria for defining the access slices and CN slices include the need to meet different service/application requirements and different communication requirements.
- Each CN slice is built from a set of NFs.
- An important factor in slicing is that some NFs can be used across multiple slices, while other NFs are tailored to a specific slice.

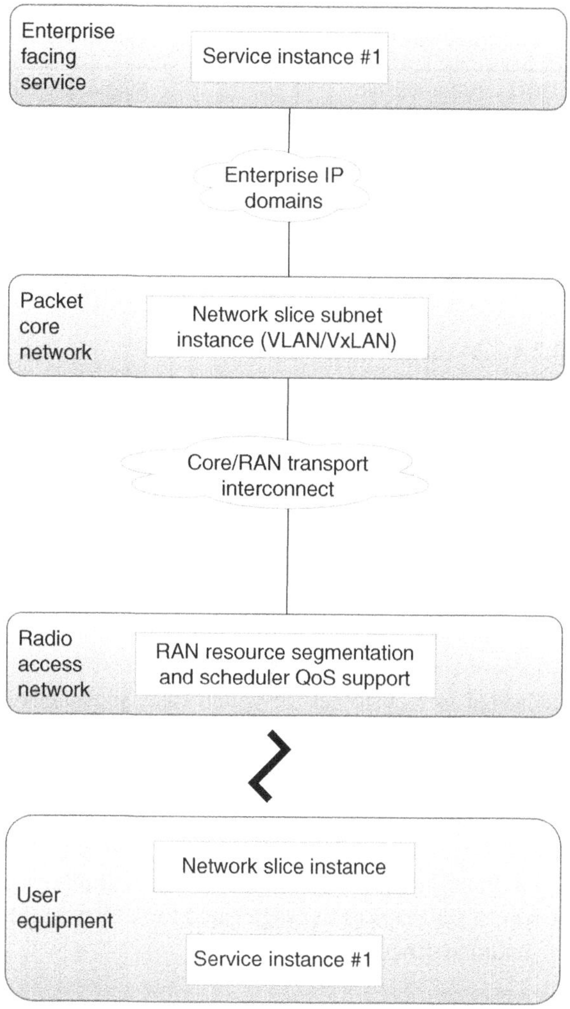

Figure II.2.4.5 NR slices usage.

II.2.4.3.4 Standards SST Values

3GPP has defined a set of well-known SSTs. The realization of the network slices is not restricted by these definitions. Even within these defined SSTs, further sub-classifications can be achieved with SD.

Slice/Service type	SST value	Characteristics
eMBB (enhanced mobile broadband)	1	Slice suitable for the handling of 5G-enhanced mobile broadband, useful but not limited to general consumer space mobile broadband applications, including • streaming of high-quality video, • fast, large file transfers, etc. It is expected that this SST will aim at supporting high data rates and high traffic densities.

(*Continued*)

Slice/Service type	SST value	Characteristics
URLLC (ultra-reliable low-latency communications)	2	Supporting ultra-reliable, low-latency communications for applications including • industrial automation, • (remote) control systems.
MIoT (massive IoT)	3	Allowing the support of a large number of high-density IoT devices efficiently and cost-effectively.

II.2.4.3.5 Slice Differentiator

There are special scenarios when differentiated behaviors are needed for a specific set of users within a defined network slice that varies only by a few subtle variations, without having to define a whole new network slice. The inclusion of a SD, in addition to the network slice request, allows for this to be achieved.

Network slices may differ in supported features and network function optimizations, in which case such network slices may have, for example, different S-NSSAIs with different SSTs.

The operator can deploy multiple network slices delivering the same features but for different groups of UEs, for example, as they deliver a different committed service and/or because they are dedicated to a customer; in which case, such network slices may have, for example, different S-NSSAIs with the same SST but different SDs.

Some sample SDs use cases include the following:

- RAN slices for different inbound roaming partners, including neutral host camping
- eMBB-type services but segregated for different application types
- For example, agreements with specific streaming service providers
- Any of the services but segregated for UEs with different subscriptions with inbound roaming (traditional/neutral host)

II.2.4.3.6 Format of the S-NSSAI

A description of the S-NSSAI is included here from 3GPP TS 28.541, section 4.3.37.

sNSSAIList	It represents the list of S-NSSAI that the managed object is supporting. The S-NSSAI is defined in 3GPP TS 23.003. Allowed values: see 3GPP TS 23.003.
sST	This attribute specifies the SST for the network slice. See clause 5.15.2 of 3GPP TS 23.501.
sD	This attribute specifies the SD, which is optional information that complements the SSTs to differentiate among multiple network slices. See clause 5.15.2 of 3GPP TS 23.501.

Figure II.2.4.6 provides the format of S-NSSAI format as defined in 3GPP TS 23.003 Section 28.4.2.

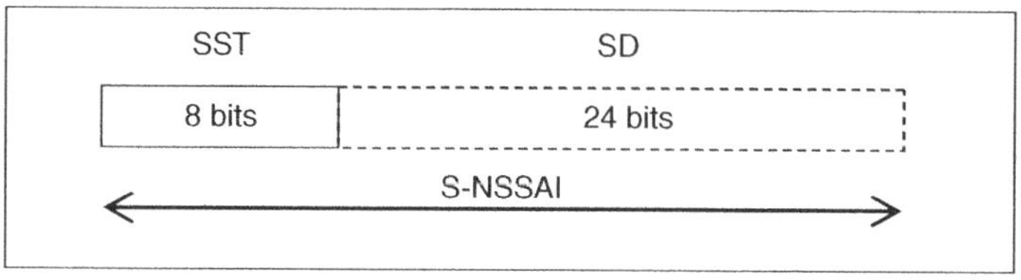

Figure II.2.4.6 S-NSSAI format (from 3GPP TS 23.003 Section 28.4.2)

II.2.4.4 UE Slice Setup/Mobility Call Flow

This section provides the over-the-air call flow between the UE, gNB, and AMF as part of the UE's association with the network. The second part of the call flow addresses the transfer of information from the serving gNB to the target gNB. Figure II.2.4.7 provides the UE slice setup call flow steps with the network, including mobility.

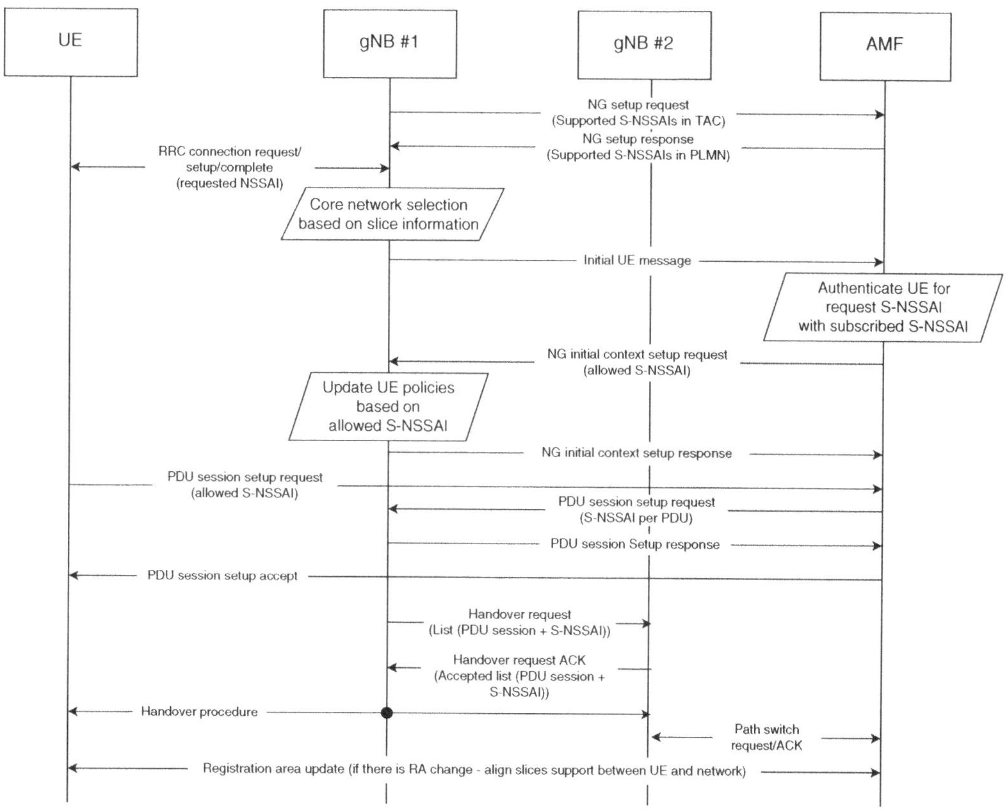

Figure II.2.4.7 UE slice setup call flow with the network, including mobility.

II.2.4.4.1 Examples of Performance Requirements

This section provides sample performance expectations based on the different scenarios that allow the reader to understand the typical network behaviors. Note that all the values in this table are targeted values and not strict requirements

	Scenario	Experienced data rate (DL)	Experienced data rate (UL)	Area traffic capacity (DL)	Area traffic capacity (UL)	Overall user density	Activity factor	UE speed	Coverage
1	**Urban macro**	50 Mbps	25 Mbps	100 $Gbps/km^2$ [a]	50 $Gbps/km^2$ [a]	10,000/km^2	20%	Pedestrians and users in vehicles (up to 120 kmph)	Full network[b]
2	**Rural macro**	50 Mbps	25 Mbps	1 $Gbps/km^2$ [a]	500 Mbps/ km^2 [a]	100/km^2	20%	Pedestrians and users in vehicles (up to 120 kmph)	Full network[b]
3	**Indoor hotspot**	1 Gbps	500 Mbps	15 $Tbps/km^2$	2 $Tbps/km^2$	250,000/km^2	[c]	Pedestrians	Office and residential[c,d]
4	**Broadband access in a crowd**	25 Mbps	50 Mbps	[3.75] $Tbps/km^2$	[7.5] Tbps/ km^2	[500,000]/km^2	30%	Pedestrians	Confined area
5	**Dense urban**	300 Mbps	50 Mbps	750 $Gbps/km^2$ [a]	125 $Gbps/km^2$ [a]	25,000/km^2	10%	Pedestrians and users in vehicles (up to 60 kmph)	Downtown[b]
6	**Broadcast-like services**	Maximum 200 Mbps (per TV channel)	N/A or modest (e.g. 500 kbps per user)	N/A	N/A	TV channels of (20 Mbps) on one carrier	N/A	Stationary users, pedestrians, and users in vehicles (up to 500 kmph)	Full network[b]
7	**High-speed train**	50 Mbps	25 Mbps	15 Gbps/train	7.5 Gbps/train	1000/train	30%	Users in trains (up to 500 kmph)	Along railways[b]
8	**High-speed vehicle**	50 Mbps	25 Mbps	[100] $Gbps/km^2$	[50] $Gbps/km^2$	4000/km^2	50%	Users in vehicles (up to 250 kmph)	Along roads[b]
9	**Airplanes connectivity**	15 Mbps	7,5 Mbps	1,2 Gbps/plane	600 Mbps/ plane	400/plane	20%	Users in airplanes (up to 1000 kmph)	[b]

[a] These values are derived based on overall user density.
[b] For users in vehicles, the UE can be connected to the network directly or via an onboard moving base station.
[c] A certain traffic mix is assumed; only some users utilize services that require the highest data rates.
[d] For interactive audio and video services, such as virtual meetings, the required two-way end-to-end latency (UL and DL) is 2–4 ms, while the corresponding experienced data rate needs to be up to 8 K 3D video (300 Mbps) in both uplink and downlink.

II.2.4.5 NR Slices

Figure II.2.4.8 NR end-to-end slices provides a pictorial representation of the user data path for the network slices. The network orchestrates the configuration of the network slices by identifying the parameters associated with each network slice.

The association of the network slice with the IP domain within the enterprise is the initial function that needs to be performed. This will be done based on the needs of the network slice and the required isolation from the other traffic types within the enterprise. The three 3GPP standards that define network slices—eMBB, URLLC, and MIoT—are shown in the enterprise core. The types of network slices required will depend on the enterprise's business needs, and one or more of the network slices may be supported within a specific IP domain (VLAN/VxLAN) in the enterprise core.

When the UE registers with the network, it indicates the requested network slices, if any. Note that the UE can connect to the network by associating itself with specific network slices and just requesting a data network (DN) connection by providing the APN. As part of the registration, the UE is authorized for a subset of the requested network slices, and the associated context is established in the network, providing the PDU connections to the UE. Once associated with the PDU, the UE or the network can trigger one or more QoS flows within the PDU session. The triggers for QoS flow establishment can be driven by specific application functions or determined in-band by the TDF recognizing Domain Name Server (DNS) queries and traffic patterns (packet size, arrival rate, etc.). As part of the QoS flow establishment, the IP flow(s) that need to be provided with this QoS treatment are recognized and configured in the UPF.

These QoS flows are routed to the RAN, and the first receiving function is the service data adaptation protocol (SDAP). There can be one or more SDAP instances established, and each QoS flow is associated with a specific SDAP instance.

On the radio interface, the RAN and UE are configured with the required set of dedicated radio bearers (DRBs). The SDAP layer is configured with the mapping between the QoS flows from the CN and the DRB(s).

The traffic in the individual DRBs is processed by the RAN scheduler to meet the QoS metrics for the admitted QoS flows. The architecture shown illustrates an open RAN model with SDAP and Layer 2 functions in the RAN, supported in the central unit, the Layer 1.5 (lower medium access control [MAC] and other real-time packet processing functions) in the distributed unit (DU), and the radio unit (RU), which supports the over-the-air transmit/receive point (TRP).

II.2.4.6 LTE Slices

From a 3GPP perspective, slices as a concept are not defined for LTE. It relies solely on the PDN connections. However, from a converged core realization, similar functions can be reused in LTE from the network perspective without the UE being aware of such realizations in the network. See Figure II.2.4.9 for a depiction of LTE end-to-end slices.

The network slice configuration from NR is replaced with a VLAN/VxLAN configuration. It performs a similar function of isolating the traffic of different users based on the enterprise needs. The traffic isolation can be done based on simple load balancing to complex behaviors that include subscription, device type, and the current operating enterprise site when the enterprise itself has multiple locations, etc. When the UEs access the network, requesting a PDN connection by providing an APN, the network is configured to associate the UE with a specific VLAN, obtain an IP address from the VLAN, and provide that assignment to the UE.

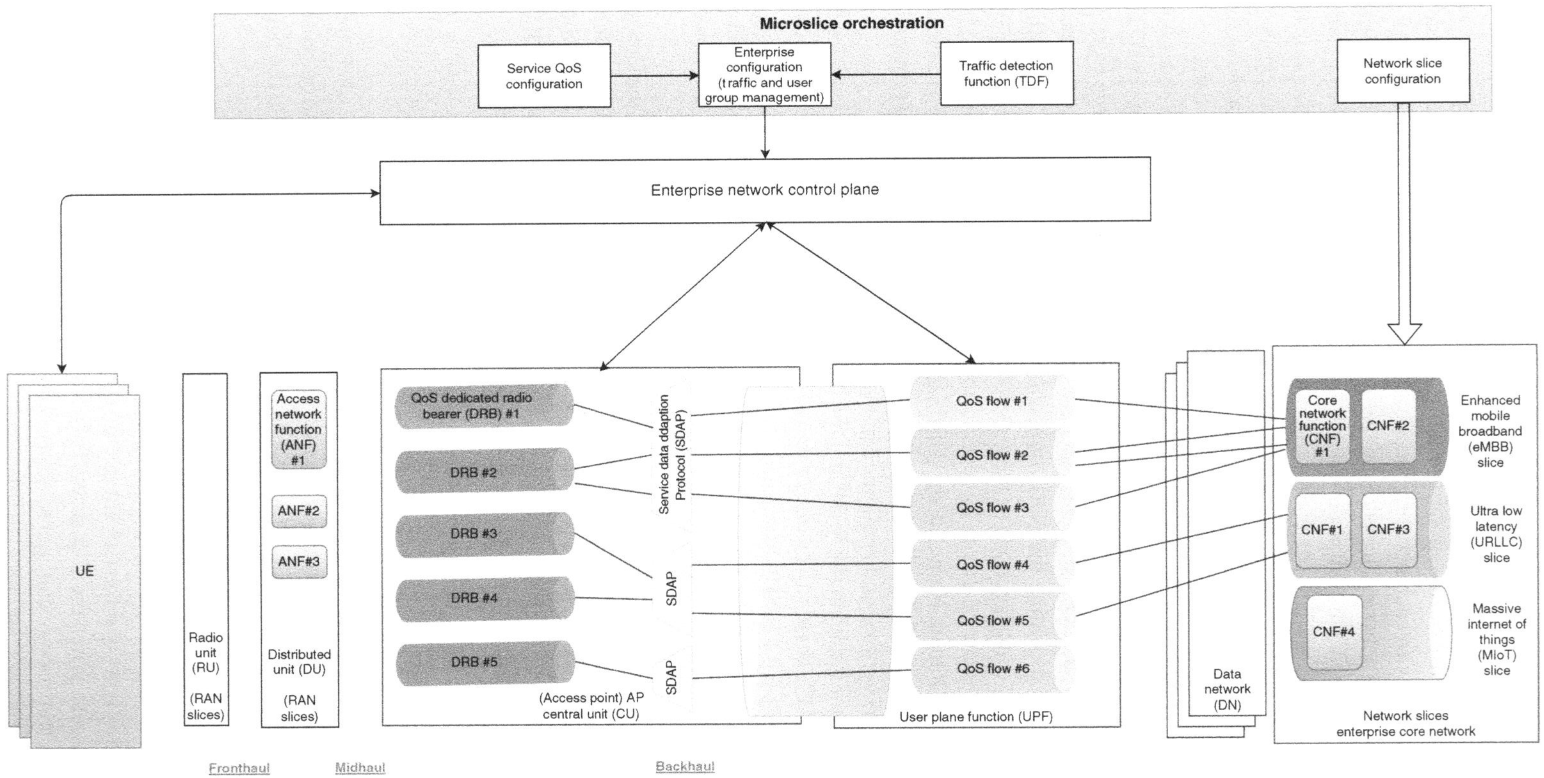

Figure II.2.4.8 NR end-to-end slices.

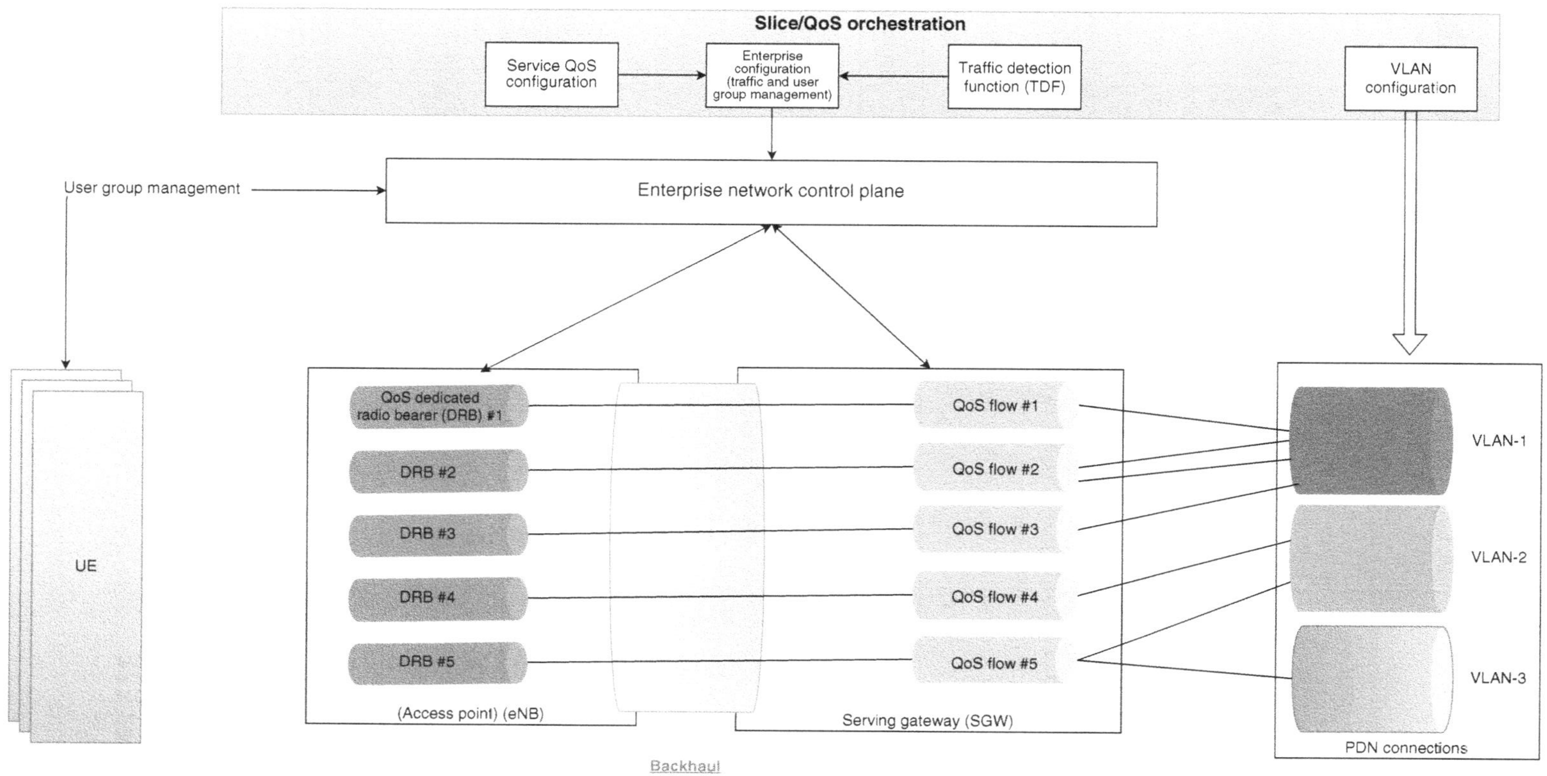

Figure II.2.4.9 LTE end-to-end slices.

As described earlier, in the LTE, there is a one-to-one mapping between the QoS flow in the serving gateway (SGW) and the eNB DRB. In a converged core, the SGW and the UPF will be supported from a unified functional node.

The triggers for QoS can be initiated from the UE side, the network service application, or the TDF.

This section's intent is to allow visualization of the LTE IP address allocation and QoS realizations as slices in the network.

II.2.4.7 RAN Slice Approaches

This section provides a high-level view of the possible approaches for RAN slice realization in the eNB/gNB. The table below provides details on the different approaches and the implications for the eNB L2 and L1 layers. This is provided here to stimulate the reader to think through possible RAN slicing approaches and weigh the trade-offs and ways to partition the RAN resources for commercial use. The use of RAN slices for enterprise private networks is in its infancy and will be shaped by market needs and evolving business cases.

See the neutral host section in the book where a practical approach to RAN slicing is discussed.

Layer	Approach 1	Approach 2	Approach 3	Approach 4
Description	Dedicated spectrum resources for each RAN slice	Combined spectrum with dedicated Radio Resource Manager (RRM) for each slice	Combined spectrum and resources with an independent scheduler for each slice	Fully shared spectrum, resources, and scheduler
PDCP	Independent PDCP for each slice	Independent PDCP for each slice	Independent PDCP for each slice	Independent PDCP for each slice
RLC	Independent RLC for each slice	Independent RLC for each slice	Independent RLC for each slice	Independent RLC for each slice
MAC	Independent MAC for each slice	Independent MAC for each slice	Independent MAC for each slice	Combined scheduler for all slices
PHY	Independent PHY for each slice	Independent PHY for each slice	Resources are managed as a combined pool	Resources are managed as a combined pool
Spectrum	Dedicated spectrum for each RAN slice (band, frequency, slots)	Combined spectrum usage across slices	Combined spectrum usage across slices	Combined spectrum usage across slices

II.2.4.8 Slices E2E

Figure II.2.4.10 brings it all together and provides a representation that includes both LTE and NR for a converged core realization. The network slices are integrated with VLAN/VxLAN. The QoS flows, with the associated five-tuple filters, are supported in the SGW/UPF, captured as a unified

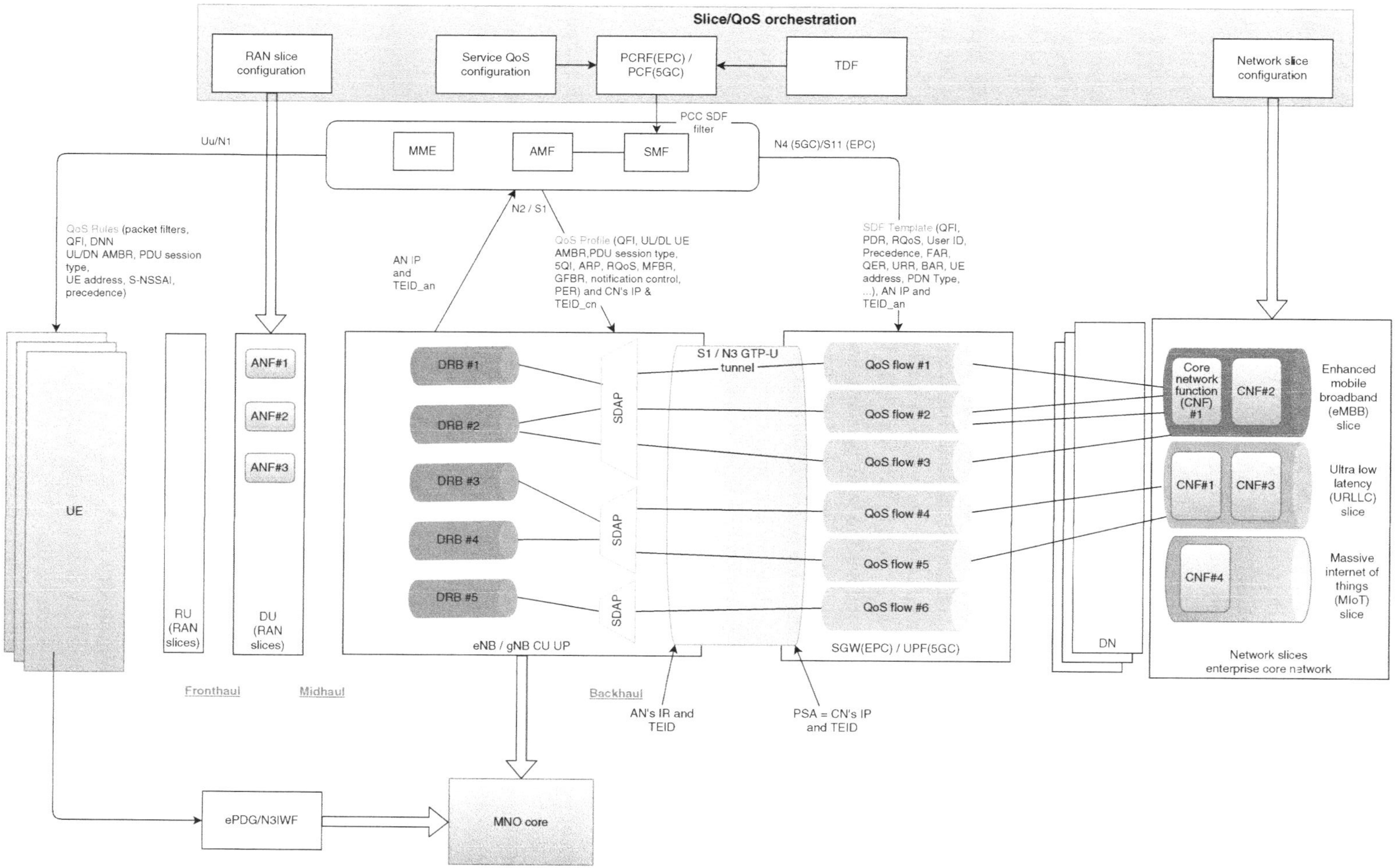

Figure II.2.4.10 Converged core end-to-end slices – a detailed view.

user plane node. The RAN nodes of LTE and NR are shown using the O-RAN architecture, which allows for a multimode access point implementation that supports both LTE and NR. The DRBs in the RAN node and the scheduler functions that enable the meeting of QoS have a similar implementation structure, varying only in how the channel estimations and modulation and coding schemes are selected to perform the transmit and receive functions.

The SDAP function is applicable only in NR, and this layer is used to map IP flows to radio DRBs. In NR, there is an abstraction and isolation of the RAN DRBs from the IP flows, and these are managed independently. In LTE, there is a one-to-one mapping between the QoS flows and the radio DRBs, and the mapping is done end to end. LTE does not have the SDAP layer as part of its architecture.

From the UE perspective, with NR, the UE can request network slices to be established over which the PDU connections are made. In LTE, it is only a PDN connection establishment process, and the network takes care of associating the UE with the appropriate VLAN. The remaining QoS procedures remain the same in both LTE and NR.

The policies (PCRF/PCF), TDF, and service configurations may depend on the radio access technology (RATs – LTE or NR) or exhibit the same behavior in both RATs. For example NR may support higher video profiles based on the increased throughput available and can differ from the performance expectations of LTE. VoIP (VoIP-over-LTE [VoLTE] or VoIP-over-NR [VoNR]) typically supports similar rates and has the same performance expectations on both RATs.

The interconnections from the UE using non-3GPP RATs (e.g. Wi-Fi) and interconnecting through the evolved packet data gateway (ePDG)/N3 interworking function (N3IWF) to tunnel into the EPC/5GC core are also shown. There are other sections in the book that cover seamless mobility across LTE/NR and Wi-Fi as part of the coexistence solutions.

II.2.4.9 Enterprise Implementation Implications

This section provides some leading thoughts on the network slices with LTE and NR for implementation in an enterprise core. This is only intended to simulate the reader into considering the aspects that may be involved and offers a starting point prior to initiating a network design for the enterprise.

Aspects to consider include the following:

- Traffic segregation = Function (PLMN, S-NSSAI(SD), 5QI)
- Like microslices, how we define/configure RAN/core slices
- QoS differentiation within a slice
  - Different QoS profiles can be applied to non-GBR bearers within a slice
  - The DRB profile can be different for the same 5QI flow type in different slices
- The granularity of slice awareness is at the level of a PDU session.
- Cloud architecture and slice-specific dimensioning to support differentiated traffic handling within the 5GS
- SDF mapping to QoS flow
- QoS flow mapping to radio bearer (DRB)
- Slice-based admission control/ARP
  - RRM needs to be studied. However, from the RAN perspective, this should be dictated through bearer configuration and treated like LTE. The implications within a RAN slice are what will be tricky, but we will likely not support RAN slices initially.

- Viable RAN slice realization
- RAN scheduler with RAN slices
  - We need to deliberate on what aspects of RAN slices we want to support. A lot of this may be determined by the market more than by a technological solution.
- Traffic separation at the transport layer (interconnect switch selection): L2VPN via VLANs; L3VPN via Multi-Protocol Label Switching (MPLS) labels.
  - Hop-to-hop behavior designs will be specific to each installation. We can study potential switches and the like to provide a recommendation to the customer, but our external messaging is that we can use the existing infrastructure to support the rollout. I agree that we need to provide intelligent arbitration and indicate where limitations with existing routers and switches can occur.
- Control loops for packet shaping across the RAN/core
- Interworking with Macro Network Operator (MNOs)
  - NH-based connectivity is possible with MNO cooperation. N3IWF is the other method to tunnel into the MNO core. We may need a slice to manage that connectivity if it helps differentiate our product more in the market.

II.2.4.10 Summary

This section introduces the concepts of network slices. The QoS realizations of LTE and NR are presented. The network slice concept from 3GPP standards is described. With that context, the use of slices for LTE, using the available techniques in that technology, is covered. With both NR and LTE, the context of QoS relative to the network slices is also presented. With these concepts expounded, the combined realization for LTE and NR to enable a converged core potentially talking to eNB, gNB, and possibly a multimode (LTE+NR) access point from a single CN is shown. The reader is further requested to consider potential aspects that will aid in the design of the enterprise network based on the demands of the campus and the RATs planned for deployment.

References

1. *3GPP TS 23.501: System Architecture for the 5G System.*

Description: This technical specification defines the system architecture for 5G networks, including key features such as network slicing. It outlines the basic principles, entities, and functional elements involved in the implementation of network slices. The specification discusses how slices can be customized for different use cases (e.g., enhanced mobile broadband, massive IoT).

Key Sections: Network slice instance (NSI), Network slice selection function (NSSF), and slice-specific resources.

Version: The document is periodically updated with newer releases.

Access: Available on the 3GPP website.

2. *3GPP TS 28.530: Management and Orchestration of Network Slicing.*

Description: This specification focuses on the management and orchestration of network slices, detailing how network slices are provisioned, configured, and monitored in real-time. It defines interfaces for the management of network slice lifecycle and describes the role of management systems like Network Slice Subnet Management Function (NSSMF).

Key Sections: Network slice lifecycle management (NSLM), monitoring of slice performance, and slice assurance.
Access: Available through the 3GPP website.

3. *3GPP* TS *28.531: Provisioning of Network Slices.*

Description: This technical specification outlines the procedures for provisioning network slices. It covers details on slice creation, scaling, modification, and deletion, as well as the assignment of resources to ensure QoS and performance objectives.
Key Sections: Slice provisioning, resource allocation, and QoS mechanisms.
Access: Available on the 3GPP FTP directory.

4. Navid Nikaein, K. Khawam, T. K. Madsen, et al. (2017). Network Slicing for 5G: Challenges and Opportunities. *IEEE Communications Magazine.*

Summary: This paper presents a comprehensive overview of network slicing, including its design principles, the challenges in creating isolated, customized slices, and the opportunities for new services. It discusses the role of software-defined networking (SDN) and network function virtualization (NFV) in enabling network slicing.
Key Topics: Network slice isolation, scalability, management, SDN, NFV.
Link: IEEE Xplore

5. Ata Khalid, Etimad Fadel, Akram Hakiri, et al. (2020). A Survey of Network Slicing in 5G Networks: Architectures, Enablers, and Future Directions. *IEEE Communications Surveys & Tutorials.*

Summary: This survey paper provides a detailed analysis of network slicing architectures, technological enablers, and ongoing standardization efforts. It also discusses the open research challenges in areas such as resource management, slice isolation, security, and interoperability across multiple administrative domains.
Key Topics: Network slicing architecture, resource management, slice isolation, standardization.
Link: IEEE Xplore

6. Kaniz Fatema Islam, Salvatore Talarico, Shuqiao Zhao, et al. (2019). Network Slicing in 5G: Survey and Challenges. *IEEE Access.*

Summary: This paper provides a detailed survey of network slicing in the 5G ecosystem, covering the design and operational challenges of implementing slicing at scale. It discusses use cases across industries and examines key issues such as multi-tenancy, dynamic slice management, and SLA guarantees.
Key Topics: Multi-tenancy, dynamic slice orchestration, SLA, slice management.
Link: IEEE Xplore

7. NGMN Alliance. (2016). End-to-End Network Slicing in 5G Networks. *NGMN Alliance.*

Summary: This paper presents a reference architecture for end-to-end network slicing and explores how to implement slicing across the RAN, core, and transport networks. It emphasizes the use of SDN and NFV to provide the necessary flexibility and control for service providers.
Key Topics: End-to-end architecture, SDN, NFV, transport networks.
Link: NGMN Paper

8. Miguel Ángel Serrano, Christian Mannweiler, Eduardo Villieri, et al. (2018). Network Slicing in Industry Verticals: Challenges and Requirements. *IEEE Communications Magazine.*

Summary: This paper discusses how network slicing can be applied to various industry verticals such as automotive, healthcare, and smart cities. It outlines the specific challenges in adapting slicing for diverse sectors and the requirements to ensure that slices can meet industry-specific demands.
Key Topics: Industry verticals, automotive, healthcare, smart cities, vertical-specific challenges.
Link: IEEE Xplore

9. Xi Li, Osama Ghazali, Christos Chrysostomou, et al. (2017). A Network Slicing Framework for the 5G Network. *IEEE Wireless Communications.*

Summary: This paper proposes a flexible framework for 5G network slicing and focuses on the efficient allocation of resources across slices. The authors also propose a dynamic mechanism for creating and terminating network slices based on service demand.
Key Topics: Resource allocation, dynamic slice management, on-demand slicing.
Link: IEEE Xplore

Part II.3

Neutral Host Networks

II.3.1

Neutral Host Network

II.3.1.1 Overview

II.3.1.1.1 What Is Network Sharing?

The fundamental concept of a neutral host network (NHN) is enabled by sharing a network deployment across users of all types and subscriptions without requiring explicit roaming agreements and supporting direct camping. Unlike macro networks, where different carriers deploy and manage the networks independently, it is harder to do that with campuses, both in-building and in the area surrounding the building. Campuses have limited space and cabling that can be accommodated to support multiple independent networks. This naturally leads to the need for supporting a neutral host that will accommodate all types of devices/users and the network resources shared among these users.

Sharing comes in different forms for a given campus network. This can be passive, without requiring active or dynamic management, for example tower, rooftop, power, cabinets, lighting, and air conditioning. The more interesting form is active sharing, which adapts to real-time conditions and the user population demanding access to the network. Active sharing involves the sharing of antennas, access network, transmission, spectrum, Radio Frequency (RF) design/planning, core network, and air conditioning. Our focus in this chapter is to cover a specific form of active sharing that is NHN.

II.3.1.1.2 Motivation for a Neutral Host Network

Lack of seamless mobile coverage and poor user experience are common in many indoor venues. Traditional indoor cellular systems are too costly and complex for enterprise deployment in smaller venues, largely relying on dynamic antenna system (DAS) solutions that have not scaled well. The gap between the top end of the indoor cellular market, directly served by service providers (SPs), and hundreds of thousands of smaller, low-traffic ("mid-market") venues is substantial. The indoor footprint has largely relied on outdoor macro network antennas shining into buildings, and the RF penetration has been weak, with many inherent coverage holes, which users have even come to accept. Aware of these coverage holes, users often step outside to make calls or primarily rely on Wi-Fi coverage, with macro network services offloaded to Wi-Fi networks, which has largely bridged the gap so far. However, Wi-Fi comes with its own issues in QoS management and extended campus coverage. The use of higher-powered and better spectrum utilization through cellular technologies has become a compelling need in the market.

Mobile Communication Systems for Private Networks, First Edition. Srinivasan Balasubramanian.

There is a growing need for an NHN operator to bridge the gap between very large projects with direct SP involvements and a large number of smaller projects that are too small for SPs to consider but too complex for enterprises to handle independently. Cost becomes a primary driver requiring a low-cost solution that eliminates the complex business models associated with the multi-operator support. An NHN with advanced sharing techniques enables such functionality for indoor and campus-wide coverage, which can be utilized by both private network deployments and potentially leveraged by macro network users to camp on the same NHN network.

It does require a business arrangement for the macro network operators to allow their network identifiers to be broadcast on the NHN. With a bring-your-own-coverage (BYOC) model, the macro network operator views the NHN as an extension of its own deployed network, avoiding additional deployment costs while leveraging the NHN when the macro network coverage is weak or nonexistent. This has become an obvious choice in the market. It allows generic users to enter in-building scenarios and benefit from this NHN coverage extension without having to leave the building or obtain an additional subscription to access the enterprise-deployed network. For example a customer walking into a big-box retail store with metal roofing that prevents RF penetration from macro networks would no longer have to leave the store just to check competing products and prices, which could result in lost business to online store. Further extending NHNs to support specific enterprise employees will enable a more proactive transition, allowing users access to specific services that are available in a walled garden within the enterprises to be accessible to the user. The enterprise users may also be provisioned with private network credentials, with devices supporting dual-SIM functionality for both macro and enterprise network credentials. With the use of enterprise-deployed networks acting as both private networks and NHNs, dual-SIM devices may use both the macro network and enterprise network simultaneously or allow for the device to use the same enterprise-deployed network for camping with both credentials on the same channels for dual-SIM dual-standby (DSDS) operations.

The goal is to achieve five-bar service from a radio perspective and to support sufficient user throughput and capacity, allowing for seamless operations across the macro, NHN, and private networks for different services.

II.3.1.1.3 Neutral Host Opportunity

Figure II.3.1.1 provides an overview of the different types of venues where enterprise-style deployment and coverage can be supported. These networks can be deployed either by current macro network operators or by enterprise entities seeking to address the coverage and service demands of the enterprise campus. The larger venues are more attractive to macro network service providers (SPs) aiming to extend their services to these campuses, with the smaller venues more likely to be supported by the smaller enterprises opting to deploy their own networks. The spectrum used will largely dictate the neutral host supportability with shared spectrum acting as a natural enabler. Even with the licensed spectrum, macro network carriers—based on agreements with the other carriers and the enterprise entity—can deploy NHNs as turnkey managed service providers (MSPs).

Each of these deployment types, apart from acting as a private network, can also be seamlessly enhanced to act as an NHN. This implies that the NHN can be used to extend the coverage for MNOs in all these types of deployments, not just in office buildings.

Carriers are still considering providing an indication to the user when camped on an NHN system, similar to a roaming indicator, with the expectation that the user will see poorer performance on these networks. From a QoS perspective, the current experience is that the NHN system is performing very well and sometimes often exceeds the performance seen on the macro network in the

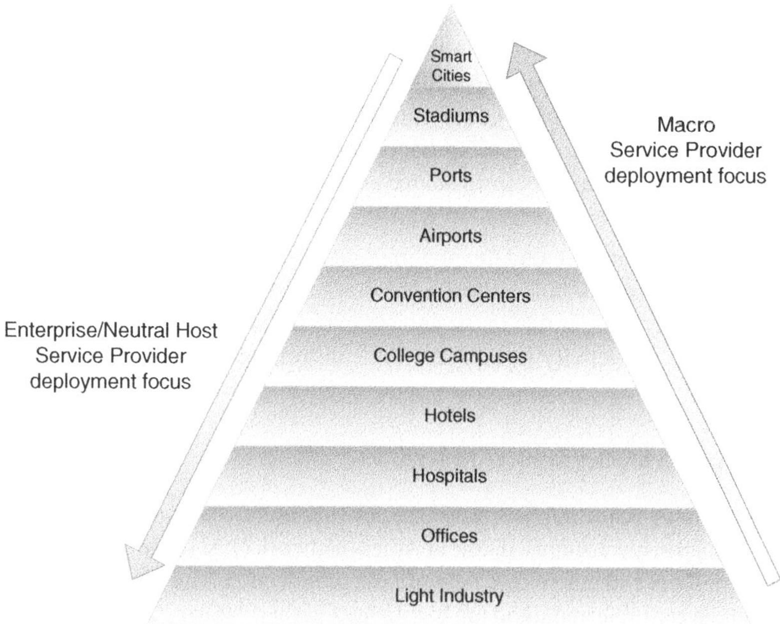

Figure II.3.1.1 NHN opportunity.

same footprint. With wider bandwidth supported on the macro networks through carrier aggregation (CA) and larger than 20 MHz supported on New Radio (NR), the throughput tends to be higher on the macro network compared to the NHN. However, with a shorter range and proximity to the cell with NHN, the device experiences reasonably good performance on the NHN, not impacting the user experience even though the throughput is not high. Based on some field experience, even when comparing NR on the macro and Long Term Evolution (LTE) as the NHN, the throughput experienced on the macro is about two times that of what is seen on the NHN. With NHN, the increased reliability of coverage for in-building use is much higher compared to the macro network. In one of the possible business models, even when the private network is extending into the surrounding areas of the enterprise, the NHN is requested for support only for in-building coverage, leaving the coverage aspects outside of the building to the macro networks. Both the seamless transitions across the macro and NHN networks are a requirement, and the grade of service will need to be on par with the macro networks for the different services. The expectation will be also to support the emergency services on the NHN, including Cellular Management System (CMAS) and Earthquake and Tsunami Warning System (ETWS) alerts and emergency calls.

There are several distinct neutral host deployment models emerging:

- The enterprise deploys private networks and also activates neutral host services on them. The MNOs for this scenario expect that the network is managed and operated by the enterprise and treat it as BYOC. The MNOs treat these networks as coverage extensions, typically for indoor footprints, and prefer to use their own macro coverage when possible. These networks operate using shared/local spectrum obtained dynamically from a central broker or statically by applying for and receiving grants to operate in specific locations.
- The MNOs themselves act as MSPs and deploy the network on the enterprise premises. This may use either shared or licensed spectrum. Agreements for other MNO UEs to camp on the network

may be negotiated by the enterprise and require the camp network to operate as an NHN or to be treated as regular roaming between MNOs that is already in place now.

- A third-party SP can install and manage a private cellular network on behalf of the enterprise. The third-party SP allows leased access to enterprise entities and also offers leases to the MNOs operating in NHN mode. This is similar to the DAS services offered today for in-building coverage to the MNOs. These deployments can be both on shared and licensed spectrums based on the site-level agreements made.

All three models will coexist in the market, and the preferred model will be location, enterprise, and MNO, dictated by the level of operational control needed among the entities involved. The economics of the situation may play a larger role in the choices made as well.

Table II.3.1.1 provides several connectivity variants for the enterprise campus network using single and dual SIMs.

II.3.1.1.4 NHN Architecture

Neutral hosts have existed for many years and have varied in network architecture and implementation, based on factors such as the spectrum used, Radio Access Network (RAN) node reuse, core network reuse, and the type of RAN and macro core network interconnection. The possible known variants and the emerging industry-preferred trend are highlighted in this chapter. As the architectural variants are examined, effective management of functional separation, on-premises versus cloud deployment, the separation of NHN and macro network functions, and the interconnection between the NHN and macro core networks are essential for NHN to succeed in the market.

Although not a neutral host of sorts, it is good to address the traditional roaming across operators that will continue to persist in the market independent of the neutral host solution realizations. The device is provisioned with the home operator public land mobile network (PLMN) identifiers in the equivalent home PLMN (EHPLMN) list. The device is also provisioned with the operator PLMN (OPLMN) list, which consists of the roaming Macro Network Operator (MNO) partners. The device will always look for the EHPLMN entries when camped on the networks from the OPLMN list. Even within the OPLMN, the entries are listed in the priority order and the device will attempt to move to a more preferred network through periodic/telescopic scans. When the home operator coverage is not available, that is, the networks identified by the EHPLMN entries are not available, the device will look for networks from the OPLMN entries and camp on them. When the device is camped on OPLMN networks, typically, the "R" roaming flag indicator is shown on the display so that the user known the user is currently roaming and can incur roaming charges. The roaming network interfaces with the home operator network to primarily authenticate the user talking from the Mobility Management Entity (MME)/ Access and Mobility Management Function (AMF) in the visited network to the Home Subscriber Server (HSS)/Unified Data Management (UDM) in the home operator network. It is possible for the Internet Procol (IP) context to be provided from the roaming operator network or, more typically, provided from the home operator network. The IP anchor is maintained in the home operator in the PDN-GW (packet data gateway – EPC) or DN (data etwork – 5GC) and the packet routed through the visited network via the SWG (serving gateway – EPC) or UPF (user plane function – 5GC). This approach required explicit interconnects to be established between the visited and home operator networks apart from the business arrangement on the roaming charges involved. It is possible for the visited operator to not use roaming charges and indicate that to the device by providing an explicit flag indicating that the currently camped visited network is an equivalent PLMN (EPLMN) and the roaming flag is not displayed to the user. Such arrangements typically exist between partners that want to mutually allow roaming between each other's networks.

Table II.3.1.1 Connectivity variants in the enterprise campus.

UE	Data connectivity	Voice connectivity	Radio	Packet core	Authentication	Enterprise interfacing with MNO core
Single-SIM single standby	Data offload to Wi-Fi	Voice services can be retained over MNO while within MNO coverage. Transitions to WFC over Wi-Fi using MNO credentials aggressively or conservatively based on policies (MNO/enterprise/user).	Wi-Fi deployed on the enterprise campus	Enterprise core for data MNO core for voice	1) MNO credentials • MNO connectivity • Wi-Fi connectivity 2) Enterprise credentials • Wi-Fi connectivity	RADIUS (S2a, . . .) interface when MNO credentials are used for Wi-Fi connectivity ePDG connectivity for Fixed-Mobile Convergence (WFC)
Dual-SIM dual standby	Data offload with alternative credential over LTE	Voice services can be retained over MNO while in MNO coverage. Transitions to WFC over LTE using MNO credentials aggressively or conservatively, based on policies.	LTE deployed on the enterprise campus	Enterprise core for data MNO core for voice	1) MNO credentials • MNO connectivity 2) Enterprise credentials • Enterprise LTE connectivity	ePDG connectivity for WFC
Dual-SIM dual standby	Data offload with alternative credentials over LTE	Voice services can be retained over MNO while within MNO coverage.Transitions to the same channel DSDS using MNO credentials aggressively or conservatively based on policies.	LTE deployed on the enterprise campus	Enterprise core for data MNO core for voice	1) MNO credentials • MNO connectivity 2) Enterprise credentials • Enterprise LTE connectivity	S1, S6a connectivity to the MNO core
Single-SIM single standby	Data offload to Enterprise LTE	Voice offload to Enterprise LTE	LTE deployed on the enterprise campus (MOCN or MORAN)	MNO core for data and voice	MNO credentials	S1 to MNO core
Single-SIM single standby	Data offload to enterprise LTE	Voice offload to enterprise LTE	LTE deployed on enterprise campus	MNO core for data and voice	MNO credentials	S6a to MNO Core
Single-SIM single standby	Data offload to enterprise LTE	Voice offload to enterprise LTE	LTE deployed on enterprise campus Traditional roaming	Enterprise core for data and voice	MNO credentials	Enterprise HSS

(Continued)

Table II.3.1.1 (Continued)

UE	Data connectivity	Voice connectivity	Radio	Packet core	Authentication	Enterprise interfacing with MNO core
Single-SIM single standby	Data offload to enterprise LTE	Voice offload to enterprise LTE	LTE deployed on enterprise campus CBRSA NHN	Enterprise core for data and voice	MNO credentials	SWa Interface (SWa), STa Interface (Sta) interfaces to MNO core for authentication (CBRS NHN)
Single-SIM single standby	Data offload to enterprise LTE	Voice offload to enterprise LTE	LTE deployed on enterprise campus	Enterprise core for data and voice	Transition from MNO credential to enterprise credential	N/A
Single-SIM single standby	Data offload to enterprise LTE	Voice offload to enterprise LTE	LTE deployed by one MNO on enterprise campus supporting several MNO PLMN.	Enterprise core for data and voice	Transition to enterprise network based on 3GPP roaming	N/A

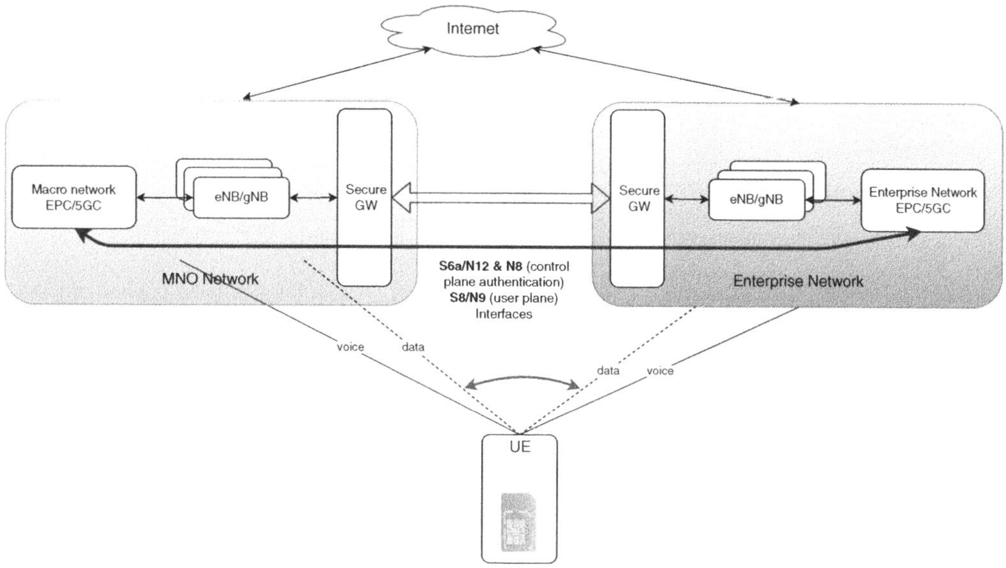

Figure II.3.1.2 Roaming architecture.

One possible configuration is to have the enterprise network act as the visited network for the MNO user to roam where the macro network acts as the home network as illustrated in Figure II.3.1.2. Note the reverse can be envisioned as well with the enterprise users roaming on to the macro network.

The multiple-operator radio access network (MORAN) architecture and the multiple-operator core network (MOCN) architecture are discussed below as possible variants for the NHN realization.

II.3.1.1.4.1 MORAN

A MORAN NHN is a system that allows for sharing certain elements of the radio base station between multiple operators. Although the hardware is shared, the component carriers (spectrum) used are isolated from each other, and each operator is restricted to using only its own spectrum allocation. The radio base station is connected to multiple core networks based on the individual operators associated with the base station. This results in shared compute resources, interfacing hardware, and site location; however, for all practical purposes, they operate as independent networks. Each component carrier is configured and managed independently. Figure II.3.1.3 provides an architectural view of the MORAN network deployment.

When shared spectrum is used, resources are equally partitioned, although other ratios, including dynamic allocations or separations, can be envisioned based on the composition of the user population, potentially adapted in near-real time.

II.3.1.1.4.2 MOCN NHN

In a MOCN NHN, the radio base station is completely shared across the MNOs wanting to participate in the NHN operations. Unlike the MORAN networks, even the spectrum resources are shared and available to all participating MNOs. The radio base station is connected to the core networks of the individual operators via a MOCN GW (gateway). From the radio base station (eNB/gNB) perspective, the MOCN GW looks like the core network, and the MOCN GW, in turn, appears as a

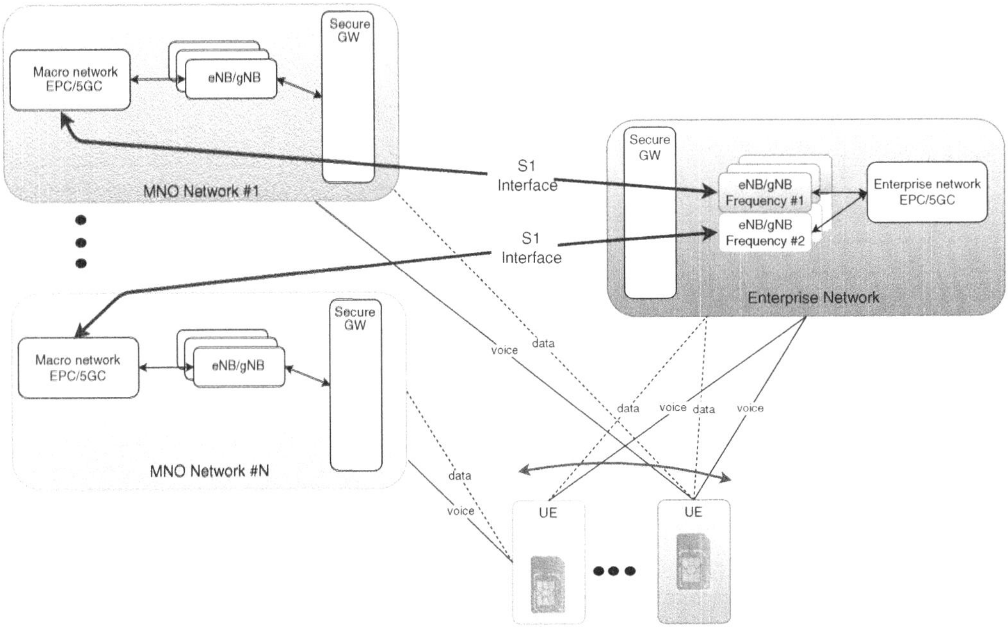

Figure II.3.1.3 MORAN architecture.

base station to the individual MNO core networks. As an example, 28-bit home eNB identifiers are used to represent the eNBs deployed in the NHN campus. The MOCN GW uses a 20-bit macro eNB identifier, abstracting all the eNBs deployed in an NHN campus as a single eNB to the MNO core networks. All mobility within the NHN campus is handled within the NHN deployment and is abstracted from the MNO core network. The user plane route path to the individual NHN eNBs may need to be updated with the MNO core network based on the packet routing mechanism utilized. Figure II.3.1.4 provides the architectural view of the MOCN network deployment for a LTE based NHN. Figure II.3.1.5 extends that to include both LTE and NR and illustrates the macro network to NHN transitions (LTE/NR multi-RAT operations).

The system information block (SIB) allows for transmitting up to six PLMN IDs and hence can act as an NHN for as many operators. Given that the enterprise network is typically deployed by the enterprise entity, which will deploy a private network and then evolve that to an NHN by supporting an MOCN GW, one of the PLMN ID entries will be utilized as a private network PLMN. This implies that five of the PLMN IDs can be available for NHN support with the enterprise network. So far, this has not shown itself to be a limitation, with the individual MNOs still working to establish relationships with the enterprise campuses. Even with the limited PLMN IDs, these NHNs can accommodate users from other operators based on the roaming agreements that they have established with the MNOs, with PLMN IDs broadcast on the NHN.

With the adaptable sharing of the spectrum based on the user population of the different MNO users, this MOCN-based approach is a much more economically viable and scalable option to pursue. Shared spectrum use, starting with the Citizens Broadband Radio Service (CBRS) definition in the USA, is becoming ubiquitous worldwide, with each country explicitly allocating spectrum for shared usage. The actual allocation, including static and dynamic methods, varies, but the process is in place to obtain localized, smaller-footprint spectrum, significantly aiding the uptick in NHN usage in the market.

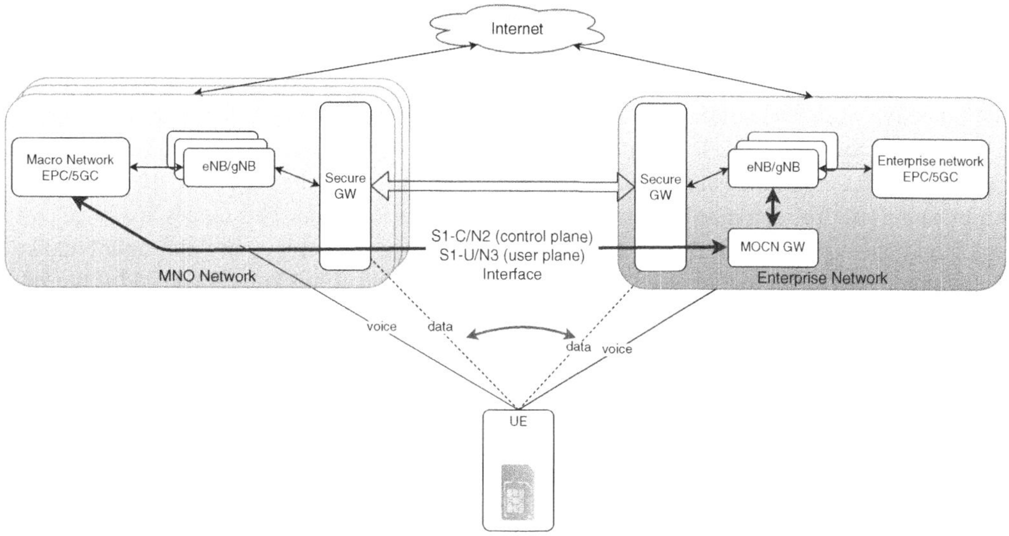

Figure II.3.1.4 MOCN architecture.

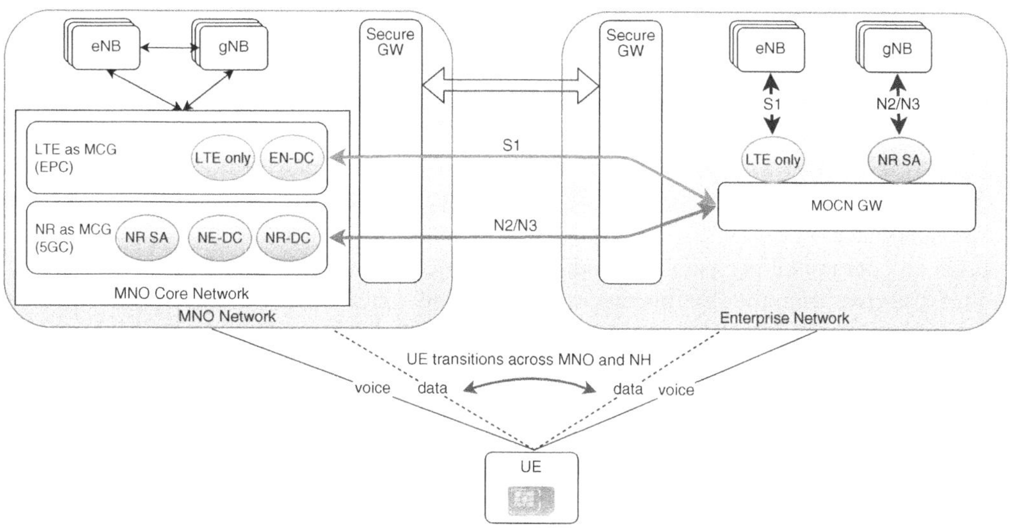

Figure II.3.1.5 Macro network to NHN transitions (LTE/NR multi-RAT operations).

II.3.1.2 Comparisons with DAS Solutions

Currently in the market, DAS is the primary in-building coverage enhancer solution that is most prevalent. NHN is positioning itself as a viable alternative and even suggests it as a preferred approach over the DAS solution. DAS has not been adopted well, even with the known indoor coverage footprint issues, due to several reasons. Some of the possible reasons are provided below, using those points to position NHN as a viable option in place of DAS to address both coverage and QoS issues.

DAS are essentially networks of antennas that are typically smaller radios deployed in buildings, acting as extenders to the public MNO networks. These DAS antennas are connected to a base station not unlike the ones used for regular macro network deployments, which is centrally housed either inside the building or in a street location near the building, and act as signal repeaters. Given the fact that these DAS antennas are only remote radio heads, they require dedicated cabling to the base station, where all baseband processing functions are supported due to the tight timing and noise-free communication that is required between them. This comes at a huge cost, requiring fiber-optic or coaxial cables to connect everything for deployment and maintenance. The dramatic price differential of NHNs primarily comes from eliminating the need for discrete fiber-optic cables to connect each DAS radio head to a central hub that house the base station. NHN deployments use small cells that typically house the radio unit, the baseband processing, and the parts of the layer 2 and layer 3 functions. This implies that these NHN small cells can receive user plane IP traffic connected through regular ethernet cabling that already exists in the enterprise. If additional capacity is needed, generic off-the-shelf routers and bridges can be supported and maintained for NHN operation, following the regular daily operational procedures of the enterprise IT team.

The DAS solutions so far have used only the licensed spectrum that is purchased and dedicated for use with the individual MNOs. This implies that to provide coverage for all the operators, the cabling and the capacity of the connectivity to the base stations associated with the individual MNOs need to be supported. All the remote radio heads use the same frequency and require careful planning, deployment, and maintenance. Mobility in-building across the DAS radio heads can be complex, and managing interference across these nodes becomes a nontrivial issue requiring extensive careful planning. The DAS solutions are typically over-provisioned to support a wider spectrum, simultaneously accommodating multiple MNO-licensed carriers. Note that DAS solutions can be used with shared spectrum as well when the deployment already supports it. Explicitly deploying a DAS solution to support shared spectrum alone tends to be prohibitive from a cost perspective.

From an operational perspective, a radio head going down is harder to detect and will also require site visits from the DAS management entity and typically cannot be locally handled by the enterprise entities. NHN networks can be deployed on licensed spectrum based on the entity deploying and managing the network. For example an MNO wanting to deploy an in-building solution with a licensed spectrum also opens it up for neutral host camping based on the agreements with the enterprises. NHN, however, typically relies on the use of shared spectrum. When deploying these NHN small cells, they are typically deployed on independent frequencies to avoid causing interference, and each small cell can be independently managed for operation apart from the mobility aspects that require some coordination. Based on this approach for NHN, it easily scales for campuses of any size, unlike a DAS solution. NHN small cells can also dynamically adapt to the available spectrum capacity and potentially even modify the individual cell capacity based on the user composition in different locations within the enterprise campus. DAS solutions can be envisioned to use shared spectrum as well; however, this will further restrict their viability due to the nature of using a single frequency across remote radio heads, significantly restricting the dynamic adaptability of the DAS network and certainly not scaling well.

DAS solutions are typically restricted in capacity by the number of radio heads that can be supported, given that the central hub and base station that support the baseband have limited capacity; to augment this, additional central hubs and base stations need to be supported. Such restrictions don't apply to NHN solutions.

DAS solutions are more rigid and lack the software-definable flexibility offered by small cells. It should be noted that most DAS deployments use passive DAS solutions that tend to utilize passive components like coaxial cables, splitters, and diplexers to distribute the signal. Passive DAS solutions are a lot easier to deploy compared to active DAS solutions, which require an independent power source for the components. Active DAS can be more flexible but comes at a much higher price point and is typically only affordable by larger enterprises like stadiums that have both the demand and need for such systems.

In conclusion, DAS solutions have one or more shortcomings such as high implementation costs, lack of scalability, limited control, and less control from the enterprises in managing the services on the network deployed on their campus. DAS solutions currently primarily rely on licensed spectrum and, hence, can claim fewer operational maintenance requirements. NHN solutions primarily rely on shared spectrum, and although they have a very low cost to deploy, they may require operational maintenance with limitations in shared spectrum availability. As noted above, a DAS solution can be deployed on a shared spectrum, and similarly, an NHN can be deployed on a licensed spectrum. Technologically, NHN offers a much superior solution as long as the spectrum availability can be guaranteed. The availability of the shared spectrum has become very prevalent across the globe, with fairly stable allocations for smaller footprint enterprise networks, and it is likely that the market will see an increased trend toward the adoption of NHN-based solutions, particularly given that it seamlessly accommodates multiple operators with minimal overhead for management.

II.3.1.3 Enterprise Network as a Neutral Host

II.3.1.3.1 NHN Deployment Architecture

Figure II.3.1.6 illustrates the view of the enterprise campus network that supports both private network connectivity into the enterprise core network and NHN-based connectivity into the MNO core network via the MOCN GW.

II.3.1.3.2 MOCN GW and eNB Functions

Figure II.3.1.7 provides the set of functions that need to be supported by the MOCN GW and eNB/gNB for an NHN realization. A description of the different functions and the possible variants is described below.

The MOCN GW appears to the MME/AMF as an eNB/gNB. In turn, the MOCN GW appears to the eNB/gNB as a macro network MME/AMF. The MOCN GW serves as a concentrator for the C plane, specifically the S1-C/N2 interface. The S1-U/N3 interface from the eNB/gNB may be terminated at the MOCN GW, or a direct logical U-plane connection between the eNB/gNB and the S-GW/UPF may be used. The macro MME/AMF may send two transport layer addresses of different version only in the case of an MOCN GW that does not terminate the user plane. Selection of an IP version to be used for S1-U/N3 is necessary if a requested E-UTRAN Radio Access Bearer (ERAB) configuration contains two transport layer addresses of different versions. The Tracking Area Code (TAC) and PLMN ID used by the eNB/gNB shall also be supported by the MOCN GW. If routing ambiguities are to be avoided, a given NHN eNB/gNB should be connected to a single MOCN GW.

Relaying UE-associated S1/N2 application part messages between the MME/AMF serving the User Equipment (UE) and the eNB serving the UE is a primary function of the MOCN GW, except

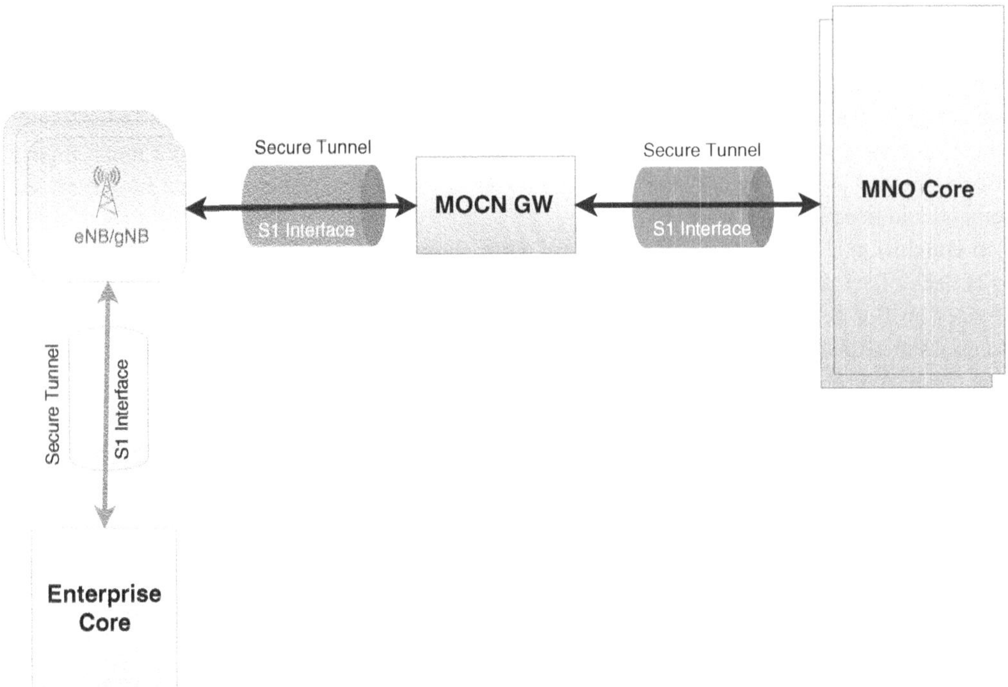

Figure II.3.1.6 Enterprise and NHN deployment architecture.

for the UE CONTEXT RELEASE REQUEST message received from the eNB with an explicit GW context release indication. In that case, the MOCN GW terminates the S1/N2 UE context release request procedure and releases the UE context if it determines that the UE identified by the received UE IDs on the S1/N2 is no longer served by an eNB/gNB attached to it. Otherwise, it ignores the message. In the case of the S1/N2 INITIAL CONTEXT SETUP REQUEST message and the S1/N2 HANDOVER REQUEST message, informing the eNB/gNB about any globally unique MME ID (GUMMEI) or globally unique AMF ID (GUAMI) corresponding to the serving MME/AMF, the MME/AMF UE ID on S1/N2 assigned by the MME, and the MME UE ID on S1/N2 assigned by the MOCN GW for the UE. In the case of the S1/N2 PATH SWITCH REQUEST ACKNOWLEDGE message, informing the eNB/gNB about the MME/AMF UE ID on S1/N2 assigned by the MME/AMF and the MME/AMF UE ID on S1/N2 assigned by the MOCN GW for the UE. Routing the S1/N2 PATH SWITCH REQUEST message toward the MME/AMF is based on the GUMMEI/GUAMI of the source MME/AMF received from the eNB/gNB.

II.3.1.3.3 MOCN Enabler

The MOCN enabler is not an explicit function but is included here to show the fundamental hosting of the compute resource, the effective interconnect between the NHN eNB/gNB and the individual MNO cores, and the handling of the scalability aspects.

The MNO core networks will not want the individual enterprises to establish secure tunnels, given that it will not be scalable to distribute certificates and maintain those many tunnels. An abstraction is needed, and the optimal choice is to use a single secure tunnel with the NHN deployment vendor or require interfacing with a common MOCN GW solution that is used by all the

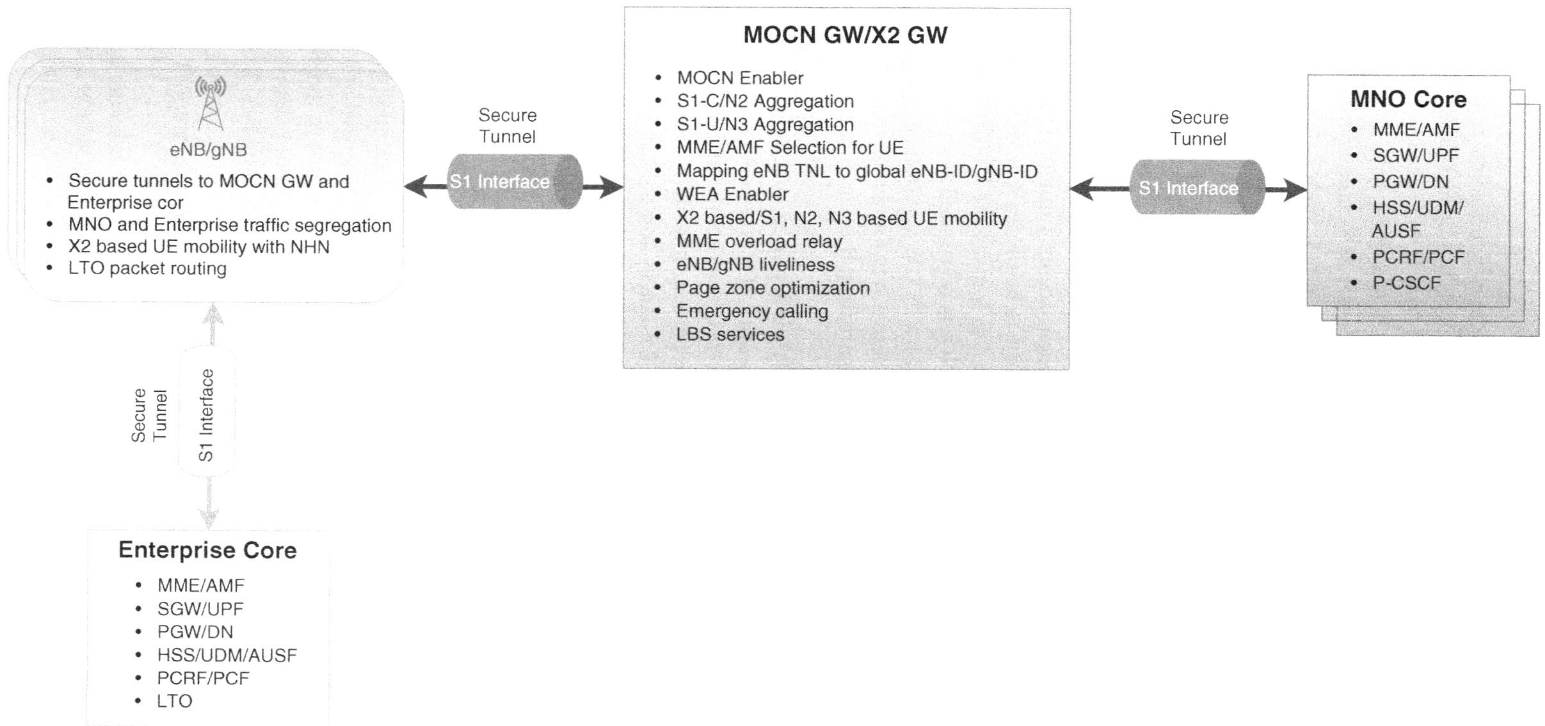

Figure II.3.1.7 MOCN GW and eNB/gNB functions for NHN realization.

NHN deployments. Given that the number of NHN vendors is not that many, this option seems to be acceptable for the market, at least for now.

The MOCN GW functions can potentially be segregated, with some functions implemented within a given enterprise campus itself and the other aspects hosted in a cloud. The cloud itself can be in the metro cloud local to the city, in a Demilitarized Zone (DMZ) used by the enterprise/MNO, and more centrally located, or even in a public cloud. There will likely be several types of realizations in the market, depending on the MNO, enterprise, and NHN deployment vendor preferences. For example the mobility within a given NHN can be supported on the campus while the remaining functions are supported in the cloud.

II.3.1.3.4 Secure Tunnels

Concerns about privacy aspects are constantly raised, and careful handling of the traffic needs to be part of the early design and deployment to prevent issues from arising later in the field. The expectation is that the enterprise traffic and the MNO traffic are separated right at the eNB/gNB. This is achieved by supporting two independent secure tunnels into the enterprise core and the MOCN GW. This still requires all MNO traffic to be routed to a MOCN GW independent of the MNO from a given NHN eNB/gNB. However, as long as the MOCN GW is implemented in a secure location, the traffic of the individual MNOs is segregated from that point onward into the individual MNO cores. The eNB/gNB and the MOCN GW solutions are typically supported by a single network vendor, and the secure tunnel between the nodes ensures that no sniffing of traffic is possible. Active monitoring of the link, apart from the certificate management, is also supported to avoid any breach.

It is possible, based on the enterprise where the NHN is deployed, that it may require a few NATs to be traversed. The choice of Virtual Private Network (VPN) tunnels used will depend on the enterprises and the MNO network operators, and this tends to be very implementation-based, requiring collaboration with the entities to establish secure connectivity. Based on experience, this has not been a straightforward process, with a lot of nuances and policies enforced by the enterprises and the MNOs. If an NHN is planned for campus deployment, the recommendation is to start by identifying the tunnel establishment and certificate management procedures as the first step, even before performing any other activities associated with the deployment, given the lead time involved in resolving the issues.

II.3.1.3.5 Control and User Plane Connections

The NHN deployment acts as an LTE-only mode or as NR SA mode, essentially implying that the UE camped on the enterprise networks will be camped on either LTE or NR at a given time. It is possible for a given campus to support both LTE and NR, but this is not yet prevalent. Given the small cell deployments involved, the benefits of NR from a throughput perspective are not very different from what can be achieved with LTE. There are specific campuses, like industrial IoT (IIoT), where delay-critical QoS support is required, and NR provides specific QoS techniques that will mandate the use of NR. Otherwise, the performance expectations from LTE and NR will be equivalent.

The eNB supports S1-C (control) and S1-U (user plane) connections via secure tunnels, one each with the enterprise core if a private network is deployed and with the MOCN GW. Similarly, the gNB will support N2 and N3 interfaces via secure tunnels with the enterprise core and the MOCN GW.

II.3.1.3.5.1 S1 Connectivity Establishment with MOCN GW

A given eNB/gNB can support multiple sectors that allow for carrier aggregation (CA) to be supported from a single site. Two levels of abstraction are possible here. The UE's operations on the individual sectors from the single site are hidden from the MOCN GW. At the second level, the MOCN GW abstracts all the eNB/gNBs deployed as part of the NHN to be abstracted from the MNO cores. Figure II.3.1.8 provides a typical private network multli-carrier / multi-sector radio base station supporting the S1-C and S1-U tunnel establishment with the core network.

The sectors of eNB/gNB will be exposed as a single eNB to the MOCN GW and MNO MME. A single S1 connection is used, and the traffic is separated at the eNB/gNB to the appropriate sector with which the UE is currently associated, based on the UE identifiers that are carried in the traffic headers. The number of carriers assigned to the UE for DL and UL operations and the actual component carrier (CC) used as primary CC (PCC) and secondary CC (SCC) are typically left up to the eNB/gNB to handle. The individual sectors will support independent eNB-ID (28-bit ID) or gNB-ID (36-bit ID).

Upon eNB/gNB power-up, the provisioned PLMNs supported are used to initiate broadcast SIBs. When the eNB associates with the MOCN GW, the MOCN GW initiates connectivity to the required set of PLMNs if it has not already been done.

The S1-C/N2 and S1-U/N3 connections between the enterprise eNB/gNB and the MOCN GW are treated independently of the corresponding connections between the MOCN GW and the MNO core.

The S1/N2/N3 connections are established on an MNO basis from the MOCN GW. Individual MNO MME failures need to be treated independently, and the outage of one should not create

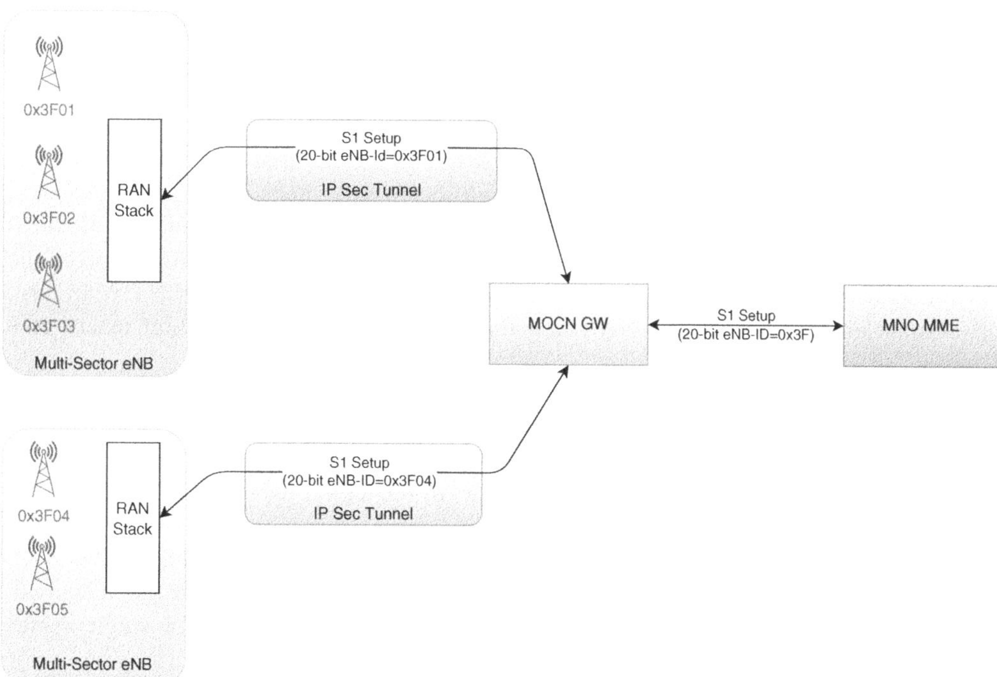

Figure II.3.1.8 S1-C and S1-U tunnel establishment.

disruptions in service for the other MNOs connected through the MOCN GW. An MNO MME/AMF connectivity failure will be propagated to the enterprise eNBs/gNB, and the failed PLMNs will not be broadcast from the eNB. From a connectivity perspective, S1/N2/N3 between the eNB/gNB and MOCN GW remains established independent of the failures that occur between the MOCN GW and MNO MME. The only regulation is to manage the PLMNs being broadcast on the eNB/gNB so that when there are outages, the availability of NHN service for the associated PLMNs needs to be turned off within reasonable time frames.

MME load balancing aspects will require explicit interactions with the MNO core, and similar to a connectivity outage, these overload triggers need to be handled when indicated by the MNO core, which will turn off NHN service for the MNO indicating an overload.

The MOCN GW will try to establish the S1/N2 connection with the MNO MME/AMF. The assumption is that the MOCN GW will be directed to the appropriate MME/AMF instance by the MNO core network when operating through a specific secure tunnel established between the MOCN GW and the MNO core.

Responses to the eNB from the MOCN GW should always be provided unless the MOCN GW is down, even when the connectivity between the MOCN GW and the MNO core is broken. MOCN GW support should be made highly available (HA) to ensure always-on service. Keep-alives can be used between the eNB/gNB and the MOCN GW, and from the MNOC GW to the MNO MME periodically to ensure link liveliness. This keep-alive can be avoided if there is already an active exchange of traffic ongoing between the nodes.

Terminating non-UE-associated S1/N2 application part procedures toward the eNB/gNB and the MME/AMF. In the case of an S1/N2 SETUP REQUEST message, verifying, as defined in Technical Specification (TS) 33.320, that the identity used by the eNB/gNB is valid. In the case of an S1/N2 PWS RESTART INDICATION message and a PWS FAILURE INDICATION message, verifying, as defined in TS 33.320, that the indicated cell identity is valid and replacing the eNB-ID/gNB ID with the MOCN GW ID before sending the PWS RESTART INDICATION message (or the PWS FAILURE INDICATION message) to the MME.

II.3.1.3.5.2 UE Attach with MOCN GW

Figure II.3.1.9 shows the connectivity aspects involved in the UE attaching to the NHN via a MOCN GW architecture. UE associates with a multisector eNB, choosing the preferred cell to camp on. From the network perspective, independent of the sector of association, the eNB abstracts it to a single sector when communicating with the MOCN GW. The link between the eNB and MOCN GW will typically use a 28-bit home eNB identifier. The MOCN GW, in turn, will abstract all the eNBs in the NHN and represent them as a single 20-bit macro eNB identifier.

The page mechanism may be supported in a subset of the sectors within an eNB based on the coverage and frequencies/channels used for operating the eNB sectors. The eNB selects the PCC assignment for the individual sectors and applies load balancing functions for DL and UL traffic based on the network and UE support capabilities for DL and UL CA operation.

For MME, services will need to take the individual sectors into consideration and use the measurements from the individual sectors for trilateration in the E-SMLC in the MNO networks. From the UE perspective, all the sectors across the different eNBs look like independent base stations, and the UE does not know the network constitution of single versus multisector eNBs.

Figure II.3.1.10 provides the call flow sequence for the UE attach procedure with the MNO core network from the NHN via the MOCN GW.

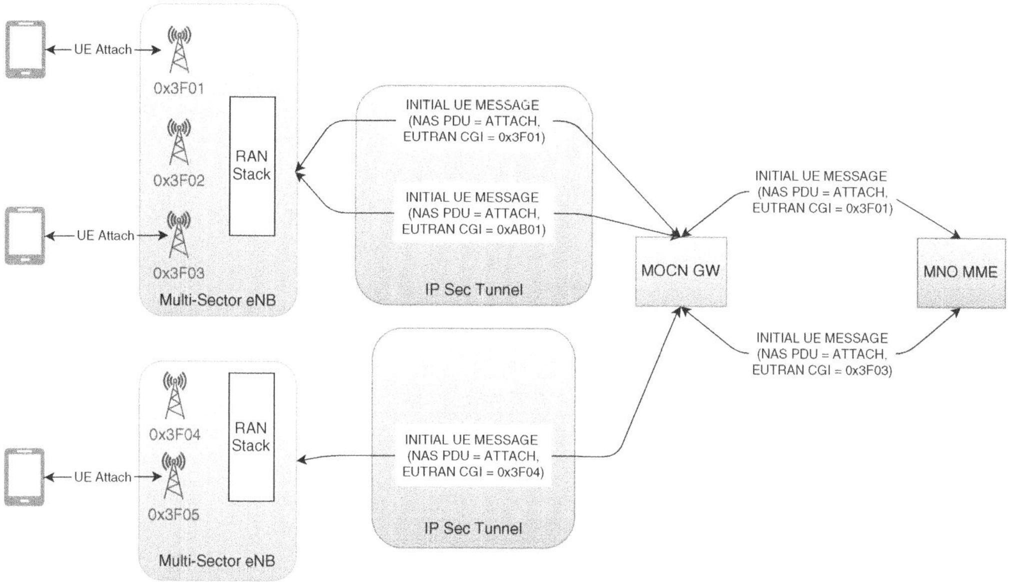

Figure II.3.1.9 UE is attached via a MOCN GW architecture.

II.3.1.3.6 Control and User Plane Node Selection in MNO Core

The NHN deployment provides the connectivity via the MOCN GW into the MNO core. The secure tunnels terminate at a point as desired by the MNO. The MNO core network is aware of the connectivity coming in from the NHN networks. The MNO core may choose to isolate the NHN traffic to independent nodes or have it generically integrated with the other macro network interaction functions. The appropriate choice of the MME/AMF and Serving Gateway (SGW)/UPF selection to provide for NHN UE connectivity and the UE identifiers assigned in the MNO core network is left as a choice for the macro core network realization.

Selection of a macro network MME/AMF at UE attachment is hosted by the MOCN GW instead of the NHN eNB/gNB. Upon reception of the GUMMEI/GUAMI from a UE, the eNB/gNB shall include it in the INITIAL UE MESSAGE. Upon reception of the GUMMEI/GUAMI type from the UE, the eNB/gNB shall also include it in the message if supported by the MOCN GW.

II.3.1.3.7 NHN Enhanced Features

Although I grouped the features below as enhanced features, these are fundamental requirements for any NHN commercialization. These are more second-level features that can potentially be ignored for the initial NHN connectivity establishment and proof of concept to demonstrate the functionality to both MNOs and the enterprise entities involved.

Relaying overload indications from MME/AMF: This mechanism is used by the macro network core to block further incoming users in the MME/AMF and can serve as a tool to regulate incoming NHN traffic. Based on the state of the MME/AMF, the NHN needs to manage incoming users and potentially reroute them to the macro network based on the coverage availability. Specific offload from the NHN needs to be further discussed with the individual MNOs regarding the specific realization requirements. Upon receiving an OVERLOAD START/STOP message, the MOCN GW should send the OVERLOAD START/STOP message toward the eNB(s)/gNB(s), including in

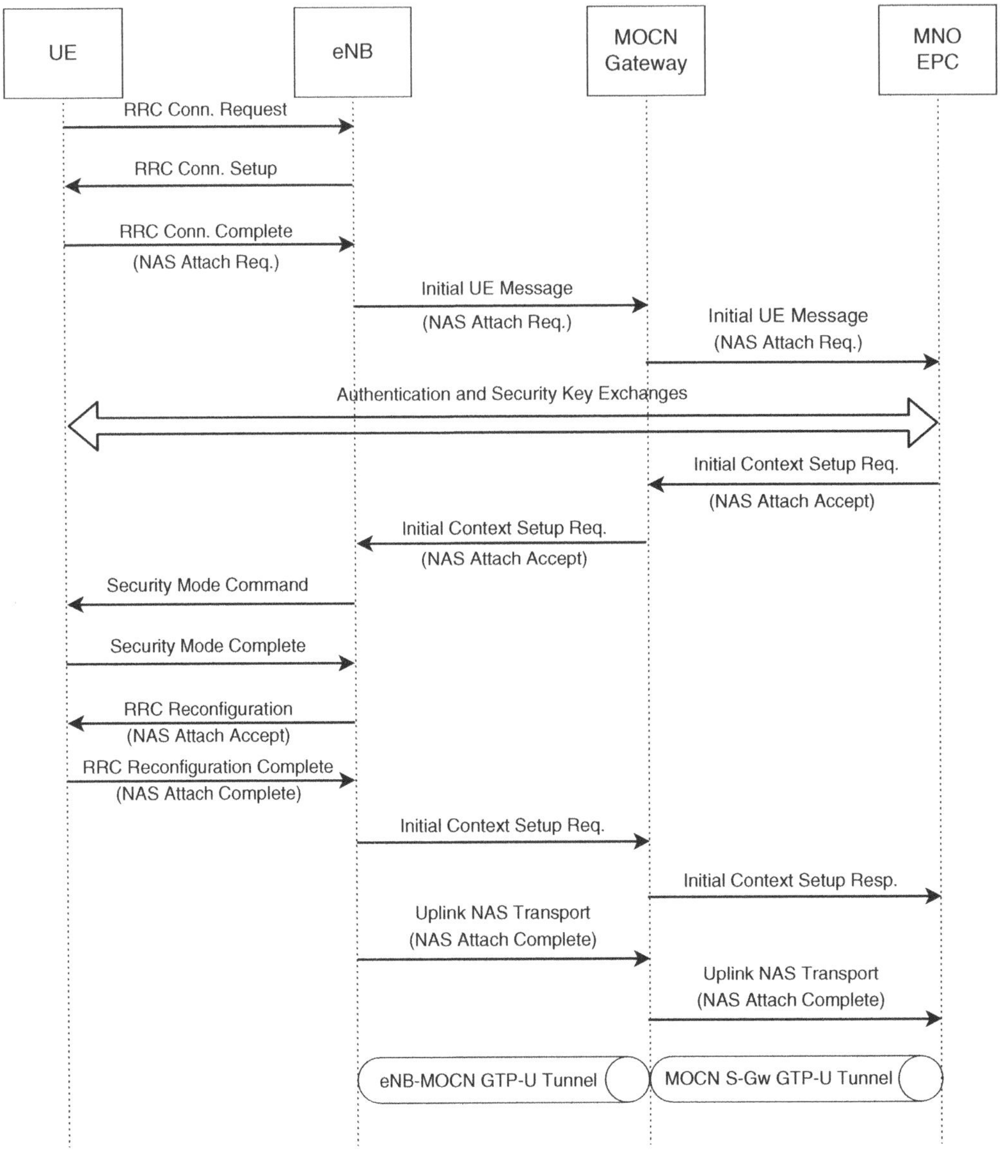

Figure II.3.1.10 UE attaches call flow via a MOCN GW.

the message the identities of the affected MME/AMF nodes. The eNB/gNB uses the information received from the OVERLOAD START message to identify to which traffic the above-defined rejections shall be applied. The eNB/gNB shall apply the defined rejections until the reception of an OVERLOAD STOP message applicable to this traffic or until the eNB/gNB receives a further OVERLOAD START message applicable to the same traffic, in which case it shall replace the ongoing overload action with the newly requested one.

NHN eNB/gNB liveliness: Each eNB/gNB needs to know if its neighboring eNBs/gNBs are still functional and whether both the radio and network connectivity are operational. This is typically done through keep-alive messages. Given that the eNBs may not talk to each other directly:

- Option 1 (centralized approach): X2GW can act as a central broker to keep track of all the eNB contexts. This has the advantage of minimizing the keep-alive control traffic; however, it requires the X2GW to retain context and be a fully functional entity rather than just a router.
- Option 2 (Distributed approach): Design it to have heartbeats go from one eNB to all its neighbors. This has the advantage of keeping the X2GW stateless; however, it increases the amount of traffic exchanged between the eNBs for keep-alive purposes.

Local Traffic Offload (LTO): Routing needs to be managed at the eNB/gNB, as the packets toward the enterprise core and MNO core are expected to be separated right at that node. It is possible to create an intermediate hub, but this will require additional maintenance and security aspects to be addressed.

II.3.1.3.8 Managing WEA

Wireless emergency alerts (WEA) support will be a fundamental requirement, given that the UEs will be camped on the NHN and will have no other source to receive the emergency alerts from. The WEA may either be obtained from the individual MNOs or directly from the emergency centers and will use geolocation information to determine if the emergency alert needs to be broadcast on a given NHN cell. Given that an NHN typically services multiple MNOs simultaneously, WEA may be received from multiple MNOs based on the MOCN GW configuration and interconnect with the individual MNO cores. Figure II.3.1.11 shows the functional nodes involved in WEA notifications on NHN.

Note that the integrated public alert and warning system (IPAWS) has been enhanced to

- increase the maximum character count from 90 to 360;
- add support for Spanish-language WEA;
- Add two new alert categories in addition to presidential, AMBR, and imminent threat:
  - Public safety message – less severe in nature than an imminent threat;
  - WEA test message – opt-in message to support state and local WEA testing; and

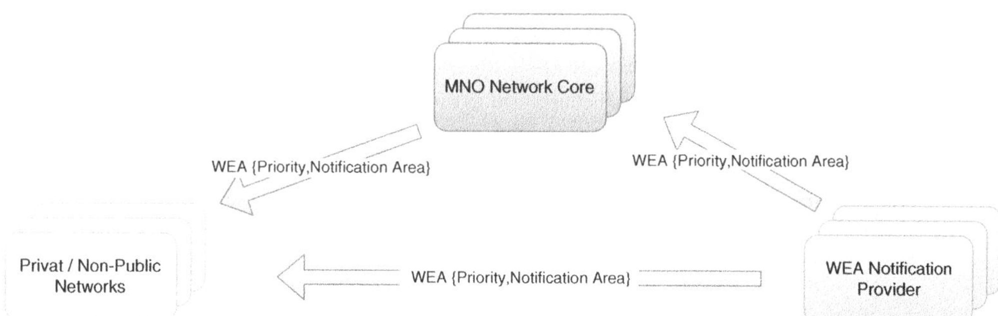

Figure II.3.1.11 WEA notifications on NHN.

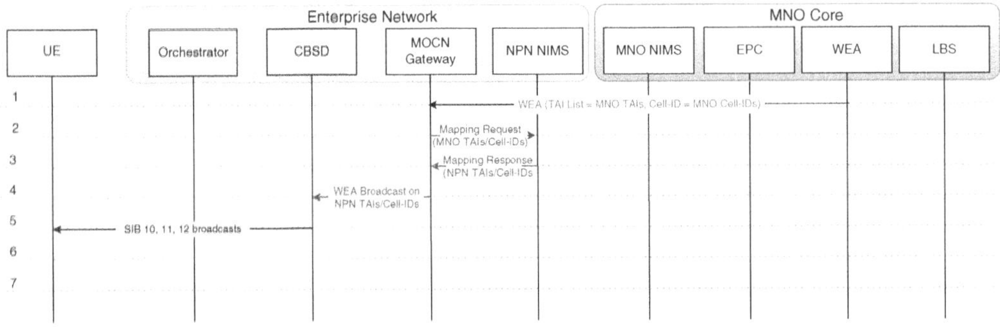

Figure II.3.1.12 Delivering WEA via MOCN GW.

- Enhance geo-targeting to reach 100% of the targeted area with no more than 1/10th of a mile overshoot.

The possible options are detailed below.

Option 1: The enterprise private network supports receiving emergency broadcast information from the IPAWS.

Option 2: Select the MNO MME/AMF to receive the emergency broadcast messages. The choice of MME/AMF will need to be decided based on the Geographic (GEO) fencing of WEA messages handled by the MME/AMF. This option should be preferred over option 1. An alternative is to process the messages received from all MMEs and broadcast only non-duplicates; this requires duplicate message detection across MNOs.

In both options, the MOCN GW needs to process the message to ensure relevance for transmission to the enterprise campus based on the indicated geo-targeting information provided. Figure II.3.1.12 shows the WEA delivered via the MOCN GW.

II.3.1.3.9 Page Optimizations

An enterprise campus can be supported by one or more TACs. Typically, a site, based on its size, will have only a single TAC. Some of the possible options for handling the page are discussed below.

Option 1: Page the UE across all eNBs in the TAC: This is a simple approach. Based on the size of the campus, the paging channel capacity needs to be managed according to the expected traffic.

Option 2: Page the UE based on previously known proximity: Select the group of eNBs relative to the previously known location of the UE based on prior accesses. Age the information and page across the full TAC after the timer expires.

Option 3: AI based: Learn the UE's patterns of mobility and page the UE first in the typical eNBs (sets of eNBs based on location) where the UE typically accesses the network. Subsequently, page the UE across the full TAC.

II.3.1.3.10 IPSec Tunnels with Integrated X2/Xn GW and MOCN GW

The primary goal is to retain the device mobility within an NHN campus to be handled locally within the enterprise network without impacting the MNO networks. With both private network UEs and NHN UEs in the mix, along with traffic separation between the enterprise core and the

MNO core right from the eNB/gNB, a simple hub-and-spoke model may not be sufficient. The architectural and packet routing options for transitioning both the private network UEs and the MNO UEs need to be considered for effective realization.

There are several possible realizations that can be done with the X2/Xn GW and MOCN GW. The X2/Xn GW is the gateway used to perform mobility across eNBs/gNBs without requiring the MME/AMF to assist in the process. The X2 interface is the interconnect between the eNBs, and Xn is the interconnect between the gNBs. For campus deployments that support both LTE and NR, the behavior of the device performing inter-RAT (across LTE and NR) is handled by using the integrated core network that supports both the MME and AMF for private network mobility. Similar integration can be performed with the MOCN GW, reflecting it in the Evolved Packet Core (EPC)/5GC core networks of the MNO.

The methods of X2-based mobility and S1-based mobility are described in the "LTE Fundamentals" chapter. Similar procedures apply for NR with Xn-based mobility and N2/N3-based mobility and largely remain the same except for the UE and radio/core bearer identifiers used in NR relative to LTE. LTO functions for NHN UEs to allow access to the enterprise services also need to be accommodated.

Mobility functions across the NHN campus need to take care of node liveliness and ensure that the UE is not asked to measure a non-functional neighbor and that a call is not handed over to that neighbor.

Handovers from eNB to another or from one gNN to another need to support the following features:

- Inter-eNB/gNB connectivity
- UE measurement configuration and report management
- Packet Data Convergence Protocol (PDCP) context transfer
- Packet forwarding and handling of DL and UL traffic
  - Minimize packet loss
  - Ensure in-order packet delivery
  - Minimize UE starvation
  - Minimize packet duplication
- Flow control between the SeGW/UPF via the MOCN GW or as independent user plane connectivity with eNB/gNB

One approach can be to rely only on the S1 and N2/N3 based on mobility and use the enterprise core for the private network UEs and the MOCN GW for the NHN UEs. However, based on the MOCN GW location, which may be in a central cloud, reflecting the mobility procedures using the MOCN GW may not be viable, and X2/Xn GW support on-premises becomes required. This will very much depend on the network architectural choices made, apart from the costs and complexity involved in the realization of the X2/Xn-based mobility versus the S1 & N2/N3-based mobility. Some of the possible variants of the X2/Xn GW and MOCN GW realizations are shown in the illustrations below. Figure II.3.1.13, Figure II.3.1.14, Figure II.3.1.15, Figure II.3.1.16, Figure II.3.1.17, and Figure II.3.1.18 IPSec present the possible variants that can be supported for the RAN nodes connected to both the private network (connected to the enterprise core) and macro network (via the MOCN GW).

II.3.1.3.11 Positioning Support on NHN

Positioning with the NHN camping requires the macro network to be aware of the NHN cell IDs. The UE measures and reports these NHN cell IDs to the E-SMLC. The NHN cell ID-related information, including the location, power level, and directionality, is either statically provisioned in the macro

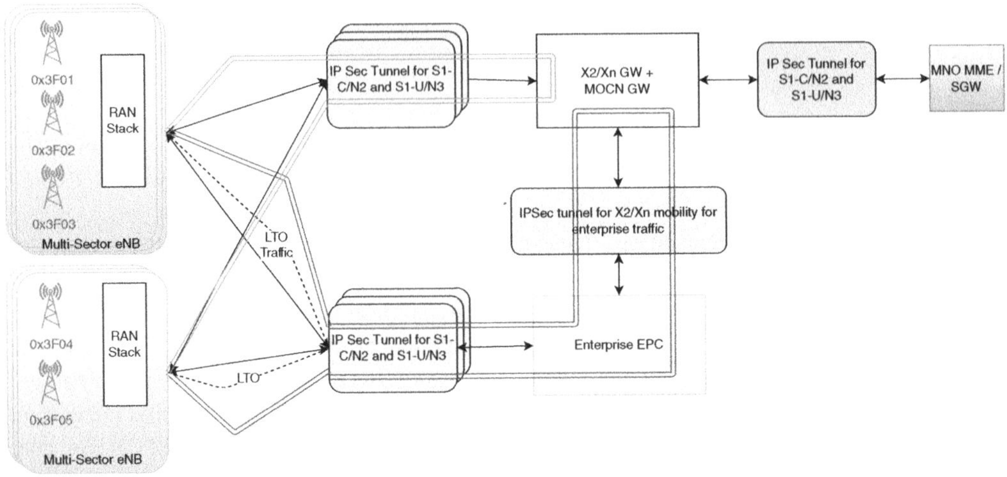

Figure II.3.1.13 IPSec tunnels with integrated X2/Xn GW and MOCN GW (variant 1).

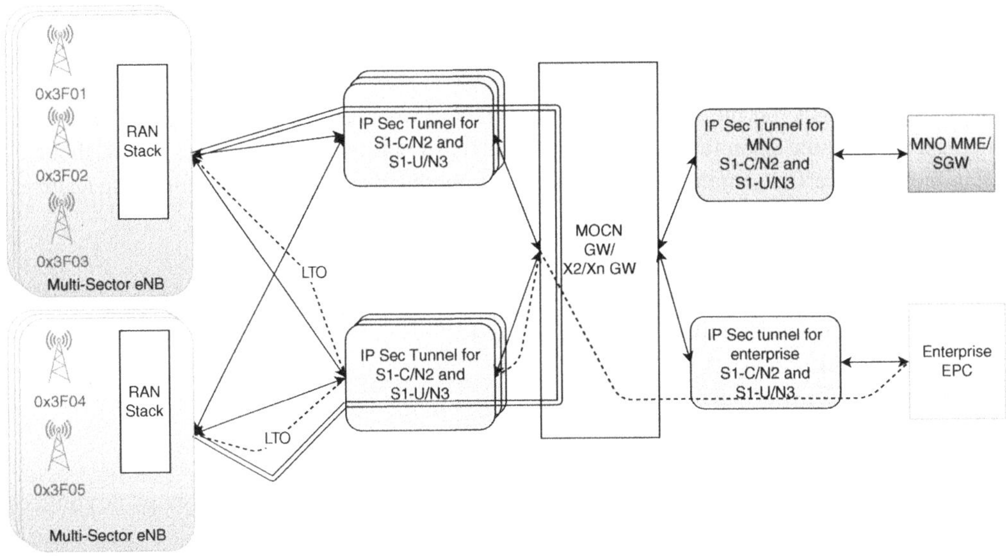

Figure II.3.1.14 IPSec tunnels with integrated X2/Xn GW and MOCN GW (variant 2).

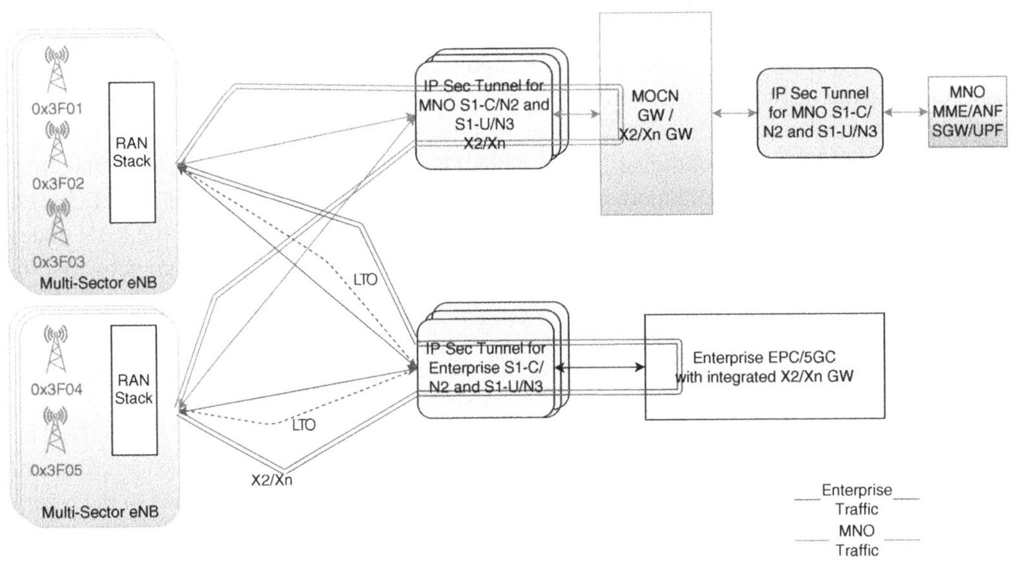

Figure II.3.1.15 IPSec tunnels with integrated X2/Xn GW and MOCN GW (variant 3).

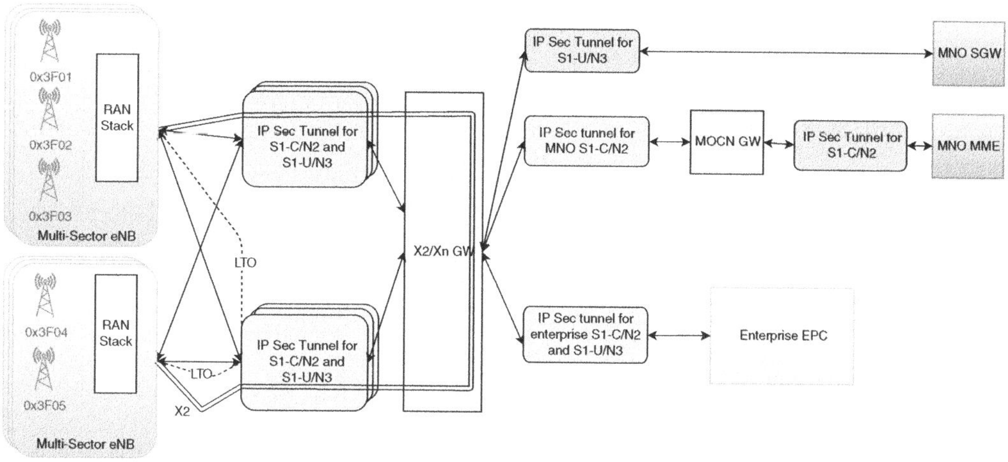

Figure II.3.1.16 IPSec tunnels with independent X2/Xn GW and MOCN GW – variant 1.

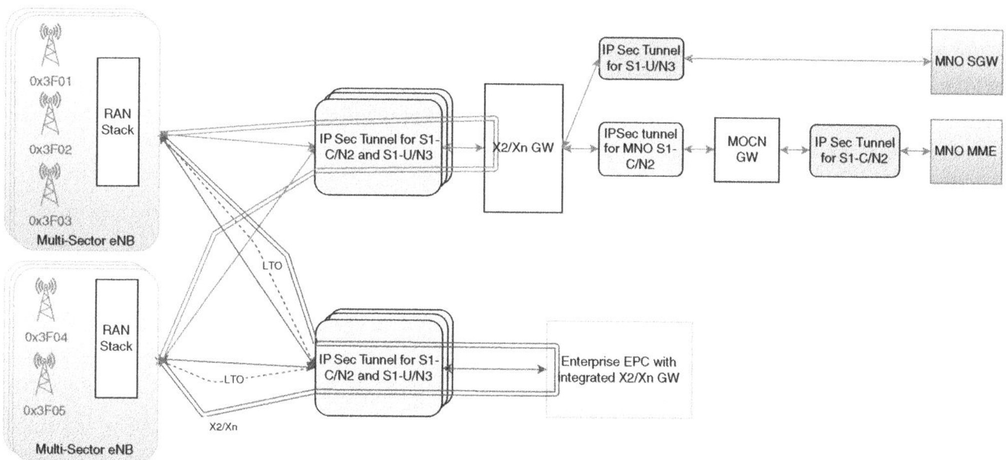

Figure II.3.1.17 IPSec tunnels with independent X2/Xn GW and MOCN GW – variant 2.

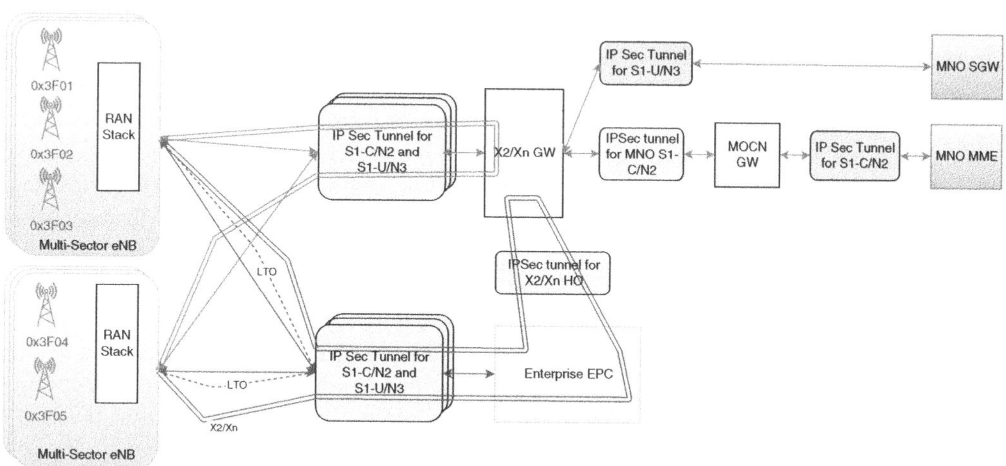

Figure II.3.1.18 IPSec tunnels with independent X2/Xn GW and MOCN GW – variant 3.

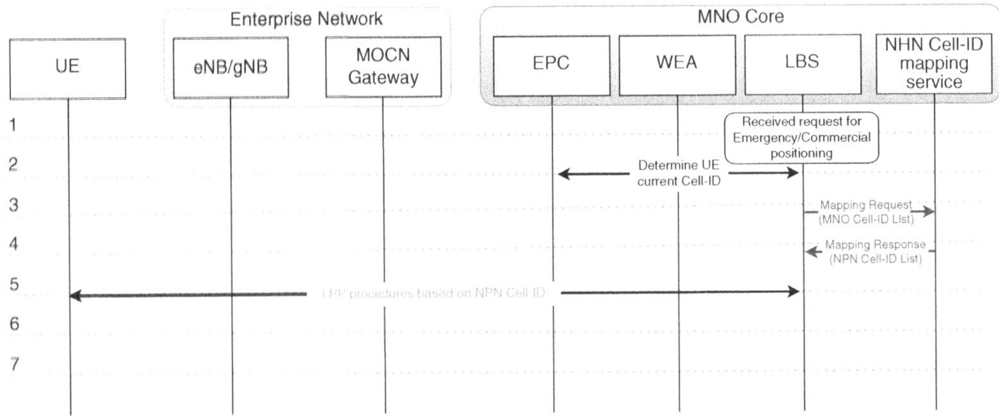

Figure II.3.1.19 Positioning support for NHN.

network or can be dynamically obtained via a mapping service that is supported between the NHN deployment and the macro network core. The E-SMLC requests the UE to measure, and this can include both NHN cells and macro network cells. Typically, only horizontal neighbors are measured, and with the smaller footprint of the NHN cells, it is usually sufficient to just measure the current serving cell alone. See Figure II.3.1.19.

II.3.1.3.12 Emergency Call Support

Based on the maturity of the NHN deployment and the integration with the MNO core, the MNOs may be comfortable allowing the NHN to support emergency calls. The integration with the MNO core requires that the NHN eNB/gNB identifiers be recognizable in the MNO core and, in particular, the E-SMLC for positioning services. The options for emergency calling, with and without NHN being enabled for emergency calling, are illustrated in Figures II.3.1.20 and II.3.1.21.

II.3.1.3.13 Mobility Transitions Across MNO and Enterprise Networks

This section provides the possible transition use cases across the macro and NHN/Enterprise networks. Both idle and connected mode transitions can be executed. Idle transitions are typically based on neighbor priority and NHN preferences for camping over the macro network, treating the NHN as merely a coverage extension or as a means for more proactive transitions, even when the macro network coverage is available. A connected mode transition moving away from the NHN into the macro network is required, given that users may walk away from NHN coverage, which is a typical scenario. Connected mode transitions from the macro to the NHN are seen to be optional, as macro coverage tends to be available, although weak, and can wait for the UE to transition to idle before transitioning to the NHN. Connected mode handover from the macro to the NHN will be required based on the location of the NHN and the macro footprint available. Such transitions require the macro network to find the appropriate smaller footprint cell in the NHN, which can be tricky to determine, and effective methods need to be addressed.

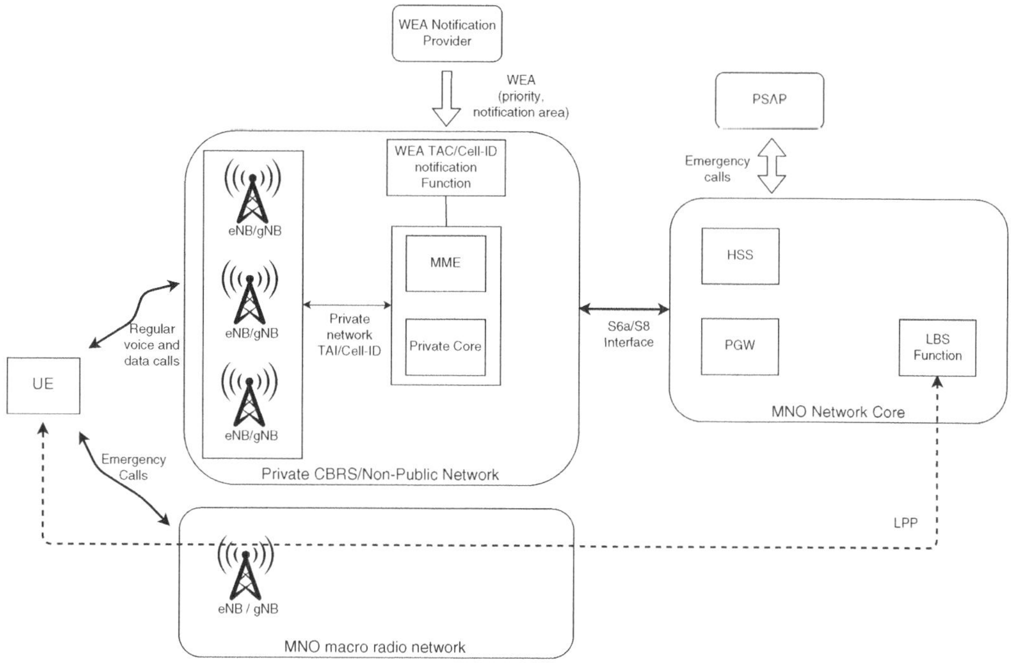

Figure II.3.1.20 Emergency calls are supported on the macro network (no emergency calls on NHN).

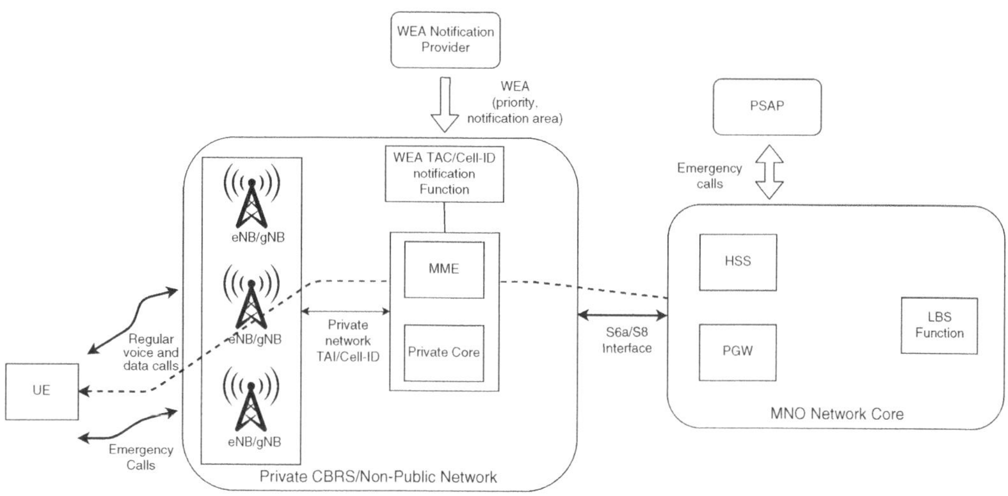

Figure II.3.1.21 Emergency calls are supported on NHN.

II.3.1.3.13.1 Idle Transitions

MNO → Enterprise: The typical behavior involves idle transitions from the macro to the enterprise NHN network. Essentially, the UE will wait until it transitions to idle and use cell selection procedures to transition from the MNO to the enterprise network. The enterprise network may be deployed on several frequencies/channels, and not all of these can be listed in the cell broadcasts provided by the macro network. UE customization will be required to scan for available cells beyond the guidance provided by the macro networks to find the NHN available cells. See the NHN geofencing section for a proposal on possible UE-provisioned methods of finding preferred NHNs.

Enterprise → MNO: The UE leaves the NHN footprint and uses the macro neighbor information provisioned to perform the scans and transitions. Given that there will be several MNOs operating from the NHN, the NHN needs to provide the appropriate macro neighbors based on the MNO association of the individual UEs.

II.3.1.3.13.2 Active Transitions

Enterprise → MNO: The UE, based on its MNO association, provided the measurement object of the macro pilots for the UE to measure. The UE performs these measurements and reports them to the NHN cell. The NHN network, via the MOCN GW, interacts with the macro core network, establishes the resources on the macro network cell, and triggers the handover process. Given that the macro cell sites have a large footprint, this is a reasonably straightforward procedure.

MNO → Enterprise: This process, going from a large footprint macro cell to an NHN small footprint cell, is a very tricky process and not easily supported. With MOCN GW, the specific eNB/gNB where the resources need to be allocated cannot be reached by the MNO MME, given that the communication is only with the MOCN GW. Specific customizations are required for the S1/N2 messaging protocol to enable mobility from the MNO network to specific eNBs/gNBs within the enterprise campus. Some possible enhancements/customizations are discussed below. Other simpler methods may be possible as well.

- Active transitions: Customization #1
  - It is based on changes to fields in the existing S1/N2 message exchange.
  - Apart from the eNB UE ID on S1/N2, the cell ID information also needs to be included in the HANDOVER REQUIRED.
  - This cell ID information is used to resolve the specific eNB/gNB for resource allocation.
  - The MNO network with the Global Positioning System (GPS) location of the eNBs/gNBs in the Serving Mobile Location Center (SMLC) is used for determining position information while on the enterprise campus.
    - Note: The enterprise networks will be neutral hosts, and the specific MNO network needs to be supported.
  - The MNO networks typically can determine the GPS location of the UE using different Location Based Service (LBS) techniques.
  - The GPS information of the UE, when accurate enough, can allow for locating the specific enterprise networks and the typical entry points and identify the specific cell ID to hand over the active connection to a specific enterprise campus.
  - The enterprise network that a given UE frequents can also be learned to aid with this mobility procedure and potentially even recognize the typical cell ID used as entry points to enter the enterprise campus.
- Active transitions: Customization #2
  - It is based on changes to the S1/N2 message exchange sequence.
  - This is based on customization #1, aiming to increase the reliability of the handover.

- Prior to the HANDOVER REQUIRED message, the MNO MME sends a message requesting the MOCN GW to provide a list of enterprise eNB/gNB neighbors to measure. The UE GPS location is included in this message as well to narrow the neighbors to a finer list for the UE to measure.
- This information is provided back from the MOCN GW to the MNO MME/AMF.
- The MNO MME forwards the measurement information to the MNO eNB/gNB to which the UE is currently associated.
- Once the UE measurement report is received, the strongest cell ID is selected for inclusion in the HANDOVER REQUIRED message.
- The remaining steps are according to customization #1.

- Active transitions: Customization #3
  - It is based on reducing the reliance on the MNO network and using the UE's preferences to find specific campuses and aiding the MNO network in performing the handover.
  - Using the closed access group (CAG) supported by the 3GPP Release-16 specification.
  - Identify a special CAG ID to be recognized as applicable for enterprise campuses.
  - The UEs allowing access on the enterprise campus neutral host are implicitly considered to be subscribed to this CAG ID without explicit provisioning.
  - Also, the MNO networks recognize this CAG ID as being intended for the enterprise campus where a neutral host is enabled.
  - When the UE is in proximity to the preferred enterprise network determined by its GEO fencing algorithm, the UE indicates the CAG-supported indication to the AMF.
  - This triggers the procedure for the MNO network to determine the UE's GPS location and employ customization #1 or #2, as per the prior description.

II.3.1.3.13.3 Geofencing for NHN

High-Level Goals to Meet

Listed below is a set of goals to meet with supporting geofencing for NHN.

- NH deployments are restricted to indoor use per MNO request. The private network itself will have wider coverage with both indoor and outdoor footprints. This will imply that we will need to manage a different geofence for private networks and a smaller one for NH. This may aid UE behavior for indoor and outdoor operations for private networks as well.
- NH will be enabled in several big box retails stores in the next few weeks and seems to be getting sufficient market traction.
- Mid year 2024, several MNOs have announced support for NHN based on LTE with support for NR introduced subsequently. NHN solution deployments globally are planned by several MNOs.
- Note that the MNOs are not funding the deployment of NHs, and they are indicating the enterprises to BYOC (bring your own coverage).
- Specific MNOs have announced plans to be an MSP for private networks using specific enterprise network vendor based deployments. These deployments may take a different form, with roaming support offered to other MNOs to camp on such private networks in both licensed and unlicensed bands.
- Transitions to NHs based on home operator and roam partner support needs to be managed as well.

Use Case for Macro Network and NHN Transitions

Figure II.3.1.22 provides a pictorial view of the use cases by defining the possible set of network identifiers used for private and neutral host networks. The required UE provisioning and network broadcast identifiers for private and NHN for UE to find and camp on the networks is shown.

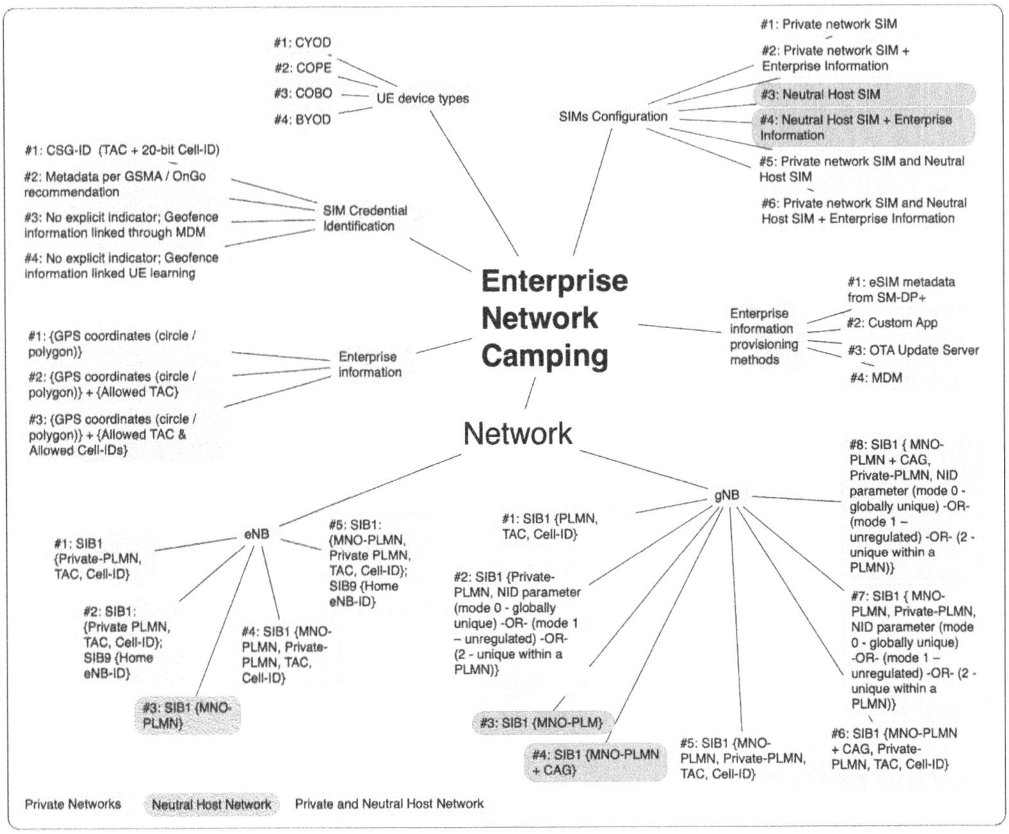

Figure II.3.1.22 UE provisioning and network broadcast identifiers for private and NHN.

Use Case: UE Entering Private Network

Use case: UE entering private network			
Purpose	**Support UE's automatic camping on multiple private networks**		
Pre-conditions	SIM configuration: #2 SIM identification: #1, #2, #3, #4 Enterprise information: #1, #2, #3 UE device type: #1, #2, #3 Enterprise eNB: #1, #2 Enterprise gNB: #1, #2	Triggers	# UE enters the geofence of the private network # Signal strength of the private network # Check against allowed TAC/cell IDs if provisioned # Check the Closed Subscriber Group (CSG)-ID against the SIB9 Home-eNB-ID, if provisioned # Check Network Identifier (NID) with SIB1 if it is provisioned

Use case: UE entering private network	
Purpose	**Support UE's automatic camping on multiple private networks**
Description	The UE enters the geofence of the private network and starts looking for private networks. It checks the signal strength of the private network before attempting to camp on the network and transition the data connection to the enterprise network. If allowed TAC/cell IDs are provisioned, the UE checks against the provisioned list. It is possible for the UE to learn from prior camping or crowdsourcing on the known TAC/cell IDs where the UE has valid private network service. For LTE, if SIB9 is broadcast, the UE checks the CSG-ID provisioned in the UE against the SIB9 Home-eNB-ID. For NR, if the NID parameter is provisioned, it checks against the provisioned PLMN and/or NID value based on the indicated mode 0, 1, or 2 for the NID.
Post conditions	UE establishes a data connection over the enterprise network.

NH Geofence Detailed Use Cases

Note on TAC/Cell ID:

The NHN can be configured to act only as an NHN or both as an NHN and a private network. When the NHN is not acting as a private network, the TAC-ID and cell IDs are negotiated and established for use within a given NHN.

However, when the UE needs to enter an NHN that also supports a private network, the typical configuration is for the network to be deployed as a private network by a given enterprise and to have additionally established a relationship with MNO(s) to act as an NHN. This implies that the TAC/cell ID included in the SIB broadcasts will be associated with the private network and can overlap with the TAC/cell IDs used elsewhere in the MNO networks. Note that the TAC-ID/cell ID could also be allocated to a completely different regional location in the different MNO networks.

This implies that the MNO-specific TAC/cell ID associated with the NHN cell needs to be provided to the UE in connected mode, having identified the MNO association of the UE connecting to the NHN.

With the use of the MOCN GW, the MNO core network will see a specific NHN as a single macro cell ID. The macro cell ID for LTE is a fixed 20 bits, and the full cell ID is 28 bits. For NR, the full cell ID is 36 bits, and a size less than 36 bits (e.g. 28 bits) is used as the macro cell ID. There needs to be assigned the full cell ID to support location services within the enterprise campus.

Refer to the OnGo Alliance specification TS-1004 on geofencing support for private networks. The same information, along with the association to MNO support of NHN agreements with specific enterprise private networks, can be leveraged to provision the UE with the geofencing information of preferred enterprise NHN deployments. For example a big-box retail store deploying NHN accommodates its employees to proactively use the NHN even when there is macro network coverage. For customers visiting the store, these NHNs are used as a macro network extension, and offloading to NHN is supported only when there is no macro network coverage. Fingerprinting can be used for customers who visit the store frequently, and this is done using user device-based logic to learn these patterns of mobility to transition to these NHN networks.

Transitioning from Macro to the NH Network Use Cases

Use case: UE is transitioning from macro to NHN in idle mode			
Purpose			
Pre-conditions	SIM configuration: #3 SIM identification: #3 Enterprise information: #1 UE device type: #1 Enterprise eNB: #3 Enterprise gNB: #3	Triggers	# UE enters the geofence of NHN # The signal strength of the macro network and NHN pilots # UE determines the available BW on the macro network # UE determines the congestion levels on the macro network # Learned throughput on the macro network and NHN
Description	The UE logic from NHN transitions from macro, as illustrated in the flow chart below (see Figure II.3.1.23).		

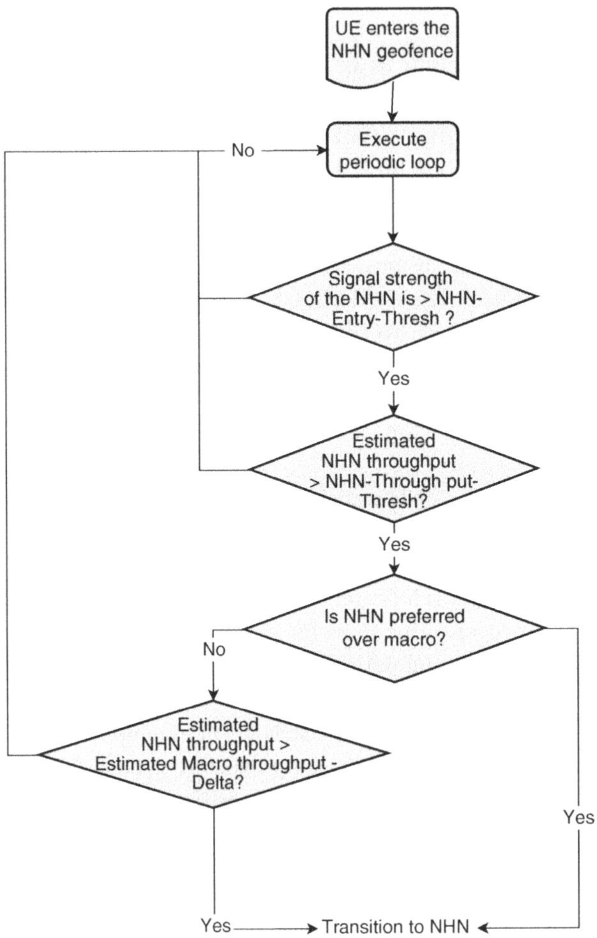

Figure II.3.1.23 UE transitioning from macro to NHN in Idle mode flow chart.

Note: The estimated NHN throughput and macro network throughput can be subject to real-time congestion estimations.

Use case: UE is transitioning from macro to NHN in idle mode	
Purpose	
	MNO-Specific TAC-ID/cell ID update When the UE establishes the radio resource control (RRC) connection with the eNB, the eNB detects the MNO association of the UE and initiates a change of TAC and cell ID that is specific to the MNO associated with this NHN cell. Once the UE receive the MNO-specific TAC/cell ID, the UE send a Tracking Area Update (TAU) with the updated information even though it has already initiated a TAU. Any Non-Access Stratum (NAS) messages initiated prior to the MNO TAC/cell ID update are dropped in the eNB to avoid overwhelming the MNO core with back-to-back TAUs. Note that this update of the TAC/cell ID is performed when the UE moves from one cell to another in connected mode with the NHN.
Sequence diagram	See Figure II.3.1.24.

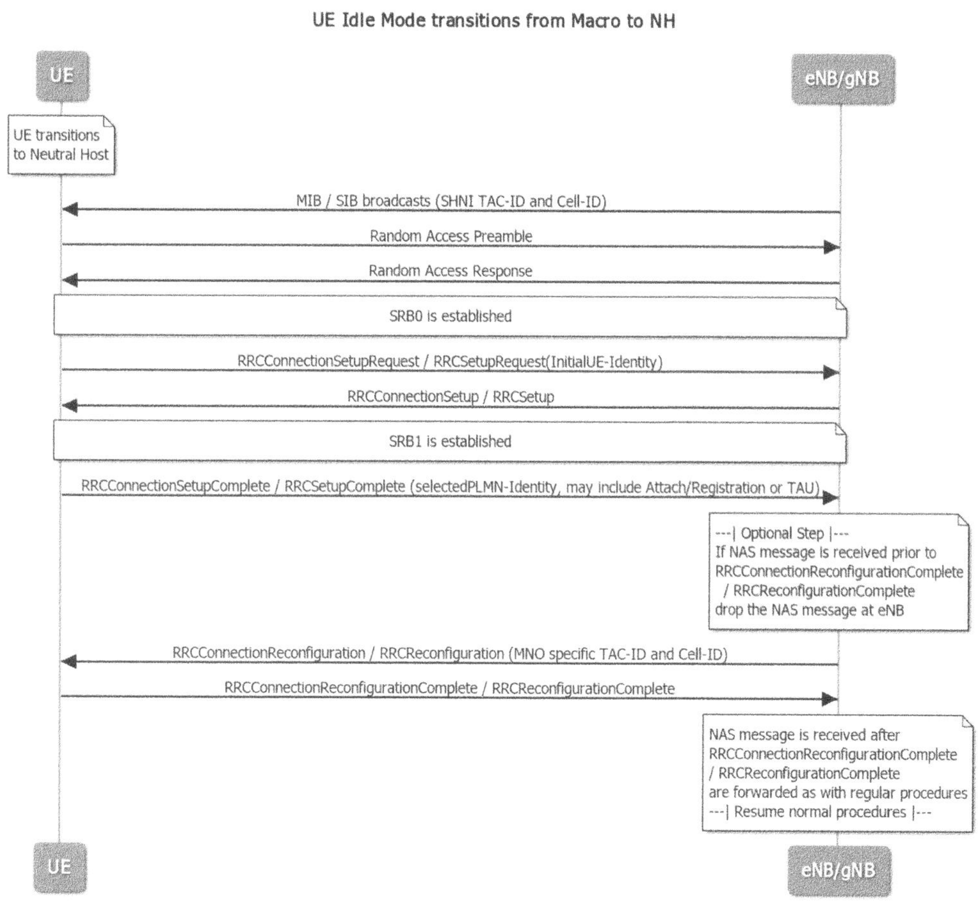

Figure II.3.1.24 E transitioning from macro to NHN in Idle mode sequence diagram.

(Continued)

Use case: UE is transitioning from macro to NHN in idle mode	
Purpose	
Post conditions	UE has transitioned to the NHN in idle mode. Given that the tracking area code will be different on the NHN, the UE enters connected mode and sends a TAU to the macro network via the NHN/MOCN GW. Based on the MNO PLMN used to access the NHN, the UE may be provided with an MNO-specific TAC and cell ID, which the UE needs to use for its TAU procedure.

Use case: The UE is transitioning from macro to NHN in connected mode			
Purpose	**The use case describes managing the MNO-based TAC ID and cell ID associated with the NHN cells.**		
Pre-conditions	SIM configuration: #3 SIM identification: #3 Enterprise information: #1 UE device type: #1 Enterprise eNB: #3 Enterprise gNB: #3	Triggers	# UE enters the NHN through connected mode HO
Description	When the UE establishes the RRC connection with the eNB, the eNB detects the MNO association of the UE and initiates a change of TAC and cell ID that is specific to the MNO associated with this NHN cell. Once the UE receives the MNO-specific TAC/cell ID, the UE sends a TAU with the updated information even if it has already initiated a TAU. Any NAS messages initiated prior to the MNO TAC/cell ID update are dropped in the eNB to avoid overwhelming the MNO core with back-to-back TAUs. Note that this update of the TAC/cell ID is performed when the UE moves from one cell to another in connected mode with the NHN as well.		

Use case: The UE is transitioning from macro to NHN in connected mode	
Purpose	**The use case describes managing the MNO-based TAC ID and cell ID associated with the NHN cells.**
Sequence diagram	See Figure II.3.1.25

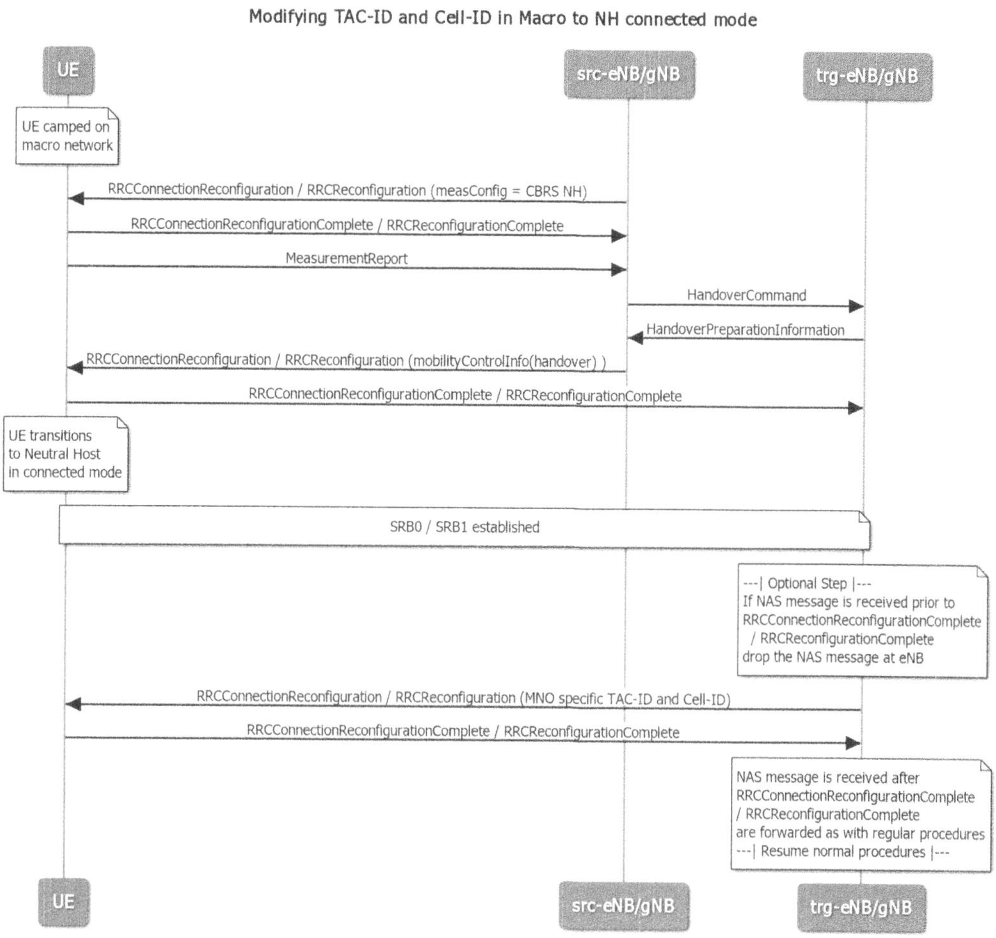

Figure II.3.1.25 UE is transitioning from macro to NHN in connected mode.

Post conditions	UE has transitioned to the NHN in a connected mode.

Transitioning from an NH Cell to Another NH Cell: Use Cases

Use case: The UE is transitioning from one NHN cell to another in idle mode			
Purpose			
Pre-conditions	SIM configuration: #3 SIM identification: #3 Enterprise information: #1 UE device type: #1 Enterprise eNB: #3 Enterprise gNB: #3	Triggers	# UE transitions to the NHN and sees a change in TAC
Description	UE transitions to the NHN and sees a change in TAC. This forces the UE to enter connected mode and perform a TAU. If the TAC/cell ID associated with the MNO for this UE needs to be changed, this is done in connected mode, and the UE sends the TAU with the information received in connected mode. Note that the SIB parameters received in connected mode override the parameters received by the UE in idle mode through cell broadcasts.		
Sequence diagram	See Figure II.3.1.26		

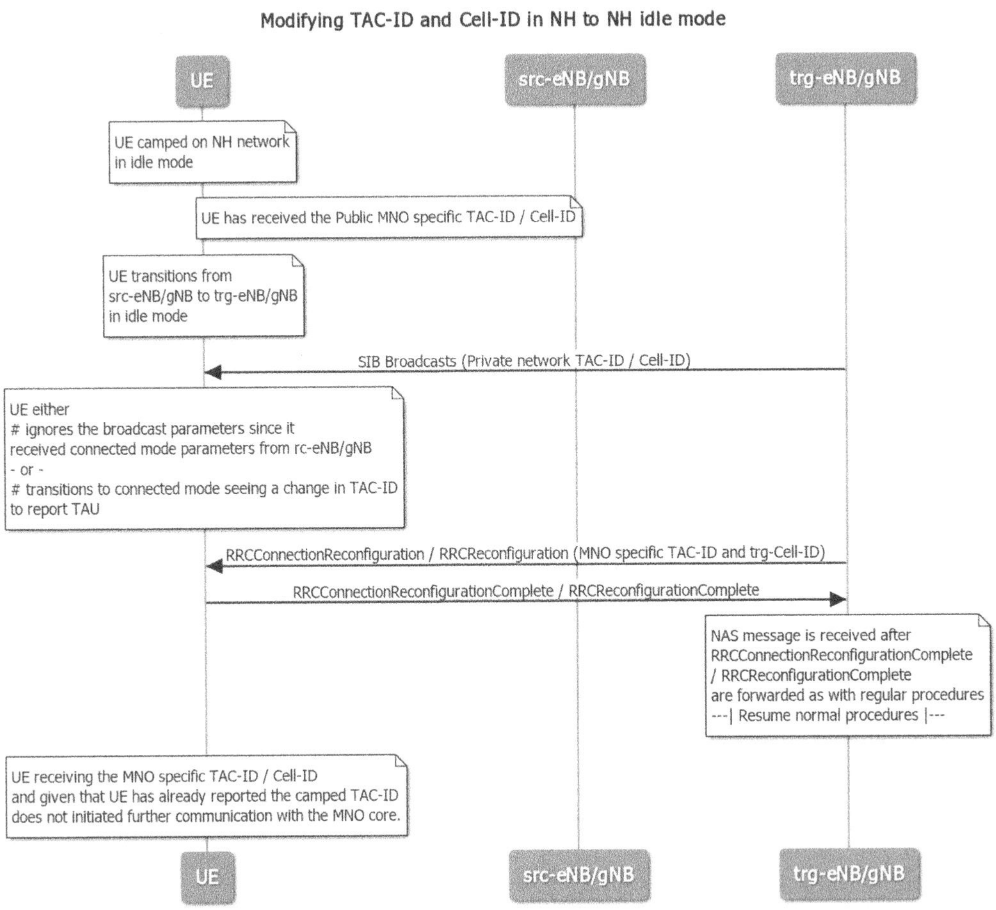

Figure II.3.1.26 UE is transitioning from one NHN cell to another in idle mode.

Post conditions	UE has transitioned to NHN in idle mode.

Use case: UE transitioning from one NHN cell to another in connected mode			
Purpose			
Pre-conditions	SIM configuration: #3 SIM identification: #3 Enterprise information: #1 UE device type: #1 Enterprise eNB: #3 Enterprise gNB: #3	Triggers	# UE moves from one cell to another within NHN
Description	The target eNB will provide the MNO-associated TAC/cell ID to the UE, if required. It is likely that the TAC remains the same within a given NHN; however, the cell ID must change. The finer cell ID information is needed in the UE to support location services within the enterprise campus.		
Sequence diagram	See Figure II.3.1.27		

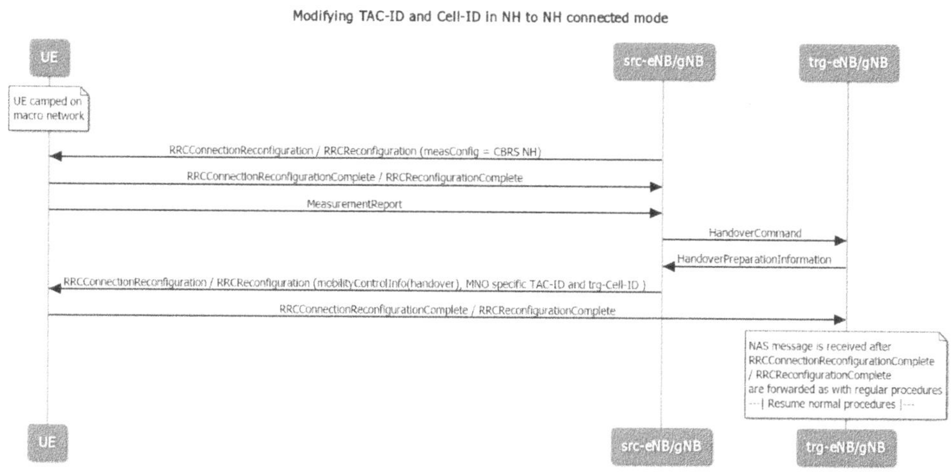

Figure II.3.1.27 UE transitioning from one NHN cell to another in connected mode.

Post conditions	The UE has transitioned to the target cell in the NHN and has received the updated TAC/cell ID associated with the MNO.

Transitioning from Macro to Wi-Fi Calling with a Private Network

Use case: UE transitioning to Wi-Fi calling over a private network			
Purpose			
Pre-conditions	SIM configuration: # SIM identification: # Enterprise information: # UE device type: # Enterprise eNB: # Enterprise gNB: #	Triggers	# UE enters the geofence of the private network # UE successfully associates with the private network # UE has signal strength below a threshold # UE determines the congestion levels in the macro network

(*Continued*)

Use case: UE transitioning to Wi-Fi calling over a private network	
Purpose	
Description	UE transitions the data connection to the private network using the enterprise SIM. UE determines it is preferable to transition the IP multimedia system (IMS) PDN connection over the ePDG to support Wi-Fi calling.
Post conditions	UE supports the data connection over the private network and the UE IMS PDN over the private network as an ePDG connection.

Wireless Emergency Alerts on NHN

Use case: UE receiving WEA on NHN			
Purpose			
Pre-conditions	SIM configuration: # SIM identification: # Enterprise information: # UE device type: # Enterprise eNB: # Enterprise gNB: #	Triggers	# UE receives ETWS/CMAS in the SIB broadcast messages
Description	A given NHN may be servicing multiple MNOs. It is left up to the network to coordinate the ETWS/CMAS messages that are delivered. There are several approaches possible: 1. The NHN registers with the Public-Safety Answering Point (PSAP) and emergency broadcast entities to receive the alerts and populate them accordingly. 2. The NHN receives the alerts along with the metadata from a specific MNO, and the MOCN GW filters the alerts that need to be provided to the specific NHN based on the zones where the messages need to be delivered. 3. The NHN received the alerts from multiple MNOs and checks for duplicates before performing the behavior described in #2 above.		
Sequence diagram	See Figure II.3.1.28		

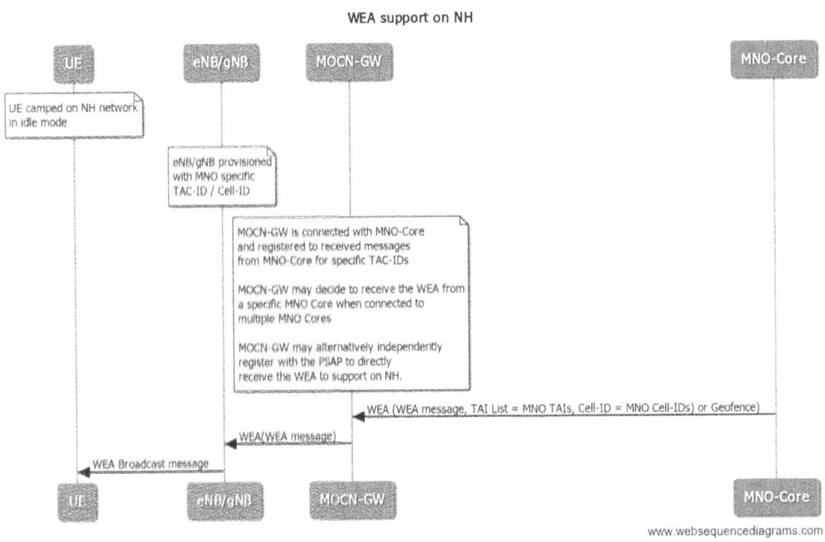

Figure II.3.1.28 UE receiving WEA on NHN.

Post conditions	UE receives ETWS/CMAS broadcasts

Transitioning from NHN to Macro Networks

Use case: UE transitioning out of NHN back into macro networks in idle mode			
Purpose			
Pre-conditions	# UE is camped on NHN (LTE or NR) # UE has received MNO-specific neighbor information	Triggers	# UE measures LTE and NR neighbors
Description	UE measures the macro network neighbors provided in connected mode as a dedicated RRC message. The UE, based on the neighbor priority indicated, determines that a macro network neighbor has a higher relative priority based on the measured signal strengths of the NHN and macro network neighbors. It is possible that the UE loses coverage prior to acquiring the macro neighbor(s); in this case, it will use the neighbor list provided on NHN to transition. If the UE is unable to find a valid cell, it performs a full band scan to find any and all available valid cells to camp on. This may result in the UE potentially finding a valid NHN to camp on.		
Post conditions	UE transitions to the macro network		

A Possible Approach to Populating Geofencing on BYOD Bring your own device (BYOD) devices are generic devices that are not managed by the enterprise, and there will be no direct control available to provision these devices with enterprise-specific details, including the geofence information. These devices will need a mechanism to learn the NHN geofence information both locally and augmented through crowdsourcing.

The UE will initially treat the NHN as a coverage extension. When the UE loses the macro coverage and finds the NHN for the first time, the UE recognizes that it is an NHN by detecting the broadcast network signature for a private network (use SHNI = 315-010 or MCC = 999/MNC, etc.) apart from the macro network PLMN. The UE uses its current location to determine the type of enterprise campus. Using that information, the UE marks geofences associated with the enterprise, including the other nearby places where the same enterprise is located. For example Walmart NHN is detected in a location, it allows the UE to mark all the nearby Walmarts to potentially also support NHN.

II.3.1.3.14 Campus Alters

- Currently, the alert systems are used only for public emergency announcements.
- The context is different for enterprise campuses.
- The alert system can be used for both public and enterprise alerts.
- These enterprise alerts could be used for emergencies or for regular announcements of importance on the enterprise campus.
- These can also be targeted to specific buildings or regions of the campus.
- Enterprise alerts could include
  - water leak in a building requiring avoidance of specific floors
  - start of all-hands meeting
  - unauthorized persons entering campus

II.3.1.4 Summary

This chapter introduced the different aspects of NHNs, describing the motivation, comparisons with other approaches, the interfaces, transition behaviors, and enablers, including the MOCN GW functions that make an NHN solution viable. The picture of NHN is evolving significantly from both technical and business/deployment standpoints. With the adoption of private networks and shared spectrum, NHN as a choice for indoor deployment is becoming an obvious one. These NHNs are typically deployed and managed by enterprises through their vendors.

There is another parallel model of using public network integrated nonpublic network (PNI-NPN) that is also evolving, which is primarily employed by the current macro network operators to deploy systems more as outdoor cells, providing in-building coverage and potentially a wider area as well, and making the connectivity services available to enterprises. This tends to be on licensed spectrum.

There is likely room for both models to exist in the market, with each solving a different set of use cases.

A summarized view of the macro network, NHN, private network, and the associated interconnects is illustrated in Figure II.3.1.29. This picture also shows the ePDG connectivity methods that are typically used for Wi-Fi calling procedures, which can establish ePDG tunnel connectivity into the MNO core for specific PDNs over the private network connectivity. This typically assumes dual-SIM support in the UE, with one SIM for private network connection, where the internet traffic is offloaded, and the other SIM for macro network connection, which is used for IMS PDN connectivity via the ePDG node with a secure tunnel between the UE and the ePDG node.

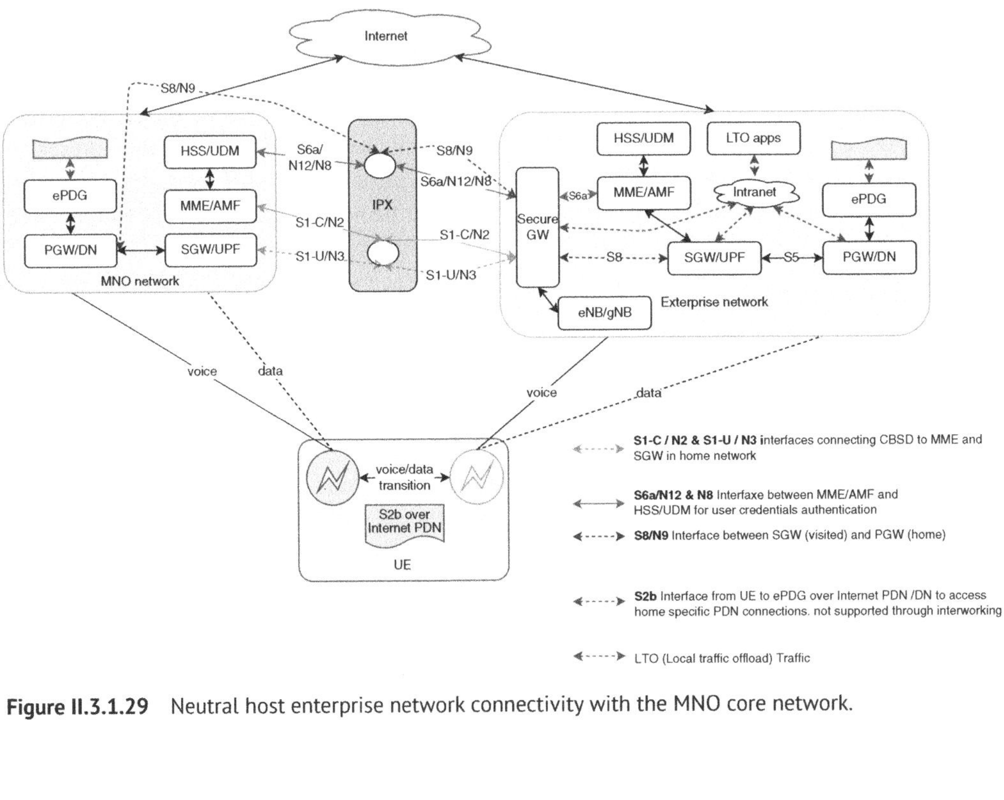

Figure II.3.1.29 Neutral host enterprise network connectivity with the MNO core network.

References

1 Evolved Universal Terrestrial Radio Access (E-UTRA) and Evolved Universal Terrestrial Radio Access Network (E-UTRAN); Overall description; Stage 2 36.300
2 Evolved Universal Terrestrial Radio Access (E-UTRA); Radio Resource Control (RRC); Protocol specification 36.331
3 Evolved Universal Terrestrial Radio Access Network (E-UTRAN); S1 Application Protocol (S1AP) 36.413
4 3GPP system - fixed broadband access network interworking; Stage 2 TS 23.139
5 Evolved Universal Terrestrial Radio Access (E-UTRA); Mobility enhancements in heterogeneous networks 36.839
6 Scenarios and requirements for small cell enhancements for E-UTRA and E-UTRAN 36.932
7 Study on Small Cell enhancements for E-UTRA and E-UTRAN; Higher layer aspects 36.842
8 Study on further enhancements of small cell high layer aspects for LTE 36.876
9 Small cell enhancements for E-UTRA and E-UTRAN - Physical layer aspects 36.872
10 Security of Home Node B (HNB)/Home evolved Node B (HeNB) 33.320
11 Numbering, addressing and identification 23.003
12 RP-142283: “New Study Item proposal: Study on further enhancement of small Cell high layer aspects for LTE.” Contribution to 3GPP TSG-RAN meeting #66
13 R3-150538: “Consideration on UE associated signaling reduction.” Contribution to RAN3 meeting #87bis
14 R3-151059: “S1 Signallng load for indoor scenarios.” Contribution to RAN3 meeting #88
15 R3-151060: “S1 Signaling load for outdoor scenarios.” Contribution to RAN3 meeting #88
16 R3-150345: “LS on Paging Optimization.” Incoming LS from SA2 to RAN3 meeting #87
17 TS 38.331
18 TS 38.304
19 TS 38.300
20 OnGo Neutral Host Network Deployment Guide
21 OnGo Neutral Host Business Update

II.3.2

Admission and Congestion Control

II.3.2.1 Introduction

Traditional admission control of individual users/services is done using static resource reservations. This typically involves allocating the maximum resource needs associated with a given service. Based on the algorithm of choice and the headroom allocated for variabilities in the services, it ends up either overestimating or underestimating in terms of the network capacity planning. The resource reservations are typically made only for guaranteed bit rate (GBR) bearers (quality of service (QoS) flows with guaranteed bitrates), apart from the resource reservations made for common channel operations for both downlink (DL) and uplink (UL). Any leftover resources during scheduling are taken up by the non-GBR bearers, and the users/flows are proportionally served in real time. The base station also reserves resources to accommodate incoming handovers from neighboring cells so that the connection does not get dropped as the user moves across the enterprise campus. This resource reservation is sometimes as high as 25–30%. There are also cell-breathing techniques that can be employed to shed users from a given cell to the neighboring cells. However, this technique is more useful from a macro network perspective that has large footprints and is typically not a viable technique with small cells. When there are multiple overlays of a cell using different frequencies within a given footprint, it is possible for a user to be moved across the frequencies to handle congestion control. This, however, tends to be not available given that cost to cover the enterprise campus with a single layer of cells is itself costly, and this technique will likely not be available for enterprise networks.

These are other techniques for admission and congestion control are known approaches used. This chapter focuses more on the enterprise networks, including both private and neutral host networks, and suggests some possible optimizations that can be considered for implementation.

A given service can be supported with several configurations, and without awareness of the potential congestion the network could face, admission control will need to be based on fixed configurations. There are also other variabilities in the system usage based on the real-time population of the users and active services. In addition, a given device/user can potentially be supported on multiple networks (e.g. macro cell, enterprise cell, Wi-Fi access point), and using a static approach both restricts the availability of the enterprise network and creates a poor user experience under specific conditions.

A lack of awareness of these dynamic conditions in the network, including the predictability aspects, limits the operability of the enterprise network.

Individual campus deployments have a lot of variability. These include campus types: carpeted/non-carpeted, types of users, types of services, times of usage, expected grades of services, device types, and types of partnerships, including interworking with macro network operator (MNO)

Mobile Communication Systems for Private Networks, First Edition. Srinivasan Balasubramanian.

networks. Several of these behaviors can be learned for optimized performance and even go as far as demand-based pricing. The intent will be to adapt the parameters as the network usage evolves. Admission/congestion control will be critical to realizing an effective network. Dynamically learning these parameterizations will be essential for a self-managed network. The goal is to manage system loading by dynamically adjusting admission/congestion control based on real-time analytics.

II.3.2.1.1 Adapting to MNO Footprint

For a neutral host enterprise network, users that have different MNO subscriptions will operate on this network. Each MNO will have a different extent of coverage within the campus, both indoors and outdoors. From an MNO perspective, the preference is to offload to the enterprise network primarily when there is poor or no coverage from their own networks. From an enterprise network perspective, accommodating the users, subject to the resource availability, is important. From a user's perspective, service availability is primary; Better or enhanced service is preferable.

Learn, for each MNO, the footprint within the campus. This includes the extent of coverage in terms of the signal strength and achievable throughput in the various locations.

Under "high" congestion, this information is used to identify the user equipment (UE) that will be admitted into the system. It is also used to determine the UE requested to transition from the system into the MNO network.

In addition to the admission and retention priorities (ARP) policies, the UE selected for transition will consider the MNO coverage in making the determination. Additionally, the active use of local traffic offload (LTO) service is used to avoid moving such UE out of the system. Priority inversion will be required under specific conditions. The UE's capability for performing inter-frequency scans, dual-Rx, and dual-Tx is used to perform system transitions, knowing it will be smoother for specific device types.

II.3.2.1.2 Recognizing Exit from Enterprise Campus

With the MNO footprint becoming more ubiquitous, entry into the enterprise network can wait for the UE to be in an RRC idle state before attempting to transition from the MNO network to the enterprise network. When the UE is exiting the campus with active service, the enterprise campus footprint will be lost, and an effective mechanism to transition the UE to the MNO network will be required.

This can be done proactively upon detecting the pattern of the UE leaving the campus by either working with the MNO network and transitioning the active RRC connection from the enterprise to the MNO network or aborting the RRC connection on the enterprise network, forcing the UE to go to RRC idle mode and transition to the MNO network. The conditions should be such that the entry criteria for the enterprise network are not met to avoid the UE from re-entering the enterprise network.

Patterns include time of day, inter-cell mobility sequence leading to specific enterprise network cells that are toward the extremities of the network, measurement of the MNO footprint, reference signal receive power (RSRP) thresholds of both enterprise and MNO cells, and service-level metrics of packet error rate (PER), delay, jitter, and throughput. The UE device capability determines both the transition point and the type of transitions to be executed.

II.3.2.1.3 Recognizing Busy Hours

Recognize the busy hours of the day and automatically restrict the QoS grants to allow for more users to be supported in the system. Identify congestion hotspots based on the day of the week and time of day. Heatmaps can be developed by recognizing population movement based on the day of the week and time of day.

The restrictions can limit the number of GBR bearers of a given type, or the bitrate granted for a QoS bearer of a certain type, e.g. video restricted to 720 kbps. Cell transmits power and allows for cell-breathing to regulate the users camped on a cell.

This can be across the entire enterprise system and for each cell within the system.

II.3.2.1.4 Recognizing Demands for Service Types

Different campuses have different applications and services that are popular, recognizing demands for service types based on the day of the week and time of day. This will allow for learning the demand patterns, which can be used to develop policies for better supporting the preferred applications on campus.

Preferences can be built based on the learned information to adjust the parameters of the application/service based on the day/time. This will allow for better regulation of the types of services that are admitted to the system, making the network more usable. It is possible for a given user to be allowed certain services while other, less preferred services are blocked under such scenarios. This can be seen as a denial of service and needs to be seen if moving the UE to the MNO will be a better option for the UE.

The service level agreements (SLA) are negotiated using multidimensional parameterization, with the managing entity establishing the allowed ranges. Relative priority of the service, ranges in the allowed QoS parameters, restricting to the minimum number of users supporting a given service, region(s) of the network, day of the week, and time of the day are some of the dimensions that need to be considered.

II.3.2.1.5 Recognizing VoIP Call and Granting QoS

There are scenarios where the enterprise network does not have direct connectivity with the MNO network. The UE has acquired enterprise credentials to allow for data offload on the enterprise network. Under such scenarios, the UE established an ePDG tunnel connectivity to reach the IP multimedia subsystem (IMS) services from the MNO network.

These are tunnel packets over the internet packet data network (PDN) on the enterprise network. Recognizing VoIP traffic and allowing for QoS to be granted will significantly improve voice quality. The signatures include uniform packets with small packet sizes (~100–150 bytes), periodic intervals (every 20 ms), and have listen, silence, and talk periods identified through DL/no-traffic/UL traffic experienced by a given UE.

II.3.2.1.6 Optimizing UE's Dedicated Bearer Assignment/RRC-Connected Mode

Two levels of control can be exercised. One mechanism is to release the dedicated bearers assigned to the UE. Another mechanism to release resources is to release the UE from the RRC-connected mode, transitioning it to idle.

There is a trade-off involved. The control signaling required to reestablish the connection and the impact to the service continuity for a given UE is traded off with the ability to release underutilized resources in the system to admit other users/flows into the system.

Determining the dedicated bearer inactivity timer to release a dedicated bearer resource assigned to a given UE can depend on the dedicated bearer type, the day of the week, the time of day, etc. Determining the RRC connected mode inactivity timer to release the RRC connection depends on congestion levels in the system. Learning and setting the "inactivity timer" for dedicated bearer and RRC connections in the system relative to the congestion levels of the system or given eNB/gNB can yield an optimal way to manage the resources in the system. The training involved is to determine the inter-burst packet arrival based on the type of dedicated bearer and the type of traffic carried. This can be used to reduce the probability of releasing the connection only to have it reestablished.

Note that modification of the bearer can be implicitly achieved by releasing the bearer and the dedicated bearer. If the UE is admitted to the system, it is either blocked or provided with more appropriate operating parameters associated with the current system congestion levels.

II.3.2.2 Summary

Some possible optimizations to the admission and congestion control for an enterprise camp network that is acting as a neutral host and as a private network are suggested. Simple learning techniques called out and additional sophistication can be achieved with AI techniques for the individual aspects, e.g. detecting walkaways. Additionally, it is not limited to the approaches listed, and this chapter is intended to trigger additional thoughts for the reader to consider optimizations to manage the enterprise network resources and radio resource management (RRM).

References

1. Core Standards for Radio Admission and Congestion Control

[1.1] 3GPP TS 38.300 - NR; Overall description; Stage 2 This document provides a high-level overview of 5G NR, including radio resource management (RRM), radio admission control (RAC), and congestion control mechanisms in the context of the NR system. It describes how the RAN controls access to the network and allocates radio resources while managing load and congestion.

[1.2] 3GPP TS 23.501 -System Architecture for the 5G System (5GS) This document outlines the overall system architecture, including the role of the core network (5GC)in supporting RAC and congestion control. It specifies how QoS flow management and policy-based control are applied in the 5G system, providing essential details on admission and congestion control.

[1.3] 3GPP TS 38.331 -NR; Radio Resource Control (RRC) protocol specification RRC plays a key role in managing radio admission by controlling UE connection establishment,mobility, and radio bearer configurations. RRC signaling is used to enforce admission control policies and manage congestion by adjusting the configurations of UEs based on network conditions.

[1.3] 3GPP TS 38.401 -NG- RAN; Architecture description It provides detailed architectural principles for the NG-RAN, including procedures for resource management, admission control, and congestion handling. It discusses how the NG-RAN interacts with the 5GC and the policy control function (PCF) to ensure resources are efficiently allocated and managed.

2. Radio Admission Control

[2.1] 3GPP TS 38.300 -NR; Overall description; Stage 2 (RAC Details) RAC is defined as the process of determining whether or not to admit a new connection or QoS flow based on the current load and available resources. It describes how the network decides whether a new user or service request can be admitted based on current resource availability and ongoing services.

[2.2] 3GPP TS 28.531 -Management and Orchestration of Network Slicing for the 5G System (Admission Control in Network Slicing). It specifies how admission control is handled in the context of network slicing, where each slice may have its own set of RAC policies to ensure QoS and resource isolation.
[2.3] 3GPP TS 23.503 -Policy and Charging Control Framework for 5G It focuses on the role of the Policy Control Function (PCF) in handling QoS and admission control. PCF decides whether a new flow or session can be admitted based on policies and resource availability in the network.

3. Congestion Control

[3.1] 3GPP TS 23.501 -System Architecture for the 5G System (5GS) (Congestion Control) It describes the mechanisms for congestion control, focusing on how the network identifies and mitigates congestion in the core and radio access networks. The document provides details on managing network congestion through traffic prioritization, QoS reconfiguration, and selective dropping of non-essential flows.
[3.2] 3GPP TS 38.300 -NR; Overall description; Stage 2 (Congestion Management) It explains how congestion in the NR network is managed through load balancing, dynamic resource allocation, and adjustments to active connections based on network conditions. The NG-RAN uses information from various layers, including the MAC layer and PDCP, to adapt resources and manage congestion.
[3.3] 3GPP TS 28.541 -Management and orchestration; 5G Network Resource Model (NRM); Stage 2 and Stage 3 It provides a framework for the management and orchestration of network resources to prevent congestion. It describes how resources are dynamically allocated and optimized to avoid congestion, using a combination of admission control and load balancing techniques.

4. QoS and Policy-Based Admission Control

[4.1] 3GPP TS 23.501 -SystemArchitecture for the 5G System (5GS) (QoS Flow Management) It discusses how QoS flows are mapped to data radio bearers, and how policies are enforced for admission control and congestion management. QoS flows with different priorities may be admitted or denied based on current network load, ensuring that high-priority services (e.g., emergency services) are given preferential access.
[4.2] 3GPP TS 38.323 -NR; Packet Data Convergence Protocol (PDCP) specification. It describes how PDCP handles QoS flow mapping and ensures that data packets are treated according to their assigned QoS class, which plays an indirect role in congestion management.

5. Specific Procedures for Handling Admission and Congestion

[5.1] 3GPP TS 38.321 -NR; Medium Access Control (MAC) protocol specification. It provides details on MAC-level procedures for scheduling and resource allocation that help manage congestion. The MAC layer plays a key role in ensuring that only admitted UEs are allocated resources and that congestion is minimized through efficient resource distribution.
[5.2] 3GPP TS 38.304 -NR; UE procedures in idle mode and connected mode. It specifies the procedures followed by the UE and the network for managing admission during transitions between idle and connected states. These procedures are critical for preventing congestion when many UEs attempt to connect to the network simultaneously.

6. Research Papers and Industry White Papers

[6.1] Qualcomm White Paper (2021): "5G NR Radio Resource Management and Admission Control." This white paper discusses the industry perspective on admission control in 5G networks, focusing on how operators manage radio resources and prevent congestion in dense deployments.

[6.2] Ericsson Mobility Report (2020): "Radio Resource and Admission Control in 5G NR." Ericsson's report provides insights into RAC strategies and congestion control mechanisms in practical 5G deployments.

II.4

Nonpublic Networks

II.4.1 Overview of Nonpublic Networks

A nonpublic network (NPN) is a 5GS deployed for nonpublic use (see 3GPP TS 22.261). This definition of NPN in 3GPP was intended to address enterprise network deployments. Given the momentum for enterprise networks in the market and the lack of availability of 3GPP Release-16-based user equipment (UEs), where the NPN feature is defined, the LTE and NR private networks were based on 3GPP Release-15 procedures. This has been fairly sufficient to address the needs of the market, and we are now at a point where the deliberations are ongoing regarding the benefits of introducing the Release-16 NPN procedures. In this chapter, we will go through the basic definition of NPN, the network architectures, the identifiers used, and the UE behaviors in discovering, camping on, and operating within these networks.

The base architecture of LTE/NR multimode, together with the core network EPC/5GC, showing the functional nodes along with the main interfaces, is illustrated in Figure II.4.1.

An NPN is either

- a stand-alone nonpublic network (SNPN), that is, operated by an NPN operator and not relying on network functions provided by a PLMN/macro network operator or
- a public network integrated NPN (PNI-NPN), that is, a NPN deployed with the support of a PLMN/macro network operator.

Note that an NPN and a PLMN can share an NG-RAN.

The procedures involved in SNPN and PNI-NPN operations are described below in this chapter.

II.4.2 Stand-Alone Nonpublic Networks

SNPNs, as the name indicates, are stand-alone networks that operate in isolation and are well suited for private network deployments. Unlike public networks, SNPNs are intended to be simplified to enable ease of network design, configuration, deployment, and management and are inherently

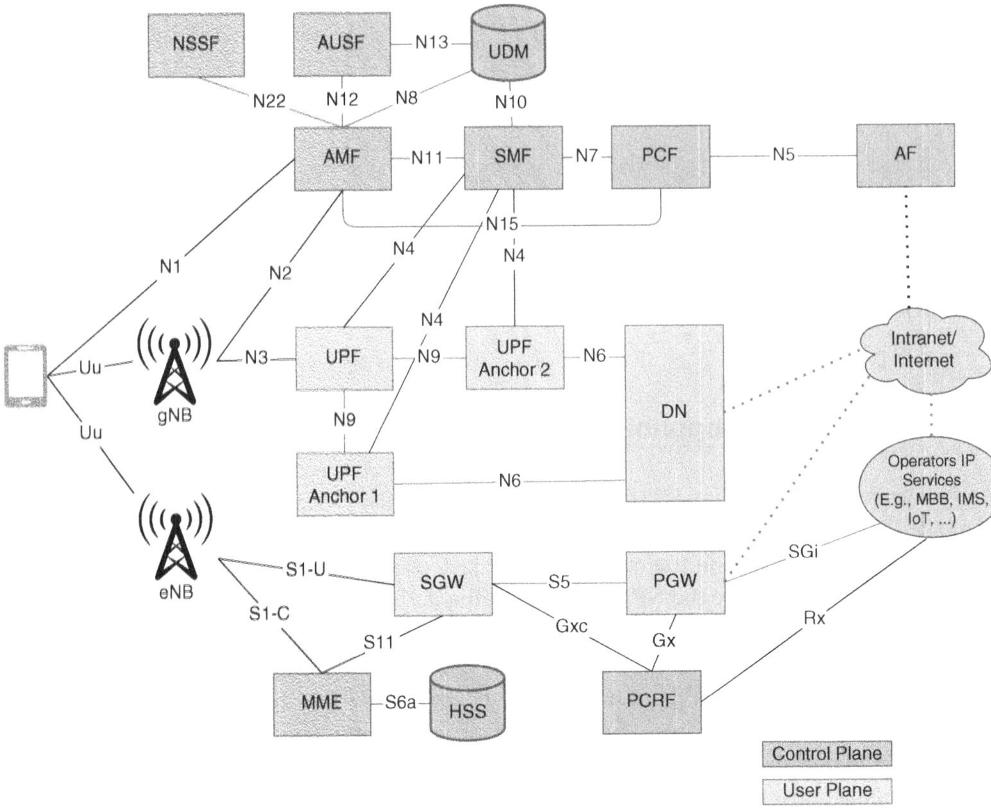

Figure II.4.1 LTE and NR multimode architecture.

defined with a set of limitations. These limitations may be removed in the subsequent releases as the market evolves, and the complexity of the demands on the SNPN networks increases. Note that the demands of an SNPN may be very different from those of public networks and may likely require a different set of features to achieve a viable realization of the requirements. Although the SNPN is initially envisioned to act as a private network, it is not restricted to that and can evolve to take other forms (Figure II.4.2).

Several restrictions are introduced for SNPN in Release-16. These include the following:

- Only 3GPP RAT-based access to SNPN is defined.
- Interworking with EPS is not supported for SNPN and operates only with 5GC.
- Emergency services are not supported for SNPN.
- Roaming between SNPNs, as defined in 3GPP, is not supported. However, proprietary approaches are emerging for common credential management and user authentication, with the data connectivity supported directly by the visited networks.
- Handover between SNPNs, between SNPN and PLMN, or PNI-NPN is not supported.
- CIoT 5GS optimizations are not supported in SNPNs.

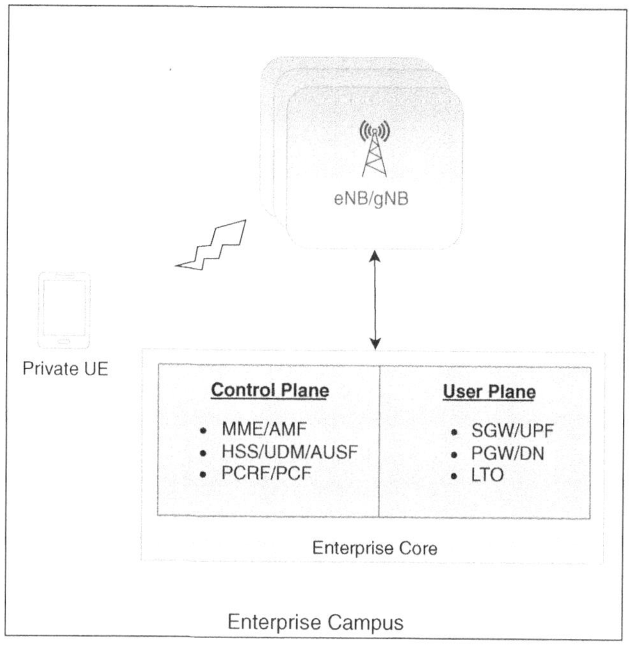

Figure II.4.2 SNPN network architecture.

II.4.2.1 SNPN Identifiers

SNPN identifier	Context	Description
PLMN ID	• Broadcast by the network • Provisioned on the UE for the subscribed SNPNs	• The PLMN ID used for SNPNs is not required to be unique. – PLMN IDs reserved for use by private networks can be used for NPNs, for example based on mobile country code (MCC) 999. – A shared PLMN ID or its own PLMN IDs for SNPN(s), along with NID(s), can be used.
NID	• Broadcast by the network associated with individual PLMNs • Provisioned on the UE for subscribed SNPNs and associated with the PLMNs when the PLMN+NID defines the SNPN.	The NID shall support two assignment models: • Self-assignment: (Mode 1) NIDs are chosen individually by SNPNs at deployment time (and may therefore not be unique), but they use a different numbering space than the coordinated assignment NIDs, as defined in TS 23.003. • Coordinated assignment: NIDs are assigned using one of the following two options: 1) (Mode 0) The NID is assigned such that it is globally unique, independent of the PLMN ID used; or 2) (Mode 2) The NID is assigned so that the combination of the NID and the PLMN ID is globally unique.

(*Continued*)

SNPN identifier	Context	Description
		The combination of a PLMN ID and a network identifier (NID) identifies an SNPN. Specific organizations such as IANA can be used to obtain unique identifier assignments. NG-RAN nodes support broadcasting a total of 12 NIDs. See TS 38.331 for further details. An indication per SNPN of whether access using credentials from a credentials holder is supported. Information, as described in TS 38.300, TS 38.331, and TS 38.304, is used to prevent UEs not supporting SNPNs from accessing the cell, for example if the cell only provides access to NPNs;
GIN	• Broadcast by the network • Provisioned on the UE if the UE supports access to an SNPN using credentials from a credentials holder – User-controlled prioritized list of preferred SNPNs; – Credentials holder-controlled prioritized list of preferred SNPNs; – Credentials holder-controlled prioritized list of GINs.	Group ID for network selection (GIN) identifies a group of credential holders that are available from an SNPN. The GIN shall support two assignment models: • Self-assignment: GINs are chosen individually and may, therefore, not be unique. • Coordinated assignment: GIN is assigned in such a way that it is globally unique (e.g. using IANA private enterprise numbers), as defined in TS 23.003. An indication per SNPN of whether the SNPN allows registration attempts from UEs that are not explicitly configured to select the SNPN, that is, UEs that do not have any PLMN ID, NID, or GIN broadcast by the SNPN in the credentials holder-controlled prioritized lists of preferred SNPNs/GINs. See TS 38.331 for further details, including the number of GINs supported. The credentials holder-controlled prioritized lists of preferred SNPNs and GINs can be updated by the credentials holder. UE parameters update (UPU) via UDM control plane procedure as defined in **clause 4.20 of TS 23.502** or the steering of roaming (SoR) procedure as defined in Annex C of **TS 23.122**.
Human-readable network name	• Broadcast by the network • Provisioned on the UE	An optional human-readable network name helps identify an SNPN during manual SNPN selection. The human-readable network name and how it is used for SNPN manual selection are specified in TS 22.261 and TS 23.122.
Subscription identifier (SUPI)	• Provisioned in the UE as part of the credentials. • Retained in the network as part of subscription response data for authenticating the UE (stored in the UDM).	A subscriber of an SNPN is either • identified by a SUPI containing a network-specific identifier that takes the form of a network access identifier (NAI) using the NAI RFC 7542-based user identification as defined in clause 28.7.2 of TS 23.003. The realm part of the NAI may include the NID of the SNPN; or • identified by a SUPI containing an IMSI. When the credentials holder is an SNPN and the MCC and MNC of the SNPN are not unique, then IMSI-based SUPI is not supported, as the MCC and MNC need not always be unique; instead, USIM credentials are supported using network-specific identifier-based SUPI.

II.4.2.2 Network Selection in SNPN Access Mode

UE uses the provisioned information to find the SNPN network. Both automatic and manual system selection procedures are supported. The UE uses the PLMN + NID or just the NID alone, along with the GID, to determine the validity of the network to camp on. The SNPN network may allow access for only SNPN camping or be open for PLMN-based camping as well. The UE can perform optimized automatic scans that are timer-based with backoff mechanisms, including geofencing provisioned to initiate scans. UE can learn the locations of the preferred SNPN network based on GPS or macro network footprint signatures from successful SNPN camping and use that information for subsequent camping. The user, based on the knowledge of the SNPN in the current location, initiates a manual scan to find available SNPN networks. The UE scans the bands that it can potentially support, restricting itself to the spectrum where the SNPN may be present, and presents the list of SNPN networks in the vicinity. The list presented to the user can also be restricted to the SNPN networks for which the device is provisioned with valid credentials. Note as well that the UE may have multiple credentials, including public network credentials and SNPN credentials. It is left up to the UE implementation when the SNPN mode is enabled, either through an automatic trigger like entering a geofence or user manual activation of the SNPN mode. When there are multiple SNPN networks in the vicinity, the provisioned priority order of the SNPNs is used to make a camping decision in automatic mode. In manual mode, the user makes an explicit decision on the SNPN network to camp on. When a UE performs initial registration to an SNPN, the UE shall indicate the PLMN ID and NID as broadcast by the selected SNPN to NG-RAN. NG-RAN shall inform the AMF of the selected PLMN ID and NID.

The UE uses the appropriate credential information to access the SNPN network. This will depend on using the PLMN/NID-based access or using the GIN, where the credential holder is independent of the deployed SNPN.

When an independent credential holder is used for authenticating the UE, Figures II.4.3 and II.4.4 describe the possible architectures used for authenticating the UE with GIN.

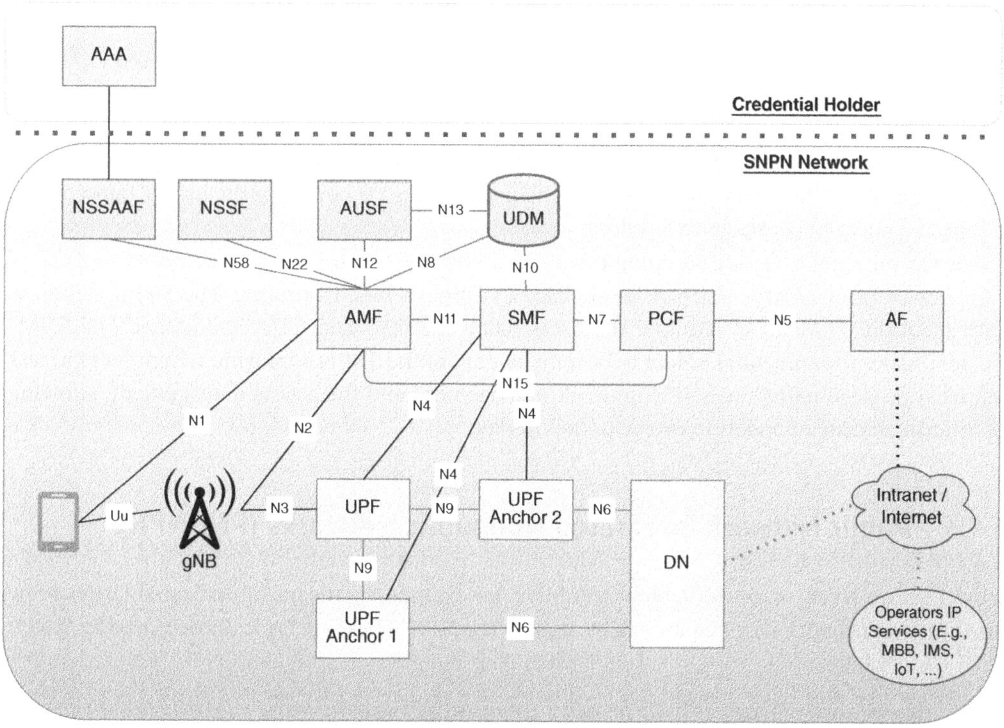

Figure II.4.3 Credential holder authentication using AAA.

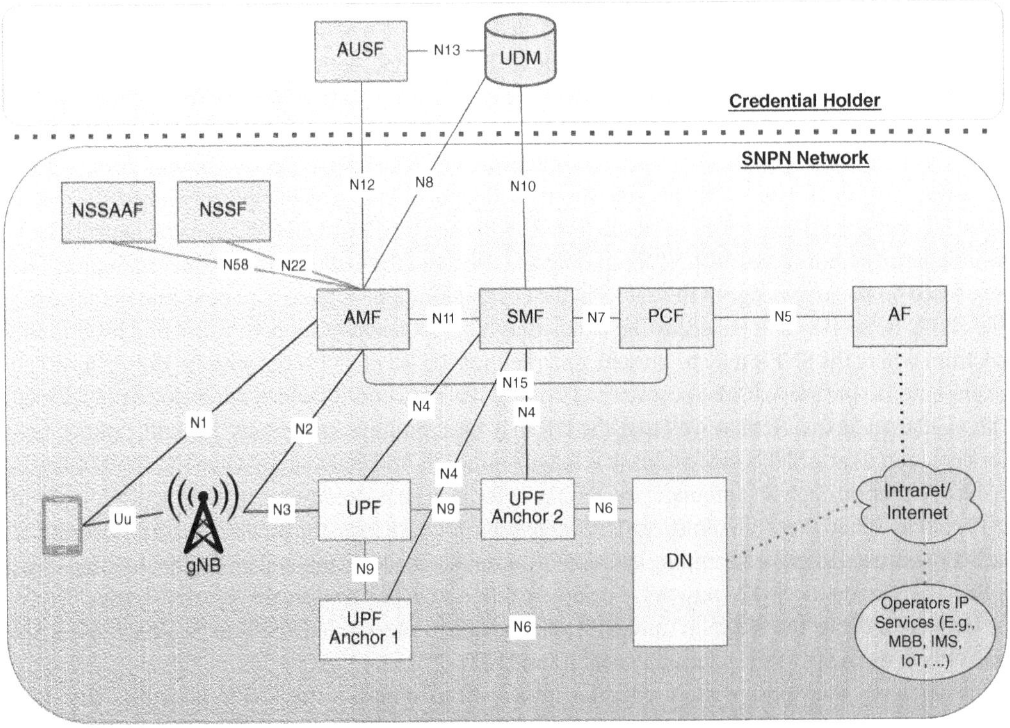

Figure II.4.4 Credential holder authentication using AUSF.

To prevent access to SNPNs for unauthorized UE(s) in the case of network congestion/overload, unified access control information is configured per SNPN (i.e. as part of the subscription information that the UE has for a given SNPN) and provided to the UE.

UEs operating in SNPN access mode only select cells and networks broadcasting both PLMN ID and NID of the selected SNPN. See **TS 38.331** and **TS 38.304** for further details on idle and inactive mode procedures for SNPN system camping.

In addition to this, specific onboarding techniques using dedicated DN to perform UE provisioning are suggested. These techniques include the use of a captive portal for the user to subscribe to the specific network connectivity services.

When comparing to legacy camping procedures, there is much finer control over the types of UEs allowed on the SNPN network as opposed to a PLMN-based camping. The SNPN camping, apart from the PLMN, can regulate the users using the NID and GIN parameters. The SNPN accommodates the credential holder to be independent of the SNPN deployment in order to access the network, decoupling the SNPN network management and the access management, allowing for differing business models to evolve in the market.

II.4.3 Public Network Integrated Nonpublic Networks (PNI-NPN)

PNI-NPNs are NPNs made available via PLMNs, for example by means of dedicated DNNs or by one (or more) network slice instances allocated for the NPN. These are typically deployed by MNOs on specific cells, potentially in the vicinity of or on the premises of an enterprise campus, allowing access for the enterprise users on these PNI-NPN-enabled cells. The existing network slicing mechanism, as described in 3GPP TS 23.501 clause 5.15, is leveraged for this function. Note that PNI-NPN can also be supported without the use of the network slicing feature. It is expected that the UEs require explicit subscription to access the PNI-NPN services. This subscription is handled by provisioning the UE with an allowed set of closed access groups (CAGs) associated with the home PLMN (HPLMN) or any PLMN. The CAG identifies a group of subscribers who are permitted to access one or more CAG cells associated with the CAG. The CAG is used for the PNI-NPNs to prevent UE(s) that are not allowed to access the NPN via the associated cell(s) from automatically selecting and accessing the associated CAG cell(s). The CAG is used to execute the required access restrictions and is independent of an single network slice selection assistance information (S-NSSAI) that identifies a specific instance of a network slice. Note that the UE always has a subscription to the HPLMN providing the PNI-NPN and has a USIM that contains primary authentication credentials. Figure II.4.5 shows a PNI-NPN architecture.

II.4.3.1 PNI-NPN Identifiers

SNPN identifier	Context	Description
PLMN ID	• Broadcast by the network • Provisioned on the UE for the subscribed PNI-NPN.	The PLMN ID used for PNI-NPN is unique and typically associated with an MNO • The MNO-specific PLMN ID • A shared PLMN ID may be utilized with the other PNI-NPN-specific identifiers regulated to create a unique network identifier.
CAG	• The network broadcasts on the PNI-NPN cell the set of CAGs associated with each PLMN that it supports. When the network is broadcasting the CAG, only UEs supporting the CAG can camp on these cells for the corresponding PNI-NPN PLMN. • The UE is provisioned with the CAGs to which it is allowed access, associated with the different PLMN IDs. An optional indication that the UE is allowed access only with a CAG may be provisioned.	Closed access group • A CAG is identified by a CAG identifier, which is unique within the scope of a PLMN ID. • A CAG cell broadcasts one or multiple CAG Identifiers per PLMN. A given PNI-NPN cell can support up to 12 CAGs. Further details are defined in **TS 38.331**. A CAG cell may also broadcast a human-readable network name per CAG identifier, presented to the user for manual PNI-NPN selection.

II.4.3.2 Network Selection in PNI-NPN Access Mode

The CAG information is provided by the HPLMN on a per-PLMN basis. In a PLMN, the UE shall only consider the CAG information provided for this PLMN. The CAG subscription associated with the UE can change, and the updates are provisioned in the UDM. The UDM informs the AMF, which in turn notifies the UE of the CAG subscription changes. For further details, see 3GPP TS 24.501. Note that the CAG information is used only for NR access and

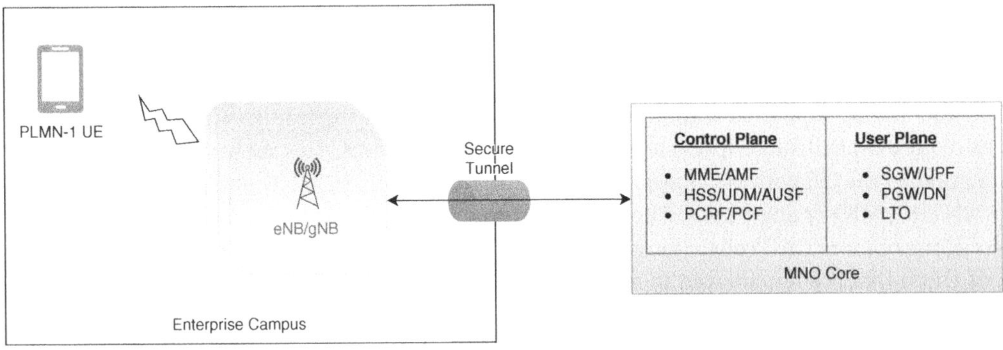

Figure II.4.5 PNI-NPN architecture.

does not apply to UE access via non-3GPP access networks. The CAG cell broadcasts information such that only UEs supporting CAG are accessing the cell (see 3GPP **TS 38.300** and **TS 38.304** for further details).

The UE supports both automatic and manual system camping procedures. The procedures remain like the SNPN procedures described above but with the use of PNI-NPN CAG as the identifier instead of the SNPN parameters. In addition to the UE autonomous procedure, the macro network can receive the UE's subscribed CAGs, and the macro network uses that information to redirect the UE to CAG-enabled cells when in the vicinity. The actual detection of the PNI-NPN network's proximity and the redirection trigger from the macro network are left up to the macro network's implementation. Apart from idle/inactive mode transitions, the macro network can potentially execute connected mode transitions in CAG cells, knowing the UE CAG subscription information. For manual system selection, the user is presented with the found PNI-NPN network filtered by the CAGs to which the UE has subscribed, along with human-readable text for the user to make a selection. Once selected, the camping procedures remain the same as with automatic system camping.

Note that a given cell can support PLMN-based, SNPN, and PNI-NPN-based camping based on the PLMN, NID, GIN, and CAG used to access the cell. All of these can coexist on the cell simultaneously. To address network congestion/overload, existing mechanisms defined for control plane load control, congestion, and overload control in **clause 5.19** can be used, as well as the access control and barring functionality described in **clause 5.2.5**, or unified access control using the access categories as defined in **TS 24.501** can be employed. Figure II.4.6 provides an integrated view of the SNPN and PNI-NPN deployment.

Figure II.4.7 illustrates a view where the user plane for a PNI-NPN is terminated closer to or even within the enterprise campus. This is done to allow the PNI-NPN user to have access to walled-garden services and to bring the traffic as close to the user as possible, placing it on the edge for faster turnaround times. This local breakout can be enabled with the same PLMN used for macro network access, while recognizing the UE's proximity to specific enterprise campuses or being explicitly enabled using PLMN + CAG or potentially an independent PLMN.

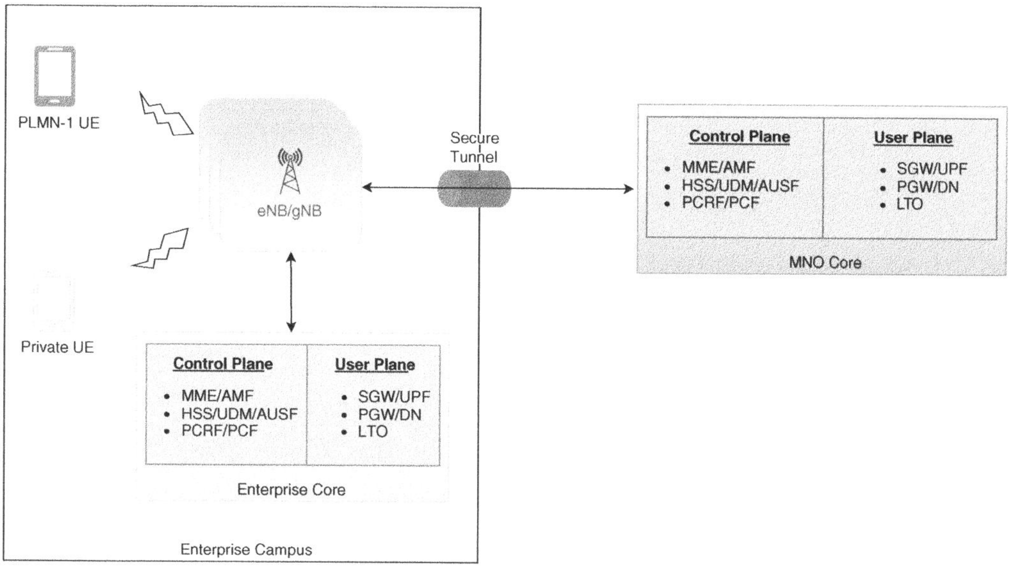

Figure II.4.6 Integrated SNPN and PNI-NPN architectures.

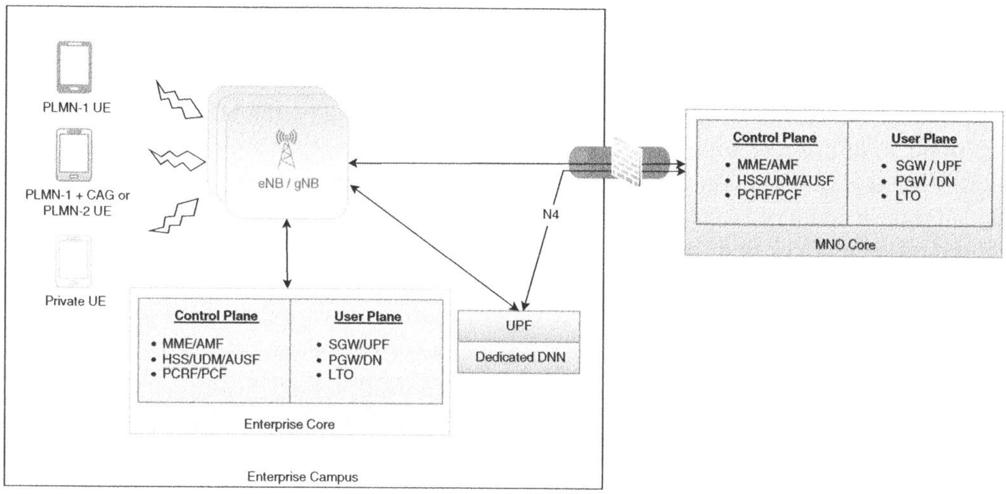

Figure II.4.7 Integrated SNPN and PNI-NPN architecture with LBO supported by independent macro core.

Figure II.4.8 suggests the use of an independent core network for the PNI-NPN system that is isolated from the macro network supporting the core. Both of these cores are associated with a given MNO; however, isolating them provides for specific PNI-NPN functionality to be supported and independently scales the PNI-NPN deployments for enterprise campuses from the macro

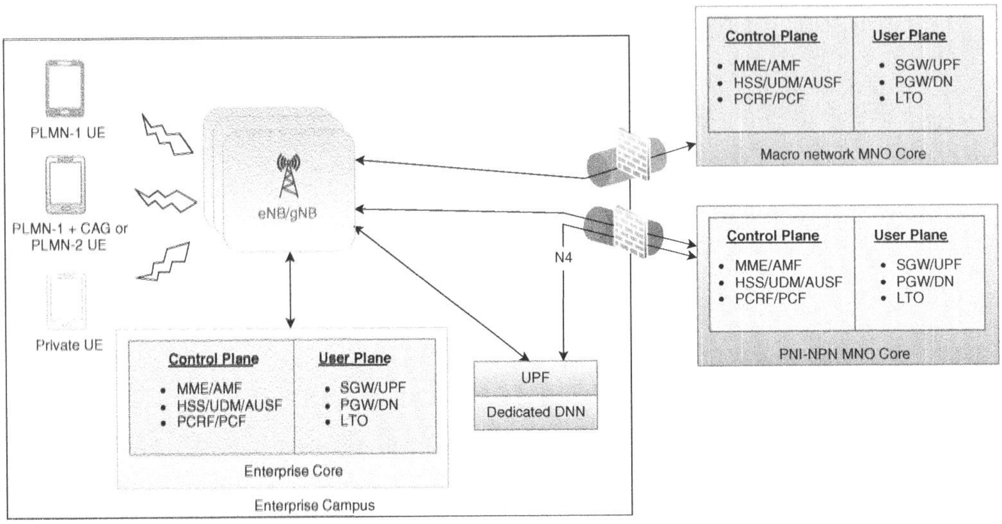

Figure II.4.8 Integrated SNPN and PNI-NPN architecture with LBO for PNI-NPN and an independent macro PNI-NPN core.

network operations. Specific interfacing between the two PNI-NPN and macro network cores is required to support mobility between the two and also handle a single credential associated with the user that will be stored in the macro network UDM.

Comparing PNI-NPN with neutral host networks, both achieve similar functions for a campus deployment. However, PNI-NPN is typically supported by the MNOs providing service to the enterprise. Neutral host networks tend to be enterprise-deployed networks that allow MNO users to camp on the network. Both solutions will be viable in the market. A lot depends on the ability to cover indoor footprints in an efficient manner while still allowing for enterprise services to be accommodated. With customization and enterprise-managed services, it is simpler to envision deploying a private network and enabling NHN services on the network, which tends to be cost-effective for the enterprises. With PNI-NPN, it enables generic macro network-supported services, including voice services, easily; however, access into the enterprise walled garden with a local breakout requires some special handling and may not be straightforward.

II.4.4 Summary

The SNPN network context, identifiers used, and the UE camping procedures are described. A comparison with the legacy network that supports SNPN is also provided.

The PNI-NPN context, identifiers used, and the UE camping procedures are described. An evolution of the PNI-NPN solution to accommodate local breakout connectivity is suggested.

Additionally, an independent PNI-NPN core network from the macro core network for the MNO is suggested for easier and independent evolution of the PNI-NPN networks. A comparison of the advantages and disadvantages of the two solutions, including NHN, is also discussed.

References

1 3GPP TS 22.261.
2 24.501

II.5

Device Provisioning

II.5.1 Introduction

For Long Term Evolution (LTE) and New Radio (NR) private networks, given that the end-user devices that operate on the macro network need to be leveraged, the same type of credentials must be provisioned in these devices, and the corresponding authentication information must be stored in the Evolved Packet Core (EPC)/5GC in the network. Having said that, there is a major obstacle that needs to be addressed when supporting the functions used for macro networks to be applied to private networks. The credential management system for macro networks is typically geared to handle millions of users, and even when supporting specific classes of users for a macro network operator, the number of users tends to run into the millions for each of those categories.

Some tricks are needed to allow this toolkit to scale for enterprises of different sizes, ranging from a few 10s of users to a few 10s of thousands of users. There are also enterprise-specific identifiers that may need to be accommodated when distributing the credentials to ensure that the end-user devices attempt access on known networks where valid attachment/registration is possible. Note that even access attempts on networks where the end-user device fails authentication leave traces that can allow for users and devices to be tracked and need to be avoided. Given the small footprint of these private networks, the user equipment (UE) on its drive route may encounter numerous private networks, and efficient methods are required for the UE to attempt association only with the "preferred" (known) network. Apart from the regular credential information that is used by the UE for macro network association, additional information needs to be provisioned with the credentials to allow the UE to discern these preferred networks. For example the network identifiers broadcasted by the private network and geofencing information of the enterprise campus aid the UE in avoiding unnecessary networks while actively finding a preferred network when the signature matches. Macro networks have clearly delineated network identifiers broadcast by their network that separate them from other macro networks. Given that each private network cannot obtain its own network identifiers due to the specific criteria and processes involved in obtaining these identifiers, such as the public land mobile network identifier (PLMN ID), these identifiers need to be shared, and other network broadcast parameters that are specific to individual cells (eNB/gNB) in the private network need to be used and also regionally separated to ensure the uniqueness of these identifiers within a given region.

Based on the entities managing the credentials for the private networks, the primary authentication credentials need to be provisioned independently of the secondary authentication.

Mobile Communication Systems for Private Networks, First Edition. Srinivasan Balasubramanian.

This section first introduces the general framework used for Subscriber Identity/Identification Module (SIM) credential provisioning and then proceeds to describe the procedures used to apply the same platform toward private networks.

II.5.2 Credential Provisioning Framework

For LTE and NR networks, the credentials used are stored in the SIM on the end-user devices. These can be on a pluggable physical card or stored in a secure location on the device as an eSIM. There is a big push in the industry to move away from physical cards and switch to eSIMs. The physical card does come with its conveniences, but these have largely been overcome with the use of eSIMs, including device provisioning, supporting credentials that can be transitioned across devices, and supporting dual-SIM operations. There are legacy devices that still operate with physical SIMs such as security cameras and will need to continue supporting physical SIMs.

Figure II.5.1 shows the architecture of the SIM credential provisioning in the UE. The SM-DP+ is the SIM provisioning server that is retained in a secure location, managing the credentials. Network vendors and enterprises establish relationships with the SIM provider. Secure channels,

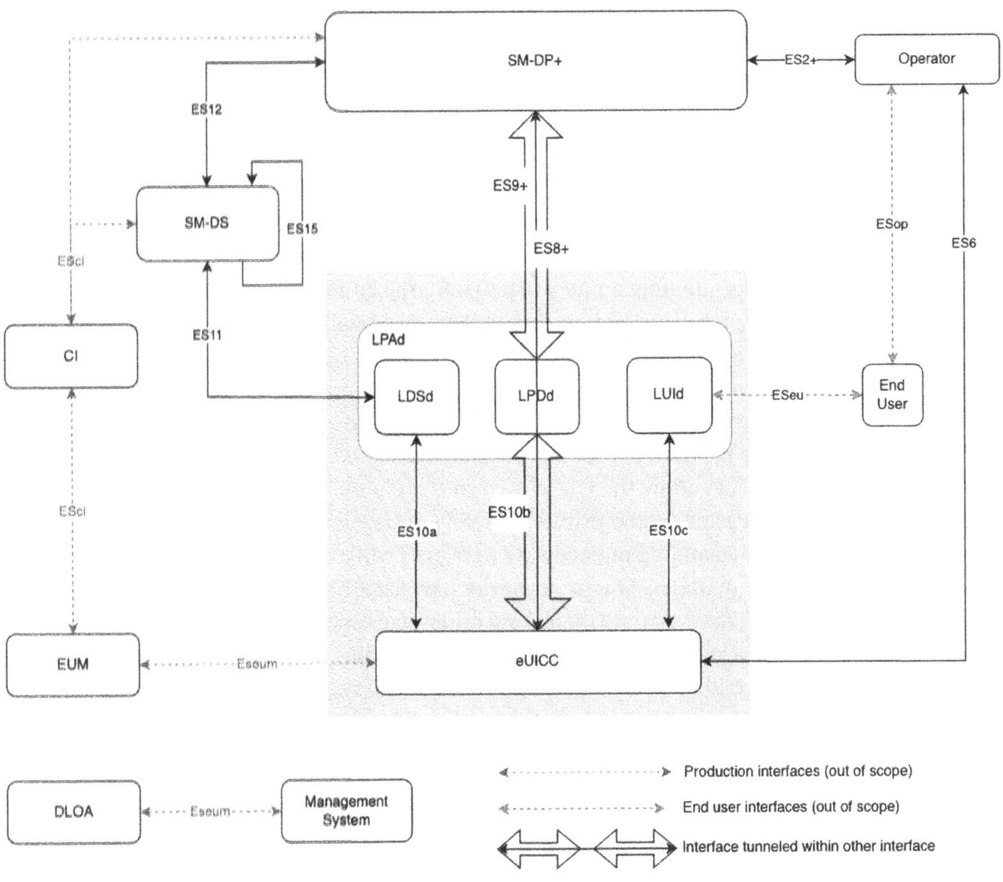

Figure II.5.1 Remote SIM provisioning system, LPA in the device (from GSMA SGP.22 – RSP technical specification, figure 1).

protected by certificates, exist between the SIM provider and the credential owners to ensure the safe transport of the credentials. The UE uses the discovery services with SM-DS to determine the SM-DP+ from which to retrieve the credentials. The SM-DP+ information may also be directly provided as part of the device provisioning of the credential. The UE uses the download services defined and stores the received credential information in the eUICC. The UE subsequently uses the information stored in the eUICC to access the network for connectivity.

Specific preferences and keys are defined as part of the SIM profile definition. The SIM profile definition is a key step in the process of identifying the elemental files (EFs) and the associated parameters that are stored in the profile. This includes information on system camping, identifying the valid networks where the UE can camp, the master keys supporting device authentication, and other operational parameters and limitations enforced on the device's connectivity. Refer to the GSM Association (GSMA) specification for the details of the different EFs and their data structures.

The specification that covers the carrier selection aspects aims to allow consumers to choose a mobile network operator from a wide range to activate the SIM embedded in a device via a subscription. It aims to simplify users' lives by connecting their multiple devices through the same subscription. It should also motivate mobile device manufacturers to develop the next generation of mobile-connected devices that will better suit the wearable technology applications. The specification that covers carrier selection for M2M devices is simpler since typically there is no subscriber involved (e.g. changing the operator in an electricity meter).

The language used to describe this specification is a little confusing since eSIM is not a physical format (or "form factor" – the phrase used to describe the various SIM sizes). The eSIM describes the functionality in the SIM, not the physical size of the SIM—and there are eSIMs in many formats (2FF, 3FF, 4FF, MFF).

GSMA has also developed a compliance framework for eSIM devices, eUICCs, and subscription management products to help with interoperability and security for products supporting eSIM. This is published by the GSMA as SGP.24. The eSIM compliance process describes common compliance requirements for

- functional interoperability
- eUICC security
- eUICC production site security
- subscription management site security

The GSMA remote sim provisioning (RSP) specification and current realizations in the market are directly used for SIM/eSIM provisioning in the UE for private networks as well. The relevant adaptations to the credential distribution for private networks are covered in the following section.

II.5.3 Credential Distribution Process

Figure II.5.2 provides a simplified view of the credential management and distribution for private networks. With legacy operations, the SIM provisioning platform has handled large macro network operators' users, and they run into the millions. The same security enjoyed by the macro networks needs to be enforced and additionally need to handle enterprises that range from a few 10s of users to a few 1000s of users requiring credentials. Also, the credentials may need to be customized on an enterprise basis, for example provisioning restrictions to ensure that the device does not access other networks within the network. The private networks' footprints are small, and will imply that as the UE moves across these networks, excessive access attempts may happen particularly when

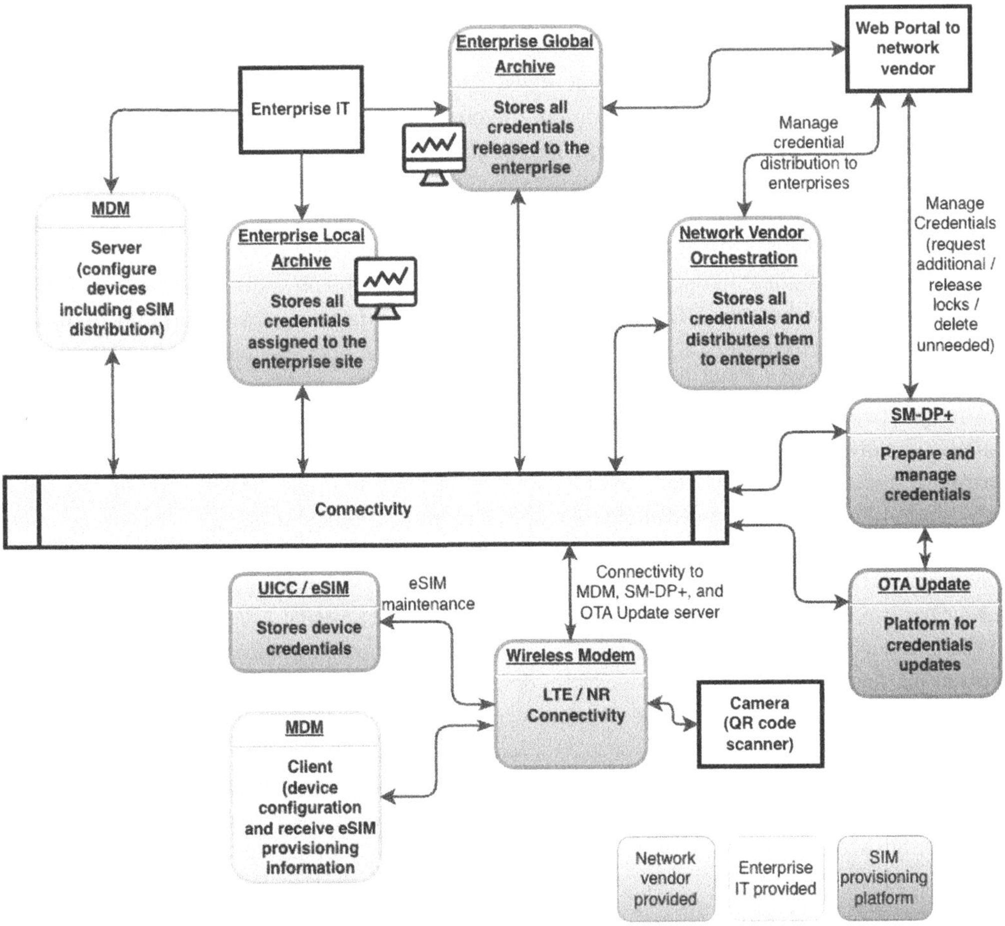

Figure II.5.2 SIM credential distribution.

common system identifiers are used for network parameters. The network vendor that supplies equipment to the enterprises typically acquires a batch of credentials and manages their distribution of the information to the enterprises. The enterprise may also require acquire more credentials, update existing ones, and release those that are no longer required. Network vendors support this process through their orchestration platforms, which enable multi-tenancy within a cloud architecture. The credentials, once acquired from the SM-DP+ by the network vendor, release a specific set of credentials to the individual enterprises. The Information Technology (IT) enterprise is responsible for assigning individual credentials to devices and managing the allocations. The credential allocation process can also be integrated with the enterprise's mobile device management (MDM), which is the preferred approach to minimize overhead for enterprise IT. Enterprise users may also provide a QR code for a specific credential to scan (e.g. an enterprise visitor or an employee with a personal device). The network vendor also has the Radio Access Network (RAN) and core networks deployed on the individual campuses, so it is best to store the credentials of enterprise employees that work at a given site, locally. This requires central management for a given multi-site enterprise, storing the credentials both globally and locally, specific to each site. An enterprise user may travel to other sites, and when the credential information is not stored locally, the enterprise's global database needs to be accessed. Additionally, the user's information should be retained in the visited site for a finite time period to avoid repeatedly reaching the enterprise's global server. Connectivity from the wireless modems is required to reach the SM-DP+ servers, which are accessible from the public internet. Specific portals that allow the device to connect and obtain credentials need to be enabled while preventing other access. At times, the enterprise may be behind a firewall that restricts public network access. Specific approaches such as isolated portals need to be available for provisioning, and in some cases, the enterprise may choose to host the entire SM-DP+ SIM platform within the enterprise to reduce the external exposure for credential management.

The IT enterprise employs MDM procedures and initiates requests for a specific number of credentials. The network vendor/credential provider receives a batch of credentials from the SM-DP+ platform, carves out the requisite credentials for the individual enterprises, and releases these credentials to the enterprise global system. The enterprise global system can then forward these to the local enterprise entity.

Any information that is included in the SIM credential needs to be keyed into the SM-DP+ itself prior to the distribution of the credential and cannot be altered by any other interacting entities in between. When the credentials are released, the enterprise-specific identifiers need to be included, for example cell ID (cell identifier list) and tracking area codes (TAC) associated with the specific private network, potentially based on the allowed enterprise locations/sites where the UE is required to be operational. The authentication information is sent to the Home Subscriber Server (HSS)/ Unified Data Management (UDM) in the core network, and only the credential identifier (metadata) is shared with the network vendor/enterprise for distribution to the UE. The MDM platform provisions the credential identifier and the SM-DP+ platform for the UE to retrieve the full credential directly from the SIM provisioning server. The MDM process provisions the UE with a specific credential identifier as a generic pointer to the SM-DP+ and also includes other related information, including the geofencing information associated with the enterprise. When the UE receives this provisioning information, it triggers the UE to reach the SIM provisioning server (SM-DP+). When an explicit credential identifier is provided to the UE, it is typically kept in a locked state and associated with the UE's embedded identity document (EID), which is the equipment hardware identifier of the (e)SIM platform in the UE. When this specific UE reaches the network, the already associated credential information is sent to the UE in a secure manner. When the generic SM-DP+ platform is specified, the UE reaches the SIM provisioning server to assign a credential to it. At this point, the SM-DP+ selects a credential from the pool of credentials created for the specific enterprise or generic private network based on the configuration, sends the credential information to the UE, and locks that assigned credential, associating it with the EID of the (e)SIM associated with the UE.

II.5.4 SIM Provisioning Models

From a SIM provisioning perspective, broadly speaking, there are two device types: those with a user interface and "headless" devices. See Figure II.5.3 SIM provisioning models.

Remote provisioning on the end-user device is initiated by the local profile assistant (LPA), a software package defined by the RSP specification. The LPA contacts a subscription manager (SM) to retrieve its carrier profile. The SM address is provided in the QR code scanned by the user, entered manually on-screen using the SM's hostname or activation code, hard-coded in the device during factory provisioning or added later, or obtained via a universal discovery service operated by the GSMA. The LPA is responsible for validating that the X.509 certificate of the SM is valid and

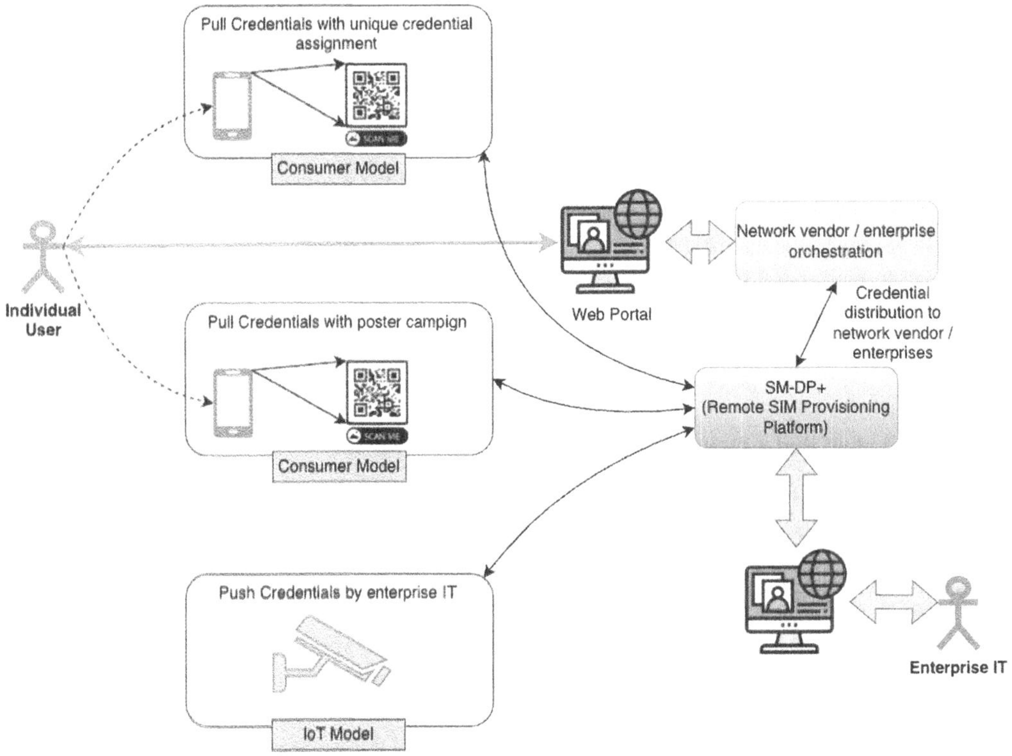

Figure II.5.3 SIM provisioning models.

issued by the GSMA certificate authority. Once validation is complete, the LPA establishes a secure channel between the eUICC and the SM. The LPA will request carrier profiles available for download, either by submitting the activation code provided by the user or the eSIM ID (EID) of the eUICC. The SM will provide the requested profile encrypted in a way that only the eUICC can decrypt/install to ensure that the network authentication key remains secure.

The device with a user interface allows user interactions that are possible and can be initiated. The provisioning for such devices is considered a "consumer model." For these devices, it employs a pull model, with the device communicating with the SIM provisioning platform to receive the credentials. With the pull model, this can be achieved by providing explicit credential assignment with the full identifier details. The device accesses the SM-DP+ and requests a specific credential stored on the server. The SM-DP+ may allow any device to download the requested credential as long as the full credential identifier is presented, or it can allow for the credential to be locked and provided only to a specific device recognized by a hardware identifier (HW-ID). The HW-ID used is the EID, which identifies the storage location of the credentials on the device. Even for the consumer model, auto-provisioning will be preferred and is employed for devices controlled by the enterprise. MDM procedures are used to assign a generic or specific credential among those distributed to the enterprise by the network vendor to individual enterprise employees. Enterprise visitors can be provided with a QR code to scan the device, which pulls the credentials into the device.

One specific application of the pull model is to use the "poster" method. For example the QR code on a poster is placed in a conference center for the attendees to scan the code to obtain a credential. The poster method only directs the device to the SM-DP+ and not to a specific credential.

The SIM provisioning platform receives a request to assign a credential; it picks one from the pool allocated for this purpose and assigns it to the device. This allows for a lightweight approach to distributing credentials to the users, although it can be employed only when the access to the network is generic, without specific differences in access and security details.

The devices without a user interface require specific approaches to auto-trigger for the device. This is referred to as the internet of things (IoT) model. The devices are typically factory provisioned to reach a specific SM. These are generic devices sold globally, and it is not known where the device will be deployed and activated or which preferred carrier services will be used (e.g. weather sensors, in-home detectors). Once activated, the device reaches the SM, and based on the location where the device is activated and the device preferences specified, it is redirected to a specific credential management platform, which pushes a valid credential to the device.

All these models are actively employed in private network deployments.

II.5.5 Summary

A basic understanding of the SIM provisioning methodology, including the architecture, credential distribution to the enterprises, and the actual provisioning of the devices, is discussed. More specifically, the consumer model and the IoT models of pull-and-push credential provisioning, respectively, are discussed. Integration with MDM for enterprise users is suggested as a preferred approach to coordinate the credential allocation to the individual devices.

References

1) Consumer and IoT (https://www.gsma.com/solutions-and-impact/technologies/esim/esim-specification/)
   Core standards for implementing eSIM on mobile devices include the following articles:[2]
   - eSIM architecture specification[4]
   - eSIM IoT architecture and requirement specification
   - SGP 22 RSP architecture for consumer devices
2) Machine to Machine (https://www.gsma.com/solutions-and-impact/technologies/esim/remote-sim-provisioning-for-machine-to-machine/)
   - GSMA publishes standards for machine to-machine (M2M) third-party provisioning of eSIM, which includes the following articles:[3]
   - SGP.01 M2M eSIM architecture v4.2
   - SGP.02 eSIM technical specifications V4.2.1

Part III

Enterprise Applications

III.1

Part III: Enterprise Applications

Part III of the book goes over some real-world private network deployment verticals and highlights the typical issues that need to be addressed for the individual verticals. The verticals called out are some of the typical types of private networks being deployed now and are by no means limited to the ones mentioned in this section. The enterprise private network applications are evolving fast, and creative ways to addressing connectivity and quality of service (QoS) requirements are actively being adopted in the market.

The two chapters on industrial internet of things (IIoT) protocols are introduced to address industrial private network deployments. One covers the support of deterministic networks (DetNet) and time-sensitive networks (TSN), which are primarily intended for IIoT deployments as private networks that meet the stringent requirements of such environments. These protocols work across multiple hops in the network and connect to the end wireless devices. These manufacturing facilities already have cabled scenarios and typically want to add or replace them with wireless nodes to allow for sensors to be places where wired connectivity is not possible. Additionally, the ease of adding wireless nodes enables more sensors to be added, allowing for better monitoring and control of the network. The second chapter covers the architectural and realization aspects of using these protocols and integrating them into a 5G local area network (LAN) wireless environment.

While introducing the use of private networks into IIoT platforms, the cost benefits and reliability of these systems play a significant role in the process. Given that each IIoT implementation tends to be very specific and proprietary, I have covered IIoT only in terms of the interfaces and protocols supported, rather than dwelling on a specific manufacturing process, deployment considerations, and optimizations that went into realizing it.

The other exemplary verticals are captured together in a single chapter. Each industrial application tends to be very specialized, and although the radio access network (RAN) and core network functions can be reused, the actual nature of the deployment will require customizations. For example, consider an assembly line with fault detection that requires active management of the pipeline to prevent wastage; this will require an understanding of the stages of the manufacturing, the functions that need to be halted, and further assistance in the quick restart of the system. Cameras are actively used in conjunction with artificial intelligence (AI) built both into the camera and the backend servers to aid real-time detection and correction. Specific applications, like turbine blade manufacturing, require the machining process to operate at a very high revolutions per minute (RPM), and sophisticated cameras are needed to detect potential issues. When caught early, these issues can avoid both material wastage and time loss. Supporting such cameras for high

Mobile Communication Systems for Private Networks, First Edition. Srinivasan Balasubramanian.

throughput in regions with harsh radio frequency (RF) environments, largely populated by metal containers, required explicit designs that include redundancies both in the RAN (multiple transmit/receive points) and core nodes to address reliability demands.

There are many verticals that are emerging that have envisioned the use of private networks. These range from simple connectivity such as offices and educational institutions, all the way to oil rigs and underground operations. It could be as simple as a set of cameras that is used for campus security or scenarios like airport hangers, where collisions of airplane wings with the walls need to be avoided through active monitoring. Asset traction is becoming a particularly important function.

Some of the exemplary use cases I have encountered, along with the typical set of requirements and problems that need to be addressed for each of the verticals, are captured. For some of the verticals, workable solutions that go beyond the current definition of the standards are suggested for realization. These solution proposals can be submitted as contributions and pursued in the standards forums.

III.2

IIoT Protocols

III.2.1 Introduction

There are several industrial implementations dating back several decades. Starting with the wired connectivity, it is evolving into a more flexible wireless connectivity. The protocol realizations and the reliability maintenance with the wireless connectivity are also evolving together with that.

This chapter introduces the communication protocols, the connectivity methods, unified architecture, and framework for reliable data exchange in industrial and automation systems. The concepts of time-sensitive network (TSN) and deterministic network (DetNet) are also introduced. The subsequent chapter discusses the mechanisms for integrating these protocols into a 5G private local area network (LAN) network.

III.2.2 Industrial IoT (IIoT) Communication Protocols

Over the years, based on the available connectivity technologies and the sensor capabilities, the extent of automation in an industrial setting has been adapted, with substantial portions of it requiring manual intervention. There has been significant evolution in both the sensors and communication mechanisms, and the IIoT automation is ripe for a sophistication not envisioned so far. The required behaviors are very localized to each specific industrial setting. However, there are several underlying techniques with sufficient commonality that can be developed with reuse in mind. The adoption of such techniques will heavily rely on the return on investment (ROI), which is hard to prove as an outside entity, like a wireless infrastructure vendor, and needs to be envisioned and initiated by the manufacturing entities themselves.

The sensors themselves have gone through a revolution, with localized decision-making leveraging artificial intelligence (AI). The sensors used to be just basic transducers based on metrics like temperature or pressure. With the introduction of high-definition cameras, recognizing faults – even with high-speed machinery – has become possible, with a reaction times of a few milliseconds through localized decisions made by the sensors. Such quick reaction time has helped significantly reduce wastage. The focus of this book is not on the sensor advancements. These sensors offer localized control within the specific location where they are installed. There are several scenarios where coordination across the factory floor is needed, employing centralized control systems with the detection and correction points being physically separated from each other. This can be achieved only with communication across these nodes. However, with the increased speed

Mobile Communication Systems for Private Networks, First Edition. Srinivasan Balasubramanian.

of manufacturing, the demands for such communication have become increasingly challenging. Drawing cables to all locations will not be possible, and wireless communication methods have become imperative. With a lot of metal used in industrial settings, this poses a huge challenge for wireless propagation and reliable communications. However, these sensors likely remain in the same location and can be fine-tuned to support the requisite performance.

There are a few fundamental aspects that the IIoT platform needs to address. Apart from using the network for regular handset-based communications and supporting commercial premise equipment (CPE) for Wi-Fi connectivity extensions, a few enablers are required, where the wireless deployment acts as network as a service (NaaS). Quality of service (QoS) functions are the primary functions that provide timely delivery of the packets both from sensors to the network and from the central controller to the individual actuators. In addition to this, based on the deployment, TSN functions may be required to allow for sequencing of activities in the manufacturing process, and realization of this requires stringent network criteria to be met. All of this is enabled using underlying protocols for information exchange.

There are several alternatives to protocols for IIoT in industrial communication and automation, each with its own features and use cases. These protocols enable data exchange, remote monitoring, and control of industrial equipment and processes. The choice of an alternative depends on the specific requirements of a given application. The following are some common alternatives to the protocols that can be employed. Among those, two protocols – Profinet and open platform communications unified architecture (OPC UA) – gain acceptance with 4G and 5G IIoT deployments in the market, and they are described in further detail in this section. See Figure III.2.1: providing a high level view of the currently available Industrial IoT (IIoT) Communication Protocols.

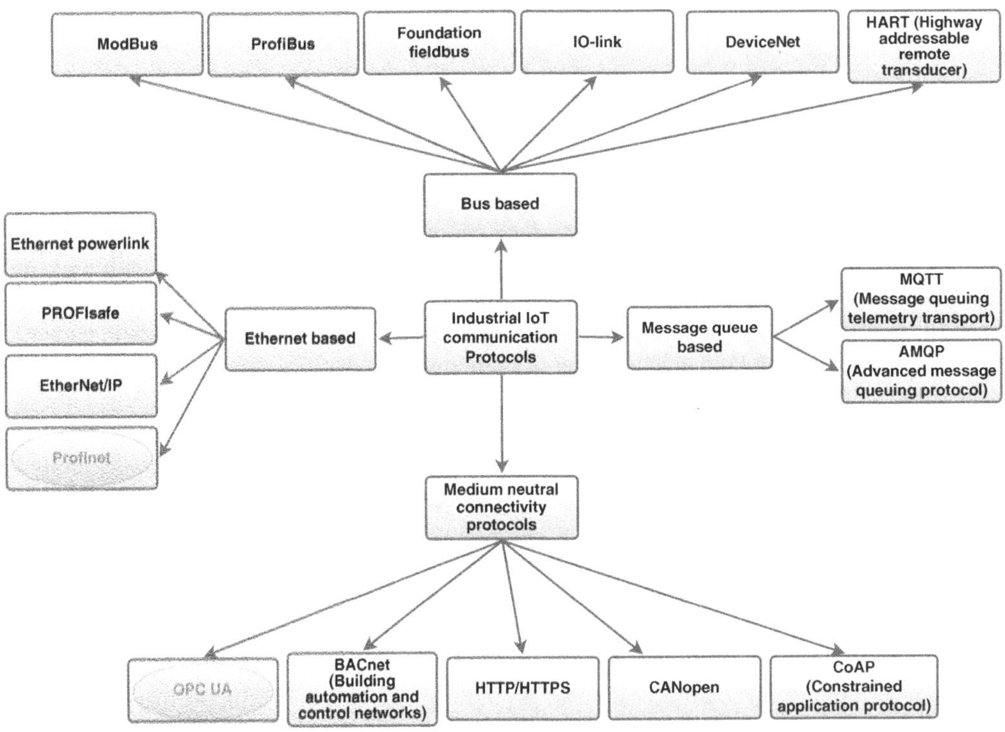

Figure III.2.1 Industrial IoT (IIoT) communication protocols.

IIoT protocol	Description
Modbus	Modbus is a simple and widely used serial communication protocol. It is suitable for connecting various devices and sensors but may not provide the real-time capabilities of Profinet.
Foundation fieldbus	Foundation fieldbus is primarily used in the process automation industry, offering advanced control and monitoring capabilities for field devices in the oil and gas, chemical, and other process industries.
Profibus	Profibus is an older fieldbus communication protocol that was widely used before the adoption of Profinet. It is still in use in some applications but is considered somewhat of a legacy system.
IO link	IO link is a point-to-point communication protocol used for connecting sensors and actuators to controllers in industrial automation systems.
DeviceNet	DeviceNet is another network protocol commonly used in industrial automation, mainly for connecting sensors and actuators in manufacturing and factory settings. DeviceNet is based on the controller area network (CAN) bus technology, which is known for its reliability in noisy industrial environments.
Highway addressable remote transducer (HART)	HART is a communication protocol used in process industries for the two-way transmission of process and diagnostic information between smart devices and control systems. HART is known for its dual-mode communication, which means that it can transmit both analog (4–20 mA) and digital signals simultaneously over the same two-wire connection. This feature ensures backward compatibility with existing analog systems.
Message queuing telemetry transport (MQTT)	MQTT is a lightweight, publish–subscribe messaging protocol that is becoming increasingly popular in IIoT applications for efficient data transfer and monitoring.
Advanced message queuing protocol (AMQP)	AMQP is a messaging protocol designed for message-oriented middleware and is used in various IoT and IIoT applications for reliable message exchange.
Ethernet/IP	Ethernet/IP is an industrial Ethernet protocol that is often used in manufacturing and process control. It is especially popular in North America and is known for its integration with Allen-Bradley (Rockwell Automation) devices.
Ethernet powerlink	Ethernet powerlink is an open, real-time industrial Ethernet communication protocol suitable for applications where precise synchronization and real-time capabilities are essential.
PROFIsafe	This is an extension of Profinet designed for safety-critical applications. It provides a safe communication layer for emergency shutdowns and other safety functions.
Process field net (Profinet)	Profinet is a real-time Ethernet communication protocol used in industrial automation and manufacturing processes. It offers high-speed communication for automation control systems.
Building automation and control networks (BACnet)	BACnet is primarily used in building automation and heating, ventilation, and air conditioning (HVAC) systems. It is a standard protocol for the control and monitoring of devices in commercial and industrial buildings.
Data distribution service (DDS)	DDS is a communication protocol and middleware standard for real-time and mission-critical systems. It is often used in applications where low latency and high reliability are essential.
HTTP/HTTPS	While not specifically designed for IIoT, HTTP and, its secure variant, HTTPS are often used to transmit data between industrial devices and cloud platforms.

(*Continued*)

IIoT protocol	Description
Simple network management protocol (SNMP)	SNMP is used for monitoring and managing network-connected devices such as routers and switches. It is commonly employed in industrial network management and remote monitoring.
CANopen	CANopen is a communication protocol based on CAN technology. It is commonly used in embedded systems and automation, especially in applications that require distributed control.
Constrained application protocol (CoAP)	CoAP is designed for resource-constrained IoT devices and is based on the RESTful architecture. It is often used in environments where low power consumption and efficient use of network resources are crucial.
OPC UA	OPC UA is an open, platform-independent protocol used for connecting industrial devices and systems. It is often used for data exchange between different manufacturers' devices and for interoperability between various industrial systems.

When selecting an alternative to Profinet, it is essential to consider factors such as real-time requirements, compatibility with existing equipment, vendor support, scalability, and the specific needs of your application. Additionally, the choice of communication protocol may also depend on regional preferences and industry standards.

III.2.3 Profinet

The use of field bus technology has been a significant development, and it has enabled a shift from centralized automation systems to decentralized ones. PROFIBUS has set the benchmark here for 25 years and has become the market leader. The use of Ethernet has become the de facto standard for information technology (IT) in general connectivity of compute nodes. Integrating IT into industrial automation systems allows for improved configuration and diagnostic possibilities, and network-wide service functionality. These functions have been integral components from the beginning. PROFINET is the innovative open standard for industrial Ethernet and is intended to satisfy all requirements of automation technology.

PROFINET is an industrial communication standard based on international standards for exchanging data between devices and controllers in an industrial control system. Here, controllers are programmable logic controller (PLCs), PACs, or DCSs whereas devices include vision systems, I/O blocks, radio frequency identifier (RFID) readers, process instruments, drives, proxies, and more. Since this is an open standard, many manufacturers have designed PROFINET products such as PACs, PLCs, robots, drives, I/Os, proxies and diagnostic tools.

Profinet technology was developed and published by PROFIBUS & PROFINET International in the early 2000s. PROFINET is an innovative and open-standard industrial Ethernet solution used for exchanging data between controllers and devices in industrial automation. PROFINET is standardized in international electrotechnical commission (IEC) 61158 and IEC 61784. The ongoing further development of PROFINET offers users a long-term view for the implementation of their automation tasks.

By using this industrial communication standard, we can connect human machine interface (HMI), PLC, distributed I/O, sensors, various transmitters, variable frequency driver (VFDs), and actuators on a single network. Profinet, together with the raw Ethernet connectivity and QoS support from 5G, provides better connectivity and quicker response time. Industrial Profinet is available with shielding, which offers superior performance in electrically noisy environments with wired connectivity when required.

To identify Profinet devices, each device should be defined by its device name and IP address. Every device within a network should be allocated by IP address to communicate. Profinet is used as a remote I/O similar to Profibus-DP to provide a very quick communication speed. In a larger network, a network switch is used for connecting Profinet for simple distribution. Profinet devices are identified through valid IP addresses. For instance, if a Profinet device has a virtual local area network (VLAN) address x.x.x.x (IP4 address), the first three digits contain network information, while the last digit is the device number. Similar nomenclature can be applied with IPv6 addressing as well.

Profinet is widely used in various industrial applications and sectors where real-time communication, flexibility, and robust networking are essential. Here are some of the industries and applications where Profinet is commonly used:

1) **Manufacturing**: Profinet is extensively used in manufacturing industries, including automotive, aerospace, electronics, and consumer goods production. It enables the control and coordination of machines, robots, conveyors, and other manufacturing equipment.
2) **Process Automation**: Industries such as chemical, petrochemical, and pharmaceuticals use Profinet for real-time monitoring and control of complex processes. It helps in managing equipment such as pumps, valves, and sensors.
3) **Food and Beverage**: Profinet is employed in the food and beverage industry to automate and control production lines, ensuring efficiency and product quality.
4) **Packaging**: Profinet is used in packaging machinery to control and synchronize operations like filling, labeling, and packaging in real time.
5) **Energy and Utilities**: Profinet is applied in power generation and distribution, water treatment plants, and other utility systems for monitoring and controlling various processes and equipment.
6) **Logistics and Material Handling**: In warehouses and logistics centers, Profinet is used to control and manage conveyor systems, automated storage and retrieval systems (AS/RS), and sorting equipment.
7) **Pharmaceuticals**: Profinet is employed in pharmaceutical manufacturing for process automation and the precise control of pharmaceutical production equipment.
8) **Building Automation**: In building management systems (BMS), Profinet can be used to control HVAC systems, lighting, access control, and other building functions.
9) **Automotive Industry**: Profinet is used in automobile manufacturing for assembly line control, quality control, and robotics in the production process.
10) **Oil and Gas**: Profinet is used in the oil and gas industry for process control, remote monitoring, and data acquisition in both upstream and downstream operations.
11) **Mining**: Profinet helps manage and control heavy machinery and conveyor systems in the mining industry, ensuring safety and efficiency.
12) **Water and Wastewater Treatment**: Profinet is used in the control and monitoring of pumps, valves, sensors, and filtration systems in water treatment and wastewater facilities.

13) **Paper and Pulp Industry**: In paper and pulp manufacturing, Profinet is employed for machine control, quality monitoring, and overall process automation.
14) **Renewable Energy**: Profinet can be used in the renewable energy sector for the control and monitoring of wind turbines, solar farms, and other renewable energy installations.
15) **Textile Industry**: Profinet is used in textile manufacturing for controlling various machines such as looms, dyeing machines, and finishing equipment.

Profinet's versatility and compatibility with Ethernet technology make it suitable for a wide range of applications in industrial automation and control systems. Its adoption continues to grow as industries seek efficient and reliable networking solutions to meet their automation needs.

III.2.3.1 ProfiNet Architecture

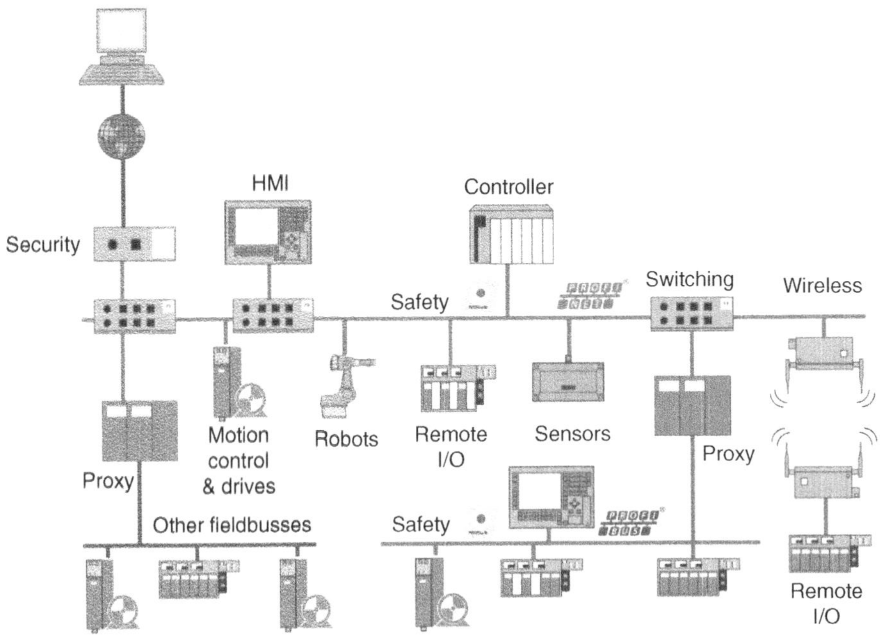

Figure III.2.2 Profinet architecture.

PROFINET is a communication protocol that is mainly designed for exchanging data between controllers and devices within an automation setting. PROFINET is an open standard that enables different manufacturers to develop products with PROFINET such as PLCs, robots, PACs, proxies, I/Os, diagnostic tools, drives, and more, which easily interwork with each other. PROFINET defines cyclic and acyclic communication between different components, including diagnostics, alarms, functional safety, and additional information.

PROFINET components [Figure III.2.2] in a network are connected by Ethernet cables, and it allows other Ethernet protocols like SNMP, OPC UA, HTTP, or MQTT to coexist in a similar infrastructure. Profinet is supported in the seventh layer (the application layer) of the ISO/OSI model (Figure III.2.3).

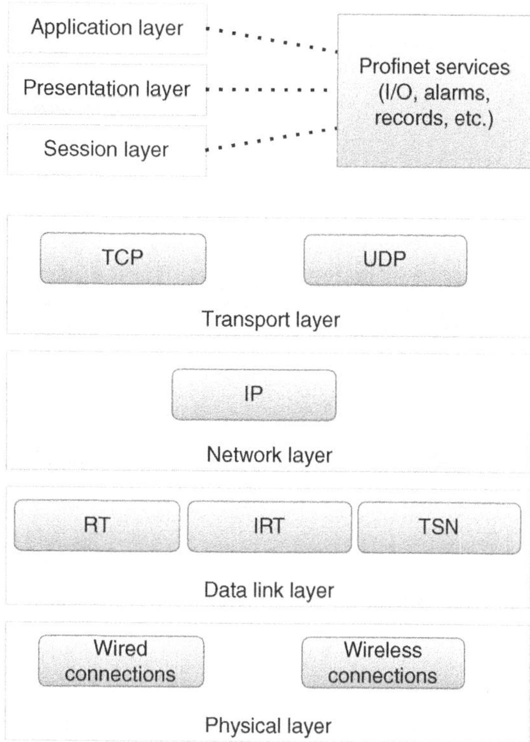

Figure III.2.3 Profinet protocol stack.

Profinet supports ease of use and a flexible network topology that is 100% Ethernet compatible. It supports integrated diagnostics, providing vital information on the status of devices and network. It uses the same cabling to support safety protocols, including high availability enabled through redundancy. Profinet supports scalable real-time solutions across a range of service and QoS requirements while also providing energy efficiency.

III.2.3.2 Profinet Conformance Classes

Profinet IO functions are supported by three conformance classes (CCs). A detailed description of the CCs can be found in the document "The PROFINET IO Conformance Classes" [7.042].

CC type	Description
CC-A	Supports basic functions for PROFINET IO with real time (RT) communication. Wireless communication is specified for this class.
CC-B	Additionally, it includes network diagnostics via IT mechanisms, as well as topology information. Redundancy aspects for process automation are addressed in the CC-B extension CC-B(PA).
CC-C	Describes the basic functions for devices with hardware-supported bandwidth reservation and synchronization (isochronous real-time [IRT] communication) Used for certification and cabling guidelines.

III.2.3.3 Profinet Standards

Figure III.2.4 provides the structure of the Profinet standards.

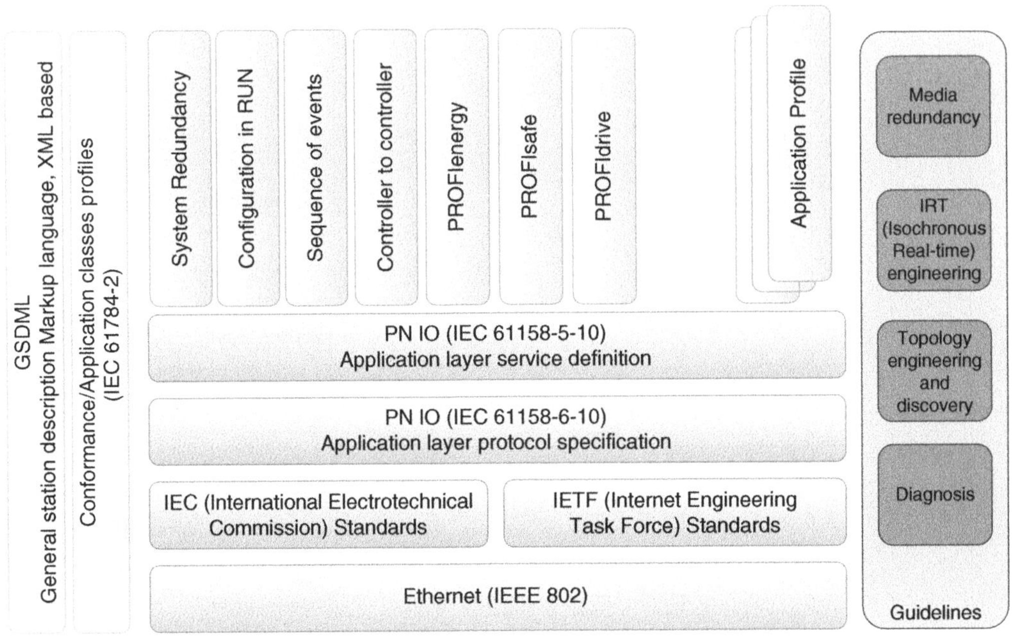

Figure III.2.4 Profinet standards.

III.2.3.4 Communication Paths for PROFINET IO

Figure III.2.5 shows the Profinet communication paths involved between the IO-Controler, IO-Device, and IO-Supervisor.

Figure III.2.6 illustrates the application relations and communication relations between IO-Controller and IO-Device.

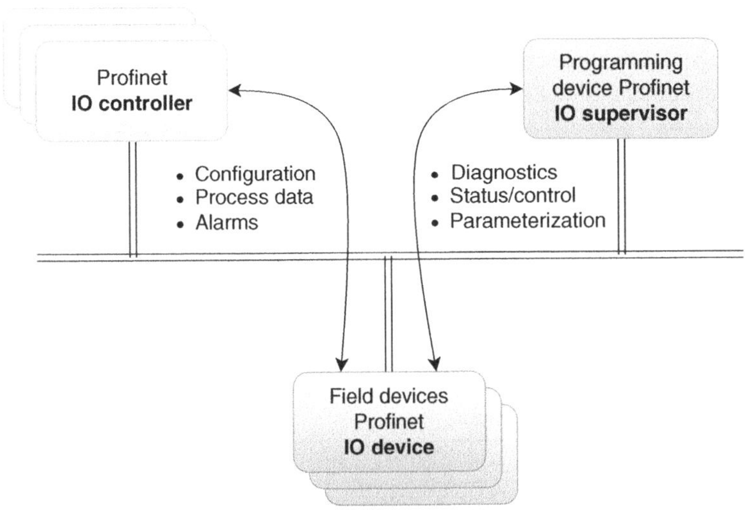

Figure III.2.5 Profinet communication paths.

Figure III.2.6 Application relations and communication relations.

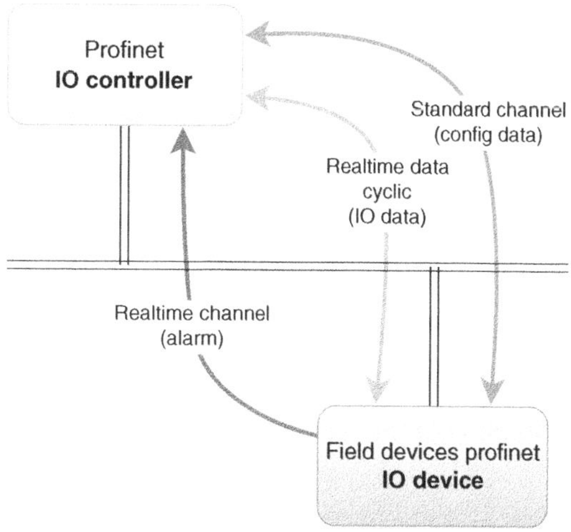

III.2.3.5 Addressing

In a PROFINET IO system, each field device receives a symbolic name that uniquely identifies it with the system. This name is used for relating the IP address to the medium access control (MAC) address of the field device. The discovery and configuration protocol (DCP) is used for this purpose.

Each PROFINET device is addressed using its globally unique MAC address. This MAC address consists of a company code (bits 24–47) as an organizationally unique identifier (OUI) and a consecutive number (bits 0–23). With an OUI, up to 16,777,214 products from a single manufacturer can be identified. The OUI is available free of charge from the IEEE Standards Department. Profinet International (PI) provides all device manufacturers who do not want to apply for their own OUI with 4 K areas of the PI OUI. This service allows companies to acquire MAC addresses directly from the PI support center. The OUI of PI is 00-0E-CF (See Figure III.2.7 and III.2.8).

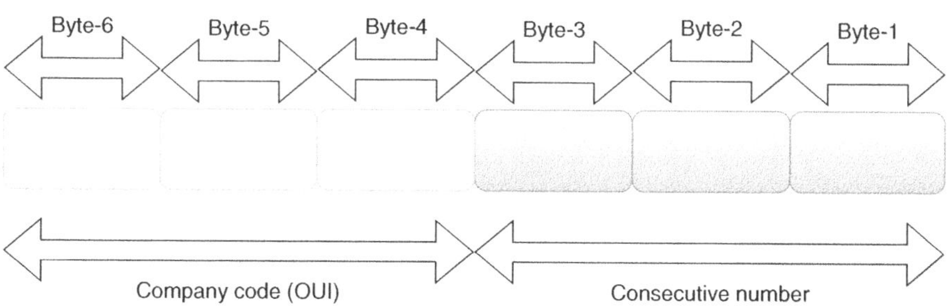

Figure III.2.7 MAC address and organizationally unique identifier (OUI).

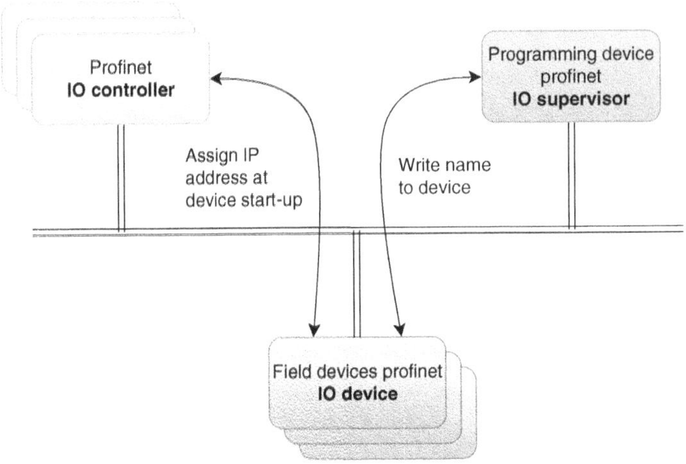

Figure III.2.8 Profinet name assignment.

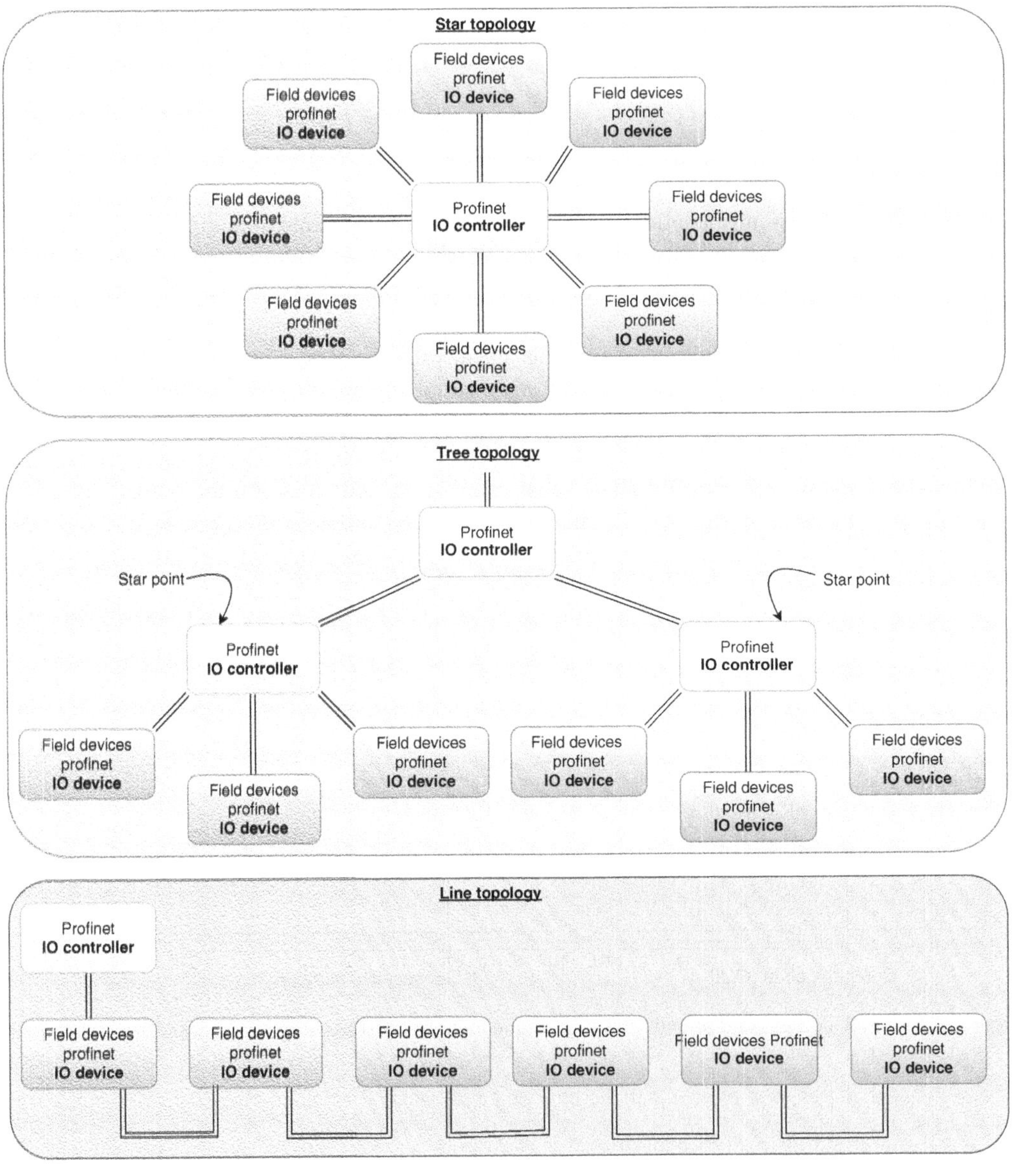

Figure III.2.9 Profinet topologies.

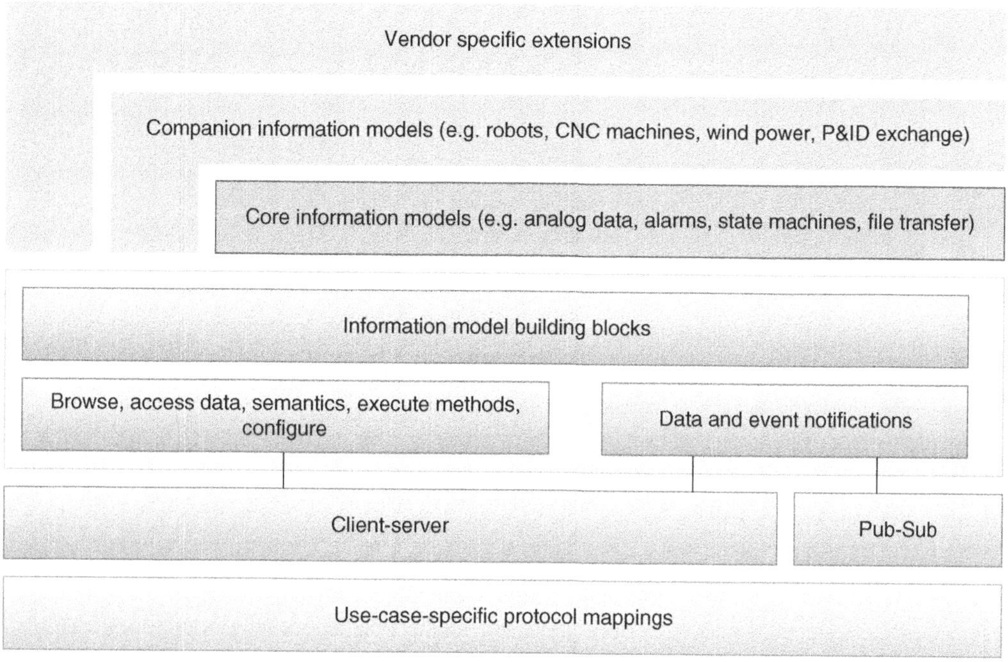

Figure III.2.10 OPC UA communication models.

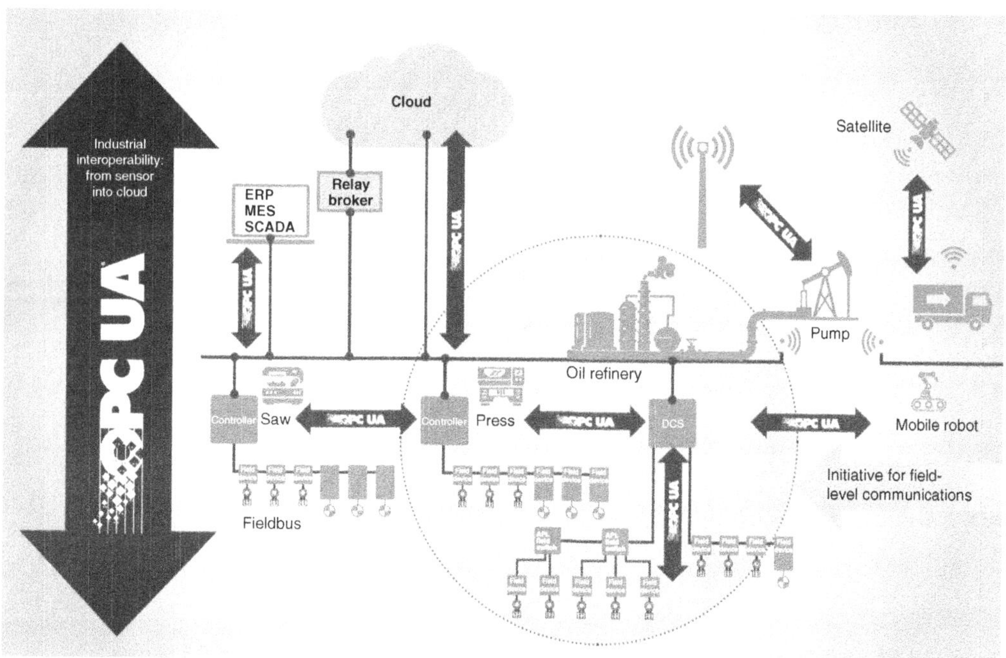

Figure III.2.11 OPC UA FLC system architecture. *Source:* Image used courtesy of OPC Foundation.

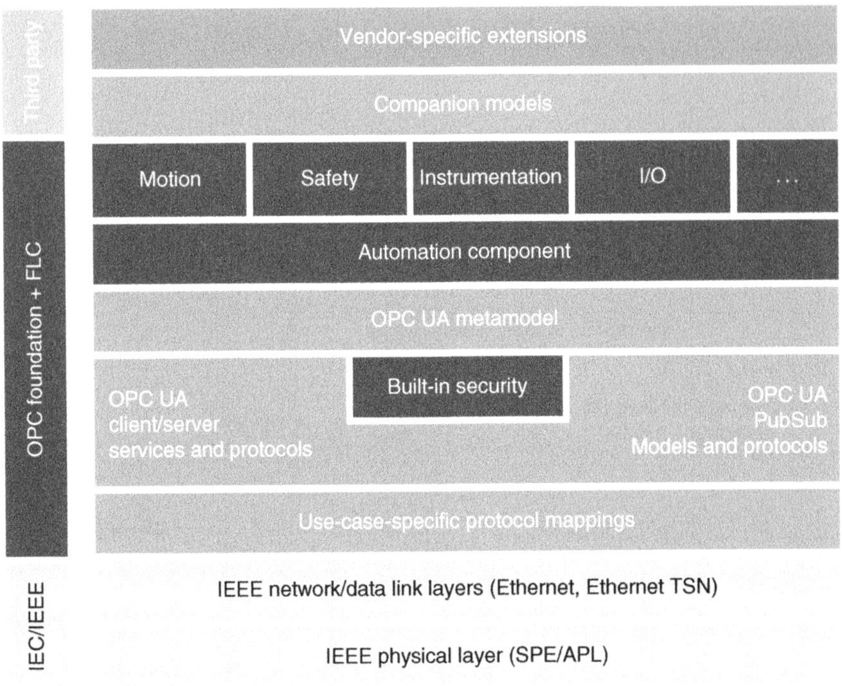

Figure III.2.12 OPC UA in the automation pyramid. *Source:* Image used courtesy of OPC Connect.

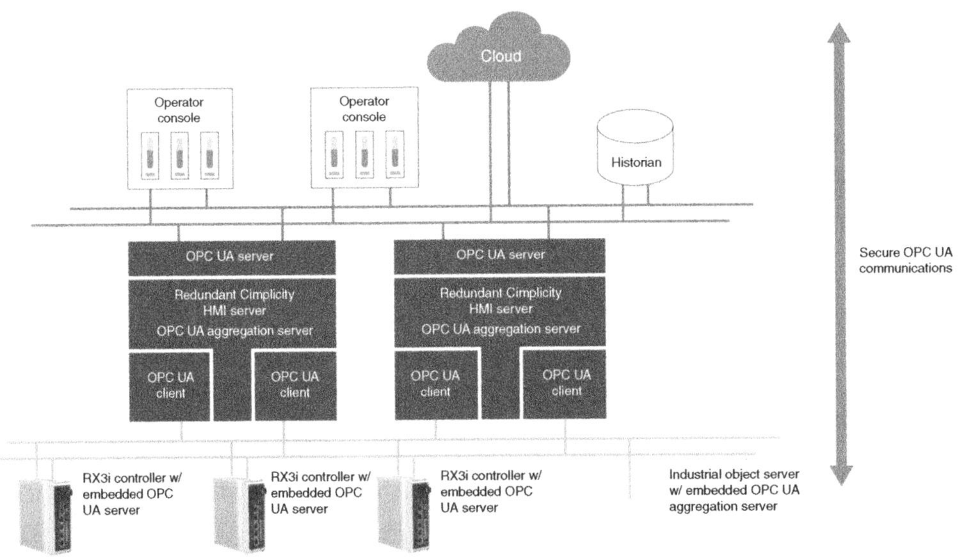

Figure III.2.13 A diagram showing how OPC UA works. *Source:* Image used courtesy of Emerson.

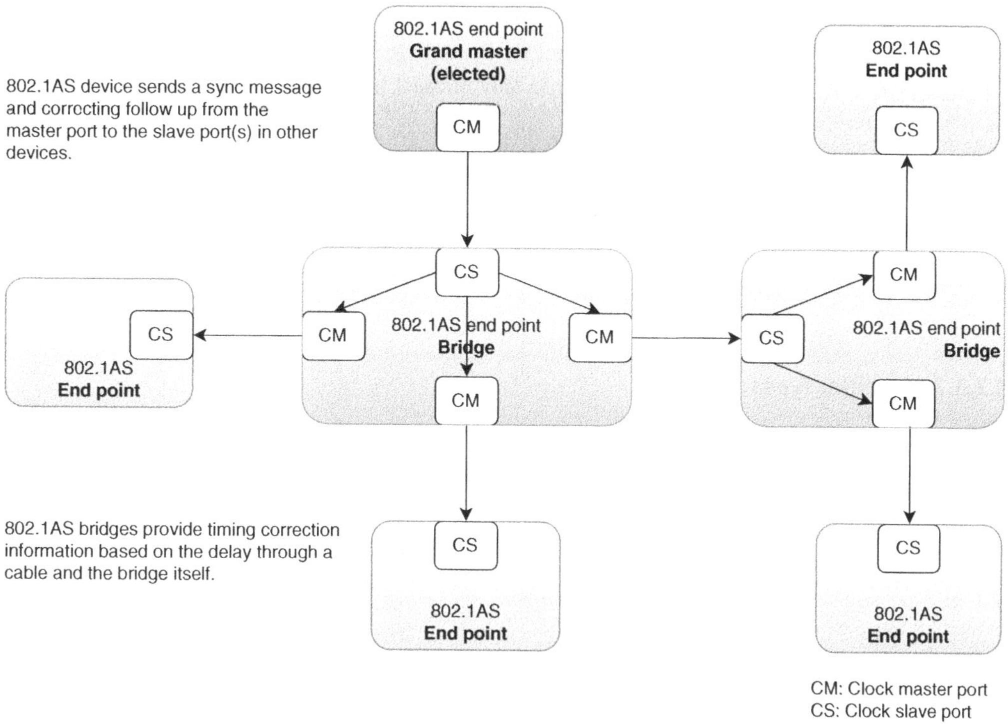

Figure III.2.14 TSN architecture.

III.2.3.6 ProfiNet Working

Industrial automation frequently needs high-speed and deterministic communication which means delivering messages precisely once they are expected. So PROFINET should make ensure that the messages are delivered at a suitable speed and determinism based on the task. However, not all applications need the same level of performance.

PROFINET delivers data using different communication channels, as shown in the aforementioned architecture, to ensure suitable performance, including TCP/IP, UDP/IP, RT (PROFINET real time), IRT, and TSN.

PROFINET uses TCP/IP or, alternatively, UDP/IP communication, especially for non-time-critical tasks such as configuration and parameterization. Due to the additional latency and jitter associated with communication based on IP, this method is inappropriate for time-critical tasks.

PROFINET uses an RT channel for delivering data in a very quick and deterministic way to use in time-critical-based applications. PROFINET RT fulfills the necessities of the majority of time-critical applications. So the overall performance mainly depends on the design of the network; however, you can attain cycle times from 250 μs to 512 ms. So special configuration or hardware is not required to utilize the real-time mechanism of PROFINET, as all PROFINET products are equipped with this capacity.

PROFINET IRT is used to enhance performance so that it reduces changeable data delays by increasing the rules utilized to switch Ethernet traffic and also creating special rules for the traffic of PROFINET. This IRT is optional and required only in exact high-performance-based applications like printing presses and packing machines.

The most recent PROFINET specification, V2.4, launches a fourth communication channel: PROFINET over TSN. This new technology operates at the data link layer of the ISO/OSI model and is based on a set of IEEE 802 standards designed to make Ethernet deterministic by default. Some of these IEEE standards include IEEE 802.1AS, IEEE 802.1-2018, IEEE 802.1Q-2018, IEEE 802.1CB, and IEEE 802.1Q-2018.

III.2.3.7 ProfiNet Types

Profinets are available in two types based on the cables used: fiber optic and copper cables.

Fiber optic cable	Copper cable
• Green colored	• Green colored
• Uses two parallel wires, which are used for the assembly of connectors directly	• Four-wire shielded cable/eight-core cable
• 100 Mbps speeds	• 100 Mbps fast Ethernet
• Full duplex communication	• Can support full duplex
• Can cover kilometers of distances	• Up to 100 m distance with four-wire cable
• Provides total electrical isolation between plant regions	• Can support up to 1 Gbps with eight-core cable
• Are resistant to electromagnetic interference	• Not resistant to electromagnetic interference
• Type B: standard flexible cable, occasional movement, or vibration	• Type A: standard permanently routed cable, no movement after installation
• Type C: special applications: for example, highly flexible, constant movement (tow chain or torsion)	• Type B copper cables are used where flexing is present. These types of cables can resist some vibrations or occasional motion.
	• Type R copper cables are used in robot applications.
	• Type C copper cables are used in specialized applications, and they can resist movement as well as dynamic environments. For instance, rotary machines.
	• Other copper cables are also there such as trailing cables used for moving parts, buried cables used in underground communication, and flame-retardant noncorrosive cables used for fire protection.

III.2.3.8 Profinet Connector

Profinet connectors are particularly designed for the terminations of Profinet cables and are both affordable and simple to use. They allow for quick connections of the components, supporting high performance with a rigid structure and shock resistance, and are typically very low maintenance.

III.2.3.9 ProfiNet Topology

ProfiNet allows for a flexible design accommodating several types of layouts [Figure III.2.9]. It supports an unlimited number of combination options when Ethernet topologies are used. The topology supported will depend on the manufacturing plant's demands and needs to be customized. The performance of the system needs to be studied, and the topology optimized to meet the requirements. This may involve adopting one or more of the topology variants, and putting in additional network switches in specific locations is needed. Some typical PROFINET topologies such as star, tree, and line topologies are described further in this section.

Start Topology: This is the most basic topological structure, where the communicating nodes are connected to a central switch. This comes with the advantage that a breakdown of a single node only impacts that node and suffers from the limitation of not being able to scale beyond a certain number of nodes. Of course, if the middle switch fails, all communications break down, but it is easy to detect and repair.

Tree Topology: A tree topology is formed by connecting various star topological networks integrated into a single network. These individual star network pieces communicate with the rest of the network through a single switch referred to as the star point. These star points are inter-networked through neighboring switches, with a given star point acting as a signal distributor.

Line Topology: With applications like a conveyor belt or a series of small machines that need to be interconnected, line topology is used to avoid drawing too many cables. An integrated switch is used to help the line topologies in node recognition. It has the advantage of not having to draw too many cables but has the disadvantage of disrupting communication for all devices along the line when one of the switches fails, which may also make debugging difficult. Ring connectivity can be used to create an additional redundant path to address a single node failure impacting other nodes.

With the use of wireless sensors, it reduces the need to create a large hierarchy connecting many devices along a single path, and the connectivity can resemble a star topology even with a large number of communicating nodes.

III.2.3.10 Comparing Alternatives to Profinet

Criteria	Comparing alternatives
Real-time capabilities	• **Profinet**: Profinet is known for its real-time capabilities, making it suitable for applications where precise timing and low latency are crucial. • **EtherNet/IP**: EtherNet/IP provides real-time features, but its real-time performance may vary depending on the implementation and network configuration. • **Ethernet powerlink**: Ethernet powerlink is designed for real-time communication and offers deterministic performance. • **CANopen**: CANopen provides deterministic communication for applications requiring real-time control. • **Foundation fieldbus**: Foundation fieldbus is designed for process control and may not provide the same level of determinism as Profinet.
Integration and interoperability	• **Profinet**: Profinet is known for its compatibility and interoperability, thanks to the efforts of Profibus and PI. This makes it a popular choice for integrating devices from different manufacturers. • **EtherNet/IP**: EtherNet/IP is widely used in North America and has good support for integration with Rockwell Automation products. • **CANopen**: CANopen is commonly used in embedded systems and may require more effort for integrating devices from different vendors. • **OPC UA**: OPC UA is a protocol that focuses on interoperability and data exchange between different industrial systems, but it may not provide real-time capabilities on its own.

(*Continued*)

Criteria	Comparing alternatives
Scalability	• **Profinet**: Profinet is highly scalable and can be used in small to large industrial automation systems. • **Ethernet Powerlink**: Ethernet powerlink is suitable for applications of varying sizes, from small machines to complex systems. • **CANopen**: CANopen is often used in applications with a moderate number of devices, making it suitable for many industrial automation setups.
Vendor support	• **Profinet**: Profinet has strong support from a wide range of industrial automation equipment manufacturers. • **EtherNet/IP**: EtherNet/IP is well supported in North America and has a strong presence in Rockwell Automation products. • **CANopen**: CANopen is supported by various vendors, especially in embedded systems and motion control.
Application focus	• **Profinet**: Profinet is versatile and used across various industries, ranging from manufacturing to process control. • **Foundation fieldbus**: Foundation fieldbus is primarily focused on process control in industries like oil and gas and chemical manufacturing.
Geographic preferences	• **Profinet**: Profinet is widely used globally, especially in Europe and other regions. • **EtherNet/IP**: EtherNet/IP is more commonly used in North America.

III.2.3.11 ProfiNet versus Ethernet

The following are the differences between Profinet and Ethernet.

Profinet	Ethernet
PROFINET is the industrial Ethernet solution that is developed by PROFIBUS & PI (PROFINET International).	Ethernet is a very famous network communication medium used for creating networks globally.
It is used for exchanging data between devices and controllers.	It is used for connecting nodes in a LAN.
PROFINET sits on the application layer of the ISO/OSI model because it is an application.	Ethernet sits on the physical layer and data link layer.
As compared to Ethernet, it runs at very high transmission speeds.	Its transmission speed is low.

III.2.3.12 ProfiNet versus Profibus

Profinet	Profibus
Profinet protocol is a control center-level and controller-level protocol.	Profibus protocol is a controller-level protocol.
It uses bus topology.	It uses a token ring topology.
It runs on Ethernet, which is a stochastic system.	It runs on RS485, which is a bus system.
The cable used in this protocol is a four-pair screened cable.	The cable used in this protocol is a twisted pair screened cable.

Profinet	Profibus
The max length of cable between two repeaters is 100 m.	The max length of cable in between two repeaters ranges from 100 to 200 m based on the bit rate used.
Profinet speed is 1 Gbps or 100 Mbps.	Profibus speed is 12 Mbps.
It has adjustable cycle times for every device.	It has fixed cycle times for every device.

Remember that the choice of a communication protocol should be based on your specific application requirements, existing equipment, and regional considerations. You should also consider factors like ease of implementation, cost, and long-term support when making your decision. Additionally, the industrial automation landscape continues to evolve, with newer protocols and technologies continually emerging, so staying up to date with industry trends is important.

III.2.4 OPC UA

OPC UA is an industrial communication protocol and framework designed for secure and reliable data exchange in industrial and automation systems. OPC UA evolved from the object linking and embedding (OLE) for process control (OPC) protocol and supports added flexibility for ease of use, integrating security for access control, authentication, and encryption, supporting end-to-end communication without the need for firewalls between the communicating entities. OPC UA supports controller-to-machine and machine-to-machine communications.

See OPC Foundation for additional details on the history and evolution of the protocol, which initially supported only a Windows PC platform and has since moved toward enabling a truly open protocol.

The first specification of OPC UA was published in 2006, and the latest version, 1.04, was released in November 2017, adding a publish/subscribe communications infrastructure and new security policies. OPC UA is an open standard that is available for anyone to use and implement under the GNU General Public License (GPL) 2.0 license. It also supports integration of the Information Model in IEC 62541, which supports integration of their information and models it into its service-oriented architecture (SOA).

III.2.4.1 OPC UA Key Features

OPC UA feature	Description
Platform-independent	OPC UA is platform-independent, meaning it can be used on various operating systems, including Windows, Linux, and embedded systems. This flexibility allows it to work in diverse industrial environments.
Vendor-neutral and open	OPC UA is an open and vendor-neutral protocol, promoting interoperability and compatibility between devices and systems from different manufacturers. It is maintained by the OPC Foundation, an independent organization dedicated to developing and maintaining open standards.

(*Continued*)

OPC UA feature	Description
Functional extensions to OPC	• Discovery: find the availability of OPC servers on local PCs and/or networks. • Address space: all data is represented hierarchically (e.g. files and folders) allowing for simple and complex structures to be discovered and utilized by OPC clients. • On-demand: read and write data/information based on access permissions. • Subscriptions: monitor data/information and report by exception when values change based on a client's criteria. • Events: notify vital information based on client's criteria. • Methods: clients can execute programs and the like based on methods defined on the server.
Unified flexible architecture	As the name suggests, OPC UA offers a unified architecture for various industrial use cases, including manufacturing, process control, building automation, and more. It is not limited to a specific application or industry. Supports multilayer future proof architecture and protocol layering. It supports both a "client–server" and "PubSub" (publish–subscribe) architecture. 1) With the client–server approach, it employs SOA where the server receives requests, processes them, and responds to the client with the required information. 2) With the PubSub approach, OPC UA applications do not directly exchange requests and responses. Publishers send messages to message-oriented middleware, without knowledge of the entities subscribing to the information. Subscribers express interest in specific types of data to the middleware platform and receive information without specific knowledge of the publishers involved. OPC UA over and above the several defined core models: individual organizations can build their models on top of these defined models allowing for exposing their more specific information with OPC UA. OPC UA supports the necessary access mechanisms for information exchange. 1) Look-up mechanism (browsing) to locate instances and their semantic 2) Read and write operations for current data and historical data 3) Method execution 4) Notification for data and events

III.2.4.2 OPC UA Communication Models

OPC UA communication model	Description
Data modeling	OPC UA uses a rich and extensible information modeling approach, allowing for the creation of complex data structures that can represent a wide range of real-world objects and processes. This makes it highly versatile for modeling industrial systems. The OPC UA information modeling framework turns data into information. With complete object-oriented capabilities, even the most complex multilevel structures can be modeled and extended.

OPC UA communication model	Description
Security modeling	OPC UA prioritizes security, providing features like encryption, authentication, and authorization to protect data and ensure the integrity of communication. It is suitable for critical and sensitive industrial systems. Security is enabled by the following security features supported in OPC UA: 1) **Transport:** numerous protocols are defined providing options such as the ultra-fast OPC binary transport or the more universally compatible JavaScript Object Notation (JSON) over Websockets, for example. 2) **Session encryption:** messages are transmitted securely at various encryption levels. 3) **Message signing:** with message signing, the recipient can verify the origin and integrity of received messages. 4) **Sequenced packets:** exposure to message replay attacks is eliminated with sequencing. 5) **Authentication:** each UA client and server are identified through X509 certificates, providing control over which applications and systems are permitted to connect with each other. 6) **User control:** applications can require users to authenticate (login credentials, certificate, web token, etc.) and can further restrict and enhance their capabilities with access rights and address-space "views." 7) **Auditing:** activities by user and/or system are logged, providing an access audit trail.
Performance modeling	OPC UA is designed for high-performance communication, capable of handling large volumes of data at high speeds. This is crucial for real-time control and monitoring applications.
Scalability modeling	OPC UA can be used in small systems and scaled up to enterprise-level solutions. It supports both local and distributed architectures, allowing for the integration of various components across different locations.
Alarm and event modeling	OPC UA includes features for managing alarms and events, enabling real-time notification and monitoring of critical situations in industrial processes.
Historical data access modeling	OPC UA supports the retrieval of historical data, allowing users to access and analyze data from the past, which is valuable for process analysis and optimization.

OPC UA includes companion specifications for various industries and applications, which define standardized data models and interfaces. These specifications simplify the integration of devices and systems within specific domains. OPC UA leverages web services standards like HTTP and simple object access protocol (SOAP) for communication, making it easier to integrate with web-based and enterprise-level systems.

III.2.4.3 OPC UA Framework (IEC 62541)

The field extensions specified by the field-level communication (FLC) initiative are based on the OPC UA framework (IEC 62541). This framework provides vendors with an independent platform that allows secure and reliable information exchange.

The OPC UA framework supports the client–server services and protocols as well as the publish–subscribe (PubSub) models and protocols. OPC UA can run on a dedicated client–server relationship. In the PubSub scenario, the server sends (publishes) data to the network, and the client (who subscribed) receives the data.

It is important to note that in the OPC UA specification, authentication, signing, and encryption of data are heavily emphasized for both the client–server and PubSub models.

III.2.4.4 The Role of OPC UA in Industrial Automation

Besides being a machine-to-machine communication protocol for industrial automation, OPC UA is also a perfect candidate to connect the machine and business networks. OPC UA not only transfers machine information such as set points, measured values, and process parameters, but it also defines and describes the data. This is done through mappings in the OPC UA specification.

With the OPC UA information model, new processes between a PLC and any higher-level, business-oriented software layer can be established very efficiently.

In an industrial process, set points and control variables can be easily and centrally maintained and controlled as part of the material master data. Even customer order-specific information can be directly exchanged with the PLC instead of replicating the data across different software layers.

Furthermore, providing measurements and processing details as enhancement to business documents for comprehensive analytics are also an easy task since the connectivity is standardized.

With Industry 4.0, the separation of the levels and the top-down approach of the information flow have started to mix, meaning that in an intelligent network, each device or service can autonomously initiate communication with other services.

PLCopen (an association of IEC 61131-3-based controller manufacturers) has collaborated with the OPC Foundation to define corresponding OPC UA client function blocks. It has created a way for PLCs to exchange complex data structures horizontally with other controllers or vertically through an OPC UA server in a manufacturing execution system (MES) or enterprise resource planning (ERP) system to retrieve new production orders or write data to the cloud. This effort has enabled the production line to act autonomously in combination with integrated OPC UA security.

Industries around the world have implemented vertical integrations using OPC UA. Each component in the industrial process, such as the controller, sensor, robot, camera, and measuring device, serves as an independent machine unit, each of which serves as both an OPC UA server and OPC UA client at the same time.

Consequently, each machine unit can make use of the OPC UA methods, events, or data points that publish its modes, attributes, and functionalities and offer itself as a service.

III.2.4.5 Industry 4.0 and OPC UA

As mentioned earlier, with Industry 4.0 and the IIoT, information can flow freely among different devices in an intelligent network. This posed a serious challenge for the secure and standardized exchange of data and information.

In 2015, the Reference Architecture Model for Industry 4.0 (RAMI 4.0) recommended only the IEC standard 62541 OPC UA for implementing the communication layer. As a result, any product advertised as “Industry 4.0-enabled” must be OPC UA-capable, either integrated or through a gateway.

In the client–server model, TCP and HTTPS are typically used. In PubSub model, UDP, AMQP, and MQTT are utilized.

It is worth mentioning that OPC UA is also implemented in chips, small devices, and sensors. Besides being used on the factory floor, OPC UA applications are already deployed in other areas, such as commercial kitchen equipment, including fryers, ovens, coffee machines, and dishwashers.

III.2.4.6 OPC UA Future Road Map

Transactions: With the increasing popularity of OPC UA in numerous industries, OPC UA is a suitable candidate for configuration. Simple configuration tasks can be solved using methods, while more complex processes will require transactions.

MetaData in the Cloud: When data is published to cloud applications such as Amazon Web Services (AWS) and Google Cloud, the data usually does not include the metadata in the server's address space. The metadata will help address this issue in the future.

Cloud Relay: The cloud-relay capability allows for connectivity between different OPC UA applications even when both the server and client are behind separate firewalls.

Deterministic Communication: In the current and past communication generations, communications are not deterministic. With 5G, the fifth-generation wireless systems will provide better performance and determinism. It will be similar to TSN, and mapping the PubSub model to 5G protocol will make OPC UA more deterministic.

Additional Protocol Mappings for Deterministic Communication: In addition to 5G, mappings to WiFi 6/7 can make the protocol deterministic for wireless and mobile industrial applications. Furthermore, mapping to the Layer 3 network technologies with QoS support is expected to enable deterministic OPC UA communication seamlessly routed over wired and wireless network segments.

OPC UA Communication Protocol: This information should help users understand the basics of OPC UA communication. The exact future of the communication protocol is not certain, but there seems to be a lot of potential for where this protocol could go.

III.2.5 TSN

TSN is a set of standards under development by the TSN task group of the IEEE 802.1 working group that defines the mechanisms for the time-sensitive transmission of data over deterministic Ethernet networks. These extensions were primarily defined in IEEE 802.1Q and addresses low-latency communications with high availability to support audio/video streaming and, in the IIoT context, real-time control streams. It provides real-time communication solutions based on switched Ethernet networks with deterministic QoS for point-to-point connections.

The TSN standards define three key aspects – time synchronization, packet scheduling, and traffic shaping in the routers and bridges – and determine communication paths to use with resource reservation and fault tolerance. Time synchronization can be achieved using global positioning system (GPS) to synchronize all the nodes involved in the path; however, this may be challenging since most nodes in IIoT will be in buildings and harsh RF environments. For time synchronization, it is sufficient for all the devices to have a common notion of time without requiring the same system time to be maintained. For packet scheduling of different traffic types, the required QoS criteria – including delay/jitter, relative priority, and preemption requirements – need to be defined, and all nodes in the communication path must treat the packets according to the same rules for processing and forwarding. Fault tolerance is addressed by reserving resources (bandwidth and time slots) and employing multiple paths simultaneously, potentially with packet duplication [Figure III.2.14].

TSN supports rate-constrained traffic, with each stream's resource utilization limited by a minimum inter-frame interval, maximum frame size, and time-triggered traffic requiring exact timing for transmission. Traffic that does not require any QoS demands is handled on a best-effort basis, with no timing or delivery guarantees.

Time synchronization: For TSN functions to be realized in the network, all devices need to have a common time reference and must synchronize their clocks with each other. This includes all devices in the communication path as well as the end devices and controllers trying to communicate with each other. As discussed previously regarding the difficulties in GPS-based time synchronization, time in TSN networks is usually distributed from one central time source directly through the network itself using the IEEE 1588 Precision Time Protocol (PTP), which utilizes Ethernet frames to distribute time synchronization information. IEEE 802.1AS is a tightly constrained subset of IEEE 1588 with sub-microsecond precision.

802.1AS device sends a sync message and a correcting follow-up from the master port to the slave port(s) in other devices. 802.1AS bridges provide timing correction information based on the delay through a cable and the bridge itself.

IEEE 802.1AS-2011 Generalized Precision Time Protocol (gPTP) is used to distribute timing information. The gPTP protocol measures the queuing delays within each bridge and the link latency of each hop, using this delay at the elected GrandMaster (GM) clock to synchronize the devices.

Packet scheduling and traffic shaping: Scheduling is used to allow for the coexistence of multiple traffic classes and to enforce the priority order for treating the packets. Traffic shaping, on the other hand, is used to smooth out the traffic and avoid bunching, creating a more uniform inter-packet arrival rate. Standard bridging according to IEEE 802.1Q uses a strict priority scheme with eight distinct priorities. At the protocol level, these priorities are visible in the Priority Code Point (PCP) field in the 802.1Q VLAN tag of a standard Ethernet frame. Due to the buffering effect within the Ethernet switches, even with the well-defined priority levels, time delivery guarantees cannot be provided. TSN enhances standard Ethernet communication by adding mechanisms to provide different time slices for different traffic classes and ensure timely delivery with soft and hard real-time requirements of control system applications. Time-sensitive traffic has several priority classes. For the credit-based shaper 802.1Qav, Stream Reservation Class A is the highest priority with a transmission period of 125 μs; Class B has the second highest priority with a maximum transmission period of 250 μs. Control traffic has the third highest priority and includes gPTP and stream reservation protocol (SRP) traffic. The time-aware scheduler 802.1Qbv introduces Class control data traffic (CDT) for real-time control data from sensors and command streams to actuators, with a worst-case latency of 100 μs over five hops and a maximum transmission period of 0.5 ms. Class CDT takes the highest priority over classes A, B, and control traffic.

The IEEE 802.1Qbv time-aware scheduler is designed to separate the communication on the Ethernet network into fixed-length, repeating time cycles. Within these cycles, different time slices can be configured that can be assigned to one or several of the eight Ethernet priorities. By doing this, it is possible to grant exclusive use – for a limited time – of the Ethernet transmission medium for those traffic classes that need transmission guarantees and cannot be interrupted. The basic concept is a time-division multiple access (TDMA) scheme. By establishing virtual communication channels for specific time periods, time-critical communication can be separated from non-critical background traffic.

See Figure III.2.15. In this example, each cycle consists of three time slices. Time slice 1 only allows the transmission of traffic tagged with VLAN priority 2, time slice 2 only allows VLAN priority 3, and time slice 3 in each cycle allows the rest of the priorities to be sent. Since the IEEE 802.1Qbv scheduler requires all clocks on all network devices (Ethernet switches and end devices) to be synchronized and for the identical schedule to be configured, all devices understand which priority can be sent to the network at any given point in time. Since time slice 3 has more than one priority assigned to it, the priorities within this time slice are handled according to the standard

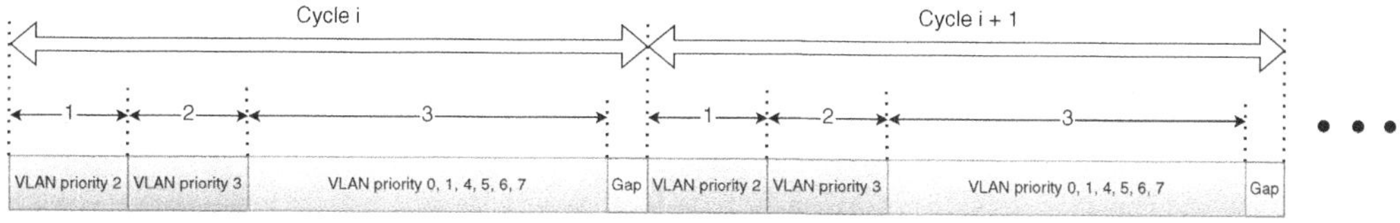

Figure III.2.15 TSN cycles.

IEEE 802.1Q strict priority scheduling. Ethernet transmissions into cycles and time slices can be further enhanced by the inclusion of other scheduling or traffic shaping algorithms, such as the IEEE 802.1Qav credit-based traffic shaper. The time-aware scheduler prevents the frame transmission from one time slot to bleeding into the next by putting a guard band in front of every time slice that carries time-critical traffic. The frame preemption approach is also possible, allowing Ethernet frames to be delivered in segments, with the time slot overrun with the current transmission, as shown in Figure III.2.16.

Figure III.2.17 shows an example of the transmission of time synchronization information for three adjacent time-aware systems. The master port of the first node (x) sends "Sync" and "Follow_Up" messages to the PTP instance at time-aware system x at local clock time "tsend,x". The time-aware

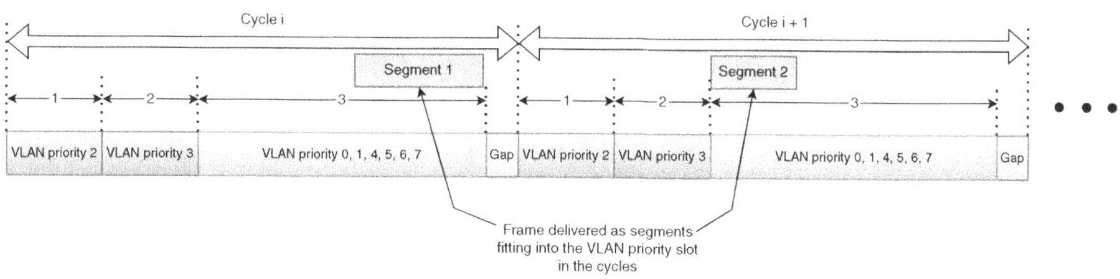

Figure III.2.16 Segmented frames transmission.

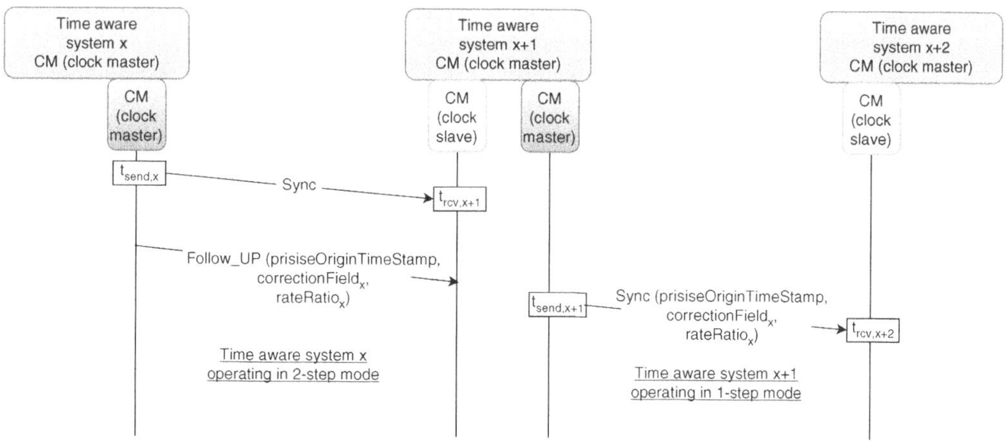

Figure III.2.17 Time synchronization across TSN nodes sequence chart.

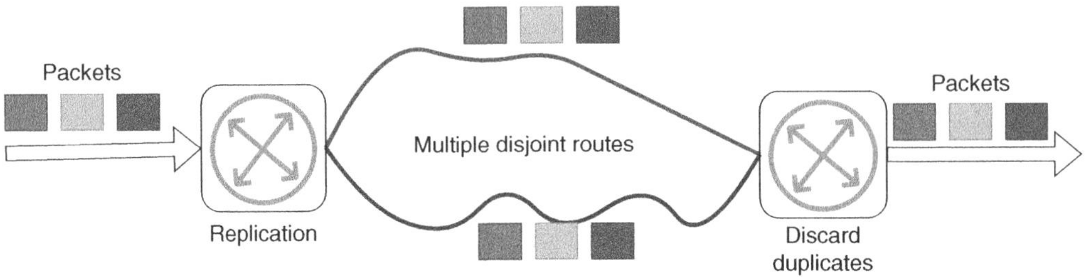

Figure III.2.18 Frame replication and elimination for reliability (FRER).

system x + 1 receives the "Sync" message from the first node, and then timestamps the receipt of the message, and the timestamp value is "trvc,x+1". After receiving a "Follow_Up" message, the time-aware system x + 1 computes the "correctionField(x+1)," which includes the residence time of the time-aware system x + 1 and the propagation delay between time-aware systems x and x + 1. Finally, the time-aware system x + 1 sends a new "Sync" message at time "tsend,x+1," with the recalculated "correctionField(x + 1)."

Frame replication for reliability: Redundancy is important for critical applications. The IEEE 802.1CB Frame Replication and Elimination for Reliability (FRER) standard defines a mechanism for multiplying packets belonging to a given stream. This mechanism ensures that the network is not overloaded unnecessarily by the duplication of all frames. Additionally, the detection of duplicates and merging of streams are possible, making redundancy transparent for the application and ensuring that redundancy exists only within the network. Figure III.2.18 illustrates the concept of FRER. The replication function sends copies of a frame/packet on two (or more) disjoint-routed paths, and the copies are assigned the same sequence number. The elimination function, upon receiving the packets, deletes extra frames/packets based on the sequence number carried in the packet. The replication and elimination functions can be either at the end stations or at various bridges in the network.

III.2.6 DetNet

The IETF DetNet Working Group is focusing to define deterministic data paths with high reliability and bounds on latency, loss, and packet delay variation (jitter) such as in audio and video streaming, industrial automation, and vehicle control.

The goals of DetNet are to migrate time-critical, high-reliability industrial and audio-video applications from special-purpose fieldbus networks to IP packet networks. To achieve these goals, DetNet uses resource allocation to manage buffer sizes and transmission rates in order to satisfy end-to-end latency requirements. It provides service protection against failures with redundancy over multiple paths and explicit routes to reduce packet loss and reordering. The same physical network shall handle both time-critical reserved traffic and regular best-effort traffic, and unused reserved bandwidth shall be released for best-effort traffic.

DetNet operates at the IP Layer 3 routed segments using a software-defined networking layer to provide IntServ and DiffServ integration, and it delivers service over lower Layer 2 bridged segments using technologies such as multiprotocol label switching (MPLS) and IEEE 802.1 TSN. DetNet aims to migrate time-critical, high-reliability industrial control and audio-video applications from special-purpose fieldbus networks (HDMI, CAN bus, PROFIBUS, RS-485, RS-422/RS-232, and I^2C) to packet networks, particularly IP. DetNet will support both new applications and existing IT applications on the same physical network.

Traffic engineering (TE) routing protocols translate DetNet flow specification to AVB/TSN controls for queuing, shaping, and scheduling algorithms such as IEEE 802.1Qav credit-based shaper, IEEE802.1Qbv time-triggered shaper with a rotating time scheduler, IEEE802.1Qch synchronized double buffering, 802.1Qbu/802.3br Ethernet packet preemption, and 802.1CB FRER. Additionally, protocol interworking defined by IEEE 802.1CB is used to advertise TSN sub-network capabilities to DetNet flows via the active destination MAC and VLAN stream identification functions. DetNet flows are matched by destination MAC address, VLAN ID, and priority parameters to stream ID and QoS requirements for talkers and listeners in the AVB/TSN sub-network.

To support real-time applications, DetNet implements the reservation of data plane resources in intermediate nodes along the data flow path, the calculation of explicit routes that do not depend on network topology, and the redistribution of data packets over time and/or space to deliver data even with the loss of one path.

The DetNet definition focuses to realize the use cases of pro audio and video (audio-video bridging), electrical generation and distribution, building automation systems (BAS), wireless industrial mesh networks, cellular radio (fronthaul/backhaul), industrial machine-to-machine (M2M) networks, the mining industry (remote vehicle control), private blockchain, and network slicing.

III.2.6.1 Rationale for DetNet

Standard IT infrastructure cannot efficiently handle latency-sensitive data. Switches and routers use fundamentally uncertain algorithms for processing packet/frames, which may result in sporadic data flow. A common solution for smoothing out these flows is to increase buffer sizes, but this has a negative effect on delivery latency because data has to fill the buffers before transmission to the next switch or router can start.

IEEE TSN task group has defined deterministic algorithms for queuing, shaping, and scheduling, which allow each node to allocate bandwidth and latency according to the requirements of each data flow by computing the buffer size at the network switch. The same algorithms can be employed at higher network layers to improve delivery of IP packets and provide interoperability with TSN hardware when available.

III.2.6.2 Requirements DetNet Is Targeted to Meet

Applications from different fields often have fundamentally similar requirements, which may include:

- Time synchronization at each node (routers/bridges) across the entire network, with accuracy ranging from nanoseconds to microseconds.
- Deterministic data flow, which shall support the following:
  - Unicast or multicast packets;
  - Guaranteed minimum and maximum latency endpoint-to-endpoint across the entire network, with tight jitter when required;
  - Ethernet packet loss ratio from 10^{-9} to 10^{-12}, wireless mesh networks around 10^{-5};
  - High utilization of the available network bandwidth (no need for massive over-provisioning);
  - Flow processing without throttling, congestion feedback, or other network-defined transmission delay;
  - A fixed transmission schedule or a maximum bandwidth and packet size.
- Scheduling, shaping, limiting, and controlling transmission at each node.

- Protection against misbehaving nodes (in both the data and the control planes): a flow cannot affect other flows, even under high load.
- Reserving resources in nodes that carry the flow.

III.2.6.3 3GPP DetNet Support

Table III.2.1 DetNet feature support in 3GPP.

3GPP release	Features introduced
Release-16	Integrated with time-sensitive networks by supporting TSN-AF, time-sensitive translator (i.e. DS-TT, NW-TT) and time synchronization.
Release-17	Extended and enhanced feature for time-sensitive communication (TSC) by supporting time-sensitive communication and time synchronization function (TSCTSF), TSCAI and hold-and-forward buffering mechanism, and uplink time synchronization (from UE to NW-TT).
Release-18	5GS architecture to support IETF deterministic networking and TSN-enabled transport network.

III.2.6.4 Operation

III.2.6.4.1 Resource Allocation

To reduce contention-related packet loss, resources such as buffer space or link bandwidth can be assigned to the flow along the path from source to destination. Maintaining adequate buffer storage at each node also limits maximum end-to-end latency. The maximum transmission rate and maximum packet size must be explicitly defined for each flow.

Each network node along the path shall not exceed these data rates, as any packet sent outside the scheduled time requires additional buffering at the next node, which may exceed its allocated resources. To limit data rates, traffic policing and shaping functions are applied at the ingress ports. This also protects regular IT traffic from misbehaving DetNet sources. Time-of-execution fields in the packets and sub-microsecond time synchronization across all nodes are used to ensure minimal end-to-end latency and eliminate irregular delivery (jitter). Jitter reduces the perceived quality of audiovisual applications, and control network applications built around serial communication protocols cannot handle jitter at all.

III.2.6.4.2 Service Protection

Packet loss can also result from media errors and equipment failures. Packet replication and elimination, along with packet encoding, provide service protection against these failures.

Replication and elimination work by spreading the data across several explicit paths and reassembling it in order near the destination. A sequence number or timestamp is added to the DetNet flow or transport protocol packet; then duplicate packets are eliminated, and out-of-order packets are reordered based on sequencing information and transmission logs. Adhering to the flow latency constraints also imposes constraints on misordering, as out-of-order packets impact the jitter and require additional buffering.

Different path lengths also require additional buffering to equalize the delays and ensure bandwidth constraints after failure recovery. Replication and elimination may be used by multiple DetNet nodes to improve protection against multiple failures. Packet encoding uses multiple transmission units for each packet, adding redundancy and error correction information from multiple packets to each transmission unit.

III.2.6.4.3 Explicit Routes

In mesh networks, topology events such as failure or recoveries can impact data flow even in remote network segments. A side effect of route changes is out-of-order packet delivery.

Real-time networks are often based on physical rings with a simple control protocol and two ports per device for redundant paths, though at a cost of increased hop count and latency. DetNet routes are typically explicitly defined and do not change (at least immediately) in response to network topology events, so there are no interruptions from routing or bridging protocol negotiations. Explicit routes can be established with Répondez s'il vous plaît (RSVP)-TE, segment routing, IS-IS, MPLS-TE label-switched path (LSP), or a software-defined networking layer.

III.2.6.4.4 Traffic Engineering

IETF traffic engineering architecture and signaling (TEAS) work group maintains MPLS-TE LSP and RSVP-TE protocols. These TE routing protocols translate DetNet flow specifications to IEEE 802.1 TSN controls for queuing, shaping, and scheduling algorithms, such as the IEEE 802.1Qav credit-based shaper, IEEE802.1Qbv time-triggered shaper with a rotating time scheduler, IEEE802.1Qch synchronized double and triple buffering, 802.1Qbu/802.3br Ethernet packet preemption, and 802.1CB FRER. Protocol interworking defined by IEEE 802.1CB is used to advertise TSN sub-network capabilities to DetNet flows via the active destination MAC and VLAN stream identification functions. DetNet flows are matched by destination MAC address, VLAN ID, and priority parameters to stream ID and QoS requirements for talkers and listeners in the AVB/TSN sub-network.

III.2.7 Summary

This chapter addresses the protocols relevant to IIoT deployments. Based on the 5GACIA and International Society of Automation (ISA)-95 standards bodies, there is a lot of convergence in the protocols being suggested for use in the industrial environment. There are many lingering protocols from the 1970s and 1980s that are implemented and actively used even today. These are not going to be replaced overnight and will require coexisting with private networks support, potentially integrated at some level. The protocols introduced here need to be adapted to the individual IIoT environment and find slow transitions ensuring usability, benefit seen, and, more importantly, the profitability of the manufacturing plant.

III.3

IIoT with DetNet and TSN

III.3.1 Introduction

3GPP specified 5G support for time-sensitive network (TSN) in Release-16, with further enhancements in Release-17, to allow seamless integration of 5G systems (5GS) with TSN networks. In integrated networks like these, a 5G system will be perceived as Institute of Electrical and Electronics Engineers (IEEE)-compliant virtual Ethernet-TSN bridges.

3GPP TS 22.104 and IEC/IEEE 60802 have described many important industrial automation use cases. The specification discusses the integration of 5G with TSN for typical industrial use cases, namely control-to-control, control-to-device, and device-to-compute communications. Industrial automation applications include safety light curtains t_o protect areas, autonomous guided vehicles (AGVs)or mobile robots, discrete manufacturing and process automation, and the coordination of multiple controllers for tasks to be executed together. More advanced use cases, such as camera-assisted robot arm-based sorting and image reconstruction for 3D analysis for AGV mobility, are supported as control-to-controller or controller-to-device functions. Information collected for offline analysis is handled as a device-to-compute function.

See [1] for more details on ISA95, Enterprise-Control System Integration with the International Society of Automation (ISA) Standards and Publications, ISA Standards Committees, and Enterprise-Control System Integration related information.

See Annex D in 3GPP TS 22.261 for a description of the critical communication use cases. This annex provides a set of clear requirements for building an industrial internet of things (IIoT) network, bringing together the required set of IIoT features, including 5G NR RAN, core network, quality of service (QoS) support, integration with Profinet/OPC UA, and TSN functions. All these use cases require clock synchronization to some degree. Some snippets from Annex D in 3GPP TS 22.261 are presented here to provide context [2].

Although the relevant pieces of the technology definitions exist, there are still gaps in terms of what is achievable relative to the actual demands of the IIoT. Deterministic networks (DetNet) bring us a little closer to enabling the integration of communication technology (CT), information technology (IT), and operational technology (OT) to meet the requirements. The ISA-95 standards body defines these aspects and supports five levels.

- Level 0: Production Process: Defines the actual production processes involving the IIoT devices.
- Level 1: Sensing and Manipulation: Sensors are used to collect data on operational aspects to assist with the manufacturing process.

Mobile Communication Systems for Private Networks, First Edition. Srinivasan Balasubramanian.

- Level 2: Monitoring and Supervision: Includes the I/O subsystems, logic solvers, and distributed control system (DCS) controllers. It communicates with the programmable logic controller (PLC) to regulate the manufacturing devices for operations within the required parameter bounds.
- Level 3: Manufacturing Operations Management: Defines workflows that help achieve production goals such as scheduling, workload balancing, and optimizing production through a manufacturing execution system (MES). It interacts with supervisory control and data acquisition (SCADA) to maintain quality and production integrity and handle maintenance aspects. It is also used to direct personnel in coordinating the plant's automated and manual activities.
- Level 4: Business Planning and Logistics: Defines administering business-related activities and plans through enterprise systems such as enterprise resource planning (ERP), computerized maintenance management system (CMMS), and customer relationship management (CRM). These systems use data from level 3 as input to make smarter decisions.

Figure III.3.1 provides the ISA-95 architecture and functions.

DetNets are used to deliver the defined service requirements as listed in the following. The demands of different manufacturing systems vary and require customization to address individual demands by performing on-site assessments. The services supported by 5G local area network (LAN) for IIoT operations with DetNet are managed based on the following metrics. Other criteria may also need to be managed depending on the specific manufacturing process, with adaptations performed as needed.

- Latency: The latency denotes the one-way and round-trip time (RTT) of the user plane, which refers to the total time it takes from the source point to the successful receipt of destination confirmation information. The guarantees on the delays will depend on the type of information being exchanged, ranging from low latency (~5 ms) with a very high reliability (99.9999%) guarantee to very delay-tolerant information with much less stringent reliability guarantees.

Figure III.3.1 ISA-95 architecture and functions.

- Jitter: This is the variance in the delays and is specified based on the information being exchanged. This tends to be an independent parameter and is dependent on the IIoT devices being managed. Of course, a smaller delay requirement will also demand a smaller jitter support requirement.
- Bandwidth: Although both downlink (DL) and uplink (UL) bandwidth have demands, the UL limitations tend to dominate network performance. The current macro networks, and even most private networks, all use a very DL-centric configuration, given that the traffic is primarily consuming information from the internet/intranet. However, the cameras, sensors, and PLCs all require a lot of information that needs to be shared, which is very UL-centric. The DL demands are determined based on the required control that needs to be performed to handle the manufacturing process. The network design is required from spectrum allocation and physical layer slot configuration all the way to QoS configuration and management from the core network.
- Availability/Retainability/Accessibility/Integrity/Usability: The network needs to be designed to ensure all of these aspects are addressed. These metrics appear on the dashboard and require proper collection to provide a true representation. Effective ways to detect the issues are involved once any one of these metrics indicates problems with the system.
  - **Availability** is the measure of the proportion of up-time of each network element (nodes, servers, base stations, etc.). With this indicator, we understand how long the functioning element was out of operation; it is the first indicator to consider when assessing the health of a system.
  - **Accessibility** measures the proportion of the ability to access the network, which, in general, is provided by the establishment rate, meaning the proportion of channels that could be accessed or used for establishing a call or a data session.
  - **Retainability** measures the proportion of calls or sessions that went undisturbed during their entirety, meaning the sessions or calls that had no drops: call drop rate.
  - **Integrity** measures the proportion of calls/session that went undisturbed during its life, where the real quality is measured in terms of clarity for calls, latency, throughput, jitter, and RTT for data sessions.
  - **Usability** is the level of usage of a network, meaning the traffic: the number of calls and their duration, the volume of data, the number of simultaneous connections, and their time and space distribution.
- Positioning: Positioning accuracy describes the difference between the estimated and actual positions. The positioning requirement for the operation of automated assembly lines can be as low as 10 cm or less.

Figure III.3.2 illustrates the IIoT DetNet/TSN high-level architecture.

III.3.1.1 Factory Automation – Motion Control

Factory automation requires communication for closed-loop control applications. Examples of such applications are motion control of robots, machine tools, as well as packaging and printing machines.

A typical industrial closed-loop motion control application is based on individual control events. Each closed-loop control event consists of a DL transaction followed by a synchronous UL transaction, both of which are executed within a cycle time. Control events within a manufacturing unit might need to occur isochronously. Factory automation considers application-layer transaction cycles between controller devices and sensor/actuator devices. Each transaction cycle consists of

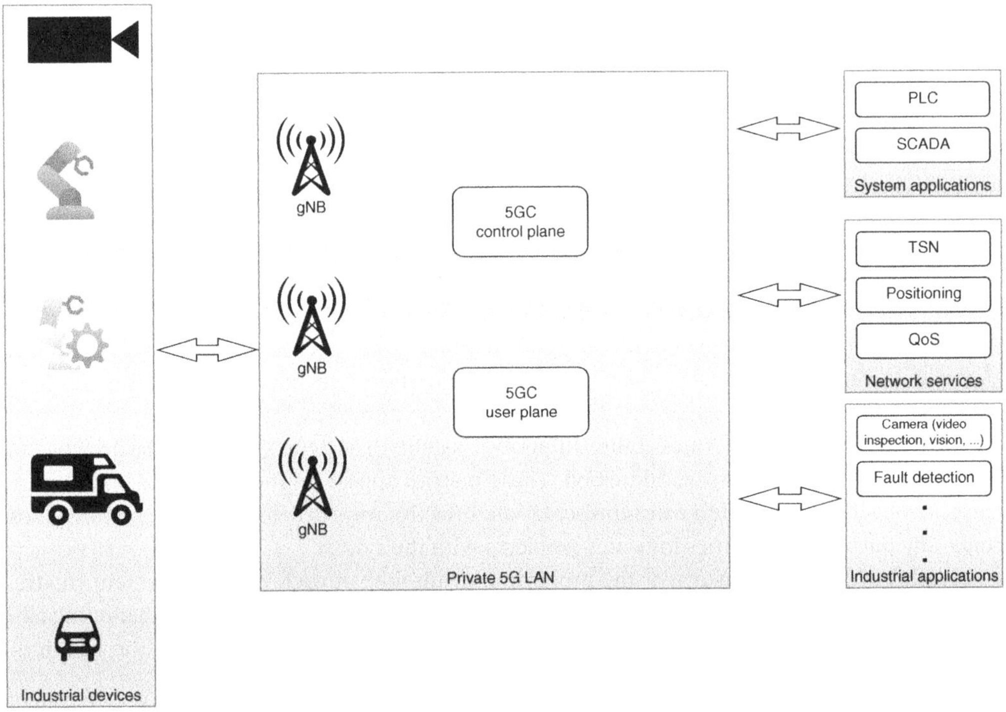

Figure III.3.2 IIoT DetNet/TSN high-level architecture.

(1) a command sent by the controller to the sensor/actuator (DL), (ii) application-layer processing on the sensor/actuator device, and (3) a subsequent response from the sensor/actuator to the controller (UL). Cycle time includes the entire transaction from the transmission of a command by the controller to the reception of a response by the controller. It includes all lower-layer processes and latencies on the radio interface, as well as the application-layer processing time on the sensor/actuator. Figure III.3.3 shows the communication path for isochronous control cycles within factory units (3GPP TS 22.261, figure D.1.0-1).

III.3.1.2 Factory Automation – Other Use Cases

Factory automation encompasses all types of production that result in discrete products: cars, chocolate bars, etc. Discrete automation requires communication for supervisory and open-loop control applications, as well as process monitoring and tracking of operations inside an industrial plant. In these applications, a large number of sensors, which are distributed throughout the plant, forward measurement data to process controllers on a periodic or event-driven basis.

For both controller-initiated and sensor-/actuator-initiated service flows, upstream and downstream transactions can occur asynchronously.

Figure III.3.4 depicts how communication can occur in discrete automation. In this use case, communication runs between the process controller and the sensor/actuator device via the plant network and the wireless (mesh) network. The wireless (mesh) network can also support access for handheld devices for supervisory control or process monitoring purposes.

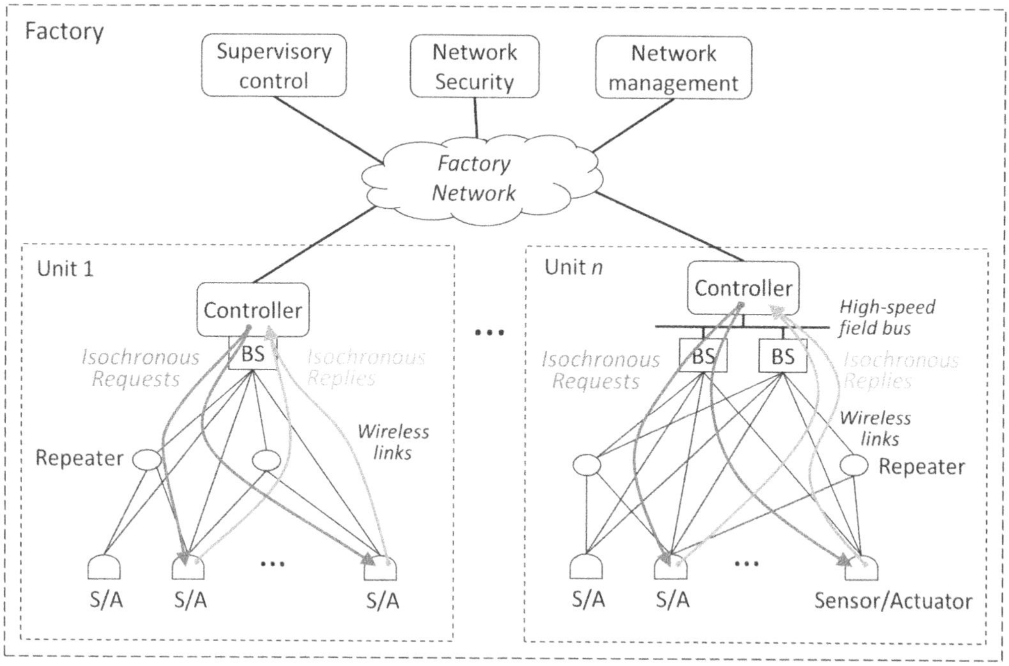

Figure III.3.3 Communication path for isochronous control cycles within factory units (3GPP TS 22.261, figure D.1.0-1).

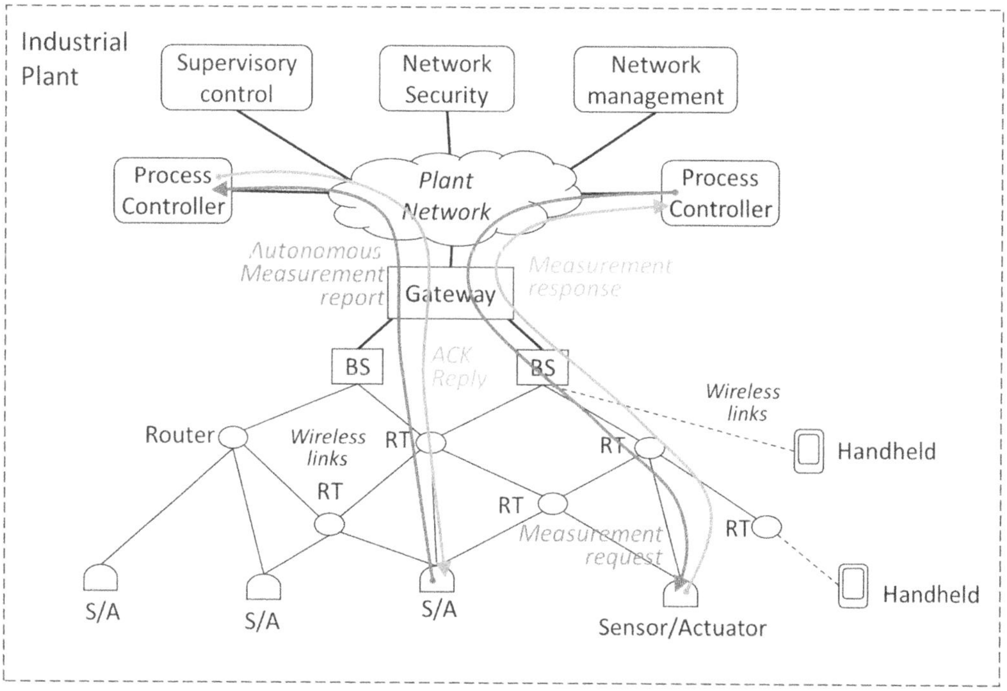

Figure III.3.4 Communication path for service flows between process controllers and sensor/actuator devices (3GPP TS 22.261, figure D.2.0-1).

III.3.1.3 Process Automation

Process automation has much in common with factory automation. Instead of discrete products (cars, chocolate bars, etc.), process automation addresses the production of bulk products such as petrol and reactive gases. In contrast to factory automation, motion control is of limited or no importance.

Some of the interactions within a plant are conducted by automated control applications like those described in the previous section. Here too, sensor output is requested in a cyclic fashion, and actuator commands are sent via the communication network between a controller and the actuator. Furthermore, there is an emerging need for the control of the plant by personnel on location. Typically, the monitoring and management of distributed control systems take place in a dedicated control room.

The monitoring of states, for example the level of the liquid in process reactors, is a paramount task in process automation. Due to the ever-changing states, measurement data is either pulled or pushed from the sensors in a cyclic manner. Some sensors are more conveniently accessed via wireless links, and the monitoring of these sensors via handheld terminals, foe example during maintenance, is also on the rise.

While, for instance, chemical plants and refineries can span several square kilometers, the dedicated control rooms are typically only responsible for a subset of that area. Such subsets are often referred to as plants, and their typical size is 300 m × 300 m × 50 m.

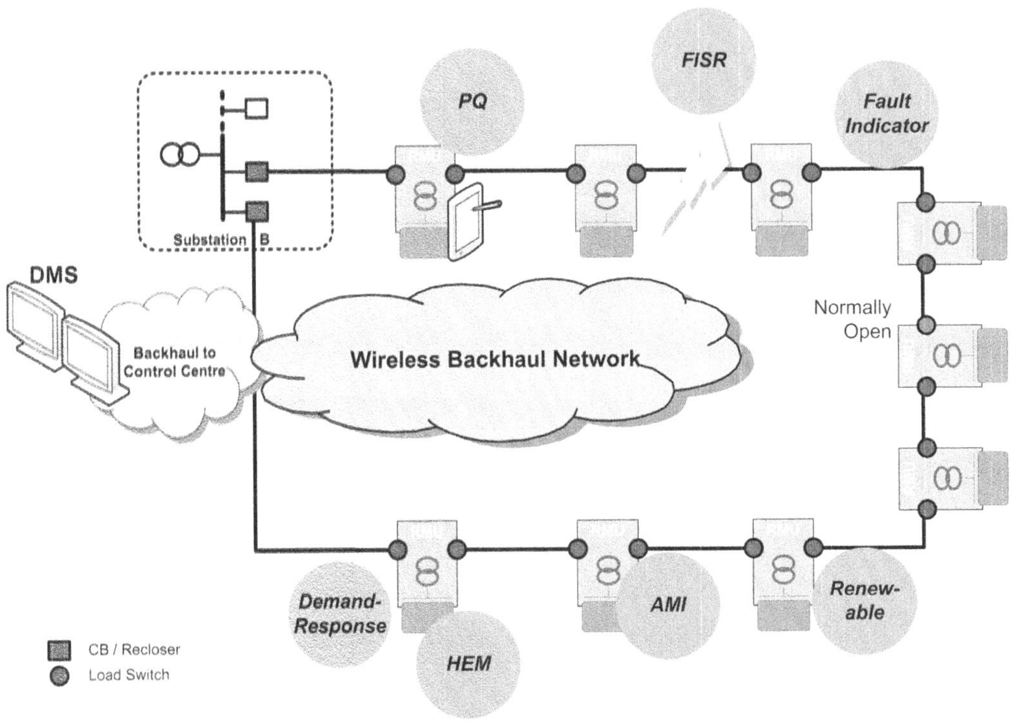

Figure III.3.5 Functional, topological sketch of a medium-voltage ring (3GPP TS 22.261, figure D.4.1.0-1).

III.3.1.4 Electric Power Distribution and Smart Grid

An energy-automation domain that now has standards-based support from mobile-network technology is the backhaul electricity grid, that is, the part of the distribution grid between primary substations (high voltage → medium voltage) and secondary substations (medium voltage → low voltage), and other smart grid services. Figure III.3.5 shows the functional, topological sketch of a medium-voltage ring.

III.3.1.5 D.5 Intelligent Transport Systems: Infrastructure Backhaul

Intelligent transport systems (ITS) embrace a wide variety of communications-related applications that are intended to increase travel safety, minimize environmental impact, improve traffic management, and maximize the benefits of transportation for both commercial users and the general public. Over recent years, the emphasis in intelligent vehicle research has shifted to cooperative systems, in which the traffic participants (vehicles, bicycles, pedestrians, etc.) communicate with each other and/or with the infrastructure.

Cooperative ITS is the term used to describe technology that allows vehicles to become connected to each other, to the infrastructure, and to other parts of the transport network.

III.3.2 Integration of IIoT with 5G System

Figure III.3.6 shows the network exposure function and integration of application functionality with the 5G system.

Figure III.3.7 shows how the TSN system is integrated with the 5G system.

Figure III.3.8 shows the architecture with the nodes and hops involved for the 5GS system to support an ethernet bridge.

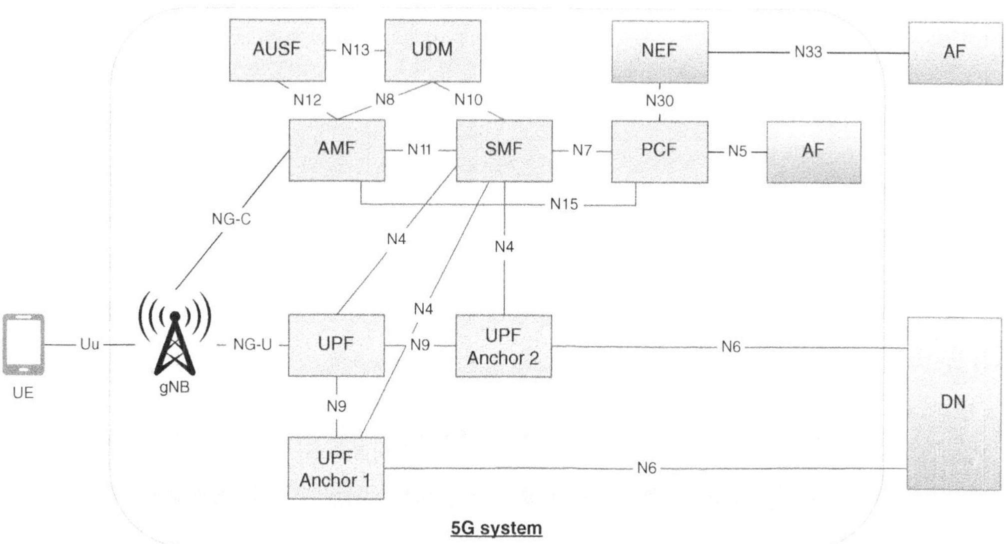

Figure III.3.6 Network exposure function and integration of application functionality with the 5G system.

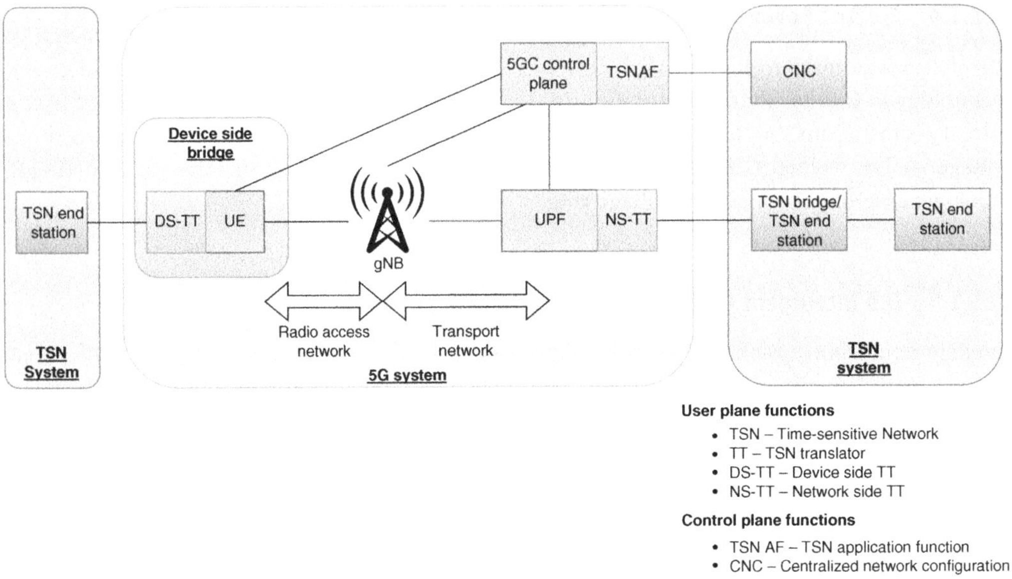

Figure III.3.7 TSN system integration with the 5G system.

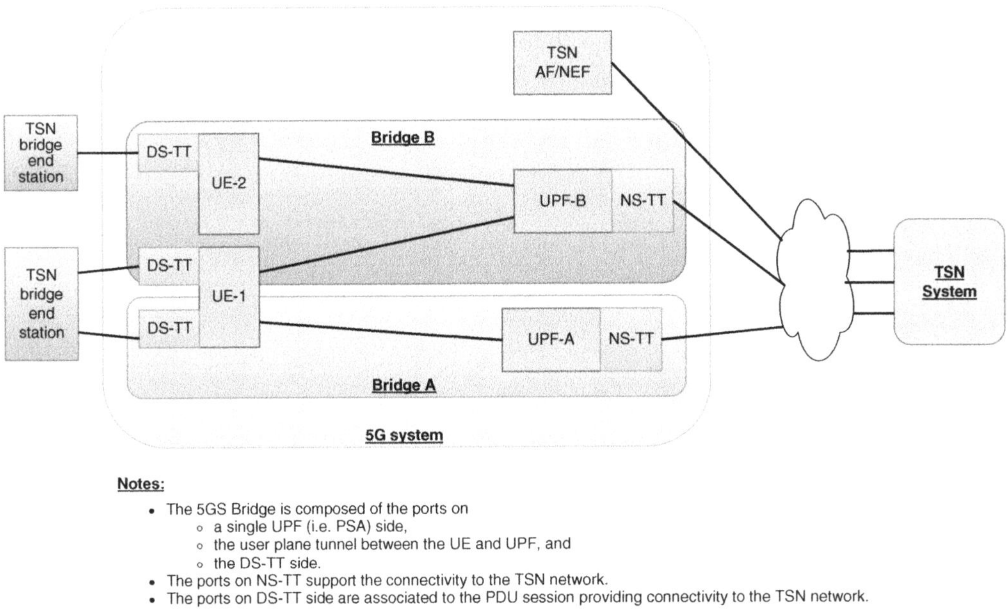

Figure III.3.8 Architecture for the 5GS Ethernet bridge.

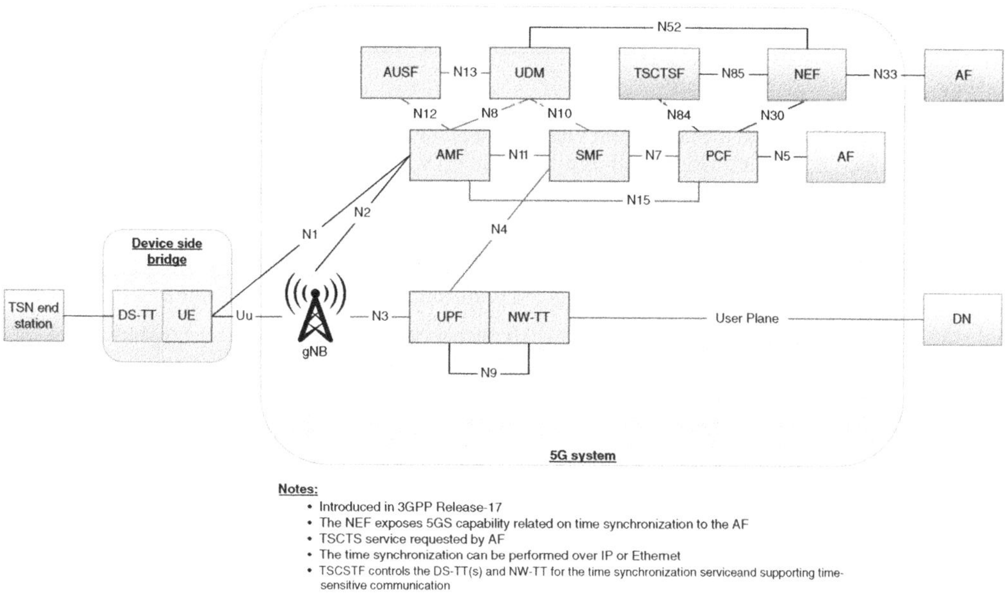

Figure III.3.9 Architecture for 5G'S time-sensitive communication and time synchronization services.

Figure III.3.9 provides the architecture for 5GS time-sensitive communication and time synchronization services functions and its association with the other 5G core network functions.

III.3.3 5G Features for TSN, TSCTSF, DetNet

Table III.3.1 5G shows the different features for TSN, time sensitive communication time synchronization function (TSCTSF), and DetNet and the support introduced into 3GPP specifications.

Figure III.3.10 illustrates the nodes and hops involved in the 5GS as a precision time protocol (PTP) instance for time synchronization.

Table III.3.1 5G features for TSN, TSCTSF, and DetNet.

Feature	Description
Delay critical guaranteed bitrate (GBR)	5QI values of 82, 83, 84, and 85 support delaying critical GBR. Its parametrization specifies a default maximum data burst volume that is supported within a default averaging window. Any throughput beyond the specified limit is handled in a best-effort manner.
A hold and forward mechanism	Performed at the DS-TT and NS-TT to de-jitter the flows that have traversed the 5G system.

(Continued)

Table III.3.1 (Continued)

<table>
<tr><th>Feature</th><th>Description</th></tr>
<tr><td>time sensitive communications (TSC) assistance information</td><td>Specifies TSC traffic characteristics for use in the 5G system. The gNB uses this information to efficiently schedule TSC traffic, including features like configured grants/semi-persistent scheduling, in addition to using dynamic grants.
<table>
<tr><th>Assistance information</th><th>Description</th></tr>
<tr><td>Flow direction</td><td>The direction of the TSC flow (UL or DL).</td></tr>
<tr><td>Periodicity</td><td>It refers to the time period between the start of two data bursts.</td></tr>
<tr><td>Burst arrival time (optional)</td><td>The latest possible time when the first packet of the data burst arrives at either the ingress of the RAN (DL flow direction) or the egress of the user equipment (UE) (UL flow direction).</td></tr>
<tr><td>Survival time (optional)</td><td>Survival time, as defined in TS 22.261, refers to the time period an application can survive without any data burst.</td></tr>
<tr><td>Burst arrival time window (BAT window) (optional)
(NOTE 1) (NOTE 2)</td><td>Indicates the acceptable earliest and latest arrival times of the first packet of the data burst at either the ingress of the RAN (DL flow direction) or the egress of the UE (UL flow direction).</td></tr>
<tr><td>Capability for BAT adaptation (optional) (NOTE 1)</td><td>Indicates that the AF will adjust the burst sending time according to the network-provided burst arrival time offset (see clause 5.27.2.5).</td></tr>
<tr><td>N6 jitter information (optional) (NOTE 3)</td><td>Jitter information associated with the periodicity in the DL (see clause 5.378.1).</td></tr>
<tr><td>Periodicity range (optional) (NOTE 4)</td><td>It indicates that the AF will adjust the periodicity and provides the acceptable range (which is formulated as the lower bound and upper bound of the periodicity) or acceptable periodicity value(s) (which are formulated as a list of values for the periodicity).</td></tr>
</table>
NOTE 1: Only one of the parameters (BAT window or capability for BAT adaptation) can be provided.
NOTE 2: The parameter can only be provided together with the burst arrival time.
NOTE 3: Only one of the parameters – BAT or N6 jitter information – may be provided for a given traffic flow.
NOTE 4: The periodicity range can only be provided together with periodicity when BAT and the BAT window are present.</td></tr>
<tr><td>TSC assistance container</td><td>TSCTSF determines the container based on the input received from AF/NED or a DetNet controller. The TSN AF can also directly provide the container information.
The policy control function (PCF) receives the container and provides it to the session management function (SMF), which, in turn, derives the time-sensitive communication assistance information (TSCAI).</td></tr>
<tr><td>Time synchronization</td><td>Enables the 5GS to operate as a PTP relay (IEEE Std 802.1AS), as a boundary clock, or as a transparent clock (IEEE Std 1588), and it can be carried over IP or Ethernet.</td></tr>
<tr><td>5G access stratum-based time distribution</td><td>Used for NG-RAN synchronization and distributed to the UE. See 3GPP TS 38.331 for access-stratum-based time distribution over the radio interface to the UE. The UE further propagates the timing information to devices connected to it.</td></tr>
</table>

Table III.3.1 (Continued)

Feature	Description
(g)PTP-based time distribution	Provides timing among entities in a (g)PTP domain, as specified in applicable profiles of IEEE Std 802.1AS or IEEE Std 1588. This method relies on the 5G access stratum-based time distribution method to synchronize the UE/DS-TT and on the 5GS time synchronization to synchronize the gNB (which, in turn, may synchronize the DS-TT and the NW-TT).
5GS modes for supporting time synchronization	• Time-aware system, as described in IEEE Std 802.1AS • Boundary clock, as described in IEEE Std 1588 • Peer-to-peer transparent clock, as described in IEEE Std 1588 • End-to-end transparent clock, as described in IEEE Std 1588

Source: (From 3GPP TS 23.501) Table 5.27.2-1: TSC Assistance Information (TSCAI).

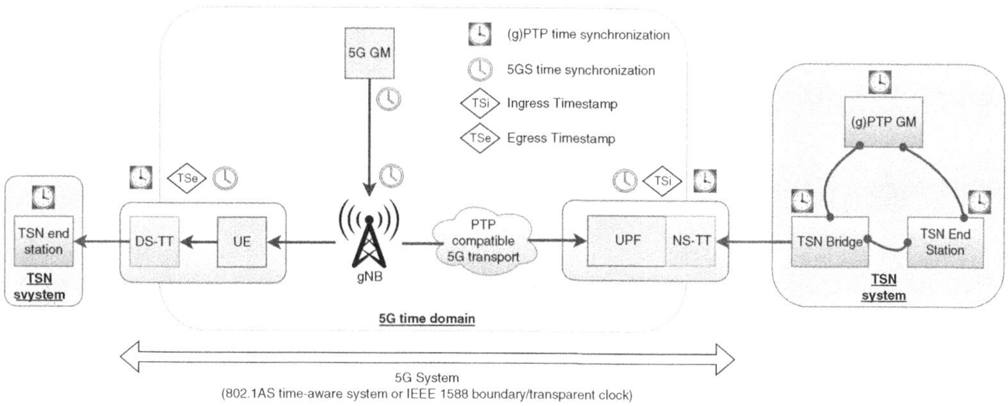

Figure III.3.10 5GS as a PTP instance for time synchronization.

III.3.4 Summary

The requirements for an industrial environment and the methods used to integrate across the CT, IT, and OT aspects are addressed in this chapter. The DetNet aspects, including the architectural integration with the 5G networks, are covered. The need for TSN and the architectural implications of interworking with 5G networks are also covered.

References

1 International Society of Automation: ISA-95. https://www.isa.org/standards-and-publications/isa-standards/isa-standards-committees/isa95

2 3GPP TS 22.261>>>

III.4

Private Network Verticals

This chapter covers several of the typical private network verticals and addresses the key aspects that need to be addressed for each. I have used a use case model to provide relevant context for each private network vertical, along with some examples. For some of these verticals, additional solutions need to be implemented, and where relevant, these approaches are discussed. Some of these can be customized using the existing standards, while others require standardization for solutions that can be applied across the industry. The necessary performance criteria for measurement and management are identified for individual verticals. Key technological concepts from Parts I and Part II are referenced for each vertical, in case the reader wishes to review them.

III.4.1 Ad Hoc Networks

Title	Ad hoc networks
Purpose	Support the dynamic establishment of networks for short periods of time.
Triggers	• Start of an event and • Individual teams arriving on-site
Preconditions	No connectivity exists.
Description	Ad hoc networks are private networks on wheels and typically travel with the individuals using the network to a specific destination. These are established with a few small cells providing coverage in the required footprint. These networks typically require connectivity only between the devices operating in the ad hoc network and can be isolated from the internet. It is also possible for one of the base stations to act as a gateway to the internet, with the other nodes reaching this node via multi-hop routing to provide internet connectivity to the user devices operating on the ad hoc network. The travel kit tends to include redundancy equipment to ensure operability upon arriving on-site.

(Continued)

Examples of ad hoc networks include sporting events like football games in stadiums, car racing events like National Association for Stock Car Auto Racing (NASCAR), and emergency personnel at disaster sites.

- Stadium events require communication between coaches and players.
  - Active coordination is required in preparation for the games. With the crowds involved, the macro-network connectivity may be overloaded, making the connection unreliable. This includes the traveling staff and the playing team while they are in the stadium.
  - In American football, there is active communication from the coach to the team on the field. Such communication is required for both teams, as well as sufficient isolation of the networks to avoid interference with each other's communications.
  - Coverage is required across the playing field and extends into the locker rooms and parking lots.
- For bike and car races, the driver and pit crew need to communicate with each other.
  - The track routes, with their curves and sharp turns, create a challenging problem for mobility and handover support. The placement of the base stations needs to be carefully planned. The speeds are also extremely high, and special radio features need to be supported to maintain continuous connectivity. Radio access network (RAN) features like conditional handover (CHO – 3GPP Release-16) or L1/L2 triggered mobility (LTM – 3GPP Release-18) can be employed. Custom solutions of pre-reserving and using fixed resources for a given user equipment (UE) (vehicle) on all the cells along the drive route can aid mobility, including quick recovery upon failures.
  - These vehicles all have several camera feeds that are sent to the crew pit. The real-time video feeds will be very uplink-centric, and an appropriate slot configuration is needed to support this traffic.
- For emergency personnel at a disaster site, push-to-talk, voice, video, and image-sharing applications will need to be supported.
  - The site planning for the disaster site will need to be figured out after arriving on-site.
  - Given the urgency, it is likely that a single radio node is brought up first, and the other nodes are incrementally added based on the coverage needed on-site.
  - It is also possible that the deployed base station is moved around as the emergency personnel are relocated within the site location.

All these use cases are extremely critical, and exceedingly high reliability is required. A single loss of communication can result in a game being lost or in timely action not being taken, with potentially huge consequences.

Each of these has specific device types and QoS requirements. Isolation between the competing teams will be required as well, and each team may travel with independent networks or share a single network.

- One of the most critical aspects will be to determine the spectrum to use. If it is a shared spectrum like citizens broadband radio service (CBRS), the spectrum acquisition status needs to be determined on-site. Internet connectivity to reach the spectrum access system (SAS) is required. This process is typically automatic and works well if there is sufficient spectrum available in that location. If there are limitations, manual configurations and grants from SAS may be required, including supporting spectrum isolation between the teams playing to avoid interfering with each other. Where dynamic spectrum is not supported, the local allocation of spectrum needs to be planned, and licenses acquired prior to arriving on-site.
- Voice, video, and text services need to be supported at a minimum. This requires QoS support. Mostly, over-the-top applications will be used and do not necessarily require IP multimedia subsystem (IMS)-based services to be enabled.

	• Cabling support to interconnect the base stations with the core network anchor node is required. Cabling to internet connectivity, if available from the site, needs to be supported, including association with the dynamic host configuration protocol (DHCP) servers to obtain internet protocol (IP) address assignments from the local network. • The ad hoc should be quick to deploy and activate. There will be literally no time to verify the operation, and the network issues need to be debugged after activation. • The travel kit needs to be modular and easily transportable. • Some understanding of the power connections available on-site and the cables needed prior to arrival will help the bring-up process.
Performance criteria	The following performance criteria will help assess the ad hoc network performance: • QoS support for voice, video, and text • Downlink (DL) and UL system throughput/capacity • Delay performance for the individual services. • Number of users that can be accommodated
Technology concepts to focus on	Revisiting the following concepts from Parts I and II of the book can be useful for network planning and operations: • eNB/gNB slot configuration to handle DL/UL traffic • Mobility and handover mechanisms • Self-organizing network (SON) for DL and UL radio resource planning • RAN and core network connectivity (interfaces) • Security • QoS behaviors
Post conditions	Support one or more private networks and the required grade of service (GoS) based on the services. The existing standard definitions can be leveraged without many customizations.

III.4.2 Big Box Retail

Title	Big box retail
Purpose	Provide coverage in in-building coverage for big box retail stores.
Triggers	• Employees carry devices to assist with sales. • Fixed nodes, such as security cameras, are deployed on campus both in buildings and outside. • Customer walking into the store with macro network operator (MNO) subscriptions.
Preconditions	An enterprise campus typically has Wi-Fi coverage for employees.
Description	Big box retail stores typically have tall ceilings with metal beams running through them to hold large lighting and fan/air-conditioning equipment. The shelves holding the items are also typically metal-based and provide coverage for users who will be walking in between these aisles. These act as radio frequency (RF) shields, causing poor in-building coverage, and careful planning for coverage is required to ensure reliable service. The point about the private network for the indoor footprint is to enable full coverage when the user is in the retail store. Ensuring reliable connectivity is the primary purpose of deploying such networks.

(Continued)

Due to the range of required coverage both in buildings and outside on campus (e.g. parking lot, tire center, and so on), using cellular technology aids in better penetration with a lesser number of nodes.

Store employees/operational equipment

- The store employees, apart from looking up information for the customer, also require point-of-sale terminals, and supporting them with both fixed and mobile terminals (e.g. tablets) makes the shopping experience for the customer much easier and more pleasant.
- There are times when employees are in audio/video calls with the customer, and having good coverage with QoS service helps provide a smoother experience potentially enabled by mobility as well.
- There are also security cameras, and supporting those with only power cabling and wireless data connectivity with QoS helps place the cameras in locations that were not possible before.
- There are vehicles used to transport articles to shelves, loading docks to assist customers in loading articles onto their vehicles, and so on. These vehicles require connectivity for both tracking and navigation if they are automated guided vehicles (AGVs).
- Deploying a private network to cover the campus, both inside and outside, provides the required coverage and QoS for the employees and operational equipment.

Visiting customers

- Customers typically have an MNO subscription and tend to want to compare other products and prices when shopping.
- Supporting neutral host services on the campus, at least in in-building scenarios where MNO coverage is likely to be weak, will provide a better shopping experience.
- Typically, when the customer must step outside just to perform comparisons, the customer tends to leave without making a purchase at the store, and enabling neutral host network (NHN) service on campus helps avoid that. MNOs treat the NHN as an extension of their networks and tend to want to use their own coverage when outside, only requiring coverage extension to be supported in-building when the MNO coverage is weak.

Performance criteria

The following performance criteria will help assess the ad hoc network performance:

- QoS support for voice, video, and text for enterprise employees and operational equipment
- Internet connectivity for customer devices
- Macro-network coverage and in-building NHN coverage; customer device transitions across macro and NHN networks
- Campus mobility for all users

Technology concepts to focus on

Revisiting the following concepts from Parts I and II of the book can be useful for network planning and operations:

- Mobility and handover mechanisms
- SON for DL and UL radio resource planning
- RAN and core network connectivity (interfaces)
- Security
- QoS behaviors
- NHN support

Post conditions	The enterprise network supports both private network and NHN services as components of the private network. Private network coverage is required both inside buildings and outside on campus. The NHN service is expected to be provided inside buildings as a coverage extension to the MNO networks. The existing standards' definitions can be leveraged. Coexisting LTE/NR alongside Wi-Fi will require customization. NHN support for transitioning in and out of the macro-network will require further extensions in the standards, and explicit work items need to be created to address these aspects.

III.4.3 Campus Emergencies

Title	Campus emergencies
Purpose	Allow the user to be tracked in real-time when an emergency is triggered within an enterprise. This is intended to address enterprise- or organization-specific types of emergencies (e.g. water leak, lost id card for building entry, and pipe breaking on an oil rig). These emergencies are not intended to be public public-safety answering point (PSAP)-style emergencies but ones that can be addressed by enterprise support personnel (campus police, security, plumber, cardiopulmonary resuscitation (CPR) support, etc.) It is also intended to address active shooter scenarios, potentially supporting commercial mobile alert system (CMAS)-style broadcasts to disperse people from hotspots. Enterprises include university campuses, offices, malls, and carpeted and non-carpeted spaces.
Triggers	User initiates an emergency and indicates the type of emergency
Preconditions	The device is provisioned with an enterprise-specific server to indicate emergencies, too.
Description	Positioning support: UE-based support for using multiple radio technologies for signal strength reporting that can be used to determine the UE's indoor/outdoor positioning in an enterprise. The intent is to enable fine positioning based on the application's needs. For example, the Tx power of the BlueTooth(R) (BT) beacons can be coordinated to ensure a tighter correlation to the current UE location. When an emergency is triggered, the UE may initiate fine-position determination using ultra wideband (UWB) signals with a paired communication device such as a phone or tablet. The UE may also retrieve position information from the paired device, which may use additional positioning mechanisms such as cellular or Wi-Fi. As such, only trying to leverage existing techniques for positioning and not reinventing them, received signal strength indicator (RSSI) is not reliable, and based on past experience deploying BT beacons, simply detecting the beacon that is sufficiently toned down in power mostly does the trick.

(Continued)

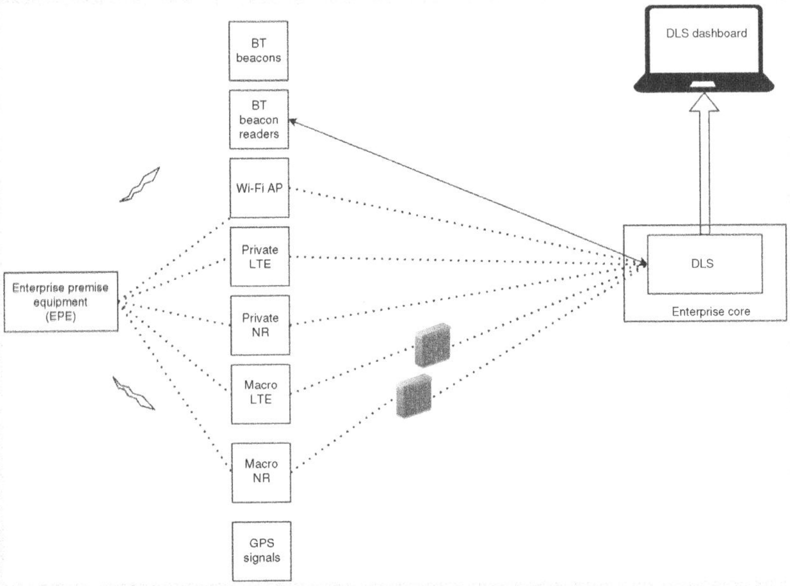

Enterprise emergency dashboard: Two-way communication chat/voice/video to provide live updates. Allow the user, in an emergency scenario, to track the arrival of the emergency assistance personnel.

Notifying specific emergency personnel based on the type of emergency.

Notify the identified set of people provided by the individual user and store it in the enterprise servers as part of the emergency management.

The enterprise emergency dashboard may be connected to the public PSAP to additionally trigger public emergency response. The external notification may provide for filtering to determine the appropriate authority to be notified depending on the emergency and to consolidate multiple calls to the enterprise system. The emergency position information conveyed to the public PSAP may be modified by the enterprise system in one or more of the following ways, including:

- refining the reported emergency position by averaging multiple coarse position inputs from various users,
- reporting a unified, larger affected area that corresponds to the union of the individually reported affected areas.

Another component of the emergency management system is event-triggered emergency notification in the affected area. When an emergency is reported by one or more user devices to the enterprise emergency management system or dashboard, it may trigger the fine-position determination procedure for all network-connected user devices. After determining the identities of devices within a certain distance from the reported emergency, the system may deliver specific warnings to the identified devices. The distance around the emergency location to which the warnings are delivered may be incident-type specific. The kind of warnings delivered may depend on the incident type and the distance of the device from the emergency location.

Additional use cases

- Chaperone mode, where the individual wants to be monitored when going from spot A to spot B (e.g. from the building to the parking lot)
- Child pickup at school to ensure the device is paired with the appropriate adult for pickup. Schools allow for such devices, even for young children, where cellphones are not allowed.

	Hardware support • Support with a cellphone through an application provided by the enterprise and installed by the user. • Support with wearables through an application provided by the enterprise and installed by the user. • Independent hardware that is low cost and also acts as a campus identity card. This allows for addressing scenarios where the use of cellphones or watches is not possible or allowed. It may also require specific enterprises to supply devices to individuals, as protection and a lower-cost option may be desirable (e.g. hospitality and school children). Connecting enterprise service to PSAP • Connecting the enterprise service to the PSAP allows for enterprise-level positioning, even for regular emergency calls • This will require tunneling into enterprise services for enterprise-level positioning Integration with cellphone • Detecting the emergency from the device to the user's cell phone • Detecting the emergency from neighboring cellphones – using reports from multiple devices to locate the emergency when there are no BT beacons nearby.
Performance criteria	The following performance criteria will help assess the ad hoc network's performance: • Internet connectivity for customer devices • Campus mobility for all users • Efficiency of positioning services
Technology concepts to focus on	Revisiting the following concepts from Parts I and II of the book can be useful for network planning and operations: • Mobility and handover mechanisms • Positioning services • Security • Bluetooth® and Wi-Fi-based positioning aspects (not covered in this book)
Post conditions	Allow for tracking the situation to ensure the issue has been resolved, mainly performed through the dashboard. This can be an especially important use case for private networks to aid in increasing awareness of the happenings on the enterprise campus and to enable easier communication among enterprise personnel. The existing standards' definitions can be leveraged without many customizations.

III.4.4 Collaborating Organizations

Title	Collaborating organizations
Purpose	Support several collaborating entities
Triggers	User moving across organizations
Preconditions	Roaming across these organizations required explicit credentials to be established with each campus where users are allowed access. This is typically handled using credentials for Wi-Fi that are provisioned on the end-user devices.

(Continued)

Description	Mobility across organizations and potentially requiring access to information from different entities with LTE/NR private networks will require many subscriber identity module (SIM) credentials to be pushed to the devices. Devices have limitations, and the seamless selection of the appropriate credential for a specific organization is not straightforward, given that the system identifiers used in these networks will largely be the same. Examples of doctors, lab technicians, medical school students, and pharmacists will, on a given day, move across these organizations. This can be addressed by using a common broker to allow for the credential to be stored in each "home" location and to enable the routing needed to authenticate the user. Roaming with private networks should not be treated like traditional roaming across the public networks used today. • Inter-private network transitions will be based on collaboration among the enterprises • The roaming indicator will not be turned on • Usage-based metrics for cross-charging will typically not apply • Routing for authentication from the visited network to the home enterprise network may need to be simplified, as traditional interfaces like the S6a are typically not supported by CBRS networks. • Local breakout for data connectivity with the visited network avoids all packets being routed to the home enterprise network. Typically, the connectivity required in the visited network will be a public internet connection, and this approach allows for local breakout to be supported, both to avoid the costs of home routing and to reduce end-to-end latency. • Allows connectivity for specific PDN/DN that requires home routing. It is used as an exception when needed. See the next section on a proposed approach for end users to move across these organizations using "collaborative camping."
Performance criteria	The following performance criteria will help assess the ad hoc network performance: • QoS support for voice, video, and text for enterprise employees and operational equipment • Internet connectivity for customers' devices • Macro-network coverage and in-building NHN coverage; customer device transitions across macro and NHN networks • Campus mobility for all users
Technology concepts to focus on	Revisiting the following concepts from Parts I and II of the book can be useful for network planning and operations: • System camping algorithms • RAN and core network connectivity (interfaces) • Security/authentication procedures • QoS behaviors • Virtual private network (VPN) tunneling (not covered in this book)
Post conditions	Support collaborative camping to enhance mobility across organizations. The existing standards definitions cannot be directly leveraged. One possible approach is for the interacting campuses to build custom solutions. Ideally, the preferred approach will be to address it in the standards bodies and have a unified solution that will allow any of the enterprises to support inbound/outbound collaborating campuses by simply managing policies with the interacting enterprises.

III.4.4.1 Collaborative Camping

UE transitions to another private network when out of the footprint of its enterprise network by using periodic scans or the geofencing feature defined on TS-1004. The UE may find a private network based on the agreements in place for UE operations and the available networks in the UE's current location.

Note: The suggested approach for collaborative camping is not addressed in the standards. This architecture proposal can be standardized with the study item/work item introduced into one of the standards forums. Any of the forums focused on private networking can adopt a viable solution, including 3GPP, the OnGo Alliance, and possibly other standards bodies as well.

System Camping to Find Preferred Enterprise Networks

System camping procedures for the UE to find preferred home enterprise and visited enterprise networks need to be detailed.

UE Authentication

The primary function is authentication for camping and routing to find the "home" domain where the credential stored is required.

Inter-enterprise authentication is addressed by using a hierarchical HSS/UDM and can be treated as a home network when transitioning across enterprises along with IBN/SUCI-based routing.

The UE operates on the visited network without the "roaming" flag turned on, given that the public land mobile network (PLMN) used to select the network is identified as the "home" or "equivalent-home" network.

Data Connectivity

The data offloads local breakout (LBO) traffic to access the internet/intranet. Any home enterprise access is supported through VPN tunnels, which will be the typical method employed.

When specialized traffic support is needed, an explicit PDN connection to the home enterprise is established. This requires domain name service (DNS) support to find the PDN GW in the home enterprise network.

Similar connectivity needs to be established for policy management functions.

The connectivity supported allows potential access to

- public internet,
- visiting an enterprise private network with restrictions, and
- remote connectivity to the "home" enterprise network, either tunneled or through implicit connectivity.

Figure III.4.1 provides a high-level view of the network, including the visited and home enterprise network architecture for connectivity.

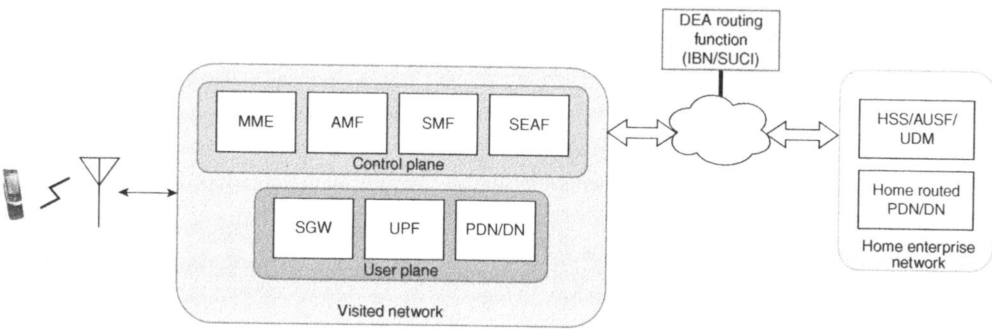

Figure III.4.1 Collaborative camping architecture.

The following aspects are highlighted as key concepts addressed by this architecture.

- Routing for authentication from the visited network to the home enterprise network.
- Local breakout for data connectivity with the visited network avoids all packets being routed to the home enterprise network. Typically, the connectivity required in the visited network will be a public internet connection, and this approach allows for local breakout to be supported to both avoid the costs of home routing and reduce end-to-end latency.
- Allows connectivity for specific PDNs/DNs that require home routing. Used as an exception when necessary.

III.4.5 Conference Centers

Title	Conference centers
Purpose	Support connectivity in conference centers for booth holders, attendees, administrators, and ground staff for the duration of a specific conference.
Triggers	Conference booth holders, attendees, and administrators.
Preconditions	Wi-Fi coverage is available on office campuses. MNO coverage may be available on the office campus.
Description	Enable connectivity in conference centers for booth holders, attendees, administrators, and ground staff during a specific conference, while making the same venue available for another conference later. The conference center may also host multiple conferences simultaneously, requiring careful management of resources and coverage to ensure that each ongoing conference is supported without interference. Connectivity is required for both internet and "walled garden" services localized to the conference. **Booth holders and administrators** • Booth holders and certain administrators require priority access over other users. • This can be enabled by supporting different grades of service for non-GBR QoS bearers such as gold-, silver-, or bronze-type users, providing prioritized access even for best-effort-type traffic. • Explicit QoS grants can be provided to enable specific services on campus by provisioning appropriate policies. • Booth holders will want to support advertisements that attract visitors to their booth. • The booth holder may have specific events planned that they will want to telecast across the conference inside and outside. This can be done through wired or wireless connectivity. The same content may be available to individual users via streaming. **Broadcast messaging** • Campus announcements are handled as described in the "Educational Institutions" use case. • The announcements sent out may be links to additional content. • Based on the demands for this broadcast messaging, additional radio resources may need to be accommodated. • User interface that needs to be enabled to display the information broadcasted.

Content distribution

- Lecture demonstrations, panel discussions, and advertisement streaming (unicast/broadcast) will be common use cases for campuses, and supporting some form of caching closer to the delivery points will help reduce the load on the core networks.
- The content may need to be displayed on different screens across the conference center. The same content should also be available via streaming (both live and offline).
- This content may be delivered only within the conference center or made available on the public internet, and appropriate connectivity and requisite QoS need to be supported.

Security

- Surveillance cameras help the conference admin manage the activity to quickly get aid where it is needed and are a great security tool.
- Given the heavy UL nature of the traffic, aligning the cell that is serving the security camera to have a higher UL capacity will allow for better management of campus resources.

Credential distribution

- The conference center will be reused for different events throughout the year, with each session supported by a completely distinct set of attendees.
- The attendees will require explicit credentials that will be granted and revoked after the conference ends.
- Supporting an eSIM push to the visitors' devices and also supporting a timer-based expiry of the credential, after which the end user clears the credential from the device, will allow the same eSIM to be reused for other visitors at a future point. Global system for mobile communications association (GSMA), in its remote sim provisioning (RSP) specification, has introduced mechanisms to send explicit messages to the device releasing the credentials. The timer-based approach will be an easier method to control, even when the device has left the conference. This timer approach needs to be proposed to the GSMA forum for adoption.
- The eSIM installation can be done using a poster method where the user scans a QR code to download the eSIM.
- Specific credentials can also be assigned to the users by sending a QR code via email or in person when they register.
- Using specific credential entries allows for better control and even caters the service based on the attendee, while the poster method allows for a more flexible approach to provide all attendees with a generic credential. The method employed will depend on the sensitive nature of the conference and the extent of control that needs to be exercised over the access control to the network.

NHN connectivity

- All the users typically have MNO subscriptions as well, and in-building coverage tends to be limited; enabling NHN on the private networks helps serve as a coverage extension for the MNO and greatly aids the conference attendees.
- This may be selectively enabled for specific MNOs supporting NHN. This requires connectivity to the established MNO core via the multiple operator core network (MOCN) GW.
- This NHN connectivity may be supported in a permanent manner or established for the duration of specific conferences at the conference center.
- The MOCN GW realization for this will likely be in the cloud to keep the functions at the conference center minimal if this connectivity is a temporary setup for specific conferences.

(*Continued*)

	LTE/NR and Wi-Fi interworking • Private networks installed in the conference center allow for all these scenarios to be supported. Wi-Fi connectivity may also be supported, and interworking with LTE/NR can be supported, as described in the "Educational Institution" use case. • Based on the available spectrum for private networks, it is possible that this private network is utilized for specialized services while Wi-Fi is used for generic connectivity.

Performance criteria	The following performance criteria will help assess the ad hoc network performance:
	• QoS support for
	  – video streaming
	  – QoS for content access
	  – security cameras with the requisite UL capacity
	• Internet connectivity delivers streaming content and also provides connectivity for all types of users
	• Macro-network coverage and in-building NHN coverage
	• Conference center mobility for all users.

Technology concepts to focus on	Revisiting the following concepts from Parts I and II of the book can be useful for network planning and operations: • System camping • SON for DL and UL radio resource planning • RAN and core network connectivity (interfaces) • RAN slices • Admission control • Security/authentication • Device provisioning • QoS behaviors • NHN support
Post conditions	Augment the Wi-Fi on campus with LTE/NR networks, potentially supporting a common interface to applications and dynamically choosing the radio access technology (RAT) to route the UL/DL traffic. Push eSIM credentials to visitors and dynamically release them if they are to be reused for subsequent conference attendees. The existing standards definitions can be largely leveraged. However, to avoid accumulating clutter of eSIM context in both the UE and SIM provisioning servers, further extensions to the standards are needed to address scenarios like the timed release of the credentials. This will allow these credentials to be revoked after a time period and rekeyed and issued to other users.

III.4.6 Educational Institutions

Title	Educational institutions
Purpose	Provide coverage for professors, students, and institutional employees.
Triggers	• Professors stream lectures, requiring access to materials and student information. • Student entering campus, accessing lectures/class material, moving from one classroom to another, and going to other campus centers (library, café, etc.). • Institution employees addressing campus administrative aspects, security, camera feeds, etc.

Preconditions	Campuses usually have Wi-Fi coverage that is uniformly available to all users, but it can become congested.
Description	Educational institutions are primarily supported by providing commercial premises equipment (CPE) for Wi-Fi connectivity extensions. Direct connectivity based on private network access is also enabled to allow for improved and specialized exclusive connectivity. Depending on the types of users, different types of access to the educational institution's servers are enabled, and separating the IP domains allows for improved security. **Professor/teacher access** • Professors and some administrators require priority access over other users. • This can be enabled by supporting different grades of service for non-GBR QoS bearers such as gold-, silver-, and bronze-type users, providing prioritized access even for best-effort-type traffic. • Explicit QoS grants can be provided to enable specific services on campus by provisioning the appropriate policies. • Classes may need to be streamed; that was a necessity during COVID-19 time frames. Students have started using these recordings even when they attend live sessions to improve their understanding and continue to be helpful. This reduces the number of questions coming to the educators and also improves the quality of the questions and comments raised. **Student access** • Student mobility on campus tends to occur in clusters and is dependent on the day of the week and time of day, typically based on class schedules or large campus events. This requires dynamic rebalancing of radio resources and allocating more resources to locations where a larger student population exists. This rebalancing can be supported by dynamic detection or by predictive techniques that learn patterns on campus. • For specific schools (elementary, middle, and high school), lacking basic internet connectivity, supporting both access to the internet and to the school's intranet,, is a fundamental enabler for these students. Access is provided through CPEs, potentially providing coverage into the residential neighborhood and not just within the school campus, so that kids can complete their homework from the comfort and safety of their homes. **Campus announcements** • Campus announcements (including active shooter scenarios, event notices, etc.) can be done through broadcast multicast services (eMBMS). However, this has not seen commercial success with the macro-networks and is not a supported feature. • A push/pull method through broadcast short message service (SMS) or notifications to the application provided by the institution and installed by the users is required to address this scenario. SMS support requires IMS platforms to be supported, which are currently not compatible with private networks and require the MNO services to be leveraged for this purpose. • The CMAS/ETWS notifications can be used to broadcast to the users using system information block (SIBs); however, the legal aspects of using this approach need to be considered. • Lecture streaming (unicast/broadcast) will be a common use case for campuses, and supporting some form of caching closer to the delivery points will allow for reducing the load on the core networks.

(*Continued*)

Security

- Surveillance cameras help the campus administration manage campus activity to quickly get aid where it is needed and are a great security tool. Given the heavy UL nature of the traffic, aligning the cell that is serving the security camera to have a higher UL capacity will allow for better management of campus resources.
- Currently, campuses have security poles equipped with cameras and a dialing facility to contact campus security or police. However, these poles are spaced at least 1 mile apart, and a lot can happen between them. The chaperone mode feature allows campus security to monitor individuals as they move from one location on the campus to another, for example heading into the parking lot and driving away, or walking from class or lab to the dormitory room. The person requiring assistance triggers the request, and the dashboard allows the user to be tracked throughout the process. The user can turn off the request upon reaching the destination. Any breaks in the routine or lack of communication will trigger campus police to initiate action.

Collaborative camping

- Educational institutions collaborate with similar institutions, while professors and students move between campuses, requiring access to their home institution's network and limited access to the visited institution's network.
- This can be addressed by explicitly supporting roaming authentication and connectivity between interacting institutions.
- Generic roaming support will require an intermediary broker to locate the "home" network for user authentication and establish the routing path for data connectivity from the visited network to the home network.
- See the previous section describing collaborative camping techniques and the suggested approach that can also be utilized by educational institutions.

Campus emergencies

- See the section on "Campus Emergencies" for details on how to trigger, locate, and follow an emergency event, including allowing the person facing the emergency to track the arrival of emergency personnel.
- It is important for the campus security or police to know the number of people in the building, on each floor and in the rooms. Tracking this information has become particularly important for addressing emergencies and ensuring the area has been cleared for further action.

Crowd awareness

- Food breaks can be brief between classes, and knowledge of the crowd at different restaurants on campus and in the immediate vicinity can be very useful when selecting a place to eat. This can be achieved either through a simple camera feed or more complex methods, such as counting the number of people at the restaurants and making that information available on a website for easy access.

LTE/NR and Wi-Fi coexistence

- Supporting a common interface through specific software solutions to allow the end devices to connect to both LTE/NR and Wi-Fi, while dynamically choosing the RAT to route traffic on the UL and DL, would be an ideal approach. See Figure III.4.2.
- A suggested method of tunnel support to enable LTE/NR and Wi-Fi connectivity is captured here as well. LTE/NR and Wi-Fi coexistence can be supported using the evolved packet data gateway (ePDG) node, but it is only supported for IMS services and is a very heavyweight function to introduce into enterprise campuses.
- This approach avoids additional authentication and encryption, given that the UE is already operating on LTE/NR and Wi-Fi after being authenticated, and both of these domains are associated with the given enterprise.

	Private networks allow for all these scenarios to be supported. There will be limitations on capacity, and users may get blocked when serving other higher-priority users/services. A combination of LTE/NR private networks, together with Wi-Fi and appropriate routing of specific traffic on LTE/NR and Wi-Fi, will help address this issue. Location services for several aspects, including emergencies and food delivery, have become essential services. The techniques defined as part of campus emergencies can be leveraged for this purpose. NHN connectivity to extend macro-network connectivity into campuses may also need to be supported based on the support coverage by these MNOs. All the users typically have an MNO subscription as well, and in-building coverage tends to be limited. Enabling NHN on the private networks helps serve as a coverage extension for the MNO and greatly aids the campus population.
Performance criteria	The following performance criteria will help assess the ad hoc network's performance: • QoS support for voice, video, and text in enterprise employees/operational equipment • Internet connectivity for customer devices • Macro-network coverage and in-building NHN coverage; customer device transitions across macro and NHN networks • Campus mobility for all users
Technology concepts to focus on	Revisiting the following concepts from Parts I and II of the book can be useful for network planning and operations: • Mobility and handover mechanisms • SON for DL and UL radio resource planning • RAN and core network connectivity (interfaces) • Security/authentication • Device provisioning • QoS behaviors • NHN support
Post conditions	Augment the Wi-Fi on campus with LTE/NR networks, potentially supporting a common interface to applications and dynamically choosing the RAT to route the UL/DL traffic over. The existing standard definitions can be largely leveraged. The LTE/NR and Wi-Fi transitions and simultaneous operations will require customizations but can be implemented without impacting the existing standards definitions.

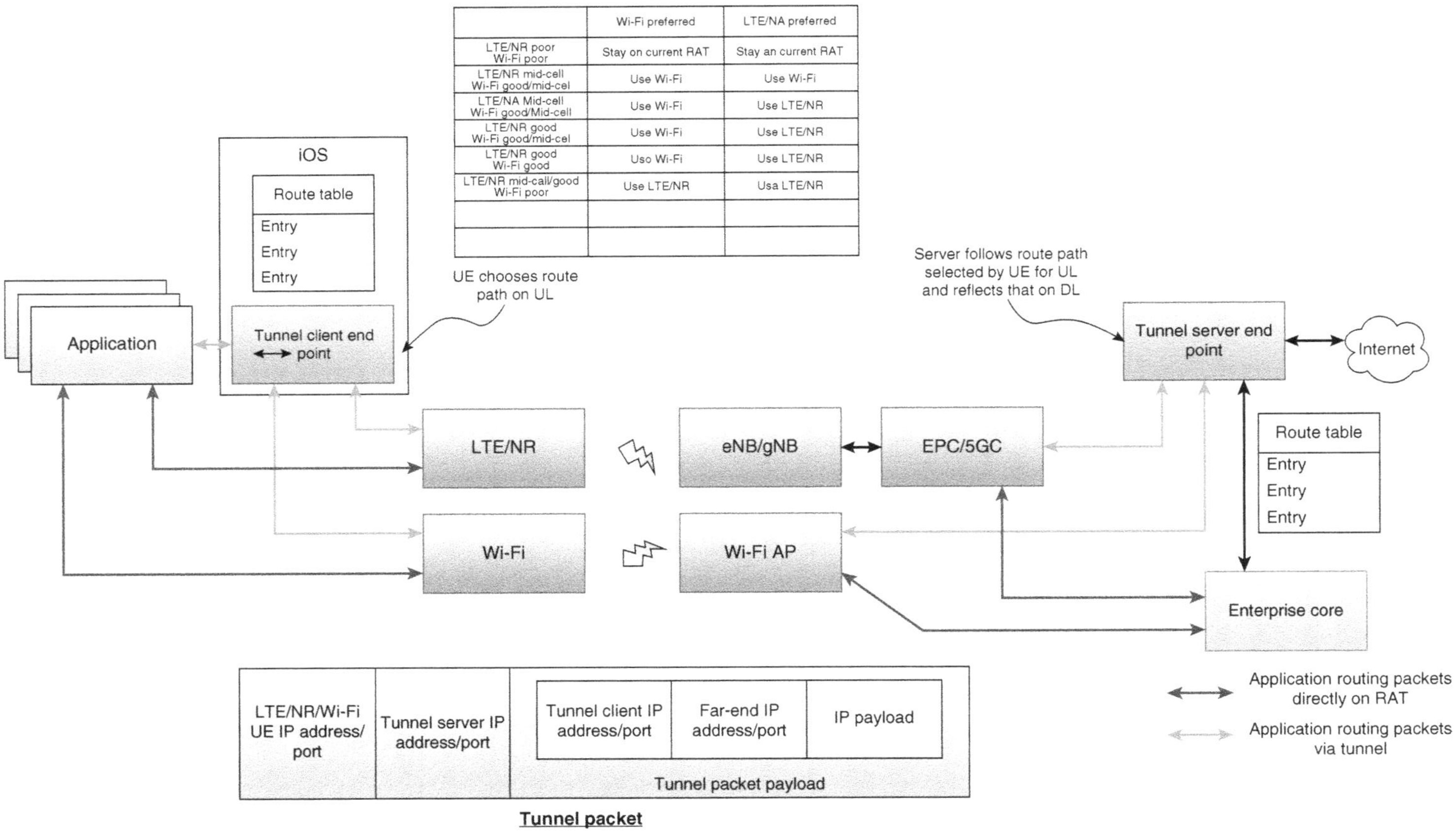

	Wi-Fi preferred	LTE/NA preferred
LTE/NR poor Wi-Fi poor	Stay on current RAT	Stay an current RAT
LTE/NR mid-cell Wi-Fi good/mid-cel	Use Wi-Fi	Use Wi-Fi
LTE/NA Mid-cell Wi-Fi good/Mid-cell	Use Wi-Fi	Use LTE/NR
LTE/NR good Wi-Fi good/mid-cel	Use Wi-Fi	Use LTE/NR
LTE/NR good Wi-Fi good	Uso Wi-Fi	Use LTE/NR
LTE/NR mid-call/good Wi-Fi poor	Use LTE/NR	Usa LTE/NR

Figure III.4.2 Tunnel implementation to support for seamless mobility across LTE/NR and Wi-Fi.

III.4.7 Offices

Title	Offices
Purpose	Support employees in an office.
Triggers	Employees are performing their day-to-day work.
Preconditions	• Wi-Fi coverage is available on office campuses. • MNO coverage may be available on the office campus.
Description	In office work environments, private networks with LTE/NR will augment Wi-Fi connectivity. The IP domains and individual service accesses on the office network need to be regulated based on the user type or group. This is typically done through user login requirements to access specific servers, files, or resources. Private networks can be used for further isolation based on the projects a person is involved in, restricting access by assigning IP addresses specific to VLANs on campus. Additionally, prioritized access may need to be provided to higher tiers of users (e.g. executive staff) to address congestion scenarios. **Executive staff** • Executive staff and certain administrators require priority access over other users. • This can be enabled by supporting different grades of service for non-GBR QoS bearers, such as gold-/silver-/bronze-type users, providing prioritized access even for best-effort-type traffic. • Explicit QoS grants can be provided to enable specific services on campus by provisioning the appropriate policies. • The access class associated with these users needs to be set to a higher-priority level to enable the preemption of other users to accommodate the executive users in the network. **Regular employee** • Employee mobility on campus tends to happen in clusters and is dependent on the day of the week and time of day, typically based on meeting schedules and campus events. This requires dynamic rebalancing of the radio resources and allocating more resources when a larger employee population exists. This rebalancing can be supported by dynamic detection or by predictive techniques learning patterns on campus. Access to company-wide calendar events will allow for knowledge a priori to plan for appropriate resource rebalancing. **Campus announcements** • See the description of educational institutions covered earlier in the chapter, and the mechanisms described there equally apply to office environments. **Streaming services** • Lecture streaming (unicast/broadcast) will be a common use case for campuses, and supporting some form of caching closer to the delivery points will allow for reducing the load on the core networks. • Surveillance cameras help the campus admin manage campus activity to quickly get aid where it is needed and are a great security tool. Given the heavy UL nature of the traffic, aligning the cell that is serving the security camera to have a higher UL capacity will allow for better management of campus resources. **Visitor access** • Visitors on office campuses will require explicit credentials to be granted or revoked. • Supporting an eSIM push to the visitors' devices and also supporting a timer-based expiry of the credential, after which the end user clears the credential from the device, will allow for the same eSIM to be reused for other visitors at a future point. Private networks allow for all these scenarios to be supported. There will be limitations on capacity, and users may get blocked when serving other higher-priority users/services. A combination of LTE/NR private networks, together with Wi-Fi and appropriate routing of specific traffic on LTE/NR and Wi-Fi, will help address this issue.

(Continued)

	Additionally, supporting a common interface through specific software solutions that allow the end devices to connect to both LTE/NR and Wi-Fi, while dynamically choosing the appropriate RAT to route traffic on the UL and DL, would be an ideal approach. See "Educational Institutions" section on LTE/NR and Wi-Fi seamless mobility. All users typically have an MNO subscription as well, and in-building coverage tends to be limited. Enabling NHN on private networks helps serve as a coverage extension for the MNO and greatly aids the campus population.
Performance criteria	The following performance criteria will help assess the ad hoc network performance: • QoS support for voice, video, and text for enterprise employees/operational equipment • Internet connectivity for customer devices • Macro-network coverage and in-building NHN coverage; customer devices transitioning across macro and NHN networks • Campus mobility for all users
Technology concepts to focus on	Revisiting the following concepts from Parts I and II of the book can be useful for network planning and operations: • Mobility and handover mechanisms • SON for DL and UL radio resource planning • RAN and core network connectivity (interfaces) • Security/authentication • RAN slices • Network slices • Device provisioning • Mobile device management (MDM) platforms (not covered in this book) • QoS behaviors • NHN support
Post conditions	Augment the Wi-Fi on campus with LTE/NR networks, potentially supporting a common interface to applications and dynamically choosing the RAT to route the UL/DL traffic. The existing standards definitions can be largely leveraged. Push eSIM credentials to visitors and dynamically release them to be reused for subsequent visitors, as extensions to the current GSMA RSP standards will better enable such scenarios.

III.4.8 Ports

Title	Ports
Purpose	Provide coverage for port employees, shipping container managers, and truck drivers to ease the process of tracking, registration, pickup, and delivery services.
Triggers	• Ships with containers arriving and departing from the port. • Port employees wanting to track specific assets (containers, items, camera feeds, trucks, etc.) • Truck driving arriving/departing from the port.

Preconditions	Port may have coverage with an MNO. Wi-Fi coverage may be available in certain locations.
Description	There is constant and heavy traffic at the ports, which includes ships, docking support provided at the port, and trucks that transport the materials brought in by these ships. The RF environment tends to be exceedingly difficult to handle, given the number of metal structures in place. This can typically be addressed by placing the base stations at a much higher elevation, allowing for a line-of-sight for devices connecting to the networks, thus largely overcoming the metal barriers. Apart from connectivity when at the port, connectivity to the port services may also need to be supported using macro-network connectivity. Specific services may be accessible only within the port, and the core network needs to be designed to allow for both macro and private network connectivity or only private network connectivity. **Ships** • Ships arriving at port can register by providing their details and the port services needed, even as they are docking. • This typically required the ship personnel to walk up to a counter and wait in line to be registered, typically manually by the port employees. • Enabling support through the macro-network and specific services at the port as the ship is docking saves a lot of time. • It also aids the port authorities in managing more easily and better catering to individual ships based on the cargo and the support each ship requires from the port. **Port employees** • The port employees need to readily track activity and specific items, in addition to monitoring camera feeds from anywhere in the port. Several accidents occur, and it requires specific port personnel to manage the movement of containers, items, and trucks. This responsibility may even put them in harm's way, as they are in close proximity to large moving objects. **Trucks** • Trucks arriving and departing from the port are required to enter the port, potentially stopping at an entrance to register. • These can be supported through the private network, avoiding long queues at entry and exit points. • Locating the merchandise and tracking it for quicker loading/offloading significantly speeds up the process. Specific tracker (IoT) can be used to aid locating of the goods. Support for security cameras similar to that of other campuses is needed. All of this can be better handled, and a simpler workflow managed, if these activities can be offloaded to a wireless network with access credentials to perform them. Ports with large containers and trucks tend to have RF coverage issues. However, cellular technology and mounting the antennas higher up (e.g. 80 m) allow for sufficient coverage directly from the cell or reflected from the surrounding metal.
Performance criteria	The following performance criteria will help assess the ad hoc network performance: • RF coverage in the port • Asset tracking • Connectivity to port services from the macro-network and the private network.

(Continued)

Technology concepts to focus on	Revisiting the following concepts from Parts I and II of the book can be useful for network planning and operations: • Mobility and handover mechanisms across macro and private networks • SON for DL and UL radio resource planning • RAN and core network connectivity (interfaces) • Security • PNI-NPN – a network supported by macro-network operations/coverage • NHN – ports enabling connectivity using macro-network subscriptions • Device provisioning – enabling connectivity using a private network subscription
Post conditions	Supporting a private network with LTE/NR provides huge benefits for port operations. The existing standards definitions can be largely leveraged. The RF deployed needs to be customized and is typically addressed by mounting the cells at a high elevation, allowing for radio propagation that avoids the metal container and large trucks.

III.4.9 Warehouse

Title	Warehouse centers
Purpose	Support robots for warehouse operations
Triggers	Robot (bot) mobility for storing and loading products on shelves/trucks.
Preconditions	• Manual operation of driving the bots. • Self-driving with Wi-Fi but encounters poor coverage and does not handle the required mobility speed of 30 km per hour.
Description	This is one of the more challenging use cases for private networks apart from IIoT scenarios. The warehouse has travel lanes and individual bays where the products are marked and stored. The loading and unloading of the trucks can be in-building, outside, or at the threshold. This implies that wireless coverage across the campus indoors, outdoors, and transitions must be handled without breaks in connectivity. The AGVs are equipped with light detection and ranging (LiDAR), cameras that enable local detection capabilities with AI or use remote assistance, travel at a top speed of 30 km per hour, and require periodic docking for recharging purposes. The AGVs exchange information with the control center every 30 ms and typically remain in radio resource control (RRC) connected mode all the time, with packet delays needing to be managed even across handovers from one small cell to another quite frequently. The docking stations for these bots tend to be clustered toward one end of the warehouse, and there will be a large group of bots that need to be accommodated for connectivity in these regions.

The AVGs use LiDAR and cameras to navigate, avoiding objects. Bays are marked with recognizable markers, and the camera system locates the bays and articles within them. Cameras are becoming sophisticated with localized AI and detection, but there are still many AVGs that operate with legacy cameras, requiring the camera feeds to be reliably provided to the control centers for both manual and AI-driven recognition in the servers.

An LTE/NR-based system as a private network with a better cell footprint greatly helps with such scenarios where Wi-Fi does not meet the needs. Even with LTE/NR networks, multiple overlays of cells are required to both address load balancing and avoid dropping connections. Even when a connected is dropped, quick recovery to reconnect is required. Transitioning indoors and outdoors across different types of cells requires careful RF planning. Mobility management becomes key to the operation. Some of the more advanced features of mobility supported in 3GPP, like the CHO and dual active protocol stack (DAPS), will further help with the management of these AVGs. The CHO feature allows the network to provide multiple potential candidates to the device, which, based on subsequent changes in the RF environment, self-triggers the transition to the target cell. DAPS allows the device to maintain the protocol stack with both the current serving and target cell as part of the mobility procedures, enabling the device to ensure that the target connection is established prior to releasing the source. Other finger printing methods to determine the directionality of AGV motion, plan ahead for the handover thresholds, detect know drop points, initiating handover transitions, are employed to overcome any post-deployment issues once the RF environment in the warehouse is established.

Performance criteria

The following performance criteria will help assess the ad hoc network performance:

- QoS support for voice, video, and text for enterprise employees and operational equipment
- Campus mobility AGVs

Technology concepts to focus on

Revisiting the following concepts from Parts I and II of the book can be useful for network planning and operations:

- Mobility and handover mechanisms
- SON for DL and UL radio resource planning
- RAN and core network connectivity (interfaces)
- Security
- QoS behaviors
- Positioning – finer positioning to identify objects and store shelf bays and trucks

Post conditions

The support for AVGs is introduced with LTE/NR private network connectivity. The network is constantly monitored for performance, and local tuning of the parameters is done to ensure the deployment requirements are met. Typically, initially, only a subset of the bots is put on the LTE/NR private networks. As the performance is understood, the migration of the other bots is done slowly. As the number of bots on the LTE/NR private network increases, the network deployment needs to be adjusted to meet the mobility, throughput, congestion, and other performance requirements. Metrics analysis becomes key to the operational maintenance of such networks.

The existing standards definitions can be largely leveraged. Having said that, indoor–outdoor transitions and fast mobility (30 km per hour) speeds require handover procedures to be optimized with much more sophistication than just the basic tuning of the handover thresholds.

III.4.10 Summary

This chapter describes some of the known verticals supported by private networks. By no means should private network applications be limited to these verticals. This is a fast-evolving field, and service demands for these verticals will only grow, including the appearance of other creative verticals in the market.

The use cases are described with the typical aspects that need to be addressed on-site when deploying each vertical. It is highly likely that custom issues will need to be addressed based on the customer, and the key to a successful deployment is finding effective ways to customize to meet the demands rather than choosing a generic, non-adaptable approach. The typical expected performance associated with each vertical, along with the possible technological aspects linked to the concepts introduced in Parts I and II of the book, is also provided to help the reader tie the pieces together.

Looking Ahead

Private networks are one of the key growth areas for wireless communications. This book has detailed the fundamentals of long-term evolution (LTE) and new radio (NR) systems, covered the key technological aspects involved in deploying private networks, and illustrated some potential use cases/industry verticals in play now. All this is very much in its infancy and will rapidly evolve as the demands of the market change. This chapter provides some leading thoughts on where the standards and the industry are heading, with pointers to where the reader can pursue further investigations.

Spectrum for Enterprise Use

Wireless real estate is all about the spectrum that is available for use: spectrum, spectrum, spectrum. Mid- or high-band spectrum; licensed, shared, or unlicensed spectrum; static or dynamic allocation of spectrum;

However nuanced and spectrally efficient the technology, the availability of the spectrum for both indoor and outdoor operations becomes essential. The demand for shared and small footprint localized spectrum allocations is not ubiquitous, and their work is progressing in other regions/countries to enable such spectrum use. Most countries are adopting bands 77, 78, and 79, with a few countries supporting spectrum allocations outside of the 3.1–4.2 GHz range.

With macro network operators (MNOs) also stepping up to become managed service providers (MSPs) for enterprise networks, they are allowing licensed spectrum to be utilized to increase the reliability of the networks. This is done in addition to the use of the available shared spectrum.

There is no straightforward way to understand the private network spectrum allocations in the individual countries other than to follow the regulatory bodies associated with each country. In places like the EU, a few of the countries are coming together and aligning on the spectrum that they plan to allow for private use to both aid the economics and gain from the common vendor pool to select for deployments and avoid fragmentation in the market.

Mobile Communication Systems for Private Networks, First Edition. Srinivasan Balasubramanian.

Standards

3GPP determines the content of Rel-19 in December 2023. The following are some of the key work items (WIs) and study items (SIs) identified:

- Mobile metaverse and extended reality (XR)
- Artificial intelligence/machine learning (AI/ML) model transfer
- Edge computing and mission-critical communications
- Satellite access, unmanned arial vehicle (UAV), and FMRC communications extensions
- Ambient IoT and integrated sensing
- Energy efficiency enhancements
- Network sharing and non-public networks (NPNs)
- Multiple studies on security (e.g. for NPN, real-time communication (RTC), satellite access, and zero trust).

Table 1 provides the list of WIs/SIs covering the NPN in 3GPP.

Table 2 provides the set of WIs/SIs on edge compute definitions in 3GPP. The evolution of this will define the effective integration of public networks into the enterprise system, leveraging the local compute close to the access point where the end-user device is camped when possible.

WinnForum is expanding on the Citizens Broadband Radio Service (CBRS)-based operations. The shared spectrum operations for Wi-Fi and 5G in the 6 GHz region use automatic frequency control (AFC), and an initial version of the specification has been defined with further evolutions being considered. Once the National Spectrum Consortium (NSC)/ Federal Communication Commission (FCC) approve the type of use allowed in the 3.1–3.45 GHz spectrum in the USA, the tiers of users and the nature of sharing will be defined in this forum.

Table 1 3GPP WIs/SIs on NPN.

Name	Acronym	Release	Hyperlink
Study on interconnect of SNPN	FS_ISN	Rel-19	SP-230236
Non-public network security considerations	SecNPN	Rel-19	SP-230523
Study on security for a PLMN hosting an NPN	PLMNNPN_SEC	Rel-19	SP-231786
CT1 aspects of eNPN_Ph2	eNPN_Ph2	Rel-18	CP-231286
CT3 aspects of eNPN_Ph2	eNPN_Ph2	Rel-18	CP-231286
CT4 aspects of eNPN_Ph2	eNPN_Ph2	Rel-18	CP-231286
Stage 2 for eNPN	eNPN	Rel-17	SP-200980
CT aspects of eNPN	eNPN	Rel-17	CP-212103
CT1 aspects of eNPN	eNPN	Rel-17	CP-212103
CT3 aspects of eNPN	eNPN	Rel-17	CP-212103
CT4 aspects of eNPN	eNPN	Rel-17	CP-212103
Security aspects of eNPN	eNPN	Rel-17	SP-210422
Study on media production over 5G NPN	FS_NPN4AVProd	Rel-17	SP-210241
NPN support of PWS	NPN_PWS	Rel-17	SP-210585
IMS emergency support for SNPN	IESNPN	Rel-17	SP-191038
Management of nonpublic networks (NPN)	OAM_NPN	Rel-17	SP-200189

Table 2 3GPP WIs/SIs on edge computing.

Name	Acronym	Release	Hyperlink
Edge computing considering the operational needs of service hosting environment	EdgeOpNeeds	Rel-19	SP-231037
Study on enhancement of support for edge computing in 5G core network – phase 3	FS_eEDGE_5GC_Ph3	Rel-19	SP-231796
Edge computing for industrial scenarios	EDGINDUS	Rel-19	SP-230229
Architecture for enabling edge applications: phase 3	EDGEAPP_Ph3	Rel-19	SP-231160
Rel-18: edge computing	–	Rel-18	–
Architecture for enabling edge applications, phase 2	EDGEAPP_Ph2	Rel-18	SP-221231
(Stage 2 of EDGEAPP_Ph2) architecture for enabling edge applications, phase 2	EDGEAPP_Ph2	Rel-18	SP-221231
CT1 aspects of EDGEAPP_Ph2	EDGEAPP_Ph2	Rel-18	CP-233114
CT3 aspects of EDGEAPP_Ph2	EDGEAPP_Ph2	Rel-18	CP-233114
Edge application standards in 3GPP and alignment with external organizations	EDGEAPP_EXT	Rel-18	SP-231156
Study on enhanced architecture for enabling edge applications	FS_eEDGEAPP	Rel-18	SP-211510
Edge computing phase 2	FS_EDGE_Ph2	Rel-18	
Study on edge computing, phase 2	FS_EDGE_Ph2	Rel-18	SP-220070
Study on stage 2 of edge computing phase 2	FS_EDGE_Ph2	Rel-18	SP-220352
Study on security of edge computing, phase 2	FS_EDGE_Ph2	Rel-18	SP-220201
(stage 2 of) edge computing phase 2	EDGE_Ph2	Rel-18	SP-230112
CT3 aspects of EDGE_Ph2	EDGE_Ph2	Rel-18	CP-233026
CT4 aspects of EDGE_Ph2	EDGE_Ph2	Rel-18	CP-233026
Security aspects of support for edge computing in 5G-C phase 2	EDGE_Ph2	Rel-18	SP-230366
Enhanced edge-computing management	eECM	Rel-18	SP-230775
Study on alignment with ETSI MEC for edge computing management	FS_MEC_ECM	Rel-18	SP-220147
Rel-17 edge computing	–	Rel-17	–
Architecture for enabling edge applications	EDGEAPP	Rel-17	SP-200109
Study on application architecture for enabling edge applications	FS_EDGEAPP	Rel-17	SP-190065
Architecture for enabling edge applications	EDGEAPP	Rel-17	SP-200886
CT aspects for enabling edge applications	EDGEAPP	Rel-17	CP-211196
CT1 aspects for EDGEAPP	EDGEAPP	Rel-17	CP-221106
CT3 aspects for EDGEAPP	EDGEAPP	Rel-17	CP-211196
CT4 aspects for EDGEAPP	EDGEAPP	Rel-17	CP-211196
Study on enhancement of support for edge computing in 5GC	FS_enh_EC	Rel-17	SP-200093
Enhancement of support for edge computing in 5G core network	eEDGE_5GC	Rel-17	SP-201107

(Continued)

Table 2 (Continued)

Name	Acronym	Release	Hyperlink
Stage 2 of eEDGE_5GC	eEDGE_5GC	Rel-17	SP-201107
CT aspects of 5G eEDGE	eEDGE_5GC	Rel-17	CP-212021
CT1 aspects of 5G eEDGE	eEDGE_5GC	Rel-17	CP-212021
CT3 aspects of 5G eEDGE	eEDGE_5GC	Rel-17	CP-212021
CT4 aspects of 5G eEDGE	eEDGE_5GC	Rel-17	CP-212021
Security aspects of enhancements of support for edge computing in 5GC	eEDGE_5GC	Rel-17	SP-210423
Edge computing management	ECM	Rel-17	SP-210388
Study on security aspects of enhancement of support for edge computing in 5GC	FS_eEDGE_Sec	Rel-17	SP-200347
Edge extensions to 5GMS, stage 3	5GMS_EDGE_3	Rel-17	SP-211336
Charging aspects of edge computing	EDGE_CH	Rel-17	SP-210861
Study on charging aspects of edge computing	FS_EDGE_CH	Rel-17	SP-200467
Charging aspects of edge computing	EDGE_CH	Rel-17	SP-210861
Study on enhancements of edge computing management	FS_eEDGE_Mgt	Rel-17	SP-200195
Edge extensions to the 5G media-streaming architecture	5GMS_EDGE	Rel-17	SP-210375
Study on streaming architecture extensions for edge processing	FS_EMSA	Rel-17	SP-200056
Study on management aspects of edge computing	FS_MAN_EC	Rel-16	SP-180390

The open radio access network (O-RAN) alliance is working toward "intent-based" RAN intelligent controlled (RIC) operations, enabling specific use-case realizations that can be directly utilized in deployments. There are also many security aspects being raised for open RAN solutions, and the O-RAN alliance is working toward specifications that provide implementation approaches that allow for improving the security postures of the individual deployments. The O-RAN alliance also maintains the eCPRI interface and will continue to evolve to address newer challenges.

The MuLTEFire alliance is working toward viable device profiles that can be utilized for private networks. This involves defining parameterizations across the wireless stack, from the radio frequency/physical layer (RF/Phy), medium access control (MAC), L2, and L3 protocols associated with the user equipment (UE) modem realizations.

Small Cell Forum is continuing to evolve the interfaces that best apply to small cells, primarily basing them on the option-6 definition of the network radio stack implementation using the nFAPI protocol.

AI/ML

Given that private networks are typically designed to meet enterprises' specialized demands, they naturally lend themselves to fine-tuning the deployment using AI/ML. This includes learnings across the private network LTE/NR RAN, core, enterprise core, and intranet and internet applications. From the 3GPP standardization process, the first release of 5G-advanced in Release 18 involves a comprehensive study, including the establishment of the data collection framework with the definition of the network data analytics function (NWDAF). This is intended to be a stepping stone toward 6G. The intent is to create a platform to normalize the information collected and use the learnings from the standardized data archives to allow for models to be trained for specific optimizations in the UE and network. See "AI/ML Management for 5G Systems," which provides an overview of the current happenings in 3GPP, including the AI/ML specifications and study item references.

See Figure 1. The different forms of AI supporting spectral efficiency, asset utilization, and enabling new applications are some high-level goals. There are several collaboration levels based on the interactions between the UE and the network. These include one-sided interactions, where each UE and network perform the learning independently, and two-sided interactions, where the learning is performed across both the UE and the network.

As such, prior to 5G-advanced, AI/ML is employed in several scenarios in a wireless network, including traffic type detection to enable specific quality of service (QoS) preferential treatments. The end-to-end behavior for an enterprise application is also emerging for a tighter integration with the wireless platforms.

The current efforts in 3GPP are focused on employing AI/ML toward radio air interface optimizations and RAN behaviors. The illustration provides the ongoing activities on the data collection, air interface, and RAN-level optimizations planned using AI/ML. These mechanisms equally apply for private network deployment as with macro networks. The learnings from the macro networks may not be directly applicable to private networks and will likely require independent data collection on the private networks for the associated optimizations. Also, note that the problems that need to be addressed in private networks will be different and potentially disjoint from those in macro networks.

The scope of the 3GPP study on AI/ML for the NR air interface included the development of a general AI/ML framework, along with the exploration of specific use cases such as channel state information (CSI) feedback, beam management, and positioning.

CSI refers to the channel state information provided from the UE by measuring the downlink (DL) reference signals and reporting in real time for the network to determine the modulation and coding used for scheduling the UE. AI/ML-based algorithms for CSI feedback enhancements of spatial-frequency domain CSI compression and time domain CSI prediction with a UE-sided model are being studied. With CSI compression, UE uses an AI/ML-based CSI encoder to generate CSI feedback information, while a corresponding AI/ML-based CSI decoder at the gNB is used to reconstruct the CSI from the received compressed information. This two-sided AI/ML model can be employed to compress either the raw channel matrix estimated by the UE or the precoding matrix derived from the raw channel matrix, which aligns with the existing codebook-based CSI feedback framework specified for the NR air interface.

For beam management support with AI/ML, two representative sub-use cases are being studied. They are "spatial-domain downlink beam prediction" and "temporal downlink beam prediction." Spatial-domain downlink beam prediction leverages measurement outcomes from a designated set of downlink beams, denoted as "Set B," to predict the best beam within another set of downlink beams, termed "Set A." Temporal downlink beam prediction harnesses historical measurement results derived from "Set B" to anticipate the best beam in "Set A" for one or more future time instances.

For positioning, two representative sub-uses are being investigated. These have been termed "direct AI/ML positioning" and "AI/ML-assisted positioning." Direct AI/ML positioning employs an AI/ML model to directly determine the location of UE. This can involve fingerprinting-based

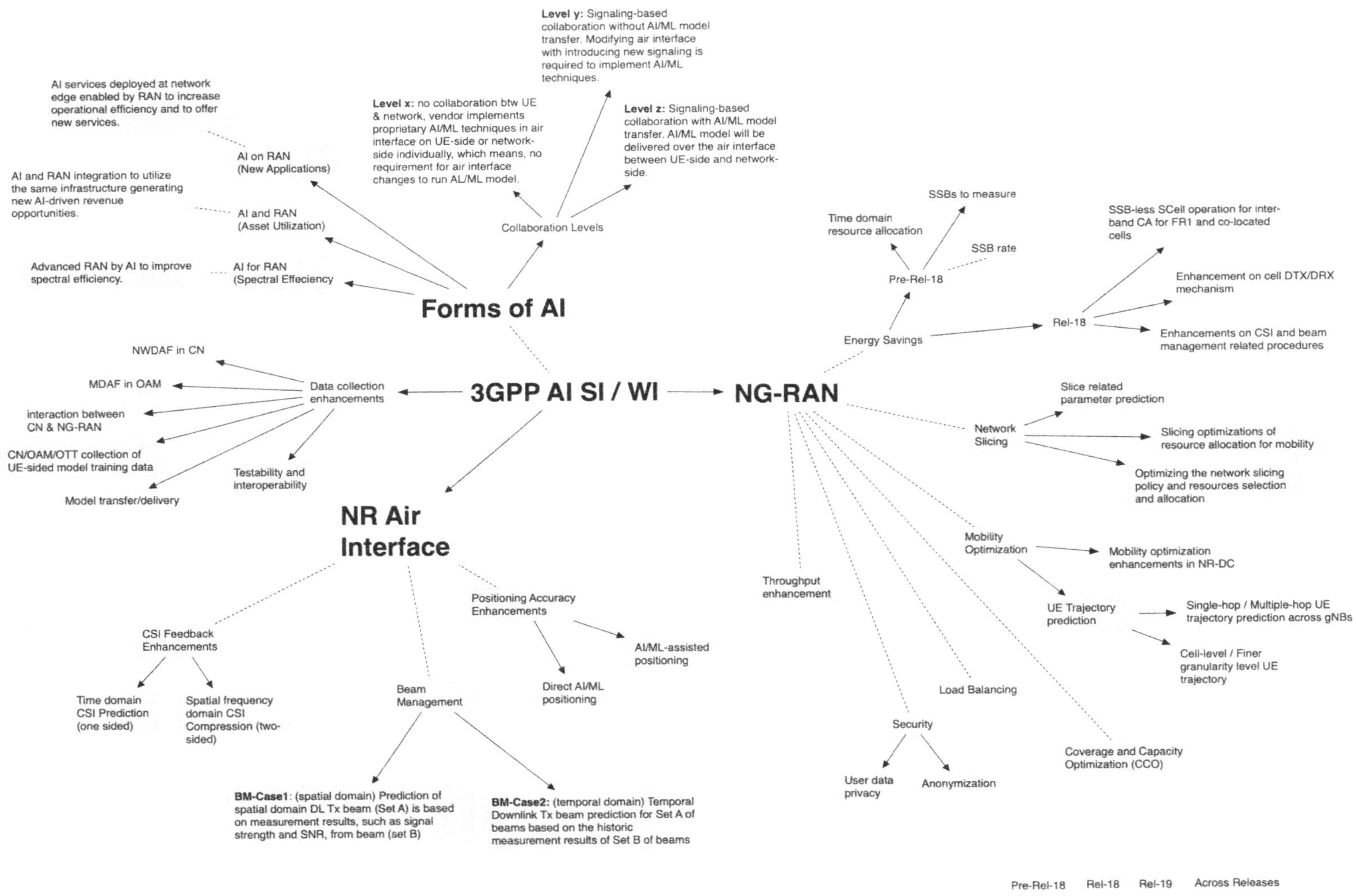

Figure 1 3GPP AI/ML focus areas.

positioning utilizing channel observations, such as channel impulse response or power delay profile, as input to the AI/ML model. AI/ML-assisted positioning involves leveraging an AI/ML model to generate an intermediate measurement statistic involving measurements such as line of sight (LOS) probability, angle-of-arrival/departure (AoA/AoD), or observed-time-difference-of-arrival (OTDOA).

The RAN optimizations using AI/ML include network energy saving (NES), mobility, load balancing, cell shaping, security, throughput enhancements, and network slice operations, which are some of the items currently envisioned.

The comfort of AI/ML is that the behaviors can be quickly trained or tuned. The downside of that is that intuition may be lost, and the total reliance on the trained models can be unnerving. All this hinges on effective data collection and clear identification of the relevant data sets to exemplify the network(s) being optimized. The information used for training and defining AI models for sharing needs to be carefully curated, and the network operational metrics should be closely monitored and adapted to prevent undesirable behavior.

Use-Case Evolution

Private Public Integration

Although 3GPP has defined NPN, all the market realizations are based on legacy approaches for system camping, association, and connectivity for private networks. For NR, it is based on 3GPP Release 15 and proprietary approaches. The MNOs have so far not enabled a path to providing support using public networks with the required isolation and local connectivity needed for enterprise network access. Multi-SIM credential provisioning, inter-private network roaming, and seamless roaming across public and private networks will determine how mainstream private networks will evolve. All this requires both creative business use cases and technically viable solutions to address those scenarios in a practical way. Given that the individual enterprises have distinct needs, a single solution that fits all will likely not be the way to go. A more flexible, modular approach that brings the required pieces together based on the scenario will be required.

If we are to follow the money on this, enterprise private network deployments are happening now and are operating well in isolated environments given the demand for indoor footprint. Traditional MNOs with the existing technology are already riding this wave using neutral host solutions, Wi-Fi calling solutions (using IP multimedia subsystem (IMS) packet data network (PDN) connectivity via the evolved packet data gateway (ePDG) node over the LTE/NR private network like Wi-Fi), and dual SIM solutions for both treating these networks as coverage extensions and offload purposes. Having said that, finding the appropriate private network-based connectivity to transition to the macro network and supporting localized user plane function (UPF) are far from reality, and significant work needs to happen on both the network and UE sides to enable seamless transitions.

Digital Twins

3GPP is working on a SI "study on management aspects of network digital twin," FS_NDT, as part of Rel-19, and is captured in SP-231428.

Next G Alliance, an Alliance for Telecommunications Industry Solutions (ATIS) initiative, is working toward defining a 6G system digital twin representation. An extracted excerpt is captured here for convenience. The paper "6G Technology White Paper on Management and Orchestration" covers the 6G system or subsystem, including physical and logical parts, digitally. A digital representation regularly synchronized with the real system is often called a digital twin. This paper discusses the operations, observability, optimization, enabling, and realization of innovations. The intent is that new functions and features will be added and tested in the twin system before being rolled out in the real 6G system. These digital representations are used for advanced modeling and simulations, allowing multiple technologies to merge and provide a truly versatile view of the ecosystem, including the propagation aspects involved, thus improving 6G network performance.

Also, refer to the following items for ongoing work on digital twins.

- Digital twin network – requirements and architecture as defined by International Telecommunication Union's recommendations (ITU-T Y.3090). https://www.itu.int/rec/T-REC- Y.3090-202202-I/en.
- Zero touch and service management (ZSM); network digital twin (European Telecommunications Standards Institute's (ETSI) group report (GR), ETSI GR ZSM-015). https://docbox.etsi.org/isg/ZSM/Open/Drafts/015_Nwk_DTwin/ZSM-015_Nwk_DTwinv002.docx
- The Network Management Research Group (NMRG) of the Internet Engineering Task Force (IETF.org). https://datatracker.ietf.org/rg/nmrg/about.

Metaverse

It is hard to talk about metaverse given the expansive scope and the nebulousness of actual realizations in the market. It is also hard not to talk about it, with a full industry focus involving many major companies, from start-ups to multibillion-dollar companies and research organizations putting in extensive resources to solve some critical problems. A lot of the focus is on the hardware aspects and supporting the camera, display, and compute environments, including distributed computation for rendering.

The 3GPP standards body has started defining stage 1 requirements for the metaverse in 3GPP Technical Specification (TS) 22.156, focusing on services and system aspects; mobile metaverse services specification as part of Rel-19.

The following is the stage 1 scope from the 3GPP TS 22.156 specification:

The present document provides stage 1 normative service and performance requirements for diverse service enablers to enhance XR-based services. The term "metaverse" in the title of the present document embraces the broader implications of AR and VR.

Service enablers considered in this document include:

- *Localized mobile metaverse service functionality*
- *Avatar-based, real-time communication functionality*
- *Digital asset management functionality*
- *Operation efficiency, exposure, and coordination of mobile metaverse services*

A lot of the metaverse depends heavily on a localized service to support an immersive experience, integrated with the other activities of the user, providing localized experiences based on the user's environment and integrating the physical world with the mobile experiences. To enable these spatial anchors, they need to be discovered and accessed. The metaverse is seen mostly as a third-party service with policies defined for access to be enabled from the operator-based connectivity. This can equally be envisioned by using private network connectivity with the enterprise supporting the required metaverse services. The fundamental operations of metaverse depend on avatars, which are digital representations of entities like organizations, individual users, groups of users, and even fictitious characters, creating the required experience for the individual user. The gestures and expressions of these avatars need to be managed by the 5G system, and capturing this in a standardized form helps with the ease of creation of an animated digital representation of the individual avatar, e.g. facial expressions. Creating predictive and contextual gestures and experiences allows for smoother rendering, even when there are glitches in information delivery across the 5G system. The device and user capability, apart from the subscription aspects, need to be accommodated through the process. Given that the operator-based services, together with a well-identified user, are centered around IMS, metaverse integration with IMS will be required for a more scalable solution. It is entirely possible that metaverse can be supported without IMS using localized credentials and an isolated service definition within an enterprise network. Effective digital asset management is required for both user and network resources so that they are uniquely recognized in the metaverse for connectivity, authentication, authorization, and avatar representation. With the metaverse services enabled, performance requirements need to be rendered effectively for end-to-end operations by the 5G system by adapting to changes in the conditions of the interconnecting networks and dynamically supporting the QoS demands to meet the end-to-end requirements.

This area will evolve in the coming years and will make viable some overly critical, innovative use cases in the market.

Block Chain – Roaming as a Service (Long-Range-Style Operations)

Helium (www.helium.com) is enabling blockchain-based CBRS networks along with neutral host operations on those cells. The access points are purchased and self-installed by generic individuals, potentially at their residences or other locations where they have access to install these cells.

These cells offer private network connectivity but will typically require the individual hosting the cell or network to support credential distribution and will be very restrictive. It is possible that the request is routed through the Helium network for access, with the individual hosting the network authorizing the credential allocation.

The typical use of these cells is to employ them as a neutral host network. The public land mobile networks (PLMNs) of MNO are broadcast based on agreements in place to act as network extensions to individual MNOs.

Blockchain-based wireless service coverage and availability are employed to verify credibility of the end-user devices wanting to camp on Helium-based cells. This should address the extent of QoS support available on these as well.

Neutral host networks require extensive certification with specific operations and are typically targeted toward enterprise deployment, with known locations of neutral host network (NHN) offload planned by the MNO. The Helium approach of deploying these cells, potentially where there may already be MNO coverage, is playing out in the market.

This is certainly an interesting approach and tries to commoditize 4G/5G coverage subject to spectrum availability. At a minimum, this approach is bound to bring about some changes to the market dynamics involved.

Leveraging Defined Technologies

Proximity services (ProSe) allow for innovative use cases to be realized with devices in proximity to talk to each other without involving the network. This allows for connectivity even in harsh RF environments and in isolated regions with minimal communication delays. Using device-to-device and cooperative communications allows for objects moving relative to each other to coordinate their movements, avoid collisions, and even perform combined tasks.

Multicast services, without having to use connectivity to individual devices, allow for campus-wide communications and alters. Although the technology has been well defined, a genuine business use case has been identified using macro networks. This can be highly effective within an enterprise campus and should be investigated for inclusion in the campus deployments.

Slicing, both RAN and network slicing, although defined in 3GPP, has seen marginal adoption in the market. Slicing allows for better partitioning and sharing of resources, and some of the techniques involved are discussed earlier in this book.

Understand high RF-constrained environments; aspects of fractional frequency reuse (FFR), both within and across private network deployments, can be employed. This requires a fair amount of sophistication, including information exchanges and cooperation across the neighboring networks to solve the resource constraints.

Effective ways to monitor the quality of experience (QoE) of different enterprise applications are required without having to only look at the link-level metrics with some implicit assumptions about the needs of the application. An end-to-end understanding needs to be developed, and the QoS adaptation should be provided based on the real-time needs, adjusting to the changes in the hops that are not directly under the control of the deployed private network in the enterprise.

Commoditizing LTE/NR

When one mentions Wi-Fi, the connotation of "free" is tagged along with it. The Wi-Fi chipset costs are also extremely low compared to the cellular modems. LTE/NR are seen to be complex technologies, and hopefully, this book will demystify some of that and everyone feels comfortable venturing into it.

Commoditizing LTE/NR will become fundamental to the traction that it is seeing. Ranging from high-complexity devices for IIoT all the way to extremely low-cost IoT devices, with a full dynamic range of device types including handsets and commercial premise equipment (CPE), a reduced-complexity integration without requiring too much sophistication and understanding of the underlying technology involved will be necessary for building a strong ecosystem of device vendors.

Every cellular-based device built now requires high integration effort with optimizations considered in the individual layers across the protocol stack and application layers, apart from high certification costs in the individual countries. An improved streamlining of these aspects will be required to enable the private network market.

The networks will need to evolve so that they can be shipped to the site and self-installed by enterprise personnel without requiring in-depth knowledge of the system. For scalability, treating LTE/NR private networks as a service is required. The RF planning aspects are challenging and now require a site visit/survey to assess. With sufficient learning from different deployments, the demands of the private network and the RF environment can be more easily assessed for the initial installation of the network. The network can be further optimized based on monitoring of the activities and the issues seen with the network as part of the acceptance tests and adjustments made afterward. This requires metrics collection from both the network and end-user devices, and such monitoring can be continually used to optimize the deployed network. Learnings from one network can also be leveraged for other networks.

Small cell deployment today remains the most challenging aspect of private network deployments. The core network and integration into the enterprise environment are also challenging, given the numerous variants and specialized choices made within each enterprise.

These aspects will need to be resolved to support with ease the integration of the different pieces to bring together a private network, particularly with multiple vendors involved. Currently, system integrators are required to address the needs of the enterprises and make multiple visits to the site to deploy private networks. Any automation introduced into the process is going to save considerable time and money and determine the success of private networks.

Redefinition of the RAN architecture, using the local and cloud compute and modular functions defined, allows for a very flexible architectural realizations. The hardware compute resources available for such deployments are rapidly evolving, with general-purpose processing units and neural network processing units from highly efficient digital signal processing (DSP) units all changing the landscape for both RAN and core network architectures. We are inching closer and closer to fully software-defined radios, which, although not very practical now, will become viable in the not-so-distant future.

Acronyms

AAA	Authentication, authorization and accounting
ABS	Almost Blank Subframes
AC	Access Class
ACIA	Alliance for Connected Industries and Automation
ACM	Association for Computing Machinery
ADC	Analog to Digital Conversion
AFC	Automatic Frequency Control
AI	Artificial Intelligence
AKA	Authentication and Key Agreement
AM	Assured Mode
AMBR	Aggregate Maximum Bit Rate
AMF	Access and Mobility Management Function
AOI	Area of Interest
AP	Access Point
AP	Application Protocol
API	Application Programming Interface
APN	Access Point Name
ARFCN	Absolute Frequency Channel Number
ARQ	Automatic Repeat Request
ATIS	Alliance for Telecommunications Industry Solutions
ATSSS	Access Traffic Steering-Switching-Splitting
AVB	Audio Video Bridge
AWS	Amazon Web Services
BAT	Burst Arrival Time
BE	Best Effort
BLER	Block Error Rate
BM	Beam Management
BS	Base Station
BT	BlueTooth®
BW	Bandwidth
CA	Carrier Aggregation
CBRS	Citizen Broadband Radio Service
CBSD	Citizen Broadband Radio Service Device

Mobile Communication Systems for Private Networks, First Edition. Srinivasan Balasubramanian.

CCS	Conference on Computer and Communications Security
CDMA	Code Division Multiple Access
CDT	Control Data Traffic
CE	Control Element
CEPT	Conference of Postal and Telecommunications Administrations
CFR	Code of Federal Regulations
CHAP	Challenge-Handshake Authentication Protocol
CMAS	Commercial Mobile Alert System
CMMS	computerized maintenance management system
CP	Control Plane
CPE	Commercial Premise Equipment
CPI	Certified Professional Installer
CPR	Cardiopulmonary resuscitation
CPU	Central Processing Unit
CQI	Channel Quality Indicator
CRM	Customer Relationship Management
CRS	Cell-Specific Reference Signal
CS	Circuit-Switch
CSG	Closed Subscriber Group
CSI	Channel State Information
CTIA	Cellular Telephone Industries Association
CTS	Clear To Send
CU	Central Unit
CUPS	Control and User Plane Separation
CW	Contention Window
DAC	Digital to Anlog Conversion
DAS	Distributed Antenna System
DCS	Distributed Control System
DFT	Discrete Fourier Transform
DHCP	Dynamic Host Configuration Protocol
DL	Downlink
DL-SCH	Downlink Shared Channel
DMRS	Demodulation Reference Signal
DMZ	Demilitarized Zone
DN	Data Network
DNN	Data Network Name
DNS	Domain Name Service
DP	Decentralized Periphery Domain Proxy
DRB	Dedicated Radio Bearer
DSP	Digital Signal Processing
DU	Distributed Unit
E-UTRAN	Evolved Universal Terrestrial Radio Access Network
EAP	Extensible Authentication Protocol
EARFCN	E-UTRA Absolute Radio Frequency Channel Number
ECC	European Consumer Centres Network
ECGI	E-UTRAN cell global identifier

ECM	Edge Computing Management
ECS	Environmental Sensing Capability
eMBMS	evolved Multimedia Broadcast Multicast Service
eNB	Evolution Node B
EPC	Evolved Packet Core
EPDCCH	Enhanced PDCCH
ePDG	evolved Packet Data Gateway
EPS	Evolved Packet System
ERP	Enterprise Resource Planning
ESP	Encapsulating Security Protocol
ETSI	European Telecommunications Standards Institute
ETWS	Earthquake and Tsunami Warning System
EU	European Union
eUICC	evolved UICC
EUTRA	Evolved UMTS Terrestrial Radio Access
EUTRAN	Evolved-UMTS Terrestrial Radio Access Network
EVDO	Evolution Data Optimized
FCC	Federal Communication Commission
FDD	Frequency Division Duplex
FDMA	Frequency Division Multiple Access
FQDN	Fully Qualified Domain Name
GAA	General Authorized Access
GBR	Guaranteed Bit Rate
GERAN	GSM EDGE Radio Access Network
GL	Ground Level
gNB	g Node B
GPL	GNU General Public License
GPRS	General Packet Radio Service
GPS	Global Positioning System
GR	Group Report
GRPC	Google Remote Procedure Calls
GSC	GAA spectrum coordination
GSM	Global System for Mobile communication
GSMA	Global System for Mobile Communications Association
GTP	GPRS Tunneling Protocol
GUTI	Globally Unique Temporary Identifier
GW	Gateway
HARQ	Hybrid Automatic Repeat Request
HDMI	High-Definition Multimedia Interface
HMI	Human Machine Interface
HRPD	High Rate Packet Data
HSS	Home Subscriber Server
HTTP	HyperText Transfer Protocol.
HVAC	Heating, Ventilation, and Air Conditioning
HW	Hardware
IBN	IMSI Block Number

ICI	Inter-Cell Interference
ID	Identifier
IE	Information Element
IEC	International Electrotechnical Commission
IEEE	Institute of Electrical and Electronics Engineers
IEFT	Internet Engineering Task Force
IMEISV	International Mobile Equipment Identity Software Version
IMS	IP Multimedia Subsystem
IMSI	International Mobile Subscriber Identity
IP	Internet Protocol
IRAT	Inter Radio Access Technology
ISA	International Society of Automation
ISO	International Organization for Standardization
IT	Information Technology
ITU	International Telecommunication Union
JSON	JavaScript Object Notation
KPI	Key Performance Indicator
LAN	Local Area Network
LAN	Local Area Network
LBO	Local Breakout
LBT	Listen Before Talk
LBT	Listen Before Talk
LCID	Logical Channel Identifier
LDPC	Low-Density Parity Check
LMF	Location management function
LoRA	Long Range Radio Access Network
LOS	Line Of Sight
LTE	Long Term Evolution
LTM	L1/L2 Triggered Mobility
LTO	Local Traffic Offload
LWA	LTE/WLAN Aggregation
MAC	Medium Access Control
MBR	Maximum Bit Rate
MCC	Mobile Country Code
MCC	Mobile Country Code
MCG	Master Cell Group
MCPTT	Mission-Critical Push-To-Talk
MCS	Modulation and Coding Scheme
MDM	Mobile Device Management
MEC	Multi-Access Edge Compute
MIMO	Multiple-Input Multiple-Output
ML	Machine Learning
MME	Mobility Management Entity
MNC	Mobile Network Code
MNO	Macro Network Operator
MO	Mobile Originated

MOCN	Multiple Operator Core Network
MOS	Mean Opinion Score
MPLS	MultiProtocol Label Switching
MRC	Maximal Ratio-Combining
MWC	Mobile World Congress
NAS	Non-Access Stratum
NASCAR	National Association for Stock Car Auto Racing.
NATS	Neural Autonomic Transport System
NB	Node B
NDI	New Data Indicator
NED	Network Element Driver
NG	Next Generation
NGRAN	Next Generation Radio Access Network
NHN	Neutral Host Network
NIST	National Institute of Standards and Technology
NLOS	Non Line of sight
NPN	Non-Public Network
NPRM	Notice of Proposed Rulemaking
NR	New Radio
NSA	Non-Standalone
NSC	National Spectrum Consortium
NSSAI	Network Slice Selection Assistance Information
NTIA	National Telecommunications and Information Administration
OAM	Operations, Administration, and Management
OCC	Orthogonal Cover Code
OFDM	Orthogonal Frequency Division Multiplexing
OFDMA	Orthogonal Frequency-Division Multiple Access
OLE	Object Linking and Embedding
OPC	Open Platform Communications
OPC UA	Open Platform Communications Unified Architecture
ORAN	Open RAN
OSI	Open Systems Intercommunication
PAL	Priority Access Licenses
PAP	Password Authentication Protocol
PATTHS	Partnering to Advance Trusted and Holistic Spectrum Solutions
PBCH	Physical Broadcast Channel
PCF	Policy Control Function
PCFICH	Physical Control Format Indicator Channel
PDB	Packet Delay Budget
PDCCH	Physical Downlink Control Channel
PDCP	Packet Data Convergence Protocol
PDN	Packet Data Network
PDSCH	Physical Downlink Shared Channel
PDU	Protocol Data Unit
PER	Packet Error Rate
PF	Proportional-Fair

PGW	Packet Gateway
PHICH	Physical channel HybridARQ Indicator Channel
PHICH	Physical Hybrid ARQ Indicator Channel
PHY	Physical Layer
PI	PROFIBUS & PROFINET International
PKI	Public Key Infrastructure
PLC	Programmable Cogic Controller
PLMN	Public Land Mobile Network
PMI	Pre-coding Matrix Indicator
PNI	Public Network Integrated
PPA	PAL Protection Area
PRACH	Physical Random Access Channel
PRB	Physical Resource Block
PS	Packet Switched
PSAP	Public-Safety Answering Point
PSCH	Physical Uplink Shared Channel
PSK	Pre-shared Key
PSS	Primary synchronization Signal
PTP	Precision Time Protocol
PTRS	Phase Tracking Reference Signal
PUCCH	Physical Uplink Control Channel
PUSCH	Physical Uplink Shared Channel
PWS	Public Warning System
QCI	QoS Class Identifier
QI	Quality Indicator
QoS	Quality of Service
QPSK	Quadrature Phase Shift Keying
QUIC	Quick UDP Internet Connections
RAB	Radio Access Bearer
RACH	Random Access Channel
RAN	Radio Access Network
RAT	Radio Access Technology
RB	Resource Block
RE	Resource Element
REST	Representational State Transfer
RF	Radio Freqency
RFC	Request For Comment
RFID	Radio Frequency Identifier
RI	Rank Indicator
RIC	RAN Intelligent Controlled
RLC	Radio Link Control
RLF	Radio Link Failure
RLM	Radio Link Monitoring
RNTI	Radio Network Temporary Identifier
RQI	Reflective QoS Indicator
RRC	Radio Resource Control

RRM	Radio Resource Manager
RS	Reference Signal
RSA	Rivest–Shamir–Adleman
RSP	Remote SIM provisioning
RSRP	Reference Signal Receive Power
RSRQ	Reference Signal Received Quality
RSSI	Received Signal Strength Indicator
RSVP	Répondez s'il vous plaît
RTC	RealTime Communications
RTP	Real Time Protocol
RTS	Ready to Send
RTT	Round Trip Time
RU	Radio Unit
SA	Standalone
SAP	Service Access Point
SAS	Spectrum Access System
SCADA	Supervisory Control and Data Acquisition
SCF	Small Cell Forum
SCG	Secondary Carrier Group
SCH	Shared Channel
SCS	SubCarrier Spacing
SDAP	Service Data Adaptation Protocol
SDK	Software Development Kit
SDU	Service Data Unit
SEPP	Security Edge Protection Proxy
SF	SubFrame
SGP	SIM Group Protocol
SGSN	Serving GPRS Support Node
SGW	Serving Gateway
SIB	System Information Block
SIM	Subscriber Identity Module
SINR	Signal to Interference and Noise Ratio
SINR	Signal to Noise Interference Ratio
SIP	Session Initiation Protocol
SL	Sidelink
SLA	Service Level Agreement
SLO	Service Level Objective
SM	Service Management
SMF	Session Management Function
SMO	Service Management and Orchestration
SMS	Short Message Service
SNR	Signal To Noise Ratio
SO	Second Order
SOAP	Simple Object Access Protocol
SON	Self Organizing Network
SR	Scheduling Request

SRB	Signaling Radio Bearer
SRP	Stream Reservation Protocol
SRS	Sounding Reference Signal
SRVCC	Single Radio Voice Call Continuity
SSC	Spectrum Sharing Committee
SSF	Special SubFrame
SSID	Service Set Identifier
SSS	Secondary Synchronization Signal
SSS	Secondary synchronization Signal
SUCI	Subscriber Concealed Identity
TAC	Tracking Area Code
TAI	Tracking Area Identity
TAU	Tracking Area Update
TBD	To Be Determined
TCP	Transmission Control Protocol
TDD	Time Division Duplex
TKN	Token
TKNMNO	Token for an MNO
TLS	Transport Layer Security
TM	Transparent Mode
TMNO	Tokens for MNO
TMSI	Temporary Mobile Subscriber Identities
TPC	Transmit Power Control
TPMI	Transmitted Precoding Matrix Indicator
TR	Technical Report
TS	Technical Specification
TS	Technical Specification
TSC	Time Sensitive Communications
TSCAL	Time Sensitive Communication Assistance Information
TSCTSF	Time Sensitive Communication Time Synchronization Function
TSN	Time Sensitive Network
TTI	Transmit Time Interval
UAV	Unmanned Arial Vehicle
UDM	Unified Data Management
UDP	User Datagram Protocol
UE	User Equipment
UICC	Universal Integrated Circuit Card
UL	Uplink
UL-SCH	Uplink Shared Channel
UM	Unassured Mode
UMTS	Universal Mobile Telecommunications System
UP	User Plane
UPF	User Plane Function
URLLC	Ultra Reliable Low Latency Communications
USIM	Universal Subscriber Identity Module

UTRAN	Universal Terrestrial Radio Access Network
UUT	Unit Under Test
UWB	Ultra Wideband
VCC	Voice Call Continuity
VFD	Variable Frequency Driver
VLAN	Virtual Local Area Network
VoIP	Voice Over IP
VPN	Virtual Private Network
VxLAN	Virtual eXtensible Local Area Network
WCDMA	Wideband Code Division Multiple Access
WLAN	Wireless Local Area Network
WMNO	Weight for MNO (Macro Network Operator)
WPS	Wireless Priority Service
WTO	World Trade Organization
XRAN®	x Radio Access Network (JMA wireless)
ZT	Zero Trust

q

t